THE FRENCH REVOLUTION
by Claude Manceron

VOLUME I *Twilight of the Old Order*

VOLUME II *The Wind from America*

These are Borzoi Books
published in New York
by Alfred A. Knopf.

The Wind from America

THE FRENCH REVOLUTION
II

The Wind from America 1778-1781

CLAUDE MANCERON

Translated from the French by Nancy Amphoux

ALFRED A. KNOPF   NEW YORK   1978

English translation copyright © 1978 by Alfred A. Knopf, Inc.
All rights reserved under International and Pan-American Copyright Conventions.
Published in the United States by Alfred A. Knopf, Inc., New York,
and simultaneously in Canada by Random House of Canada Limited, Toronto.
Distributed by Random House, Inc., New York.
Originally published in France as *Les Hommes de la Liberté II, Le Vent d'Amérique,*
by Editions Robert Laffont, Paris.
Copyright © 1974 by Editions Robert Laffont

ILLUSTRATION CREDITS

Bibliothèque nationale: pages 3, 23, 29, 34, 39 (Mirabeau), 49, 55, 62, 68, 84 (Versailles), 133, 139, 157, 164, 182, 193, 204, 233 (Mme. Helvétius), 241, 250, 294, 300, 315, 321, 332, 348, 362, 369, 394, 421, 429, 435, 442, 454, 460, 494, and 508; *Bibliothèque nationale, Photo H. Roger-Viollet:* page 257; *Centre Culturel Americain, U.S.I.S.:* page 473; *David Lindroth:* page 476; *Musée de Blevancourt:* page 488; *Musée Carnavalet:* pages 18, 99, 109, 117, 148, 226, 233 (Franklin), 263, 271, 277, 308, 356, and 403; *Musée Carnavalet, Photo Lauros-Giraudon:* page 408; *Musée Condé, Photo Giraudon:* page 39 (Sophie); *Musée Coppet, Photo Lauros-Giraudon:* page 399; *Musée de Versailles, Photo H. Roger-Viollet:* page 121; *Musée Mozart:* page 9; *New York Public Library Picture Collection:* page 382; *Photo Bulloz:* pages 76 and 199; *Photo Giraudon:* page 84 (Fersen).

*Most of the illustrations were provided through the courtesy of
the Service iconographique of Editions Robert Laffont.*

Library of Congress Cataloging in Publication Data

Manceron, Claude.   The wind from America.
(His The French revolution; 2)
Translation of *Le vent d'Amérique.*
Includes bibliographical references and index.
1. United States—History—Revolution, 1775–1783—French participation.
2. Necker, Jacques, 1732–1804.
3. France—Politics and government—1774–1793.
4. Yorktown, Va.—Siege, 1781.
I. Title.
DC145.M3513   1977, vol. 2   [E265]   944.04s   [944.04]
ISBN 0-394-49883-6   78-054928

1-16-79

To Salvador Allende,
Martyr to Liberty—
Santiago, September 11, 1973

We owe to the dead only what is useful to the living.
                    —CONDORCET, Preface to the *Eloge des Membres*
                              de l'Académie des Sciences de Paris, 1781

The true way to serve the Revolution is to continue it by bringing a free soul
into its course.
                    —EDGAR QUINET, *Critique de la Révolution*

Coincidence plays a great part in the history of the world. The acceleration or
delay of events depends to a large degree upon such accidents, which also
include the personalities of those at the head of the movement.
                    —KARL MARX, letter to Kugelmann, 1871

The dons, the bashaws, the grandees, the patricians, the sachems, the nabobs,
call them by what name you please, sigh, and groan, and fret, and sometimes
stamp, and foam, and curse, but all in vain. The decree is gone forth, and it
cannot be recalled, that a more equal liberty than has prevailed in other parts
of the earth, must be established in America. That exuberance of pride which
has produced an insolent domination in a few, a very few, opulent, monopolizing families, will be brought down nearer to the confines of reason and
moderation, than they have been used to. This is all the evil which they
themselves will endure. It will do them good in this world, and in every other.
For pride was not made for man, only as a tormentor.
                    —JOHN ADAMS, letter to Patrick Henry,
                              Philadelphia, June 3, 1776

Contents

Acknowledgments

I'm not one of those people whom gratitude humiliates. That is why I keep writing. What should I say today? Words weigh down the heart's song. How can I thank Robert Laffont more or better for having done more and better? All I can do is point out that I don't find it easy, and remind everyone that those thanks go to the whole team at the Laffont publishing house, who are joined with him in the agonies and delights of *The Men of Liberty*. However, I must mention the work of Mme Claude Chapuis, who has seen every page of the volume through the making.

The Wind from America owes its title, the image I was looking for, to Max Gallo.

To all the friends, known or unknown, who have encouraged my efforts by saying kind things about *Twilight of the Old Order*—the critics, readers, booksellers—I can only say that they have made it possible to transpose a great dream into reality. They are forcing me to go on, with them.

Jacqueline Barde died before I could tell her all I owed to her. That is the first thing she ever did to cause me pain. But there is no remedy for that remorse.

The Historian and His Pemmican

Some of the shortcomings which the reader will not fail to detect in this book can be blamed on my pemmican.

"Pemmican [Webster's Third New International Dictionary]: *1 a:* a concentrated food used by No. American Indians consisting essentially of lean buffalo meat or venison cut in thin slices, dried in the sun, pounded fine, mixed with melted fat, and packed in sacks of hide   *b:* a similar preparation (as of dried beef, flour, molasses, suet) used for emergency rations (as by explorers) *2:* information or thought condensed into little compass." Milton and Cheadle observe, on page 55 of their *North-West Passage by Land,* that "the pemmican used in the Arctic expeditions was manufactured in England of the best beef, with currants, raisins, and sugar; very different to the coarse stuff which is the staff of life in the Hudson's Bay territories."

In other words, a historian's pemmican is the card-index belonging to any man crazy enough to set out on a solitary paddle through a quarter of a century in the hope of re-creating it through the biographies of its contemporaries, navigating blind between the death of Louis XV and the death of Babeuf with the sole aid of *portolanos* inherited from his predecessors. All will be well, he trusts, because he has farsightedly thought to bring along an ample supply of pemmican. Nothing could be more reassuring, and less space-consuming, than the card-index perched on a corner of his desk. The only item to be rescued in case of fire. So long as you've got that, you'll never run short of material. And when your index is well filled, it's as though your book were already written. All you have to do is copy it down.

For instance: using my index I drew up, at the end of my first volume, a provisional summary of this one, the menu for the pemmican then in the pot: 1778 to 1788—plenty of provender for all! The paths were marked out, the passages programmed. It was all down on cards, ready to be run through my pocket computer-brain. Card X: "The Rolands get engaged"; card XX: "The Rolands quarrel"; card XXX: "The Rolands make it up"; card XXXX: "The Rolands get married." Reckoning an average of six pages per card, that makes twenty-four pages, or three days. Say four, because Saturday comes in the middle and that's *aiguade* day, I mean market day in Lodève. Four days for the Rolands. Card ZX: "Necker resigns." Two days and twelve pages. The stack of cards on the American war was a little heavier, because of all those naval battles and their casts and crews—d'Estaing, Suffren, du Petit-Thouars, Bougainville, La Pérouse, de Grasse—call it forty-eight pages and fifteen days, long enough to get your sea legs.

I stowed my pemmican in a corner to rise. When I looked back it was spilling over the gunwales of my canoe. Full of fat, nice and glossy—the best kind, like Milton and Cheadle's, crammed with raisins and spices. I should have chucked half of it overboard before tasting. But I'm the type of man who, although conceivably capable of not going out in search of temptation, is totally unable to resist it when the good Lord sets it in his path. In the margins of Mme Roland, for instance, a big chunk came floating up on François de Neufchâteau and Pache. I took a bite. I met Dom Gerle in the forest of La Double, and Saint-Simon (not the duke—the count, that weird prophet-to-be) in a trench at Yorktown, and I collided with Jacques-Robert Coquille Dugommier in Guadeloupe on the way to pick up Marie-Josèphe Rose Tascher de La Pagerie in Martinique. I must have followed twenty or more detours like these.

Worse yet, two pieces of perfectly innocent-looking pemmican swelled to such enormity that they nearly scuttled my little craft: the rebellion of Tupac Amaru and the radical revolutionary swing in Diderot's thought in response to the *Histoire des Deux Indes* and Necker's fall. And as for that fall, once you begin to take a closer look at it, there's so much to see and understand! The seeds of the crisis of July 1789 . . .

Thus I became a victim of the density of the event. The alleged vacuum of the reign of Louis XVI proves to be a plenum instead. The base of the iceberg whose tip will be the Revolution takes on dimensions not apparent even to a cruising aircraft. As I paddled on into the abortive invasion of England or the progress of Sieys's thought, untreated crates of pemmican got shoved into corners. One of them, however, was beginning to emit ominous rumbling noises—the one labeled 1782: the débuts of Robespierre and Barnave, the old age of Frederick II, the *Liaisons dangereuses,* the Geneva revolution . . .

I was headed for shipwreck from overweight: eight hundred pages and two years behind schedule. I took the only way out, and I beg all those who are following my expedition to forgive the jolt: a crash landing on the near shore of 1782, clinging for dear life to that vivacity of style which, in the author-in-labor, is something akin to the fixed grin on the face of a circus acrobat clambering up for one more try at his death-defying leap without a net.

—C. M.

The Wind from America

JOHN PAUL JONES

I

APRIL 1778

Mean Distinctions of Country

April 18, 1778. The night over Whitehaven ends endlessly. The little west-coast port is deep in slumber, and all England with it. America? As far away as the moon. Who between Blackpool and Glasgow could care about the Rebels? Who has ever heard of Philadelphia or Saratoga or what's going on there? All that is the king's business, and the Lords'. Cumberland peasants and fishermen don't read gazettes. They don't know how to read. Their one enemy, from time immemorial, is the Irisher over the way, a hundred miles across the Irish Sea. But for the time being those damned papists are quiet.

When suddenly . . .

"Here we go, boys!" cries out John Paul Jones, "commodore" of the young American navy.

Thirty men swarm out of two longboats that have just grated ashore at the foot of a little fort. The time is well chosen—low tide, at the turn of the night. No watchman could have seen them coming; but why should there be a watch? The *Ranger,* which brought them within a mile of the coast, two masts and twenty guns, is cruising out there in the shadows like a ghost in search of a horizon to haunt.

The little troop divides. John Paul leaves a detachment of a dozen men and two officers at the base of the high walls: they're going to slip down the shore, creep up, almost dry-shod, to the ships grounded by the ebb, and try to set them afire. Meanwhile, he and the rest of his men . . .

He knows every bend of the wall, every possible chink in the stones to cling to and swarm up like a lizard. He falls back into the gestures of his youth fifteen years ago, when he used to play war with the Whitehaven striplings, egged on by the local soldiers. But this time the boys giving him a leg up are giants, a crew out of Babel, the crew of every pirate ship afloat. Blacks, Spaniards, Swedes, French escapees from the convict galleys, and a few Americans for good measure.[1] They get along like a house afire, talking their universal lingo peppered with a hail of English oaths of incomparable obscenity. In two shakes they're on top of the rampart walk, facing "the fair mole within which ships lie protected at low tide,"[2] but its thirty cannons could pulverize the longboats, and the *Ranger* too. So the idea is to put them out of commission and their men as well, but not too nastily: John Paul Jones can't bear the sight of blood. The sentries, hugging the stove in the guardroom, gape at these fifteen men fresh from hell and let themselves be overpowered without a scratch, "before they had time to say 'oof' in English." There's a lot of noise now, but it's all coming from the assailants, clattering out to spike the cannons. John Paul Jones takes a hand himself, just to show them how to go about it. You pull some thick square steel rods from a bag and you wedge them into the priming holes* of the guns, using a hammer at the back and a rammer at the front. It's like working in a forge. Get it down there fast, for Christ's sake!

"Soak those nails in tallow! Bend the tips with your rammers!"

One last, more violent blow of the hammer breaks the nail off level with the priming hole. The Whitehaven lads will have one hell of a job unconstipating their guns now! We'll be miles away. But all the nails won't fit all the priming holes. Some rattle in the openings, others are too thick. Never mind:

"Take some cannonballs from those stacks. Wrap them in these gentlemen's hats to make them thicker. And shove them down the front end of the guns. Force them in with rammers, all the way back, right to the end! They'll have to sweat to pry them out again! Now, what the devil are the others up to? We should be seeing the fire by now."

The town is all aquiver. Flutterings at every window. Next thing, we'll have two or three thousand people on top of us! John Paul Jones runs to the port, where the men from his sabotage detachment are floundering in the mud around their ships and wasting time looking for tar and pitch and fagots. Their lantern's gone out. The oafs: we won't have time for more than one boat. At last a flame snakes up and along the rigging, transforming a large merchant ship into a torch. And the red sun of war rises on an illuminated Whitehaven, where the bells are clanging and a terrified crowd huddles at the edge of the quay long enough to watch the boats row out of sight and to squint after the silhouette of the ship that is about to carry the pirates away. But first, true to the grand tradition, their leader, the last to go, turns back to face the foe with a pistol in each hand covering their retreat, and tomorrow all England will see him through the eyes of the good people of Whitehaven, "a gigantic, hairy monster, ferocious and armed to the teeth"—John Paul Jones.

"Had I been able to disembark a few hours earlier," he writes to Sar-

---

*That is, the aperture at the rear of the cannon through which the burning wick is passed to set fire to the powder charge.

tines,* "not one of the two hundred ships anchored in the port would have escaped me, and no power on earth could have saved the town. Nevertheless, what has been done is enough to show that the much-vaunted English navy is not capable of protecting its own coasts, and that the scenes of distress occasioned in America can be repeated closer to home."[3] There's the crux of it: inaccessible Albion has felt the sting of retaliation. In all those years since the Royal Navy began bombarding and raiding Rebel ports at will, who could ever have foreseen this incredible event: the Americans striking back at the English coast? You mean they actually exist, those people? Tomorrow everyone will be filling in walls and building barricades all over Ireland, Scotland, and England, and all because of a little pinprick in the neck of the United Kingdom. John Paul Jones and his one *Ranger* have brought American Independence home to the English.

He's a genius—making them think he commands a whole fleet. Almost before the inhabitants of Cumberland have time to catch their breath he's seen across the channel on the Irish coast, where he surprises the *Drake,* a twenty-gun frigate like the *Ranger,* in Belfast lough.† One hour and forty minutes of battle, flashes and explosions, observed from the shore by the population of Carrick-fergus, who can't believe their eyes. Unmasted, its canvas dragging over the waves "like broken wings," the *Drake* surrenders and is sailed to Brest by a capture crew, the first English combat ship taken in this war. Then John Paul Jones fades into the heavy mists of the Irish Sea, as though playing hide-and-seek with three kingdoms. Will he get back to France before King George's ships close the Channel to him? Patience. He has one more thing to do, this time in Scotland, at Kircudbright. Due north, straight up from the Isle of Man. Ostensibly he's going there to avenge America, but his real object is to settle accounts with his own life. He needed to cancel out his undistinguished youth in Whitehaven. Now that's done. But he still has to settle the score of his childhood farther north, in the little bay of Kircudbright where a drab gray castle, like a thousand others in Scotland, stands alone atop a minute island, St. Mary's. It was there, almost thirty years ago, that little John Paul . . .

In those days he had no other name. He was the son of William Paul, a gardener on the estate of Arbigland, where he was born in 1747. But he never knew his father. Why did they move him, when he was hardly more than a baby, from the upland heather country clear to St. Mary's Isle, to live with his uncle who was Lord Selkirk's gardener? They might as well have thrown him in the sea. The interminable chatter of the servingwomen put some funny

*French minister of the navy.
†*Lough* is the Irish term for firth or loch, a sea arm.

notions into his head. Such a handsome child, so well-made, just look at those slim ankles, that lad could never have been a peasant's son. With Lord Selkirk the skirt-chaser he is! And didn't he used to be going up to hunt in Arbigland just around the time the little chap was born?

"Here we go, boys!" John Paul Jones cries out once more. He wants to get to the bottom of it. In the icy dawn of April 24 (the coasts of Scotland lie buried in snow) he leaps out of the same longboat, with the same men, for a mission he has assigned himself, and why not, it's a pirate's privilege. We're going to surround this castle in the sea. We'll kidnap Lord Selkirk and take him hostage, and then exchange him for some American prisoners. That's what he tells his men. But why choose this lord, out of the hundreds in Britain? Because John Paul knows the place like the inside of his pocket? Maybe.

It's true, he cuts a fine figure and he has a noble air, pacing up and down the beach while he waits for the men to come back; but why hasn't he gone with them? Shy? Intimidated? In fact, the ogre of Whitehaven is a short, red-haired man of middling height and delicate build, with clean-cut but wiry limbs and arms too long for the rest of his body; and nobody could have guessed the strength of his fist.[4] He is neat and well-groomed. He's fond of reading and silence. Women have been looking for—and finding—him since he was fifteen. Now he's thirty. At thirteen he was a cabin boy. He would have done anything to settle his ambiguous status, and there wasn't a hope that his naval genius would ever be recognized as long as he was in it, for His Majesty's ships were not given to commoners to command. The colonies beckoned; so farewell, Whitehaven! *Au revoir,* rather; but he couldn't have known that at the time. Then came ten years of shuttling back and forth across the Atlantic on brigs and brigantines engaged in every form of trade, until the day the slave trade made him sick: this sea hawk is a delicate bird. As if a sailing man could be delicate! He can go to hell. He almost got there once, in Virginia, when he collapsed in the doorway of a tavern in Halifax like an Arctic tern at the end of its odyssey.

That was in the spring of 1775. America was just emerging from the primal ooze, and one of the men hacking out her features happened to be inside the tavern that day: Willie Jones, from North Carolina, a prominent member of Congress. "Ultra-democratic in theory, he was an aristocrat in his habits, his pursuits and even his prejudices. He lived ostentatiously, wore fine linen, adored racing and played cards"[5]: an ideal Pygmalion for the unformed youngster to whom he was to give everything, including his name. And so John Paul Jones was born at last, the product of an adoptive father who resembled the one in his dreams if not in reality, and of a mysterious male tenderness that interfered in no way with his other loves. For the wind from America was blowing wild and free among the daughters of the southern planters. Rebecca and Mary Montfort, two pretty brunettes, didn't even bother to argue over John, they simply shared him. Then Dorothy Dandridge, Washington's cousin by marriage, came along and played the third thief. But not for long: the law of John Paul was the law of the sea, demanding all things and promising none. By this time he had won the respect of the gentlemen in Congress. War broke out. They began trying to form a Rebel navy, without either ships or men. One sailor they must have, though, a man as crazy and cocky as America herself. On June 14, 1777, Congress published two resolutions. The first decreed that "the flag of the thirteen States shall be thirteen stripes, alternate red and white, with a union of thirteen stars of white on a blue field." The second, that Captain John Paul Jones was to be "commodore"* of the *Ranger*, 6 the frigate about to be launched into the hazards of the chase. December 1777: he lands at Paimboeuf, below Nantes, bringing news of Saratoga, and celebrates the victory by drinking the wine of Jesus (Muscadet), among the Bretons. Franklin recommends him to Sartines. So now he's half-French, half-American, going off to insult England on his *Ranger,* newly fitted out by the shipyards in Brest. Nobody could guess he was trying to solve the secret of his birth.

In vain. He never does find out. The men come back frustrated, bearing bulging sacks but no prisoner: Lord Selkirk is in London. All they found were his wife and servants, so to save the day's work from being a total loss they overrode the commodore's orders and took the silver. (Perhaps that's why he didn't want to go up to the castle himself.) But according to the elementary code of pirate democracy the men were entitled to compensation. And the *Ranger* sails away to the south, toward France, abandoning the scene and secrets of the infant John Paul Jones.

Inside the castle on St. Mary's, things were done in the English manner. And the next day it is with a wholly English pen that Lady Selkirk, never dreaming of the true designs of her persecutors' chief, writes to her husband:

> I do not know whether or no you have heard talk of this American invasion? Thursday, just after breakfast, Daniel [the butler] told me that a horde of people had landed on the island, and that several of the gardeners had fled from their work. I could do nothing about it. A few minutes later they were surrounding the house and their officer asked to speak to me. I went down to the drawing room. As I was about to open my mouth to tell him what I thought of him:
> "Madam," he said, looking me straight in the eye, "we thought to take you by surprise but that is needless. We have come from a frigate belonging to the United States of America. We meant to deal with the master of this house and

---

*A purely honorary title, but it gave him precedence over other ship's captains and opened the way for promotion to the rank of admiral whenever the United States should finally possess a fleet.

to take him prisoner. Since he is absent, we have orders to ask for your plate. Please to have it handed over to us immediately. We are masters of the place and everything inside it. All resistance is vain."

"I am perfectly aware of that," I replied. And I called Daniel to tell him to give them the silver. I followed him to the pantry, where I found him filling the chambermaid's apron with objects he wished to secrete. I had everything put back in its place, determined to argue over nothing and to withhold nothing. They then called for sacks and demanded more:

"Where is the teapot? The coffee-pot?"

As I gave them over, they insisted again. Was there no other? One of them said he had orders to go through the house, and did so but took nothing. In short, they behaved civilly. The men who remained outside were armed with muskets and bayonets and wore a brace of heavy pistols in their belts. Although the doors were open, none tried to come inside . . . It is rumored that their captain, Paul Jones, is a certain John Paul, allegedly born at Arbigland . . . A villain if ever there was one, guilty of several murders and great crimes. The truth is, however, that the sailors standing guard swore to our people that their captain knew you, had a high opinion of you, and for that reason had given orders that no harm was to be done to us. They thanked me politely for the glass of whiskey which hospitality compelled me to have served to them.[7]

Perhaps she is not utterly amazed, a month later, to receive a letter from this terror of the seas, via Holland. In it John Paul Jones apologizes for the theft of the silver, which he had been forced to "wink at," but which his "heart cannot approve." His intention had been merely "to have him taken on board" and "make him the happy instrument of alleviating the horrors of hopeless captivity, when the brave are overpowered and made prisoners of war" (hold him as hostage for an exchange of prisoners, in other words). Furious to find him absent, the sailors demanded the silver as compensation, and afterwards reminded him that "in America, no delicacy was shown by the English, who took away all sorts of moveable property—setting fire, not only to towns and to the houses of the rich, without distinction, but not even sparing the wretched hamlets and milch-cows of the poor and helpless, at the approach of an inclement winter." He then trots out his pretty little dénouement: "I had but a moment to think how I might gratify [my men], and at the same time do your ladyship the least injury" and hit upon the idea of buying back the silver when it was sold, after which he will "gratify my own feelings by restoring it to you, by such conveyance as you shall please to direct."* Then come three pages on the horrors of war, his loathing of all forms of cruelty, and his opinions as "a citizen of the world, totally unfettered by the little, mean distinctions of climate or of country, which diminish the benevolence of the

*Lady Selkirk's silver is in fact returned, down to the last teaspoon, but only after the end of the war, when communication becomes easier.

heart and set bounds to philanthropy." And he closes by hoping that "the amiable Countess of Selkirk" will not regard him as an enemy, for "I am ambitious of her esteem and friendship, and would do anything, consistent with my duty, to merit it."[8]

THE MOZART FAMILY

2

JULY 1778

People of No Understanding

Jean-Jacques Rousseau dies at Ermenonville on July 2, 1778.* The news hasn't reached Paris yet by the time Mozart's mother dies there on the 3rd, attended only by her son, a friend, and a nurse, in a humble room in the Hôtel des Quatre Fils Aymon on the Rue du Gros-Chenet† where the poor woman has spent the past three months in utter misery. The catastrophe came without warning. Madame Mozart was not ill. She was simply languishing, for Salzburg, for Germany, for her beloved husband Leopold: they've been cooing like turtledoves for thirty years, the pair of them, in a conjugal complicity from which their children are excluded.** A good woman, Anna Maria Pertl, of old peasant stock. A solid female of no great wit. Her nice hen's head, with its pointed nose and clean white hair always skinned tightly back, has only three or four ideas in it: family, neighbors, Church, and money. She doesn't understand much about what her husband and son are up to. All she knows is that music is one means of gaining the patronage of the Great when you start with nothing. And she has only come to this horrid Paris, where she huddles like some old stray bird, because you couldn't let Wolfgang loose on his own there at twenty-two, and such a baby he is, just imagine, and already after the girls—why, it would have been the end of him. But far better to have sent Leopold, he has so much more control over the boy, and he could have advised Wolfgang in his quest for a place at Paris and Versailles.‡ But Leopold was

---

*Here I resume the sequence of events in exact chronological order [following Volume I], from which I departed to place the John Paul Jones episode as a prologue to this book.

†Now the Rue du Croissant, on the right bank. Mozart and his mother moved into it in mid-April, three weeks after arriving in Paris on March 22.

**They lost five in infancy. Only Wolfgang and his older sister Marianne, nicknamed Nanerl (born in 1751), survive. In 1778 Anna Maria is fifty-eight and Leopold fifty-nine years old.

‡Leopold Mozart is vegetating as "Vice Kapellmeister" to the Prince-Archbishop of Salz-

unable to get leave from that nasty prince-archbishop in Salzburg, so he asked his beloved spouse to make a sacrifice for the cause. How could he have guessed?

"How often we talk about Salzburg, in the evenings when we dine together,"[1] she wrote him on May 29. At that point her ailments were almost reassuring —eyes, teeth, migraines: female complaints. The pains in her stomach began on June 15. The hotel people advised an enema, which she refused in horror: only the French could advocate such diabolical practices; no German could bring himself even to mention them. Bloodletting was the absolute limit ... She took to her bed on June 19. Fever set in. An "antispasmodic powder" had no effect. Wolfgang fought for two days to get his mother to consent to see a French physician. "I was rushing about as though I had lost my wits." The doctor prescribes powdered rhubarb. No result. At his second call, on June 29, he shrugs: "See that she has a priest." Her guts are rotten, the infection is spreading all through her. Paris bread and Paris water have poisoned her, like so many other people from the country or from small, clean towns. In those days the Parisians ate and drank their own excrement carried by the water running in the gutters of the streets. Anyone who didn't die in childhood was immunized for life. But when you come from Salzburg, where you get your water pure and fresh from the mountains ... Anna Maria remains conscious long enough to take confession and the last rites. The idea of death hasn't seeped through to her brain. She doesn't understand. She goes into a coma on July 3 at five in the afternoon. "I was holding her hand. I talked to her, but she didn't hear me, said nothing." She dies quietly, at 10:21.*

At midnight Mozart writes to his father: "My dear mother is very ill ... She is delirious, I am told to hope but have little." At "two o'clock in the night" he writes to a friend in Salzburg, a priest, and asks him to break the news to Leopold. "This was the saddest day of my life ... I bore all with fortitude and complete acceptance, by the special grace of God." Not until six days later does he write to his father again: "Weep, weep your heart out. But, in the end, be comforted. Think that Almighty God has willed it. And what can we do against Him? We will pray to Him, that is best, and thank Him that it happened so painlessly ... So let us say a fervent Paternoster for her soul. And now, we will move on to other subjects; to everything there is a season."[2] His letters are full of God but the words ring like a gesture of courtesy to fate,

---

burg. He has no hope of promotion. For the past ten years Wolfgang has also been bound to the same petty sovereign by contract, with the title of Hofkonzertmeister—an unremunerated and menial job which has earned him nothing but a commission two or three times a year. This trip to Paris is intended to relaunch his career.

*Brigitte and Jean Massin say she probably had typhoid or paratyphoid fever.

and no tears are welling in his eyes; in fact, this ordeal has made him feel sorrier for himself than for the loss of his parent—not that he's insensitive, he vibrates all over, with everything: grief, wrath, creation. But Mozart did not love his whiny nursemaid mother. And he's about to lose patience with his fussy, self-seeking little tyrant of a father, who has forbidden him to dream of his first true love, Aloysia Weber, found and abandoned in Mannheim at the beginning of his trip.*

This second trip to France is so unlike the first! Fifteen years ago he was conquering Europe. "I saw him give a concert as a child of seven," Goethe wrote.[3] "I was about fourteen then myself, and can still clearly recall the little fellow with his wig and sword," Leopold Mozart's goose that lays the golden eggs, the clever puppet being toured around by its daddy to gain money and fame. Queen Marie and Madame de Pompadour congratulated him at Versailles, but so did Maria Theresa in Vienna, and King George and Queen Charlotte in London. Grimm's *Correspondance littéraire* put him in the European orbit on December 1, 1763: "True prodigies are sufficiently rare that one makes a point of speaking out when one has an opportunity to see such a thing . . . [The young Mozart] is so extraordinary a phenomenon that one can scarcely believe what one sees with one's own eyes and hears with one's own ears. It is as nothing for this child to perform the most difficult pieces with the highest degree of precision . . . What passes belief is to see him play out of his head for an hour on end, abandoning himself to the inspiration of his genius."[4] Even then a composer, not just a virtuoso. The catalog of his works contains some ten titles from that period, mostly minuets, but also two sonatas for harpsichord and violin composed at Versailles.†

How far away all that is today! Now he's become a real composer—now that nobody listens to him anymore. In this month of July 1778 he passes the 300-mark in his numbered works: fifteen concertos, thirty-one symphonies, thirteen masses, and seven operas** on subjects imposed upon the gilded lackey by his patrons' whims. But he's already bursting the seams of that straitjacket, and Mozart is about to rise from the ashes of Mozart. "What pains me most here is that these doltish French *will* imagine that I am still seven years old, because I was when they first knew me."[5] They adored the child and petted him because he didn't bother anybody and sat quietly in his place at the harpsichord, among the little blackamoors and lap dogs. But how are they

---

*The daughters of a Mannheim "music copyist," Aloysia and Constanze Weber (Mozart later marries the latter) are the nieces of a musician whose son, Carl Maria, to be born in 1786, will write *Der Freischütz*.

†Marking, in the words of the Massins, "the decisive step by which Mozart publicly proved himself a composer, in all the fullness of his eight years of age."

**La Finta semplice; Bastien und Bastienne; Mitridate, re di Ponto; Lucio Silla; Thamos; La Finta giardiniera; Il Re pastore.

supposed to enthuse over this gawky, unclassifiable young man; just looking at him makes one cringe from the combined assaults of his adolescence and his genius. Mozart is no beauty, with his heavy blond head, oversized nose, and clumsiness, and his Teutonic accent in which every *e* is stamped out as though by a die—it's an absolute scream listening to him, my dear. In fact, he looks common. He *is* common: the lineage of the peasant Pertls lies just beneath his skin; and that of the Mozarts, too, stonecutters or bookbinders in Bavaria, none of whom ever set foot in a court, until Leopold—and can one really call the menagerie of a German archbishop a court? Can one conceive of such a person at Trianon? And now Leopold's son is driving his father to despair: "You're too ready to answer back in a jesting tone at the first opportunity. That is the first step toward familiarity. And if one wishes to keep people's respect in this society, familiarity is not a thing to be too much sought after . . . You are rather too proud and self-concerned, and then you are too quickly intimate with people, you open your heart to everyone; in short, wishing to seem free and natural, you become familiar."[6] And on such subjects! Faugh! Worse than Rabelais—when Mozart puts his mind to it he's a match for Hieronymus Bosch at scatology. As, for example, when he writes to the little cousin in Augsburg whom he used to tease so impishly: "Ah, turd! What a delicious word! Turd, herd, that's good too: herd, turd—Turd, furred, oh, charming! Turd, furred, that's what I like! Turd, heard and furred, heard a furred turd . . . Is your belly well relieved? . . . Our assholes ought to be the emblem of peace . . . But I must shit one more time today."[7] There's an echo here of his bassoon concertos of 1774 and 1775, where the bassoon gambols and crashes into the four corners of the orchestra like a great lolloping puppy dog. But the young man who relieves himself in such graceful prose professes other opinions of no less elephantine conventionality—you might think it was Maria Theresa moralizing: "I'm always at my best at home, or when visiting some good, genuine, honest German who, if a bachelor, lives like a decent Christian or, if married, loves his wife and brings up his children properly . . . That miscreant, that master scoundrel Voltaire has died, like a dog one might as well say, like a beast."[8] He infuriates Baron Grimm, who was his protector fifteen years before—a true Parisian German. The leading fop of Europe, in his red-heeled pumps, now finds Wolfgang "over-candid, inactive, too easy to gull, too inattentive to the means that lead to fortune. To make your way here you must be devious, enterprising, bold. For his own good, I could wish him half his talent and twice his tact."[9]

Half his talent? Small chance of that: Mozart already knows he's Mozart, the secret's choking him. He'd like to share it with a universe whose door Paris is slamming in his face. Perhaps that's why he can't stand Voltaire, the mirror of that same Paris. "So they suppose that, just because I am humble and young, there can be nothing great inside me, nothing ripe? Well, they'll soon learn

otherwise."[10] "I am surrounded by brutes and animals, as far as music is concerned, I mean. But how could it be otherwise? They behave no differently in all their actions, their pursuits, their passions. There is no place on earth like Paris!"—where he cannot even go to call on people: "every time, it's too far or too filthy, because Paris is indescribably full of shit . . . The French have lost all semblance of their manners of fifteen years ago. Now they are almost coarse, and abominably proud."[11] At this point he has just been humiliated at the home of Mme de Chabot, where he was kept "waiting in a huge, icy hall, with neither fire nor fireplace, at least half an hour" before sitting down, shivering with cold, to play some of his *Variations* for the duchess and her table mates, who were "all seated in a circle around a big table," drawing . . . "The most amazing rudeness of all was that Madame and all the gentlemen never stopped drawing for one instant, but kept straight on, so that I was forced to play to the seats and tables and walls . . . Give me the finest pianoforte in Europe, but if my only audience are people of no understanding and no desire to understand, and who do not feel what I am playing the way I do, then I shall lose my joy."[12]

They invite him, and then they pay him not to be listened to. That spring Paris would not hear Mozart; Mozart will never forgive it. The Paris of the Rohan-Chabots and of Grimm, at any rate. He has taken the full measure of its futility.

So much the worse: "I shall make my way as I can . . . provided I escape [from Paris] unscathed . . ." "I am a *composer* [his italics], born to be a Kapellmeister. I must not and cannot bury the composer's talent God in his magnanimity has given me." He has just completed a symphony for the feast of Corpus Christi. "For the small number of intelligent Frenchmen who will be there, I am very sure it will please them. As for the imbeciles, it will be no great loss if they don't like it. And I still have hope that even the donkeys may find something to their taste in it."[13]

3

Between Fear and Hope

On July 10, 1778, Louis XVI writes a letter, published the following day, to the Admiral of France, Jean-Marie de Bourbon, Duc de Penthièvre; it confirms France's declaration of war on England following the battle between *La Belle-Poule* and the *Arethusa*. "The dignity of my crown and the protection I owe to my subjects demand that at last I make reprisal . . . I therefore send this letter to tell you . . . to order the commanders of my squadrons and my ports and the captains of my ships to give chase to those of the King of England . . . I am trusting principally to the protection of the God of armies"[1]—the same one King George and the bishops of the United Kingdom are simultaneously exhorting to chasten both Rebel dissenters and papist French. Poor old Jahweh's going to be scratching his head again—but the sailors are jumping for joy!

Penthièvre, to whom this letter is addressed, is a freshwater admiral with an old honorary title. Last descendant of the bastards legitimized by Louis XIV, governor and lieutenant general of a Brittany nearly half of which belongs to him, he took both his own name and that of his son, Lamballe,* from the region. Having withdrawn into a dignified and devout old age, he spends his time every day winding up and synchronizing his passion—one hundred watches. He once actually did navigate, it's true, for the sake of his title: with a miniature fleet launched on the canals of his Château de Rambouillet. But he married his daughter to the first prince of the blood permitted to venture out upon a real sea: the Duc de Chartres.† Times are changing.

For Philippe de Chartres, it's now or never. He's about to make his mark or sink out of sight. He is thirty-one years old but everybody talks about him as

*Dead of syphilis at twenty-one. His young widow, the Princesse de Lamballe, is one of the queen's favorites.

†Louis-Philippe-Joseph, born April 13, 1747, who will become Duc d'Orléans when his father dies in 1785 and take the name of Philippe Egalité in 1792. His eldest son, after serving his term as Duc de Chartres and Duc d'Orléans in turn, becomes the last king of the French, Louis-Philippe. [See genealogy, page 20—*Trans.*]

though he were a perpetual infant condemned to idleness and kept on a short rein by his cousin's ministers. An Orléans can't even sneeze without asking permission. Thus far he has been noted for little but libertinage. The hour of his adulthood strikes on July 8 when he sails out of the Brest Channel roads on board the *Saint-Esprit.* At three in the afternoon, after long and arduous maneuvering to catch the wind, he has established himself in his proper position as sternmost ship in the formidable alignment of Admiral Comte d'Orvilliers's forty-three rated vessels.* A ship of the line was an armed vessel fitted out to fight in a line of battle (from which *battleship* is derived) or formation commanded by the fleet leader. Frigates and corvettes were lighter and fought singly. For the French navy too, it's the big league at last, the adventure of the high seas. Resurrection. The navy is out to "give chase" to the English—Philippe, to life.

He's Duc de Chartres, and so descended from Henri IV in the male line and Louis XIV in the female, and he is heir to the one domain still unannexed by the crown: not only Chartres, but Orléans, Nemours, and the Valois as well. When his father dies he'll be as rich as the King. And if the Comte d'Artois's two babies are carried off by disease, and if the Queen is only pregnant with a girl child, he will become fourth in line for the throne. And at last they've given him something better than a rattle to play with: the title of lieutenant general of the naval armies, with responsibility for the "blue squadron"— one-third of the whole fleet. He cuts a fine figure in his superb white and gold uniform, contrasting with the dominant scarlet of the other officers. It makes him today the target of every eye, tomorrow of every trigger. He has an extremely pleasing appearance; he's tall, with shapely legs and black, laughing eyes that enable you to avoid dwelling upon the rest of his face—all unrelieved bonelessness, nothing to catch hold of, a mouth less sensual than fleshy, nothing aggressive, nothing dominating: a thirty-year-old youth who'd be glad to make himself useful—but are they finally going to let him? Philippe glances anxiously at the mentor planted at his side, post captain Toussaint-Guillaume de La Motte-Picquet de La Vinoyère, a smallish fifty-eight-year-old, a leathery veteran of twenty-two campaigns, "loving fame and his calling as much as he hated the English, brave as his sword and stubborn as the devil; a man who, when he had his enormous hat on, would have made hell itself shudder."[2] What's he here for anyway, except to get in Philippe's way? All the requirements for total confusion have been united on the *Saint-Esprit,* where the Duc de Chartres, as "lieutenant general," is theoretically in charge of the eleven ships of the "blue squadron" which La Motte-Picquet effectively commands, where both must relinquish control of their own ship to "flag captain" Montpeyroux-Roquefeuil,† and where all three are compelled to keep their eyes

---

*Thirty-two ships of the line and eleven frigates.

†The "flag captain" was the officer in command of a ship flying the flag of—or in other words

glued to the signals of the "general of the naval army" far in the distance on board the *Bretagne* in the center of the "white squadron": Louis-Jacques-Honoré de Guillouet, Comte d'Orvilliers.

Well, time will tell. Meanwhile, it's all so grand between Brest and Ouessant, the heavy sea, ten-foot troughs, a southwest wind—the first foe to overcome if you hope to keep off the Molène shoals. The ships don't dare lay on any upper sails; the quarterdeck is covered with spray and the fleeting sun brushes long streaks of gold down the gilt of the sculpted poops. Philippe, standing tall at the stern of the *Saint-Esprit,* is the privileged witness to a scene that all the Opéras and Trianons in the world can never show him: the deployment of the Ponant fleet.* Forty-three monuments harrow the field of waves in a formidable silence peopled by a thousand intelligent noises: the murmur of sailors like big birds among the rigging, the snap of wet canvas, squeak of yards and creak of planking, and the pipes and long rising and falling cries of the boatswains passing the orders of those gentlemen in scarlet, the officers, from one ship to the next. For the officers themselves never raise their voices except in battle: their words are low and few, like God's, and are amplified and hurled out to the winds by the hundred throats of their sea monks.

Never have ships of war been so beautiful: wood reaches its apotheosis in the days of sailing ships, like stone in the age of cathedrals. Philippe can only dimly discern the eleven ships of the "blue and white" squadron in the vanguard, commanded by old du Chaffault.† But with the naked eye he can make out, there in the middle of the "white squadron," the hulk of the *Bretagne,* France's largest ship, three decks, one hundred and ten guns, a crew of a thousand, built twelve years ago by subscription among the states of Brittany and newly refitted at Brest. Its somewhat ponderous outline makes it the focal point of the huge moving body, with an armament of two thousand pieces of artillery, whose compact symmetry the signals of "General" d'Orvilliers are struggling to maintain. Surrounding the *Saint-Esprit* are the *Sphinx, Roland, Fier, Zodiaque, Intrépide, Triton, Solitaire, Conquérant,* and *Diadème,* which, along with the *Robuste,* commanded by the Comte de Grasse, form the "blue squadron." In bright sunlight they make a carnival of color against the

---

carrying—a general officer (Chartres in this case).

   Ponant (from the Latin *ponere*) was the naval term for *couchant* [setting], or the west: the Atlantic war fleet. Its corollary, the Toulon fleet, was called the *Levant* [rising; cf. *Levantine*], destined since the Crusades to fight the Infidel, although lately it's been doing so from an increasingly defensive position, trying to ward off the "barbaresque" jabs of ships from the "échelles" (*escales* [ports of call]) of Tripoli, Tunis, Algiers, and Morocco, still nominally subject to the Grand Sultan.

   †The pennants flying from the flagstaffs at the stern bore the colors of each squadron and thus showed to which any ship belonged.

emerald backdrop of the sea; a palette gone mad, from the dark brown hulls to the chalk-white sails and the gold of the carved fore and aft castles where unicorns, gargoyles, and dragons stretch out their gaping man-sized maws to devour the English.[3] We're going to deliver Dunkerque, the demolished port where an English garrison gloats over its razed jetties. We're going to avenge La Hougue.* The officers of the French navy are well past the flash point. "It is deeply humiliating for us to have ships lying at anchor and to be insulted at our very doors, because we are always the weakest," du Chaffault wrote to Sartines last October 3.[4] "For my part, my blood boils in my veins." And on October 6: "England mistakes our courtesy for cowardice . . . The entire department [of the navy] suffers from our consideration for people who never show any for us. It has a lowering effect on the men's spirits, and when the time comes to make war every man must think himself better than his enemy, or he is good for nothing." After all these years of stagnation the moment has finally come to shake off the dust. Sartines hasn't made too bad a job of it, as a magistrate whose transfer from police to navy was received with great misgivings four years earlier. But it was high time: the end of Louis XV's reign had done more to deplete the arsenals than ten campaigns. For one *Bretagne* built by regional initiative at vast cost, twenty or thirty ships sat rotting in the roads. And not only their hulls corroded: their very souls were rotten, their skeleton crews weren't even going out on maneuvers anymore. "Of the midshipmen, a good half are useless because of their want of years," moaned du Chaffault again from the height of his three-score-and-ten.[5] One reason for the reluctance of Vergennes and Maurepas to give the Americans any effective assistance was this great penury in Brest—the one possible crucible for revenge, after the peace of 1763 had left the Channel to the English.† Three months ago the authorities in Brest were still deploring the shortage of seamen owing to "insufficient conscription,"** but they were also bewailing a general scarcity of carpenters and caulkers, wood, iron, and ammunition.[6] "When the King came to the throne," Vergennes confessed, "everything needed to be done. Not one ship was fit to sail, not one warehouse filled. Everything had to be found at once."[7] Sartines worked like a Trojan. They fetched elms all the way from the park at Trianon and sent to the Black Forest for pine for the mainmasts. "It has not been possible to see to everything at the same time, and

*Where, on May 27, 1692, Tourville suffered the most glorious defeat imaginable, off Cotentin, at the hands of Admiral Russell's Anglo-Dutch fleet. Between then and Ouessant, there had been no naval battle on this scale.

†Le Havre served merchant ships only, Cherbourg was still on the drawing board, and Dunkerque was dismantled and under English surveillance.

**Since Colbert, the fleet's crews were recruited by compulsory conscription among the coastal parishes, often drawn by lot. Thus the Ponant hands all came from Brittany, Charente, or the Vendée, and those of the Levant were Provençal.

if anyone had known the condition of our navy last spring, he would not have believed we could rebuild it from its ashes in so brief a time," again according to Vergennes,[8] as he trumpets his joy to learn that at last Louis XVI can call upon "forty-two ships of the line in good condition and all things needful to put them to sea."* But "this tableau, pleasing as it is, does not provide a consolidated force: for at the end of one campaign this squadron would be worthless unless there were a second set of ships and rigging to send in its place, and these are things which money cannot buy if they have not been undertaken in good time."

In July 1778, with one double cast of the dice, France decides to back the sea, winner take all: the Ponant expedition coincides with the departure of the best ships from the Toulon or Levant fleet, which Admiral d'Estaing is taking across to the American coast in an attempt to prize open the jaws of the English reconquest. Double or nothing. The situation is tense enough to make d'Orvilliers proceed with caution despite the bloodthirsty blustering of his officers. His real mission is to nail the great English fleet down off Ouessant long enough for d'Estaing to get through farther south, and out of sight of the Azores. D'Orvilliers will have to behave himself, as behooves a power that simply cannot afford any deeds of derring-do. The dilemma of all commanders of big fleets. Here he is, suspended "between fear and hope" like Vergennes back at Versailles, waiting for the news.[9]

LOUIS PHILIPPE,
THE DUC DE CHARTRES

4

JULY 1778

A Sort of Cheerful Viciousness

Philippe is suspended meanwhile between the fear of vegetating indefinitely and the hope of becoming something more than an Orléans. The sailors are beside themselves with impatience, no doubt; but what about him? There has been a thriving tradition in the French monarchy for the last hundred and fifty years, and its aim is the gradual extermination of the Orléanses. They turned Monsieur into a pederast so he would be less of a menace to his brother, Louis XIV, than Gaston d'Orléans had been to Louis XIII. Since then, kings and

*The *Bretagne,* then still in dry dock, made the forty-third; the Ponant had thirty-two and the Levant eleven.

their coteries had been trembling nonstop at the thought of this ever-possible cloud on the horizon: the popularity of a prince in the younger branch. They were not mistaken. The regent was better loved than the old king he replaced, and better loved than the brat in whose name he was ruling, and if it hadn't been for the Law catastrophe . . .* But in the fifty years since bankruptcy and debauchery made an end of that other Philippe, his two descendants have been reduced to walk-on parts. One, a bigoted nut, a sort of gloomy, ill-tempered saint, "Louis-le-Génovéfain," withdrew to a monastery after the death of his wife. The other, a "German to his very fingertips,"[1] Louis-le-Gros, has fallen under the distaff of a clandestine spouse, the Marquise de Montesson. The Duc d'Orléans in 1778: an ailing wine butt whom everyone is waiting to see choke on his own fat—Egalité's father.

His turn to be Duc d'Orléans must come soon; but for how long? Monsieur died at sixty, the regent at forty-nine, Louis-le-Pieux too. The present duke, the fat one, is getting on toward sixty now. Will he make it? Philippe at thirty-one, on board his *Saint-Esprit,* has some reason to fear that he's already passed the halfway mark. Unless . . . He has often been told, most emphatically —too emphatically, as though there were some doubt in the matter—that he has his father's fleshy features. But is that really so certain? His mother was a Conti, she had the devil in her flesh and was glad of it; and the "devil" had made his first appearance shortly before Philippe's birth. So? The Comte de Melfort, maybe? Abbé de Martin? Lacroix, the coachman? When her friends teased Louise-Henriette d'Orléans on the subject of her son's paternity, she would shrug: "When you fall into a briar patch, can you pick out the one that scratches you?"[2] But maybe Philippe was the Fat Man's own, after all . . . There was that resemblance. Although, from infancy, there had also been intermittent fits of energy, and his official father certainly never suffered from them.

But "in monarchies, a man of energy often has no resource but pleasure," as the intendant† of Marseilles has just written—Sénac de Meilhan, who fancies himself a moralist.[3] "His infancy over,** Monsieur le Duc de Chartres commenced his education, and then his governesses were men; for between his nursemaids and his first teachers there was scant difference, other than that

*John Law (1671–1729) was a Scottish monetary reformer who obtained permission in 1716, a year after Louis XIV's death and hence under the Regency, to try a plan for banking reform in France, where the government was heavily in debt. His plan, involving the program known as the "Mississippi Bubble," ran foul of speculative complications and political intrigue, and Law was forced to leave France in 1720.

A brief Bourbon genealogy may be of use here—see page 20. All wives, and children not immediately relevant, are omitted. Reigning monarchs are italicized. [*Trans.*]

†Intendant: an agent of the king, responsible for justice, police, and finance in each of the thirty-four districts of France. Their powers were limited but enormous, and they were unpopular. [*Trans.*]

**According to Talleyrand, who later becomes Philippe's friend and confidant.

THE BOURBONS

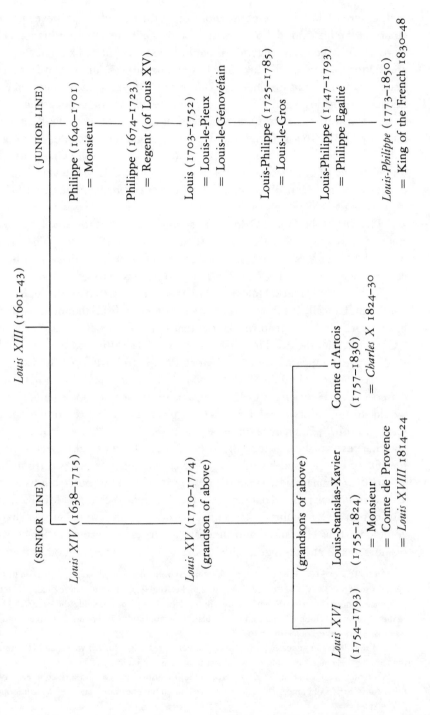

Louis XIII (1601–43)

(SENIOR LINE)

(JUNIOR LINE)

Louis XIV (1638–1715)

Philippe (1640–1701)
= Monsieur

Philippe (1674–1723)
= Regent (of Louis XV)

Louis XV (1710–1774)
(grandson of above)

Louis (1703–1752)
= Louis-le-Pieux
= Louis-le-Génovéfain

Louis-Philippe (1725–1785)
= Louis-le-Gros

(grandsons of above)

Louis-Stanislas-Xavier
(1755–1824)
= Monsieur
= Comte de Provence
= *Louis XVIII* 1814–24

Comte d'Artois
(1757–1836)
= *Charles X* 1824–30

Louis-Philippe (1747–1793)
= Philippe Egalité

Louis XVI
(1754–1793)

Louis-Philippe (1773–1850)
= King of the French 1830–48

between the frailty of women and the indulgence of men."[4] His long adolescence is nothing but an apprenticeship in appearance-making, the sole function permitted to princes of the blood. Baptism at twelve, admission into the order of the Holy Spirit at fifteen, a regiment at sixteen, and tours of his little kingdoms of Villiers-Cotterêts, Nemours, and Chartres, where he is suzerain.[5] "At that time, his character gave no promise of anything remarkable. It was observed, however, that he took a kind of sly pleasure in embarrassing those who approached him, and had a sort of cheerful viciousness, elusive and arrogant, which the well-disposed call mischievousness. It was also noticed that from early childhood he never showed the least gratitude to his parents or teachers, and felt no affection for his playmates." Maybe so; but "he would never suffer the most insignificant of animals to be maltreated in his presence,"[6] and his servants loved him.

When he was nineteen people began to worry: an Orléans, and still a virgin? His father intervened personally to put a stop to that, by entrusting him to Rosalie Duthé, a "completely new mistress," a girl of fifteen who was already an expert but guaranteed syphilis-free by the matrons of the laboratories in which Jeanne Bécu* and a few others had also been trained. "Extremely thoughtful and tender concern for his son's health."[7]

Once initiated, he conscientiously performed his princely duty. Using the aforementioned matrons and employees as informers, Sartines's inspectors followed the boy's progress step by step through the drab orgy of the sixties, the reverse side of life at court. They kept an inventory for the delectation of that great voyeur, Louis XV. On February 27, 1767, "Monseigneur le Duc de Chartres finally made his début in the house of Dame Brissault. He came to her at seven in the evening and she offered him the choicest morsel in her larder; this was the demoiselle Lavigne, known as Durancy; it was she who had the pleasure of entertaining His Highness, and they did not part until after the third embrace. This prince seemed delighted with his mount and gave fifteen louis† for its hire; he has since sent word to Dame Brissault that he would be pleased to run the race again, but the Durancy girl would not join him. She finds the caresses of this prince far too coarse, and says that he has no refinement and swears like a fishmonger. Several other young women have also found him so, and everything about him gives promise of a temper well suited to foul libertinage."[8] The stoolie who ran off this kind of report knew the right way to go about pleasing his betters. On March 27, the same year: "M. le Duc de Chartres persists in his career. On the 24th of this month a young gentleman of his court came to Dame Guérin's at three in the afternoon, to fetch Emilie and Zelmire; he took them to a small suite of rooms in the Palais Royal

*Who became Comtesse du Barry in 1771.
†Equivalent to 1,500 new francs [$300].

... Emilie had the honor of entertaining His Highness, who charges straight through the cabbage patch,* while Zelmire amused herself with two other gentlemen whom she did not know, one of whom was addressed as 'Vicomte.' The young women were sent away, with six louis, at five o'clock in the morning. This young prince often indulges in similar sports; he will be fortunate indeed if he emerges from them unscathed [by venereal disease]."9 Louis XV was fond of this kind of nonsense, and Louis XVI is even fonder of it. Sartines's entire fortune has been built upon such tittle-tattle. He's still at it today, behind his desk in the ministry of the navy—working through Le Noir, his chief-of-police henchman.

After two or three years Philippe swam relatively clear of these murky waters. His marriage to Louise de Penthièvre, a child bride clever enough to be not only the richest heiress in France but also tolerable at sixteen, permitted him to achieve a degree of calm to which he was naturally predisposed. He continued to attend the parties of the playboys in his gang—always the same, Lauzun, Coigny, Rohan-Chabot, Fitz-James, Fronsac, the Prince de Ligne.10 Beginning in 1771 he held open house, open bed, and open board for them in his "folly" at the Mousseaux gate,† which the spy calls "a true den of voluptuousness." But from then on Philippe was more a host than a participant, his heart wasn't in it anymore. One feels the police are having to rack their brains to squeeze out any fresh tidbits for Louis XVI. The bulk of his debauchery took place during those indecisive years when he was being forced to sow his wild oats. But it was sufficient for people on the King's side to think they could write him off; and he had been supplied with enough talkative girls to give him a world-wide reputation as a monster of depravity. Just another Orléans ...

He has fought back, however, in fits and starts, hard enough to stay in the running. He reads nothing to speak of but he's restless, and he's picked up one or two ideas through his travels and sailing and by taking his role as a seaman seriously, at Toulon, Cadiz, and in Brest last year, where he was one of the first to back John Paul Jones and give him help. Bougainville found him an apt pupil at compass-reading. Since June 24, 1771, he has been Most Serene Grand Master of the Grand Lodge of France, a sophisticated and snobbish Freemasonry, more of a club than a movement, in which his duties are confined to presiding solemnly over an esoteric liturgy. But through it he has dimly begun to scent the sea breeze: a confused aspiration toward universal brotherhood. Now his lungs ask only to expand. He has taken the oath of "Chevalier Kadosh";** this is the time to remember it: "All men are equal.

---

*What would we do without *Littré* [venerable French dictionary]? "To charge straight through the cabbage patch: to act in a scatterbrained manner, without examining anything."

†Which later becomes the Parc Monceau.

**The degree of "Chevalier Kadosh" in the "Ancient and Accepted Scottish Rite" adopted

None can stand above another or command him; sovereigns must belong to the multitude. Peoples bestow sovereignty where they please and retract it when they please. Any religion claiming to be the work of God is an absurdity. Omnipotence that calls itself spiritual is an abuse."[11] Onward, *Saint-Esprit!*

THE BATTLE OF THE OUESSANT

5

JULY 1778

The Signals Could Not Be Seen

July 9, 1778. Calm sea, hot sun; a sapphire world. The Comte d'Orvilliers can hold a high council on board the *Bretagne,* the entire fleet being "hove-to" under almost bare poles so that its general officers and post captains can join their admiral. Now: when are we going to start eating up those English? The scene under the huge striped marquee where the footmen are busily serving up a collation looks more appropriate for a wedding reception than a military tactics meeting. But don't trust appearances: if you look again you'll notice a hand missing here and there, or a couple of fingers or an eye, and the one dream beneath the powdered curls of all these tall red and gold gentlemen is flashing swords and gore. The Duc de Chartres, in white, speaks for everyone when he implores the "general" to obtain permission from Louis XVI to go and ferret out the enemy in his Channel ports. Did he or did he not order them to "give chase" to the foe?

That kind of talk sends shivers up and down d'Orvilliers's spine. The greatest danger facing the "naval army" he's supposed to be baby-sitting is the pugnacity of its junior officers. He knows that his English counterpart, Admiral Keppel, is cruising off Portsmouth with two squadrons of ships "superior in numbers and in strength." He has just written to Sartines: "In the event of an encounter [with Keppel], which I shall still try to avoid, I flatter myself that I shall, if not beat him, at least put up a strong resistance . . . If nothing else, we shall gain some most necessary experience for our crews and their leaders."[1] He's not what you'd call overconfident, this supreme commander, but he's right. He knows how puny his armada is despite its fresh coat of paint.

by the Freemasons of the Grand Lodge was the thirtieth, almost the summit of the hierarchy. "Synthesis of all other degrees," it taught "the path of realization of the human order in harmony with the universal."

And there's nothing wrong with his courage: d'Orvilliers has fought over many an ocean in the last half-century. But he is sixty-eight years old and has turned crabbed and despondent—maybe for want of a good battle. He's rusty. All last winter, in Brest and Paris, he was fidgeting around "like an old man afraid of the cold, who isn't up to a hard day's work anymore."[2] He's one of those men who gouge their way to the top only to turn yellow with terror of a disgrace that can no longer touch them. D'Orvilliers is apprehensive as a bishop being called to account by the pope; he fears Sartines worse than Keppel, and he is disappointing his officers badly:

"My advice is not to bring the [naval] army into the Channel, where we have no port that can contain it and where it would be in danger of being driven to the leeward by a west or southwest gale, and would inevitably be cast aground upon the English coast. We will cruise at a suitable distance from the canal so as to avoid being drawn into it by the currents."[3]

So all they can hope is that the English will come out after them. Meanwhile, they tack back and forth within reach of Ouessant as the sky begins to fade. The weather seems as perplexed as the "God of armies"—a misty sun, not enough wind to get under way until July 11, when a light northwest breeze enables d'Orvilliers to try a few general maneuvers and brings a smile of bleak satisfaction to his pessimistic face. Undertake a major engagement with these greenhorns? It's all he can do to keep them from ramming each other! "This maneuver, which was executed either badly or not at all, has confirmed my previous opinion that the greater part of the captains have no experience and little knowledge of most of the ships . . . It is too important that they should at least be able to assume their battle positions and maintain the proper distances before any encounter with Admiral Keppel."[4]

Not surprising: the King's ships have only been going out on maneuvers for a year, after spending the previous twelve lying at anchor developing arthritis. How many days has d'Orvilliers got left to haul his novices—like Chartres—over the hump from theory to practice? A naval officer is a mathematician, as far as compass, wind science, and sail physics are concerned; but he has to forget his textbooks and get the feel of the sea or he'll never be able to decide in a split second which sails to reef and which to furl, which are the best men to send aloft and which should stay with the guns.

And the French navy is rotten from stem to stern. The crews are undermanned and underfed, and suffering from endemic scurvy. The officers are a body weakened by a graft that failed to take: Colbert firmly established the "blues" (the non-noble captains of the merchant ships) or "paper officers" in positions as port officials and intendants, and Sartines has just stripped them of their privileges by merging "blues" and "reds" into a single rank in which blue takes precedence—but only as a color of blood. Neither seniority, efficiency, nor merit is any use to a commoner now; he is condemned never to rise above the rank of lieutenant commander of a frigate. The aristocrat-officers, sharing the same families, pleasures, and upbringing, have slammed down on top of the rest of the navy like a marble coffin lid—pink Trianon marble. Cold comfort to those who, like Malouet, have to sail all the way to Guiana to try—and fail—to achieve something. "On land as at sea, general, commander, sublieutenant, and naval guard, all [of the young aristocrats] mingle in a single group; they say 'tu' to each other like pals,"[5] and applaud the maneuver decided by their superior/pal/second mate as though it were a stroke of genius. This isn't even *esprit de corps* anymore, it's *esprit de classe,* the narrowest of all. The disgusted plebians were biting their tongues or disappearing. Philippe de Chartres (perhaps some masonic influence here?) is shocked to see the upper-crust nitwits treating the ex-"blues" who were holding the fort at Brest like some species of lower ape, and reminds them that Duguay-Trouin and Jean Bart* came out of the merchant navy. He invited "blues" to his table and told them, "Prince of the blood I may be, but I am honored to serve at your side."[6]

A "people's" prince? The fops begin looking at him askance. This must be another Orléans demagogue, you can see his game a mile off; d'Orvilliers gives him the cold shoulder, La Motte-Picquet starts gunning for him. He should learn his business instead of preaching to us. Just let us get him in a tight corner . . .

July 23. The English! There's a momentary lull in the heavy weather that has kept everybody quiet since the 13th: a bouquet of sails springs up on the horizon—Keppel ahoy! But the English admiral shows symptoms of suffering from the same obsession as the French, for both fleets hasten to envelop themselves in the squally mists—hide-and-seek, loser wins. The "generals" are in perfect agreement about "avoiding"—but some of their subordinates, who call it a crime to waste such an opportunity, decide to cheat. At first the admirals heave a sigh of relief, although they know it can't last forever. Then d'Orvilliers becomes increasingly anxious: five of his vessels have gone astray in the dark, and two, the *Duc-de-Bourgogne* and *Alexandre,* are among his most powerful ones; their absence will be cruelly felt by the "white and blue squadron." "The sea was too rough and the night too dark when the general ordered us to come about. The signals could not be seen by the entire army."[7]

From July 24 to 26 the supreme commanders cudgel their brains over a thorny problem in applied physics: knowing that the enemy fleet is, or ought to be, in a given direction, how does one "get the weather gauge of him" in order to have the advantage at the beginning of an engagement? Ever since

---

*Jean Bart (1650–1702), son of a merchant family from Dunkerque, began as a seaman and worked his way up, did service for Louis XIV, was ennobled in 1694 and made a squadron leader in 1697. Duguay-Trouin (1673–1736) had a somewhat similar career. [*Trans.*]

Tourville imposed the line-of-battle formation, the entire conduct of naval warfare has hinged on that. It can take days and days to catch the southwest or northeast breeze that will enable one line of twenty or thirty ships to bear down on another line at a faster clip, choosing their moment and angle of attack. It's a little as though thirty Bastilles were circling around thirty Châteaus de Vincennes, where Mirabeau was imprisoned. The connoisseurs sniff the wind like bad cooks: if God is with us, it will drop from heavy to moderate, passing through stiff, stormy, and fresh . . .[8]

"Fresh," from the west, on a fairly clear day, July 27. But Keppel's ships are to the west of the French fleet, and can steal their wind. Keppel has 2,284 guns, the French only 1,934. The two fleets rotate ponderously, following courses plotted on the ships of each of their "generals." Signal flags go zipping up and down the masts. Two herds of marine monsters, jockeying for position.

Eleven o'clock. Advantage to Keppel: his fleet has managed to catch the wind best, not full astern, when some of the sails cancel each other out, but on the quarter, between stern and beam. Every sail stands at an oblique angle to the ships, heeling slightly under the powerful hand of the wind that drives them toward the enemy at the speed of a galloping horse. The French see the English bearing down on them at the worst possible moment: they're in line too, but running before the wind, with their poops open to the assailant. He's going to overtake us! Faster and better placed, he'll run right down our line letting off his broadsides. The *Saint-Esprit,* sternmost ship of the "blue squadron," which is still at the rear, will take the first volleys, but we'll all be riddled . . . D'Orvilliers hasn't a moment to lose. Every commander aims his glass at the *Bretagne*'s mainmast, where the plays for the counterstroke are being called: two yellow pennants, one blue, one red. Zounds! Confounded tricky maneuver for such ill-trained crews: we're coming about! They mean to attack us from behind: we turn head on.

Every ship rotates almost in its tracks, nearly 180 degrees. The commands come cascading down from the quarterdeck of the *Saint-Esprit* and every other ship, hurling all available hands aloft. The mastodons shudder under the pressure of the strain imposed by rudder and yards, turned by hand so as to hug the wind, get as close to it as possible, master it, ravish it. And all the time taking care not to collide with the next ship and to keep together with everyone else in the line; for if any are outdistanced they'll be isolated, cut off from the main body, and swallowed up by the English pack like so many stray sheep.

Noon. The two vast moving curtains draw together, flags high. That of the French navy is a simple white rectangle.* Now Philippe, aboard the *Saint-Esprit,* is at the front of the line, the fleet's about-face having placed the

---

*Which later becomes the "white flag," emblem of the Royalists. At this time there is no "French flag" as such.

"blue squadron" in the vanguard. He is first to see the foremost English ship driving at him. All the others are sailing in single file behind, "jack over poop," that is, with the bow of one ship so close to the stern of the next that no other ship, however swift, can pass between them without being crushed to bits.*

The suspense is unbearable. Ordering his port guns to open fire as he draws level with the *Prince George,* the Duc de Chartres begins the Battle of Ouessant.

That one gesture, that little finger lifted between two nations, the opening of an artillery bombardment, is the only one he's allowed to perform. Did he suppose that in mid-ocean he'd be free? Why, he's almost as much a prisoner here as at Versailles; he's ruled by the mechanisms of naval warfare, which function without him and hold him up to the public eye as the high priest of this improvised liturgy—another stage performance. Making appearances, milord, always and forever, making appearances is the fate of princes of the blood. D'Orvilliers works out the overall strategy, La Motte-Picquet determines your squadron's tactics, and Montpeyroux-Roquefeuil commands the movements of your ship. You are left with one word to pronounce: "Fire!" A brutal thunder roars over the waves. The flames of parting shots, puffs of acrid smoke, and the thuds of impact. The two lines cross within firing range, each ship receiving in turn the courtesies of every one it passes. Kneeling in the bulwarks, sharpshooters fire on sight at the crews across the way, trying to pick out their officers. The English fire is more effective, again because they are better placed in relation to the wind: heeling slightly toward their firing side, and thus toward the enemy, their shots travel downward straight into the hull, and they're doing a lot of damage, even though they've had to close their bottom row of portholes because the sea was washing in. The French balls, inclined in the opposite direction, fly upward into the English sails, but when they hit a mast they can make an awful mess. Also, the French can spare far fewer people to man the guns because they need twice as many to sail against the wind. And their guns recoil onto the feet of the men serving them. And the searing cartridges roll back between-decks, where the smoke hangs heavily. The French are firing into cotton, the English are in the clear: all their rubbish, smoke included, goes into the sea. When the *Saint-Esprit* finds itself out of range, everybody is amazed to discover that this parade of death has lasted nearly half an hour.[9]

Philippe is less lucky than La Fayette: not even a scratch to show for his baptism by fire. Nevertheless, he is covered in compliments. Standing on the

---

*The distance between warships in line of battle was sixty meters, or the average length of one ship.

bridge, with the wide blue streamer of . . . the order of the Holy Spirit—that's a nice coincidence—cutting across his tall white silhouette, he has exposed himself to the enemy in true princely manner, chatting nonchalantly with his friend the Comte de Genlis and La Motte-Picquet. ("An admirable bravura," exclaims d'Orvilliers in his report.) It's not his fault if the English musketry and balls merely grazed his ship: only one man dead and four injured on the *Saint-Esprit*. Besides, Chartres thinks he's still on the hors d'oeuvre and is dying to get back in for the main course. The two lines, reeling slightly from their impact, initiate a fresh series of complicated movements in order to make contact again after this first-round draw—which will remain the substance of the match. "The Battle of Ouessant was nothing but a volley of shots."[10]

Three o'clock. Into the ring again, from a greater distance and in some disorder. The "blue squadron," back in the rear, strains every sail to regain its place in the line of fire, where the two control towers of the edifice, d'Orvilliers's and Keppel's admiral ships *Bretagne* and *Victory*,* trade some nasty blows in passing. A general hesitation ensues, long enough for both sides to relax their tight formation. A gap opens up between the main body of the English line and its last five ships. The chance of a lifetime. Was it La Motte-Picquet or the prince who was inspired to seize it? Both at once, no doubt. The "blue squadron" draws level with the laggards. All it would have to do is leave its own line, swing over to starboard† and plunge into the breach in the enemy ranks, attack their ships from astern and immobilize them in a cross fire . . . Five English cruisers out of commission, prisoners, maybe . . . A triumph.

No time to ask d'Orvilliers's permission, he's got more than he can handle back there on the *Bretagne*. Philippe takes it upon himself to give the order to his eleven ships. "According to this signal it was for the leading ship [the *Diadème*], commanded by M. de la Cardonnie, to begin the maneuver which the remainder were to follow."[11] Yes, but the smoke of battle, the misty weather, and then the jangled nerves . . . The message doesn't get through. The *Diadème* sails straight on and the *Conquérant* after her. Are they blind or stupid? They plod after the rest of the fleet like sheep, paying no heed to the orders of the *Saint-Esprit*, which has been placed at the rear of the line by the change of tack. One last resort: set them an example. The Duc de Chartres, "absolutely determined that his fleet should undertake this operation, fell off four points."** He breaks ranks. He prepares to head for the enemy. But he never makes it: d'Orvilliers has now shaken off the *Victory*—another draw—and is watching over his fleet like a mother hen; his jaw drops when he sees

*The famous ship on which Nelson will win and die at Trafalgar.

†Facing forward: starboard, the right side; port, the left.

**Meaning: veered about forty degrees away from the line. In naval terms the compass was divided into thirty-two "points," by which a ship's direction was determined.

the *Saint-Esprit* taking such a risk. Does he think it has made a false maneuver that will lead the isolated ship to its grave? Or maybe he realizes that Chartres is trying to set an example for the rest of the fleet to follow, and resolves to put a stop to any initiatives that might turn the prince into the hero of the day? A flock of signal flags scurries feverishly up the mast of the *Bretagne,* pulling back the pawn. To their intense annoyance, the *Saint-Esprit*'s officers see them, and Philippe obeys before any other ships have time to follow his lead. After one ten-minute lurch toward an inaccessible glory, he drops back in line.

The ships continue sniffing at one another and launching occasional volleys all through the endless summer afternoon, but without conviction. The "generals," meanwhile, are doing their sums: 1,196 men out of action on the English side, 407 of them dead. Less than half as many among the French: 517 wounded, 163 dead. No ships lost on either side. During the night Keppel slips away and returns to Portsmouth to lick his wounds, so the French proclaim themselves victorious—but they also head for Brest.*

FREDERICK II OF PRUSSIA

6

AUGUST 1778

The King's Eyes Were Moist

Nevertheless, the battle isn't a total loss for the King, since it gives him an opportunity to perform an exemplary figurative murder: the English may live to fight another day, but for Philippe de Chartres it's all over.

Who could have foreseen it on the evening of July 27 when he draws back into line, proud and angry? And at Brest, on the 29th, his longboat is cheered at the quay. "The thirty-two army staffs unanimously paid tribute not only to the excellent conduct of the Duc de Chartres, but even to the ability he displayed."[1] He ought to have been on his guard, though, against the flattering words of the Comte d'Orvilliers, who needs a scapegoat to cover his own inglorious attitude toward the battle. In the chronology of this triumphal march for a sick stomach, we can follow every step

*These figures make the battle sound like an English defeat, especially considering the English advantages of wind and angle of fire, but one-third of the English casualties are on board the *Victory* alone, which came off a very poor second in its bout with the *Bretagne,* and if that is left out of account the figures are much closer.

of the two-phase demolition—first the puffs of praise, then the pinprick
that spells death to the balloon.

July 30. D'Orvilliers sends Philippe to Versailles bearing official tidings of
the battle. Everyone agrees he's the right person for the job, and no one
thinks so more than himself. He's jubilant, so jubilant that he forgets his
humiliation and begins to take himself for a conqueror. But on the very
next day d'Orvilliers stabs him in the back with an unofficial report to Sartines in which he makes Philippe the cause of the semi-defeat: "I have
every reason to believe, considering the reverse order in which we fought,
that if the leader of the 'blue' squadron had responded to our signals more
promptly, Providence would have crowned our labors with a most glorious day."[2] A drop in the ocean; yet this tiny tinkle skipping along the
waves is a big fat lie. D'Orvilliers's version turns the facts back to front,
just as he turned his fleet back to front for the battle. After being prevented from making a bold bid with a strong hand, Chartres now becomes
the bungler who lost us the rubber.

But he is unaware of this reshuffling of the cards when he reaches Versailles during the night of August 3–4. Louis XVI is asleep and doesn't receive
him until eight in the morning, and then apathetically. The prince is struck by
the discrepancy between the vibrant world of the past few days in which he
finally felt he was *living,* and the disenchantment of Versailles. The distance
between life on shipboard and this debilitated court can only be measured in
light-years. Here, everything remotely connected with America is regarded
with suspicion or, worse, indifference. The important news here is that while
the king's ships were on the high sea between Brest and Ouessant, he "was
greatly incommoded by a sore throat which gave rise to some anxiety but
which terminated in a cold and colic lasting but a short time. The Queen also
suffered greatly from heart palpitations and difficulties in breathing, but she
is now better."[3] Is it her pregnancy? "My child moved for the first time on
Friday July 31 at half past ten in the evening. Since then it has been moving
frequently, which gives me great joy. I have not words to tell my dear maman
how much each movement adds to my happiness."[4] But this is not the only
reason for her jumpy nerves, and the happiness she speaks of is extremely
relative, for in the same letter she goes on to moan, "My head could not
contain all the thoughts assailing me" on the subject of the war that has just
broken out between Austria and Prussia. The queen's true malady is Bavaria.
"With the aid of the *philosophes**   and every manner of intrigue, the King of

---

Philosophes: loosely, the philosophers of the Enlightenment, who were not congenial to
traditional Christian beliefs, wanted tangible evidence and clarity of thought, respected science
and sympathized with humanist ideals, and believed that the moral nature of man could be
compassed in scientific terms. In particular, a group of French writers of various persuasions,

Prussia has ultimately contrived to win a great many supporters here, and at times I find myself compelled to put on a cheerful face when I assuredly have neither cause nor desire to do so." She can plainly see that everybody at Versailles is against her. The French have gone to war for the King of Prussia too many times in the past, and they're not eager to start again now for the Emperor of Austria—who has just put himself in the wrong, moreover, as his own mother admits, by acting like a sparrow with pretensions to eaglehood.

Maximilian Joseph, Elector of Bavaria, died with the year 1777 and left no direct heir. The senior branch of the Wittelsbachs is extinguished. The throne of Munich reverts to the Palatinate elector, Charles Theodore, who hates the thought of leaving his cosy little court in Mannheim, so Joseph II slips him a solution: why doesn't he just pass, as at whist? Through various cousinships, the Hapsburgs have as many claims to Bavaria as he. But it takes more than two to play whist, especially in central Germany where Prussia isn't about to buy the idea of an expanding Austria: Frederick, therefore, says thumbs down to that particular arrangement.

Joseph overrules him and sends his troops to occupy lower Bavaria—not because he wants Munich, but because he wants war; he's been driving for so long with the brakes on that he's about to set the whole machine on fire. Thereupon, his mother begins uttering loud cries in pacifist tones seldom heard among sovereigns: "What an ugly occupation is that of war, so contrary to humanity and happiness! . . . We have been a great power but we are one no longer. We must resign ourselves . . . Unfortunately, it is we who are at fault, for not speaking plainly, and indeed we are unable to do so because what we want is unjust . . . Better a mediocre peace than a victorious war."[5] Her forthrightness would be even more admirable if its object were not to humiliate that son of hers who was simultaneously declaiming, "If the Prussians take up arms, we shall teach them how to behave."[6] The instant Frederick hears that old refrain his aging bones stop aching. He grumpily hauls himself out of the big lumpy armchair which has grown into the shape of his body and which he deserts increasingly seldom. Since that youngster Joseph was provoking him . . . By July two wars have broken out, one between Prussians and Austrians and the other between Maria Theresa and her son. Frederick invades Bohemia. The empress asks nothing better than to yield to his superior forces. "We are the King's inferiors by forty thousand men."[7] She has long since measured the ineptitude of her totally decrepit generals Lascy and Laudon. As

influenced by seventeenth-century theorists such as Descartes and Locke—Diderot, Voltaire, Rousseau, d'Alembert, and many others were *philosophes* or related to them—who became increasingly concerned with social problems. Their writings were extremely controversial and influential. [*Trans.*]

for Joseph, she is not mistaken when she says he's bluffing. He's overreaching himself: he only really loves war in his dreams, and drops back into character at the sight of his first battles (and they are innocuous enough, but the Austrian army is being ravaged by a typhus epidemic). "It is certain that war is a horrible thing; the evils it causes are frightful. I can assure Your Majesty [his mother] that, whatever idea I may have had of it before, it fell far short of what I am seeing now."[8]

Maria Theresa doesn't need to be told twice; she sells out. Without asking her son's opinion or even letting him know, she sends an emissary, Baron von Thugut, to offer Frederick peace, or rather sue for it. "I should throw myself at his feet if that could bring him to end it."[9] "Wishing to save my States from the most cruel devastation, I must, at all costs, seek to withdraw from this war . . .* By making peace now I shall be charged with great pusillanimity, and I shall also make the King [of Prussia] seem even more grand . . . I own that my head spins from it all, and my heart has long since been utterly annihilated."[10] The conflict between this Oedipal mother and son is finally out in the open. Wild with rage at her interference, "the most mortifying imaginable," Joseph starts dreaming of wounds and fractures again, halts his retreating armies, and tries to mobilize the Empire with a series of extraordinary measures: conscription, new taxation. Maria Theresa digs in her heels: "Having begun this thankless task, I shall see it through to the end as I see fit, for it concerns you," she writes to the emperor, "and the monarchy. My old gray head can bear all. All blame can be laid upon it."[11]

Frederick II sits on the sidelines keeping score, and finds it all highly diverting. He lets the two heads of the Austrian eagle peck away at each other, and keeps Thugut dancing on a string. It looks as though Austria can only be saved by the intervention of her ally—France. Mercy-Argenteau† is trying to sell Louis a package deal: armed mediation, to be transformed into belligerence in the event of Prussian noncooperation. Wasn't it for just such occasions that an Austrian queen has been set upon the throne of France? Your play, Marie. Fine; but there's the rub: "The Queen continues to be gratified by expressions of deep affection on her husband's part, caresses and consideration and the most anxious concern. The King has entreated her to think of nothing but her own amusement, to banish any thought that might trouble the serenity of her heart and mind. To satisfy her desires he has given her freedom to spend whatever she likes, but this princess is forbidden to involve herself in affairs of state; and when, impelled by covert sentiments, she reveals her longing to speak of the war between her House and the King of Prussia, her husband intervenes, changes the subject or leaves the room." He's taken a dislike to

*Letter of August 6, 1778, to Marie Antoinette.
†Austrian ambassador to Versailles and secret adviser to Marie Antoinette.

Austria since his marriage, and nary a one of his ministers would dream of trying to talk him out of it. Necker and Vergennes have already let themselves in for one war, with England, and that's more than enough for them. France can't afford to fight on two fronts. Maurepas himself, although anxious to keep on the queen's right side, is immovable on this subject—even if it means incurring her permanent displeasure, which it does: she never forgives him. "M. de Maurepas still has a little of that accursed fear which has done so much harm in our affairs." (From Marie Antoinette to her mother, August 14.) She puts up the best fight she can, as a loyal servant of Austria who would gladly send her subjects to be slaughtered for the sake of "her House." She shakes Maurepas like an old plum tree; the days when she took only a timid interest in politics are long since gone. "The Queen, raising her voice,* said to him: 'This, sir, is the fourth or fifth occasion on which I have spoken to you of serious matters, and you have never been able to make me any other reply than your customary subterfuges. I have kept patience until now, but things are becoming too serious, and I no longer wish to put up with such refusals.' "[12] Afraid she'll have to, poor dear! She's got more than Maurepas to contend with: there's Louis XVI himself, who takes advantage of this opportunity to refine his natural style by meeting her demands with an opacity that becomes increasingly impenetrable as she becomes increasingly insistent. If he finds her in mid-tantrum after receiving some dispatch from Maria Theresa, for example, as happened on July 13, why, he gently plays her along, he sheds a little tear, but he doesn't budge. Observers note that "the King's eyes were moist." "I would do anything in the world to relieve your distress, but my ministers have stayed my hand. The good of the realm will not permit me to do more [for Austria] than I have already done."[13] For Marie Antoinette, these days may have marked the peak of her purdah phase: shut up and have that baby.

*Mercy-Argenteau's official report to his government, on July 17.

7

OCTOBER 1778

You'll Be Immortalized Fore'er
At the Opéra

As a result, this is not the right moment for an enthusiastic reception of Philippe de Chartres. It's the Danube Louis XVI has got on his mind, not the Atlantic. If the messenger were at least coming to announce a triumph—but is that all? A couple of sword thrusts? "Our victory did not delight the King excessively, and still less M. de Sartines. They would have preferred the enemy ships to have been captured and sunk, and the enemy to have been pursued into his very retreat."[1] "The day after the arrival of the Duc de Chartres, a *Te Deum* was sung at the Court parish church. Many people imagined that it was in honor of our little naval victory. They were mistaken, however, for it was only to give thanks to God for the Queen's pregnancy, which has now reached the fifth month without mishap."[2]

Versailles, thus, takes no notice. But there's still Paris—that will be a different story. On that same day, Philippe reaches the Palais Royal, and this Versailles of the Orléanses, at least, responds with the long-awaited acclamations. A shade lacking in spontaneity, no doubt: "The cafés of the Palais Royal district and the Swiss at the gates* sent a letter around that morning to all the houses overlooking the garden, inviting them to illuminate their windows and roofs, as they themselves were doing, in honor of the Duc de Chartres."[3] On the right bank of the Seine, a considerable population lives off the Orléans family, from day laborers and *oublie*†-vendors to booksellers, café-keepers, pimps, prostitutes, and gambling-house managers, not counting the thousand and one parasites directly employed by the Household. They've been so yearning to have a reason to cheer one of their own princes, for once! As he alights from his coach Philippe is presented with the *Bulletin de Parnasse,* the first Parisian newspaper to publish details of the operations at Ouessant. It

---

*The hundred-odd men in uniforms, like those of the Vatican Swiss Guards, who stood at the gates of the Palais Royal and acted as go-betweens for the people of Paris and the House of Orléans.

†Little cylindrical waffles, the French fries of that age.

greatly exaggerates his role, depicting the *Saint-Esprit* as fighting off "seven large enemy ships" single-handed and Chartres as urging his men forward in the teeth of death . . . He doesn't contradict the story, and he's wrong; it's asking for trouble—but this long-deferred incense has gone to his head. "The prince had great difficulty making his way through the crowd that had come to greet him and the throng of courtiers on the main staircase. The people would not disperse until he and the duchesse appeared on the balcony, to cries of 'Long live the conqueror!' "[4] Is it his fault if they're giving *Orphée* that evening at the Opéra? All he has to do is go through a door and he's in his private box. "He was received with cheers, swelling up so repeatedly that there was scarce time to hear the opera. In the evening, while Their Most Serene Highnesses were at supper, the musicians of the orchestra played a concert during which messieurs Larrivée, Gelin, Moreau and all the ladies of the chorus sang this fine passage from *Pyrame et Thisbé:*

> Honorez un héros, digne sang de vos rois,
> Honorez un héros que la gloire couronne . . .

> [Honor a hero, worthy blood of your kings,
> Honor a hero crowned in glory . . .]

In the heat of the moment Moliné, Gluck's librettist—"such a nice little poet"—improvises a couplet for them to the tune of the chorus of *Vertumne et Pomone:*

> Grand héros que la gloire guide,
> La France te revoit vainqueur . . .
> . . . Nos plus beaux jours sont dus à ta valeur.[5]

> [Great hero by glory led,
> France sees you victor once more . . .
> . . . Our finest hours are owed to your valor.]

At Versailles the following day these improvisations cause an unpleasant itching in the ears of the King and princes of the senior branch, already aching from the din of the fireworks set off under Philippe's window at the expense of Sophie Arnould, the actress. "The illumination blazed most brightly, and the promenade walk, always much frequented in this season, drew even more people than usual that evening . . . His Most Serene Highness responded most touchingly to all these homages, and kindly allowed all the young ladies to embrace him."[6]

He can keep the kisses, it's the crowds we don't like. The reality gap now is not between Brest and Versailles, but Versailles and Paris. For a century and a half, coinciding with the permanent castration of the Orléans family, the Court of France has succeeded in stifling the capital by reducing its functions

to merrymaking and executions. Now, has this Orléans taken it into his head
to play at being "king of Paris"? God alone knows what might be born of such
a union.* "[At Versailles] the young prince is criticized for having sought the
adulation of Paris . . . It is felt that M. d'Orvilliers did not dare refuse him
permission to bring the news."[7]

Whereupon, enter Sartines. That's what he's there for, he's built his entire
career on a few gestures like this, easing out of the shadows at the right
moment to do a favor to the person with the most power. D'Orvilliers has
given him the ammunition. He orders the *Gazette de France* to print "An
Extract from the Journal of the King's Naval Army" which sets the story
straight, at least according to the version of the court and "red" officers. This
is an exceptional procedure, for custom forbade any reference to the words
and deeds of princes of the blood in this sort of unofficial journal without first
obtaining their approval. The unprecedented publication fires the opening
shot in the new war between the King and the House of Orléans. It hits its
target, knocking off balance an impulsive young prince who was unable to
keep his modesty in the face of his sycophants' praise. Calumny breaks into
couplets of heroic doggerel. The counter-story is accompanied by a counter-
song, twelve or fifteen verses, possibly from the hand of Maurepas himself:

Chers badauds, courez à la fête,	[Beloved idlers, run to the feast,
Pâmez-vous, criez à tue-tête:	Roll your eyes, scream like a beast,
Brava! Brava!	"Brava! Brava!"
Cette grande action de guerre	At this heroic feat of war
Est telle qu'on n'en voit guère	Of a kind you'll witness never more
Qu'à l'Opéra . . .	Outside the Opéra . . .
Grand prince, poursuis ta carrière,	Noble prince, surge to the fore,
Franchis noblement la barrière	Nobly fling back the noble door
De l'Opéra.	Of the Opéra.
Par de si rares entreprises	By endeavor so high and rare
A jamais tu t'immortalises	You'll be immortalized fore'er
A l'Opéra.[8]	At the Opéra.]

The escalation is swift: first Chartres is accused of nothing worse than
lending a complacent ear to words of praise. Next, of having fished for them.
It is affirmed that he forced d'Orvilliers to return to Brest on July 29, because
all he could think of were his laurels at the Opéra. But did you know that he
actually aborted the battle? Why, you can read it in *Gazette de France,* where
it tells how he sent his squadron off on a different tack. Vergennes authenti-
cates that rumor in a letter to his ambassador in Spain: "It is most unfortunate

*What is born is the 1830 July monarchy, brought about, through a convergence of the
people of Paris, La Fayette, and the son of Philippe Egalité, by the stupidity of Charles X—and
the intelligence of a few bankers.

that the ships of the squadron of M. le Duc de Chartres either did not perceive or did not understand the signal of M. le Comte d'Orvilliers; the enemy's rear guard would have been cut off."9 D'Orvilliers's lie becomes the minister's official version; Philippe's courageous gesture is turned into a blunder. And then—what could his motive have been? Another two or three steps and we get the illuminating answer, which explains everything and closes all accounts: cowardice. If Philippe didn't see his general's orders, it was because he didn't want to see them, and if he didn't want to see them, it was because he was afraid to get involved in a battle.

A cowardly Orléans. Divine surprise, gift of heaven! It had never been possible to blacken them on that score before, because their princes, however vulnerable they might be in other areas, always fought like lions. Homosexual, womanizing, corrupt, devious, avaricious, dim-witted, that'll do for a start; but nobody could deny they were brave in battle. At last, somebody's going to be able to deny it: signed d'Orvilliers, Sartines, Maurepas, Vergennes = Louis XVI.

The calumny invades Versailles on August 10, occupies Paris by the 15th, and surrounds the Palais Royal where the prince's partisans, who had been about to hoist him onto their shoulders at the beginning of the month, are now forced to defend him with blows of unsheathed libel. It pursues him to Brest, to which he returns on August 8 in hopes of another battle, and finds himself treated with the frigid respect accorded to the contaminated. From August 17 to September 18 he can do nothing to defend himself, the *Saint-Esprit* having gone out again with the "naval army," for a long, vague, and vain excursion "in the season of mists and gales."10 On September 21 he rejoins an about-faced Paris.

Greeted icily by most of those who were hailing him less than two months before, Philippe clutches at half-smiles and begins to be haunted by whispers. His father-in-law the "Grand Admiral," jealous of a son-in-law with pretensions to actually *sailing,* does not take up his cause. The fact that "M. le Duc de Penthièvre, rather than attending the Opéra with his son-in-law and daughter, went to give thanks to God at St. Eustache"11 is carefully publicized. A few friends in the Palais Royal, however, especially the Comte de Genlis, swim steadily against the stream. He was standing at Philippe's side on the deck, he witnessed his bravery, and he trumpets it aloud. From Brest, La Motte-Picquet and most of the officers echo him. They would gladly let Philippe be accused of flustering, but not cowardice—it's too idiotic. Louis XVI sends the Chevalier d'Escars* to Brest to look into the matter and bring back, if possible, enough evidence to hang Philippe; but the chevalier (although an intimate friend of the

*Duc des Cars and minister of Louis XVIII under the Restoration.

Comte d'Artois) returns bearing reports that are, on the contrary, highly injurious to d'Orvilliers. He whitewashes the Duc de Chartres of every charge against him, including the famous allegedly abortive maneuver. He is an honest man. His friends berate him:

"You have just proved yourself a poor courtier, Chevalier, by acquitting a prince whom everyone else convicts . . ."

"Upon my soul, then, let the Court and Town reform the opinion of the entire naval army, of the navy itself . . . [He was forgetting d'Orvilliers; but d'Orvilliers was playing a double game, and only accusing Philippe in secret.] All I have done was be its echo."[12]

A swiftly muted echo: Chartres is given no chance to speak in his own defense. After belling the cat in the *Gazette de France,* Sartines forbids publication of a revised version, which might be prejudicial to d'Orvilliers's reputation. "The King gave out that he wished nothing to be printed on the Ouessant affair."[13] Philippe is cornered between a fleet condemned to idiocy by its "general" and a public opinion that is making him look ridiculous. He escapes by sidestepping the issue, by abdication; it suits his dilettantish style. The one positive act he ever perpetrated seems likely to ruin his career: they've managed to make him well and truly seasick—he capitulates. In October he writes a bitter, dignified letter to Louis XVI. "As the result of my desire to serve Your Majesty on the seas, I see my father-in-law's good name compromised, together with my children's future, my wife's happiness, my fame, my reputation." He asks leave to resign from the navy and enter the land army. In order to command a position worthy of his rank, he suggests that the office of "colonel general of light regiments" be created for him.[14]

Jubilation at court: why didn't you say so! Louis XVI signs with both hands. It's a bauble, they invent them every year to flatter somebody or other. An honorary title giving no chance for action, hence for real popularity. Let him be honored in it, forgotten and buried in it. We'll be calling him "colonel general of light regiments," will we? Well, everybody knows which regiments *that* means: the next time he appears at the Opéra, where nobody cheers, "people had the unkindness to point out that the Duc de Chartres, speaking scarcely a word to his adorable wife the duchesse, left his box to go gadding from place to place, and finally settled in the box of the Prince de Soubise, which is ever filled with dancers and other nymphs from his seraglio."[15] A far cry now, the shoals of Ouessant. He's toeing the line again, their line. Back in the fold, the kennel of princes: a box at the Opéra. The Battle of Ouessant may not have been a great victory over the English, but it has made possible the conquest of an Orléans. One more out of the way.

MIRABEAU/JUPITER,
WIELDING THUNDERBOLTS

8

OCTOBER 1778   SOPHIE IN COSTUME

All That Was Estimable in Me

A heartrending cry reaches Maurepas's ears in November 1778—it's Mira-
beau-the-desperate, beseeching from the fastness of his prison tower: "The
political events which have occurred since my detention assuredly require
that troops be sent to America, perhaps to the Indies. I implore you to
have me transferred to one or the other of those countries. There can
never be too many men for such deadly work and I must be worth as
much as a common soldier."[1] He's been shut up in the Donjon de Vincennes since June 7, 1777—another one who needs to live so badly that
he's ready to die for it. But Maurepas will give him no answer. "Ministers
nowadays are like walls," the Marquise de Sade writes to her husband,
who is Mirabeau's cousin—also locked up, a few cells down the corridor,
although neither is aware of the other's presence, and also vociferating:
"When, great God, shall I be extracted from this tomb in which I have
been buried alive? . . . For me here, I have nothing but my tears and my
cries, and no living soul to hear them."[2] Because no living soul wants to
hear them. There's none so deaf . . .

"The unfortunate are always in the wrong," Mirabeau writes to Sophie
de Monnier. "Wrong to be wrong, wrong to say so, wrong to need others and
wrong to be unable to do anything for them in return."[3] It would be obtrusive
to inform the king that the involuntary guests he is harboring in his châteaus
carry ingratitude to the point of complaint. "The great and the princes are
lying children who say unto those who have eyes: See not! . . . Tell us things
that are pleasing to us."*

The King and his ministers are not the only ones who will not hear the
lamentations of Gabriel-Honoré.† There is also his wife, Emilie de Covet-
Marignane, Comtesse—oh, so slightly?—de Mirabeau. Her husband's public

---

*Allegedly but unidentifiably biblical, quoted by Mirabeau in *Des Lettres de cachet,* p. 34.
†Gabriel to Sophie de Monnier; Honoré to everybody else.

adultery with Sophie has given her the leading role. And then her temperament inclines her to forgetfulness. When she went home to her father at
Marignane, she was putting two hundred leagues* between herself and her
husband, but she was removing herself from far more than his person—it was
all the desolation of failure she was leaving behind. In 1778 it is hard to believe
they had been living together four years before.

And yet she wasn't overjoyed to turn her back on Bignon, she had grown
fond of its rustic little aristocratic society. And then the proximity of Paris
. . . But in the end she got on the Friend of Man's nerves. He doesn't care
for birdwomen and, although he wouldn't admit it, he resents the fact that she
doesn't stand up more staunchly—even to him—for the husband he has pater-
nally determined to destroy. The day of their separation he makes no attempt
to hide his relief. "The countess left yesterday, at long last . . . She became
entangled in her own snares, wanting one thing, no longer wanting the other,
but in truth she was in agony at having to leave this place, and employed every
little ruse of her sex, illness, etc., in the hope of being asked to stay . . . It will
be a cold day somewhere before I begin playing chaperon to a young woman
again."[4]

She quickly readjusts to her little Provençal kingdom, nestling back into
her cosy niche as a virtually widowed only daughter, more or less mistress of
herself. Her father never forbids her anything; she gets her inconsistency from
him. "I do not deny that there is something noble dangling about his person,
like the abbess's psalter that can't find anywhere to perch, but I see no jot or
tittle of character . . . He is neither the beginning nor the middle, nor yet the
end of a man."† Emilie might well be glad to be back in his lap again: in
Holland Mirabeau had published a memorandum in which he swore that she
had been unfaithful first, with young Gassaud; and the Friend of Man, a
thoroughgoing phallocrat, had given his daughter-in-law to understand that he
held this against her—meanwhile pursuing his fugitive son as hotly as ever.
Back at home, nobody dreamed of criticizing her. There were many young
men who aspired to follow in Gassaud's footsteps: Emilie was only twenty-six.
The tone of her letters begins to raise eyebrows at Bignon, when she describes
herself as "surrounded by fresh bridegrooms and eligible young men . . . One
feels that everybody here is full of joy. And consequently there have had to
be countless horseraces, dances, charades and amusements . . ."[5] Summer finds
her fluttering from château to château in the foothills of the Provençal Alps:

---

*A league is a somewhat indefinite linear distance, say 2 1/2 to 3 miles; it was the ordinary
unit of measurement in those days. [*Trans.*]

†According to the Marquis de Mirabeau, in one of his ineffable letters to his brother the bailli.
A psalter is a large monastic rosary. [A bailli was an agent of the king whose powers were very
broad, entailing supervision of local officers, centralization of revenues, convening of quarterly
court sessions, etc.; but by this time their functions were largely honorary.—*Trans.*]

Tourves, Tourrette, Vence—and Le Tholonet, whenever she wants to be near Aix or Marseilles.

Another butterfly, a huge, shuddering one—her husband Mirabeau—is pinned down in the outskirts of Paris on the second floor of the Donjon de Vincennes, to which Isabeau de Bavière used to repair four hundred years earlier in order to debauch in peace. The setting is almost unchanged, except that what represented the ultimate in comfort for a queen in 1350 has become a Gehenna for the noble prisoners of the eighteenth century. On that day when he first climbed nearly half the two hundred thirty-seven steps "of a tortuous, narrow, precipitous staircase . . . lit by the feeble gleam of a truly sepulchral lantern, seeing bolts and bars on all sides," Gabriel felt as though he were leading his own funeral procession and that behind him marched the ghosts of all the famous people who had been imprisoned there: that king of Navarre who was later to become Henri IV; then the two Vendômes, his bastards; and Beaufort, "king of the markets"; and the cardinal de Retz, and the grand Condé, and a Conti, and a Longueville; and Fouquet for his wealth, and Madame Guyon for her piety, and Diderot for his impiety. Mirabeau is no exception. That's his one consolation in this living death. He describes in minute detail, and not without pride, that tall tower* "built so stoutly that it still shows not the faintest trace of wear; it would take battery cannon, of the largest caliber, to breach it;[6] the moats are forty feet deep and twenty paces wide, the walls sixteen feet thick, the vaults thirty"; the complicated system of doors barring the only entrance to the halls: "each, armed with two bars having three locks apiece, opens across the one after it, so that the second door bars the first and the third the second." Depression gets the better of pride, however, when he comes to "the dark panes that let through only a few weak rays of light" and "the intersecting bars, crossing and recrossing beyond reach." "At last the poor wretch comes to his lair; in it he finds a pallet, two chairs with seats of straw, often of wood, a pot which is almost always cracked, a table smeared with grease. And what else? Nothing."[7] This is Mirabeau's sixth prison.† Apparently it has finally taught him what PRISON is.

Emilie, meanwhile, has chosen the Château du Tholonet** as her favorite, and placed it at the increasingly confined center of her graceful gyrations. An immense estate covered in dark green pine and cork oak, like a huge verdant pool surrounded by the scorching rocks. The main building is all bumps and

*Fifty-two meters.

†After the Fort of Ré, the Château d'If, the Fortress of Joux, the Château de Dijon, and the Veerbeterhuis of Amsterdam.

**It still exists and can be visited, by taking the D17 eight kilometers out of Aix. In summer a festival is held in its celebrated paved courtyard, as part of the festival of Aix-en-Provence.

lumps, no style but every convenience: twelve three-room suites heaped together any old how lodge the guests who foregather in the drawing rooms, armory, and principal apartments of the owners, the Marquis de Galliffet (Prince de Martigues), and his son the comte*—two men wholly engrossed in the arduous task of spending five hundred thousand livres a year† amassed for them by the Negroes deported to their plantations in Santo Domingo. They're only two leagues east of Aix, from which Emilie can come in an hour by coach, along the Saint-Maximin road. She turns right into a long avenue shaded by tall elms, "whose curve unfolds nobly across a graceful vale cheered and refreshed by a slender brook."[8] At the end of the drive she finds a waterfall and Roman ruins fancied up in the taste of the day. Next, defended by a superb wrought-iron grill, comes the vast paved courtyard, with the chapel on the right (for servants), and on the left—brand-new, bright and shiny—the trinket-theater (for gentlefolk). Coming down the stone steps, arms outstretched to Emilie, the man who had it built: Comte Louis-François-Alexandre de Galliffet, thirty years old, "a man of fine manners, an accomplished dancer, who dotes upon display."[9] The chosen one. The young woman seems to have a penchant for musketeers. First Gassaud, now Galliffet. This one, it is true, no longer has the right to call himself a musketeer because they have ceased to exist: the Comte de Saint-Germain abolished them in one of his fits of reformitis. The King's Household nowadays is composed solely of his personal guards (noble), the French Guards, and the Swiss Guards. Galliffet has no cause for complaint, however: he was demobilized at the age of twenty-six, with a pension—in case he ran short, maybe? He has been competing for her with another needy soul, the Comte de Valbelle, who has reconstituted the opulence of the High Middle Ages in his Château de Tourves; he even holds a court of love there, but the scepter passes from one fair hand to the next a little too quickly for Emilie's taste—she aspires to a more durable sovereignty.** Galliffet won her by offering her the pretty theater of Le Tholonet, where he hires professionals partly to act with Emilie but mainly to boost her ego by enabling her to outshine her girl friends, all of whom are slightly dizzy—the Marquise de Clapiers, Madame de Boisgelin, the comtesses de Grasse and du Bausset. She performs twice a week, she is admired, she is

*The famous general and grand butcher of the Commune descends from a junior line of this family. [The Commune of Paris was an insurrectionary government that took over Paris from March to May 1871.—*Trans.*]

†2.5 million new francs [$500,000]. [A livre was a French money of account, divided into twenty sous or sols.—*Trans.*]

**The courts of love, held chiefly in the regions of the *langue d'oc* from the twelfth to the fifteenth century, were sorts of tribunals of amorous casuistry whose supreme judge, always a *châtelaine,* handed down verdicts on issues of amorous or even amical conduct arising between barons, poets, and *précieuses,* in a kind of permanent party. This one was a reconstruction, like the balls at which people dressed in the style of Henri III.

applauded. At last she is the queen of a court of love, and she owes it all to Galliffet. Why should she be ungrateful? After all, the "code of courtly love" established by the decrees of those intensely languishing assemblies of the thirteenth century has acquired force of law for these latter-day ladies, and it tells us that on the question of whether love can exist between lawfully wedded persons—one of the major causes at issue—the court of love of Champagne replied in the negative.[10]

Everything Mirabeau has to eat at Vincennes "is horribly nauseating, and for that very reason positively unhealthy . . . Tough veal, boot-sole mutton, beef that has been cooked twice, or else is half raw when it has been used only once for the soup; this is the prisoner's unvarying fare, if you except Thursdays when pastry is given, which, thanks to the sloth of the servants, is never more than half-baked. These dried-up and ill-chosen viands are always drowned in a quantity of vegetables and lumpy sauce devoid of all seasoning . . . The very sight of the sauces makes one's stomach turn . . . Three-fourths of the week, the prisoners are given pieces of neck of beef for the soup course, and the first course on a certain day each week is beef liver swimming in onions, and on another day it is tripe . . . I say nothing of the lean* diet. Anyone knows that even more skill is required to combine the ingredients properly then than on meat days. They give us vegetables, herring, ray . . . The wine is not drinkable."[11]

After a year and a half of this diet he can take no more. "My health is not good. My circumstances are too violent, especially considering my age and physical and moral temperament, for me not to suffer. The soul is wearing out its envelope." He is racked by attacks of colic nephritis and nasal hemorrhages, and the worst of all is that he is going blind, or at least he seriously fears so. "It is hard to be compelled to don spectacles before the age of twenty-nine. But it is harder still to see through a maze of black specks, the imminent and virtually infallible harbingers of blindness. I own that I cannot calmly contemplate the loss of my sight,"[12] even though having it gives him no greater joy than to read "a small number of frequently mismatched volumes lent by an old Jesuit father. It is forbidden to show the list of these books; the prisoner must name one at random."[13] At least the officials have deigned to supply him with ink, a pen, and paper. "All the fire of my heart is confined and cannot break out, and all my ardent and almost unrestrainable faculties are in chains and have no nourishment; and this only makes my head the more active. Work is my only means of staving off the horde of feelings and sensations that course through me . . . Whatever I do is too far beneath my themes, my ideas and

---

*That is, the 120 to 130 days each year, counting Lent, Fridays, Ember Days, and the feasts of Corpus Christi or the Virgin, on which meat was not eaten by Roman Catholics.

my views, and the little decent work I produce is purchased at the cost of my life . . . It is cruel to have to tell oneself: *E fornito il mio tempo a mezzo gli anni,* * but such is my fate. My career has reached its term at an age when other men are but commencing theirs. Nature bestowed upon me faculties for traveling farther and higher than they; but if adversity fortifies strong souls, it slays the genius."[14]

All the same, he makes full use of the weapons they've left him. For La Fayette the sword, for Mirabeau—the pen. "I scorn my birth and every man of quality in the world. I know not one who is worth the great writers who won their living by their pen."[15] "Without books I should soon be dead or mad."[16] "Therefore I write, or read fourteen or fifteen hours a day."[17]

What does he write? Letters to Sophie—sizzling, nagging, domineering, full of drivel. A very lengthy *Mémoire à son père* containing, beneath the defendant's plea, the elements of an autobiography on which later historians will draw. Translations of Homer, Ovid, Tacitus. A treatise on the French language. A scheme for the improvement and embellishment of Paris, calling for sidewalks and a system of plumbing. "Care must be taken of those who cannot work . . . The true poor in the capital city are those one never sees. Who imagines that the district authorities ever probe those labyrinths of pain? . . . I have always believed, and always shall, that indifference to injustice is treason and cowardice."[18] But his major work in 1778, for its import if not for its literary value, is *Des Lettres de cachet et des prisons d'Etat,* the third revolutionary book of his life, following the *Essai sur le despotisme* and the *Avis aux Hessois.*†

A shapeless heap with no head or tail, an outline improvised as he goes along, two unequal sections, a perpetual turning back on himself: the exact opposite of a great book. In it, Mirabeau gives final proof that he is no writer —and he also gives the prison system a beating. Part of his depression stems from the fact that in this field he can't measure up to his father, and his critical faculties are too keen for him not to be aware of it. Many of the chapters in this relatively short work (235 octavo pages in large print) are devoted to settling the hash of M. de Rougemont, the prison governor, who was feathering his nest on the side and took fright at every exception to the rules—but that was why he'd been put there, after all. Mirabeau focuses so much of his resentment on him that he transforms the man into an ogre; he dissipates his

---

*My time is run ere half my days.

†*Des Lettres de cachet* is published by Fauche at Neuchâtel in 1782, subtitled: "posthumous work composed in 1778," bearing no signature, and mendaciously claiming to have been printed in Hamburg. It is curious to note that under nobiliary privilege Mirabeau, who was otherwise rather harshly treated by the governor of Vincennes, was able to keep this load of dynamite in his cell and walk out with it in his suitcase.

rage over a great cause by hurling insults at a little man. What remains is a volley of poignant outcry and an attempt to write a documented indictment of the growing abuse of the royal "gracious pleasure" obtaining in France— as opposed to the *habeas corpus* and inalienable rights of the English citizen. The *Essay on Despotism* stuck to generalizations and could be applied to any tyrant. *Des Lettres de cachet* aims at a target as precise as Damiens's* blade: the régime of Louis XVI. "As though man were not entitled to use EVERY MEANS, without exception, to break his chains!" Sentences like that are written in blood. They vibrate like eyewitness accounts. This is a failure as a book, but it bears the stamp of human experience—whence the force of statements in which a legal dispute becomes the foundation for a political demand. Mirabeau's historical character is born with the turn of a page, when he affirms that "to be just, legitimate, binding, in a word truly law, the law must bear the seal of free and general consent," and calls for nothing less than free assemblies of the people: "In any State whose citizens have no share in the legislative power, through the delegation of representative bodies freely elected by the greater part of the nation† and subject to control by their electorate, there is and can be no public liberty."[19]

Des Lettres de cachet: less a book than a gesture—the only political act a prisoner can perform.

And as though to bestow exceptional solemnity upon his gesture, Gabriel-Honoré dedicates it to his son. Not to Sophie; leave the women, those adorable and cumbersome creatures, out of this—we'll keep it among Mirabeaus. "And you, my son, whom I have never embraced since you were in your cradle, you whose anguished lips I watered with my tears on the very day of my arrest,** with a pang in my heart that told me I should not see you again: I can have little claim upon your affections, as I have had no part in your education or your happiness . . . I do not know if I would have been a good father . . . When you read this I shall probably be no more, but in this work you will find all that was estimable in me: my love for truth and justice, my hatred of adulation and tyranny. O my son, avoid the failings of your father, and let his faults be lessons to you . . . But imitate his courage. Vow eternal war on despotism. Ah, if ever you can compose with it, flatter it, invoke it, serve it, may death strike you down before your time! Yes,

---

*Robert-François Damiens (1715–1757), wanting to "warn" Louis XV and recall him to his duty, gave him a slight prick with a knife in 1757; he was arrested, subjected to appalling torture, and drawn and quartered. [*Trans.*]

†Not "the whole nation," we note: this patrician qualification maintains the dispossessed status of those who are not eligible to vote. Nevertheless, the term *electorate* is striking.

**At Manosque, on September 18, 1774, after the fracas at Grasse. Mirabeau's little Victor was then eleven months old.

it is with a firm voice that I pronounce this dreadful vow."[20]

According to Mirabeau these lines were written during the summer of 1778, thus *before.* If he wrote them *after,* what an incredible ham! There's no way of knowing for sure. However, he adds a note by way of postscript at the foot of this high-flown tirade: "My child had already ceased to exist when I dedicated this work to him! And I did not know it! And the first news I ever heard of my son was that he was dead!"[21]

The last of the Mirabeaus dies on October 8, 1778.

People had forgotten they ever had a son. Only one person in both their families gave any thought to little Victor, and that was the boy's grandfather, the Friend of Man; but even his interest was dictated by nothing but "postero-mania"—the child remained the sole heir to the name. The virility of Honoré's younger brother Boniface seems to have been absorbed into his fat.

We catch glimpses of a long-term plan filtering through the Marquis de Mirabeau's persecution of his elder son. The Friend of Man never cared two hoots about him except as the indispensable progenitor, and the instant Gabriel-Honoré had legally procreated his father fell on him like a ton of bricks, and would have had him strangled if they had been living in Turkey. Not that Vincennes is a whole lot better. The child alone matters, and it, at least, doesn't have a swollen head; the Friend of Man is going to be able to turn it into an "oeconomist," fashion it in his own image. Therefore, he mustn't be too nasty to his daughter-in-law, the genetrix; he'll confiscate her, if possible, to serve as a tame wet nurse. But she isn't having any. She fancies a life of her own, she takes lovers, she gives out that she wouldn't mind being free to remarry. She's gone over to the rebels too. He packs her off back to her father, but wrapped in layers of tissue paper, because he's got plans to retrieve little Victor—whom he has never seen—and bring him up in his hothouse at Bignon.

Biography of a wisp of grass: Victor-Gabriel-Emmanuel de Mirabeau* was born at Marignane on another October 8, in 1773. Six months later, at Manosque, somebody else was already looking after him—the family of his mother's lover, the Gassauds, while his parents tore each other apart or made love to pass the time. Once the father was in the Château d'If and the mother at Bignon, the Gassauds kept him. He was nicknamed Gogo. He was endearing. He showed, it seems, that precocious gravity which is seen, after the fact, as a portent of early death. His father had known only a tiny babbling creature, and hardly had time to bother about him during his subsequent adventures.

---

*Christian names stamped children with the mark of family domination (at all levels of society) as firmly as the shoulder-brand of galley slaves. Victor is the paternal grandfather, Emmanuel the maternal grandfather; Gabriel, sandwiched between them, the father.

After leaving Bignon, his mother picked him up like a discarded toy. "I found my child more or less as I could wish him, that is, large, fat, tall for his age [three years], robust, and with a very good appetite . . . He is very gentle, loves everyone around him, even all the little girls in Manosque, however dirty they may be. He is not at all difficult, although he is very particular about his person, and washes his hands every time he remembers. He very sweetly does not demand as much of his little mistresses (that is how he calls them); and I assure you nothing can entertain me more than to see how respectfully he offers them his arm when going for a walk. He greeted me coldly."[22] How was he supposed to understand that she was his mother? So far Emilie was just another of the grand ladies who patted him on the head and dragged him from château to château. He is fond of Le Tholonet, because there he can "try to play the fop on stage whenever he manages to crawl across it with Galliffet's little girl." They give him lots of little parts to play. Nobody ever mentions his father. They prepare him for the idea of going to Bignon to meet his grandfather. And from Provence to the Gâtinais, Marignane and Mirabeau teeth begin to bare in preparation for the big battle for control of the vast "properties" piling up on top of his small head. Wasted effort: in the spring of 1778 he falls ill.

Apathy, fever, impossible to find out anything more. Emilie's letters to the marquis and to Caroline du Saillant* are nothing but a recital of her own sufferings. One wonders if there was a doctor at Le Tholonet, or if Victor didn't die from a sort of incompatibility with life. He had matured a great deal in the last year. "He seldom laughed, and could not understand how anyone could do an unreasonable thing. He was utterly amazed at me for laughing out of turn, or being frivolous. At the beginning of his illness he saw one of the women near him laughing. He thought it was at him, and said to her, 'What is there to laugh at in a sick child?' He had a Bible, which he loved the way other children love their toys."[23] His mother is heartbroken at the thought of having to cancel the grand entertainment planned for the little patient's fifth birthday. She is to be the star of the occasion. For weeks she's been rehearsing a leading role in honor of the day. The child does his best to make her believe he's getting better. On the morning of October 8, "he was completely out of danger." That evening he's asleep. The tapers are lit. Emilie, costumed and bejeweled, glides on stage to the sound of applause. But at the first-act curtain they come to tell her that Victor has been seized with "convulsions." She hesitates to change her clothes and go to him. The audience is gallantly clamoring for her. Second messenger. The child is dead. She faints. She is carried away, in her costume for "La Belle Arsène." "Life has become intolerable to me, now that I have lost everything it stood for . . . My tears for my poor child will never cease to flow. I lived only for him and through him. Since

*One of Mirabeau's sisters.

his death I merely vegetate."[24] There is not one word in her letters about Victor's father; you might think the poor creature was a product of partheno-genesis. Less than a year later, Emilie's back on the boards at Le Tholonet.

The Friend of Man is more deeply shaken. By disappointment rather than grief. For him the child was an abstraction, but even so, who would have thought him capable of this glimmer of emotion? "I am brought news of the death of our child, the last hope of our name . . . After bearing up under so much, I had supposed myself strong. It has pleased God to undeceive me. I was unable to prevent myself from summoning him, with more sobs than I have allowed to rise in my entire life, either to judge me that very moment, or to give me some counter-conscience [sic] that would enlighten me as to the failings which have merited so unexampled an accumulation of misfor-tunes."[25]

His son "merited" *his* misfortunes before reaching manhood. He is not told the news until mid-November. It grieves him as it should, neither too much nor too little. A frigid misery. By dying, this child of an arranged marriage, this trump card—first his own hostage, then that of others—becomes an ele-ment in the dispute. From Mirabeau fils to his father, written in the Donjon de Vincennes on November 16, 1778: "I loved my son, Sir, and so I was to lose him. This misfortune quite entirely fills my cup."[26] He's wrong, though, or else he's pretending: in fact, it's the first good news he's had since his internment. As long as Victor was alive the Marignanes and Mirabeaus could carry on their game of leapfrog using the captive's back as their frog; nobody needed him anymore—except Sophie of course, but her purposes were not those of the family and its interests. They were on another planet.

His Sophie? She's in a prison-convent. She spent the last seven months of her pregnancy in conditions of captivity almost worse than those of Gabriel, at the "pension" of Mademoiselle Douai near Mesnil-Montant. After her confinement she was transferred to the Poor Clares of Gien on the banks of the Loire. The little girl born on January 7, 1778, and begrudgingly given the Christian names of their sin—Gabriel-Sophie—naturally was taken from her. Sophie feels ashamed at having given Gabriel only half a child. She sends him groping letters, letters which search like a blind man's hands, feeling for a pain she is unable to locate, a frightening pain.

She has reason to fear. Now they're going to need him again, because he's the only man capable of perpetuating the Mirabeau name. Providing he ditches Sophie. And Gabriel is shrewd enough to be aware of it. His son's death pries open a crack in the door to his cell, but it walls up Sophie's last air hole.

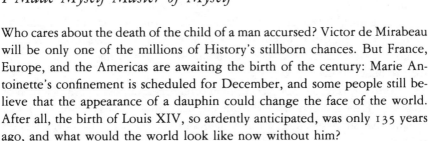

9

I Made Myself Master of Myself

Who cares about the death of the child of a man accursed? Victor de Mirabeau will be only one of the millions of History's stillborn chances. But France, Europe, and the Americas are awaiting the birth of the century: Marie Antoinette's confinement is scheduled for December, and some people still believe that the appearance of a dauphin could change the face of the world. After all, the birth of Louis XIV, so ardently anticipated, was only 135 years ago, and what would the world look like now without him?

On September 27, 1778, Abbé François-Gabriel Secrée de Penvern, priest of St. Etienne-du-Mont on the Montagne Sainte-Geneviève, preaches a panegyric to Sts. Como and Damien, the martyr twins during the reign of Diocletian who became the patrons of medicine and surgery. To them the preacher attributes what he considers to be the dazzling progress made by those two sciences. "To whom do we owe all this, gentlemen? To whom! Can you even ask! To the blessing, the invocation, the protection of our twin saints, our glittering stars whose light is incorruptible . . ."

May they now, up there in paradise, guide the hand of the Queen's obstetricians. "Thanks be to Heaven, she is young, she is well-made, and of a family, moreover, to whom childbirth comes easily. We can but trust that St. Como and St. Damien will preserve her from the pains of such a great operation. It is in the name of these two twins that we address our prayers to God for the safe delivery of our young Queen."[1]

Even the "so-called Reformed" are praying for her, in those temples* which they have been permitted to keep; the very Jews are praying; and Rabbi Mordecai Venturi, leader of the Avignon Israelite congregation that fled to Paris and stayed there after their persecution in the time of the Papal States, has an advantage over his Christian colleagues: he can pray that the awaited child will be a male, for his theology, unlike the other two, does not compel him to believe that the sex of a child is determined in the embryo.[2]

Marie Antoinette gives them all the help she can with their supplications.

*Protestant churches in France are called temples. [*Trans.*]

"Not only has this princess ordered the release of many poor fathers incarcerated in the prisons of Paris for failure to pay their children's wet nurses, but she also said, 'If heaven blesses me with a safe delivery, I shall see that there are no more such unfortunate persons.' "[3] And to M. de Lassone, her chief physician, she says, "Since God, as it appears, is granting me the grace I have so longed for, I wish hereafter to live very differently from the way I have done in the past. I want to live as a mother, feed my child myself, and devote myself to its upbringing."[4]

The selection of an obstetrician is an affair of state. It makes the chosen one's career for the rest of his days, and the choice finally falls upon a M. Vermond, who just happens to be the brother of Abbé de Vermond,* "in preference to MM. Levret, Andouillet and Milot, obstetricians of Paris and the Court. The King did not approve the choice [Why not? Because it was that of the Austrian "party"?] but contented himself with saying, 'I do not wish to see the man.' "[5]

Vermond is no sooner elected than submerged in gossip. He's "a man of no birth." He has dared to tell the Queen, who thinks she has put on too much weight, that she is "naturally full-bellied and heavy-breasted"[6]—which is no more than the truth, and responsible, moreover, for part of her rather ponderous charm. But can you picture it! If he messes up this delivery, you can be sure they'll mess him up good and proper. "There are three hundred women of divers origins applying for the position of wet nurse to the royal child,"[7] in spite of its mother's vague idea of breast-feeding it herself, which she is finally talked out of by universal agreement—too many great ladies would have to imitate her. Meanwhile, every imagination is encouraged to blossom in an effort to make Marie Antoinette forget about her pregnancy and Bavaria. The court spends the early part of the autumn at Marly, where the "young" can set the tone, as opposed to Versailles, where the dowagers are still influential. "In the last days [at Marly] the Queen set up a sort of café,† to which the lords and ladies repaired of a morning, dressed in chenille.** All etiquette was banished. Everyone behaved with the freedom that is customary in such places. One sat at a little table and was served whatever one asked for."[8] Even at Versailles, during the dog days, the Queen and her attendants went for walks along the illuminated terraces "in the cool of the evenings," wearing simple white muslin gowns. They mingled with the guards and common people, who are sometimes allowed inside the grounds. The style of the reign is changing, and a few retarded courtiers are convinced that the whole world is coming to an end because their own little world has begun to sway. But criticism of this at-long-last fertile queen is no longer voiced above a whisper.

*The "reader" sent by Maria Theresa to advise and spy upon her daughter.

†Coffee has been drunk in France for only a century (and only by the rich). A few high-class taprooms are just beginning to rebaptize themselves "cafés."

**"Informal garments worn before *la toilette.*"

Even the Comte de Provence is wearing a smile.* Just in case, and out of pride. As heir to the throne until a dauphin is born, he's well aware that his features are being scrutinized for the smallest trace of jaundice. And it's true enough that he's got a load on his mind. "But very soon I outwardly made myself master of myself and always went on in the same way as before, showing neither joy, which would have been taken for insincerity and would have been so—for to be truthful I felt none at all—nor sorrow, which would have been put down to weakness of character."9 He writes this confession on October 5, 1778, during the seventh month of the pregnancy, in a long letter to King Gustavus III of Sweden, with whom he is carrying on a secret correspondence.† They met in 1771 when Gustavus, casting about on all sides for allies for his coup d'état, stopped off at Versailles. Even then, at sixteen, Provence was already cultivating his reputation as the one-eyed man in this kingdom of the blind. Being a venerable twenty-five-year-old himself, Gustavus III, glad to secure a useful antenna in France, treated him as an adult and future sovereign. Today they are twenty-three and thirty-two respectively, Gustavus has become all-powerful, and Provence is threatened with a return to total obscurity. They write each other empty, rather solemn missives, in which they exchange more good advice than information in the tone of elderly adolescents and with affectations of equality. Nevertheless, this letter of October 5 brings us a little closer to one of the most impenetrable psychologies of the age.

Louis-Stanislas-Xavier** has a rather pretty doll-like little mug, with well-drawn lips and large, wide-awake, sometimes coaxing eyes.10 But he's more than that. The rest of Provence, body and complex-ridden soul, is pure monster. He's shorter than Louis XVI, and already almost twice as fat; he has the obesity of the sedentary man, "library fat," enriched by a glandular deficiency. His brother's corpulence is relatively muscular, and kept within limits by physical exercise. But in Provence it is an infirmity, so distressing that one has to look away every time he undertakes to shift his bulk, which is as seldom as possible; he has "some imperfection in the hips that, although he did not actually limp, gave his gait a strained appearance."11 "He had an unhealthy constitution, and this obliged him, even as a youth, to resort to pharmaceutical potions in order to activate the circulation of the blood and elimination of the

*As younger brother of the king, he was called Monsieur; as Louis XVIII, he will reign over France from 1814 to 1824, except for the Hundred Days.

†Through the Comtesse de La Marck, a Noailles who had married a German. She traveled a lot and liked playing the go-between.

**Louis was the first name of all the Children of France. Stanislas was his great-grandfather and godfather, Stanislas Leczinski; Xavier was his uncle, the brother of Crown Princess Maria Josepha of Saxony.

humors. This morbid condition was further aggravated by want of exercise. His bad posture rendered him unfit to mount a horse; he was very clumsy at it. Never did royal prince have a more awkward walk. He possessed to a supreme degree that swaying gait peculiar to all the Bourbons, and it was not possible, despite his refinement and elegance of dress, to overlook his unfortunate appearance."[12] Artois alone, the youngest brother, has been spared this deluge of fat that has also swamped their sister Clothilde and is threatening Elizabeth. It comes from their father the dauphin, "almost obese at twenty, with puffed-up face, broad girth, and slow and fumbling figure which made him appear older than his years," and enabled the svelte Louis XV to look like Apollo when compared with this son who complained "of dragging painfully behind him the ponderous mass of his body."[13]

Louis-Stanislas makes up for it as best he can with conversational charm, skill at vicious caricature, and an imposing natural loftiness that gives him the "princely look," the absence of which in the King is so greatly to be deplored. His company is by no means disagreeable provided you never ask him a favor: he is utterly devoid of any sense of friendship, or even common decency. Avarice is his one confessed vice, all the more sordid for somebody rolling in gold. Not only is he Comte de Provence, but also Duc d'Anjou, Duc d'Alençon, Duc de Vendôme, Comte du Perche, du Maine, and de Senonches, and, since 1774, Duc de Brunoy: a sumptuous estate with a fine château southeast of Paris in the forest of Sénart, which he was able to buy for a song after having its owner declared insane—the Marquis de Brunoy, a harmless religious maniac whose spectacular processions were highly diverting to the good people of Brie.* The income from all this land brings in a goodly sum, but never enough—to hoard, not to spend. So in the last few years he has been trafficking on a large scale in Santo Domingo plantations and Negroes, and is now trying to branch out into Guiana.

These are his successes. The rest of his youth is a series of setbacks, the cause of the sourness that is beginning to corrode the very depths of his nature.

First disillusionment: in 1761 his stupid jackass of a brother plays a filthy trick on him by refusing to die. Provence was only six, but he already knew that he alone was fit to reign. His parents lost two children in infancy. He is the third of the survivors; then the Good Lord comes to his aid by carrying off Bourgogne with consumption. That leaves Berry, and Berry is languishing, Berry is at death's door. His hopes soar wildly. Provence sees himself crowned dauphin. But the other fool pulls through. Provence never forgives him. The lodestar of all his actions is his hatred and contempt for Louis-Auguste, and

---

*To show Wellington his gratitude for the victory at Waterloo Louis XVIII gives him the title of Marquis de Brunoy.

his fierce longing to see him disappear. He grows taciturn and secretive, and shines at his studies because his older brother is a poor scholar. The Other has no gift for expression, so Provence slaves away at Latin and rhetoric. He may say little, but he says it well. People begin to notice him, and he does not long remain the only person to tell himself that if, after all, some poor marksman were to hit Louis-Auguste by mistake out hunting one day . . .

But the second blow comes when they marry the ass, now dauphin after their father's death, to a pretty Austrian girl whose fine breasts have caught Louis XV's eye. One more rival on the road to power. And if she lives up to the reputation of the Hapsburg wombs . . . At the end of a year hope rises anew: the Austrian belly stays flat. Provence is also married, as a diplomatic maneuver, to Marie-Josephine-Louise of Savoy, whose mafia-dynasty has seized Sardinia and the Piedmont. The princes of Savoy have become Italy's protection men in Europe: there is no way to reach an understanding with Rome or Naples without going through them. The family auction off their children, and the Bourbons are high bidders.* This marriage might have put Provence back in the running. But alas, the Princesse de Savoie is ugly, stubborn, small, and swarthy, with "a beard even on her chest and shoulders."[14] How are you supposed to produce a child with *that,* especially if you turn out to have no more talent for the job than your father the dauphin? Seven years go by with Louis-Stanislas and Louis-Auguste still neck and neck in their childless marriages; the Comte d'Artois, meanwhile, is in there making babies.

But at least Provence remains the heir. He grows fatter in his well-furnished shadows, at the head of a little coterie that works overtime manufacturing poisoned darts. He has his familiars, part highwaymen, part frustrated noblemen: a certain Comte de Modène, a Montesquiou, a Montmorency-Laval, a Comte de La Châtre, a Lévis, a Chabrillant—not to mention his steward Cromot, more of a speculator than a valet, who earns money for his master by earning it for himself. This little clique thrives on the golden promise of Louis XVI's death, or at least sterility. At his brother's accession, Louis-Stanislas tries to get himself admitted to the Council, the "Council of Ministers" or cabinet as it is later to be called. From time to time, depending on sovereigns' whims, crown princes have been given access to it. But on Mercy's advice Marie Antoinette implores her husband not to give so much power to a brother who is perfectly capable of eclipsing him, and whom Austria does not trust. The door to affairs of state is shut in Monsieur's face. "It is said he shows a little too much impatience to be called to the Council . . . On this occasion the Queen had to express herself . . . in a manner which led one to think that she might secretly oppose the desires of this prince.

*For a time a sort of osmosis develops between Bourbons and Savoys. Four marriages in five years: a Savoie-Carignan to a Lamballe, two Savoy girls to Louis XVI's two brothers, and a Daughter of France (Clothilde) to the Prince of Piedmont.

Thereafter, his jealousy resumed its sway."[15] Jealousy—the word is a vast understatement: Provence has now become pure molten hatred. In 1777 he writes to Gustavus III: "I continue relatively at ease as regards minor harassments, but only too much so as regards important affairs: my whole being rages at the uselessness in which I am left, but I possess myself in patience and live on hope."[16] Marie Antoinette was dead right. They smile and nod, the pair of them, while waiting for the poison or the noose: "We continue [Provence and I] on terms of friendship and cordiality; to tell the truth, I see it is no more sincere on one side than the other."[17]

He consoles himself with bits and scraps. By helping to bring down Turgot. By moving into the Luxembourg, one of the handsomest palaces in Paris, where he can throw a few monkey wrenches into Orléans's works. Now there are two little Parisian courts mirroring the Court of Versailles: that of Provence on the left bank, and that of the Orléanses in the Palais Royal on the right.

And by proving that he is not so impotent as those slanderers were calling him, because he has just taken a mistress, yes, sir, a real one, and set her up in the Petit Luxembourg like a second wife—Anne de Balbi, née de Caumont de La Force. "My sister is a slut," is the comment of her brother, the Duc de La Force.[18] Tut, tut, always those nasty names . . . The truth is, she simply knew how to go about it, skillfully, without fuss, in two moves. First, by playing upon the lesbian propensities of the poor Comtesse de Provence, becoming her "lady-in-waiting" and then her favorite; and second, by retrieving Monsieur, in the nick of time, from a penchant for young page boys that was beginning to create problems for his entourage. In 1778 she is twenty years old, lively, witty, and wicked; ugly too, but with "fine eyes above ghastly teeth," and next to Madame she seems like a very Venus. That leaves Balbi to be disposed of —the Italian gentleman she has saddled herself with by marriage. The Comte de Provence is preparing to work the same trick on him that he used for the Marquis de Brunoy: we'll just have him declared insane and put away.* Meanwhile, the threesome moves into the finest rooms in France—Madame in the Grand Luxembourg, and Monsieur and the Comtesse de Balbi in the Petit. A caricature of happiness, but not exactly the vine-covered cottage type: the Household of the Comte de Provence numbers seven hundred sixty "holders of office," from the first gentleman of the chamber down to the four "chest bearers."† In his wife's there are over two hundred. Together they spend 3.5 million livres a year,** one-third of which comes from his various estates and interests, and two-thirds from the royal treasury.[19] That's almost enough to keep you in patience while you wait for heaven to make up its mind to remove

*This is done in July 1780.
†Little chests used to transport hot dishes.
**Nearly 18 million new francs [$3.6 million].

Louis XVI. In this case, Provence can't even help God to help himself by applying his usual treatment and having his brother declared insane, for the King shows heartrending evidence of gross common sense. Oh well; as long as he stays childless . . . But here it comes. The final blow.

"You know what change has been wrought in my fortunes.* It has made none in my heart . . . At present I can tell you, like Zamore [in Voltaire], 'Formerly at thy feet I laid my empire . . .' You were the friend of a man who one day, through his power, could be of use to you: now I have nothing to offer you but an affectionate and faithful heart . . . You may think, from these words, that this traverse has grieved me; I may nevertheless assure you it has not. I have been affected by it, I make no attempt to conceal that; but reason, a little philosophy perhaps, and trust in God have come to my aid and brought me to accept the thing, as the expression is, 'like a man.'" And so Provence has outwardly made himself master of himself, etc. "The inward part," however, "has been more difficult to overcome. It still rebels occasionally; but with the help of the three comforts I have just named to you, I contrive to keep it in check, though I may not subdue it utterly." Like everybody else, he goes on waiting, through the longest months of his life. He has two things left to hope for: an accident in delivery or a girl-child.

THE BIRTH
OF MADAME ROYALE

10

DECEMBER 1778

These Masks Did Dance

November 25. "All the Great who are to attend the Queen's confinement have assembled at Versailles, and nobody stirs from Court again until after the event, which it is hoped will take place very shortly."[1] By some curious phenomenon, Louis XVI is as pear-shaped as his wife: "The King grows stouter every moment, and his physicians have ordered him to drink Vichy water so as to arrest, if it be possible, an excessive and dangerous condition of overweight." "The layette for the royal child and those of its nurses were brought in" from Paris to Versailles on December 1, "with great ceremony; they are magnificent. The carriage was escorted by guards." This ostentation

*From the same letter to Gustavus III, October 5, 1778.

is not to everyone's taste. "An unpardonable atrocity has recently been committed in the gardens of Marly. Seven of the superb antique white marble statues, admired by all connoisseurs, were hacked and mutilated with axes." This was put down as the work of the English. "But one of the culprits was apprehended, and denounced two accomplices. These three poor wretches are laborers customarily employed in the gardens, who were intoxicated when they perpetrated the offense. It is thought that an exemplary punishment will be meted out to them," and nobody is going to lose sleep over such a trifle. "The King has caused one hundred thousand livres* to be taken to the chief almoner, to be distributed among the poor after the Queen's delivery . . ." "The Paris town corporation† has also decided to provide dowries for one hundred marriages of poor people." "Independently of the nation in general, which is praying for a prince, there are over a thousand persons at Court who have a particular interest in the question: the King's Household, which serves the young prince. Twice as many women will be employed for him until his seventh birthday, and larger and more numerous gratuities and rewards are to be distributed, including those of the obstetrician himself, who automatically receives forty thousand livres annually if the child is a boy, but only a single payment of eight or ten thousand if he delivers a girl."** And since the first of December comes and goes and the queen is still making us chew our nails, what can we do but dance? So we dance.

A little gesture of affection from Louis XVI. For Antoinette, he sets the old folks spinning. "In a span of twenty-four hours, and in deepest secrecy, with the help of the wardrobe collections of the Menus-Plaisirs,‡ the entire Court was disguised and masked . . . M. de Maurepas was Cupid and Mme de Maurepas Venus; M. de Sartines was Neptune, with a trident in his hand. M. de Vergennes had a globe on his head, a map of America across his chest and one of England on his back. The Prince de Soubise came as a Chinese Mohammedan [sic] monk; the Maréchal de Richelieu was Cephalus,†† with the old Maréchale de Mirepoix on his arm, dressed as a Huron [Indian]. This couple trod a measure as lightly and gracefully as youngsters of twenty . . . The Maréchal de Biron was a druid, the Maréchal de Brissac a dervish, the Duc de Cossé a vizier, the Duc de Lauzun a sultan, the Duc de Fronsac a pilgrim, the Duc d'Aumont a Swiss; other lords and ladies formed quadrilles

---

*500,000 new francs [$100,000].

†Composed of merchants and magistrates; a sort of embryonic town council.

**An illustration in hard cash of the position assigned to women: for a dauphin, 200,000 new francs [$40,000] a year until the obstetrician's death. For a princess, a paltry 50,000 francs [$10,000] at most . . . a good tip.

‡"Small pleasures"—almost like a ministry of entertainment. [Trans.]

†† A mythological hero, undoubtedly a sun-figure, of whom the goddess Aurora was enamored.

of rabbis,* soldiers, hussars, sailors, huntsmen, couriers, etc. All the page boys were disguised as jockeys. These masks did dance, and when the clock struck one, the King (in his ordinary dress) gave the signal to withdraw and led the Queen to her bedchamber. Everyone was regaled with hot chocolate and ices.

". . . the Duc de Coigny came as Hercules, and was the first person recognized by the Queen."[2] Is it mere coincidence that the author of the *Correspondance secrète,*† who dispatches his weekly gossip in the direction of Warsaw, allows this allusion to slip off the end of his quill? Just lately, with the first rumors of adultery beginning to eddy round Marie Antoinette's skirts, Provence has glimpsed a third ground for hope: what if the child is not by Louis XVI? Oh, to be able to proclaim *that* one day, to wrench the throne from its grasp . . . But that day's a long way off. For the time being the rumor is nothing but a wisp of smoke trailing along the waxed parquet floors; Monsieur doesn't even need to blow on it, however, it's spontaneous combustion. There aren't ten people in the world who know the part Joseph II played in the private life of the royal couple; so what's happened, after seven years of a virtually platonic marriage? One can quite reasonably entertain some curious suppositions without being disloyal to the young Queen, especially when one sees her in such pleasant company. Always the same stableful of purebred pretty-boys. Lauzun is slowing in the turn, but there are plenty more breathing down his neck: a noble Hungarian, Esterhazy; "fair Dillon," fat Guines, Besenval—even the Comte d'Artois, who is displaying such ostentatious camaraderie toward his sister-in-law that some people have not hesitated to proclaim him the father of her child—and above all, the big winner that autumn, Coigny.

François-Henri de Franquetot de Coigny is forty years old. "He was not a very handsome man, nor a man of great wit. He had better qualities than those: an excellent bearing, an exquisite tone, a prepossessing figure, a simple and straightforward way of thinking, poise and courtesy . . . Beloved by all, the Duc de Coigny hated no one."[3] Why should he? He's Master of the King's Horse, about to become a lieutenant general,** worth millions, and he's the lover of the Comtesse de Châlons, *née* d'Andlau, one of those good-looking girls the Queen is so fond of; and soon, as soon as his first wife has finished discreetly dying,‡ he'll be able to marry her. What need could he have to run

---

Sic. This is not the only illustration of the prevailing anti-Semitism of the French aristocracy. A rabbi was a grotesque personage: who could conceive of a parish priest dancing in a ballet?

†Almost certainly a Toulouse pen-pusher, Jean-Louis Favier, who had been a vague secret agent under Dumouriez and ended his days with a pension paid by the Comte de Vergennes. He may have been writing for the King of Poland, Stanislas Poniatowski. The correspondence came to light in Saint Petersburg and was published in 1866 by Lescure.

**Equivalent to a four-star general.

‡The daughter of this first marriage, Aimée de Coigny, will be the model for André Chénier's poem *"La Jeune Captive."*

the ghastly risk of becoming the Queen's lover? There are a dozen drawing-room roosters who'd like nothing better than to add this pretty, frustrated young woman to their list of conquests; but all, like him, cringe at the thought of the complications. We will understand nothing of Marie Antoinette's latent hysteria unless we see that her rank, and the unrelenting domestic espionage to which she is subjected, create inhibitions in any would-be lover almost as crippling as those of the King. Beyond all doubt, she resents her suitors being so universally and eternally respectful, and would gladly see them drop it now and then. But so far there's nothing to prevent her sexual conscience from being pure as the driven snow. She has slept with nobody but Louis XVI, and he happens to be the only one she really can't stand. She doesn't care much for Artois, and there's nothing between them. She hasn't slept with Lauzun, although she loved him, and she's quite fond of Coigny but is not sleeping with him either. It has just given her a real pleasure to see Axel Fersen again, that brilliant Swedish officer whom she teased, when she was still dauphine, at the Opéra ball. "All Versailles talks of nothing but a Count Fersen who has come to Court wearing the Swedish national costume; it is true that the Queen is said to have studied him most attentively."⁴ This is not gossip, as confirmed by Fersen himself. He returns for a second visit to Paris on August 22, after four years spent in England and, mainly, Sweden, which strengthens his reputation as confidant of Gustavus III. On the 25th he's at Versailles "to be presented to the royal family.* The Queen, who is charming, said when she saw me, 'Ah, this is an old acquaintance!' The rest of the family did not speak a word to me." So Marie Antoinette hasn't forgotten him, and finds him even more agreeable than before. In September, "the Queen, who is the prettiest and most amiable princess I know, has been good enough to inquire after me on several occasions. She asked Creutz [the Swedish ambassador] why I did not come to her games on Sunday, and learning that I had come one day when they were not held, she made a sort of apology. Her pregnancy is coming on, and is very visible."⁵ In November, "the Queen always treats me kindly. I often go to pay her my court at her games, and she always speaks to me. She had heard people speak of my uniform and expressed a great desire to see it at her levee. I am to wear it there on Tuesday, not to the levee but to the Queen's apartments. She is the most amiable princess I know [again]."⁶ But she hasn't gotten any further than the uniform. As for Coigny, who's been claiming for two years "that he has access to the apartments of this princess at certain hours which give rise to much comment,"⁷ the spectacular degree of favor he has been enjoying during the pregnancy has given rise to a comment currently attributed to Chartres: "Coigny's child will never be my king."⁸

---

*Who already knew him. But he was first "presented" under Louis XV and it all had to be done again, à la Louis XVI.

Provence keeps mum. He waits. For once he lets the others do the talking
—loudly enough, in the last few days, for Marie Antoinette herself to get wind
of certain echoes and to confide in Mmes de Lamballe and de Polignac: "I must
own that I am most unhappy to be so ill-used."

Then, recovering her usual good humor, she adds, "But if it is wicked
of other people to suppose I have so many lovers, it is even more singular of
me to have so many charged to my account and yet to do without them all."[9]

The august infant, meanwhile, seems to be taking his time. Is he coming or
not? Fifteen days overdue, then twenty. Who knows why we finally do resign
ourselves to set foot in this inhospitable world. "Some have claimed that it was
want of nourishment that caused the fetus to seek a way out. Others, that the
child detached itself from the womb in the same way as the fruit detaches itself
from the tree. The latter maintained that the bitterness of the waters enclosed
in the membrane forced the child to move and seek the way out, and the
former thought that its urine and excrement formed a certain mass and that
their acridness, incommoding the fetus, compelled it to move."[10]

The contractions begin at half past midnight on December 20, and proceed in a specially prepared room on the second floor of the palace of Versailles, at the end of the long file of vast, boring, and public chambers which
Louis XV used to flee. At first they are mild and infrequent, allowing intermittent periods of rest and sleep, all the signs of a normal delivery; then, some
time around eight, they become more intense and the bag of waters breaks.
Obstetrician, surgeon, physicians, apothecaries, and midwives bustle about the
large bed "composed of numerous mattresses garnished with sheets doubled
over several times." A flood of white linen. Vermond, the obstetrician, has
"anointed his hands with some fatty substance like lard, liquid butter, or some
oils, to lubricate the passage." At the proper moment he places "the tips of
his fingers inside the vagina, spreading them apart as far as possible during the
contractions."[11] In addition to his professional duties, he must order the
double doors flung open when he feels the head about to emerge, "for it was
then customary for the public to witness the opening of the womb,"[12] a
tradition dating from Merovingian times, when people feared the substitution
of one baby for another to the benefit of a rival dynasty. The strange ritual
of the papal high mass at Rome dates from the same period—a deacon tastes
the wafer chosen at the last moment from a sample of three, so that the pontiff
will not be poisoned.*

That absurd respect for tradition is about to endanger Marie Antoinette's
life. Until eleven o'clock she suffers bravely, like a woman, like a Hapsburg,
kneading the hand of the Princesse de Lamballe in her own, while "the King

*This liturgical detail persisted until the pontificate of Pius XII.

paced heavily and mopped his brow, the ladies of the Palace fanned themselves," and she endures, like a long-awaited trial, the gaze of all those witnesses who despise her: the princes and princesses, the chancellor Maupeou, making his first appearance in public since his disgrace. The Queen's real friends aren't there. Can you imagine a Coigny at her bedside? All of a sudden, everything starts spinning round in her head, Vermond cries out, and "the doors of the chamber open upon the tumult of a delirious crowd" which has collected in the galleries. Mostly household servants, but a few anonymous citizens of Versailles as well, who wouldn't for the world miss this relatively rare opportunity to inspect the Queen's private parts. "Courtiers, lackeys, townspeople, fishwives, chimney-sweeps, all rush forward." The chimney sweeps, two "Savoyards," climb onto a table to get a better view. "With no distinction as to rank, and no consideration for the august victim, all the places are taken, people climb up the fireplace (one of whose torches is shattered), and all, in a murmuring silence, intoxicated with the most unwholesome concupiscence, shiver and gape at every cry."[13] The Queen, meanwhile, is being asphyxiated.

The crowd alone wouldn't be too bad. All part of the job. Marie Antoinette holds out through those final minutes when her body breaks under the public gaze: after all, there's a sort of primitive communion in this public disemboweling. But the oxygen in the unventilated room is beginning to give out as her apprehension mounts—please, God, let all this not be for nothing, that is, for a girl! Fifty or sixty pairs of eyes are riveted upon her sex, waiting to see that of the child. Double or nothing.

France is one of the few countries in the world in which the Salic law turns princesses to dust. Women can, have, and do reign in Muscovy or England, Austria, Sweden, Portugal, Spain, or Madagascar. But they have been excluded from the French throne since the grand maneuvers of Philippe VI, three pitched battles of procedure won in 1316, 1322, and 1328 with the help of the aristocracy, bishops, and learned doctors of the Sorbonne. His problem was how to set aside the legitimate and direct Capetian descendants in favor of their cousins, the Valois. To solve it, the old barbaric text of the Salic law was dug up in some monastery—a sort of Deuteronomy of the Salian Franks,* 408 articles forming a rough-and-ready code establishing penalties for the theft of horses, oxen, or swine, and setting the amount of damages owed in case of mutilation. "If the bones are visible in a wound to the head, the culprit will pay thirty sous; if the brain is uncovered and three bones protrude from it, forty-five sous."[14] The Valois had drawn upon a combination of this hodgepodge and the Gospels—"Consider the lilies of the field, how

---

*Saliens meant conquering. The Salic land was that which they conquered by armed force, and a warrior's arm was needed to defend it. By extension the whole of France became Salic land.

they grow; they toil not, neither do they spin"—to conclude without a blush that "the kingdom of the *lis* [French for lily] must not fall to the distaff side." The Salic law "is in conformity with the law of nature, which, having created woman imperfect, feeble and sickly in both body and mind, made her subject to the force of man, whom she [nature] endowed for that purpose with greater strength of judgment, resolution in courage, and robustness of body. Thus we see that divine law wills woman to acknowledge and make obeisance to her husband as to her chief and king. And it is seen in Isaiah, Chapter 3, that God threatens to set a woman to rule over his enemies, as an intolerable curse."[15]

The final acts of suffering, the first of life. Vermond pulls forth into the world a bloody, mute bundle. Provence is on the rack: stillborn? First cry, the child lives. Sounds of applause from birth-chamber to kitchens, everybody thinks it's a boy. Provence is lost. No: a girl! Provence breathes, for the first time in six months, but there's never a twitch in the folds of his fat face. A girl, hallelujah, a lousy little skirt, one more womb to auction off around Europe. They'll name her Maria Theresa,* as a nod to Austria—just another Austrian, let's forget about her. Silence falls like a trap upon the lying-in room, now the room of disappointment, while King and courtiers move next door to see the child washed, and perhaps also to avoid its mother, who's begging them to tell her, boy or girl? As if she didn't know! No one has said a word, but their silence is more eloquent than speech. She understands. Back to the drawing board.

"During this time the Queen was fainting and saying, 'I'm dying. Hurry . . .' And indeed she was turning cold and lifeless."[16]

Vermond earns his ten-thousand-livre tip by having her instantly bled from the foot by the surgeon, who removes five *palettes* (over half a liter) of blood. "The incident was over in four minutes."[17]

From the Comte de Provence to Gustavus III: "My sister-in-law did well this time; it is to be feared things will not be so satisfactory on another occasion . . . By dint of reasoning with myself, my sacrifice was made, and when my niece came into the world I was well content, I confess it, but less than I might have supposed."[18]

---

*And also Charlotte, in homage to King Charles III of Spain, who will be her godfather; her godmother is her grandmother, the empress. The child born on December 20, later known as Madame Royale, is the sole survivor of the royal family in 1794. In 1795, after his release, the future Louis XVIII marries her to her first cousin, the Duc d'Angoulême, son of the Comte d'Artois. History knows her as the Duchesse d'Angoulême.

II

DECEMBER 1778

La Libertà o la Morte

While people at Versailles are praying for the birth of a Louis, a Louis is born in Corsica; but why should France take any notice of that? Nevertheless, the baptism of Louis de Buonaparte, celebrated with great pomp in the cathedral of Ajaccio on September 24, 1778, is quite an event in the region.[1] The French, breathless in anticipation of their dauphin, may pass it by, but the Corsicans are vastly impressed. A sign of the times. The fourth son* of Carlo Maria de Buonaparte (Charles-Marie, to the Continent) is given the French-est name there is, that of the king.† He is suspended over the baptismal font by the governor of Corsica, Louis-Charles-René, Comte de Marbeuf, and by Jeanne de Buocheporn, the wife of the intendant. The "cathedral" of this almost-new little burg is no more than a big shapeless church crammed full of gilt sculpture and pompous paintings, an explosion of decadent baroque; and the Bishop of Ajaccio is a parish priest with a congregation of three thousand souls. The ceremony is typically Corsican in its combination of improvisation and solemnity. Shuffling feet, a procession, discordant chanting, salvos, incense, organ wheezes, and a big picnic under the tall chestnuts standing on the waste ground between the cathedral and the Buonaparte house.

The crowd is smaller than expected: many Ajaccians have refused to attend this baptism of French Corsica pretending to be the baptism of a child —mostly those who, unlike the Buonapartes or the Pietra-Santas, are in no hurry to worship what they once abhorred. In the first row of the congregation sits a little fellow of nine, this one bearing the true Corsican name of Napoleone, very dignified beside his father Carlo Maria, his mother Laetizia, and his brothers Giuseppe and Luciano. Maria Anna, just a baby, has been left in *la casa*.** Napoleone feels very much at home, a young big fish in a middle-sized

---

*But tenth child; five have already died in infancy.

†After the accession of Napoleon, Louis Bonaparte becomes "connétable de l'Empire" in 1804, then King of Holland from 1806 to 1810. He marries Hortense, the daughter of Joséphine de Beauharnais, and is the putative father of Louis Napoleon (1801–1873), last sovereign to reign over the French, with the title of Napoleon III.

**Napoleon is Emperor of the French from 1804 to 1815; Giuseppe (as Joseph), King of

pond, destined for the churchwarden's pew. He knows that in three months he'll be going to the Continent with Giuseppe, where they will be the guests of the King of France, or so they've been told, and that seems perfectly natural to them. In their eyes their father is the Prince of Ajaccio, if not of Corsica itself. It's all in the family . . .

There's some good sense mixed with the child's conceit. Marbeuf is not playing godfather out of the kindness of his heart, it's a calculation, a political gesture. The first Louis of French Corsica deserves a little special attention. From the silences and stares of the local gentry—including its hostile members —Napoleone has understood that the French need his father. A convert is something you pay for: it's only taken Carlo Maria two years to desert Paoli for Marbeuf. Since 1771 he has been salaried assessor* to the Court of Ajaccio, a sort of justice of the peace in the service of the occupying forces. He's begun a little game between the French leaders, playing off Marbeuf against Narbonne-Paoli, and, by provoking a slight shift of opinion in a dozen patrician families, has helped to increase the power of the former. He's carving out a handsome future for himself, here and on the Continent—and he's only thirty-two. Who thinks kids don't notice these things? Everything in Napoleone's little world is shaping up very nicely: in wartime his daddy was a hero, in peacetime he's becoming a top dog. And his children firmly believe that he's making no concessions to the French. On the contrary, it's really very kind of us to forgive them for the Niolo.

The Niolo repression. His first childhood memory. The conquest, in 1769, was history as ancient as his mother's womb, "which he went into a Corsican and came out of a Frenchman." But Napoleone was five years old in March 1774, when nearly half the island was up in arms to the old battle cry they'd used against Genoa before—*la libertà o la morte*—and the Comte de Marbeuf and the Marquis de Sionville put down the last Corsican rebellion. For forty years they'd shouted for *libertà* and all they got was *morte.* The only difference now was that it was France's turn to occupy the ports and aim the artillery. Because after failing miserably to gain a foothold on the island, the Genoese, the Dutch of Italy, had sold it off cheap. The Corsicans changed hands "like a flock of sheep"—it's always the proudest peoples who are humiliated most, perhaps because they're poor, and that's where they get their pride. Yet Paoli had given Corsica a face of its own, with the blessing of Voltaire and Rousseau.

Naples from 1806 to 1808, then King of Spain from 1808 to 1814; Maria Anna, renamed Elisa, becomes Princess of Lucca and Piombino, then Grand Duchess of Tuscany. Luciano (Lucien) has no imperial title. The first name should be pronounced *à la corse:* Napoléoné.

*At 900 livres, or 5,000 new francs [$1,000], a year. Almost a token salary, but an office that puts his foot in the stirrup.

It was an ideal democracy. The *Consulte* of Corte, an example for the entire world: a permanent forum of free men. Brushed aside by the back of Louis XV's hand. Paoli fled to England. And when the Niolo district rose up in his name . . .

Sionville had eleven of the rebels hanged from the same branch of a tree; he had a connoisseur's eye when it came to judging the strength of a piece of wood. At La Rocca, he ordered the arms of a woman who had hidden the rebels to be fractured with iron bars. At Oletta, five patriots were broken on the wheel. Marbeuf decreed that any "bandit" taken with arms in his possession—in Corsica!—would be punished by "death without remission." One hundred "bandits" were slaughtered the same day in the Fiumorbo region. Six were executed at the gates of Ajaccio where the Buonapartes, barricaded inside their house, heard the drum rolls and the single word uttered by one of the six, who screamed *"Pazienza"* as his bones were being crushed. The other five were mute. The Corsicans are not chatty people. Twenty-seven of the more fortunate were chained together and shipped to the prison of Toulon. At the time of the conquest, the Comte de Vaux had warned Versailles: "The bandits' numbers will continue to increase unless you authorize the burning of their houses . . . It is therefore essential to allow the [military] commands to destroy the homes and possessions of the guilty and of their relatives."[2] The flying columns spared neither crops nor vines nor olive groves. Some imagined even more drastic measures: the Corsicans lived almost exclusively on chestnuts. What luck—"Somebody put forward the singular scheme of cutting down or burning all the chestnut trees, whose fruit is the chief sustenance of the mountain people.[3] 'You will force them down to the lowlands, to beg for bread and peace.' "*

It couldn't be done, though, there wasn't enough manpower. So they confined themselves to razing the homes of all suspects and burning harvests all over the Niolo, as they had done five years before at the time of the conquest—Mirabeau's one campaign before beginning his career in prison. "My early youth was blighted by my participation in the conquest of Corsica."[4] Some French soldiers had a thoughtful look on their faces when they came back from this war against shepherds and fishermen. "Never have I seen anyone maintain such serenity and resolution as those six unfortunates, before and during their torture," one officer in the Royal Picardie wrote from Ajaccio; "not complaining, not betraying either their accomplices or their leaders, and never seeking to make amends to the King or to justice, but insisting throughout that they had committed no crime save that of defending their freedom."[5]

*According to Napoleon, on St. Helena. "Fortunately," said the emperor (to Las Cases, as reported in his *Mémorial de Sainte-Hélène*), "it was one of those impractical schemes which exist only on paper."

This is the environment in which Napoleone's intelligence begins to function. He's a quiet boy. He thinks too much. People say there's no such thing as a pessimistic child. Yes, there is: him.[6]

It's time to go now, Napoleone, the King of France is expecting you; not in his châteaus just yet, it's true, but in his collèges,* so that you can learn how to do him the honor of commanding his armies. It's high time, in fact, because Ajaccio's getting too hot for you. The first real battles of his life, those that begin at the age of seven—the "age of reason" as they call it—have left him bruised and bleeding. They were between gangs of kids that tangled, twenty or thirty at a time, using sticks and stones for weapons—the *Ajaccini* against the *Borghigiani.* Napoleone's place is with the former, of course, with those who've been in Ajaccio for two centuries, the sons of nobles and bourgeois who were hospitable to the Genoese, converted to Paoli long enough to clean their slates with him, and are now backing the French: what the hell, you've got to live. But the *Ajaccini* often come away the losers from their skirmishes with the *Borghigiani,* the children of sailors and shepherds and craftsmen who've come down from the mountains to settle in the Borgo on the outskirts of the port, and are waiting their turn to follow the greatest man that ever lived, Sampiero Corso.† Napoleone lost the first real battles of his life, those he fought against the Corsicans. His loyalty is to Ajaccio, and Ajaccio is not the island, only a knot tying it to the rest of the world; it's the place of subtlety, diplomacy, lies, and concessions. Since 1536 the Buonapartes have been "Genoese citizens," as Paul of Tarsus was a "citizen of Rome." In those days, when people in Italy talked about Ajaccio they called it "Genoa's colony." A short time before Marignan,** one of its colonists was a man named Francesco Buonaparte of Sarzana, a crossbowman, a Tuscan. Thirty years later, his son Jerome became an "elder" of Ajaccio—other parts of the world would have called him a senator—one of those who, in 1536, demanded that the Corsicans be run out of town.[7]

On December 15, 1778, Carlo Maria leaves Louis (whom everybody calls Luigi), Luciano, and Maria Anna in the care of his wife and the nurses. He

---

*The collèges were secondary schools; initially, in the Middle Ages, they were residences for poor university students, and were later used by abbots for young members of their orders. Those of the Jesuits were particularly well-organized and important, until the expulsion of the Order in 1763. Before the fall of the monarchy, there were virtually no other non-military schools in existence; all collèges were run by the clergy. [*Trans.*]

†Sampiero d'Ornano (1501–1567) came to Corsica to fight the Genoese, strangled his wife who wanted to make peace with them, and was killed by his in-laws who had sold out to them. [*Trans.*]

**Battle won by François I against the Swiss in 1515. [*Trans.*]

sets off for the Continent with his two oldest boys and two cousins: the Buonaparte's second migration, and Napoleone's first trip. He's thrilled to death. Until then he's never been any farther than from Ajaccio to Corte—with his father or some cousin, uncle, or friend, most often riding pillion on a half-saddled horse in a whirlwind of dust along the rutted roads. He's never been in a carriage, let alone a boat. And here they are taking ship at Bastia, a town he's never seen and is astonished to learn is almost as big as Ajaccio. Bastia is already a foreign country to him because they have to sleep in an inn there—another first in his life. No relatives to give the travelers a bed. His father says the inn is no good, but could there be any good inns in Corsica? *He*'s got no complaints, however: he gets both boiled and roast meat for supper! He's even allowed to drink a glass of Uri wine mixed with water, like Giuseppe. He also shares a mattress with Giuseppe in the room where all five of them sleep, after some old man comes to spread three mattresses on the floor—one for his father, one shared by cousin Varese the sub-deacon and uncle Fesch who's going to enter the seminary, and one for Giuseppe and him, but there's nothing new about that: ever since leaving his cradle Napoleone has shared a bed with Giuseppe. As always, he takes advantage of the fact to pummel and scratch him in the morning because the great lump never wakes up fast enough.[8]

The crossing to Leghorn takes almost two days. What a weird sensation, to have the full sea all around you! And this port, where he's dazed by the noise and bustle and sees his first English ships, so full-bellied, so high, and with so many cannons sticking out of their sides that he wonders why they don't just sink . . . Then Genoa, then Marseilles; they make him forget all about Leghorn. In Marseilles somebody has to hold his hand so he doesn't get lost along the boulevards which M. de Meilhan, the intendant, has lined with four rows of trees. And then the fountains of Aix make him forget the white houses of Marseilles. They leave uncle Fesch at the seminary there, without even exchanging a kiss; the two children have scant affection for the tall silent young man, a mixture of Swiss and Corsican, whose dream is to end his days as canon of the cathedral of Ajaccio. In Lyons, on the Place Bellecour, Napoleone asks if Louis XIV was really twice as tall as other men on account of the size of his statue, but he's already less intimidated by the crowds of people. One hundred thousand inhabitants! gasps Giuseppe. He retorts that Marseilles has just as many and they hadn't seen anything yet. Even so, all along the Burgundy road he makes no attempt to hide his curiosity about the changing of the horses at every posting station, the arguments between his father and the postilions, the first winter snowfall frosting the road—although he's already seen snow twice in Corsica. Villefranche, Mâcon, Tournus, Chalon; and then, late in that gray afternoon of December 30, they come into a landscape of little bare hills, tightly fenced skimpy fields (what're the fences for, to keep the dandelions from running away?), and he catches his first glimpse of the town in which he is going to become French: Autun.*

It's all up and down hill, even the main square. It huddles close around its cathedral, so beautiful and strange: Napoleone is shocked at the sight of naked cherubs and devils sticking out their tongues. The streets swarm with priests: Autun is one of the most flourishing bishoprics in Burgundy, and cousin Varese is glad of it, since he's come there to be sub-deacon. The first French to have any dealings with Napoleone are also priests, of course—the faculty of the collège (directly attached to the bishop), who've just taken over from the Jesuits. They will keep Giuseppe, who is also to become a priest, and knock off a few of Napoleone's rough edges while waiting for a place to be found for him at the Tiron military academy. But why Autun? Because its bishop is the Comte de Marbeuf's brother, and he rather fancies the idea of sending one or two Corsican cuttings to blossom in his family greenhouse. The prelate sees them in person the very day after their arrival, and gives them an approving benediction, laying his hand on their foreheads. That means the teachers will treat them decently, at least, in spite of their sparse attainments and outlandish lingo. On this occasion, Giuseppe and Napoleone can admire their father's nonchalance in his handsome embroidered uniform and with his new sword that is so becoming to him—for the Chevalier Charles-Marie de Buonaparte has just obtained a ruling from the magistrates' council of Corsica, proclaiming "the Buonaparte family noble, of proven nobility for more than two hundred years."†

Two days later they watch him set off for Versailles and Paris, where he will heckle the ministers until he can extort a few more favors for his family, his clan, his friends. The boys are not wildly grieved by his departure: he's always been rather remote, even at home where he speaks kindly to them but hurriedly, as though in passing, between his Corsican tours and his travels on the Continent. It's no wonder to them to see him swallowed up by the world that has always been his—the world of favors and frustrations, the world where people talk French. But Napoleone continues to be dazzled by the newness of things, although he doesn't feel lost so long as he still has his beloved brother with him, his constant companion since birth, his good old Giuseppe who'll be sleeping in the same dormitory. True, they tell him right away on the first of January that he's got to call him Joseph from now on, and that's hard on account of the accent.

Nor are they overcome by sorrow at being separated from their mother,

*The Burgundy road, now overlaid by the N6 over almost its entire length, used to make a detour by way of Autun, leaving out Arnay-le-Duc. Fesch, by the way, becomes a cardinal and Archbishop of Lyons.

†Commoners did not wear swords. [*Trans.*]

a mother who never kisses or cuddles, beautiful as ice and prolifically silent. The only tenderness Napoleone has known in early childhood is that of nannies; and is a Buonaparte going to cry over a petticoat?

THE DUC DE LAUZUN
TAKING SENEGAL

12

JANUARY 1779

Monsieur de Lauzun Has Taken Your Senegal

The Duc de Lauzun was also on the scene at the conquest of Corsica, where he became a friend of Marbeuf—and of "Mirabeau *fils.*" "I did not leave Corsica without regrets, for I spent there what may be the happiest year of my life."[1] Lauzun was still a very young man then and not head over ears in debt, and he "fought with the fervor and energy of an active man seeking to prove himself." Now he's thirty, ruined, and broader around the waistline. On the quarterdeck of the *Fendant,* a fair seventy-four-gun vessel, he turns the heavy gaze of a ladies' man toward the coast of tropical Africa. The eyelids droop from boredom, lassitude. But a steady fire still burns behind them. January 28, 1779. Is Senegal about to offer him a second Corsica? Here's another one trying to escape. He's eight hundred leagues from Versailles.

When the artillery salute announcing the birth of a royal baby which was not his rang out all over France, twenty-one guns instead of the hoped-for hundred and one, he was in Quiberon making preparations for his expedition, and paid little attention to it. He's starting to take himself seriously again. We're off to see the Wizard and to hell with all beauties, royal or otherwise. The very next day after that ball where he turned up disguised as a sultan, the least aged of those aged masks, he left court. Even then he was laying careful plans for the blow he is about to try to strike at his darling England.

Without the slightest remorse. All's fair in war, including cheating. For the last two days the ships in Lauzun's mini-fleet have been ordered to run up the British flag. His fleet: two ships of the line—the *Fendant* and the *Sphinx* —two frigates, three corvettes, one schooner, and ten or so big troop-transport barges, that flounder through the waves like a herd of marine cattle and have ruined the trip because everybody's had to spend all his time prodding them along. Not a bad idea though, eh, to fly the British colors? The English garrison at Saint-Louis in Senegal will mistake us for those reinforcements they've been fretting for. They'll send us a pilot to help our longboats over that cursed river bar. We'll seize him and force him to lead us up close to the fort by night, then we'll give the enemy a touch of the old John Paul Jones at Whitehaven. Lauzun isn't far from taking himself for a military genius, and he's looking forward to recapturing not only the river delta but the whole coast of Senegambia for his king, without striking a blow. Ours, the leather and ivory, the gold dust and ostrich plumes which the English have been stealing from us for fourteen years! Ours, the miraculous substance that oozes from the flanks of wounded acacias—gum arabic for our plasters and physicians! And above all, ours the new wealth of Africa, its fast-expanding commerce: the Negro for our Islands [West Indies].[2]

But first of all, ours, Saint-Louis! The "supreme commander of the Africa volunteers," that's his official title, aims his glass at the coast, fizzy as green champagne where the foam of the estuary meets the foam of the trees, the baobabs looking as though they grew straight up out of the water. Here and there, basalt rocks reflect the sun like echoes, so pure they're almost blinding. It is no accident that our ancestors gave the name "Cap Blanc" to one of the few points on the coast where a ship can come in to harbor, way up north at the edge of the Sahara,* there where the cliffs are so white you'd think it was Dover in Africa. Now Lauzun has come well to the south of it, opposite the enormous opening that marks the first break in the line of the coast after Morocco, "like some obscene vent in the belly of Africa." It is one of the mouths of that "single river" indiscriminately known as the Senegal, the Niger, the Gambia, the Casamance, or even the Guinea, why not? It depends on the point at which you encounter it, because four or five of these Gargantua's maws are spread over five hundred miles on the way down to the equator and people still believe they are arms of the gigantic estuary of a single waterway, and this region—Senegambia—is the delta of some Rhone or Rhine on the scale of the rest of Africa. The geographers aren't compulsive about accuracy: "Between Cap Blanc and Cape Verde at sixteen degrees north lies the river of Senegal, or Niger, and five leagues upstream of its mouth is the isle of Saint-Louis."[3] They're even wrong about the five leagues: the fortified warehouse planted there by men from Dieppe sometime around 1650— France's first even slightly firm harpoon in the flank of West Africa—crowns the islet of Saint-Louis a bare league upstream. Lauzun can see it with the naked eye, beyond the surf of the bar. A wart of white civilization which he intends to remove, the first stone dwellings he's seen since Mogador, squeezed up against the squat fort in a profusion of grasses and water. Inside it, a handful of English at bay.

*Today Cap Blanc lies on the frontier of the Spanish Sahara and Mauritania, whose capital and only decent port—Nouakchott, which didn't exist in those days—lies 120 miles farther south.

Captain Eyriès's corvette, the *Lively,* goes as close to the bar as it dares, the Cross of St. George prominently displayed, and makes the customary English naval signals to request a pilot. Lauzun wasn't poring over all those issues of the *London Magazine* just to while away the time: English freedom of the press makes espionage a cinch. He's even copied the plans of the fort. But the fort is in no hurry to reply. Twice, three times, the corvette ventures out from the fleet to the reefs, at the risk of running aground. Are they blind in there, or what?

No; just taking time to load their guns. Boom. We see the smoke of a dozen shots before we can hear them. No danger: the fort was firing at random and the balls come down somewhere in the river. All the same, the *Lively* makes fast tracks back to the *Fendant,* where Lauzun's face is such a study in astonishment that the Marquis de Vaudreuil, the Vicomte d'Arrost, Robert Dillon, Sheldon, and Miewkovski, his little gang of officers, burst out laughing. Here's a fine master stroke unstruck, Your Grace! We needn't have bothered mustering our troops at Oléron and Quiberon instead of Brest, and calling you the "Chevalier de Saint-Pierre" in Brittany just to put the English spies off our scent! Some stoolie has been sharper than yourself. They were waiting for us. Never mind; we'll fight them tomorrow. It's better for our reputations not to have sailed so far, such countless cables, without even drawing our swords.

On January 29 it takes the whole morning to get the longboats ready, sort out the uniforms and arms, and load the ammunition and a few supplies, just in case. The fort has withdrawn into stubborn silence. The fleet now flies the white ensign. We'll fight in the open. The plan is simple: the fusiliers will be put ashore as close to Saint-Louis as possible. They'll move up, hauling the longboats along the shore, then cross the river arm at its narrowest point and invade the islet while the ships bombard it, but more to keep the fortress occupied than do it any damage, because our guns will be out of range beyond the bar—which the French fear far more than cannon fire. "Despite the pilots' skill, the river channel is a daily witness to fresh incidents; the waves there are short, choppy, and rapid; they break so violently that any longboat meeting them broadside is capsized on the spot."[4] And we haven't even got a pilot!

At three in the afternoon, here we are at last, piled into sixteen boats and pulling away toward the bar over a sea as gray as that of Ouessant—we might as well have stayed on the other side of the Tropic! Lauzun at the front—*noblesse oblige*—in the *Fendant*'s longboat, is expecting heavy losses but doesn't know whether they'll be from drowning or gunfire: those who get across the bar will be exposed to shelling from the fort for almost an hour.

One bit of luck: everybody gets over the bar. "A few boats were in danger, but mastered it successfully." Now all we have to do is keep from being blown over in the wind of the cannonballs . . . But, in the image of so many other crazy things that happen in the craziness called war, here's the craziest of all: not one sound comes from the fort. Strange people, these English; one day they fire on the English flag and the next they miss the chance to sink half a dozen French longboats on sight! Oh well, it's a day gained, we've been neither drowned nor bombarded, but it's too late to attack now, we'll pitch camp where we land, in this calm pool formed by the crook in the shoreline "just after crossing the critical passage"—this limbo between two worlds.

To the north, "Barbary, flat, naked, barren," the Moors' country, the Sahara, Islam—and to the south, "verdant Guinea, heavily wooded, bristling with palms and baobabs." The Senegal is like an ethnic watershed. Above, they're still whites, the Arabian kind; below, the blacks begin. Two worlds, and they don't get along all that badly. The Senegal has been the boulevard for their commerce since time immemorial, and who would believe its balance could be upset by a microscopic infiltrate of bacteria seeping through this seam of Africa: three hundred Poles, Germans, and Irishmen raked up along the cowpaths of Lorraine and towed out here by sailors from Brittany—Lauzun's volunteers? Big blue-red-and-yellow bacteria. "The uniform was of sky-blue broadcloth; the footsoldiers wore a lemon-yellow braid on their jacket and scarlet breeches."[5] They've come "to conquer Senegal." Some specimens—will they even be capable of shouldering the English out of Africa, and putting a handful of blue uniforms in place of a handful of red ones?*

For the moment, it's the cold they seem most likely to die of: they've been engulfed by a glacial fog. At the latitude of the Cape Verde Islands, you must be joking! The men from East and North sit shivering in their wool from Lodève. Just stick close together and make a fire, that's the thing. No shortage of wood—baobabs, acacias, terebinths, and scores of nameless bushes enclose the myriad sounds of a different night: secret Africa, swarming along the banks. Huddled around the fire, the intruders sense the presence of "the lion, the hyena, the panther, the jackal," and crocodiles, and snakes of every description. "Toward the island of Kuma a few hippopotamuses have posted themselves, gigantic pachyderms which heave their monstrous heads to the surface of the water now and then, and whinny like horses . . . These beasts only come ashore toward the middle of the night, to seek their food, which

---

*This expedition of January 1779 illustrates the basic difference between eighteenth-century colonialism and the variety practiced in Africa after the beginning of the nineteenth century. The former merely set up forts here and there on the outskirts of civilizations which it left intact, the better to trade with them. The latter, starting with the conquest of Algeria, aimed at confiscating the land and dismantling the civilizations. With one exception, however, in the period we are concerned with: the "Islands" which were doomed to total conquest because of their diminutive size.

consists of grasses, roots and branches." Until now Lauzun has never seen anything bigger than the animals at Trianon, and this gives him very different sensations: nature is not, it appears, a toy farm. Who would want to penetrate any deeper into "the African continent, which is nothing but an immense menagerie of wild animals? An excursion into its hinterland offers more opportunities for drama than poetry. To venture upon such an undertaking, one must be endowed with all the enthusiastic courage of the naturalist, or with that morbid cupidity of the merchant which is stronger than fear."[6] Better to stay on the edge of it, and continue the elegant square dance of West Indies companies, with or without four-day warlets: French, English, Dutch, Portuguese, and Spaniards, all exchanging their trading posts like figures in a dance along the Senegambian coast which they have mistaken for a ballroom floor. The waltz of the colonies, a European entrechat.

Besides, who needs to push farther inland? In the morning, Africa comes out to us. The natives here aren't like the ones in America, they have no fear of these well-mannered whites laden down with iron and trinkets for trade.* And the French have a better reputation than the rest—that is, they pay more for their gum arabic, in the only legal tender on the coast: the iron bar, worth six ox-hides.† Lauzun has filled his longboat with these bars and uses them as ballast, and as the sun rises the banks of the Senegal are seen to swarm as thick with men by day as they swarm with beasts by night. First there are the "Negro fishermen" who emerge from their nearby huts, very black and frizzled, draped in cotton loincloths "tinted blue or undyed. The women wear handkerchiefs on their heads. They wear rows of glass beads at their waists, and around their necks are strings of amber or coral," which they will be only too happy to supplement with the latest mode from that incomprehensible beyond whence come the ships and thundersticks of the whites. Lauzun has a hard time keeping his Polacks in order when they find themselves surrounded by platoons of completely naked statuesque Negro adolescents: the girls don't "dress" until they reach sixteen and begin nursing. "Their hair, like that of the men, is done in rows of tiny plaits and oiled with butter." Looks good enough to eat. These first arrivals are Mandingos; but how are we supposed to talk to them? They don't speak, they bark, according to the interpreters, and it's not a whole lot of help to us to learn that "their language is a corrupt form of Bambara mixed with Sarakolé."[7] To them, Saint-Louis is

---

*Nor, apart from a few exceptions at points along the coast where pirate slave ships had made forays, were the coastal blacks afraid of "official" European slave-traders, who did not organize the deportations themselves. It was the blacks' own chiefs who sold their subjects, often after a raid in the hinterland.

†This was a flat iron bar, 9 feet long, 2 inches thick, and 4 inches wide. It was divided into twelve "legs," each containing three "dialots." In other words, it was a genuine currency, valued in 1787 at four livres sixteen sous the bar, or approximately twenty-five new francs [$5].

N'dar, we figure that out when they point to the ever-silent fort. They jig for joy when they identify these whites as "French." Let's not confuse the issue by trying to explain to them what an Irish mercenary is. The Moorish chieftains are already coming in from nearby Barbary, majestic and bronzed, "their heads also anointed with a coat of grease." They bring fresh vegetables and livestock, what a treat after two months of salt pork. Toward noon a cortege fit for an oriental emperor winds out of the south, and in fact it is an emperor, or almost: the brother of the King of Kayor or *Akkayor,* who rules over a vast unspecified domain, the black lord of the unexplored expanses beyond the peninsula of *Dakard.* News travels quickly across the savannah: the king, who is also called the Damel, has sent his brother "to this minister of the King of France" whose arrival is known throughout the kingdom; here's our Lauzun upgraded, and solemnly bowing to the Monsieur of another sovereign, "escorted by a large following of Negroes mounted on horseback and on camels."[8] Two civilizations brush wingtips: an overripe lily of the valley from the oldest monarchy in the world and one of the heirs to those red mud cities where the black Mohammedan marabouts have been chanting evening prayers for a thousand years. They contemplate each other with courteous contempt, without enmity, without curiosity. They shake hands from one world sidewalk to another as they exchange their little gifts.

The English, already short-circuited inside their fortress, would almost have disappeared from memory if the Damel's brother, who can speak a little French, hadn't finally provided the key to yesterday's enigma: of course they fired on the English flag—because they've mutinied! There've been some fine goings-on at Saint-Louis these last few weeks. Out here, on the coast of Africa, the garrison seems to have been more or less forgotten by the bigwigs back home. Fever, hunger, plague last winter, a hundred dead; the handful of wretches still on their feet, less than a score of hardened louts, finally did away with their governor, a brute named Fall, and replaced him with another brute named Stanton. Then, curled up like porcupines, they awaited the gallows, glad to live a few more hours on their own terms; and when they first saw Lauzun's pseudo-English fleet they thought it was King George sending out some very big guns just to punish little ole them. One corvette would have done the job. They bravely fired upon this "punitive force"—but ever since the word came in that the ships were French, they've been dead drunk. Prisoners of war instead of hanged, that's worth celebrating! Oh, for honor's sake they'll make the French twist their arms a little, ever so little . . .

Decidedly, Lauzun's volunteers aren't going to be able to lose a single man in this affray. The rest of the day is spent in virtually diplomatic negotiations: the fleet fires a few symbolic volleys in the general direction of the fort, which symbolically returns them before striking its flag. A proud and ragged delegate turns out to parley with the assailants as they invade the island.

"Surrender unconditionally, and commend yourselves to the magnanimity of the King of France."

That's all they're waiting for. Out of the fort straggles a small band of
famished buccaneers brandishing their few remaining weapons—the English
army in Senegal. They are loaded on board the *Fendant,* and Lauzun takes
possession of the first conquered stronghold of his life, an indescribable mess
of wormy biscuits, empty bottles, newly dug graves, and occasional smears of
English blood shed by other Englishmen. Nevertheless, on the following day,
Sunday, January 31, he presides over mass in full pomp and ceremony, flanked
by his officers in the friendly little bustle of his new allies—the mulatto traders
who are permanent residents of the place and the Peuls who have poled down
the river in their dugouts, bringing sheep and goats. The *Te Deum,* in the
presence of the new garrison in parade dress, is quite impressive. "One round
of cannon and three of musket were fired, then the duke was officially invested
as governor. The inhabitants were inexpressibly overjoyed at the restoration
of the Roman Catholic faith."9 This colorful mumbo jumbo is more their sort
of thing than those pallid Anglican services.

One last ordeal remains, more challenging than any battle: the solemn
interview, a week later, with the Damel in person, a huge character paralyzed
by fat, borne on a litter which he never leaves; with his two thousand horsemen, he practically takes over Saint-Louis. He has come to negotiate a new
trade agreement—new governor means new treaty—which requires eight
days of palaver. The sixty-two wives, "who never leave their sovereign, consume quantities of strong spirits," offered by Lauzun, of course, in return for
a palm wine that makes French, Irish, and Poles alike regurgitate with a single
nauseous surge. It's like syrup with red pepper in it. Fortified by booze, the
Damel finally signs, and starts guzzling all over again. "To show their contentment, the king and his favorite queen each drank off a score of glasses of
eau-de-vie." Lauzun is in training, all right, but he begins to wonder if he'll
last the course, and doubts his senses when he witnesses the strange phenomenon of these blacks whose complexions veer to white when they turn gray.*
One ultimate test awaits him: "The queen sent me her favorite slave," a sort
of walking beer barrel a couple of ells high, coated in oil and rancid butter,
not exactly Lady Bunbury or the Princesse de Guémenée, "assuring me of her
complete good will toward all whites, and myself in particular. She also made
me a present of a fine ox. I parried this courtesy by sending her a drum, an
instrument for which she has great affection."10 As for the young lady, if any
of you gentlemen would care to try? His aides-de-camp flee in terror, but come
nightfall, the Polish under-officers . . . Fifty days since Quiberon without a
woman. War's war.

* *Gris* (gray) is French for tipsy. [*Trans.*]

Boufflers, the governor who will take Lauzun's place, can think of no better
way to please his mistress, Eléanore de Sabran, than to announce "the dispatch
of a product of my government." "You cannot conceive of our surprise when,
a few days later, a little Negro no bigger than your thumb and black as ebony,
was delivered to Paris."[11] He's worth a pretty thank-you note to the Chevalier
de Boufflers. Senegal is not a total loss:

"I must tell you about your little savage, which my children have named
Friday,"* just as Mme du Barry, six years before, named another little depor-
tee Zamore. "They are absolutely enchanted with him, and no joy could equal
his when he first saw himself with a fine blue costume on his body; he puts
on such airs in his new attire that he makes us all nearly expire with laughter;
he resembles those cats who have frills tied to their tails; he twists and turns,
he looks at himself, he doesn't dare stir for fear of making himself dirty; he
can scarcely walk in his pumps; in short, he provides us with day-long entertainment, and seems all the more piquant to us as, in the way of pleasures and
distractions, he is our sole resource."

As she says, you could die laughing.

From Paris, with a more consciously cruel snicker—the habitual grimace of
such people—Mme du Deffand, whom no war would keep from her letter
writing, informs her old friend Walpole in London, on March 21, 1779, as
follows: "M. de Lauzun, with two ships and a very small number of troops,
has taken your Senegal, where you had your trade in Negroes; yesterday M.
de Choiseul was telling how M. de Sartines, reading to the King the details
of this expedition, was somewhat reluctant to relate all the circumstances of
it; but M. de Maurepas insisted he should leave nothing out, and so he
informed the King that the English garrison consisted of four men, three of
whom were ill, and M. de Choiseul tells us that the one who was left apparently
surrendered with good grace, and he had no doubt but that he would be
accorded the honors of war. If in this exploit M. de Lauzun had also found a
few gold mines, they would be quite as useful to him as any glory he may
derive from it."[12]

That's the line their intelligence always takes: denigration. After all, Lauzun
has just recovered Senegal for them, so they can have a steady supply of pet
Negroes. It's not a far cry from this to the people who insist that the Duc de
Chartres was hiding in the hold of the *Saint-Esprit* throughout the Battle of
Ouessant.

Robinson Crusoe was published in France in 1719.

13

FEBRUARY 1779

As a Soldier on Furlough

On February 11, 1779, a Philadelphia gazette, *The Pennsylvania Packet,** publishes one of those rectifications that are news in themselves: "We can assure
the public that the Marquis De Fayette's† having taken his leave of Congress
to take his departure for France, by way of Boston, is not owing to any disgust,
or public reason of a political nature, but flows from the earnest solicitation
of his private connections."[1] Now there's an item likely to cause several ears
to prick in both worlds. So he's already clearing out, is he, the little marquis,
before anything has been settled, while everything's still in a mess? The
desertion of a dilettante . . . In Paris, where they're gunning for him, some
people say they're not surprised, and the *Correspondance secrète* of January 10
intimates that no one there is deceived: "The Marquis de La Fayette has
written to a friend, 'I begin to realize that, misled by false enthusiasm, I erred
in leaving everything to rush to America; but it would be a still greater error
to come back. The cup is filled, and must be drained to the dregs, but one
already begins to taste the dregs.' "[2] A perfect example of a manufactured
quotation: the gossip writer has picked up a drawing-room witticism uttered
by some so-called friend of La Fayette attributing to the marquis what he
himself would feel in his place, and transformed it into a transatlantic confession. In other words, that's what Versailles thinks he's thinking.

He *is* mildly fed up with America, as a matter of fact, but would let himself
be cut in half sooner than admit it. On October 13 he applied to Congress for
"furlough," taking a large wad of precautions. Official motive: he might be
needed in France. "Now, Sir, that France is involved in a war, I am urg'd by
a sense of duty, as well as by patriotic love, to present myself before the King,
and know in what manner he judges proper to employ my services . . . I dare
flatter myself that I schall be look'd on [by the United States] as a soldier on
furlough, who most heartly wants to join again his colours, and his most

*This was also the name of the "packet" that brought Franklin back from England.

†All variants in spelling and names, when quoted from texts originally written in English,
are as given in Charlemagne Tower or other sources. [*Trans.*]

esteemed and belov'd fellow-soldiers."*[3] He leaves in a haze of incense: *"Resolved,* That the marquis de la Fayette, major general in the service of the United States, have leave to go to France; and that he return at such time as shall be most convenient to him . . . That the president write a letter to the marquis de la Fayette, returning him the thanks of Congress for that disinterested zeal which led him to America, and for the services he hath rendered to the United States by the exertion of his courage and abilities on many signal occasions . . . That the minister plenipotentiary of the United States of America at the court of Versailles be directed to cause an elegant sword, with proper devices, to be made and presented, in the name of the United States, to the marquis de la Fayette,"[4] and the finest frigate in the American navy, renamed the *Alliance* in his honor, was put at his disposal.

She was waiting for him in Boston.† On October 26 he leaves an exhausted Philadelphia in which the embryo of a Congress (reduced to twenty-two members) is squatting in the houses that are left standing, not knowing whether the English will be back next week or in three months **. . . . Four hundred miles to cover on horseback, through a bruised and bleeding country lashed by the late autumn storms. He's at the end of his tether. He doesn't even have the strength to swagger anymore: the fatigue and disappointment of the wasted summer have taken the stuffing out of him. D'Estaing has failed. Far from pulling the Rebels out of the mire, France's first gesture in their support has only pushed them a little deeper into it. He's not too proud of his homeland just now, is Gilbert de La Fayette; and as for being proud of his own services . . . "courage and abilities," sure—but results?

A driving, icy rain along the sloppy roads; he's skinny as a rail, exhaustion has pared him to the bone. In Rhode Island last July he went eight days without sleep, while he was shuttling back and forth between d'Estaing and Sullivan. And during the interminable match between Washington and the English in the four corners of New Jersey he never got time to make up for it. He sways with weariness in his saddle, and in the evening, stiff as a real soldier, he sways in the corner by the fire, reeling from the beverages they keep serving him to warm him up in every deadly bead of this rosary of little towns all exactly alike, all longing to toast the one nice Frenchman in two continents. Bristol, Trenton, Princeton, Somerville—he loses track. Grog, white rum, mulled

---

*La Fayette's English made rapid strides but at this stage it still shows signs of strain in spelling and expression. They disappear as time goes on. [*Trans.*]

†One of the few ports from which people could try to get through the British blockade and leave the continent. You had to sail either from the extreme north (Boston) or south (Charleston).

**On June 20, 1778, the Americans reoccupied Philadelphia, plundered and deserted by the English troops who had evacuated it to march through New Jersey to New York because, a little like Napoleon evacuating Moscow, they had been unable to establish themselves firmly in Pennsylvania.

wine, tea. Somerset, Plainfield, Chatham, Livingston, tea, mulled wine, white rum, grog. All Hallows isn't a holiday here (yet), nor is the Day of the Dead. You cross it without noticing, like the Hudson, well above New York, where the English are carousing. The yellowish river, mournful as all America this winter, trundles its mud down toward the English fleet. And those colorless girls in white, they're all alike too, and their grogs all taste exactly the same. Make a wide detour to the north, to escape the English outposts. Up the left bank of the Hudson. Funny: when you go away from New York, you enter the state of New York. But Massachusetts is still a long way off. Distance is the greatest ordeal in America. Gilbert is hardly halfway. Mulled wine, rum, grog. His beloved general is waiting for him two leagues from Fishkill, in his winter quarters. Little mountains. The town of Fishkill, one last grog—and La Fayette collapses, a few miles from headquarters, convinced he's going to die. He could be right. He's in far greater danger now than he was after Brandywine.

Dysentery? Intestinal flu complicated by gastritis, caused by bad food and alcohol burn? They call his affliction "a diarrhoea of the gut," they bleed him, they stuff him full of quinine bark because he's delirious with fever, they wait for him to get better or die. Twenty days abed in November, dreaming in the din of the little town which is also delirious because of the proximity of so many officers. Cavalcades, parades, shrill laughter of girls, regular appearances of Dr. Cochran, the army physician-in-chief whom Washington sends every day to take La Fayette's pulse and look gloomy. The winter wind blows, down the Hudson from Canada and on, to become the wind from America on the far side of an ocean Gilbert fears he may never cross again. The storms fling fistfuls of dead leaves against the panes in his bedroom window. A year of his life.

In November of the year before, everything was going so well. He was getting over his good wound. He had gone back to fight in a jolly little battle that was a tie all around, at Gloucester, one foot shod and the other bare like Diddle, diddle dumpling, my son John. Washington got Congress to give him a real command: "major general of the Virginia division." He had a long winter to break in his Virginians, at Valley Forge where the Americans had gone to earth—seven leagues [about 21 miles] from Philadelphia where the English were holed up—after "having skillfully erected, in a few days, a city of wooden huts,"[5] little barracks hardly more cheerful than prison cells—images of America's one remaining trump card: the endurance of Washington. The men "were in want of everything; they had neither coats, nor hats, nor shirts, nor shoes; their feet and legs froze till they turned black, and it was often necessary to amputate them."[6] The last bastion of freedom, five or six thousand fighters with the weight of a world on their backs, so stubborn and set that Washington himself, oh wonder! begins to betray an affection for them: "No history now extant can furnish an instance of an army's suffering such uncommon hardships as ours has done, and bearing them with the same patience and fortitude . . . their marches might be traced by the blood from their feet . . . [This is] a proof of patience and obedience which in my opinion can scarce be paralleled."* But at what cost! "The arms at Valley Forge were in a horrible condition, covered with rust, half of them without bayonets, many from which a single shot could not be fired . . . A great many of the men had tin boxes instead of pouches, others had cow-horns; and muskets, carbines, fowling pieces, and rifles were seen in the same company . . . The men were literally naked, some of them in the fullest extent of the word . . . I saw officers, at a grand parade . . . mounting guard in a sort of dressing-gown, made of an old blanket or woollen bedcover."[7]

There he was, La Fayette, right in the thick of it and as though enthralled. "I read, I study, I examine, I listen, I reflect, and upon the result of all this I make an effort to form my opinion and to put into it as much common sense as I can. I am cautious not to talk much, lest I should say some foolish thing,"[8] but he writes a fair number of them. He's meddled a little too much in everything, it's an itch with him. The worst of it wasn't the winter and the deprivation at Valley Forge; it was this great depression into which it seemed the whole of America had sunk, the doldrums of the war. Where was the Land of the Saints they were preaching in Europe? "This land is as ours, subject to the same passions, except that the passions here are naked, and that art is lacking which at least renders ours tolerable."[9] Defeatism was sprouting fast beneath the snow, and La Fayette made Washington smile at his naïveté: "You can conceive my astonishment when I saw that Toryism was as openly professed as Whiggism itself: however, at that time I believed that all good Americans were united together . . . It would be . . . a great pity that slavery, dishonour, ruin, and unhappiness of a whole world should issue from some trifling differences between a few men."†[10] Was he pretending to be, or was he really, such an innocent? The men engaging in what he calls "trifling differences" are a pack of cutthroats. Even Washington's hide is rubbing thin. Gates, the victor at Saratoga; and a general of Irish origins, Conway; and

*Letter from Washington to John Banister, delegate in Congress, April 21, 1778. After drawing attention to the precarious circumstances of his officers, who must "break in upon [their] private fortune for present support, without a prospect of future relief," he adds that "Men may speculate as they will; they may talk of patriotism; they may draw a few examples from ancient story, of great achievements performed by its influence; but whoever builds upon them, as a sufficient basis for conducting a long and bloody war, will find himself deceived in the end," and says there is all too much reason to fear that the very existence of the army will be shaken "unless a remedy is soon, very soon, applied. There is none, in my opinion, so effectual as the one pointed out"—i.e., an establishment of half-pay for officers after the termination of the war.

†Letter from La Fayette to Washington, December 30. 1777.

Charles Lee, who commands one army, are all in cahoots to get rid of their commander-in-chief, "who had won only a single battle one evening in the snow [Battle of Trenton], against a few drunken Germans."[11] And the loyal, the devoted, the crystal-pure Gilbert himself has been performing an impressive series of pirouettes among them all, while aiming a stream of letters of adoration in Washington's direction. True, Conway had given him hopes of commanding a whole army which was going to conquer Canada. Gates had even written out his orders: "In taking possession of Montreal . . ."[12] La Fayette avenger of Montcalm! It was enough to turn a steadier head than his. "How happy I would be had I the satisfaction of being an instrument of such a revolution." In January and February (1778) he was signing his letters "Commander of the Northern Army"—which consisted of his escort and aides-de-camp.[13] Washington made him a ceremonious reply, but between the lines one glimpses his perpetual mournful smile, and in March Washington was feeling abandoned by Congress, public opinion, and his subordinates too —all he had left were his trapper-soldiers at Valley Forge. He thought he might soon have to give La Fayette the *et tu, Brute!*

When the bubble of Gilbert's dream bursts it relieves him of having to face a cruel moral dilemma. This is the springtime of dejection: first come two weeks of sledges and horses up to Albany, the northern town where he was to meet his troops. "I go on very slowly; sometimes drenched by rain, sometimes covered by snow."[14] The Susquehanna is packed with floating ice. In Albany, not a thousand men and not a thousand dollars. Nobody has ever heard of the scheme. "I have been deceived by the Board of War . . . I confess I was perhaps too sanguine in my hopes . . . I am afraid it will reflect on my reputation."[15] No, no, not at all, calm down—Washington soothes him in mildly patronizing tones: "I . . . hasten to dispel those fears respecting your reputation, which are excited only by an uncommon degree of sensibility. You seem to apprehend that censure, proportioned to the disappointed expectations of the world, will fall on you."[16]

Then, farewell Canada and back to Valley Forge, where he finds the nucleus of the army stronger than before, thanks to some more foreigners: Baron von Steuben, the Prussian; Kalb, reprieved at the last moment; du Coudray's French artillery, and the cavalry under Armand de La Rouërie; and Pulaski and Kosciusko, the Poles serving their apprenticeships in freedom. As Washington's mistrust of his own men grew, he began turning increasingly to these others. Eleven thousand men, at last! Against sixteen thousand English, but the latter were divided: four thousand in New York, two thousand in Rhode Island, and ten thousand making ready to leave Philadelphia. "Up to this time, we have always supposed that troops should be disciplined and equipped before going into battle, but what has happened here disproves this theory; for the Americans, by their courage alone, without training and without breeches,* have whipped the British who had both."[17]

May 18: Barren Hill, La Fayette nearly gets caught going too close to Philadelphia, which was in the process of being evacuated. Flight across the Schuylkill, with only his men's heads showing above water, like "the corks of a fishing seine."[18] Anxiety: if I'm a prisoner tonight it's the end, La Fayette will never get off the ground. An irrepressible roar of laughter at the sight of the double flight of his Iroquois conscripts in terror at their first encounter with a cavalry, and the English dragoons in terror at the war cry of the Iroquois. His relief at getting back to camp.

Then his grief at learning that his first daughter died six months before: the letter from Paris reaches him at Valley Forge "only after passing through the sticky hands of all the Spanish postmen" and being rolled and pitched across the ocean and laboring all the way up river from New Orleans.[19] The consolation of knowing that another daughter, Anastasie, featureless for him, has replaced his little Henriette. Homesickness. "When I go home, we shall be old enough to establish ourselves in our own house,† to entertain our friends, build a sweet freedom and read foreign newspapers . . . I love to build châteaux in France, castles of happiness and pleasure . . . We are not so feeble that we shall need a miracle in order to produce another child. And this one will absolutely have to be a boy."[20]

He begins pestering the English between Philadelphia and New York. Then, on June 28: Monmouth, a battle of madmen, with both sides announcing they'd won and fearing they'd lost. We nearly had them, though, but then everything went wrong on account of the mistake, or treachery, of General Lee. "Why are the troops retreating! By God, they are flying from a shadow!"[21] Court-martial for Lee. Laurels for Washington, who turns the tide at the last moment. "Washington became Washington at Monmouth." No time to hang around: the fleet from Toulon is outside New York. France on our side, at last!

Then, on August 4: the longboat out to the *Languedoc,* the awesome bulk of the great ship, the Provençal sailors shouting "Vive le Roi!" and the tears, Admiral d'Estaing's great carcass hugging the frail little twenty-year-old general, his cousin: "You have won the opinion of the public to your side, you will spur us into action."

---

*I can resist the temptation to italicize, fourteen years before Valmy, but not the temptation to point out that I have resisted it. [Valmy was a battle won in September 1792 by the French revolutionary forces against the Prussians. At that time revolutionary soldiers (and civilians) wore striped trousers and were thus *sans-culotte* (without breeches); the name became applied to all supporters of the Revolution—*Trans.*]

†La Fayette and Adrienne de Noailles, a pair of infants married off at sixteen and fourteen respectively, had been compelled to live "in a nursery" with the Noailleses until La Fayette's departure for America.

"I have never wished so much for the ability that I have not, or for the experience that I shall obtain in the next twenty years, if God spares my life and allows us to have war. No doubt it is amusing to you to see me presented as a general officer; I confess that I am forced myself to smile sometimes at the idea, even in this country, where people do not smile so readily as we do at home."*

Amen! They share "our common origin as Auvergnats." Before they even mention America, hours are spent talking about "our lands in Auvergne, my Château de Chavaniac, the fine estate of Pont-du-Château and the excellent salmon-fishing that belongs to M. de Montboissier, my aunts and the marriage of my cousin [his love at fifteen] with M. d'Abos . . ." Somebody to talk to at last, after all these stand-offish Americans: "My purpose is, to leave at once for the Islands, for Europe, even for India, if in any one of these three portions of the world we are going to make war . . ."[22] War, war for war's sake, his eternal refrain since Metz and Bordeaux; and the war here is in a bad way, d'Estaing grim, always bad-tempered, a land officer gone to sea too late in life and disliked by his sullen officers; and the crews are like ghosts, what's left of them, that is, those who've survived the scurvy. A fleet worm-eaten under its fluttering flags, a hand stretched out across the ocean only to be snatched back again. Impossible to make a frontal attack on New York: the ships can't get past the bar. All right, then, what about coming ashore farther east, at Newport: with one cast of the net we can scoop up six thousand English who've hurried up here and cut themselves off in their eagerness to keep ahead of General Sullivan's militia. It would be all glory to the French, and that's what we're here for.

Young Colonel John Laurens, son of the president of Congress, has never heard of allies like this, he can't get over them: "This measure gave much umbrage to the French officers. They conceived their troops injured by our landing first, and talked like women disputing precedence in a country-dance, instead of men engaged in pursuing the common interest of two great nations."[23] Then everything comes to a halt at the end of two days—because the English fleet is on the way, thirty-six sea lions, quick, about face! D'Estaing hoists his battle flags, we'll show 'em. The last happy memory of La Fayette, left ashore: at ten in the morning of August 10 the French ships parade past accompanied by the futile barking of the Rhode Island batteries; seventeen vessels so resolute—and so well-placed in the wind—that the English "cut their cables, and stood out under full sail, leaving behind many of their ship's boats,† which, in their haste to get away, they had not stopped to pick up, in

*Twenty years . . . 1798. The year of the Egyptian campaign; La Fayette is an Austrian prisoner at Olmütz.

†The unloading boats which were to put ashore four thousand men to reinforce the English garrison at Newport.

the most beautiful weather in the world, and in sight of both the English and the American armies. I never was so happy as upon that day,"[24] the day when our dream comes true and the English flee before us after fifty years of keeping us on our knees. But after every dream comes the awakening: this one, on August 11, is a storm like the wrath of the gods unleashed upon these mortals, these children playing hide-and-seek with the prettiest toys in the world, and suddenly the inky sky splits open.

In Rhode Island tents are blown away, hail chops the countryside to cole slaw, the soldiers are soaked to the skin, and the natives have never seen anything like it. And when at last you can stand upright in the soaking fields again, where the devil have the ships gone? Not fleets now: corks bobbing in the ten-fathom swells. For a dollar, French and English would be going to each other's rescue. War? Bullshit. The *Languedoc*'s masts and rudder are gone, she has to be taken in tow. The *César* went down with all hands. Pitiful return of the grand most-Christian expedition to Newport: a procession of cripples limping up to say good-by. We've just come to tell you that we can't do anything for you, we're off to convalesce in Boston, like the English in New York. Outburst of anger from the Americans, you can't mean it, d'Estaing can't let us down, at least let him unload his troops, he's in cahoots with the Tories, for sure, do something, Monsieur le Marquis! La Fayette on the rack, ambassador of the impossible.

Then, days of toing and froing over the still heavy sea between these allies who are beginning to loathe each other, before being finally washed ashore among Americans wild with rage—d'Estaing has sneaked off during the night; well, he'll get a warm welcome in Boston, the shipyard workers'll be trying to hurl his sailors overboard, what a mess! General Sullivan's protest makes the rounds: "No possible reason can be assigned for the Count d'Estaing's taking with him the land forces which he has on board . . . We, therefore . . . do, in the most solemn manner, protest against the measure, as derogatory to the honor of France."[25] How could a La Fayette not accept this challenge? He nearly fights a duel with these people he's supposed to be helping, "myself, the friend of America—the friend of General Washington. I am more upon a warlike footing in the American lines than when I come near the British lines at Newport."[26]

And then, the evacuation of Rhode Island with clenched teeth, like that of Philadelphia a year before, and no chance of a wound to let him catch his breath, after one last fruitless approach to the Comte d'Estaing. "The Marquis de Lafayette arrived about eleven in the morning of August 31 from Boston; where he had been, by request of the general officers, to solicit the speedy return of the fleet," which is making ready, on the contrary, to sail for the Islands; and so the first French expedition to America ends before it ever started. "He had ridden hence to Boston in seven hours, and returned in six and a half—the distance nearly seventy miles. He returned in time enough to bring off the pickets and other parties which covered the retreat of the army."[27] Some mission. What a way not to get famous. Exhaustion or revulsion? Both, each feeding the other. "One half of the Americans say that I am passionately attached to my country, and the others say that since the arrival of the French fleet I have gone mad, and that I neither eat, drink, nor sleep but according to the direction of the wind."[28] From that point on he wants to get out, to escape from the sight of this limping alliance more than from America itself. Two months of letter writing. And now this last journey that really looks like the last one of all, the dead leaves of Fishkill. "I am hideously unlucky, and it makes me wretched and miserable . . . I feel all too well that I do not deserve to be pitied. Why was I so eager to come here? I've been sufficiently punished for it. I must be too sensitive, dear heart, to bring off such tours de force."[29] A year of his life . . .

At the end of November a hemorrhage "empties him of his entrails." It could kill him. It cures him. He manages to drag himself to headquarters to bask in the comforting pessimism that radiates from Washington. December 18: Boston, "where his recovery is completed with the help of Madeira wine."[30] January 10: The *Alliance* sets sail, a fine thirty-six-gun frigate with a crew of one hundred thirty-five commanded by a native of Saint-Malo who has defected to the United States. "Farewell, my dear General; I hope your French friend will ever be dear to you; I hope I shall soon see you again, and tell you myself with what emotion I now leave the coast you inhabit." Does he really? What he mostly hopes is that he'll get home in time for that descent upon England everybody's talking about. "If they went without me I should hang myself."[31]

COUNT HANS AXEL FERSEN

14

MARCH 1779   SCÉNE GALANTE AT VERSAILLES

The Cost of a Single One of Our Entertainments

But he's got to get there first. The storm pursues him—storm or his bad luck?—and nearly drives the *Alliance* aground off the coast of Newfoundland. He hasn't gotten his strength back yet, and a queasy stomach inclines him to moroseness: "What a brilliant idea I had, at twenty, with my name, my rank, my fortune, and after marrying Mademoiselle de Noailles, to leave it all and come here to be turned into luncheon for the cod!"[1] The storm is followed by mutiny. He'll have had the lot. The *Alliance*'s crew was taken on in Boston, barrel-scrapings, English deserters, gallows bait. They couldn't care several thousand damns less about the United States and freedom in the world—anything to eat a square meal once in their lives. And King George is promising a very high price, as war booty, for any American ship brought into his ports by a mutinied crew. The leaders work out a good plan: give the alarm at four in the morning, "Ship ahoy!" All the officers would turn out on deck and a gunner in on the plot would mow them down with a single burst of grapeshot. But an informer decides it's worth even more to spill the beans, so the *Alliance* sails into the Brest roads on February 6 with thirty-three men in irons for ballast at the bottom of the hold. Gilbert abandons them to their fate on a convict ship without much moisture in his eyes: "There was not a single Frenchman or American among the conspirators."[2] So his honor's safe. And his life too, by the skin of his teeth. And he's going to be able to savor a small revenge. The Recouvrance guns fire thirteen rounds to salute the thirteen-star frigate, and Gilbert takes them as a salute to himself. "It was in recollecting the position of my country, of America, and of myself at the outset, that I watched the port of Brest welcome and salute the flag flying on my frigate."[3] From France, America was already beginning to look good again.

One hundred forty-one leagues from Brest to Paris—no, Versailles, for he goes to the King and his ministers before going to his wife; ambition before love, it's becoming second nature to him. He's received there by his childhood —and barracks—friend, the Prince de Poix, known as "le petit Poix."* There's a bevy of beauties at his levee: the "combined princesses" de Poix and d'Hénin, as those inseparables are called. And my dear, do you know, the Queen is more beautiful than ever since her confinement, and she's wearing ribbons created specially for her, two colors on each lapel? That's the big news here, the same as ever, while elsewhere half the world is changing. Gilbert was expecting to be congratulated and embraced by the King on his first day back; hold your horses, boy. Maurepas deigns to see him, and even that's a favor; the court is still annoyed with him, or rather it pretends to be for convention's sake, because he was disobeying orders when he left. But Maurepas is fond of La Fayette who reminds him of his own youthful dreams. For two hours he listens to him reel off all the news he's already heard, along with a hodgepodge of plans, secrets, and little digs against the Quakers. Then he gives the hero of two worlds a pat on the head and sends him to stand in the corner.

Petit pois: green pea; *poix* is pronounced like *pois.* [*Trans.*]

A penalty, just for form's sake: a week under house arrest at his father-in-law's, the Hôtel de Noailles, where he is allowed to see "only the people of his own family."* They're delighted to pull him up a bit, put him back in step. No official triumphs for him. All he gets, in the way of laurels, is a token punishment for having gone over the wall—their wall, the one that protects Versailles from the march of time. Maybe he's right and they're wrong, but where would we be if we didn't punish people who are right before their time? La Fayette, go to your kennel.

There's one person, at any rate, who won't complain. Adrienne is almost twenty now, and in her husband's absence, after the birth of her second child and the death of her first, she has finally begun to grow into a woman. To her, her husband is God. His return overwhelms her with a happiness "easy to believe, impossible to express. M. de La Fayette has come back as modest [*sic*] and charming as you left him.† Just now he is in disgrace with the King, and forbidden to show himself in any public place. The most distinguished and agreeable person in the world, that is whom God has preserved for us from a host of the most awesome perils . . . When I think upon my lot as his wife, I am very grateful to God. I find myself so far from being as lovable as he is that I feel positively wretched."⁵ To think he's been dreading a fit of the sulks for having left without giving notice! She'd gladly beg his pardon instead. Magnanimous, he grants her these few days, a present from the king, before padding eagerly off to see Aglaé d'Hunolstein, whose handsome body has become so expert in the hands of Philippe de Chartres at Mousseaux. Aglaé doesn't talk to him about God when they're in bed, and she doesn't keep him hanging around waiting. She's the eager one here, and she's not alone. Gilbert discovers the erotic virtues of glory. "Upon my arrival I had the honor of being consulted by all the ministers and, which is worth a great deal more, kissed by all the ladies."⁶

But he can no longer be satisfied with them. There's a part of himself that is irrepressible. Letters to Maurepas, letters to Vergennes, letters to Franklin, letters to the king—the last one as from a schoolboy asking please, how much longer does he have to stay in after class? In this cockeyed world, La Fayette tenders his apologies; he's got to—it's the rule. "Love of my fatherland, a desire to see its enemies debased, a political instinct which seems to be justified by the latest treaty;** these, Sire, are the reasons which determined the course I have followed in the American cause . . . The nature of my faults entitles me

---

*"In other words, the whole Court," comments Maurois.⁴

†Letter from Adrienne to Gilbert's two aunts, who lived in the château where he was born —Chavaniac, in Auvergne.

**Treaty of alliance between France and the United States. Indeed, this letter is not without a certain embryonic political "instinct." Not one syllable to Louis XVI about those bugaboos Independence and Republic. La Fayette sticks to the old elements of European strategy.

to hope that I shall be able to efface them. It is to the goodness of Your Majesty that I shall owe the joy of removing them, by whatever means Your Majesty may deign to offer me of serving, wherever the lands and whatever the manner of that service,"[7] the descent upon England, or failing that the Indies, East or West, who cares, or Senegal or Gibraltar, or Canada, his fond old dream of Canada . . . Vergennes and Maurepas are beginning to know their man. We'll just let him flap around in midair and cool off a little in the whirligig of festivities.

At last he is received at court, where the King listens to him and says nothing in reply, where the Queen holds out a hand for him to kiss in passing, where he melts into the corps de ballet and the habitués of the gaming tables. He is metamorphosed back into the slightly provincial young nobleman he was a couple of years ago. All America has done is to give him self-confidence. No lanterns, no cheering, a few balls, eight lines of doggerel sandwiched into the script of one performance of the deathless opus of somebody called Rochon de Chabannes given at the Comédie-Française—"*L'Amour français,* comedy in one act." The "Marquise de Sernette" crosses downstage and, pointing at La Fayette who's very much in view in the front row of the Noailles box, says to "Damis":

> Voyez ce courtisan à peu près de votre âge.
> . . . La gloire seule échauffe, embrase ses esprits.
> Il vole la chercher sur un autre hémisphère.[8]

> [Behold this courtier, almost of your years.
> . . . Glory alone heats, inflames his spirit.
> In search of it he flies to other hemispheres.]

And that is the full extent of his "triumph," far smaller than the one for which Chartres was forced to pay so dearly six months before. The common people pay no attention to him. Three or four two-line squibs in the newspapers. And that's all. He's kept well away from politics and strategy. The Maréchal de Broglie is on maneuvers in Normandy, we've just recovered Senegal but we've lost Pondicherry, and since the Comte d'Estaing was unable to do anything for the Rebels, who could succeed where he failed? But *he,* at least, can occupy himself looking after our Islands. Well, then, what about Canada? No, no, heaven forbid! Don't touch it! La Fayette is the only man in the world who wants to march on Quebec and Montreal. Neither the King of France nor the American Congress has the slightest desire for an expedition to the north, and for similar although diametrically opposed reasons. The French are already becoming alarmed by the burgeoning of the monstrous American dolly. In his diplomatic correspondence, Vergennes is busily arranging for it to be held in check to the south: the Spaniards will keep Louisiana.

And far be it from us to rescue those saber-toothed republicans in the north! Far better for the English crown to keep its Canadian possessions, like a sword of Damocles over the head of New York and Boston, a *cordon sanitaire* of monarchist colonial troops to quarantine the seat of infection. And the Rebels aren't eager to offer any footholds to an avenging French army, either. Washington has already sounded the alarm,* after hearing his little marquis's fantasies: "France . . . possessed of New Orleans on our right, Canada on our left . . . would, it is much to be apprehended, have it in her power to give law to these States . . . Let us suppose that, when the five thousand French troops (and under the idea of that number twice as many might be introduced) had entered the city of Quebec, they should declare an intention to hold Canada, as a pledge and surety for the debts due to France from the United States . . . what should we be able to say? . . . I fancy that I read in the countenance of some people, on this occasion, more than the disinterested zeal of allies . . .† Hatred to England may carry some into an excess of confidence in France"[9]; some, maybe; but Washington certainly isn't one of them. A fine lot of allies! France is at war with England and at the same time wants to keep her in a strong position to the north of America, while America is bristling with mistrust of that same France. And the diplomats, in their gilded cages in Madrid and London, go on spinning the wheel like so many squirrels.

We'll just keep him well away from all that, Jocrisse** de La Fayette. He's got America on the brain. "Amidst all the different whirlpools drawing me along I was not losing sight of our Revolution; having gotten into the habit of great causes sustained by small means, I told myself that the cost of a single one of our entertainments would have outfitted the United States army."[10] We really must calm him down and get him out of here, or he'll be seeing himself as a minister of American affairs. They give him a regiment—the king's Dragoons—to take the edge off his appetite;‡ and they contrive to make him think it comes as a special favor from the queen, that'll flatter him. The garrison is at Saintes, true, which is a dull enough place when you've just left the banks

---

*In a letter to Congress, on November 13, 1778.

†This was not aimed at La Fayette, but Washington wasn't far from believing him "manipulated" by the Versailles government, at least as far as his Canadian designs were concerned. In this instance he was well off course, and endowed Vergennes and Louis XVI with more imagination than they possessed. To be sure, they might well have considered seizing this magnificent opportunity, and Beaumarchais may conceivably have suggested it to them. The historians who never fail to sneer at Voltaire for his blindness on the subject of those famous "few acres of snow" ["You know that these two nations are at war about a few acres of snow in Canada . . ."—*Candide,* Chap. 23] thirty years before offer no explanation of this oversight on the part of their precious Vergennes.

**Jocrisse: a comic character who gets led around by the nose. [*Trans.*]

‡Or rather, they "consent to allow him to purchase it" from its owner, the Marquis de Créquy, for 80,000 livres—around 400,000 new francs [$80,000].

of the Hudson—but colonel at twenty-one, he could do worse. And they let him hope that one day soon he'll be able to load his soldiers into two or three ships under the command of John Paul Jones, and swoop down on some English town like a falcon. He sets out for Saintonge on May 20. All in all, he hasn't done too badly out of his return. And his wife is pregnant.*

But the Queen is cross with him. On May 15 she had to confess to Mercy-Argenteau that she was unable to tell her mother anything at all concerning the French preparations for war. "The Queen confided to me that she could see very well how anxious people were to persuade the King to speak as little as possible of serious matters with his august spouse, that M. de Maurepas was the author of this reticence, that he had forbidden the Marquis de La Fayette to speak to the Queen on the subject of the expedition which is to be entrusted to the said marquis, that the said La Fayette [Mercy wields his pen like a bulldozer] had confessed this fact to the Queen, who was greatly incensed thereby at the old minister."[11] Is Maurepas the only subject of her irritation? All year long Marie Antoinette treats La Fayette as though he didn't exist. Even before that she was not wildly fond of him because he's such a weedy type: she prefers fleshy men, like Besenval or Guines, like her father. And Gilbert, by refusing to share his secrets, has just lost his only chance to gain favor with her; to hell with him! This American business is all such a bore!

. . . The Bavarian business, meanwhile, is over. On May 13 a slapdash peace is signed, at Teschen, to end a non-war. A great many sword thrusts gone astray in the Danube. The Wittelsbachs will reign in Munich, and Austria will not get Bavaria. For Frederick it's half a victory, and for Maria Theresa it's almost a whole one over her son, who's choking with rage. The eaglet is not allowed to become an eagle. Marie Antoinette might have spared her tears last year. For consolation, she has just treated herself to a case of the measles—a real holiday because it means three weeks away from Louis XVI. "I would not let him come with me into quarantine. He has never had the measles and, especially now when there are so many pressing concerns, it would have been regrettable for him to contract this illness. We write to each other every day. I saw him yesterday, from the top of an outdoor balcony"[12] at the freshly decorated Petit Trianon, where she goes to spend these three weeks "for a change of air," but also so that she can finally use the place: she's never been able to sleep there before. The court promptly goes into a tizzy because her four "sick nurses," those who "took over the Queen's bedchamber from seven in the morning until eleven at night and only emerged from it for their meals," were the ducs de Guines and de Coigny, the Baron de Besenval, and Count

*And by October 1 he has to pay off 190,000 livres in promissory notes signed by him before leaving Bordeaux, the equivalent of a bare million new francs [$200,000]. His fortune can stand it.

Esterhazy. That's the kind of crime the Queen is being accused of now—being sick in the company of men she fancies. "The Court debated which ladies would be chosen to look after the King should he fall ill,"[13] and Maria Theresa starts moaning again: "The company of these four men whom my daughter selected during her illness has greatly distressed me."[14] What a lot of fuss about nothing! The only person (female) who has a real hold on her heart so far, Yolande de Polignac, is shut up in the Muette with another case of measles, and the only person (male) who is about to gain hold of that same heart—without wanting to and perhaps without even being aware that he can—isn't close enough to the inner circle to have acquired access to her intimacy. Nonetheless, this is the one important secret event of the spring of 1779, fleetingly glimpsed by a few expert observers such as Creutz, the Swedish ambassador, who writes to Gustavus III on April 10—that's his job, after all:

"I must tell Your Majesty, in confidence, that the young Count Fersen has been so well treated by the Queen that it has given umbrage to several persons. I confess I cannot help thinking that she showed a leaning toward him. I saw signs too certain to doubt it."[15]

She hasn't toppled. But she's leaning.

15

APRIL 1779

Avenger of Every Ignominy

In March, in the fair town of Alençon, "two poor devils accused and convicted of having forced open an alms box in a church"[1] have been hanged. And forgotten—except by Jacques Hébert, who is outraged at the disproportion between the crime and its punishment. True, he's expecting to feel the heavy hand of justice on his own head one day soon, and it's his own case that has diverted the public's attention so quickly and so thoroughly that it seems quite oblivious to the present war.

Yet Normandy has again become the springboard for a conquest of England. Rouen and Le Havre, packed with soldiers, are a long way off to the north, but Saint-Malo, the third rallying point of the army of invasion, lies west of Alençon, and the town has been crossed and recrossed for weeks by divisions from Navarre, Touraine, Normandy, and the King's own, coming all the way from the frontiers.² It's the vast ebb and flow, the trampling herd driven by an about-face of History, marching from east to west across "middle Normandy," the little land of the Marches squeezed between Perche, Houlme, and Auge, between hedgerow and plains. Neither riches nor poverty: comfort. "Good land, well-enclosed, well-built, and tolerably cultivated, with marling."³ Alençon, heavily seated on both banks of the Orne, is a fat mother-hen town whose citizens' one topic of conversation these days is Jacques Hébert. And his big worry is the two courts in Alençon—that of the bailiff's judges who are to pass verdict on his case, and that of the twelve thousand voices of public opinion. The war can wait; besides, England's waiting too. But the decision that will make or break his youth is to be taken any day now.

But what has he done, this Jacques Hébert, to come up before the judges at twenty-one? The eldest son, and such a good family! He's from "the upper portion of the third estate,"*⁴ the bourgeoisie of prosperous craftsmen whose corral is beginning to seem increasingly confined to them when they see what a huge pasture the aristocrats are still monopolizing. His grandfather—another Jacques Hébert—was apprenticed to a master goldsmith in Grenoble under Louis XIV, but left when still a very young man and came to settle here in this fine town of fairs, markets, and nascent industries, where trade was booming. It was a good life, cutting the jewels, real or false, that went so well with Alençon lace and the cuffs people wore in the winter, a single pair of which could cost as much as two thousand livres.† "In the Hertre mine two leagues from town false diamonds are found among the quarry stones, called Alençon diamonds. Some have such fire that even connoisseurs have mistaken them for real gems."⁵ Jacques Hébert the elder had cut out his life on the edge of that quarry, and faceted it by marrying a girl who was a daughter of some big tradespeople and sister of a priest. Four girls were born—that meant litters of goldsmiths, but magistrates too—and a single son, another Jacques, the father of our lad, who became, of course, a master goldsmith and took off from there to soar from strength to strength. First alderman, then deputy mayor, lieutenant of the bourgeoisie, and parish treasurer, he ended his days as "prior consul" (later known as "chief magistrate of the commercial court") or, in other words, as arbiter and chief among his peers. All of which were valid reasons for his marrying the high and noble lady Marguerite Beunaiche de La Houdrie, born in the pretty manor house of a hamlet in the Lower Maine

---

*The third estate (in French, *tiers état*): under the monarchy, or Ancien Régime, this was the section of the population that had no "privileges." The other two estates or orders were the clergy and the nobility. In other words, the third estate contained the bourgeois (bankers, painters, and writers as well as merchants, craftsmen, and shopkeepers), laborers, and peasants—almost everybody. [*Trans.*]

†10,000 new francs [$2,000]! At that price they went to court. But you could find a pair for 100 or 200 livres.

district, Izé. She was thirty, he sixty. On November 15, 1757, this classic association of bourgeoisie and nobility, classic even to the generation gap, produced a child of his old age, Jacques-René Hébert. Godmother: his mother's sister Anne-Marie, spouse of squire Louis de Bastard, lord of La Paragère and des Hayes and lord of Boissy-en-la-Pallu.* This couple, by the way, could show their in-laws a thing or two in the way of retarded fertility, for when Hébert's cousin and contemporary Louis-Estienne de Bastard was born two years after Jacques, his father the squire was eighty-eight. This cousin, also childhood playmate, has just married a demoiselle Challemel des Moulins.† Almost a wedding of aristocrats, with a hundred guests, among the front row of whom the pretty, slightly girlish features of Jacques Hébert could be observed; neatly dressed, pleasant manners, "a good-looking lad in spite of his small stature." You're willing to bet he'll soon marry some aristocrat too? Keep your money in your pocket. Nothing is less certain; you know he's been "involved" for the last two years. Who would want to get mixed up with him after that scene in the apothecary shop over the widow Coffin? And especially after that shocking broadsheet he put up, that claw-scratch across the walls of Alençon? Why, he's started behaving like a pamphleteer. He won't live that down so soon. And true enough, if you look again, there's something about him, some part of him that isn't even at the wedding, that has escaped them all, an insolence in his look, something brooding. He's going to make trouble for somebody, is Jacques Hébert.

His early years didn't make too much, though, despite the death of his aged father while he was still a child, too young to step automatically into the line of goldsmiths. But that was almost a blessing for his mother, a pious woman who longed to have a bishop or lawyer for a son. She sold off the family business and legally undertook "to have him taught the Latin language, and to send him to class in the collège of this town [Alençon]. After which, should he not enter the priesthood or go on to study law, the said lady under-takes to put him to learn a trade befitting his estate and condition."[7] The poor woman was out of luck: the Alençon collège had been renowned in the days of the Jesuits, but since their expulsion the instruction was fumb-lingly dispensed by an ill-tuned chorus of ill-assorted priests. Nevertheless,

---

*In the present-day department of Mayenne. The name "Pallu" shows that there were once brine pits there, and hence brine-pit workers *(paludiers)*.

†In 1792 Hébert's noble cousin Louis-Estienne becomes an émigré. "I never knew he cared so much about his gentlemanliness," sighs the editor of the *Père Duchesne.*[6] [Hébert *is* the Père Duchesne, whose radical paper has enormous influence later in the Revolution. Titles of his editorials often begin *"La Colère"* or *"La Grande Colère du Père Duchesne"* ("The Wrath" or "The Great Wrath of Père Duchesne")—whence the inspiration for the running head for this chapter. *Trans.*]

Hébert manages to pick up some Latin along with a few useful notions of rhetoric. He likes talking in public, and his friends like listening to him; they find him "amiable and distinguished." He describes himself as "lazy and mischievous";* it makes a rather nice combination. The priesthood? He doesn't fancy it. The bar? We'll see. Politics? The barest tinge, a mere twitch of interest in Turgot's attempted reforms and the Grain War, which had singed Normandy just badly enough to leave a holy fear of fire. Turgot remains the downtrodden hero of his youth. He later admits that for a time he had hopes of Necker: *"I don't set myself up to be a man of wit, but damnation! when I saw that honest man, that good intendant of Languedoc,† that Turgot whose soul was so fine and whose views were so just, hell's fire and brimstone! when I saw him driven out of the ministry, I swore like holy blue blazes . . . They told me . . . there was a diabolical plot that would infallibly set some foreigner, a Genevan, at the head of our finances . . . And in a trice, we began imagining, like confounded street-corner loiterers, that the Genevan was going to make larks drop ready-roasted into our open beaks. Damn me, we deserved the fate we were preparing for ourselves."*[8]

The great event of his teens was Denise Coulombet, Coffin's wife, one of those providential hussies who save provincial towns from total somnolence and are the despair of respectable mothers and prostitutes alike because they lure the youths away from both. She was married to Coffin the apothecary long enough to give birth and vogue to a couplet that ran through the streets of Alençon:

Si tout cocu avait des cornes,	[If simple cuckolds wore one horn,
Coffin serait un vrai bigorne.	Coffin'd be a real *bigorne*.**]

Then, as a merry widow, she throws herself into the part. Since it is true that "them that has gets," she's blamed for debauching half the young blades in her part of town. Now, her part of town is the area bounded by the Church of Notre Dame, the town hall, and the collège, where his status as day pupil offers Jacques Hébert plenty of opportunity to saunter back and forth with his hands in his pockets in front of the dispensary that Denise Coffin is still managing without the slightest difficulty: men are falling all over each other to help her. She's thirty-six, just twice his age, and she has a penchant for striplings. An easy meeting, a benign initiation. To her Jacques Hébert owes

---

*A remark he makes in 1793 to Desgenettes, a former fellow pupil who becomes one of the great physicians of the armies of the Empire.

†*Sic.* Turgot was intendant of Limousin, never of Languedoc. In this text, written in 1790, Hébert shows his hazy knowledge of the events of his youth. Here, as with Sade, passages not contemporary but directly relevant are italicized. The italicized passage and those that follow it are taken from the newspaper *Père Duchesne* and are directly inspired, eleven years later, by the events related in this chapter.

**A *bigorne* being a two-horned anvil.

an auspicious sexual awakening; but he's a romantic and has to spoil it all by
mixing up dalliance and love. Ah, sweet eighteen . . . she's touched, and puts
up with him for a couple of months, making an attempt to hide the other side
of her life. Until April 14, 1776.

That day, two of her other lovers come to blows inside the shop: a doctor
named Clouet, arguing seniority, and Latour, the apprentice apothecary, who
has replaced the late lamented Coffin at his mortars, cauldrons, alembics, and
elsewhere. Latour is on the way up. Clouet finds it intolerable to be out of the
top ten. An apothecary's shop, filled with breakables, is not an ideal place in
which to settle a point of honor. These worthy characters proceed to play out
the last scene of an act by Molière, hurling pottery jars filled with "confections,
compositions, balms, plasters, unguents, perfumes, syrups, oils, preserves,
sugars, waxes, other drugs and groceries" at each other. Demijohns of oil
explode. Clouds of powders gush from gutted sacks. It's Low Sunday morning
and the neighbors come running; among them, three houses down the street,
is young Hébert, who gets the full picture from one earful of the adversaries'
insults. Naïve he may be, but a dunce he's not. There's no time to weep over
shattered illusions, however; he has to leap in and try to avert disaster. Doctor
Clouet has the advantage in weight and is now working little Latour over with
whatever he can lay his hands on, bottles, pestles, spatulas—Hébert and Latour
later testify it was a knife, but Clouet swears it wasn't. He's also shouting,
though, and there's no doubt about his words:

"I'm going to kill him, your little fancy boy!"

Maybe he would have, except for Hébert. They're a bloodthirsty lot,
those Normans . . . But he doesn't need to go that far. The widow Coffin is
a female down to her toenails, she reacts like the doe in front of the old stag
and automatically sides with the strongest. She sends Latour packing. She
eludes Hébert and tries to play on their recent idyll to persuade him to give
false evidence in Clouet's favor, but Clouet just manages to settle out of court,
with Lawyer Desgenettes;* he'll pay for Latour's medical expenses—the boy's

*Father of the future physician. And cousin of another young Alençon student, Valazé, whom
we will meet again among the Girondins at the Convention. This may be as good a place as any
to identify a few of the terms relating to the Revolution proper, to which the author alludes in
this volume but which won't become realities until future ones. (For those readers, that is, whose
French Revolution isn't exactly at their fingertips anymore.) The body of men who actually
governed the country while bringing down the monarchy was known by various names at various
periods, the main ones being as follows: the *Estates General,* who met in May 1789 and argued
over what kind of representation the third estate should have until a decision was taken on June
27, when the *Constituent Assembly* came into being and, while the first paroxysms were taking place,
worked out and enacted the foundations of a constitution. This was accepted in September 1791,
after which the Constituent was replaced by the *Legislative Assembly.* It is this body that was also
known as the *Convention.* Depending on who had the upper hand in it, moderates or extremists

covered in bandages, they had to shave his head—yes, and he'll pay damages too . . . But please, please, no scandal!

Fine. But a month later the doctor still hasn't forked out so much as a sou, and the two younger jilted lovers find themselves companions in misfortune. Their lust for vengeance has cooled, and is ready to serve up in the form of six large anonymous handwritten broadsheets stuck up during the night of May 16–17 on the doors of Notre Dame, the intendant's offices, the finance bureau, and two houses on the Porchaine crossing. Alençon awakes all atwitter at Jacques Hébert's first pamphlet, every copy of which is surmounted by two knives dripping in laboriously painted gore.* This fruit of several days' labor is a model for the birth of *Père Duchesne*—the birth of a wind of wrath.

"On May 16 in the year of grace 1776 before us appearing: Honor, avenger of every ignominy and all sentiments degrading to man, hear! hear! the cry of the public and the laments of the oppressed innocent: Gilles Fiacre Barrabas Clouet,† physician, they say, of the Faculty of Montpellier, guilty in fact and in law of having, by unprecedented actions, determined to add the title of murderer to that of poisoner . . . we have declared and do hereby declare the said Gilles Fiacre Barrabas Clouet unfit for all human society and to this end have sentenced and do hereby sentence him to banishment from all places in which honesty, humanity and reason foregather; and do hereby order the said Clouet to respect his ban, under pain of being compelled to cohabitate with the savage beasts whose bloodthirsty temperament he shares."9

There isn't enough powder in this prank to blow up a teaspoon, but the solidarity of right-minded people works against Hébert and Latour, and especially the former, as the only person capable of conceiving and penning such a broadsheet. Clouet takes his suit to the magistrates. Hébert and Latour plead not guilty and guffaw. "We, the authors of that broadsheet? Prove it!" Somebody actually tries to: a weird coalition that could be found in no other environment, composed of the judges, the priests . . . and the butchers. At the request of the first, the second issue admonitory imprecations from their pulpits so that the whole town will know what's up. The chief vicar of Alençon solemnly pronounces the *monitory* three Sundays running before the sermon

---

or reactionaries, it was the *Girondin Convention* (until June 1793), the *Montagnard Convention* (until July 1794), or the *Thermidorian Convention,* which ended in the *Directoire.* [*Trans.*]

*Meant to represent the weapon that Clouet's accusers say he used against Latour.

†The future Père Duchesne's first target is actually named Michel, but Hébert is also showing intimations of his future skill at turning popular sayings to his own ends by attributing three Christian names to the doctor which were insults in those days [as "nance" in a later era, for example]: Gilles—"the nincompoop who gets stung"; Fiacre—the man who messes up everything he does (derived from the name for a poor coach, or fiacre); and Barrabas—the man "known as Barrabas at the Passion of Christ."

at high mass: under pain of excommunication, the faithful are enjoined to tell the religious authorities anything they know concerning the authors of the broadsheets. The priests will subsequently transmit the information to the magistrates.* The priests! What a bunch of bastards! Beginning with those Sunday masses when he unexpectedly finds himself entangled in the machinery of the Church and thus threatened, denounced, spewed forth by the universal Mother, it's all over between Jacques Hébert and religion. All against one. "Both God and the devil were called in to confound me."†

"Damnation, we're not going to let ourselves be diddled by a pack of good-for-nothing skirtwearers. Their confessions, their purgatory, their absolutions, and their indulgences are nothing but pap for idiots today. The so-called keys of St. Peter, with which the Popes' pimps unlocked and flung open the double doors of our heavenly Father's drawing room, now seem to us as picklocks, which the Roman pontiff would still like to use for breaking into our houses and strongboxes and taking away all we possess."[11] "O God, deliver me from mine enemies: therefore, deliver us from those buggerly priests who used to take our wheat from our fields, our wine from our cellars, our daughters and wives from our houses, and then gagged us when we tried to open our mouths."

In the same breath Hébert conceives a loathing for his enclergified compatriots. The only thing worse than a Norman is a Norman priest:

" 'Hast lost thy soul?' said the first Norman to the second Norman, who had just sworn a false oath.

" 'And thou thy oxen?' retorted the second.

"Well, hell and damnation, almost every skirtwearing priest thinks like the second Norman."[12]

"As for the butchers, all we have to do if we want them to toe the line is let everybody sell meat; then there will soon be plenty of it, and cheap enough too."[13] The butchers are the most powerful guild in Alençon, a major stock-trading center in which "this brutish and even ferocious species of men" carved out a filet for themselves way back in 1560 when they helped the Catholics to annihilate the Calvinists, who were "then very numerous and powerful in the region," in a massacre twelve years prior to the famous one on St. Bartholomew's Day. This earned them the right to march at the front of the Corpus Christi procession

---

*The monitory was a great boon to secular detectives, who could use it to make up for their own dearth of numbers by regimenting the flock with a combination of fear of the devil and fear of the gendarme. Recourse to it was current practice in Normandy, where the *cahier* [notebook listing grievances] of the clergy of Evreux at the Estates General in 1789 protests against "the trivial and indiscreet grounds on which monitories are ordered, even in ridiculous cases, thus exposing to contempt and derision censures designed to be employed only in the gravest matters."[10]

†From a confidential statement to Desgenettes.

with their cleavers in their fists and at their heels their hounds, "who became frightened and began biting because people trod on their paws, or howled terrifyingly every time the château culverins were fired to salute the Blessed Sacrament."[14] The butchers and their hounds take the monitory very much to heart, and spend whole nights stalking the streets of Alençon, only too content, on the pretext of looking for broadsheet-posters, to affirm their supremacy in a town in which they see themselves as the priests' militia. Hébert will never forget those baying dogs.

Pious but prudent, the burghers bolt their doors and keep their mouths shut. Then, just as Hébert thinks he's wriggled off the hook, the bitch comes out of her hole. Denise Coffin, last season's good fairy, ruins him by showing the judge a love letter he wrote her on February 14, 1776: "Madame, in vain, far from your charms . . ."[15] A comparison of his handwriting with that on the broadsheets convinces the experts. That's one boy who'll never forget his first love! Don't let anybody ever talk to him about eternal vows again. *"If all the husbands and wives who quarrel publicly were burned, not to mention the ones we do not know about, the firewood would come to a hundred francs a load . . . That's what our stinking marriage is."* He becomes a fierce champion of divorce, which *"will reduce by three-quarters, hell and damn, the numbers of bachelors and spinsters, prostitutes, cuckolds and legitimate bastards. The papish buggers and the cursed harasstocracy* [sic, more or less], *who cling together at the asshole like cockchafers, are against it. But for sweet shit's sake, that alone is enough to prove that divorce is good."*[16]

Meanwhile, here he is, dragging this business around behind him for three years like a frying pan tied to a dog's tail. When he leaves the collège there's no place for him among the Alençon attorneys. His mother doesn't want to know him because he hasn't lived up to her expectations. His family has abandoned him to the priests and butchers. People point at him in the streets. He feels himself being slowly squeezed out of his birthplace, like some foreign object embedded in its flesh. He's floating between two lives. His one last hope is acquittal, which would rehabilitate him.

But on April 17, 1779, "the said Hébert and Latour are declared to be violently suspected of having written the libelous broadsheets; in reparation for which they are jointly sentenced to pay all legal costs; forbidden to commit any further offense under pain of more severe punishment; and ordered to pay one hundred twenty livres* for the report and deliberations herewithin."[17] Not too bad; they might have fared much worse. Others might shrug off this rather mild correction, but Jacques Hébert is neither rich nor loved; so he overreacts to the humiliation. As he sees it, this sentence, defamatory in spite of its leniency, may well ruin his chances for a career in law. One unfair

*600 new francs [$120].

judgment can break his life line, as it has those of Beaumarchais, Linguet, Fabre d'Eglantine, Mirabeau. Besides, everybody's disappointed: Hébert because he's been convicted, Clouet because he was demanding thirty thousand livres in damages, and the good townspeople because the trial has fizzled out. Both parties appeal to the Parliament* of Normandy, which sits in Rouen— Clouet for more and Hébert for less. A perfect opportunity for him to leave Alençon without a fuss. One of his cousins, Germaine Massieu, has married an attorney in Rouen. Maybe they can help him? He leaves at the end of April, burying his childhood in the dust from his bootsoles. As he approaches Rouen, "where they are working night and day to get ready 10 million cartridges," he begins to realize that things are happening in Normandy. On the road that takes him from Bernay to Rouen, "artillery trains, war ammunition, supplies of every description, remounts, etc., are pouring in from all sides . . ."[18] Maybe we really are going to invade England, setting out from Le Havre under the command of the Maréchal de Broglie. Hébert passes the Broglie château on the road, an estate as vast as Versailles, "surrounded by such a multiplicity of clipped hedges, double, treble and quadruple, that he [the Duc de Broglie] must half maintain the poor of the little town in clipping."[19]

The current of the Seine sweeps Hébert on into the mainstream of the century. Which doesn't prevent him from thinking: *"How many honest families despoiled, how many innocents sacrificed! How many of the great favored, enriched at the expense of others! How many scoundrels running scot-free! For f. . .'s sake! At all these ideas my blood boils . . . F. . . this whole army of attorneycrats! . . . F. . . all Pettifoggers, that breeding ground of rapine and piracy!"*†[20]

---

*Parliament: essentially a body of jurists, not legislators. Initially (Middle Ages), a high court of justice. The most powerful one was in Paris, but provincial parliaments existed from the fifteenth century. Through the play of legal formalities, the Parliament of Paris could become a serious adversary of the throne; and as seats could be bought, it grew into an assembly of the upper middle classes, who protested against excess taxation by the crown, etc. It had considerable importance in the prerevolutionary ferment. [*Trans.*]

†Modern renditions of F . . . *(au foutre),* written out in full by Hébert, would be "get stuffed" or "up yours," rather than plain "fuck."

ROLAND

16

AUGUST 1777

MANON

O Liberty, Idol of Strong Spirits!

In the heart of Paris, Manon Phlipon is echoing the Alençon youth's complaints about "the ecclesiastical tribe, on the whole but feebly human, and feebly deserving of respect.* All this popery, preaching about a God of love, shows scant charity itself: indifference, pride, intolerance, selfishness, those are its characteristic features. I might also add, for many of its members, the most frightful baseness and corruption it is possible to imagine."[1] She's not writing this to Jacques Hébert, of course, but to the two witnesses of her life, her correspondents in Amiens, Henriette and Sophie Cannet. Week after week these two young women, themselves haunted by the dread of eternal spinsterhood in the swamps of Picardy where suitors are scarce as hens' teeth,† share in every secret twist and turn of a sedentary odyssey: the inner emancipation of a twenty-year-old girl. Manon has burnt the bridges that link all young people, especially girls, to an ethics of obedience: daddy, husband, king, our heavenly Father. It took her at least three years, 1776 to 1779. But she's reached the end of it, and it all happened within the four walls of her little bedroom next to the studio of her engraver-father. "Hard night. The dried blood still smokes on my face; combats with the angel are fiercer than battles among men."** She's finding it increasingly difficult to breathe in this setting, it's too narrow to let her spread her wings. She's like a seagull in a chicken coop. "I confess I find it a great trial to be a woman: I should have had a different soul, or a different sex, or a different century. I should have been born a Spartan or a Roman woman, or at least a French man ... My ill-humor may well look like madness, but I really do feel as though chained to a class and manner of being that are not mine. I am like those animals from burning Africa which, transported to our menageries, are compelled to enclose within

*At this point, for the sake of the intelligibility and coherence of her biography, I must make an exceptional excursion backwards in time: August 1777 will enable us to understand more about April 1779.

†They were the daughters of one of the richest merchants in Amiens, and lived with their widowed mother.

**Arthur Rimbaud.

a space that scarce contains their bodies, faculties designed to expand in a happier climate with the vigor of a strong and free nature. My mind and heart encounter the fetters of opinion, the irons of prejudice, on every side, and all my strength is spent in vainly rattling my chains. O Liberty, idol of strong spirits, nutriment of virtues, for me you are but a name!"[2]

As it stands, her spiritual itinerary has carried her far beyond all the girls of her day and most of those of our own, along the path that begins with Rousseauist devoutness and ends in an agnosticism inclined toward tolerant atheism. "Sometimes great surges fill me, and they carry me with amazing rapidity, but nearly always to advantage. It is a ship driven by powerful winds over an immense surface . . . I grow increasingly convinced, through my own experience, that the unity of the inner self is the pivot of felicity."[3]

"The first thing that struck me, when I thought about it calmly, was that religion, properly understood, could and must have no other goal but human happiness . . . With this one stroke, how many things were shaken to their roots for me! I could not bear, among other things, to think that all who did not believe as I did should be lost eternally; that so many innocent beings, good men, peaceful peoples, should be delivered up to the cruel flames because they had not heard of a Roman pontiff who preached a stern morality he seldom practiced himself. I found this principle absurd, atrocious and impious." Therefore: "if the intolerance preached by my church is an abominable dogma, then that church sometimes teaches what is false and is not infallible . . . What! is this entire system, whose binding,* and most of whose morality at least, I did admire, founded upon a rotten apple? What good was served by sending a God incarnate to save a few men from the universal shipwreck, with no regard for the greater number! . . . The edifice crumbles before my eyes . . . It is society, the establishment of property, it is laws, governments, prejudices that alter man, corrupt, perfect or degrade him . . . The deists bring man onto the stage, but then they cripple him in a thousand ways, they make him as miserable as they please, and on this depravity of human manufacture they erect a necessity for a Revelation and a Redeemer."[4] "I meditate peacefully and I sail among my thoughts, seeking truth sincerely and remaining steadfast as to the principles of morality.† Each day I feel the need to keep them separate from any religious system."[5]

This is no pure victory of reason, however. A large part of herself remains all sensitivity, highly vulnerable to the seduction of church organs and incense. "A few days ago I was at a church ceremony: I reflected upon the power of the things that impress us through our senses, and I felt how strongly they

*Coherence.

†The strictest little bourgeois morality that ever was, too: virginity, chastity, sobriety, thrift, self-respect. Where morals are concerned her mind is as timid and caged in by traditional ideas —even reflexes—as it is free and fearless on questions of religion and philosophy.

tugged at the imagination and spirit . . . If I were forced to live in a convent, I should become as religious as St. Theresa." But humor tempers the whole; as, for instance, when she goes to the hospital for the blind to hear "a certain Abbé Beauregard who is all the rage today. There was a ghastly press. Duchesses, priests, foolish women, people of every description, it was asphyxiating, and all to listen to the most unpleasant orator I can think of, the tone extremely artificial, the look of a charlatan, in every respect despicable. Such is the man of the day. Whenever he uttered some very forced screech, without saying a meaningful word, I saw women gaping in admiration, and a person beside me exclaimed half aloud, 'Ah, how he sweats!' I burst out laughing, and returned home unedified to a degree."[6]

At twenty-two she takes stock, like a little captain of herself, in a text dated May 10, 1776, which she keeps and parsimoniously shows to special friends: "Extract of my soul, or, the point of view of the moment."[7] In it she sets forth, in a coherent system, all the things she had been letting trickle out in the course of her confidings. She waves good-by to her childhood and devotions, not without indulgence. "I entered into myself, I questioned nature, I looked about me, I listened to experience: I saw my road and followed it . . . I want to be happy, in the manner most conducive to the welfare of my fellows, most in conformity with the established laws, most firmly founded for the duration of my happiness. I believe that I cannot be so, save by listening to reason and practicing justice. That is my desire and my faith." And since adherence to the truth means exposure to persecution, she will use cunning, she will cheat—but quietly, like Galileo or Father Meslier.* On April 12, 1777, for example, "I contrived to leave the house alone one morning. I went into a church, where I was presumed to be making my Easter devotions, and I let people think so. If it had been absolutely necessary I should have gone through with them to make people happy, on the same principle that would make me go to the mosque if I lived in Constantinople . . . As for my confessor, he will not have been surprised by my absence, for he knows how I think."[8] Nevertheless, she's laying no bets on the future. She doubts her convictions, like everything else, without panic: "Thus, resolute forever where the principles of my conduct and happiness are concerned, for the remainder I navigate among uncertainties."[9] "I am still poised in the scales of doubt, and I sleep there calmly suspended like the Americans in their hammocks."[10]

Fine; but woman does not live by platonic speculation alone. What about love? Or at least, since that word is not admitted, "an establishment," as a young

---

*The incumbent at Etrépigny, near Mézières, from 1689 until his death in 1733, Jean Meslier was an excellent priest and loved by his parishioners, whom he consoled in their beliefs. But he left a will and papers revealing that he had long since lost his own faith and become a convinced atheist of revolutionary cast. Voltaire was fascinated by this character.

woman's marriage is known by the middle classes? Unclaimed at twenty-two, twenty-three, twenty-four, she's beginning to think she's an old woman, and her father makes no attempt to undeceive her. But she's just as determined not to marry someone she doesn't like as she is to keep feeling and reason separate in religion. And since she's hard to please, it's none too clear how she's going to manage. During those three years, 1776 to 1779, her history is one unending calendar of hesitations, from Pahin to Roland, not forgetting —among others—Sainte-Lette and Sévelinges; but without conceding so much as the tip of her little finger. What's happened to her famous clearsightedness here? She's "dabbling," as she calls it. We'll have to be clearsighted for her.

At the beginning of 1776 it's all Pahin, as we already know—or rather M. de La Blancherie, who has followed the fashion by ennobling himself thanks to the name of the laundry district in Langres where his mother lived. You get your nobility however you can these days, and an engraver's daughter is entitled to take this form of escutcheon seriously. It's even one of the reasons why she goes on lending an ear to Pahin de La Blancherie, until that great crisis in the winter of 1775–76 when suddenly she knows she loves him, she's caught, it gives her the shivers, she confesses, it's him and him alone—only to take it back via Sophie Cannet as soon as the letter has been sent. From paroxysm to collapse almost in the same breath. The next spring we find Pahin waning apace—not because of the first visits of Roland, who is making no headway, or even the growing influence of Sainte-Lette—but because Manon exorcises the full charge of her attraction to him by revealing it. An expulsion. Delivery. She's slightly ashamed afterwards, as though she had made an exhibition of herself, and starts looking for all sorts of faults to find with him. That's not hard, you can't miss them: a coarse poltroon rather than an author, a pedant rather than a scholar, less amorous than opportunist. And anyway, the whole thing took place in writing, he stayed walled up behind his studies at Orléans instead of running to throw himself at her feet; what kind of a suitor is that? Old Sainte-Lette slips easily into the vacant place; now, there's a "philosophe," a real one. "He came to dine with us on Holy Thursday. Our conversation was of a kind that makes me want to see him again." He submits a few lines on Le double tableau de la vie par un homme de cinquante ans [The twofold scene of life by a fifty-year-old man]* so pedestrian that had they come from anyone else she would have sneered, but there we are . . . "After reading these lines I was walking up and down one side of the room in a revery. M. de Sainte-Lette was walking along a parallel line." No danger here of any

*Joseph-Charles de Saintelette (the name used to be written as one word), born in 1717, was actually crowding sixty. He came from Lorraine and was a colonist by inclination, having traded in a little of everything, particularly Negroes, from Louisiana to Pondicherry, where he was ending his days as "lieutenant of police [a more important rank than it sounds—commissioner, perhaps] of the town and surrounding districts."

terrifying assaults, kisses, or even a squeeze of the hand. It's the tranquillity of the Affectionadian Great North. "He has a proud walk, an eagle's gaze, a somber and earnest air; his voice is sonorous, his pronunciation clear, strongly accented; every word that issues from his mouth conveys some thought, or image, and their energetic expression goes to stir the soul in every direction." The soul, always the soul—all is well. "I was plunged into my musings, and in an unassuming voice uttered a few thoughts to which he replied. Our conversation was interspersed with silences that composed a pantomimed scene about which an intelligent onlooker would have wanted to learn more."[11] You said it, lady. She possesses the art of transforming us into intelligent onlookers at the scene of her little Easter parade for the season of 1776 in the company of "this aged gentleman" "with a soul of fire, saltpeter and sulfur" and therefore so unlike her own father, the mild Phlipon, yet all the more reassuring as no faintest shadow of any other emotion can darken their friendship: he is to go back to the Indies almost immediately. By the end of the summer of 1776, "M. de Sainte-Lette has become my regular fare. I see him three or four times a week . . ." But not only him. Roland has managed to regain some lost ground, even though she has perceived that with this one the dividing line between friendship and flirtation is not so clear. "I must confess to you that Sainte-Lette and M. Roland are two men who spoil me; I see in them that elevation of soul, that sensibility, that uprightness of heart, that turn of mind which I have ever judged to be alone worthy of fixing my esteem. By what singular chance do I, in my relatively solitary existence, come to know two beings so rare of their kind?"[12] Roland's stock has been mounting steadily ever since the mortification of their first contacts. On May 2: "M. Roland has this moment left, after spending nearly two hours here. During that time I acquired a greater portion of esteem for him than I previously entertained. I admired the rightness of his reasoning, the pleasure of his conversation, the firmness of his mind, and the quantity of his attainments."[13] On June 24: "The acquaintance of M. Roland flatters and interests me . . . To me, he seems to combine an honest and sensitive soul with an enlightened and forthright mind . . . He is truthful and frank . . . He has a tranquil and true philosophy . . . In a word, he seems perfectly fitted to become a firm friend."[14] On July 5: "I laugh to myself when I think of the impression left by his first visits and the tone I took in speaking to you about him. He must have been courageous indeed to brave the revulsion of those first efforts."[15]

No, Pahin de La Blancherie definitely can't measure up to that. When he makes his belated return to Paris, he goes to the Place Dauphine only to get a reception so frosty, so far from Manon's January letter, that it becomes plain to him she's now on a different planet. In July she meets him by chance in the Luxembourg gardens. "I saw him with a plume in his hat. Ah, you cannot imagine [to Sophie] how that accursed plume tormented me. I twisted myself in all directions, trying to make it concur with his philosophy, with that manner of thinking that had made me love him . . ."[16] Wasted effort. On July 25, "the enthusiasm is gone, and for me he re-enters a class* to which I could not ally myself without apprehension."[17] On December 21, 1776, when a feeble revival brings him back again, she courteously shows him the door, "and I ended by saying that in wishing him success in his affairs I hoped that someday, when each of us would perhaps be otherwise committed, we might be friends." Exit Pahin.† But even now, although she supposes she has opted for that reassuring relationship called friendship, Roland has actually become the source of her serenity. She thinks about him, and for a girl of her age and condition that in itself means a lot. As his visits become more frequent, she begins to see more in this fellow whom she first took for a pompous small-town dignitary. He's got something.

The image of him she succeeds in portraying during the first seven months of their relationship, before he leaves for his long trip to Italy, already has political, or at least economic and social overtones. What Manon likes about Roland is that he's always doing or planning something interesting. His occupation puts him right in step with his time; a little more, and she could pretend she was being courted by a mini-Turgot.

He was born in the Beaujolais country. His large and many-branched family, or his mother at any rate, still lives there, not far from Lyons. Four priest-brothers. He refused: industry, "the arts," that's what he wanted. The year Manon was born, he was already "supernumerary pupil in the Manufactures** at Rouen, authorized by the minister of commerce to become a member of the Manufacture inspectorate." But first he had to spend ten long years going gray—or rather yellow, since it's Roland we're talking about—drafting memoranda on raw materials for fabrics, the bleaching of linen, and cotton dyes, before being appointed under-inspector of manufactures at Clermont-de-Lodève‡ in that corner of southern Languedoc where a goodly share of the cloth that dressed the army had been woven since Colbert's day. Trudaine was

*"A kind of person."

†Pahin de La Blancherie had personality, however, and Manon wouldn't have been bored with him. As the founder of a "salon de correspondance," a sort of open-door academy, he goes through numerous ups and downs between 1778 and 1788 but never achieves stability. At the end of his rope, he emigrates to England around 1791. There, he goes mad, takes himself for a reincarnation of Newton, has himself called "Newton La Blancherie," and dies (in London) in 1811.

**The manufactures were the works attached to certain crown monopolies, especially arms, ammunition, and tobacco, but also tapestries and porcelain, etc. Being state industries, they involved more bureaucracy and officialdom than we usually think of when using the term. [Trans.]

‡Today Clermont-l'Hérault.

pleased by his capacity for overwork and his passion for cataloging techniques. "I understood that all the productions of nature, like those of the Arts [as employed in the *Encyclopédie,* of course: Arts and Trades], lay within the compass of an inspector. I believed that neither his assiduity nor his knowledge should be exhausted until nothing remained to be done."[18] He was trying to kill himself and nearly did, in 1765, with a sort of endemic jaundice. He went on overworking at Amiens, where he was appointed inspector of manufactures in 1766. Broadcloth, linen, wool, and indigo had no more secrets from him, and he could talk about them by the hour with that fervor that renders anyone interesting who is obsessed by his subject. More than that: he was opposed to routine, encouraged innovation, made war on waste, and tried to protect the workers. The Amiens manufacturers disliked him: another point in his favor in Manon's eyes.

And then, like herself, he so loves the Ancients! "Ah, for the love of the Greeks . . ." Roland presses his advantage and lets her go on thinking friendship—friendship to her heart's content—while he, already in March 1776, is toying with the idea of something more. Neither libertine nor prude, he likes women and has no desire to end his days an old bachelor. He has already missed two or three opportunities to make a marriage "of interest and inclination" which mildly terrified him. Just on the off chance, he's also paying a tepid court to Henriette Cannet; but at this stage, out of pathological indecisiveness, and also because he senses that a Manon Phlipon is not to be had with a bunch of violets. He hasn't yet tipped his hand, if he has one.

On August 7, 1776, he sets out for a long study-journey in Italy, a sort of commercial and industrial survey for Trudaine. Not before staking out a small claim: "The day of his departure he dined at my father's with Sainte-Lette; taking his leave of me, he asked permission to kiss me; and, I don't know how it is, but that favor is never granted without blushing by a young person, even when her imagination is calm. 'You are happy to be going,' Sainte-Lette said to him, in his grave and solemn voice. 'But hasten back to request another!' "[19]

He won't see her again for sixteen months. But the claim remains staked.

A fine kettle of fish, to have all these earnest gentlemen courting her and then going off to the ends of the earth! Roland in Italy, Sainte-Lette in Pondicherry . . . But it's as though they can't leave without passing on the torch. Manon Phlipon's little theater might have had to close for the season if Sainte-Lette hadn't introduced Firmin de Sévelinges to her, "his good friend, who has just lost his wife [in September 1776]. I never saw a widower so imbued, so stricken with grief; he has one of those exalted souls that can contain no ordinary sentiment. His pain is mute and still, but he is engulfed by it. His aspect is like that of the sky before the storm."[20] A minor aristocrat from the

Soissons region, where he was "collector for the tobacco farm."* Fifty-six, *philosophe,* and bruised: just the thing for an interlude.

On October 27, 1776: "M. de Sainte-Lette is about to leave. I shall sincerely miss him; it is fortunate for me that this man is not ten years younger, or I should have cared more for him than I wished . . . He bequeaths me the acquaintance of his friend, his other self. I shall cultivate it with pleasure."[22] On November 9, a farewell that she knows will be forever: "All M. de Sainte-Lette's fine projects cannot prevent me from looking upon his departure as the moment of eternal separation; at his age one does not cover six thousand leagues with impunity."[23] Last dinner at Manon's, together with Sévelinges and two others of their generation. A micro-academy, aging and melancholic, presided over by a girl. "M. Roland's absence was felt. I missed him. My imagination carried me after him, for some moments I was rather distracted. We chatted cheerfully nonetheless, and, which is most agreeable, parted more or less in the same vein, M. de Sainte-Lette kissing my hand, and myself in a very gay mode."† Apparently not a word is said about the war whose shadow darkens this departure: how long will the English let us keep Pondicherry? Sévelinges is going back to Soissons, less perilous and less remote. They agree to write; Manon deigns to entrust him with "a few of my notebooks . . . I mean to say, my scribblings . . . They contain some of those rather bold philosophical reflections that in this country are made beneath the chimney . . .** There are a million worthless trivialities in them, and none of it was ever written for anyone but me; but it's done."[24] True, she's abandoning something here, but it's something innocuous, as always, not at all what Sévelinges would already be overjoyed to see abandoned, and will soon be dreaming of.

1777, a long, flat year. Letters to the Cannet sisters, armfuls of them, equivocal letters to Sévelinges, no letters at all to Roland. Where would she send them? It would be his place to write, and he doesn't. Sévelinges's philosophy isn't up to embracing his widowhood; with a little help from Manon, he simmers slowly away in his corner until mid-July, when he suddenly boils over and is undone. With about as much sense of psychology as my shoe, he bluntly suggests that she come to live with him at Soissons. "It would be an act of philosophy," he says, "to make up your mind to do it; you are free to bring a friend; you will be lodged far away, close to the garden, etc." This timid shuffle forward sends her leaping ten paces back: "It is the prettiest thing in

---

*The tobacco farm was a company that had a monopoly on the import, manufacture, and subsequent sale, at a taxed price, of tobacco in France; profits went to the royal treasury, but not before lining the pockets of regional delegates. Yield in 1777: 23 million livres, or 115 million new francs [$23 million].[21]

†Sainte-Lette dies a year later, on November 17, 1777, in Pondicherry.

**Beneath the chimney: "in secret, in the silence of vigils beneath the chimney mantelpiece."

the world, but circumstances, fathers, their prejudices, oppose innumerable barriers."[25] No more of that. "Farewell, my dearest friends. I dreamed of M. Roland. I dislike being without news of him."[26] His name recurs eight or nine times in her letters between January and August, and always in connection with her anxiety about his silence. Still, she is learning more about him: he has left some manuscripts with her for safekeeping, and she very nearly knows them by heart. "The naïve growth of your soul," she will write in May 1779, "as it appears in the works I pondered over and savored, has elevated, nourished, and fortified the opinion you had given me of yourself."[27]

But if Roland doesn't write, it's because he wants to be straight with her. He knows that the noises he would make could no longer be noncommittal, yet he's not ready to commit himself. His relatives have proposed an "arranged" marriage with a young woman of good family. He argues heatedly, as a thrifty Lyonnais, about dowries, trousseaux, "expectations," and the business drags on all the way from Turin to Naples.

Aggravated by this silence, the crisis of 1777 is a severe one; Manon Phlipon is alone and unaided the day she has to tackle her father head-on in an attempt to avert disaster. "Nothing is worse than to be compelled to lose respect for what one loves . . ." "If there are evil days ahead, as I have reason to believe, I shall learn a trade." But what trade? Reading and writing are no use to girls. "If we have enough left, I shall ask to be allowed to enter a convent."* But Gratien Phlipon himself doesn't know how badly off his business is. At the end of July his daughter sends for an accountant to take an inventory that is like to be the poor man's death. "We never ate and scarcely slept . . ." "My father hates me." The balance sheet is disastrous: little mother Bimont's dowry, theoretically inalienable, has melted from twenty thousand to six thousand livres.† Not the poorhouse yet, but a dead end. On that kind of money, you can't even afford to escape.

It's no picnic, Manon Phlipon's twenty-fourth year on the Place Dauphine. After the collision, father and daughter resume their tête-à-tête, but it has been fractured. "I preserve, as I have always done and as I must, the appearances and gestures of respect, but I catch glimpses of a kind of resentment that he feels toward me. He fears me, as some meddling supervisor . . . We are like so many husbands and wives who behave decorously, feel scant affection for each other and know it full well, but hide it from the rest of the world . . ."[28] "You don't know what it is to sit by the fireside every evening playing hands of piquet with one's father, without uttering a word except to count one's points. I'd as soon tell my beads."[29] It can't have been much fun

*Even that required some money, the dowry one brought for one's marriage to Christ and the convent. [*Trans.*]

†From 100,000 to 30,000 new francs [$20,000 to $6,000].

for her poor dad either, who was only trying to live, after all, with that gimlet-eyed little gendarme watching him every minute and never missing a trick, not even his syphilis: "It is the second of August, seven in the morning; I am already alone with my faithful Mignonne [her servant]. My father went out over an hour ago. It is the same eternal story, alas! his health, his money, his happiness . . . all lost. A hidden poison is running through his veins, whose ravages he palliates by secretly taking ineffective drugs. She whom he goes to see morning and night is infected with this poison."[30] It's quite true, the Phlipons are beginning to sound like a marriage gone sour.

Summer goes, the year turns, still no word from Roland. Manon is on the verge of depression. "To make the crisis worse, a new marriage must needs be dragged out for discussion,"* but nothing doing. "I am fond of the species, but I loathe its thousands of individual specimens. I should ask no more than to despise them if they would leave me in peace. The quest made for me by those I could never care for renders them hateful to me. I must restrain my soul with both hands to prevent it from expressing itself too forcefully . . . I do not know whether this comes as the result of an exalted imagination, or illusion, or enthusiasm, but I confess I do not feel myself made for common things."[31]

"Against my will I sacrifice time, which is my most precious possession, in dressing and preparing myself, a thing I hate, to see people I care hardly more for. Light and teasing words issue from the same mouth that sobs on the pillow at night. Laughter dwells on my lips, and my tears, confined within my heart, affect it in the end despite its hardness, like drops of water imperceptibly wearing away a stone. Courage does not destroy sensitivity,"[32] and it's courage that's holding her together, her fine little mother-naked courage, without God, without man. Nothing but books, in a now balanced assortment: "I retire with a thrill into this little room where Montaigne, Massillon, Bossuet, Rousseau, Fléchier, Helvétius, Voltaire take turns keeping me company."[33] "Recently I opened Pascal; I was a little taken aback by the despotic tone with which he presents his thoughts. I was even more so to see him bitterly condemning Montaigne after making use of one of his ideas."[34] Her armor's solid. "The tranquillity which I have preserved, and which I hope always to enjoy, is quite independent of the revolutions of life . . . I appreciate, as I should, the advantage and usefulness to be derived from the trials to which I am subjected at an age when, ordinarily, one has known only happiness. I began philosophizing very young, and had no choice but promptly to put into practice the principles I adopted so early."[35]

For a bit, oh such a little bit of diversion, she makes the acquaintance, at

---

*With a Rheims lawyer; it was an aunt who recommended "this fine cloth to cut a husband from."

her bookseller cousins, the Trudes, of one of those weird and bashful admirers she finds it so hard to do without, Abbé Bexon. "He's a small, hunchbacked priest, quite young,* witty, a great connoisseur of letters, the author of a new *Histoire de Lorraine* dedicated to the Queen [Marie Leczinska]; he corresponds with M. de Buffon, has little fortune, and lodges rather by accident in a small furnished apartment that Mme Trude thought to take for him."[36] He falls ill. She pities him. Too much; there she is again, having to back-pedal. "The little hunchbacked priest is much better. I have not been to see him. Firstly, because he was beginning to get up and the servant's care sufficed. Secondly, I feared from his slightly self-satisfied air that he might have thought himself more sought-after than he would in fact be, by me." This backtracking motion prevents her from taking proper notice of a friend of Bexon's, young François de Neufchâteau, an odd bird from Lorraine. His reputation is of the kind that ought to interest Manon, though; when people in Paris talk about him, they call him the "littérateur." But he's only twenty-seven, and he associates with someone to whom she has just taken a dislike. "The result of all this was that I did not make the acquaintance of the 'littérateur,' who often goes past saying good day and good evening and nothing more."[37] That was a mistake on her part, but how could she know?

NEUFCHÂTEAU

17

AUGUST 1777

The Battle Cry of Reason

That young man to whom Manon Phlipon didn't give a second glance on her cousin Trude's staircase is living through a curious adventure, half literary anecdote and half news item. The drawing-room babble is full of it. François de Neufchâteau is achieving notoriety in a rather novel way—by vanishing.† In August 1777, a lot of people are wondering whether he's still alive. He's asked for it, he has cultivated his living-dead image. Even before,

*He was born in 1748.

†François de Neufchâteau becomes president of the Legislative [Assembly], minister of the interior, member of the Directorate and thus "king of one-fifth of France," and finally president of the Senate during the Empire. A member of the Académie Française, he hails Victor Hugo in 1817 and encourages his early work. My object in continuing this digression into 1777–78 is to maintain some degree of unity in the tale of the débuts of the future revolutionaries (François, Pache).

however, he was by no means unknown. People call him the Mozart of literature, the child prodigy of Lorraine.

François is actually his family name, that of his peasant ancestors and of his father, a "little schoolmaster" who taught a sprinkling of children how to read, write, and sing mass in the village of Saffais, somewhere between Lunéville and Nancy in what will later be the Vosges [department]. Our François was born there in 1750, and the locals would have hooted if they were told he would one day be calling himself "de Neufchâteau," seeing as that little burg of two thousand souls, which seemed gigantic to the insects in a Lorraine hamlet, is a long way to the southwest, and his parents had never set foot in it. His Christian name is "Nicolas, legitimate son of Nicolas François, schoolmaster at Saffais, and of Marguerite Gillet, his spouse,"[1] of the bell-founders' family in Sommerécourt. There must have been a good fairy hanging around the Saffais baptistry that day, because things go like a charm for him, just as they did for that little girl from Champagne—allegedly Lorraine—born 340 years earlier in Domrémy, which was actually closer to Neufchâteau. Both were put into orbit in the kingdom of France by the same launching stages, the successive rockets of priests and influential country gentry.

Stage one: the Lorraine of good King Stanislas, father of Marie Leczinska, who was sedately ending his days embellishing the city of Nancy. François was born a Frenchman in abeyance, for Lorraine had been "loaned" to Stanislas and did not technically become a French province until his death in 1768, although it was already subject to Louis XV in fact, and part of his realm.

At eight François follows his father to Liffol-le-Grand, at the confines of Barrois and Champagne. This time Neufchâteau is less than three leagues away and it becomes the "big town" on the horizon of his childhood. There's a priest from nearby Rouceux who just happens to be an enlightened spirit, and spends his time industriously "causing walnuts, chestnuts, elms, and ash to be planted along the roads, setting the example, at his own expense, on the stretch between Neufchâteau and Nancy." But there's a whiff of heresy about Abbé Huel, too. He has published a book that created a bit of a stir in those parts, on the *Moyens de rendre nos religieuses utiles et de nous exempter des rentes qu'elles exigent* [Ways of rendering our nuns useful and relieving us of the pensions they exact].[2] In Lorraine! The devil is gaining ground on all sides.

Abbé Huel takes an interest in the alert little mug of Nicolas François, recommends him to the nearest lord, Claude-Antoine Labbé, Comte de Morvilliers, who passes on the recommendation to a "high and potent" protector, the bailli of Alsace. We're also not far from Vaucouleurs, whose squire decided Joan's fate by lending her three nags and two soldiers. And thus, passing from hand to hand like the ring in the children's game, Nicolas François rises above his obscure origins.

This bailli is about as much of an Alsatian as Leczinski is a Lorrain. He's a descendant of the Hénin-Liétards from French-speaking Flanders, where a little town called Alsace, which had fallen into their estate, made the confusion possible. Everybody thought they came from the east, where they have been gradually taking root, starting in Neufchâteau, for the last two generations. Seeking to relieve the provincial monotony with literature and good works, the bailli of Alsace, a man of the Enlightenment, takes François's cause so much to heart that people begin whispering he's the boy's natural father.[3]

So that gives him a head start. 1764: the bailli has him sent to the Neufchâteau collège and pays his tuition there. The local priests, Jesuit-trained and good rhetoricians, infect him with a love of literature. 1765: Monnoyer, "printer of the town and collège," publishes a slim volume (forty-four pages) of the *Poésies diverses du sieur François, pensionnaire au collège de Neufchâteau* [Miscellaneous verse by Master François, boarder at the Neufchâteau collège], before his fifteenth birthday. The author turns it into a homage to his "illustrious protector," the bailli of Alsace:

> Je viens, sur mes pipeaux sauvages,
> Pour t'offrir un tribut que mon coeur a dicté.[4]

> [I come, with my wild reed pipes,
> To offer you a tribute dictated by my heart.]

Not so wild as all that, his pipes. Well-regimented, carefully adjusted to the current fashion. Just the thing to send the salons into ecstasies. He's a Mozart, I tell you. Promise of talent? No, revelation of genius! The *Almanach des Muses* brings the glad tidings to France: "The child always replies with modesty and precision, speaks with familiarity of all ancient and modern authors, and reasons with much good sense on politics, morality and history, and even on war. He says, and instantly executes, the prettiest things in the world for the ladies,"[5] who promptly begin dreaming about this Cherubin. The bailli is proud of his prodigy; he sends him on a tour of France and exhibits him in Dijon—where the academy receives him on June 28:

> Quelle vaste carrière à mes yeux se présente!
> Des sages rassemblés par l'amour des beaux-arts
> Sur les faibles essais de ma Muse naissante
>   Jettent de propices regards.[6]

> [What a vast career spreads before my eyes!
> These sages assembled by love of the arts
> Look on as my Muse begins to rise
>   With indulgence in their hearts.]

After the Academy of Dijon at Midsummer, he gets the Academy of Lyons for a Christmas present and the Academy of Marseilles in mid-January. But what about Lorraine? Don't rush him, don't rush him. Upon his return, François is elected to the Academy of Nancy on June 7, 1766. That makes him four times an academician at the age of fifteen. In the general euphoria it becomes easy to overlook a comma, so Nicolas François, de [from] Neufchâteau, is changed into François de Neufchâteau [the particle implying nobility] for the rest of his days and by the grace of the gazettes, and nobody has a word to say against it.*

He sends his poems to Voltaire, who politely writes back:

Il faut bien que l'on me succède   [Somebody has to come after me,
Et j'aime en vous mon héritier.[7]   And in you I love my heir.]

From his provincial launching pad he is now aimed toward the Jupiter of letters, Paris. He nips into the entourage of Palissot the pedant-king, "enemy of Jean-Jacques"; and Palissot, in *Mercure de France,* really lays it on: Rouen may have given France Corneille, La Ferté-Milon Racine, Château-Thierry La Fontaine, and Paris Voltaire, but:

Enfin c'est aujourd'hui le tour de la Lorraine:
Son âge d'or commence à vous.[8]

[Today, at last, comes the turn of Lorraine:
Her golden age begins with you.]

With this kid of seventeen? François, not to be outdone: "Palissot is a very fine mind and, what is more, a very good heart . . . I shall owe to his advice a manly way of thinking."[9] Says you. François's poems are sexless, his operas cloying, and his plays deadly. At nineteen he's the quintessence of a literary epicurean, a chimney-corner cockchafer.

Sophie Arnould undertakes to loosen him up. "She loved François de Neufchâteau as Aspasia loved Socrates,"[10] in other words not as a courtesan nor yet as an initiator; but, like any other interesting man, he was thrown off balance by the reflection in her vast mirror-eyes. He believes, he plunges, "forgetting everything to think only of her, and, upon my soul, that is the same as thinking of everything."[11] She, however, never goes beyond that seemingly exclusive attentiveness that has bred so many illusions in so many other men. Her lover that year is the Prince d'Hénin, a relative of the bailli of Alsace. What does little François think he's doing in that league? "I love without hope. Pity me" (July 13, 1769). That was the most useful birthday present Sophie Arnould could give to a spoiled nineteen-

---

*Ten years later, however, the Parliament of Nancy asks François de Neufchâteau to justify his "title"—just a formality, you understand. He placidly replies that it's an old usage.

year-old:* his first failure. Paris turns his stomach. A jolt. He suddenly notices all the town's bad smells. Oh, to see the banks of the Meuse again, to breathe "the chill, biting air" of his country, "pernicious to the delicate," as the hunchbacked priest assures Manon Phlipon, and "this is caused by the Vosges mountains, which send an almost perpetual north wind there . . . The pine-covered mountains detain the fog and increase the cold. There are few or no villages to be seen. The houses are scattered far apart . . . An air of independence and fertility . . . Simple, pure customs . . ."[13] He goes back. "I am shouldering my pack, I am leaving Paris" in 1770, but not for a vine-covered cottage: the Bishop of Toul becomes his host at "Moselli," his country place, a little paradise filled with footmen and pretty women who make him forget all about Sophie. He toys with the idea of becoming a confessor to such parishioners. The seminary at Toul offers him a chair of eloquence, poetry, and history, on which he seats himself (at twenty) with restored aplomb. "I emerged from my [first] lecture very weary, much applauded, and very modest [*sic*]." But not wary enough. The seminary is not the same as the Toul drawing rooms in which he can "speak impiously on certain points of Holy Scripture." He is blamed for "the manifold perturbations" infecting the pupils that year. Dissonant notes are heard in the choir: the trainee priests would rather live at Thélème.†[14] François giggles during vespers, he shrugs at a sermon. But nobody's going to begrudge him his dog collar for that; or rather, the bishop doesn't dare refuse it to a protégé of the bailli of Alsace. So he becomes a graduate "in theology, albeit having never studied philosophy in Latin." He takes advantage of it "to inject several of his fellow students with the poison of incredulity, thanks to his seductive chatter." Some theologian! At Toul he makes friends with another young deacon, Bexon, the one whom Manon Phlipon, that true Parisian snob, calls "the little hunchback priest" without perceiving the hidden qualities of this provincial "possessed by the demon of celebrity and brochurism [*sic*]," but above all by that of agriculture —on which François and he write a "dictionary for the use of country folk: *La Botanique mise à la portée de tout le monde*"[15] [Botany Made Easy, we might say]. Bexon goes on to enter the priesthood, but François decides to quit. Paris again, and that no man's land between Church and literature: the law. March 1772: "I am a lawyer. I am anxious to unite the roses of literature and the thorns of jurisprudence."[16] He works with Panckoucke, as something of a

---

*As related by Gaston Lenôtre, this four-month flirtation becomes a Pygmalionesque adventure: "The indulgent Sophie took an interest in this peasant from the Vosges, badly dressed and gauche to a degree . . . In a twinkling, she transformed him into a discreet, polished Parisian who knew how to listen."[12] The "peasant from the Vosges" had been a member of four academies for three years when he met Sophie, and all she really gave him was a disappointment.

†The Abbaye de Thélème figures prominently in Rabelais's *Gargantua* as a voluptuary's ideal retreat. [*Trans.*]

bookseller and much more of a journalist. He works with Linguet, as something of a law clerk and already a polemicist. But he no longer feels comfortable in his Paris persona. "This mixture of glory and gain wearies me."[17] He
quarrels with the bailli. Finally resolved "to climb less high, perhaps, but
alone," he tries to find some small job near Nancy.

Comes the shakedown. 1775: "M. François de Neufchâteau was summoned by the council of attorneys. He attended and was reprimanded on
several counts, such as his connection with Maître Linguet [French lawyers are
addressed as "Maître"], his affection for poetry, etc."[18] He kicks against the
traces, and balks at all the "annoyances," that's his word for them. So his
beloved poetry is held against him, is it, and he's not supposed to marry the
—well-endowed—daughter of Dubus, a dancing master at the Opéra? Well,
he'll show them. I'm marrying her. "Misalliance!" cry the lawyers, and slam
the door in his face. His wife dies "of a putrid fever" (Linguet later writes "of
grief") after three months of matrimony, during which François finds time to
buy a position as lieutenant general of the King in the bailliage of Mirecourt*—with money from his mother-in-law, with whom he's almost in
love. Married, widowed, consoled, and a civil servant in less than a year,
he remains chained to his Lorraine, and to "belles-lettres."

So soon . . . Is this rest without labor, retirement before employment?
These days so many men lean back in their armchairs before the age of thirty!
François is twenty-four when he first becomes interested in "the principles and
virtues of the mineral waters of Contrexéville,"[19] which rise near Mirecourt
and have cured a few people (of gallstone, they say): first Turgot, then Necker,
refuses the money to develop them. Even so, a good hundred or so people
crowd into squire Brunon's field every season, near the shed-covered springs
and the two hundred yards of brook they feed. Cool water, pine trees everywhere, the great forest, what more could one desire to treat that "gout in the
left heel" with which poor François has been afflicted so young. "I suffer
abominable pain." All right; am I supposed to throw in the towel?

Not so fast, the sap is still flowing. In 1777, the year in which he meets
Manon, François publishes "a daring tale" in the *Almanach des Muses,* about
"The Thorny Consultation" given by a spry attorney to a not very strait-laced
client.[20] Between two cures, Mirecourt and Contrexéville, the imagination
begins to bubble. And what about a little jaunt to Paris? Such is life for all
prosperous provincials, regular as clockwork: home for the fresh air and Paris
for adventure. His latest one, between two drawing-room doors, resembles a
scene from Sedaine or Beaumarchais. Who is this "young lady of the Court,
very pretty in sooth," whose name no newspaper pronounces, not even
Linguet's *Annales,* while revealing to all Europe, in the spring of 1777,

*A minor sort of deputy-mayor job.

that François de Neufchâteau is about to marry her, when . . . Impossible to identify her.

. . . When he slams into reverse at the last minute. "The bride and guests were about to sit down to dine" in the presence of notary and priest. Thank God for François, tough luck for the historian—not a trace; neither marriage contract nor registry entry. Whoever she is, her "groom" doesn't show. He vanishes. *La Gazette française de Londres* turns it into a cruel little tale: if he broke it off it was because he had discovered he was a cuckold before ever becoming a husband. Filled with chagrin and spite, "he lives in Paris like an anchorite, seeing almost no one and going almost nowhere."[21] François emerges from the shadows to confirm the rumor, more or less, in a letter published on July 10: "It is all too true, sir, that on the eve of abandoning myself to motions which were to make my life's delight, I learned to my peril that one could rely upon nothing. Believe me, were I free to reveal the injury to my fate, I should interest, I should soften the hearts of, I should cause mingled shudders of horror and pity to course up and down the spines of, those same readers whom you proposed merely to divert." And as if to prove that it was no laughing matter, he does drop out of sight in Paris, but lets it be known that he is a totally broken man and has gone much farther away: "Reversal of his fortunes and violent persecutions having left him without resources, he thought to sail for the New World. But his ship was capsized by a squall in the Bordeaux River. There are thought to be no survivors."[22] What a pity! "He wanted to publish a *Histoire universelle* of the puns of every nation." This is signed Linguet, who, being inclined by nature to dramatize, doesn't waste time checking up on Paris rumors bruited about in London, especially when they're juicy ones. The government of Louis XVI has driven a young author of note to drown himself, it's a natural function of that body which has just banished Linguet. One more victim . . .

And it is no lie that François de Neufchâteau hits bottom in 1777, his every certainty demolished. Unstrung from top to toe. He really does run all the way to some friends in Bordeaux, a town well outside his regular circuit. He spends some months there in a state of suspended animation. He writes to Voltaire: "An evil turn of fortune, added to cruel persecutions, has taken me far from my country and leaves me very unsure what the future will bring."[23] When, in September, the *Correspondance secrète* has no alternative but to resuscitate him, the explanation it offers is as good as any other: "It occurred to him to try what human shortness of memory would be, by putting about the rumor of his death."[24]

It isn't until the beginning of 1778 that he cautiously creeps back inside himself, taking up a career as "periodical contributor" to the *Journal de Paris* and knocking off billets-doux to "Mme la Comtesse de C . . .":

Lorsque des gazetiers maudits
D'un trait de plume me noyaient,
. . . Blessé même par l'amitié,

Je doutais presque de mon être.
J'étais presque un homme enterré.
Mais, puisque vous m'avez pleuré,
Je sens qu'il est doux de renaître.[25]

[When the damned gazeteers
Laid me low with one pen's stroke,
I groaned if even a friend's voice spoke,

And could scarce believe I trod this earth:
A man for whom day would no more break.
Yet since the tears made your throat to ache,
I feel full sweet could be my rebirth.]

Meanwhile, he crosses Manon Phlipon's path without noticing. He has set his sights higher. A little later she takes more note of him, but nothing excessive: "He is a mild, timid, sensitive, interesting man, but of highly unstable character, whimsical and inconstant, perhaps as a result of overrefinement . . . I learned from the abbé [Bexon] that his friend had found out that the one he wished to wed was pregnant . . . Deceived and betrayed, desperate, he could but flee."[26] She moves on to other matters, forgets him, and says no more about him. Their destinies will have barely brushed wingtips.

He gets over it. He's happy to see his Lorraine countryside and drawing rooms once again, to scan them with his large, slightly protuberant eyes set above a big, solid, sensuous nose, a nose made for finding out which way the wind blows. He'll live. He'll work. He'll write. He regains his appetite for everything. "I want to do something about the country police [at Mirecourt]. Farewell, my friend. Ours must be an offensive and defensive league against the wicked, and the devil take all stupid fools. That is the battle cry of reason, and we shall utter it as softly as need be in order not to have too big an army to fight."[27]

GREUZE

18

SEPTEMBER 1777

A Glass of Water and One Red Apple

From time to time Manon Phlipon tries to shake off her blues. A change of scene, a chance to forget about her father and her "elderly" suitors. "We have been for a walk along the boulevards, which I hate, and through that district where the Pardons procession passes . . . I was diverted by all the stir, which gave me much to think upon; it is a singular thing indeed, this huge crowd made up of all manner of persons brought together by the desire to see . . . what? One admirable man? some amazing deed? some curious monument? No; to see a few hundred rascals dressed as priests occupied in gracefully swinging censors and casting flowers in front of the God of the Faith, who is the pretext for the fête, true, although by far the least fêted. People clapped their hands when the censors swung in time together; then they all knelt down as the dais passed, and stared at the beautifully dressed hair of the women at the windows.

"I spent a long time admiring the handsome Porte Saint-Denis: it is an exquisite work that I had never before observed.* Toward evening we went out beyond the barriers, where it gave me an exquisite pleasure to see the greenery, and inhale the fresh air."[1]

That quest for fresh air, the perennial obsession of all Parisians, who ordinarily breathed the delicate perfumes of the gutter as soon as the weather turned warm. Whenever she gets the chance, Manon airs herself in the country —that is, Vincennes. Abbé Bimont, an uncle of whom she is fond, is canon of the Sainte Chapelle there, a few steps from the prison in which Mirabeau and Sade are stagnating. At Vincennes Manon finds "a certain indolence in the air which alters all who breathe it."[2] "I play the clown, to amuse us; I take up a violin, while a good canon in spectacles seizes his ancient bass and makes it resound with quavering bow. A third accompanies us on a yapping flute, and

*And she lives and has spent almost her entire youth within a mile of it. There can be no better proof than this of the insularity in which Parisians lived, each in his district knowing nothing of the rest of the town. In the absence of any form of public urban transport, those who had no horse or carriage had to travel on foot, and did so only for utilitarian purposes.

we play a concert fit to drive away every cat alive. Nevertheless, delighted by his prowess, each of the little priests concludes and applauds himself. I run away to the garden, to pick roses and parsley . . ."3

One day in September 1777 she makes another of these little escapes, but this time to hop over the north branch of the Seine and call on Greuze. She has already known him for two years, through Pahin de La Blancherie. The painter had received her with the special attention he bestowed on any pretty girl of the "French type" who seemed capable of inspiring him; and one of his honeyed compositions, *La Bienfaisance* [*Charity*], prompted her to utter those compliments without which he could tolerate no human company: "If I did not already love virtue, this painting would give me an affection for it."4 They have met two or three times since. He teases her by being catty about Rubens, the anti-Greuze. She is no longer a stranger; and then, she's the daughter of a colleague: there is a guild bond between painter and engraver.

She turns left at the end of the Pont Neuf, follows the quay along the imposing façade of the Old Louvre, "broad and heavy," and goes under the enormous vault to cross what have always been called "the wickets" on account of the grillwork behind which the Valois kings used to lurk. The grills are gone now, the entrance to the great courtyard is open, there are no frontier police in the little artists' republic you can recognize instantly thanks to the motley of their canvases and prints hanging all askew on the thick damp passage walls. A little corner of Florence in Paris: the Louvre, for once useful and cheerful. At last a palace that's good for something! It's been a century and a half since good King Henri gave "basement, ground floor, mezzanine and first floor" of the new gallery to those artists his gracious pleasure had selected "in order that they might there exercise their talents and industry freely, with the possibility of teaching apprentices who might afterwards settle throughout the realm."5 Starting with that, and taking advantage of the Louvre's desertion by the kings of France after the Fronde, the artists had gradually devoured the entire palace like ancestors of the squatters, or descendants of beavers, whichever you prefer. Not just painters and architects, but a whole swarm of grasshopper-locust cabinetmakers, sculptors, tapestry-makers, goldsmiths, and writers. "When they got permission to use a room or two they built their homes in them, each according to his own taste and means. They put up brick walls, dug chimneys and staircases out of the thickness of the monumental walls, divided their rooms into levels."6 They glued balconies on here and there, and planted terraces on the roofs using soil poached from the gardens; stovepipes stick up everywhere and in the middle of the courtyard, which now looks like a gypsy encampment, stands a conglomeration of crooked shanties, hencoops, stables, wash-houses, and ropes with laundry flapping as it lists. The Louvre dances; it laughs.*

Manon dives into this echo of her little inner bazaar as though she'd been born there. She follows the endless corridor, as long as the Grande Galerie, onto which open twenty-six little Gardens of Freedom. Fragonard's in number 2. Pigalle used to live at number 3 before he moved farther afield. Young Hubert Robert is at number 10; his wife, later Madame Chardin, looks after the lanterns and cleans the hall. Joseph Vernet lives way down at the end. Manon finds Greuze at number 7.

Fifty-two years old. Big Burgundian features that would look right at home in Restif,† ploughing or coupling loads of wood. A heavy, forward-jutting chin, the better to tell you to go to hell with, my dear. Compromise is not his forte—in art, at any rate. For fifteen years now he's been the scandal of the Court, for refusing the dauphin, Louis XVI's father, when he tried to commission his wife's portrait: "I crave your dispensation, Monseigneur, because I do not know how to paint such heads."[7]

And crude, too. Ah, that's the way they make 'em in Tournus. Aggressiveness is a form of coquetry with him. Yet all that churlishness, all those angles, that great mass of knotted muscles: it all culminates in a bashful brush. Greuze the Violent paints sweetly, mutes his tones and drowns his contours. Not exactly a simple man. He serves up boatloads of lavender and lace to the very same people he's forever insulting. He's been dishing out *La Cruche cassée* [*The Broken Jug*] for eighteen years now. Look: he's showing yet another version of it to Manon Phlipon, "with a very special sincerity. It depicts a naïve, fresh, charming little girl who has broken her jug; she holds it in her arms, next to the well where the accident has just taken place; her eyes are not too wide-open, her mouth still half agape; she is trying to understand the implications of the event, and is not sure whether she has done wrong. Nothing could be more piquant or prettier." That's just what he expects from her and from the world he lives in: adjectives with ruffles on. Tough-boy Greuze has deliberately chosen to be cute for the cuties. "He seemed flattered [by my compliments]. This year he did not criticize Rubens. I was better satisfied with his person. He told me rather smugly what obliging things the Emperor had said to him [during his visit to Paris]. I stayed three-quarters of an hour . . . There was but a scattering of people, I had him nearly to myself,"[8] freed for a few minutes from the monster who was devouring his life—his wife, his demon, his open sore with her cosmetic-covered face, her blood-red lips and terrifyingly blued eyes . . . that very same Gabrielle Balbuti whom he immor-

*Napoleon, shocked by this spectacle, puts everything back "in order" in May 1806. "Those devils will set fire to my conquests before they're through!" Order to vacate within the week. The Louvre goes back to sleep.

†Refers to the phalansterist (agricultural commune) works of Restif de La Bretonne. [*Trans.*]

talized as the original model for his broken jug, painted on the Rue du Petit Lion-Saint-Sulpice the first time he made love to her for his damnation on earth: marriage ensued. Is it she, Gabrielle, making all that ruckus on the floor below, Gabrielle and her "callers"? He no longer ventures to disturb her when she's receiving, he feels out of place in those canvases by Fragonard or Boucher. She never bolts the door. How many times has he already surprised her, and uttered not a word but, "Oh, madame, oh, madame . . ." He would retire in tears, his long arms dangling, and go on painting her as he had loved her, all silly and innocent, in order to sell her, sell her, and sell her again; because she needs more money every day.

What a pity he didn't insist on painting Manon Phlipon's portrait, too, what a loss! But no; he lets the ideal model for an incarnation of the *petite bourgeoise* of the reign of Louis XVI, copyright by Mr. Greuze, fly back to her nest on the Place Dauphine. "Ah, if I ever could have a hand in dressing you [to Sophie], you would be so pretty sometimes. I am quite mad about *rémotis*** and simplicity, but combined with a little *je ne sais quoi* of piquancy. There is a certain art (which is not quite an art) of inspiring or discouraging ideas at will by means of the appropriateness of a color, the form of a garment, the look of a hairstyle, and then the matching of all together . . . Who knows? Don't you find me terribly profound on the subject of appearance, I who spend the entire year in my housecoat and do my hair, *escaliers* and *chiens couchants,* † etc., notwithstanding, in the same two fat curls as of old?"9 Lord above, if only Greuze had wanted to! "It is so hot [on July 19, 1777, at eleven in the evening] that I am very nearly in the state in which nature made me; my window is open, but fortunately there are no neighbors across the way. It is sultry and heavy outside, not a breath of air. My only refreshment is a tall glass of water, which I am continually emptying and refilling. I am impatient for morning, when I can go and bathe"10 in a big tub of cold water which constitutes the "water chamber" of Parisian apartments. So much for the summer, Greuze. And in the winter: "The day has been clear and serene [on December 17, 1777, at six in the evening]. I am living in the little cell you know; fortified with a piece of bread, a glass of water and one red apple, I chew, I munch, I write a few words and, in my daydreaming, I have just put my finger into the inkwell, meaning to do something else. I am in good health, and would be gay if I had someone to be gay with."11

*From the Latin *removere.* The term was becoming obsolete; it meant things that had been discarded or set aside, out of fashion—"retro."

†"Staircases" and "sleeping dogs," two new hairstyles brought from the Court to Paris in 1776–78.

19

APRIL 1779

I Stifle My Thoughts

He's on his way. When she writes "someone" she's thinking of Roland, and he, throughout his long trip to Italy, hasn't forgotten the young woman in the housecoat of the summer of 1776. He arrives back in the lap of his aging mother at Villefranche-en-Beaujolais* on September 16, 1777, and writes to Manon the following day. The scheme for an arranged marriage has fallen through again. His prospects are not rosy: Trudaine has died, Roland is without a protector. Necker doesn't seem too keen on manufactures inspectors. The one comforting address: "Mademoiselle Phlipon, in care of her father, engraver, Quai de l'Horloge du Palais, Paris."

"Mademoiselle, after so long an interval, a sequence of so many events, and crises of so many kinds, may I hope it will not be found unreasonable in me to remind you of my existence?"[1] Six pages. She's on fire in a second, and for the first time she keeps something secret from the Cannet sisters, because of the vague hint of an understanding between Henriette and Roland. But her joy squeezes through between the lines: "I have not seen M. Roland yet. I am awaiting him with something akin to eagerness. I feel esteem and affection for him. So long an absence adds interest to his return."[2] She's unable to repress a quivering reply: "Paris, October 2, 1777. I am overjoyed, ravished, despairing: I pity you, I scold you, I . . . I should like to know several languages and use them all at once."[3] She can't stand any more solitude. She has suddenly realized that Roland is her last chance—but it's a mistake to admit it so soon. Any form of transport scares the life out of him. He falls ill, true, a backlash of fatigue after his long journey, but not so ill that he couldn't scribble a few lines from his bed. Yet he does nothing of the sort. She's expecting another letter within two weeks. What she gets is two months of silence, followed by a few prudent little notes. Their grand adventure has now begun all right, but it looks more like an unwilling business deal, and at times like a fencing match —two steps forward, one step back. Is this love? . . .

*Villefranche-sur-Saône.

They spend the whole of 1778 playing hide-and-seek. February: he finally comes to Paris and calls on her right away. Once they're actually face to face cheating is impossible. He makes an offer; now it's her turn to draw back, on the pretext that it would be unkind to Henriette Cannet, who is completely bewildered by Manon's allusions: "What would you say, my dear, if I told you I had found a second [*sic*] who is all I could wish for, eagerly desiring to give himself to me, but that delicacy has made it my duty to refuse him, out of considerations resulting from a prior engagement on his part,* and also owing to my lack of fortune? This is not the least of the ordeals I have had to endure, and it is only just past [on February 24], I should rather say, present."

Every time they meet Roland burns and Manon chills; the moment they're apart, she heats up and he grows tepid. In this game, he's the one with the most elementary reflexes, when they're together at least. Do you or don't you? She takes refuge in amorous friendship. "At M. Roland's return I found myself a friend; his seriousness, his manners, his ways, so wholly devoted to his work, made me think of him as sexless [*sic*], so to speak, or as a philosopher who existed only through his reason." Baby, it's cold in here . . . Not the shadow of a response to the other's honestly acknowledged desire. She does have the excuse of clearsightedness. Her eyes took the measure of him once and for all two years before, and she can never idealize the physique of that "man of forty years and more, tall of stature, negligent in his attitudes, with a sort of stiffness the result of spending so much time in offices . . . His leanness, a yellowish complexion owing to illness, hair already thinning at the top of a brow that is very high in itself do not spoil his regular features, but have rendered them respectable rather than enticing." We're at the North Pole. If you look hard, though, there's "an extremely delicate smile and a lively expression . . . a manly voice"[4] that brings a blush of warmth to her vision. But it's still well below zero. She is desperately hoping that this man will provide the only release now possible for her: a marriage of inclination and that's the word for it. If affection comes on top of it, nobody's going to say no. We'll see.

From February to June 1778 Roland muddles along in his role as unofficial suitor. He visits her often, tells about his travels, and discourses on the ancient Romans. But Manon is keeping Sévelinges in reserve, like a second iron in the fire—or a sort of defense, maybe, against Roland's urgings. And just to complicate matters, Sévelinges, who has been writing faithfully from Soissons, tosses

---

*Who's fooling whom? There was never any "engagement" between Roland and Henriette, only "overtures."

on the scales an offer by which she might conceivably be tempted: an unconsummated marriage. "I had had intimations of M. de Sévelinges's wishes before he explained himself clearly; in his proposal I saw a touching proof of the deepest esteem . . . Celibacy in marriage . . . How chimerical this notion would be for three-fourths of my fellow creatures! M. de Sévelinges and I seem to be the only ones able to visualize it . . . Putting it into effect would seem delightful to me . . . I shall soon be twenty-four, I am in a position to know myself. I also know how the affections of the heart and preoccupations of the mind may distract one from all other things."[5] Roland, luckily, has no inkling of this aberration. Be he ever so *"philosophe,"* he'd have walloped her for it, and we could forgive him. Manon's inability to make up her mind begins to be exasperating. "I have portrayed myself more unconcerned than I really am; with all my moderation I sometimes feel very strongly that the day is only half of life, yet I should gnaw my nails to the quick sooner than allow anything approaching a man, even if he were my husband, to learn aught of this." Looks like fun ahead.

In March, Sévelinges has second thoughts. He's erratic: "One ought never to promise, Mademoiselle, more than one is certain to provide."[6] She's annoyed, reprimands him, sulks, and forgets him. Roland, after all, is definitely something else . . .

. . . Yes, but Roland's going back to Amiens in June, with everything left hanging except that they will write, keeping it secret from the Cannet sisters. He's the one who asks for secrecy, which is proof that he wants to keep himself free for other possibilities. She rather resents his imposing this dissimulation upon her: "You have come to set up a guarded camp in the heart of limitless trust."[7] Their letters are stiff, the frost is still on the ground. And then Roland, searching for a steady job, goes from Amiens to Rouen, where, as a repeat of the Cannet sisters, he frequents two Miss Malorties whom he met ten years earlier and who've been waiting for him ever since, just on the chance. It seems this valetudinarian has been sowing old-maid seeds in all the fields of Picardy and Normandy—it's his devastating side.

For Manon Phlipon the last six months of 1778 are one long tunnel, an age of suspense, the worst part being that it could last forever. If Roland doesn't come back the horizon will remain clouded. Resignation has become the modus vivendi of her relations with her father, as in so many families. And so many girls have slipped gently down that path into a rancid life . . . Only one fact worth noting: in passing, she meets Jean-Nicolas Pache.*

---

*Who is minister of war from October 18, 1792, to February 2, 1793. After that, he is elected mayor of Paris, representing *Montagnard* and even Hébertist tendencies [roughly, radical or extremist], from March 1793 until March 1794.

Another one plotting his escape. But not as a solitary navigator, like François de Neufchâteau. Pache is the take-the-whole-family-along type, children, books, and dog. Manon makes his acquaintance at the home of a certain Gilbert, who works at the post office (a friend of her cousins the Trudes), but she feels lukewarm about spending time in his company because his wife has "more bearing than sweetness." "At M. Gilbert's I saw the most interesting sight: a happy couple. It is the first my eyes have ever beheld. I saw a married *philosophe,* an enlightened husband, a tender and wise father, a man of thirty-two who has lost all his illusions, even those of knowledge, who has been tempered by adversity and become learned through the study of all subjects, through experience, travel, observation, sensibility, good sense; who has become master of a middling fortune and is satisfied with that, renouncing all expectations and the faculty of amassing a more considerable capital, choosing a homeland in the Vaud country on the shores of Lake Geneva where he intends to live the life of the patriarchs, with a virtuous companion who has little wit and still less knowledge or chatter, but a smiling nature, unswerving mildness, an impulse toward the good, simple tastes, sound judgment, a passable appearance and the greatest veneration for her dear husband." They were setting out, thus, on a sort of inside-out adventure: half a century of contented tedium, Swiss bliss.

Manon fails to note—but perhaps she didn't know?—that there's nothing remarkable in this choice of destination: Jean-Nicolas Pache's parents are Vaudois and have steadily instilled this very vision of happiness into him in the guard's lodge of the handsome mansion on the Rue de Varennes where they lived as doorkeepers for the Maréchal de Castries, one of the men on his way up at court, with his eye on the ministry of war. The maréchal took an interest in young Jean-Nicolas, such a mild, well-mannered child. Not a word of reproach in his entire youth; ah, they don't make them like that anymore. He took pains with the boy's education and sent him to good masters, but this wasn't totally disinterested for he then employed him as tutor to his own children, only slightly younger than Pache himself. Like Dupont, Pache is one of those lower-middle-class boys whom discerning aristocrats carefully set apart to cultivate in hothouses. A human investment. In Pache, though, something goes wrong somewhere, for he refuses Paris and leaves, like Dupont chasing off to Poland. At least he's capable of dissatisfaction. But even his departure is such a sedate affair . . . It leaves Manon Phlipon thoughtful: "I dined [at the Gilberts'] with them before they left . . . There exist good people to whom happiness has not been refused . . . The husband's physiognomy bears the stamp of a noble and strong soul, the gravity of reason and sentiment joined to an indefinable honest sweetness that is conferred by refinement, enlightenment and courtesy. The wife's features are those of naïveté: interesting. Possessing no more beauty than adornment, pale and modest, she is ingenuous candor and kindly nature in all its simplicity."[8] A la Rousseau.

As it turns out, Pache doesn't go to Switzerland after all. Setting off from Paris on October 27, 1778, in a carriage laden with trunks, he heads south instead, along the Rhone valley. In December Manon learns that "the place of his retreat is not the one he had initially chosen. Particular reasons have turned the steps of this interesting man toward the southern part of Languedoc. He has reached the place of his residence and is beginning to carry out his projects"[9] at Castries, north of Montpellier, where he exchanges his benefactor's Parisian mansion for his superb country château. Part manager, part public scribe, part housekeeper, he sincerely believes he is retiring for life to the sunny south. At thirty-two.

1779. At last, with the new year, the temperature starts to rise. On January 3, Manon writes Roland a long letter, ending with a bit of banter in Italian, which becomes their code language. *"Quando voglio servirmi di quel agradevole linguagio [sic], balbetto, bisbiglio lentamente com'un bambino,"** and on she stutters for page after page until her farewell, which is an appeal: *"Addio! v'aspetto con letizia.†* My father sends you all manner of good wishes."[10] On January 24 Roland arrives in Paris and takes up his abode in the Hôtel de Rome, Rue de la Licorne, in the Cité's maze of alleyways between Notre Dame and the Palace of Justice, or in other words, just around the corner from her. He comes to pay his respects at once. He sends Phlipon senior a gift of Amiens ducks in pâté, which is about the only decent thing he can find in Picardy—where he has never managed to feel comfortable and which he calls "Boeotia." Manon thanks him in tones that leave no room for misunderstanding: "Monday [February 8] at three in the morning . . . With the thoughtful sincerity that accompanies all your actions, you have enlisted the aid of Boeotia, and wrung her most renowned possession from her grasp to offer to your friends."[11] On February 21 she illustrates her letter with images well calculated to move a bachelor: "From my bed . . . It is not yet seven. I wake, and the first emotion I experience carries me back to its object . . . Take care of your health and your happiness; it would be unforgivable should you cloud the felicity of those who cherish you."[12] The kettle's boiling. He's at the door every day. The first love letter, in which Italian makes possible the transition from *vous* to *tu*, is dated March 16: *"Che fai tu adesso, mio amico? Pensi tu a mi, che t'amo, che te [sic] scrivo? . . ."*** He thinks it must be safe to make a move. Clumsy oaf!

"Questo primo dolcissimo bacio ["That first, sweetest kiss"], impetuously

*"When I try to use this delightful language I stammer and falter like a child."

†"I await you with joy."

**"What are you doing just now, my friend? Are you thinking of me who loves you and writes to you? . . ."

stolen [in the first week of April], has pained me dreadfully. The repetition
of the offense, too feebly resisted, increased my agitation and regrets."[13] For
one last, face-saving salvo she runs away to Vincennes, ostensibly to see "her
little uncle." The kettle's cold again. Infuriated, Roland huffs off to Amiens.
She comes crawling: "You drive me to despair, you make me hate life; learn
to know me better or let me die . . . Blind and ungrateful! Could I be happy
if you were not? Yet you tell me so without blushing!" On April 22, his
response: "I have neither metaphysics to deploy nor antitheses to fabricate;*
I have only a heart, and even that is no longer free to offer. It is sincere,
oversensitive, and it loves you. That is all I am worth, and I am content to be
worth that."[14] She comes back to Paris to nurse her maid, afflicted with an
"inflammation of the lungs." She breaks into a twenty-page defense, although
she's not very clear what it is she's defending: "Do not hope to bring me to
the point of responding to your transports with that perfect return which I feel
must be the accompaniment of physical pleasure. I am passive in spite of
myself. I should prefer not to be and, in my vexation at finding myself so, I
fiercely forbid myself to become anything more."[15]

"It is past midnight, all is still and dead, I hear nothing but the moans of
suffering." Mignonne, her almost-mother, the maid she "took along under her
arm" when she went to bother Greuze or Rousseau, is dying. Is this a sign of
change in her own life? There are those faithful dogs and nannies who know
how to make their exit at the right moment, marking a transition as in the
theater.

Manon has never concerned herself very deeply with the inner life of
soldier Mignon's widow, whom they hardly paid for keeping the house clean.
Does a servant have a soul? Class feeling among the Phlipons is almost as
strong as at Versailles. You take up the cause of Kaffirs or Hottentots with
passion, but it never occurs to you to wonder what Mignonne is thinking, and
you were on the point of firing the poor creature. Maybe it's better that she
should die after all, better for her and for us. "I knew the decision to get rid
of Mignonne had been taken . . . My heart ached while I nursed her; I was
both longing for and dreading her recovery. Extreme unction was administered Monday. Her mind was clear and conscious. She knew very well what
was happening. I always hoped, she told me, to die with you [sic], I shall be
happy"—and perhaps Manon realizes that something of herself is dying too,
with Mignonne: her unmarried life, that long infancy in adulthood. "Yesterday [April 27], at ten in the morning, she sank into a painful death agony, her
skin imperceptibly darkened around her eyes, her nostrils widened and her
sight was extinguished. As long as she could murmur, she called my name,
wanted me to be at her side, took my hand in hers. They soon grew wrinkled

---

*In our day he would have written, "I have no gift for high-flown, flowery speech."

and yellow, all strength left them, consciousness vanished completely and the teeth clenched . . . The surgeon and confessor who had come to attend her bade me a final farewell."[16]

Every week Roland sends her letters, letters which have at last become ardent, but written in a disguised hand so that the senior Phlipon will think they come from the Cannet sisters. Not just her father but her grandparents and cousins, too, are sniffing at her suspiciously. Intimates have a vulture's flair for scenting the flowering of something new, anything, in a young woman. Her joy is carrion for them to peck at. "I do not know how to hide the light in me, and escape the vigilance of my well-meaning nuisances. I stifle my thoughts, I feel constraint in every word I write . . ." "If you could see [to Roland] how severe they look! It rends me and makes me indignant."[17] She is overwrought rather than moved, and Roland shatters her nerves worse than Mignonne, whose funeral oration she rather skimps: "I employed her own [religious] opinions to console her and relieve her last moments; but after a harsh and laborious life, dying, for a simple soul with a narrow mind, does not require much effort."[18] For a complicated soul with a broad mind, on the other hand, becoming engaged—if you can call it an engagement—apparently requires a great deal. However, here it is, for what it's worth.

Ultimatum from Roland, on April 30: "I demand, with all of friendship's prerogative to ask and to obtain, that you tell me *yes* or *no.*" Capitulation from Manon, for form's sake, on May 6, 1779: "If you can't hear this *yes,* what other can I give you?"

20

JULY 1779

Some Boys Had It in for Him

Sleep doesn't come easy to Angoulême, that July 18, 1779. The summer heat wave has prolonged the day's prostration into the depths of the night. Not one breath of air in these twelve muggy leagues of swampy ground lying between the Garonne, the Dordogne, and the Charente. And the few meager yards of elevation of the "mountain" of Angoulême are enough to raise it above the flatlands, but not enough to bring a breeze to the twelve thousand inhabitants of the rock-clinging town.[1]

Quarter to twelve.* With a resigned sigh, both the people who still haven't gone to sleep and those wrenched from their fitful slumbers by the racket listen to the youths thundering through the narrow, sloping streets (everything in Angoulême slopes, though) around the seminary walls, near the ancient, tumbledown Cathedral of St. Martial. Stones fall off its façade at the feet of those rowdy boys who've been coming every night for the last three months just to drive the Lazarists† mad. "They made it a cruel game to break the seminary windows with stones so large [including those "quarried" from the old church nearby] that the casement wood was shattered as well. The police officers had done nothing to remedy these abuses."[2] For good reason. In the first place, Angoulême has no more "forces of law and order" than any other provincial town in France: at most, a few constables and a watchman or two. And in the second place, everybody knows that the gang of troublemakers are the prosperous sons of the up-and-coming bourgeois, the men who distill and sell liquor, the golden liquor of Angoumois. "The local wine is so inexpensive that a two-hundred-bottle keg costs twenty-four francs;** this wine is consumed in ordinary households as commonly as beer among the Dutch."[3] The young people must have been elbow-bending a shade too actively for such a sweltering day, and it's Sunday besides, what else is there to do except pretend to quench your thirst with wine served straight from the cellars, so cool you'd think you were drinking green grapes and currants? And we're not going home to roost like a bunch of chickens until we've taken care of those black skirts. Let's have a little action in this deadly hole! "Angoulême had neither academy nor literary society nor newspaper; in this area the town was dependent upon Bordeaux, La Rochelle or Limoges."[4] Behind double-bolted doors, the folks on the Place du Minagé grind their teeth and swear; but after all, it's a break in the monotony for them too, sitting with their ears pricked for the clatter of the rich men's sons who've been calling themselves "the gunners" ever since they started bombarding the seminary. Their ringleader is Thiron, who still acts like a kid at twenty-seven, isn't it a shame, but there's Merchadier too, the lawyer's boy, and Maulde d'Anais and the Mioulle brothers. The "libertines," that's the word. That's where the spirit of the century has gotten us. In our day they taught them how to behave. Oh, in one way the papists are getting no more than they deserve, so they say. "The

---

*Jacques Roux states the exact time in his *Letter to Marat* in July 1793. Known as "the red priest," Roux is one of the leaders of the Enragés of Year II. [The "Enragés" were the ultrarevolutionaries of 1793; with the foundation of the Republic in September 1791, the French decided that recorded time should also begin over again, and the following years were called Year I, Year II, etc. Year II is synonymous with the second and most notorious *Terreur,* during which Marie Antoinette, Philippe Egalité, and Mme Roland were guillotined.—*Trans.*]

†Name of a religious order. [*Trans.*]

**Which puts the price of a bottle of table wine at sixty 1975 centimes [about fifteen cents].

superior of the seminary fed the pupils very badly. He had no consideration except for canons and nobles."⁵ Those fellows are only getting even for us, after all. Thus Angoulême's third estate washes its hands of the youngsters' vandalism, and now they've broken into the seminary itself "by means of a breach in the surrounding wall of the house."⁶ And smash, crash, bang, the cannonade, the waltz of stones on the windowpanes, the symphony of broken glass, shouts of joy, it's a party.

One shot rings out and the party's over.

Somebody at the corner of the building fires blind into the mob of youths. One shot from a loaded gun, like using a machine gun to kill a fly, just to drive away these boys who've been annoying us. One body left on the ground with a nasty wound in its side, the youngest of the Mioulle brothers, he's only twenty. He was only twenty.⁷

His father is a lawyer. He lodges a complaint the next day before the funeral of his son, whom they brought home to him, dying, through the stillness of the shaken town. Suing the authorities of a seminary: another sign of the times. In such a Christian country! But the bourgeoisie closes ranks around the injured family. The priests have committed a murder, there's no way to avoid an investigation. Who was holding the weapon? Who gave the order to fire?

Arnaud de Viville, criminal lieutenant of the Angoumois district,* is a man to be pitied. There is no nobleman here to impose his arbitration upon priests and plaintiffs: the Duc d'Angoulême is only a child, the oldest son of the Comte d'Artois. And the most influential family in the region are the La Rochefoucaulds, whose name lives on in the goodly town six leagues to the northeast, and who once entertained Charles V; but "the family rarely are here for more than a few days in the year, having many other and more considerable estates in different parts of the kingdom."⁸ The poor officer is overwhelmed by his omnipotence. Afraid he'll just have to use it; Père Collot,† the superior, is "ordered to be taken into arrest" along with the warden and secretary of the seminary. They are circumspectly conducted to a place that's hardly ever used anymore: the *official,* or ecclesiastical prison (associated with the court of the same name), which has been kept dusted just in case, ever since the not so long-ago days when it used to be stuffed full of Protestant heretics. You can't put priests in a civilian lockup, heaven forbid! With the bishop's permission, their interrogation begins.

Nobody can try to pretend that they did the shooting, "because the clergy are forbidden to carry firearms." No, the man who pulled the trigger was the

---

*Today he would be called "chief commissioner."

†No relation to Collot d'Herbois. [Another important character in the Revolution, president of the Convention and opponent of Robespierre—*Trans.*]

seminary cook, André Eloy Ancellet, a lay brother—now there's one we could hang in a pinch, except that he fights like a tiger to save his skin and the victim's father stands up for him. It was the priests who put him on guard with a loaded gun and instructions to intimidate the upstarts once and for all, and Attorney Mioulle insists that the real architect of the ambush is missing—a man being loudly accused by public rumor, a certain Abbé Roux, the philosophy teacher.

Of all their professors he probably is the one "the boys most had it in for," if we can credit the testimony of Pierre Gillardie, "son of Rivaud the wine and spirit merchant."9 The pupils dislike him. A cold fish. He admits it: "It is true that I am extremely severe in my principles, that I carried severity to the point of dismissing from my philosophy class pupils who did not have the necessary abilities although they happened to be relatives of persons who treated me with respect. It is true that my love of justice has made me irreconcilable enemies . . ."10

The name of Abbé Roux kept coming back like an old refrain during those three months of vituperation and vandalism; and the cook doesn't deny that the decision to arm him came from Roux—as much as anyone else. But where has he gone, this bogeyman? He left the seminary during the night and went to stay with his parents not far from Angoulême. It looks suspicious, almost like a confession of guilt. Was he afraid of being manhandled? Let him be arrested and questioned, too.

He isn't hiding. He's waiting. They look for and they find Jacques Roux on July 31, in the village of Pranzac where he was born twenty-seven years before and baptized in the Church of St. Cybard, "on the twenty-third of August, 1752, legitimate son of M. Gratien Roux and Marguerite Montsalard."11 This is four leagues to the east of Angoulême on the Limoges road, after passing through the poor village of Touvre, which has had a curse upon it since 1610 because Ravaillac* was born there. To the north lies the forest of La Braconne, all of which belongs to the La Rochefoucaulds. To the south, the forest of Horte and Bois-blanc. The country is greener than the Saintonge lowlands on the other side of Angoulême, where the Charente, dotted with islets, has to force its zigzag course through the limestone near Jarnac, Cognac, and Saintes. Jacques Roux spent a quiet childhood in this network of little pathways bordered by tiny patches of vineyard, "a chalk country well-wooded," well-populated, in fact too well-populated to feed everybody: the peasants are treading on each other's toes in the crowd of tiny hamlets ending in -ac. In the immediate vicinity of Jacques Roux alone you find Bunzac, Ronzac, Mornac, Marsac, Magnac, Grassac, and Souffrignac. Four houses at every cross-

*The assassin of Henri IV. [Trans.]

roads, where you starve to death at the larder door: the soil is good and would yield in abundance but its owners have prohibited its cultivation, apart from tiny plots allotted to the peasants, those tenants in perpetual insecurity of tenure. "The quantity of waste land is surprising: it is the predominant feature the whole way . . . Thus it is whenever you stumble on a Grand Seigneur, even one that was worth millions, you are sure to find his property desert . . . All the signs I have yet seen of their greatness [that of the nobles, observes an English traveler on the road between Barbezieux and La Rochefoucauld] are wastes, *landes,* desert, fern, ling. Go to their residence, wherever it may be, and you would probably find them in the midst of a forest, very well-peopled with deer, wild boar, and wolves. Oh! if I was the legislator of France for a day, I would make such great lords skip again!"*

Pranzac was a tiny marquisate that had fallen by marriage into the estates of the Pérusse des Cars, lords of the Limousin who had struggled fiercely against the diabolical machinations of intendant Turgot. François-Marie des Cars, present head of the family, has allowed his château at Pranzac to fall into ruins and spends most of his time at Jolignac, near Limoges. In other words, Officer Gratien Roux,† magistrate's assessor enforcing signorial rights by proxy, is the big man in Pranzac, or at least he tries to look like it, with the help of his wife who styles herself "de Montsalard"—it's the latest fashion, as we already know.** The man's one noteworthy feature is a want of imagination in an area highly regrettable from the historian's point of view: he names four of his daughters Marie and four of his sons Jacques, with the result that archivists have taken to numbering them like kings: Jacques I, Jacques II, etc. The tangle becomes even more inextricable when the older ones begin acting as godparents of the younger, and the baptismal records cheerfully mix them all up together. Anyway, with the death of the first Jacques, our Jacques became Jacques the First. Did anyone consult him about his future? He never complains of having been railroaded into the priesthood along with another of his brothers, thanks to the favor of Comte François-Marie. That's the most Gratien Roux can hope for by way of "preferment" for his sons, since a military career such as he himself pursued with great difficulty has become a dead end for commoners. Jacques works hard. The Bishop of Angoulême—who just happens to be a Broglie: the family had vast estates around Ruffec—ordains him in 1776. Abbé Roux becomes "canon of St. Cybard" (an ecclesiastical dignity attached to the church of his baptism), auxiliary serving in the parish of St. Martial, almoner of the St. Louis Collège, and, finally, professor of philosophy and physics at the seminary

*After this outburst, worthy of Jacques Roux's later writings, Arthur Young placidly reports, "We supped at the Duke de La Rochefoucauld's."

†His lieutenant's "license" was bought for a good price during the Seven Years' War.

**In 1787 her son himself signs his first published pamphlet "Jacques Roux de Pranzac."

where the Lazarists, who aren't very gifted teachers, have been limping along since taking over from the Jesuits.*

Hours and hours spent reeling off Aristotle and St. Thomas Aquinas by the yard, to form a generation of little priestlets descanting inexhaustibly in the wilderness on essence, existence, substance, and grace. No connection with the Encyclopedists' idea of philosophy. In this sector of education, Descartes is still viewed as a dangerous innovator, to be handled like dynamite. In the record of his interrogation, Jacques Roux, himself a manufacturer of windbags, gives ample proof that he too knows how to talk without saying much, and how to head off direct questions. As for humor, he doesn't deal with it conspicuously better than many people from Charente; but unlike them, he also turns out to be utterly lacking in charm. Prickly as a hedgehog, is Abbé Roux. Is overwork to blame for it? Or is it just his nature? Maybe some outside pressure has set him on edge? Or maybe it's simply the fact of being detained for over a month in an upholstered prison where he is carefully turned once a day, sunny side up then over, on a tepid grill.

By September 21 the criminal lieutenant is enlightened, and that's the word for it, as far as religion is concerned: he'll get nothing out of the accused. They admit to giving the cook a firearm, and yes, it may possibly have been Jacques Roux who first suggested it, and that's all. From that point on they collectively plead legitimate self-defense. Those hoodlums were threatening the lay brother, and who was to know they weren't trying to invade the collège. He fired to scare them off. He didn't mean to kill anybody. Nobody told him to shoot, and is there any real necessity to beat our breasts over this lesson administered to a bunch of youngsters who think they can get away with anything? The town dozes off again. Jacques Roux sourly orders the clerk to put it on record that he personally has always "striven against the vices of the day, combated the distribution of seditious works among his pupils,† and taken the bishop's part against the town in their quarrel over the administration of the St. Louis Collège." Even so, if somebody twisted his arm a little, he'd have a word or two to say about this business of the school food and the precedence given to the children of aristocrats . . .[12]

Are the accused going to start fighting among themselves now, at the risk of stirring everybody up again? Let bygones be bygones, the bishop said, and if we don't muffle the echo of this one rash shot and a lawyer's complaint over

---

*Jacques Roux, as a secular priest, does not belong to the Order of Lazarists, therefore, but is "on loan" to it by the bishop. The regular clergy is that which follows a rule [*régle*] laid down by the founder of an order, for example, "the rule of St. Benedict," and the secular clergy are priests who live "in the century" [*siècle*] and are attached to their bishop.

†In the context, the records would appear to be incriminating the *Philosophical Dictionary*, but Voltaire's name was too hot to utter in an *Official*.

his son's dead body, we'll soon have not only bishops but Broglies, ministers, and Court on our necks as well; why didn't Mioulle teach his boy better manners?

"A month and a half after this event, the superior, the priests and myself were released and resumed their [*sic*] work."[13] He's stretching the facts a bit there. Work, yes, but not the same work. It's a big diocese, and the Lazarists have many houses in it. The transfers are performed quietly; let's just keep this in the family. Superior Collot resigns. His successor, Père Poirier, "reorganizes" the curriculum and "releases" Abbé Roux from his philosophy course. He still gives a few physics lectures, but only from time to time. The bishop also "releases" him from his parish duties in Angoulême. And it just so happens that they need a priest at Varaignes, not far from Pranzac; he'll be closer to his parents there, and the country air will be good for his nerves. And if anybody tries to say that Ancellet the cook's shot cut off the career of schoolmaster Jacques Roux no less than the life of young Mioulle, let him be told that the ways of the Lord are unfathomable.

SUFFREN BEING HONORED

21

JULY 1779

The Finest Opportunities

June 27, 1779. If it gets any hotter we'll all keel over. Bailli Pierre-André de Suffren de Saint-Tropez is indulging his perpetual tantrum in the gloom beneath the *teugue,* the canvas awning stretched over the poop of the *Fantasque,* anchored in the roads of Fort-Royal in Martinique.* What the f . . . are we doing here, for Christ's sake, screwing around for six whole months. He's got a giant-sized chip on his shoulder against his "general" of lost opportunities, that lousy d'Estaing who has apparently dragged the entire Toulon fleet over here just to stuff it in a drawer at the edge of America. We chickened out at New York, we collapsed in Newport, now we're snoring in the Windwards. That's what you get for entrusting Provençal ships to an Auvergne man.

*Since 1848, Fort-de-France. Suffren was born on July 13, 1726, at Saint-Cannat, near Lambesc. "Most important: pronounce the name Suff*rin* and not Suff*renn,* in the Provençal manner," implores Jean de La Varende.[1] [In English, it's pronounced more like Syoofran— *Trans.*]

D'Estaing drives his fleet around like a herd of cattle. At least, that's the opinion of the most irascible man in all France and Navarre. It makes you wonder—has Suffren caught sight of his temper once since he began knocking around the four corners? That makes thirty-six years now, and he's only fifty-two; the sea has been his fatherland, his cornfield, his convent, his rose of Sharon, and still he has to put up with the command of a sixty-four-gun ship ruled by the eighty-gun *Languedoc,* on the top deck of which that asshole of a d'Estaing is airing his self-satisfied face! Suffren knows perfectly well that he's being punished for his impossible temper and foul language. At Versailles they don't like people who call a spade a spade; well, they'd better not count on him to gild his language, or geld it, it's the same thing. And as for making them *caguer* a bit, as they say in his part of the world, the word comes from the Italian *cagare,* making them shit . . . That's all they've ever done to him, so he's not about to start acting sweet and sickly for them.

"Our general is inept, lazy, and incompetent. The only thing wrong with our sitting in this port is the fact of being here in the first place. We are starving the colony.* Hunger will soon drive us out, and if the convoy we are expecting [of supplies and reinforcements from France] does not arrive, I do not know how we shall manage." He's writing this to his mistress, Marie-Thérèse de Saillans d'Alès, a handy widow for the only form of love permissible to a Knight of Malta who had to take a vow of chastity: a few holidays-for-two at the Château de Bourigoille whenever Suffren puts into Toulon. You'd think he was chewing his letter; he writes the way he talks, and he talks the way he chomps his tobacco:

"Imagine a sea general the least of whose shortcomings is that he cannot sail . . . Our second general officer is the Comte de Breugnon,† who has grown out of imbecility into second childhood. And with that one is supposed to smile and say thank you? . . . Never has there been such a tedious campaign. We have had the pain of seeing the finest opportunities arise without taking advantage of any of them, and we are fully convinced that we are capable of nothing."[2]

"Monsieur de Suffren had genius, creation [*sic*], any amount of ardor, a justified ambition, and an iron will. He was one of those men whom nature prepares for everything and anything. Very hard, very eccentric, extremely egotistical, ill-tempered, a bad friend . . ."[3] So writes the young cadet Las Cases,** who will soon come to serve, although still almost a child, under this

*He means that the requisitions to keep d'Estaing's ten thousand men in vegetables, fruit, and especially fresh meat are ruining the island's economy, which was already damaged as a result of the English blockade.

†Commander of the *Tonnant,* also an eighty-gun ship. In d'Estaing's absence he would have assumed command of the whole fleet.

**Future author of the *Mémorial de Sainte-Hélène.*

mountain of flesh who stinks so badly that some of his more delicate officers are seriously incommoded at his approach. Suffren never washes. After venting his spleen, he wrenches his 330 pounds out of the rattan deck chair in which he has been wallowing and lobs his wad of chewing tobacco into the face of one of the two or three sailor-valets he always has around—they're so young and comely, "Suffren's cuties," because that's the way he likes them and he doesn't give a damn what people say. The only thing he likes better than pretty boys is pretty girls, but as you only get them in port you've got to make the best of it among yourselves at sea, and he energetically exhorts his sailors, by word and deed, to follow suit. He systematically promotes "cruise or campaign marriages," facilitated by the fact that the men have to sleep two to a bunk. Their captain prefers to match them according to age and experience, pairing a veteran with a novice as the Greek generals used to do. Something novel in the way of a matrimonial bureau, the *Fantasque.* When the men "set up house together" they "don't mind so much being abroad without a broad,"* Suffren placidly declaims to his most stiff-necked officers, not hiding a grin when they blench. "Everything aboard, gentlemen, nothing for the bordel. Less danger of syphilis; no children; no more despondency: the married lads do best in a battle. They help each other out. They are always cheerful."4 For those who cannot bring themselves to participate in this system, Suffren has ordered three well-greased barrels full of tallow to be stood in a corner near the toilets. Holes of three diameters—"Grandmother," "Girl," and "Nymphet"—have been bored in them at varying heights. The bailli lets loose his huge, mournful guffaw as he brags, for the pure pleasure of shocking, that by means of these contraptions he can "offer a ride on horseback in mid-ocean, and with no horse on board, gentlemen."5

Whenever he emerges from under the awning, the crew's most urgent task becomes to find something essential to do at the other end of the ship. He radiates the peevish temper of the great man deprived of great actions, and woe unto anyone who comes within range of his cat-o'-nine-tails, or even his stevedore's fist, when he decides that a piece of rigging is filthy or a knot badly tied. "Who says sail says force." The other day he split the skull of one poor bugger, grabbed him by the throat and flung him against the gunwale clear across the deck. He moves fast, too, on those piano-leg stumps of his, with that unexpected agility of the obese—fortified by years of standing upright in the teeth of the roll and pitch—and that makes them even more afraid of him.

But his lieutenants can't run away. Besides, they need have no fear that he will ever raise a hand against a gentleman: his verbal assaults are enough to flatten them. The Chevalier de Campredon and the Marquis de Sérignan, compelled to appear before him with curled and powdered hair, smothering

---

*The words in French are *"luttent contre le mal du pays et celui de la payse"*; "broad" is of course a more modern term, but it makes the pun possible. [*Trans.*]

in their white knee-hugging breeches and triple-tied cravats over their long satin coats, stoically await their daily dose of tirade from the most slovenly captain in the king's navy. "Eccentric in dress and figure, Suffren looks more like an English butcher than a Frenchman. Five feet five inches,* extremely corpulent, balding . . . Although he was quite gray, he used neither powder nor pommade, wore no curls and had a short pigtail, three or four inches, tied with a bit of old rope. He wore a pair of old shoes with the heels cut off, unbuttoned breeches . . . Cotton or linen hose, never clean, hung about his legs. A sweat-soaked shirt of coarse cloth"[6] gaped open over his gorilla's chest. To protect himself from the Caribbean sun, none of your regulation tricornes: screwed onto his pate he wears the ancient wide-brimmed gray felt that his brother, the Bishop of Sisteron, had given to him. And if anybody doesn't like it . . . Who's the boss here? Them or him?

"Anything in sight, gentlemen?"

"Nothing, sir."

Ritual dialogue. It might be Columbus and his officers on the *Santa Maria,* lost between two worlds. But that bunch was looking for land, whereas here, on every one of the thirty French ships immobilized in the vast natural harbor dominated to the north by the dark green mass of Mount Pelé, the spyglasses are all trained seawards, awaiting the appearance of the convoy from Brest. If we spend much longer looking out for La Motte-Piquet, who's been promised since Christmas, we'll be in time to sight Admiral Byron and his English heading for us.

So far this latest war between France and England is being fought only in the Islands, where the Powers, as they call them—that is, the countries with ships and powder to waste—have been trading pawns for two or three centuries now, every time they come to blows back on the Continent. This time it's a real game of leapfrog through the Lesser Antilles, the ones they call the Windwards because their chain, shaped like a shield in front of the Americas, takes the full brunt of the trade winds' blast that brings the gifts of Europe all the way across the Atlantic: Christianity, slavery, alcohol, syphilis, hard labor, and guns. The Windwards' misfortune is their diminutiveness, which enables a handful of colonists and soldiers to overpower them,† whereas it's a very different matter invading the Greater Antilles up there to the northwest: Havana, Hispaniola** (where the French hold Santo Domingo), Jamaica, and Puerto Rico. Sitting on the balcony in the Lesser Antilles, the few native Caribbeans who survived the great massacres of the conquest are used to looking on at the internecine throat-cuttings of those who once cut the

---

*In fact, he was taller than that, over five feet ten inches.

†Unfortunately for the aspirants to independence on Guadeloupe and Martinique, this is still true.

**Today, Cuba and the island divided between Haiti and the Dominican Republic, respectively.

throats of their ancestors in order to replace them with slave-trade blacks. French, English, Dutch, Portuguese, Spaniards . . . even the Danes got into the act.

For the past few months it's been French and English only. Leapfrog, hide-and-seek, or tag? Which island belongs to whom and for how long? The continental ports aren't safe anymore, since Rebels and Tories have started tossing them back and forth like hot potatoes. Where can you revictual, repair, caulk, remast, and rearm except in the Windwards, within reach of the open sea? That's fine, if you're at home there. But the hazards of battle and treaty have sprinkled the ocean with a scattering of different-colored marbles. The two firm French bases are Guadeloupe and Martinique. The English are holding Dominica in the middle, Grenada at the bottom, and Antigua way up top. In the absence of any major campaign the sailors, abandoned to their own devices by their ministers in Versailles and London, are trying to rearrange things a little. In September 1778 the Marquis de Bouillé sends three frigates to take Dominica. Six hours of fighting for twelve square leagues of tropical forest. France then holds three "big little islands" in a row. But in December Admiral Barrington evens up the score with St. Lucia, captured in one day. So now the English fleet can anchor in the excellent harbor of Gros-Ilet, five leagues below Martinique. At this point, along comes d'Estaing fresh from his pitiful performance in the north, his ears still ringing with American jeers from Boston. He sets his ships circling around St. Lucia for three days. Suffren, driven wild by this merry-go-round, writes to him: "We can still hope for success. But the only way to achieve it is to attack the enemy fleet with energy . . . Let us destroy it! The [English] land army, with no supplies, would have no choice but to surrender."[7] Attack, dive in, smash everything—that's all Suffren has been living for ever since he joined the naval guard in 1743. And for thirty-six years fancy-pants like d'Estaing have been keeping him treading water. What are warships made for, war or pleasure cruises? Meanwhile, in the other camp, a twenty-one-year-old cadet named Horatio Nelson is growing ulcers from frustration at the pusillanimity of his own superiors.

D'Estaing's one overriding object, like that of d'Orvilliers, is to preserve his fleet. By December 30 he has abandoned St. Lucia and gone back to curl up at Fort-Royal in Martinique, imploring Sartines to be understanding and pity him after this campaign that has led him "from fall to fall, and from one misfortune to the next."[8] Months of bickering ensue between d'Estaing who, crybaby though he is, still prides himself on his resounding title of "Vice-Admiral of the Asian and American Seas," and the handsome forty-year-old brute who governs the Lesser Antilles with an iron fist, François-Claude-Amour de Bouillé, a cousin of La Fayette.* They spend six months writing angry letters to Versailles saying nasty things about each other. Neither will consent to obey the other. Meanwhile, Byron's fleet has arrived to reinforce

---

*He leads the massacre of the Swiss at Nancy in 1790, and "engineers" Louis XVI's escape attempt, foiled at Varennes.

Barrington at St. Lucia, and the small detachments of de Grasse and Vaudreuil (four and six ships respectively) have joined d'Estaing. The storm clouds are piling up in the Caribbean, they'll have to break one day. But d'Estaing keeps hanging back, waiting for La Motte-Piquet.

"You can wear your eyes out staring into your blasted glasses," Suffren snaps at the lookouts in his provoking nasal voice. When you see the English, let me know. I'm hungry.

He's always hungry. He goes back to his open-air chamber and slouches over the table at which he has to eat sitting sideways because there isn't enough room for his stomach. No fork: "Is it the custom to use an instrument when you caress a woman?" He dismembers his fowl with his bare hands or a crunch of his jaw, and liberally spoons the sauce over his food—his one consolation around here is that it's spiced the way he likes it, lots of ginger and saffron, dill and garlic brought from Provence, and stiffened with hot red peppers which they deliver every morning from Derrière-le-Bois or Petit-Paradis, and all of it more certain to tear your guts out than any cannonball. So much the better: he rinses his with white rum. He stuffs himself *"à la grosse mordienne,"** in the style of a gentleman of the century of the Valois. For a snack, in case he feels a twinge of hunger during the night, he has a pyramid of bread stuffed with onions, chives, and hunks of suckling pig placed next to his collection of history books—nothing but history, contemporary if possible, not one book of poetry, not one novel. Between gorgings he lights up a huge cheroot, of which he laid in a good supply on his way through Havana. His officers are also being converted to the enormous cigars, but Suffren doesn't smoke his, he eats it, and then he says, "a cheroot is a good way to make you thirsty"[9]—as if he needed any help!

Suffren: a perpetual-motion gratification machine. From dinner table to his cuties' buttocks, from cheroot to combat—but the last is the one he needs most of all and its scarcity has made him melancholic. Slaughter—that's what gives him his real kicks. It's coming, my captain.

Shouts along the surface, running from ship to ship: "A sail, a sail!" Thirty vessels on the horizon. Byron's English? No, the long-awaited reinforcements are actually here. La Motte-Piquet's arrival is going to enable the French fleet in the Windwards to get under way at last. We're going to fight.

*Without fuss or bother.

22

JULY 1779

We Have Washed Away Our Ancient Wrongs

There's a little of everything in Louis XVI's navy—Gargantua, but also Eliacin.* The young midshipman Aristide Aubert du Petit-Thouars, on board the *Fendant* (one of Vaudrueil's ships), is among the first to spy the sails of La Motte-Piquet. In delicacy of feature, elegant grace of limb, and moderation of speech, he is a sort of anti-Suffren. To each his pleasure: Aristide's big thrill is serving at the almoner's mass every morning. But the approaching battle sends him into ecstasies too: "I burn to write you† that we have washed away our ancient wrongs. I am so happy to be in the navy! . . . Time is short; I fly to glory."[1] He's nineteen.

He sounds as though he's never had time to live and is afraid he never will. His fever betrays the anguish of all younger brothers in the aristocracy: Aristide is the last of the four sons born to Gilles Aubert du Petit-Thouars. In the senior branch they all bear this Christian name which has now become a family name; one of his brothers, the one who's so crazy about botany, was actually baptized Aubert Aubert. A tribe of hardworking nobles sprouting from the sands of the Loire near Chinon. Their lucky break was the favor of Mme de Montespan who, still rich and powerful after her repudiation by Louis XIV, was running short of charitable deeds to perform at the Abbey of Fontevrault. She paid their debts, gave the girls dowries and the boys a leg up into the saddle of war. The du Petit-Thouars became lords in the Saumur region. Gilles Aubert gave them a fresh thrust forward by marrying Marie Gohin de Boumois, the heiress to a magnificent château on the Angers road.** A marriage in the best literary tradition: Gilles was pleading the cause of a rich suitor, his friend, in whom Marie was not at all interested. He himself,

*In Racine's *Athalie,* Eliacin is the alias of the nine-year-old King Joas, a prodigiously good and devout child. [*Trans.*]

†Letter to his uncle, then governor of Saumur. Aristide du Petit-Thouars walks onto and off the stage of history as "the hero of Aboukir" by getting himself heroically killed on the bridge of the *Tonnant* at the famous battle on August 1, 1798.

**Where I located the (imaginary) plot of the third part of *A peine un printemps* [Just barely a springtime—*Trans.*].

in his opinion, was too poor to try for her. But Marie de Boumois cut him off in mid-sentence:

"Well, sir, when one can talk so well for others, why not speak for oneself?"[2]

Seven children. Enough to liquidate the combined assets of the du Petit-Thouars and Boumois. To add insult to injury, not one of the four Aubert-whatchamacallits would consent to be a priest: it really was a waste of time for a devout family to work so hard on such pious ground—that corner of Anjou where crosses grow like apple trees—only to produce such barren fruit. All in the army, and all in halfway ranks because there wasn't enough money to buy anybody a regiment. Luckily, there was that uncle in Saumur, slogging his guts out to find a niche for one, give the next a little push, guide the third in the right direction. From early childhood Aristide knew nothing but boarding schools because his parents both died young, end of romance, luck's run out. The first one wasn't too hideous a place. "I had the good fortune, when I was six years old, to study at La Flèche in the home of Mme G . . . , the virtuous wife of an honest schoolmaster. She never whipped me but once, the day I called the headmaster Mr. Sausage when his real name was Boudain."[*][3] At the age of nine there was worse to come: still at La Flèche, he was transferred to the school in which the sons of impoverished nobles were trained for the military career—the ideal preparation for which, of course, is floggings, dry bread, and prison. At twelve he tried to run away and failed, because he stayed too long on his knees praying to the Virgin and patroness of the school to forgive him before decamping. But he had read *Robinson Crusoe* and so he was saved: in his dreams, at least, he could escape. At fifteen he wrote the history of *Barbogaste-le-Hérissé* [*Barbogaste-the-Prickly*], a stalwart lad whose runaway attempt does not fail, and who becomes cabin boy, then mate, and eventually, of course, admiral of the fleet.[4]

Next, Aristide is exiled to Thionville and Metz as a paltry second lieutenant, but he hates the land army and pins all his hopes on the sea. The threat of war is the answer to his prayers: the king's warships need officers who are good at arithmetic, and Aristide, who graduated second in his class at the Rochefort naval academy,[†] feels himself following in Barbogaste's footsteps. The author is catching up with his creation. "I thought myself a maréchal de France when they made me a midshipman" and permitted him, at seventeen,[5] to don the beautiful blue and red uniform with the gold-embroidered tricorne, the crowning glory of his youth. He fights at Ouessant on the *Gloire,* and

---

[*]*Boudin* is a common kind of French sausage (black or blood pudding, in England). [*Trans.*]

[†]Colbert set up three companies of "gardes-marines" at Brest, Rochefort, and Toulon, to serve as nurseries for naval officers. While acting as ordinary seamen or mates, they continued their studies.

skirmishes under the Marquis de Vaudreuil on the Senegambian coast. Then he and Vaudreuil ricochet from Africa to the Antilles, following the trade winds on board the *Fendant,* while Lauzun goes back to Versailles, but only as an overnight stop on his way to London. They've all made a date to drink champagne with the vanquished English at the victory banquet.

Aristide-the-Prickly has never lost that fragile look, marveling but uneasy, of the child who has just barely managed to shape fate to his ends: he casts on all and sundry the critical gaze of someone who reads a great deal and thinks for himself. He's one of the first to reject the slander against Philippe de Chartres, whom he saw on the job at Ouessant, and he has scant affection for the "system of circumspection" adopted by d'Orvilliers that day.[6] His assessment of d'Estaing, moreover, whose shilly-shallying makes his officers' blood boil, tallies almost exactly with that more vehemently expressed by Suffren: "Our arrival [that of Vaudreuil's division] restored M. d'Estaing to a position of equality; since coming to this area he has been superior and inferior by turns, but has not known how to use his strength in the former position, and has been left in peace in the latter only because of Admiral Byron's want of ability and energy. And yet this Admiral Byron has sailed around the world; well, he is not the first person to whom this great journey availed little. Byron has no energy, M. d'Estaing no judgment; two generals most fit to match strengths with each other."[7] But he too senses that things are about to start moving at last, and readies himself for those few moments toward which a sailor patiently marches year after year in order to burn out his life in them. Always a slender youth, he's emaciated now, nothing but skin and bones since catching dysentery or typhus, nobody knows which, somewhere between Africa and the Islands. "A cruel epidemic that laid waste to three-fourths of our crew.* I will spare you that most affecting scene," since, after all, sailing men are made to die in silence, not one of them knowing how to read or write —are the brutes even able to speak? "I myself fell victim to the contagion and was delirious when we reached Martinique."[8] Now recovered, he's about to discover the Antilles in the heat of battle.

Such is the lot of a fighting seaman; and why shouldn't his nerves be on edge? First it's dead calm as far as the eye can see, then all of a sudden everything starts moving at once, the scene springs to life like the automatons on Vaucanson's great clocks. Twelve noon, and everybody piles out together, no more afternoon naps. "The convoy has come," chortles d'Estaing; "those four words tell all."[9] *They* don't know, the others, those babes-in-arms of all ages, how much it has cost him to sit there and be called a coward just because he had no ammunition, no cables, no second set of sails. Replacements and supplies

*360 dead on board the *Fendant.*

are an admiral's obsession. Until now a battle—even if he won—would have reduced his fleet to a heap of empty seashells. It's not La Motte-Piquet's eight little fighting ships that count, it's the forty-five merchant vessels they're escorting, seven of them filled to the gunwales by Beaumarchais, like a huge floating department store.

Council of war the following day on board the *Languedoc,* between the two thin men and the three fat ones: d'Estaing and La Motte-Piquet, like beanpoles alongside de Grasse, Vaudreuil, and Suffren. Suddenly it's d'Estaing, of all people, who has ants in his pants: he orders the decks cleared for combat then and there. For three sous the other four wouldn't mind waiting a bit now, especially La Motte-Piquet: "to set out three days after a long crossing, despite the shortage of water and refreshment, and with no regard for the number of sick among my crew . . ." But La Motte-Piquet has never put off a battle in his life. After all, taking this particular risk "is one of the most beautiful naval actions a general officer can perform."[10] Strike while the iron is hot. The great July storms will soon be rising, and after the débâcle at Newport, d'Estaing fears them worse than the whole English navy.

Okay, so we go: but where? Barbados would be useful, that fat pearl unstrung from the Antilles necklace far to the east; we could hold it as an outpost . . . But nobody commands the wind, and the wind just happens to be coming from Barbados. You might as well try to climb a greased pole. All right, we'll let the wind carry us along, cheating a little, and head due south for Grenada; there we'll have good anchorage within reach of the Spanish in Venezuela (one of these days they're going to have to make up their minds to give us a hand). We'll take Grenada to even up the score for St. Lucia.

On July 2, twenty-five ships weigh anchor and bring up that same evening in front of their objective, opposite Molenier cove, at the back of which lies Grenada's only port, named St. George, of course, by the English. A day spent skating across a mirror; nowhere on earth is the sea so pure and the sky so clear, each reflecting the other, as they are here. The Caribbean is a bottomless pit encircled by the tips of thousands upon thousands of submerged peaks, the Islands. Why do people always imagine Eden in some oriental valley? It's a handbreadth away in Grenada, for instance: three leagues by three of raving green paradise, the same scent of vanilla and lemons as in Martinique—you inhale the island before you see it. Looking like little moving islands themselves, gilded by the setting sun as they awkwardly gird their loins to ravish the slumberer, the French vessels maneuver slowly, keeping clear of the coastal batteries.

"And all is done in the greatest possible disorder," du Petit-Thouars complains, "for that was M. d'Estaing's weakest point." But, disorder or not, they can't go wrong now. The capture of Grenada is a body blow aimed by two thousand men at a garrison of seven hundred huddling at the far end of a blue tongue stuck out by the sea into the throat of the cove: St. George's "hospital," which is actually a fort surrounded by a few wooden houses (without any glass in the windows, like everywhere else in the Antilles). And on either side of the sea roads the little fortresses perched on the bluffs do their duty and have no illusions about it: they are grains of sand lost in the sea.

July 3 is spent rowing longboats ashore and back again under their noses as d'Estaing unloads his soldiers, if you can call them that—"bag and rope" men, rather (that is, those who were being stuffed into bags and dumped overboard not so long ago)—half-breeds, Spanish bandits, pirates, privateers, escaped convicts recruited on sight in the ports of America or the West Indies to make up the numbers of the epidemic-depleted crews from France. Kept vaguely in order by the surviving officers and sergeants, they're just as hot for action as the conscripts in the Hainaut regiment except that they can't shoot straight, and their ardor is all the more heartfelt because they're being led into battle by the big chief himself, finally released from his own prison ship— Jean-Baptiste-Charles-Henri-Hector d'Estaing, drawn sword in hand and looking twenty years younger in his red uniform that marks him as a target for the English sharpshooters. You'd think he was his cousin La Fayette; those men from Auvergne never seem to grow old. He's shed his sailor's skin somewhere between the *Languedoc*'s poop and the gangway, and been metamorphosed back into the infantry colonel ready for everything—Sumatra, Madras, Bender —back in the days when he was conquering the Indies for his king and being congratulated, half-naked in his scorched coat on the debris of Fort Marlborough, by the big chief of his spring years, M. de Lally, whose head that king was later to cut off . . . D'Estaing should never have let himself get dumped into this navy where all the officers look down their noses at him. It's all so easy on land, none of these winds and supplies to worry over, all you have to do is run, dragging a thousand brave boys after you, through sand so fine and soft that you sink into it as into the snow you used to play in when you were a child outside the Château de Ravel. But the soil of Gévaudan will never be planted with these weird star-shaped trees, the coconut palms bending double in the wind, that's for sure. At least you know their name; but what are you supposed to call these other things that you have to fight tooth and nail, hacking your way through their purple, pink, and orange spikes? This assault is embalmed in colors and smells, and the cannonballs are swallowed up by giant ferns. It's like a battle that nobody takes seriously. "The longboats sped along as though at the races, while thousands of multicolored birds rose from the trees at the sound of the cannon and musket fire and flew away inland."[11] They aren't the only ones: the civilians too—that is, the planters, their families, and their slaves—are pouring into the center of the island in a motley little exodus, waiting to see which way the war blows. Some families don't know

whether they're English or French anymore, the islands have changed hands
so many times. We'll find out tomorrow.

. . . French. It's all decided during the night of July 3–4. D'Estaing and his
officers hurl themselves up the "hospital bluff" in a vast muddle of shouting
and firing. Among them are some who were dancing at Trianon six months
ago, the Dillon brothers and the Vicomte de Noailles, loving every minute
of this game of cowboys and Indians; at last we'll have something for the queen
to sink her little teeth into when she's bored next winter. The Comte de Vence
leaps into a trench alongside d'Estaing, the English gunners surrender but one
of them aims his pistol at Vence; grenadier Houradour, a boy from Hainaut,
clobbers him with a metal plate lying on the ground. D'Estaing embraces him:
    "You have saved my friend. I promote you officer."
    Houradour becomes a lieutenant, and stops there, of course; but that
lethal blow saves him ten years of waiting to get even that far.* The four
cannons that those slow-witted *"Rosbifs"* [from "roast beef"] haven't had time
to spike are seized and "turned around toward the fort into which the governor had retreated. Thus threatened with being struck down at any moment by
the artillery covering the exit from his hideout, Lord Macartney† was compelled to surrender unconditionally two hours later. Seven hundred prisoners
were taken; and three flags, one hundred two cannon, and sixteen mortars
were seized."12 The local residents cautiously begin edging back toward the
beach.

. . . Stop! It's not over yet—English sails are sighted at dawn on July 6! Who
knows, maybe Grenada will only have been French for twenty-four hours?
Byron's naval army is out scouting for the fleet of Louis XVI. Now back on
his admiral ship d'Estaing, so happy ashore, becomes a poor addled nincompoop again. He can't make up his mind to order the fleet under way. "The
lack of wind prevents this maneuver and his ships remain in fairly considerable
disarray";13 Suffren is within an ace of apoplexy, de Grasse talks of going to
ram the English with a fireship, while du Petit-Thouars phlegmatically observes: "And yet we were twenty-four to twenty-one [ships]. The match was
unequal." And that damned "calm" that's keeping the French penned up
inside Molenier cove stops where the sea begins: outside, there's a nice fresh
breeze that lets the English draw in at a good clip. Are they going to catch us
like rats in a trap?
    Chin up, lads, everything's going to be all right—because the admiral on
the other side is just as great a ninny as our man. Byron has gotten it into his

*This incident becomes the subject of a great many colored prints the following year.
†We shall meet him again as English ambassador to China.

head that Macartney is still holding out, and comes steaming up to catch d'Estaing in a cross fire. Which earns him and his *Princess Royal* a nice peppering from the forts where the Hainaut gunners are ready for him. The formidable ninety-gun ship has to come about under fire, and the English line of attack is broken. Thus the French have time to rush out fifteen ships, enough to give battle just off the island, with d'Estaing making the most of the help from the forts. It's short but not sweet at all. Much rougher than Ouessant. A chaos of sails, wood, powder, salt spray, yells, bosuns' pipes, and blood on the decks. Two hours of dueling sea elephants, *Languedoc* against *Princess Royal, Tonnant* against *Prince of Wales, César* against *Conqueror.* La Motte-Piquet, his thigh shattered by a ball, lies on a mattress among the sixty dead and hundred injured on board the *Annibal* and gives orders to fire. Captain Montaut lurches into the melée with a merchant craft so heavy and unwieldy that she was originally christened *Hippopotame.* Nobody but Beaumarchais could have bought such a thing, armed it with sixty cannons, made it the protector of his convoy fleet, and renamed it *Fier-Rodrigue.* One of La Motte-Piquet's officers, a certain La Pérouse, requisitioned it in passing and prevented it from going to North America. Montaut squealed like a stuck pig . . . but since you've got to fight when there's a fight on out he comes, and dies on the poop at eleven in the morning that July 6, with as good grace as any gentleman in red. Here's the chance of a lifetime for the son of a "blue" officer who happens to be on the spot: Honoré Ganteaume, hitherto doomed to rot in La Ciotat where he was born twenty-four years ago without a particle to his name, which means that the only way he can get out of the merchant navy and into the "royal" is by the grace of God. This is it. Ganteaume had signed on, for the hell of it, as "prize chief"* in the merchant fleet of Roderigue, Hortalez, and Company. He is standing at Montaut's side when he falls. By rights the command should go to the dead man's brother, an incompetent. Ganteaume takes over and manages to bring into port a half-unmasted, smoking, blind *Hippopotame.* Montaut's brother, a nobleman, gets the cross of St. Louis. Ganteaume gets into the royal navy.

By noon things are really hotting up. The generals of both fleets are struggling halfheartedly against the whims of the winds, with great displays of brightly colored signals whizzing up and down the halyards, but their monsters are out of their control, and it's every man for himself, or almost. Suffren, on the *Fantasque,* is in heaven at last: he's taken advantage of the general melee to "attack a post of honor not intended for me" and has "endured, for an hour

---

*Meaning that he would take command of the captured crews of any intercepted ships. Ganteaume, whom we will meet again briefly in Year II, becomes vice-admiral, count, peer of France, and all the rest of it through Napoleon's favor. He was, "of all the officers in the French navy, the one who, in our time, amassed the greatest number of titles and honors," according to Lebas's dictionary of 1842.

and a half, the fire of all twenty-one English ships. Disinterested people will speak well [of me], and even my enemies will not dare speak ill."[14] The *Fantasque* alone has fired 1,654 cannonballs. It has forty-three wounded and twenty-two dead on board, and among the latter is the Chevalier de Campredon, Suffren's affable second-in-command. His chief's funeral oration is brief and to the point: "My heart is torn by the loss of my second-in-command, who played the pianoforte so well." Beaumarchais has even less trouble resigning himself to the loss of Montaut. He writes to Sartines: "The good Montaut thought he could find no better way of proving to me that he was not unworthy of the post with which he was honored than to get himself slain at it . . . I see the English biting their nails over their defeat, and my heart leaps for joy."[15]

Amidst all the confusion one of the few officers to have a clear notion of anything is du Petit-Thouars, who manages to record the instant in which d'Estaing wins the naval battle of Grenada, but wins it wrong. The English are abandoning the field, only too glad to get out of it so cheaply. "We had disabled and unmasted several of the enemy ships, and had only to close in on them"—the *Grafton, Cornwall,* and *Lion* in particular. "Byron had already decided to cut his losses and, without offering them the slightest assistance, was making off at full speed." Not only does the English commander seem disposed to leave his rear guard behind, he's forsaking half a dozen troop transports as well, which have been waiting out the battle farther away. "M. d'Estaing held back eleven frigates that could have seized these defenseless ships, and this prize would have ensured the conquest of all the Windward Islands which had been stripped to come to the aid of Grenada. But instead of following up a victory that might have had such decisive consequences, our general began to worry about his latest conquest. He turned back . . . fearing that Grenada might drift away in his absence, as though the best way of ensuring our possession of it were not to pursue the only enemies that could attack it . . . In joining the navy M. d'Estaing imagined that he possessed the talents of Tourville and Duguay-Trouin combined. As a result, instead of learning how to sail, he dreamed only of his future victories and conquests . . . It seems to me that the more ready one is to admire a good general, the more severe one should be in one's judgments."[16]

Anyway, it's over. Back at Versailles, we can sing out loud and clear that we won the first Franco-English battle off the American coast, however much de Grasse, Vaudreuil, and Suffren go around muttering that "never, never in a thousand years will France have such an opportunity again." "If d'Estaing had been as good a seaman as he is a brave one, we would not have allowed four unmasted ships to escape."[17]

Oh, who cares, it'll make a splendid print: two grinning soldiers brandishing the captured English flags above a fruit split open to reveal its scarlet seeds.

Les rieurs sont pour nous. L'Anglais est bien malade.
Et, grâces au Destin, nous tenons la Grenade.[18]

[The laughing men are ours. The Englishman is sick.
And, thanks to Fate, we've got Grenada island on a stick.]

The fact of the matter is that the Island match between France and England is a draw.

The score is totted up. The French have fired more than twenty thousand cannonballs. They have one hundred seventy-six dead and almost a thousand injured. Cadet Besson de Ramazane, wide-eyed with wonder to find himself still alive on the deck of the *Diadème,* writes to his "chère maman": "This is the first battle that I have seen but I may tell you that for a first, it was a good one. Everybody allows that it was extremely destructive . . . The balls fell on board the ship and hissed like hail. A battle is a fine thing; but only afterwards."[19]

"The men," as they say on the quarterdeck; oh, the men . . . Eight or nine thousand of them *did* it, with only a dim notion of what the five hundred-odd gentlemen who pretended to know what was happening told them to do . . . They burned the skin off their hands and feet maneuvering in the tops, they burned their throats and lungs shuffling around the guns amidships, their carcasses were ground to a pulp in the mill of masts that mowed them down and the shells and wooden splinters that tore through their skin. Those still on their feet get a double ration of rum. The wounded are transported to the Fort-Royal hospital on Martinique, "the largest in the Antilles. The crippled received six hundred écus or six Negroes."* When all is said and done, the Negroes are the ones who understand least of all.[20]

---

*To be precise: payment from the governor of Martinique, in money or in human kind, to disabled veterans who consented to settle in the colony.

23

The Spirit of Rebellion Sets a Dangerous Example

On July 19, 1779, the Parisians are treated to a most intriguing sight—what are all those nice boys doing paddling around in the Seine, they look like Jesus walking on the Sea of Galilee. They're practicing crossing the Channel. "From the Pont Neuf to the Invalides divers water exercises in cork vests were performed to demonstrate the safety and usefulness of such corsets. It is certain that this garment would be most helpful if it allowed full freedom of movement" to the infantry who are soon to march on London, "as there is much talk of a Descent upon England."[1] They're even gaily sharing out the Lion's pelt: "The public are already making appointments to the seats on the British government. The Comte de Vergennes is to be Viceroy of all England; M. de Sartines, Lord Mayor and First Lord of the Admiralty; M. Necker, First Lord of the Treasury. The King [of England] and the entire British royal family are being sent to Chambord, where they will be treated with all the honor befitting their rank . . . The kingdoms of England and Scotland, and Ireland as well, are to be added to the estates of the Crown of France."[2]

This effervescence is not, however, universal—the "people," for instance, remain unmoved because their only source of information, the Sunday priests, have never heard of any plans for a Descent and have therefore made no mention of it. And the newspapers, which might arouse the bourgeois, are also silent. But in the drawing rooms of Versailles and Paris, where "the public" is, there is that "intoxication that mounts to all French heads whenever there is a war against the English."[3] And what if it were true? What if William's adventure were to begin again seven centuries later? French soldiers in London, the face of the world altered . . .

Even those who're dreaming don't know anything. The summer of 1779 is the summer of the great fog. True, there is a vague rattle of weapons in Normandy, but who, what, how? In Paris a Comte d'Egmont gropes after the event like everybody else. He writes, to a Duc d'Harcourt: "To me it seems quite impossible to grasp anything of all that is going on and being planned . . . Time will elucidate these enigmas, for everything seems enigmatic to me."[4] The Chevalier de Kageneck, a Swede in Paris who, as a member of Louis XVI's household guard, is fairly close to the horse's mouth, nevertheless writes to his Stockholm friend Alströmer, on July 10: "If you expect to learn from me where M. d'Orvilliers has gone with his great fleet, or what he has done since leaving Brest or even what he intends to do, you are misled: we have no idea, and perhaps M. de Sartines knows no better than we do. This uncertainty is not reassuring."[5] The court's chief sin, exaggerated beyond measure by the debility of Louis XVI, is one of omission—omitting to provide any information—to such a degree that even the people who ought to be informing other people are not informed themselves. The snake biting its own tail.

Anxiety is redoubled among those who, knowing nothing, suspect. Montmorin, the young French ambassador in Madrid, takes his job seriously;* his mission at the heart of the "family pact" between French and Spanish Bourbons makes him Vergennes's most assiduous correspondent. "I am constantly awaiting a messenger from you, and every time I hear a galloping horse my heart begins to race. It is a painful condition, when one is so far away."[6] There's one man, at least, who knows what's at stake.

Now then, where are we on the world chessboard? Stalemate in America between Rebels and English, stalemate in the Antilles between English and French. Lauzun has recaptured the African forts. The English have brought down Pondicherry by raiding the French East India Company warehouses one after the other. Without more troops or allies, England is incapable of carrying the war into Europe as she has done so many times before. Your move, France. In America? The failure of d'Estaing is no encouragement. What about Egypt, if only as a pawn on the road to India? The idea has been mooted, everything's ready, on paper—but only on paper.† "The time has come to acquire this healthful [*sic*] country three thousand leagues from Provence," affirms the French ambassador at Constantinople. It will become "the commercial storehouse of the universe."[7] Vergennes is lukewarm: too many interests would be affected. It would annoy Russia, even Austria. And the Turks aren't helpless.

Well, then, if we must make war on England, why not aim for their head?

The King's Council sways right and left, limply, with no view of the whole, no muscle, and no guiding brain. Louis XVI is waiting for other people to decide for him. Maurepas is wasting away; he's always cold, even in July. Sartines is obsessed by the frailty of the recently consolidated navy: if the fleet is destroyed it means disgrace for him. Miromesnil, the Keeper of the Seals,

*Armand-Marc, Comte de Montmorin-Saint-Herem, born in Paris in 1745, becomes minister for foreign affairs from 1787 to 1791 and dies in the massacre at the Abbaye on September 2, 1792.

†Less than twenty years later, Bonaparte bases his scheme on the plans drawn up at this moment.

hides his head in his files, and Necker takes refuge behind his ledgers. He's not indifferent, though: the abasement of the greatest Protestant power would make him vulnerable, at least morally. All the more reason to pipe down; the heretic is kept under close surveillance by those who put him in the treasury but won't let him sit on the Council. His job is to fill the coffers. He's filling them. "This Monsieur Necker, of whom it has so often been said that he would not last a month,* is still enjoying the confidence of both King and mentor [Maurepas] . . . In Madrid and Lisbon, people are convinced that M. Necker is such a man that, so long as he remains at the head of our finances, the royal treasury will be full . . . This good reputation has already procured great credit in the two capitals, on the simple signature of the director of finance."[8]

Turgot, on the other hand, was not rich; one now sees that that was his greatest mistake.

What about the minister of war? That's Montbarrey, prince of a few furlongs in the labyrinth of estates in the Franche-Comté, where everybody's a prince without a principality. He has replaced the cantankerous Saint-Germain, who had shaken up the army for both better and worse with his reforms based alternately on bigotry and common sense. No danger of Montbarrey reforming anything; he's a playboy, a cynic† who publicly exhibits, in his very offices, "a Renard girl, contemptible in every respect," according to Artois and Chartres—a deed which might arouse our sympathy for him except that he's got the support of the skeptics, Monsieur and Maurepas. Anyway, this minister has too much else on his mind these days for him to bother about the war: he is marrying off his daughter, "aged twenty-one, to the son of the Prince of Nassau-Saarbrück, who is only thirteen. The marriage is causing a great deal of comment."[9] Now there's a real affair of state.

"The inactivity of so many assembled forces has not failed to incline many people to murmur . . . It is even alleged that the King, fearing that the Queen might force the secret from him, has asked not to be told what operations were being planned, and they are known only to the Comte d'Aranda [the Spanish ambassador] and to MM. de Maurepas and de Sartines, but not to the Prince de Montbarrey."[10] Court rumors, silly and false. But si non è vero . . . it signifies a state of mind—and a real go-get-'em morale at Versailles.

We were almost forgetting Vergennes. Partly because he's fond of shadows and silence, but also because Charles Gravier de Vergennes merges into his own gray mists "like a coat hanging on a wall." Nevertheless, so long as things

*He has been in sole command of the economy since July 1777, but without actually holding the title. Taboureau finally got fed up with playing doorstop and resigned; and in order to avoid giving a minister's portfolio to a Protestant, Necker has been appointed "director general of finance," not "comptroller"—there's a nuance.

†For people who like an "easy read," he leaves some pleasant Mémoires.

are in the stage of diplomacy, that anteroom of war, he's the one who really counts. And he, Vergennes, has no desire to see a single French soldier in the streets of London. He's the least anti-English foreign minister the French have had for a long time. He has blocked every scheme to reconquer Canada. As for the Descent, "why strike at the heart of a nation which is indispensable to the balance of Europe?"[11] Harass her, humiliate and thwart her, certainly. But destroy her? Never. Vergennes, the most timorous of precursors, a man whom prudence has made a prophet, expresses the sentiments of that "civilized" France which is beginning to cherish toward England the amorous rancor of a partner in a marriage of reason, resigned for better and for worse—divorce at a pinch, but no homicide.

At Chanteloup, Choiseul was complaining:*

"All my life I have treated women very well; I neglect one [du Barry] and she becomes queen of France, or the next best thing . . . As for ambassadors, all I have done for them is public knowledge, done for them all, save one. But there is one whose work is slow and heavy, whom all the rest despise, whom they wish to see no more because of a ridiculous marriage: that one is M. de Vergennes, and he becomes minister of foreign affairs!"[12]

What's his secret, Milord? He works. That's all he does, for ten or twelve hours a day in the left-hand wing of the Château de Versailles, on the sidelines of the perpetual party. A slave more resigned than zealous: "Every instant is a step toward old age; that is the universal fate of mankind; it is less dreadful when our lives have not been entirely idle and futile. The life I have led should put me beyond reach of any indictment . . . At the end of the day I find that I never noticed it passing. I have work enough in my study to keep me from conceiving any fancy to join in the whirlwind of societies, pleasures and, perhaps, slander. Walking is good for me; more of it might occasionally be necessary, but the opportunity is not always given. Matters pile up around me and, despite the speed with which I expedite them, I must fear their weight will one day bear me down."[13] It'll take a lot of pounds to do it, though, because the "life he has led" isn't making him any slimmer; the jowls are there, the double chin, the spare tire—but he's got a frame that can carry some extra weight, good solid timber from Burgundy where he was born sixty years ago.† Everything about him is broad, solidly based, firmly drawn: the high forehead, the pursed mouth, the neat but unstarched curls, the scrutinizing, slightly defensive gaze, and the big nose dropping far and straight to balance the rest. Tedium flows from him in waves. The Prince de Ligne couldn't get

---

*According to Chamfort, a disillusioned bohemian semi-aristocrat, wit, and man of letters who loved the Revolution until it got too hot for him and he committed suicide to avoid prison. [*Trans.*]

†In Dijon, on December 29, 1719, into a family of judges. The lesser nobility of the magistracy.

over it when he heard Vergennes was using Beaumarchais: "Is it not curious to see the least frolicsome minister France has ever had employing a jester?"[14] Least frolicsome, heaviest . . . fortunately, he keeps his mouth shut most of the time. It's worse when he tries to open it: "In public, he had a passion for telling stories, making witticisms, and a forlorn hope of causing people to laugh; but his unending tales made people yawn and his joviality cheered nobody, especially when he began rehearsing his reminiscences of Turkey." And when he writes he breaks all records: in ton after ton of concrete, his pen painfully extrudes the scaffolding of the Europe that is slowly rising inside his heavy skull. Vergennes's style is that of the Grand Panjandrum. Would it be to the advantage of France and the United States to establish permanent, amicable relations? On your marks, get set—here we go! "No question of interests being able to divide two peoples who communicate with each other only across vast expanses of sea, the necessary commercial relations which would develop between them would form a chain which, if not eternal, would at least be very long lasting; the which, animating and reinvigorating French industry, would bring into our ports those ingredients, essential rather than precious, which America produces, which she has hitherto poured into those of England and which, by nourishing the industry of that nation, have contributed so much to raising it to that astounding level of wealth at which we now behold it."[15] Oof. Does he never breathe?

We begin to see why he needs to spend so much time at his desk, and why Louis XVI admires him. Choiseul must have dismissed him in sheer exasperation, after a career ploughed straight as a furrow through diplomatic posts of increasing importance: Lisbon, Trier, Hanover, and then the embassy in Constantinople, where he nearly lost everything by winning his wife. He boasts about it: "It is a rare occurrence, in this century, for a wife and husband to love each other; and, what is more, to dare profess it."[16] Indeed, the Vergenneses do purr solemnly away, but it's not quite Tristan and Isolde: before marrying Anna du Viviers in the Church of St. Louis of the French at Constantinople he waited until the pneumatic widow had given him two sons, Constantin and Louis, and the elder had reached the age of reason. Their affair, meanwhile, was reaching danger point: in choosing between the scandal of a break and the scandal of a marriage, without the King's permission, to the widow of Testa the surgeon, Vergennes opted for honor and comfort no less than love, and was faithfully rewarded by this beautiful female cushion—the daughter of a minor Savoyard gentleman, but born in Turkey and bred to the Ottoman softness. She was enough for him.

At that point he was presumed finished, and presumed so himself. He embarked upon a career of retirement in Burgundy, where he would become a lord of the vineyard and forest. He emerged from it because he kissed the hand that hit him. Monarchist to the point of imbecility, Vergennes came crawling back through an interminable maze of adulation . . . Louis XV was fond of prostrate people. He needed someone to supervise the young King of Sweden, some mildly conniving French minister who could guide him in preparing his coup d'état. Vergennes managed to make himself useful to Gustavus III and to bend Sweden in the direction of France. A job for an expert. His docility subsequently found favor with the dauphin, whom death short-circuited out of the century but who was taking his revenge by tele-commanding his son's choices from Paradise.

Thus, one thing leading to another, France's foreign affairs have drifted into the hands of the man least capable of understanding the American upris-ing. Occasionally, when his obsession gets the upper hand, he can express himself succinctly enough: "The spirit of rebellion, wherever it breaks out, always sets a dangerous example. Moral afflictions are like physical ones: both may become contagious. This consideration must prevail with us to make certain that the spirit of independence, which is in the throes of so terrible [*sic*] an eruption in northern America, cannot be communicated to the points of our concern in that hemisphere."[17] Apropos of those "points of our concern," he somehow finds time to administer his fortune, which, like himself, is tranquilly swelling and which consists of large interests in the slave trade.*

However, once war has been declared Vergennes has to do his duty whether he likes it or not. His most urgent task, in the face of English naval supremacy, is to knock the rust off that ancient, creaking "family pact" and get it back into working order. But in trying to thaw out a frozen contract, all he does is stir up a hornet's nest. "It is affirmed that the [Spanish] Catholic King has fallen prey to dementia, the onset of which was marked by irresponsible concessions resulting in the rebirth of the Inquisition, the relegation to Paris of the Comte d'Aranda, and the useless equipping of the fleets at great expense . . ."[18] Charles III isn't going crazy, only senile. It's that old reflex of the Bourbons, shriveled up inside their hunting and their devotions: let me die in peace! He passes the buck to his minister Florida-Blanca, who's playing petty dictator in the shadow of the king—something of a tradition in Spain. He's the one who gets to keep Montmorin dangling while Vergennes implores him "to prise open M. de Floride-Blanche [the name is Frenchified north of the Pyrenees] and extract from him an approximate date upon which we may hope for Spain to show herself,"[19] in other words, officially enter the war against the English and send her fleet to join ours. But how are you supposed to "prise open" a man as prickly, sarcastic, and insulting as that; he treats our ambassador the way

*At his death his fortune is found to have tripled during his term in office, thanks to the kind of speculation which is always less risky for someone receiving inside information.

he treated the pope and the cardinals. He finds the alliance with the United States "quixotic": it would really be asking too much to expect Spain to "pull France out of the mire yet again [sic]."[20] "He is attached to his system and I believe [dixit Montmorin] that no one on earth is capable of persuading him to abandon it. By turns violent, cold, or phlegmatic, in the extreme forms of his opinion he remains unswervingly committed to it,"[21] and it isn't all that inconsistent: nothing for the Rebels, everything against Great Britain—on condition that Versailles agrees. Spain can feel her own powder-keg in the Americas heating up, and would gladly see those Boston witches burned at the stake. She won't lift a finger to help them. But she'll take advantage of the fact that England's hands are tied out there and give her eternal rival a good thrashing! Oh, to avenge the Grand Armada! . . . "If we were to make war upon the English, it must be done as the Romans did against Carthage."[22] No fussing with details. No procrastinating. "My view would be that the two Powers should unite their naval forces, which would form a naval army of sixty ships of the line or more, invade England and treat for peace in London."[23] As a preliminary snack we'll take back Gibraltar, that wart on the honor of Spain. In July the mountain is blockaded on land by (Spanish) soldiers under the command of a (French) duke working for Spain, Crillon, and at sea by a fleet of clumsy whales carrying masses of machinery on their backs: M. d'Arcon's *prasmes,* convoyed from Toulon by the ships d'Estaing left behind with the Comte de Sade.*

It's almost a year now since Florida-Blanca began prodding and Vergennes holding back. *He* just doesn't believe in the Descent: "We must not flatter ourselves that it could be attempted with fewer than seventy ships of the line and at least seventy thousand in troop forces, with ten thousand horse. If one thinks what that would mean in terms of transport ships, artillery, supplies, ammunition and all other manner of paraphernalia of war and personal service, it is enough to make one shudder with dread."[24] And yet he knows perfectly well that the spies placed long ago by the Comte de Broglie have made a very exact reckoning of the English forces: at most, the French would have to fight no more than fifty-four thousand men, only four thousand two hundred of them mounted, and they are divided, "some in England and Scotland and some in the Guernseys."[25] After the drain-off to America, that's all that's left of the English army at home.

And as for their morale . . . Well below zero. England, or at least its governing class, is worm-eaten. Old Chatham has just died, prophesying like Jeremiah; king and Tories, looking for scapegoats, are resurrecting antipopery. The Catholics, in turn, are ready to revolt and form a "fifth column."

---

*A cousin of Donatien-Aldonse. The *prasme* [Dutch: "barge"] was a flat-bottomed boat that could transport heavy artillery.

In Parliament, Fox and Burke are attacking the government so violently that Lord North bursts into sobs on the front (ministers') bench. "The most regrettable part of the whole scene for him was that his tears aroused no one to compassion."[26] George III closes the session immediately after Spain's official declaration of war on July 3. Even before that, a howl from Burke: "Oh, Sir [Mr. Speaker], what a long and dismal, what a dark and sad night has this session been, to leave us at the end of it engaged in war with the House of Bourbon, and America joined to her against us!"[27] Lord Shelburne is bubbling over with optimism: "I make no doubt that we shall be able to defend the two small islands of Great Britain and Ireland in a manner that will astonish all Europe. But what will be the fruit of this latest struggle? We shall nonetheless emerge from it a dead people, stricken from the ranks of the powers of the earth."[28] If we can trust Beaumarchais, all in a flutter and full of financial gossip as usual, even St. George's cavalry is at bay: "All the London café patrons are bandying the question whither they should retreat in the event of a Descent. The consensus is in favor of Scotland, because the invasion of London is feared and in that case everyone would be wanting to convert his holdings into gold. A very profound man who has been passing these things on to me says, 'I'll lay ten to one that the Bank will be brought down three days after the Descent by a run on hard money.' "[29] Lady Rivers, a close friend of Pitt, writes to a French correspondent: "The moment you have disembarked on our coasts, the discouragement of the Nation will be as great as was its former security. Your invasion plans, which everyone is talking about, make any attempt at secrecy pointless: England is lost."[30]

Is this one of those moments in History when all that's needed is for someone to push open a door? For Vergennes, the answer is no and no again. "Were it in my power to annihilate England I should avoid it at all costs, as the greatest possible folly."[31] But since he cannot silence the bellicose, he tries to sidetrack them, at least, toward Ireland. Ever since the days of the Stuarts it has been part of Court dogma in France that there's a sleeping beauty out there beyond the mists, who will leap up in arms against the Anglicans at the first glimpse of a few friendly ships. Today, it would also be possible to mobilize the Presbyterians, "by tempting them with the establishment of that democracy which is the idol of their fanaticism."[32] And it's true enough that the 3.5 million Irish Catholics, driven to desperation by the pressure of taxation and British persecutions and infected by the contagion of *Independence,* are on the verge of insurrection. Who are these "Whiteboys" ranging through the southern part of the country near Waterford, where they could be so helpful to a French landing force? A peasant revolutionary league? The authorities rename them American-style: "These *Insurgents* began appearing ten or twelve years ago, at first in small numbers, and in a short time this secret society has grown by slow degrees to have members in virtually every province of Ireland. In its alarm the government has opposed them with force and ruthlessly, but its harshness and persecution are merely swelling their ranks . . . They convene several times each winter, summoned together by fires which they light at night on high ground. The signals are seen all over the province and in a trice they have seized all the horses and weapons of the Protestant lords, and, thus mounted and armed, ride off to perform what they call acts of justice."[33] Florida-Blanca has sent an emissary to the Irish Catholics, "a zealous priest, well suited to infuse the people with that spirit of fanaticism that produces Revolutions."[34] An Irish revolution? Vergennes goes gray at the very word. Even here he moderates and temporizes. "It should be prepared in such a way that we cannot be charged with having fomented it and are not committed to its support."[35] If *he* ever had a Grand Design, it could only be to lure every hothead in the universe out of his den so they could all throttle each other at once. The planet purified of weeds . . . In May 1779 Paris is singing:

Vergennes gobe-mouches,	[Vergennes sits and swats flies,
Ministre sans talents,	A minister fit for dogs,
Laisse l'Anglais farouche	While the Insurgents rise
Battre les Insurgents;	And are beaten down by hogs;
Valet bas et soumis	The black coward's in fee
De toute l'Angleterre,	To the whole English land
A George III il a promis	And has promised George Three
Qu'on serait toujours de	His pals we'd e'er be
ses amis	While the ship's in his hand.]
Pendant son ministère.[36]	

"It is affirmed that, before coming out in favor of the Americans, Vergennes offered his services to the court of London to assist in bringing its colonies back under control; that he verbally proposed to help Lord Bute to reduce his opposition party, and to render the King of England as wholly sovereign as is our own."[37] Nasty rumors,* with no more substance to them than those beginning to circulate around Marie Antoinette; but in her case as in his they are the result of behavior that leaves their subject open to calumny. This constant in Vergennes's life—a man who contributed to the restoration of absolute monarchy in Sweden by armed force—makes him the very essence of an antirevolutionary. Whence "the rumor that secret negotiations are in progress between Vergennes and King George III with a view to establishing a treaty that will be advantageous to the House of Bourbon if an absolute monarchy were to be restored in England."[38] Everybody knows that this is George III's ambition,

---

*Which no reliable document can confirm.

so why shouldn't these two "great minds" meet, in their dreams anyway?

Some rumors may be false and yet truer than truth. In this case, they reveal the discrepancy between the intentions of the principal French minister in charge of coordinating the Descent and those of the men who are rushing out to the coasts of Normandy and Brittany, seeing themselves as the crusaders of 1779.

THE ASCENSION
OF THE CHEVALIER D'EON

24

APRIL 1779

In My Female Position

"Retirement will be the death of me," moans "Charlotte-Geneviève-Louise-Auguste-Andrée-Timothée d'Eon de Beaumont, formerly consulted Doctor, listened-to Censor, quoted Author, feared Dragoon, celebrated Captain, experienced Negotiator, accredited Plenipotentiary, respected Minister, and now a poor girl come of age,"[1] or at least *she* consents to pretend to be so and to feminize her Christian names and sign herself "la Chevalière d'Eon," just as *she* also wears wimple and coif.* Just as she would gladly play the Maid of Orléans on this crusade! Stick her sword into a few of those English who have made such fun of her . . . She'd show them whether she was a man or not.

D'Eon keeps nagging Maurepas: "I am obliged to submit to you, in very humble and very forceful terms, that, the year of my novitiate as a female now being completed, it is impossible for me to pursue this profession any further . . . In my present condition I can be of no use or service to either the King, myself, or my family,† and an excessively sedentary life is destroying the elasticity of my body and mind . . . I renew my plea, Monseigneur, that you obtain permission from the King for me to go as voluntary with the fleet of M. le Comte d'Orvilliers. In peacetime obedience enabled me to remain in skirts, but in time of war I cannot do it."[2]

I mean, who does the silly flittermouse think he is? He's beginning to get on their nerves. Can one imagine this creation in petticoats consorting with the sailors of the King? There'd be a mutiny. And as for resuming his masculine status, the answer is n-o, No, forget it. Two years ago he lost a last-ditch

---

*Physiologically speaking, we recall, this is a man.

†"My mother, sister, brother-in-law and three nephews in the King's service."

offensive—although not, as was his wont, before filling columns in every gazette—in his unending quarrel with Beaumarchais. It was in the cards: each tried to outwit the other with such flagrant insincerity that they became positively honest about it. A pair of robbers scrapping over their plunder: the secret papers of Louis XV* against the écus of Louis XVI. There were months of wrangling, with each conceding as little as possible as they gradually slid from a comedy of love into a comedy of rage. But in the end it was no, Beaumarchais definitely would not marry the demoiselle d'Eon, he'd forgotten all about that little business and was now paying court to America. So the "chevalière" kept his man's garb and dug him/herself in in London for eighteen months just to annoy them all. But d'Eon had signed his own abdication. They held him by infamy. He had no choice but to return to Versailles, worn out and infuriated—but still in his dress uniform as a captain of dragoons. Of *what?* Vergennes holds the pen with which Louis XVI slaughters the upstart:

> By order of the King
> Charles-Geneviève, etc., d'Eon de Beaumont shall forthwith abandon the uniform of dragoons which she has been affecting, shall resume the garments of her sex, and shall appear no more in this realm in any raiment other than that befitting a woman.
> At Versailles, the 17th of August, 1777.[3]

D'Eon goes down on his knees, like those condemned men who are forced to make a public retraction before being broken on the wheel. The Queen sends him a fan as a present, and dispatches her dressmaker, Rose Bertin, to prepare his maiden's trousseau. Is he supposed to thank them? "It would be easier for me to play the lion than the lamb, and a captain of volunteers in the army than a sweet and obedient maiden . . . After Heaven, the King and his ministers, it is Mlle Bertin who must be credited with my miraculous conversion." And he signs, "le chevalier d'Eon, for a few days more,"[4] long enough to receive, in masculine attire, his native Tonnerre's homage to its hero, "over twelve hundred persons with cannons, guns and pistols" tumbling along the narrow streets of a little high-perched town with blue roofs on its peaked houses. The echoes of the celebration are heard clear to Auxerre. The dilapidated old family house "presently resembles the château of Baron Tundertrumtrum;† all that is left of it are the doors and the windows, and the Armançon flows through the gardens"[5]—but it's in Burgundy, and every night two *feuillettes* of one of the finest wines in the world** are

---

*Including those containing the plans for the Descent, which it was becoming a matter of some urgency to recover.

†A character in the *Adventures of Baron Munchausen,* better known to the children of that time than were Perrault's fairy tales.

**Depending on the region, the capacity of a *feuillette* varied from 114 to 140 liters.

broached outside this ruined house, to partake of the blood of the good god of Tonnerre who burns your throat out and sends you to heaven. After all, we have won some kind of victory together, I and "my fellow countrymen both of the town and neighboring countryside, from the greatest to the lowliest," over those ministers of cruelty who would like to pretend that the adventure of the Chevalier d'Eon is nothing but an anatomical curiosity. "The common people showed their joy with such enthusiasm, letting off such salvos of musket fire and petards, that they set fire to the stables and nearly burned the nearby granaries."[6] Tonnerre: the one place where everybody knows his mother and his nurse and will never take him for a girl, even if he is forced to wear a disguise.

So there are fireworks to bury his bachelor days, but they are not followed by a wedding. Back at Versailles, he "donned a girl's habit" as one might a nun's, on the morning of October 21, 1777, "on the feast of St. Ursula, patron saint of the eleven thousand virgins and martyrs of England," and proceeds to take communion in numerous churches the same day* . . . And as for being a female: "I hope in this way to divest myself of all the flaws and dangers inherent in the masculine condition."[7] He must have felt himself a near neighbor of Sade and Mirabeau that day, in the only form of protest open to them: blasphemy.

He spends a year trying to get used to his new position as a zoological oddity, in little apartments on the Rue de Conti or the Rue de Noailles at Versailles. "In my retirement, I endeavor to inure myself to my sad lot." He has to change "clothes, shirt, lodging, convictions, opinions, language, color, face, fashion, style, manner . . .† Ever since giving up my uniform and saber I have felt as foolish as a fox without his brush! I try to walk in pointed pumps and high heels, but have nearly broken my neck on more than one occasion. Instead of making my curtsey, I doff my wig and three-tiered headdress, taking them to be a hat or helmet."[8] People come running to get a good look at this phenomenon on November 23, 1777, when *she* presents herself at Court. What's the good of all that hard work when the result is so unconvincing? "She often forgets to put on her gloves, and bares Cyclopean arms. Her bosom is covered up to her chin, so that no one can see whether or not she has one. All of which goes no little way to confirm the doubts of the incredulous."[9] He's after them, he's trying to provoke them.

They wanted to manufacture themselves a *chevalière,* did they? Well, he'll show them a grenadier in long gowns. As such, he becomes a star attraction of 1777–78. People send carriages to fetch him, like an opera singer. The La Rochefoucaulds, the Polignacs, the Breteuils, the Rohans, the d'Aguesseaus,

---

*D'Eon was—among other things—a doctor of canon law, and had written—among other things—treatises on the Church Fathers.

†This letter to Vergennes, dated November 1777, is written entirely in the masculine.

etc. Nevertheless, he's a little too much in evidence at Versailles, so they relegate him to a gilded hermitage at Petit-Montreuil, a stone's throw away.

They were paying him to keep quiet, were they? Well, he'll write to them. His logorrhea only flows the faster; twenty pages to Vergennes, sometimes, just to unburden himself at Beaumarchais's expense, having come in time to hate the man with an almost amorous loathing. "I shall always remain fit enough to beard every Barber in Seville."[10] But he's beginning, if not actually to get inside his part, at least to make use of it. The feminine endings begin pouring from his pen like so many more reasons to call the whole world to witness: "I am outraged by a ham actor who would not have dared to look the Chevalier d'Eon in the face, by a plebian who used to be a bell-ringer when Europe was resounding with my feats of war and politics . . . I denounce him, and deliver him up to every woman of my century, as a person seeking to raise his own credit by lowering that of a woman, to obtain wealth at the cost of a woman's honor, and in the end, to avenge his own thwarted hopes by crushing a woman." Is he rising to the bait? He's rising, all right, as to every other experience in his life—in seven-league boots. He publishes "Open Letters to Women" in the gazettes: "Victory! my contemporaries, victory and four pages of victory! . . . Shades of Louis XV, know the being your power has created! . . . Women, take me to your bosoms, I am worthy of you!"[11] They're not likely to miss an opportunity like this. Fashionable convents go to war to admit *her:* the ladies of Hautes-Bruyères, the daughters of Ste. Marie, the sisters of St. Cyr . . . A dragooness in a convent! What novels might have been written, if d'Eon had been interested in sex! One Lady de Durfort, a nun at St. Cyr, writes to him on October 20, 1778: "When one has as much courage as you have, as much strength of purpose, constancy, intrepidity, quality; in a word, when one is as great as you are, Mademoiselle, it requires but a little effort to become a saint." He couldn't agree with her more. Like many famous men, he has to have mountains of compliments, even if it means distributing them himself when they don't come fast enough from others. His answer to the nun: "All my life, like a foolish virgin, I have run after the shadows of things. My one consolation is that in the very core of the disorder of camps, sieges and battles, and in the horror of political meeting rooms, I have been fortunate enough to preserve my inner peace intact, together with the purity of my conduct and my faith. I alone know what it has cost me to rise above myself . . ."[12]

He might have gone on slowly inflating and begun a new career as a fat canoness gorging on incense and pastries. But "I am only happy as a wisp." D'Eon could never settle down. He is irrepressible by vocation, and not totally unlike Beaumarchais himself, the man he so yearns to send to the devil because he sees in that commoner a mirror image of himself. Tranquillity is something he's never experienced. He hasn't a clue what it might be like. People assume he's content: "I am filled with shame and sick with grief to find myself in skirts just when we are beginning a war [to Sartines, on June 7, 1778] . . . I have neither the soul of a monk nor that of an abbot, that I can eat up in idleness the allowance which the late King deigned to grant me." He tries to cheat, to bend the rules of this condition in which he lies hamstrung. Couldn't they at least authorize him to resume a man's clothing "on the working days of the week, so that I may keep up my health by riding, hunting and sword practice, and be obliged to wear my woman's clothes on Sundays and holidays?"[13] Not likely.

Silence. Gently, without a sound, the gears of state grind him to a pulp. He implores: "Just for the duration of the war?" . . . Silence, silence, and more silence, the régime's one answer to every supplicant. The monarchy can be a wall or a tomb, depending; but either way, you only bruise your fists beating at it. D'Eon hurts himself again, badly enough to make another awkward outburst. But when is an outburst not awkward, unless it's calculated? What a blunder, that letter to Maurepas, that outcry of February 1779, which he ends crescendo: "In my female position, I am reduced to poverty even with the blessings of the late King, which would be sufficient for a captain of dragoons [that remains to be seen; he always was a big spender], but are not sufficient for the estate I am forced to assume. M. le Comte de Maurepas must understand that the part of Maiden to the Court is a supremely silly one for me to play when I am still able to play a lion in the army."[14] Never mind the way he writes, they're used to that by now, they've seen so much of it. It's his methods they can't stomach: for instance, he turns this letter into a sort of high-society tract, has forty copies of it run off by a Parisian printer, and sends them to all the princes of the blood and "to several great ladies at Court." Is he trying to found a "d'Eon Party"? For the deaf-mutes who govern this realm, Louis XVI, Vergennes, and Maurepas, nothing could be more unpardonable than an appeal to public opinion, whatever its source.

March 2: Order from the king to "la Chevalière d'Eon" to return to Tonnerre. *She* gives the messenger a receipt, promises to obey the moment she is better, but just now she's suffering from an inflammation of the chest . . . which doesn't prevent her, a week later, from strolling through Versailles in dragoon's uniform. D'Eon's had enough of his circus sideshow act. He's worth more than that. Anything would be better than the squirrel cage they've been keeping him in for the last two years. He comes looking for them again. He finds them again.

On March 20, early in the morning—the scene begins to be a trifle repetitive, the same walk-ons, the same script, only the leading role changes: Beaumarchais, Mirabeau, and Sade before him have already heard that heavy tread on the stairs, that clank of weapons.

"Open in the King's name!"

The Sieur de Vierville, major of military police of the King's Household, accompanied by five or six guards, barges into the little apartment in the Pavillon Marjou on the Rue de Noailles which d'Eon has decorated like a jewel box in highly effeminate taste. The gendarmes advance cautiously over the oriental rugs, skirting the rosewood furniture and the Italian draped curtains and the marquetry tables . . . In the shadow of an alcove hung with toile de Jouy, near a scent-bottle-covered dressing table worthy of a courtesan, a half-naked body, a shrill voice:

"What do you want?"

"Mademoiselle, I have received orders to secure your person."

Yesterday the "demoiselle" was "bled in both arms," but today, strong as a stevedore, she turns on them, brandishing a carbine "loaded with case shot"—d'Eon having kept his old spy's habit of never going to bed without it. The assailants valiantly try to rush him. *She* does for two of them. What a Hercules, this maid! The others "search the bed and drawers, repeatedly touch her body," not without perplexity, and "seize her papers." "They left her nothing but her innocence." It would have been a scene worth watching if they'd tried to take that too![15] The prisoner is bodily carried downstairs and stuffed into a six-horse carriage. Drive on, coachman, farewell, Versailles. His roaring has aroused the whole neighborhood. It's the Chevalière, the Chevalier, d'Eon, whatever you call him, being cut down to size.

It won't kill him. The ensuing weeks give royalist historians another opportunity to insist that Louis's prisons were inoffensive places. As it happens, his hijackers have some trouble finding one for him. They have orders to put him wherever they please, provided the ministers never hear of him again. He's not ill treated. He's left to howl his lungs out, both proud of and enraged by the incident, in the heavy carriage cracking along the Burgundy road, where it stops that same evening at Joigny. One night in a hotel. Then a pause at Auxerre, where they try to unload him onto the Cistercians. Isn't he supposed to be a convent-lover? But the ladies who longed to have him while he was free want no part of him a prisoner. The party has to push on to Dijon, where the château drawbridge drops in front of his coach as it dropped three years before in front of "Mirabeau fils." And inside it we find the same nice governor, the Comte de Changey, dragged out of bed in the middle of the night to take delivery of "a female prisoner who is a captain of dragoons and Chevalier de Saint Louis."[16]

He might have fared worse. D'Eon is treated—at his own expense—like a lord. Every day for dinner (that is, around three or four in the afternoon) he has soup, boiled meat, a fish course (trout, eels, salmon) or crayfish, wild or domestic fowl (hens, woodcock, or snipe), vegetables, dessert, coffee, and the local spirits, which tasted like burning wood—the whole washed down with the Cistercians' Clos-Vougeot.* You can survive on a diet like that, especially if you're fairly certain it won't last. D'Eon is kept locked up just long enough for one last negotiation, so that everybody in Tonnerre will know, when he turns up there again, that he has been sent against his will and by the King's hand. The halo of persecution will help his neighbors put up with his woman's headdress. Nobody will laugh at him in his own home, they'll feel sorry for him. And that's all he wants—now that he has no chance of wanting anything else. A padded downfall. Broken, but gently. He'll be able to brag, and for him that's very important. "I was put into the rooms formerly occupied by the Duchesse du Maine, the Marquis de Nesle and the Comte de Laura-guais. I remained there only nineteen days, because the Comte de Changey sent word to M. de Maurepas that all the nobility and officers in Dijon and for twenty leagues around, both men and women, were coming to beg a meal from him in order to have the pleasure of dining with me, and that he would be ruined if it went on much longer; that, furthermore, every day, and even more on Sundays and holidays, crowds of up to two thousand assembled in the courtyard of the château to see me;† and that all the officers and men in his garrison were more ready to obey me than himself."[17] Meanwhile, his brother-in-law O'Gorman is dealing with his case, assisted by the Marquis de Vergennes, brother of the minister, and the Bishop of Mâcon. Once more they alternate threats and promises to this nervous wreck on the verge of a break-down. Does he really want to be shut up in a convent for the rest of his days? That's what they pretend to prepare him for. And he pretends to be dreading it, and once more lets them extort a solemn promise from him: "my submission to the King's orders that I wear my women's clothes all my life, and stay at home with my mother." He is back at Tonnerre on April 10.

The Chevalier d'Eon will never go to war again. The Descent will take place—or won't—without him.

*The total cost of the Chevalier d'Eon's "board" for his three weeks of detention in Dijon: 476 livres, or approximately 2,500 new francs [$500].

†The courtyard in question cannot conceivably hold more than two or three hundred. And to think that d'Eon despised Beaumarchais as a braggart.

25

APRIL 1779

A Nation's Rabble

Rushes in two parts: 1778 and 1779, the year they played make-believe and the year they started believing what they played. To see what really goes on we have to back up a year and get both campaigns in the same frame.

Fersen is one of the first to volunteer, in September 1778. Does he need to escape the melting eyes which the Queen is beginning to cast his way? Some say he does, but this is unlikely. There's nothing serious between them. He's simply continuing the endless "travel-is-broadening" tour of his youth. Now there's a war to visit, like another new country. "I thought of going into Normandy to see the camp there under the command of the Maréchal de Broglie. I asked Steding to come along.* He consented and it was decided that we should set out on the 10th [of September]. We had our uniforms made according to the new model. Madame de Boufflers expressed a great curiosity to see them and we went to her home wearing them a couple of days before our departure. She found the style very dashing, but said only that my uniform was pretty."[1] The path of the amateur warrior resembles that of the truant schoolboy: two weeks of dawdling in Normandy. Caen, Lisieux, Bayeux, the orchards, the land of cows and apples, and also of textile works in every town. Near Bayeux all the roads are rutted by caissons. The hay has been mown too early, the farms are gutted by requisitions. The army destined for England is camped on two square leagues of ground around Vaussieux. The blue and white of its uniforms contrasts sharply with the Bessin green, deepened by torrential rains that have been flooding the pastures for weeks. We're not likely to get any wetter than this even if we have to swim the Channel. But rain or no rain, here is the rigorous order of the army on maneuvers: cannons, stacked arms, tents lined up in rows as though to compose some huge geometrical figure, and men moving among them in equally perfect alignment. And where Broglie commands, your leather gleams as if on parade. You'd think

*A Swedish colonel and one of his best friends. The new uniforms mentioned in this paragraph, both less cumbersome and more luxurious with their gilt overstitching, were introduced by the Comte de Saint-Germain. But nobody's wearing them yet . . . except in Paris.

he had transformed the very mud into wax. Forty-eight infantry battalions and thirty cavalry squadrons, making at least thirty thousand men in all; the entire "Brittany division" is concentrated here, ready to sail from Le Havre and Saint-Malo at three days' notice.* Fersen paces between the hedges of saluting men who conduct him to headquarters as to a supreme drawing room at the end of a long string of lesser ones, where this over-shy youth, obsessed by his terror of being laughed at, is intimidated at the thought of being presented. "We stayed with the maréchal at his headquarters. The weather was dreadful, horribly rainy and piercingly cold. Both of us were exceedingly embarrassed to show ourselves in such a state, known to nobody and in such extraordinary costume, and our unease increased considerably when we saw what a large number of people were there, who would all be scrutinizing us. The first moment, when we entered the room where all the aides-de-camp and officers were assembled, was awful, and I should have given a great deal of money not to be there. However, we had to go through with it." He's got nothing to worry about: his name is an open sesame. Every man who fought in the Seven Years' War knows that old Count Fersen was the leader of the pro-French party in Sweden. "We said that we were Swedish and had letters for the maréchal. A moment later the doors were opened and the officers went in for their orders.† We were told to enter too, and I found a small man, extremely carefully dressed, who had a most alert look about him": Victor-François, Maréchal-Duc de Broglie, Prince of the Holy Empire, conqueror at Bergen, champion of an old lost war in which France gained what heroes she could. And it is true that Broglie was the least obtuse of Louis XV's generals and might have become a man of destiny had it not been for his fishmonger's quarrel with the Prince de Soubise and the whole Pompadour clan: the Rohans, the Choiseuls . . . His disgrace in mid-celebrity sixteen years earlier— a little like that of Maurepas—recommended him to the favor of Louis XVI, in this seesaw régime. Fersen meets him, a sixty-year-old straining at the bit, in a fleeting return to glory.** The future belongs to the Broglies, they're positive of it, and although they may have missed Germany in 1765 and America two years back, they're damned if they're going to miss England now. Victor-François knows how to be nice to foreigners who can increase his popularity in Europe, and he turns on all the overpowering affability of a small man ashamed of his size. Fersen is charmed by "this little fellow bursting with spirit. His vitality is most in evidence at the head of his troops. He sheds years and has the energy of a man of thirty. He is never tired. His conversation was

---

*The "division," a new term brought in by Saint-Germain, didn't yet mean a mobile military unit; it signified a combination of three branches—infantry, cavalry, and artillery—within a definite geographical area.

†Nowadays known [even in French] as briefing.

**The Duc de Broglie was born in October 1718, his brother the comte in July 1719.

entertaining. He has an excellent memory and tells a very good story."

This war is being prepared to the tune of a minuet. Since we can't fight yet, we may as well dance. "The maréchal introduced us to his wife, his daughter, his sister, etc. To pass the extremely long afternoons on days when there were no maneuvers, the maréchal ordered dancing. All the ladies whose husbands were at camp came in from the neighboring country." Many of the senior officers have châteaus in Normandy; so handy, you know. "There were Mmes de La Châtre, de Simiane, de Navarès, de Villequiers, the Marquise de Coigny . . . Madame de Cajol and her three charming daughters were the chief adornment of the ball . . . A kind of court was paid to the maréchal during his supper. I found this a rather curious fashion, but grew used to it after a time." The service is excellent, too: just whistle or snap your fingers, and your soldier-dog is at your knee, the lackey-soldier who has made the stuff of slapstick for as long as the world has been world and the army army. Men without names—the Negroes aren't the only ones to be debaptized. La Verdure–La Rose–Joli-Coeur–La Jeunesse–Beauregard–La Grimace–Sans-Souci–Champagne–Picard–Le Lorrain belongs to his colonel body and soul, like the slave to his planter, and has belonged to him for thirty years in some cases, purchased by a sequence of signatures starting with the enlistment which the recruiting sergeant extorted from him in a half-drunken stupor on the corner of a tavern table.* He never loses that comical look beneath the impeccable acquired style of his uniform and gestures. Two out of every three soldiers are products of these regular bloodlettings effected, by means of *capitulations* between recruiter and recruit, in town and countryside alike, "in the mob of good-for-nothings, starvelings, vagabonds, and marauders."[2] Two birds with one stone: society is rid of, and the army's ranks augmented by, "for their own good and that of the public, all the layabouts, vagrants, and wastrels able to bear arms,"[3] and you can always hang them if they engage in unauthorized looting. "The army is the gutter into which all the offal of the body social is swept." Indignation at this state of affairs is beginning to be voiced by those people who are always so down-in-the-mouth about everything, the Encyclopedists, the "Turgotians," those party-poops who're trying to spoil our wars. How does it happen "that a society scoops up all its basest elements to turn them into soldiers?" Before leaving the ministry, the Comte de Saint-Germain gave deep thought to this question, and came up with an unimpeachable answer: "It would be desirable for armies to be made of reliable men, well chosen and of the best sort. But a nation must not be destroyed to make an army, and taking its best would mean its destruction. In the present state of affairs, armies can scarcely be otherwise composed than of a nation's rabble,

---

*There were special taverns, called *fours* in French, to which recruiting sergeants lured the young men, often with the help of paid girls, to get them drunk and make them sign on. In 1779 there are over fifteen such taverns in the vicinity of the Pont Neuf in Paris.

of all that is useless and harmful to society. Then it is for military discipline to purify this corrupt mass, to knead it and render it useful."[4] And so we have the camp of Vaussieux, where, moreover, the men have no complaints. At enlistment a recruit costs ninety-two livres in the infantry, one hundred and eleven in the hussars.*Not too stiff a price for a man's hide. As for his pay, in theory he earns six sous a day† but he seldom sees the color of them because his food and tobacco rations are deducted from them.

"Poor soldier." What a pleonasm.

Mmes de Broglie, de Simiane, or de Coigny run no risk of incurring the penalties inflicted upon the "girls of ill repute" against whom the Duc de Broglie "waged unremitting war. Rather than having them flogged, as was the previous custom, which did not prevent them from coming back again four days later, their faces are blackened with some preparation which, I am told, lasts more than six months. If this be true, it is certain they will not reappear, for it is dreadful to see but at the same time does them no harm."[5] Far, far from such trollops, the comely Swede, now reassured, begins to feel quite at home in the ducal tent: "When supper was finished a chess table was brought; the maréchal began to play, and we made conversation with the ladies . . . In short, people could not have been more kind to us, we were looked upon as French, and I should gladly have spent a month or so in this manner, but the camp was to break on September 30," like a wood fire that smothers for want of air to burn in. 1778 is too early. Will 1779 be too late?**

Too late for the Broglies, at any rate. When the Descent scheme finally does begin to shape up they've already been sent back to their beloved studies.

It's as though these two poor brothers, almost twins, are destined to get nothing from History except kicks in the behind. But maybe they've asked for it—judging from the position they assume on the podium . . . Fersen, as a superficial observer, is unable to see all the sand in the gears backstage at Vaussieux, that operetta that flopped during tryouts. First of all, the second lead is missing: the duke is deprived of his count, Broglie is parted from Broglie, and it leaves him one-armed. Victor-François wants his alter ego, his double, his chief of staff; their team worked so well in the other war, with one showing and the other doing. At the right moment the duke would launch the forces which his brother decided were necessary and supplied. And that amiable little fellow, the count, leaves a shadow three times his height wherever he walks: the King's Secret. He commanded a Europe-wide spy network while his brother was storming towns with tangible men. By rights the Descent is

*500 and 650 new francs [$100 and $130] respectively.

†About two new francs [forty cents].

**The total cost of the Vaussieux camp in 1778 was 11,644,835 livres, or a little over 58 million new francs [$11.6 million].[6]

his: ten years earlier he outlined it down to the quarter inch, marching up and down the Channel coasts. If there's one man who is indispensable at that moment, it's he.

But no. Louis XVI appoints one Broglie, not two. A whim of the King, Maurepas, Montbarrey? The duke pleads and storms: "Your Majesty is too sensible of the claims of fraternal affection not to end a separation which is cruel on so many counts . . . How could Your Majesty bring yourself to cause the despair of two brothers who will not long withstand it?" But maréchal-duc though he is, it avails him naught against our gracious pleasure. He's sent off to prepare an attack "which concerns lands, coasts, and resources that are totally foreign to me, whereas a mission performed under his direction by order of the late King, and carried on over a period of fifteen years, has made them familiar to my brother"[7]—who is dispatched to replace the duke in Metz, as a sort of booby prize.

The Comte de Broglie has borne all until now, but you can have too much of a good thing . . . Do you treat a dog like that? The peaceable man blows up. He resigns, there's a scandal, a lawsuit (lost) against the Cardinal de Rohan's secretary, Abbé Georgel, whom he accuses of slander; followed by escape into heartbreak in the Ruffec swamps on the far side of the Charentes, where he pretends to be an iron-master after dreaming of ruling London. He goes with iron in his soul.*

This separation is not conducive to optimism in the duke. Even without his brother's brain to help him, he realizes that he's only being asked to command a dress rehearsal. With no fleet and no Spanish reinforcements, the summer is spent thrashing out an academic dispute between Guibert, champion of the Prussian-style "shallow formation" in battle, and Mesnil-Durand, spokesman for the traditional "deep formation." Is one to attack in wide, broad lines of soldiers, following the relief of the terrain and the enemy's resistance, spaced so far apart that artillery fire can hardly make a dent in them? That's how Frederick won his battles, those are the tactics of the future. But some people see the devil when they hear the word "new," and the Duc de Broglie is one of them. Long live the assault in battering-ram columns, with the men crammed one behind the other in serried ranks! If the shells carry off the first lot, why the rest get through, and every officer keeps his men well in hand. The shallow formation would transform our compact battalions into flocks of riflemen lost in the cornfields, you can't be serious, young man.

The linear-vs.-perpendicular dispute rages through all the drawing rooms, which hold out for Guibert. "Although the quarrel between Gluckites and Piccinnites is still our chief subject of discussion, a little diversion from that

---

*And dies on August 16, 1791, in an inn at Saint-Jean d'Angély, of a "stinking fever" contracted in the bogs around Rochefort; but also of grief.

mighty interest has been allowed in favor of the Deep Formation versus the Shallow Formation . . . The shallow formation, adopted by the greatest man of war of our times [Frederick], is said to be like that ultramontane music which might well suit every other nation on earth but would never suit ours."[8] Mesnil-Durand and Guibert bombard each other with octavo volumes, refutations, retorts to the refutations, refutations of the retorts. The Maréchal de Broglie shuts his door to Guibert, even though he has been detailed to his own staff. From his self-imposed exile the Comte de Broglie tells the world "that in his book M. de Guibert had called M. de Mesnil-Durand a rascal, and his brother [the duke] a fool. It is true, then, that intolerance adheres so closely to human nature that there is no opinion or condition but is susceptible to it." Intolerance among the military! What is the world coming to?

Thus the war of 1778 takes place on the prairies of Vaussieux between one half of Broglie's troops, commanded by himself according to the principles of the "Deep Formation," and the other half commanded by the Marquis de Rochambeau, following the gospel according to St. Guibert, prophet of the linear attack. Fersen and many another gaze upon all this fuss with startled eyes. The drawing rooms award the victory to Rochambeau. Everybody knows that maneuver battles are won on paper; and since Rochambeau writes better than his general, he doesn't waste this opportunity to argue his case and judge it too: "Nonetheless [sez him], every time the two troops maneuvered together, the one in shallow and the other in deep formation, the advantage unvaryingly appeared to lie with the shallow."[9] Not so sure, not so sure. The specialists are unconvinced, and one of the most clearheaded bystanders, Dumouriez, who is commanding at Cherbourg, sensibly observes that Guibert and Mesnil-Durand are wrong, "both of them, because each was defending his own system to the exclusion of all else."[10] Now, Dumouriez might be supposed to have reasons for being partial to Guibert, a friend of fifteen years' standing. They met during the Corsican campaign and "their liaison [*sic*] was never crossed by jealousy."* We'll just see about that: "Guibert showed more, Dumouriez did more; one always in Paris, opulent, sought-after; the other always in the country, in straitened circumstances, solitary. Guibert's pleasures were more brilliant, those of Dumouriez more solid. He often told his friend, 'We are like the two mice in the fable. You are city mouse and I am country mouse . . .' "[11]

In other words, a friendship flavored with the customary sauce brewed of bitterness and envy. The only gifts either partner gives are poisoned ones: "Guibert aspired to the honors of the Academy; Dumouriez [still according to himself] never regarded the arts of writing and speaking as more than a

---

*According to Dumouriez, who speaks of himself, in his memoirs, in the third person. The next quotation is also by him.

vehicle for ideas." The country mouse probably rather enjoys standing Mesnil-Durand and his "friend" back to back with guns in hands. All the same, he's right when he says you don't fight with systems.

For want of an enemy the men eventually return to their quarters, Fersen to Versailles, and the Duc de Broglie to the Château de Broglie, there to spend, as he thinks, the winter. Nay, nay, Your Grace, this time it's for good, unless something very unforeseen happens. The court deems this campaign of the French army against itself to be a failure. In the spring of 1779 the command of the Brittany troops—the England troops, as they're also called—is given to the Comte de Vaux, "who is under Guibert's thumb and allowing it to be too plainly seen," dixit Dumouriez. The Duc de Broglie, without anyone deigning to give him an explanation, is left sputtering with rage in his Norman Versailles.

26

SEPTEMBER 1779

Disgust and Disease

1779 is more serious. We have a first-rate witness in the young Chateaubriand, brooding over the narrowing of his life, after so much freedom and merriment at his Saint-Malo grandmother's, under the shroud of paternal neurosis in the massive Château de Combourg.* "Troops were billeted at Combourg. Out of courtesy, M. de Chateaubriand† entertained the colonels of the Touraine and Conti regiments, each in turn . . . Twenty officers were invited to my father's table every day. I disliked the jesting of these strangers; their movements disturbed the peace of my woods. It was after watching the Marquis de Wignacourt, second-in-command to the colonel of the Conti regiment, cantering under the trees, that the idea of travel first entered my head . . .

"One thing delighted me, however: the parades. Every day the change of guard filed past, led by fife and drums, at the foot of the steps in the Green courtyard. M. de Causans offered to show me the coast camp [at Saint-Malo]. My father consented . . . I ran along the streets of the camp. The tents, stacked

---

*He is ten years old in 1779.

†François-René always speaks thus of his father in the *Mémoires d'outre-tombe*. And he calls his own wife "Madame de Chateaubriand."

arms, and picketed horses composed a beautiful scene, with the sea and ships, the wall and far-off bell towers of the town. In a hussar's uniform, going at a round gallop on a Barb,* I saw pass one of those men in whom a world was ending, the Duc de Lauzun."[1]

Is he here too? Of course: this is the great spring rendezvous. Lauzun is back from Africa with his Senegal, for which nobody is grateful, under his arm. He was expecting to be complimented; all he gets is a cold shoulder. "I was not too well received at Versailles when I arrived . . . The King was pleased by the Senegal expedition, but others [the ministers] were displeased; they nearly begrudged my having undertaken it . . . I got neither promotion nor increase in pay. M. de Sartines wanted to give me a sort of gratuity, which I refused . . . He scattered my corps [the "Lauzun legion"] to the four corners, I had not enough funds left to serve decently . . . I tendered my resignation, and made no further attempt to see him."[2] He drops in at Marly in the course of the customary "journey" and finds a change of scene. Yolande de Polignac and her clan are reigning over Marie Antoinette who, after staring so long at Coigny, no longer has eyes for anyone but Fersen. Lauzun? That was three years ago, you might as well call it three centuries. "One cannot conceive how I was treated by the Queen, and consequently by everyone else. They scarcely looked at me." With one fortunate exception: Lauzun gets a bellyful of looking from the fine eyes of Louise-Marthe de Conflans d'Armentières, Marquise de Coigny,† one of the prettiest and liveliest women at court, to whom the Prince de Ligne has just predicted that in fifty years' time she would have the "piquancy of a Madame du Deffand, the sense of a Madame Geoffrin, and the taste of a Maréchale de Mirepoix." She steps forward, in that desert of illuminated mirrors in which everyone turns his back on anyone on whom the queen turns hers. She sits beside him, smiles, listens to him. He's forty. She is twenty-six. He's caught. Nobody has ever made such an impression on him, not even the Princess Czartoryska. It's high noon for him, the hour for grand passions. "Madame de Coigny spoke to me. I was absurdly grateful to her. I found her most witty and graceful . . . Everything else ceased to matter to me . . . She filled my mind, it was folly to think of it."

But that doesn't cure him of his enterprising spirit, nor does it soften the cruelty of his gaze as he contemplates the officers of a Descent which is finally on the agenda. So Vaux has taken over from Broglie as chief of staff. Some chief, to hear Lauzun talk, and some staff! "M. de Vaux was, as usual, pedantic, flat and mediocre, and, for all his airs of austerity, he remains the basest currier of favor.

"This army was so oddly composed, as to its general officers, that I cannot

_____

*From "barbary," a horse from North Africa.
†In 1775 she married the Duc de Coigny's younger brother.

forbear to speak of it . . . M. de Puységur, major general, laughed at his generals and colleagues and shook his head over them at least a hundred times. M. le Marquis de Crécy, confidential aide de camp of the commanding general, assisted him to provide us with poisoned fare and occupied the remainder of his time in petty nastiness, some of which was entertaining enough. M. le Comte de Cergny . . . smoked in the general's antechamber so that he would be taken for an old partisan, and lapsed into reminiscences of the war the moment one entered his room. M. le Marquis de Langeron, lieutenant general, a faithfully dull fellow and great maker of digs, would say, when inviting someone to dine with him, "Would you care to dine with me on one egg quartered on the ass of a pewter plate?" M. de Rochambeau, camp maréchal commanding the vanguard, could speak of nothing but deeds of war, and would plan maneuvers and describe military positions in the field, in the room, at table, on your tobacco pouch if you drew it from your pocket; exclusively filled with his trade, he knows absolutely everything about it. M. le Comte de Caraman, dressed to kill, honeyed, fastidious, would stop all the men who had done their buttons up wrong in the street and eagerly deliver small military homilies to them; he was constantly showing himself to be an excellent officer, full of knowledge and enterprise. M. Wall, camp maréchal, an old Irish officer, closely resembled Harlequin-as-Yokel except that he had more wit, was a fine trencherman, drank punch all day long, said that everybody else was in the right, and kept out of everything. M. de Crussol, camp maréchal, afflicted with a disreputable disease, had a crooked neck and a mind not much straighter."* Could he be any nastier about the English?

La Fayette wouldn't have missed this rendezvous for an empire. "My blood boils in my veins [June 10] . . . My imagination often advances into the enemy country at the head of a forward guard or light body of grenadiers, dragoons and riflemen . . . The thought of seeing England humiliated and crushed makes me quiver with joy."[3] One of the first to arrive at Le Havre, to await the embarkation of his regiment, he finds something American in the little town "neatly aligned and well built; there are even quite a goodly number of houses worth remarking. The streets are wide,"[4] but it's the port that draws him every day, and above all, beyond the port, "the large and very safe sea roads affording excellent anchorage, well sheltered by high cliffs."[5] "Here I am within view of the port, Monsieur le Comte [to Vergennes, on August 13]. Judge of my contentment, and whether my heart yearns for the south wind that will bring Monsieur d'Orvilliers to us . . . So here we are, at last on the

*The caricature of Wall, notably exaggerated, does not inform us that in the event of an Irish expedition, he was to be the man for it. He fought there in 1745 in the ranks of the Pretender. The extremely detailed plans he is now drawing up for Maurepas will be used in preparing Hoche's abortive expedition to Ireland in 1796.

threshold of great events."[6] But alas, the roads are empty, or almost, and even when the wind does blow from the south all it brings is the smell of hay being scorched by the August sun. It would have to give a good puff from nor' norwest first, to catch the errant armada somewhere in mid-ocean, funnel it into the Channel, and bring it to its post beneath the cliffs.

They wait. Everybody waits. La Fayette champs and Lauzun curses. Chartres, too, has been gnawing his nails in these parts, but in vain. The office he was patronizingly tossed last year has assumed no concrete form; officially he's still "colonel general of light troops" . . . but his troops are so light they don't exist. Flanked by his inseparables, Genlis and Fitz-James, he has been scouring the coast since spring under the name of the Comte de Joinville, trying to net a few soldiers in Le Havre, but also in Saint-Malo and Saint-Servan. He swore that in order to be in the vanguard he would march up the gangway with one manservant if he could get no other troops of his own. The rest of the army is clearly hoping he's already back in Paris. His quarrel with Sartines has grown more bitter in the course of the year, and begun leaking into the gazettes; and Louis XVI revels in humiliating his cousin to the benefit of his minister. In fact, this is the one decision taken during the entire summer by this evanescent king whom nobody, and especially not himself, could ever imagine going to inspect his armies, at one day's remove from Versailles, before the great attempt: on July 20 Louis XVI instructs the Queen to write Philippe a "friendly" letter (oh, what a loving family) in which, "in order to spare him the more severe form of an order," she announces that he is forbidden to join the army.[7] He's being sentenced to his box at the Opéra; it's a *lettre de cachet* in sheep's clothing.

Farther out, farther west, at Cherbourg, Dumouriez is waiting too, but without too many illusions, as befits an old hand at grand designs gone sour. He has philosophically drawn up the plans he's been asked to provide for the organization and order of events of the Descent—because it's all very well to set sail for England, assuming we get that far, but then where do we land, where do we dig in? Dumouriez answers: on the Isle of Wight. "It is terribly important. All the timber used for building their frigates was at Cowes," the northernmost port on the island. An England deprived of the wood she needs to build her ships would be like a blind man without his cane. "The hospital, containing over two thousand sick sailors, was at Newport, in the center of the isle. All the grain and flour for Portsmouth was at St. Helen's," a little port on the northeast side. "Once ten thousand French were established on this island England would need to raise an army to drive them off it."[8] And Wight is already a bridgehead, in the immediate proximity of Portsmouth, which could easily be put out of action by filling up the passage that separates the island from the Portsmouth roads. Dumouriez, painstaking as always, calculates the number of ships that would have to be sunk there, "secured to heavy cables," down to the last ton. But to what purpose? By July 21 he gets the picture: "The tide is gone. No news of M. d'Orvilliers. The Spanish delay will be the last straw . . . Are our own naval officers so eager to enter the Channel at the onset of the rainy season? I foresee a bad end to all this. We shall be caught with our breeches down. The English, who are already almost over their surprise, will be able to reckon quite accurately how little they have to fear from this gathering of ill-aroused forces, from our lack of determination, from our languor . . . I would that I might sound less like a Cassandra, but my letter has been tainted by the morbid hue of our headquarters." By August 1 the only change is for the worse: "Time drifts by, the season draws to a close, disgust infests the officer and disease the soldier."[9] It infests the sailor worst of all, that sailor whom the soldiers are so desperately awaiting. "Admiral Scurvy" is in the process of saving the English more surely than all their fleets combined could ever have done.

In the spring of 1779 the London Admiralty has only thirty-five ships left in the Channel.[10] Sartines is hoping to add twenty Spanish ships to the thirty French ones on tap at Brest. They could fight almost two against one. French and Spanish choose the Sisargases as their rallying point—a handful of rocks off the coast of Galicia near the port of La Coruna. First the Brest fleet has to come southwards, as though to collect its blushing partner for the ball—those Spaniards who need so much begging and imploring—and then they all have to trip up northwards again, arm in arm, hundreds of leagues. So much time and so much good wind wasted! Even before they set out, an epidemic of *"flux intestinal"** hits four thousand of the crew. Two thousand soldiers are taken on board to make up their numbers. But what happens when landlubbers have to start shifting the sails . . .

D'Orvilliers on the *Bretagne,* followed by the entire fleet, sights the Sisargases on June 10. The old admiral is feeling quite chipper: "The change of air has swept away every trace of the epidemic that was wreaking so much havoc in Brest. This early sign of divine good will has enlivened my confidence." But "the number of mediocre captains is even greater in this campaign than in the last."[11] And his morale sags again during the nineteen mortal days they spend tacking around in circles on the sea while they wait for the Spanish, who are waiting for themselves, in a series of maneuvers as intricate as sea turtles', between Cadiz and La Coruna. Ten ships are sighted on July 2. Is that all? Never fear: the other half are coming. But when, for pity's sake! All this aimless cruising has made the ships anemic. "It is to be feared that disease may spread through our ships, where we have stinking fevers and smallpox [July

---

*Probably a sort of dysentery, perhaps combined with typhoid fever. It is raging in every part of Brittany in 1779.

12]." Anything else would be a miracle, which is more than divine good will is prepared to vouchsafe. "Men had been taken on who were unfit, and there were large numbers of convalescents, and sick men too; water had been drawn from tainted springs. We set out with no sorrel and no lemon. The catastrophe is inevitable." Then God definitively defects to the English by striking d'Orvilliers's only son, who was serving as ensign under the supreme commander. On July 22, "the Lord has taken from me all that I had in this world" just as the monstrous silhouette of the *Santisima-Trinidad* heaves into view in the distance —the Spanish admiral-ship, armed with 114 guns, one of the most formidable monuments afloat, displaying half the gold of Peru on her poop, the only effect of which is to make her even heavier. A moving temple to pride, and its high priest is a little old man who's even more of a dead loss than d'Orvilliers. The Admiral Don Luis de Cordoba y Cordoba is seventy-three; and according to d'Estaing, "the only time he ever fought as commander was against the Moors and, by the Spaniards' own admission, as a person he does not exist."[12] "His moral qualities can be seen in the slump of his head, and his firmness has become mere obstinacy." On July 30, two senilities, one of them prostrate with grief, finally set sail for a mirage, bearing with them the most imposing fleet assembled since the Invincible Armada. One hundred four sails on the ocean, counting the corvettes, the mortar-bearing *bombardes,* the fire ships, store ships, and hospital.[13] It gives Montmarin—at last!—a shiver of hope: "Never has the House of Bourbon deployed such a considerable force upon the sea."[14] But there's a cold breeze blowing from an unexpected quarter: Beaumarchais, the eternal enthusiast, the man who makes the world over every morning, is convinced that nothing good can come of those Spaniards. The time he spent in Madrid disabused him for good on their account: "I always have a little icicle in a corner of my brain labeled *Spain.* However I try, I cannot make it go away. May God prove me mistaken."[15]

God doesn't. To begin with, they travel so slowly, too slowly. Heading straight for the Channel is out of the question. They have to learn to understand each other first, so they undertake "a vast writing of documents, to standardize the signal system: for the Spaniards, to d'Orvilliers's vast surprise, had not even been made familiar with the French code of maneuvers"—which Sartines might easily have sent them any day in the last year. "An entire signal corps had to be improvised" under the direction of the major general of the fleet, whose very name, du Pavillon, makes him the ideal man for the job.* "D'Orvilliers's ships, most of which were good goers, were slowed by the necessity of letting the ponderous Spanish vehicles keep up with them." This is no fleet of war, it's a parade, which the northwest wind is, as usual, driving back toward Spain: "It is the customary ascendency of the English star over

---

*"Pavillon": "flag" or "colors" in French. [*Trans.*]

ours.''[16] On they go, round in circles. And when the wind does come from the right quarter they still don't get anywhere, because the admirals chicken out within range of a huge English merchant convoy, four hundred sails, a dead cinch; first they elude it, then they miss it. Another ten days lost. "Time is passing . . . Water and provisions were not stocked for such an extended period. They have to be rationed" within a few hours of the French ports, that really takes the cake. Every vessel is harboring a sewer. "Cattle, sheep, pigs, and fowl were taken on board, for the captains' tables more than for the crews', and turned loose among the men. Many an epidemic could be traced back to this cohabitation with animals. Water supplies were speedily expended on the livestock, to the detriment of cleanliness and health"[17]—water which was already fouled in the casks six hours after being taken on board, and which has to be filtered three times through napkins to get the sludge out of it.

The *Curieuse* puts in at Vigo to deposit twenty sick men. Then the *Couronne:* forty. Fifty on board the *Saint-Esprit* in mid-ocean, too late to put them off. Sixty on the *Bretagne.* At the beginning of July the average is sixteen deaths for every ship in the fleet. Nobody can fight in this condition: they stop again, off Ouessant, to await a convoy of water and supplies from Brest. The French ships have only ten days' water left. They beg some from the Spaniards. On August 8, d'Orvilliers tolls the knell: "The *Ville-de-Paris* alone is two hundred eighty men short, and for combat I shall have her furnished with one hundred men from the frigates in her division. But that resource is not open to me as regards surgeons;* this species [*sic*] is in short supply on every ship, and they are consequently unable to assist one another."[18] On August 12, when a good southwest breeze springs up at last and pushes history's largest floating hospital ever into the vicinity of Portsmouth, there are at least as many ailing sailors as able-bodied. Is the Cour des Miracles† about to conquer England?

On the French vessels alone there are 23,750 men; and 12,000 of them are dying—the deportees of the high seas.[19] Fewer than 10 percent are volunteers, and even then the word is a euphemism: at the age of twelve, boys who were orphans were forcibly transformed into *mousses* [cabin boys]—from the Italian *mozzo,* meaning a fresh youth—both apprentice sailor and manservant.[20] "Ruyter** began as a ship's cabin boy, which makes him all the more estimable," affirms Voltaire. Later they grow into full-fledged sailors and earn the right to die together as *classés* [ratings, or rated crewmen], or seamen ravished from the coastal parishes under the "system of classes" instituted by Colbert

---

*Term used for the physician-apothecary on board; nothing to do with a surgical operation.

†A Cour des Miracles was any place in which cripples, ne'er-do-wells, and other flotsam lived together. All the big towns of France had them. In the seventeenth century there were a dozen in Paris. [*Trans.*]

**Great seventeenth-century Dutch naval captain. [*Trans.*]

to supply crews for the king's ships. Kidnapped by the sergeants from their fishing, farms, and families. "The advantages that Colbert tried to secure for them had virtually disappeared or become illusory, and the system only survived in its abuses. Even in time of service* crews were paid very irregularly. The poverty of the coastal-town populations was another factor."[21] Gabriel Mirabeau's uncle the bailli had been scandalized by it, even though his own hide was well tanned by life on the Malta galleys: "Gravelines looks like a town ravaged by a long plague; all the houses are intact, but empty . . . On three or four occasions I saw flocks of sailors' wives throw themselves at the governor's feet to beg for mercy, holding out pallid, fleshless infants. Their husbands are dead or prisoners in England; many have run away to avoid conscription . . . The thought of being removed from their homes and sent to the war causes some to die of broken hearts . . ." "All the authorities, whoever they may be, countermand each other in this matter. Commanders, intendants, inspectors, mayors, aldermen, tax-collectors, all proceed against these wretched people."[22] Those in the great fleet of 1779, Bretons for the most part, "are overcome with exhaustion and lassitude when they put into port. They know not where to go or where to stay. They overrun the cabarets, drown themselves in wine. They sleep for nights on end in the streets of Brest, and finally fall sick or become unfit for service."[23] Any who are still on their feet are signed on. Now they've spent two months between-decks in the stench of the animals and their excrement. Smells, microbes, and mildew filter through the partitions, which are unpainted, not even whitewashed.† Most of the men have but one set of filthy clothes that stick to their skin day and night. When the spray soaks them, they dry on their bodies. No bath or toilet or razor. The bunks are alive with vermin. "Poor sailor"—another pleonasm.

Take Jean Guénolé, who just happens to hail from Saint-Guénolé, back there near Penmar'ch, where there are seventeen families with the same name. He's thirty-two. He's been *"classé"* since he was twenty-five and has seen his wife six times in six years, long enough to start six children.[24] Other times it's the arsenal of Brest or Rochefort, maneuvers, and now this cruise on the *Triton,* a new sixty-four-gun ship commanded by M. de la Clocheterie. Jean Guénolé is proud as a peacock, it's his captain who was piloting *La Belle-Poule* at the beginning of the war. He'll know how to talk to the English. War, politics, everything, for the Brittany sailor, boils down to a hatred of those people he's never seen and identifies with the devils in the Dance of Death painted on the walls of his church. The hereditary foe, it's in his mother's milk, his catechism. To accost them at last, get his hands around their throats . . . It would almost

*Apart from short periods spent at sea, combat seamen were parked on shore in barracks. Sometimes, when they became a nuisance, they were sent back to their homes on "permission."

†After 1780 they will be, precisely because of the disaster of this epidemic.

make Jean Guénolé happy. If only he could stop stewing in this shit. But it's too late, poor Jean!* He's having a hard time breathing. There he lies, "breathless, almost suffocated by the slightest effort; the thighs inflate and deflate, showing red, brown, hot, livid, purple patches . . . The gums swell painfully, they itch and are feverish, and bleed at the slightest pressure. The teeth grow loose and wobble. Vague pains are felt in every internal and external part of the body."[25] No doubt about it: he's got the scurvy, one of those diseases manufactured by man for man. Animals don't get it. It is caused by the state of hygiene on shipboard. Or rather the total absence of hygiene. "The scurvy is a dreadful affliction once it has taken hold; it is highly contagious, and when the corpse of a man dead from the scurvy begins to putrefy, it is a frighteningly efficient breeding ground for spreading the infection far and wide. It is often mistaken for the hypochondriacal disease"† or "rich man's scurvy, produced by vapors, which can be cured by bleeding, careful diet, and evacuants [sic]"; not to be confused with "poor man's scurvy." The former is a bonus of good living. "It was previously unknown in our regions," for "it comes from England, with the spleen."

Poor man's scurvy, a very different matter, does not affect seamen alone: "misery, famine and public calamities also engender this disease," which gives the anonymous author of the *Encyclopédie*'s article on scurvy** an opportunity to embark upon a period worthy of Bossuet. One sentence, all of a piece— but what a gorgeous sentence for an ugly disease! "The English, the Dutch, the Swedes, the Danes, the Norwegians, those dwelling in Lower Germany, the peoples of the North, those who live in very cold climates, especially such as are near to the sea or the places it waters, or lakes or swamps; those who live on land that is low, spongy, flat, lying between high ground and the banks of rivers and streams; idle people who dwell in stony places during the winter; seamen who live on smoked salt flesh, biscuits, stinking and foul water; those who eat too many seafowls, or salt fish hardened by smoke and wind, or beef, or smoked salt pork, or farinaceous matter which has not fermented, or peas, or broad beans, or cheese which is salty, bitter, or old; those who are subject to melancholy, to mania, to hypochondriacal and hysterical conditions and to chronic illnesses, and principally those who have consumed too great quantities of quinine; all these, I say, are subject to scurvy."

Jean Guénolé of Saint-Guénolé is not going to see the battle. His teeth have turned black. All the blood in his poor body is seeping out of him as from

---

*Victor Hugo thinks of calling the hero of *Les Misérables* Jean Jeanjean. The bad-luck name. "They called him John without asking his advice," goes the old saying.

†For neurasthenia, in other words. Scurvy is actually caused by a nutritional deficiency of vitamin C (ascorbic acid), leading to generalized decalcification accompanied by increasingly severe hemorrhage, particularly from gums and teeth.

**Undoubtedly Dr. Bordeu, the physician of Louis XV and Mme Pompadour.

a sponge, through his lips, his mouth, his gums, his esophagus, his stomach, and through those ulcers that have grown on his skin in the last week. Fever, "hot, malignant, intermittent," is his one opiate, and it carries him over nightmare and death toward the sea. The commander of the *Triton*, missal in hand, presides while the body is stuffed into a bag and dumped overboard almost before its last breath. The ship's chaplain himself is out of the action. In one month Jean-Timothée Chadeau de la Clocheterie has buried nineteen of his sailors in the great salt shroud.[26]

In Madrid Montmarin is sick too—with "rich man's scurvy." "Rather than that celerity on which we were counting, contrary and obstinate winds have made us lose much precious time . . . All this has spread a blackness through my soul, which has become so ill that it is affecting my body."[27] Vergennes's afflictions are less forthright: "My citizen's heart is suffering from all these curbs upon the glory of its fatherland . . ." No doubt; but why is he in such a hurry to cry defeat? "What a fine moment we had, and it escaped us through nobody's fault." He writes this on July 23, the day after the Spanish make contact with the French off the Sisargases. Nothing is decided yet, and maybe the fight's only beginning? No. "The elements are at arms against us, they restrain the blows of our vengeance . . ."—still on July 23. For the Comte de Vergennes, that summer was over in a hurry.[28]

And yet, on August 16, d'Orvilliers sends him what might be the beginning of a victory dispatch: "Monseigneur, the combined army is at present anchored in calm waters within sight of the tower of Plymouth . . . It is most important to hasten the battle, particularly as the condition of the French ships is worsening daily, as regards both the disease running rampant in them and the small quantity of water and rations they possess."[29] This is the real turn of the summer. "Faced with the advancing Gallispan [*sic*] fleet, the English squadrons, inferior in number, were falling back toward the Scilly Isles. The British coasts were unprotected. England spent three days in a most worrisome predicament; it was on the 13th, 16th and 17th of the month [August] that trouble, terror and consternation were rife."[30] There is a beginning of an exodus inland. The French prisoners in Plymouth revolt. They believe, the poor suckers. They're brought back under control with the greatest difficulty. The London stock market nosedives.

Pointless panic. The French have been beaten before they begin. On August 17, d'Orvilliers learns that there has been a last-minute change of plans. Forget the Isle of Wight, the Comte de Vaux's troops are to be put ashore in Cornwall. We'll get a foothold there, fortify ourselves over the winter, and emerge next year to march on London. This new scheme is the brainchild of the Comte d'Aranda. Dumouriez, in a rage, goes back to his dredging in Cherbourg. Cornwall! A peninsula of pebbles! "You will never kill the enemy by stinging his toe."[31] And how're we supposed to land there? The French sailors haven't been in these waters for decades and are navigating blind. They know less about its ports and shallows than those of the Antilles; and Sartines has naturally forgotten to equip his ships with pilots. D'Orvilliers tries to abduct them on the spot. But "I have met no fishing boat from which I could take useful pilots . . . With the result that we are navigating by conjecture, and with no knowledge of the dangers and currents of the coast; the Spanish are lamenting the fact even more than we, and we are never out of earshot of their complaints."[32]

And yet everything is virtually ready, on the other side of the Channel: there are scores of barges sitting in the mouths of the Seine and Rance, crammed with victuals, ammunition, and equipment for war. All they're waiting for is the go-ahead, to start loading on the troops. But who's going to give it? Vergennes or d'Orvilliers? They keep passing the buck. In Honfleur the Duc du Châtelet decides that the only thing to do is laugh: "Amidst all this ambiguity one thing is clear, and that is that the minister has no definite scheme as yet . . . The Court, which has changed its plans and was unwilling to make any decision (a state most congenial to the ignorance and indecisiveness of our ministers), wanted to play on two strings, Wight and Falmouth, and left M. d'Orvilliers to make up his mind which should be set vibrating first . . . Our ministers have acted as weak people do, who are never able to want things more than halfheartedly when the time comes for taking them, and are delighted to give only provisional and muddled orders to others . . . I swear to you that they are in a worse state than we will be [in the event of a debarkation], because they are holding the handle of the frying pan! It is true, though, that they run no risk of being fried in it."[33]

Just for good measure, here comes heavy weather. "Decidedly, the sea is the great saint of these heretics."[34] A storm forces d'Orvilliers to put out from Plymouth. He wanders through the Channel like some giant Tom Thumb looking for a sign. The only thing "more sad than the condition" of his fleet is that "of his soul." "What with the heavy seas, the gales, the lightning [which has just done serious damage to the *Protée* and *Conception*], communication has been rendered impossible, and it is by means of hermetically sealed bottles strung on buoys that I am seeking to have these letters conveyed to you."[35] Lost sails can no longer be replaced. There are not enough men left to carry out maneuvers. "The 'tween-decks are infected." The sailors are dying off like flies. The *Actif* can no longer drop its big anchor: it would have no means of weighing it again. The question is no longer where we are going to strike England first, but how we are going to get back to Brest.

Council of war on August 25, on board the *Bretagne*. We're going home; but not before making a show of force, for honor's sake, in the direction of the Scillies, just to intimidate Admiral Hardy. If he only knew! Even one against three he could have cut the French to shreds. But he's put off by their numbers and ducks out. Between September 10 and 14 d'Orvilliers brings the most beautiful fleet ever seen by living Breton into the roads of Brest; but every one of the monsters is rotting and the spectators' admiration changes to consternation when they see what the pageant looks like backstage. One little cadet from Picardy, the Chevalier de Mautort, will never forget the contrast: "We saw the return of the combined French and Spanish army. It was composed of more than one hundred ships of war. It would be impossible to imagine a more majestic, more imposing sight. But it became doubly affecting when one learned that our squadron alone was bringing back over eight thousand sick men. The first problem was to get them ashore, and a great many perished in no time. I watched the covered wagons carrying the dead to their graves, they passed under my windows in a steady stream."[36] As for the ill: the population of an entire town. They had to be transported all the way to Landerneau, where the nuns were evicted from their convents to make room for them.

D'Orvilliers has just enough strength left to drag himself to Moulins and bury himself "in the most profound retirement."* Now, after making the Duc de Chartres into the butt of the street singers, it's going to be his turn. "Greatly pious, yet but a little man—Vice-Admiral of the Capuchins."[37]

Preparations are made to break camp at Le Havre and Saint-Malo, where the Comte de Vaux is bedeviled with prostate trouble, providing Maurepas with material for a witticism: "The only Descent that took place was inside M. de Vaux's breeches." Vergennes heaves a sigh of relief: "I cherish the equinox, not [only] as the end of the sea campaign, but as the date on which any great undertaking against England becomes morally [sic] impossible." Marie Antoinette shrugs: "The public is much annoyed that M. d'Orvilliers, with forces so far superior to those of the English, was unable to join battle with them or prevent a single one of their merchant ships from returning to its port.† It will have cost a great deal and accomplished nothing, and as yet I see no indication that peace can be treated this winter." One consolation: "The health of the King and my own are very good, and we are living together in such a way that I might soon have hopes, although I cannot yet be certain of anything."[38]

An heir would make everything right again. Who knows?

But who can we blame for this whole huge fiasco? Well, why not take it out on a Negro? Extract from the *Correspondance secrète:* "Scipion, the little Negro of the Duchesse de Chartres, was given twenty well-placed lashes with the

*And die there, on April 14, 1792.

†Letter to her mother, September 15. It is significant that Marie Antoinette never even mentions the Descent itself; her correspondence contains no trace of the scheme.

bull's pizzle for having spread a rumor about the gardens of the Palais Royal that the Comte d'Orvilliers was dead and sixteen ships had been captured by the English. This little wretch,

| . . . animal inutile
Malin, gourmand, saltimbanque,
indocile, | [. . . useless, cunning,
greedy, clowning, cheeky
beast,] |

and mischievous as well, and ill-mannered, had meddled [*sic*] in misleading the public curiosity by this means. Half of Paris was duped by him for two days."[39]

"Half of Paris"? That's four hundred thousand souls. Not bad for a pickanniny.

ABBÉ SIEYS

27

SEPTEMBER 1779

You Cannot Pull the Wool over My Eyes

They'll call him "Abbé Siéyès" but maybe he never did have the faith. He hadn't had it for a long time, anyway, when he was ordained on the feast of the Most Holy Trinity in the year of grace 1772, at the age of twenty-four.[1] "The alleged truths of history have no more reality than the alleged truths of religion"[2]—and, more than that, "The moment that my reason emerged sound and healthy from the distressing prejudices in which it had been shrouded, the energy of insurrection entered my heart,"[3] and that was long before the summer of 1779, the summer of the big breakthrough for this obscure young priest buried in the Brittany hick town of Tréguier, so near and yet so far from the rumble of the army camps he couldn't have cared less about.* What was the invasion of England to him—it was his youth that was being murdered.

He was suffering from the melancholia of all transplants. What has Tréguier got in common with Fréjus except the sea, and even that's not the same. The Channel winds chill him to the marrow. It's healthy, though,

---

*Sieys, one of the most neglected figures of the age, is "the man who opens the Revolution [with his famous pamphlet] and closes it" (with the 18 Brumaire). In the interim he plays a far larger part than has been recognized. He dies, after refusing last rites, on June 20, 1836.

invigorating, that sting that hurtles down from the northwest from Perros-Guirec. The moors of Tréguignec or Penvénan have no more effect on it than on a runaway horse; and it's strong enough to sweep all the swamp gas out of your brain and put some flesh on your bones—except that the little priest keeps himself shut up in his library, building walls out of books. He was born in a stagnant country—Fréjus, the Forum Julia so dear to Caesar. The only joys the infant Sieys ever knew tasted of sea slime. "The port, once large enough to shelter the fleets that fought at Actium, is three-quarters silted up. The sea has retreated half a league. Bulrushes are choking the harbor, which no longer communicates with any moving water, so that the heat, by attracting fetid exhalations, spreads disease through the country . . . The air there is so unhealthy in the summer that in the last fifty years* the population of the town has fallen by one half or three-fourths, which makes a great loss, even to the State, because it reduces the number of able arms and taxes. In the time of the Cardinal de Fleury† Fréjus counted for seventy fires** on the State rolls. Today, it has not fourteen. The streets are small, dirty and badly paved"[4]; but it was so warm there! And the ruins at every street corner so awesomely recited a forgotten tale: the Golden Gate where Caesar ordered huge golden nails driven into the stones; "the arena where wild beasts fought"; the aqueduct that brought water from eighteen leagues away . . . "Today the aqueducts are broken and the conduits blocked, and one small fountain supplies the whole of Fréjus. This fountain is dried up during half the year, and then the people drink brackish water from the wells."[5] To Emmanuel Sieys, no water will ever taste so sweet. Giants had built that fallen land where his dream was born. A strangled dream of wild rides and conquest . . . He awoke from it a priest, wheedled out of life and into the folds of a bishop's train. "Embittered," they'll call him, already are calling him. The label is made to order. It's been stuck on him since his seminary days, when his teachers all sang the same song: "Sieys shows quite considerable aptitude for the sciences; but it is to be feared that his private reading will give him a taste for the new philosophical principles." "It will be possible to make a decent man and learned canon out of him. However, we must warn you [this to his "protector," Mgr. de Lubersac] that he is entirely unfitted for the ministry." Why so many precautions? The record books of the *petit séminaire* of St. Sulpice don't mince words: "He's a sly-boots."[6] Sounds like the opening phrase of a peroration by the chief justice of a supreme court summarizing the life of one of the defendants in the trial

*From a travelog written in 1782.

†Prime minister in Louis XV's childhood, after being Bishop of Fréjus from 1698 to 1715.

**Not to be confused with hearths [households]; the "fire" is a fictitious unit invented for purposes of taxation in urban communities. In Provence, according to Marion's *Dictionnaire des Institutions,* a fire was "what was reckoned to be worth 50,000 livres" (250,000 new francs [$50,000]).

of History. "Rise, Siéyès, mole of the Revolution!* Even at the age of fifteen, those responsible for your education . . ."

If you're going to indict him, you might at least start by getting his name right. Emmanuel-Joseph Sieys was born in Fréjus on May 3, 1748. The orthography of his name was as uncertain as that of Robespierre or Bonaparte. Toward the end he even signs himself Siéyès now and then. In any event, it was always pronounced without the accents, and was commonly written Sieys,† following the easier pronunciation.

His father Honoré Sieys is almost fifty when he's born, and is going to die two years from now.** A product of the *petite bourgeoisie:* Sieys senior was both collector of royal taxes and director of posts, a dual position well chosen to line a man's pockets—except in Fréjus. Further back we find Sieyses who were goldsmiths and painters. His mother was a notary's daughter and that's all there is to say about her. Emmanuel is going to have a hearty laugh a few months from now (in February 1780), when old Honoré takes it into his head to dream up a coat of arms for his family: "What proof have you that your arms really were those of your ancestors? Do you even know where your father was born? . . . To the best of my knowledge, your honored father and your honored uncle were small-town painters, from which it is hard to see how anyone can derive much conceit."8 Even as a youth, he wanted people to be known only as "John son of Peter or Lewis son of George, etc."9

He's the fourth of six children: three brothers, two sisters. The latter "are what I love best in the world"—but from afar, for they have taken the veil. By his very existence his older brother bars Emmanuel's way to civil or military service.‡ The fact that his father oozes piety and likes to play patriarch makes him doubly destined for the priesthood. His affection for this father is only skin-deep; the relationship is one of frigid respect not wholly free from irony, as when religious questions crop up in their correspondence—the priest is the one who steers clear of pious expressions. He'll never forgive Honoré for driving him into the Church: "You have started me on this path. All I expect is that you should not now abandon me by the wayside . . . Moreover, I have your letters, which I deeply treasure, and can always put your own words before your eyes,"10 words relating to the money problems which darken his

---

*Expression attributed to Robespierre.

†From Camille Desmoulins to his father, on June 3, 1789: "The priest whose name you couldn't make out is the author of the thrice-reprinted book *Qu'est-ce que le Tiers?* [What Is the Third (Estate)?]. Abbé Syeyes. Pronounced See-ess."7

**On December 24, 1782.

‡Joseph-Barthélemy Sieys becomes a delegate to the Estates General for the Tiers de Draguignan, and later mayor of Fréjus. He openly takes advantage of his younger brother's fortune and reputation.

years at school. Not without hypocrisy, his father exhorts him to practice an evangelical simplicity which he firmly rejects for himself. As a child, Emmanuel goes from the Fréjus Jesuits to the Draguignan Doctrinaires before having the "good fortune," by which he is none too thrilled, to be recommended for the seminary of St. Sulpice by some auxilaries in the bishopric of Fréjus who are looking for respectable clerics. He comes up to Paris at seventeen, unwillingly. "There he was, totally severed from all reasonable human society,* ignorant as any schoolboy at that age, having seen nothing, known nothing, heard nothing; and chained to the core of a little sphere of superstition which was meant to be the whole universe for him. He let himself be borne along by events, as one is borne by the laws of necessity. But in this position, so contrary to his natural inclination, it is not remarkable that he should have contracted a sort of wild melancholy, accompanied by the most stoic indifference regarding his person and his future. Here, he must forego happiness; he is outside nature."[11] Stoic, are you sure? Not stoic enough to refrain from "bemoaning his sacrificed youth, and so many tyrannous bonds that were yet to pinion his bleak future . . . And how is one not to pity that multitude of tender infants whom one ancient and powerfully rooted error seemed to await upon their arrival in the world only to brand them the property of a superstition which was assuredly not of their making? No sooner did these innocent creatures reach the age at which they might benefit from an individual culture, than barbarous and much-praised attentions and paternal prejudices ruthlessly wrenched them from the course of their nature; in order, it was said, to bring them up, but more truly to cast them down and sacrifice them, far from any ray of wisdom, to an inhuman, sepulchral discipline in which the most abysmal masters diligently tortured them, both physically and morally, and assiduously molded and trained them to serve some incomprehensible chimera. And this crime was committed in the name of Divinity, as though God needed the service of men, as though he could wish his house, his seraglio, to be built like unto that of a king of the earth! Oh weakness of reason! Oh force of habit! And the Government bore it!" We can hear Sieys boiling under his frigid veneer—the veneer he laid on during those years, his St. Sulpice years.

He endured his youth in one of the three schools established not far from the left bank of the Seine by the disciples of Cardinal de Bérulle and Monsieur Olier. Three priest factories designed to outflank the Jesuits' novitiates. The *grand séminaire* for aristocrats; the *petit séminaire* for bourgeois who could pay, but not so much; and the *robertins,* where grains of saintliness were winnowed out from the chaff of the clever poor. Sieys landed in the *petit séminaire.* Every day he was paraded off to the Sorbonne, already bundled up in his cleric's

---

*Sieys's text on the training of priests, written in Year II; a self-portrait of himself at twenty.

gown, to receive an education that was "solid rather than brilliant, and deep rather than extensive."[12] The seminary itself was simply a boarding school governed by a maze of entangled regulations, in which the Sulpicians served as drillmasters rather than teachers: the bulk of the actual learning was ingurgitated at the Sorbonne, in ton after ton of theology and religious history. Jesus Christ and the Gospels? Never heard of them. But five years of abstractions and hairsplitting, culminating in the defense of three theses—minor, major, and Sorbonnic—after which one had earned one's degree: "six hours on the sacraments in general, and each one in particular; twelve hours on the Incarnation, Grace, the theological virtues, human actions, sins, laws, and conscience; ten hours on religion, the Church, Scripture, and the major events of ecclesiastical history."[13] A strong tinge of Gallicanism; some Leibnitz-inspired efforts among the less backward professors "to establish a sort of bridge between metaphysics and religion"[14]; a solid armature against Jansenism, which gave the Church worse chilblains than the freethinkers, for Jansenism was tantamount to ascesis, and totally opposed to the lifestyle of the upper clergy and the opulence of this excremental baroque age.

Sieys drinks it all in, easily but absentmindedly. "He's a slyboots." His real life is elsewhere. Here, but further on. An inside-out school, a secret collège in which he is his own sole professor. The seminary is no convent, and boarders who keep their noses clean are left in peace. The main library, shared by all three schools, is the grand tour of his twenties, just as it is for a young priest called Talleyrand-Périgord, haughty and lame, who sat reading alongside Sieys back in 1770. "Endowed by Cardinal de Fleury, it was large and well composed. I used to spend my days there* reading the great historians, the personal histories of statesmen, moralists, and a few poets. I devoured travel journals . . . Sometimes it seemed to me that there was something less irrevocable in my situation when I contemplated these great voyages and these great collisions whose descriptions fill the writings of modern navigators."[15] They've taken the same escape route, the great lord and the commoner cornered in the same cul-de-sac, although they may never have exchanged a word. But Sieys goes deeper than Talleyrand. No travel tales are enough to take him through his prison walls. "Guided only by his tastes,† and perhaps obeying no other dictate than a need for distraction, for some means of consuming his energy, he traversed all the regions of literature indiscriminately, following no rule, studying the mathematical and physical sciences and even seeking to initiate himself into the arts, more particularly music."[16] Yes, music; that will have a great place in his life. "He has a charming voice, somewhat weak and muted in conversation, but gentle and expressive in song,"[17] especially when

---

*This is Talleyrand speaking.

†Another passage from the autobiographical text, in which Sieys speaks of himself in the third person.

he hums "the tune of the *Village Divine* by Jean-Jacques Rousseau, which has only a few notes."[18] The quarrel between Gluckites and Piccinnites is an open book to him. He amasses mountains of notes "on music and the notes of the scale, an outline of a musical language, two notebooks filled with tunes, and their corresponding notes and index"[19]—and that's only one wall of his world. This lean student in the dog collar is also a glutton for modern learning. When, one day, he imagines his ideal library—the one he'll never own, he's certain of that, because where would he get the money?—his catalog "embraces all subjects, all countries and all ages": sciences, law, history, poetry, theater, novels. From the Jesuits to the Encyclopedists, from the Germans to the Italians, Spaniards, and a biggish heap of English. Already, grabbing whatever comes to hand, he navigates without instruments, an autodidact abandoned to himself. The only help he gets from his teachers is in theology. Sieys at twenty-five is more highly cultivated than most of the aristocrats of his day, but his learning is less refined. As he goes along, he also acquires the habit of trusting nobody's judgment but his own. "I attack no man's opinions. I merely seek my own, and I may be mistaken. Hence I make no claim to indoctrinate anyone. This is for myself alone," he's writing just about now, in 1779, when we find him at Tréguier filling a thirty-two-page notebook on *Dieu ultramètre et sur la fibre religieuse de l'homme* [*God the Ultra-standard and the Religious Fiber in Man*].[20] This God, a sort of supreme standard or "ultrameter," is far more akin to that of the Savoyard curate than to the one of the Sulpicians. It is restful to the mind to plant him there at the end of the quarrel —physical or metaphysical, a provisional solution to all enigmas—and forget about him. This is lip-service religion, if you like, but not of the ordinary Christian variety. Turn the other cheek? Never! "Wotan's religion* of combat prepared generations of men for courage and strife," observes the little priest lost in the depths of the great book-lined hall reeking with the perfumes of Sulpician virtue: wax and incense.

Could any contrast be more strident than that between this solitary highwayman of the library stacks and the masters of a world which they presume will stay as it is for all eternity—while Sieys is already penning reams on its reform? "Every section of Europe, every district should have its temple of humanity, where the unhappy would go to receive aid and the happy to dispense it."[21] Sieys in 1770 . . . the days of the Chevalier de La Barre, the follies of Mousseaux and Bagatelle, and La du Barry's diamonds. The lands he explores, since he can't sail on ships, are these: Locke first, the simplifier of Descartes, "the greatest manipulator of ideas of his century . . . because with one blow he annihilated the old rhetoric and grammar . . . and because he gave

---

*Odin or Wotan, a Teutonic and Scandinavian god, gave crowns to kings and strength to warriors.

to impressions and sensations a place previously denied them"[22]: the Newton of philosophy. But already, in the same niche, Sieys is discovering Condillac, a disciple of Locke who has gone further into "sensualism"—and does he know that in 1779 Abbé Bonnot de Condillac, a priest of his own breed—one who never celebrates mass although he makes his servants attend it—is still alive, or rather surviving, huddled inside the handsome shell of his Château de Flux near Beaugency? Antoinette, his favorite niece, is all his family and friends. Wasn't it a little for his sake that she left her husband? "Forbidding in aspect, ponderous and slow in conversation, he was humane and compassionate to the poor and sought to raise them up from their misery through labor."[23] Another of those icy hotheads, doing battle from the parapets of their reading-stands.* The Sieys-Condillac link is forged when the former reads the *Cours d'Etudes* which the latter wrote for the Infant of Parma, on "all the things which have conspired to form civil societies, to perfect them, to defend them, to corrupt them, to destroy them." In it Sieys finds "governments, customs, opinions, abuses, arts, sciences, revolutions, their causes, the degrees of greatness and the decadence of empires."[24] But by then Sieys has already left St. Sulpice: Condillac was forbidden to publish his course for ten years, and it is Turgot, in 1775, who finally brings it to the light of day. Emmanuel Sieys, son of Locke and son of Condillac, proceeds from the abstract to the concrete, from soul to body, and from the individual to the social. It is seven years now since he wrote (when he was twenty-four, in the year of his ordination), for his eyes alone, "that belated reason will one day preside over the constitution of a humane society, and I want to offer an analytical table of its composition. I shall be told that it is a novel I have undertaken to write. I shall reply: so much the worse . . . Many another man has busied himself putting together servile ideas, always agreeing with events. When one reflects upon them, filled only with a concern for the public interest, one is obliged at every step to tell oneself that sound policy is not the science of what is, but of what should be. Perhaps one day the two will become one: and then it will be possible to separate history from the human foolishness of political science."[25]

In 1776 Sieys is one of the first to get hold of a translation of a treatise by an obscure "professor of moral philosophy" at the University of Glasgow, Adam Smith, whose *Inquiry into the Nature and Causes of the Wealth of Nations*† will appear in France twenty years after its original publication. If there was ever one book that was Sieys's mentor, it was that one (even though, having trained himself never to swallow precooked lessons, he promptly sub-

---

*Condillac dies on August 3, 1780, "of a putrid, bilious and verminous fever very widespread in the canton of Beaugency." It was known as the "Loire fevers."

†Adam Smith was born in 1723 and dies in 1790. His *Theory of Moral Sentiments* has already been translated—and sniffed at—in 1764, under the pompous title *Métaphysique de l'âme*. His treatise on the *Wealth of Nations* establishes him as one of the precursors of Marxism.

jects it to his criticism and commentaries). Adam Smith, too, moves from the abstract to the economic. His entire life has been a journey from philosophical speculation to the study of the actual conditions in which men live. "He began with Nature, like everyone [of his day]. Man had only to comply with Nature's code. Only [in Smith] Nature's code spoke a different language. Labor becomes the supreme value. The rattle of the weavers' looms was already audible. The cell had already ceased to be the family, and become the factory."[26]

1779. If the good people of Tréguier only knew what a cutthroat crew had been smuggled into their midst inside Abbé Sieys's suitcases! Far more deadly than the bunch that went raiding with John Paul Jones: Adam Smith, Locke, Condillac; but also Helvétius, Diderot, Montesquieu (whom he demolishes), Rousseau (from whom he keeps his distance); Descartes, whom he is constantly giving as his authority if only in opposition to his professors, since "in the University courses the work of Descartes was summarized cursorily at best,* and then only in order to refute it"; Voltaire, whose polemical and critical phases Sieys prefers; and even the early works of an elder brother of Condillac, Abbé Bonnot de Mably—what a fine brace of philosophers in this Dauphiné family! Upper-crust critics are forever taking potshots at Mably because he presumes to preach—in writing—to kings. A utopian, just another dreamer!† But Sieys quite likes the denunciation of the abuses of Louis XIV in his *Droit public de l'Europe fondé sur les traités* [*European Public Law as Derived from Treaties*]. And *he* doesn't find Mably's text out of order. He's even beginning to follow in his footsteps, scribbling page after page inspired by his ideal portable library for the home dynamiter.

John Paul Sieys, fireside pirate, has brought all the devils of hell into Tréguier with no one the wiser. A perfect example of a Trojan horse, or the worm in the apple. Who would look askance at one more canon in this "nest of priests and monks, this exclusively ecclesiastical town, where trade and industry were unknown, a vast monastery into which no sound from without could force its way, where what others pursued was called vanity and what other men called chimeras passed for sole reality"?[27]

For he's been made a canon, or in other words one of those fifteen to twenty thousand parasites who combine all the pleasures of the century with the security of monkhood. Who are paid to celebrate mass in a cathedral in which they may never set foot, and only one string attached—celibacy—but that's almost like an added perk. Sieys spent a year or two twiddling his thumbs

---

*According to a remark by Paul Bastid. (Sieys is later called "a Descartes of politics.")

†And Sieys, like everyone else, doesn't know that Mably has been keeping the manuscript of *Des Droits et des devoirs du citoyen* [*On the Rights and Duties of the Citizen*]—far too hot to publish in those days—in his desk drawer since 1758.

in Paris, waiting for his name to come up on the *Feuille,* or roll of livings, that magic list on which prebend candidates jockey for position pending the gracious pleasure of the king, who is himself pushed and prodded by the allocating bishops. Disappointment in 1773: "If the thing had been successful I would have become everything, instead of which I am nothing."* Luck in 1774: a living in the collegiate church of Pignans, near Fréjus. Even that is symbolic, though, because, owing to a kind of life-tenure arrangement, he has to wait until the canon-in-office dies. However, it puts Sieys's foot on the ladder; then the young Jean-Baptiste de Lubersac, "almoner to the King"† at thirty-five, takes a liking to him and gets him another living, this one at Tréguier. It coincides with the period which the court prelate needs to spend in the country in order to earn his bishop's miter—a sort of episcopal retreat. In Brittany and Provence there are "certain unfavored seats which, in the space of eighteen years, have been occupied by at least five bishops; as much as to say that they had none at all. They are called seats of passage."[28] Tréguier is one of them, a waiting room in lower Brittany for the bishop and the little Provençal priest he's brought with him for one doesn't know quite what purpose—secretary, factotum—who now finds himself a double canon until something better comes along.

How he despises them! Ever since his seminary days, since Paris; "I truly believe I am traveling among a foreign people. I must study their customs. In my solitude I trained myself to love truth and justice. At first I understood nothing of the oblique language of society or its uncertain ways."[29] Ah, all those things he's got in his head and is teaching himself to hide!

Sieys unnoticed. Average height, brown hair, long aquiline nose, intellectual's pallor, thin and inexpressive mouth, slow shambling gait, narrow shoulders, an expression "devoid of fire and as though turned inwards."[30] A shaky constitution: already, in every letter, he's complaining of his bladder, kidneys, varicose veins, hernias. He's half bald and his scalp, "covered with floury scales," strews dandruff all over his cassock. Anything but a seducer, but then whom would he seduce? He knows nothing of women, of woman. "A natural indisposition in him forbids all commerce with them."** "I know not what iron-fisted destiny, that has never left me since birth," watches over him to

---

*Letter to his father, June 25, 1773, sixteen years before his famous expression: "What is the third estate? Everything. What has it been until now? Nothing."

†Under the "grand almoner" there were, in addition to the king's confessor, eight almoners like Lubersac, serving in pairs to bless the king's meals, hold out the holy water when he prayed, and look after his gloves or hat during mass.

**According to Talleyrand, and confirmed by Etienne Dumont: "He had little sensitivity toward women, perhaps as the result of a weak and sickly constitution." Théodore de Lameth maintained the contrary, on the strength of unsupported drawing-room gossip.

keep that particular paradise well out of his reach. He doesn't mind too much. He is sufficient unto himself.

But what he does mind, and openly grouses about, is when the grass is cut from under his feet. Having no strong sexual urges, he has wed ambition. Does he imagine they'll let him get away with it? Already last year he had one big setback: Mgr. de Lubersac, who is also first almoner to Madame Sophie, Louis XV's youngest daughter, allowed his protégé to apply for a job as chaplain in the house of that poor limp, colorless princess. Versailles! The court! He's all aquiver. But "my bishop played me false.* He is not enough of a gentleman to do me any favor that he cannot turn to profit for himself. His design is to make me his *âme damnée* in Tréguier. That is the only reason that can have brought him to break his word to me in such a flagrant manner, and cause me to miss Madame Sophie [*sic*] . . . I pretended not to understand, but you cannot pull the wool over my eyes . . . If it were not my intention to secure the canonry of Tréguier at any cost, I should have spoken my mind to him. Patience! I put no more faith in the promises of all these people than in the predictions in the almanac. But I look as though I believe them, for I cannot do otherwise."[31]

He does well to possess himself in patience: a short time later we find him appointed to a sinecure as "ordinary chapel cleric" to Madame Sophie, with a dispensation from active duty so long as he remains attached to Mgr. de Lubersac.† Not quite the sort of dispensation he was hoping for. But at least he's inching his way up, by his bootstraps.

His worries all come from the usual source: father, brother, family, Fréjus —whence letters take a month to cross France—if only they could get lost on the way! He's still not firmly in the saddle and they're already deafening him with calls for help. Old Honoré has taken it into his head to start the third son, Jean-François, on the same path as Emmanuel. Now if he could be gotten into the seminary at Tréguier, under his older brother's tutelage . . . Now if Emmanuel could cede the canonry of Pignans to him . . . "It is only right that you should present a respectable appearance at Versailles," Honoré plaintively writes, "but it is also right that Jean-François should have some shelter against the storm." Poor Emmanuel, head of a family and he hasn't even got a wife! He maneuvers as best he can, he plays deaf: "I am sorely distressed by the poor state of my good mother's eyes . . ." You won't fool the old man as easily as that. Paternal ultimatum: "Write me immediately [concerning Jean-François]. I am in my eightieth year." . . . "I earnestly hope, my dear father, that the summer heat is not damaging to your health . . ." On August 5, 1779, the dear

*Letter to his father, April 3, 1778.

†When Madame Sophie dies in 1782, Sieys retains the title of "retired chaplain" to the princess and continues to receive 767 livres a year (4,000 new francs [$800]) in that capacity until 1789.

father blows up: "Your reply of May 6, on the new estate which your brother Jean-François wished to assume, was not satisfactory to me . . . The indifference with which you seemed to treat it, and the difficulties it seems to have created for you, were a polite pretext for your being unable and unwilling to deprive yourself of a single one of the advantages you have received . . . Your neglect of the friendship you owe your younger brothers, and the gratitude you owe to me, has been like a sword thrust to us; it made me ill for the entire month of July."[32] Emmanuel is not the man to come bouncing back with a "So die and be damned!" He promises, he commits himself to everything and nothing, and somehow he manages to avoid a family row. He's got other things on his mind, mainly getting out of Tréguier. Any excuse will do to extricate him from this hole. Mgr. de Lubersac, in his march toward greater glory, has just captured the bishopric of Chartres. Magnanimous, he offers to take Sieys along, which means Sieys must have done a good job of hiding his loathing. Chartres is an enormous diocese, its cathedral is within reach of royal excursions—Henri IV was crowned there—a pilgrimage town almost as well supplied with priests, deacons, monks, and nuns as Lyons. The bishop has a substantial administration to run: eighty canons and sixteen general priests. Would Abbé Sieys like to be one of them, and a bit more: one of the six grand vicars who form his mini-government? He doesn't need to be asked twice, he grabs his chance by the hair. "The stormy cape has been doubled at last."[33] "For myself, I am so ambitious, I long so passionately to have a condition, by that I mean a manor house and my stew in the pot inside it, that you must not be surprised if you see me take a parish, I mean a rich parish, especially as I will lay you odds that it would not interfere with any of my plans"[34]—plans that are still vague for the moment, but beginning to creep out of his notebooks: he envisages a career as a political philosopher, a diplomat, or a counselor to the mighty. From the northwest he descends to the west, and edges a little closer to his goal during those weeks when France is giving up the idea of invading England. "As yet I have no cause for complaint, for my race is not run. Either I shall give myself an existence, or I shall perish."[35]

28

SEPTEMBER 1779

Beyond the Blue

This could begin like a parable: "In those days a holy man set forth for the place in which the Lord was appearing to a young woman . . ." Dom Gerle's first meeting with the visionary Suzette Labrousse takes place in September 1779.* She is thirty-two. He is forty-three. He's almost a neighbor, and has been promising himself for many a day to conduct this little inquiry into the events at Vanxains and sort out how much of them is the devil and how much the good Lord. Not that he has any authority to decide the matter in the name of the Church: regulars don't compete with seculars, and the decision in this case lies with the Bishop of Périgueux. But Dom Gerle is one of the most respected figures in the diocese, the priests invite him to preach on feast days, and he himself has been more than intrigued by the echo of Suzette's vaticinations. They have a certain ring that calls forth a responsive vibration in him. He wants to see for himself.

So he sets out on muleback from the Carthusian monastery of which he is prior, Notre Dame de Vauclaire, *Vallis Clara,* a little building that fully deserves its name, round and humble, hooked onto a prominence above the spilling waters of the Isle. He'll have at least seven leagues to go, northward along the Angoulême highway, to bring himself to Vanxains, a little before Ribérac. A day's journey through this blessed bit of Périgord, already warmer and more southern in aspect than Jacques Roux's Angoumois a little higher up. All the peasants in these parts greet the handsome white monk as their lord: on official visits he comes to collect the tithe, or tenth of all the grain, wine, and livestock produced annually on the land between Aubeterre and Ribérac that belongs to the Carthusians, who have no difficulty reconciling this situation with their vow of poverty. The great forest of La Double, too, which

*Ten years later Dom Gerle has a fleeting moment of glory as one of the most picturesque figures in the Constituent Assembly. David sets him in the foreground of his painting of the Jeu de Paume oath.

Dom Gerle crosses to get from one valley to the other, from the Isle to the Dronne, from Montpon (the town beneath the priory) to Ribérac: part of it belongs to the Trappists of Bonne Espérance d'Echourgnac, where he is fraternally invited to lunch. Brawny bearhugs between the great mutes of the Church: the Trappists, who never speak, but cheat by gesticulating in their deaf-mutes' sign language; and the Carthusians, whose granite stillness is broken by the weekly babble of the *spaciment,* the relaxation-stroll during which they are released from their vow. After that, Dom Gerle, as superior of his microscopic community (a priory is not an abbey, and his whole kingdom amounts to six fathers and eight lay brothers, who nonetheless address him as "Révérendissime"), treats himself to a little private *spaciment* in the service of God as he clops along under the fronds, scarcely russet-tinged by the August heat, between Mussidan, Brantôme, and Périgueux. It's a happy forest, from which you emerge to see those towns blessed by man's madness —the wars of religion, as they termed their massacres a couple of centuries ago. The soldiers of Charles IX didn't leave one wall standing in Mussidan when they tore it from the heretics in 1569; but it's been quickly and sturdily rebuilt since then. "The countryside around Mussidan is delightful. All along the road there are hedges and homes of a cleanliness that bespeaks prosperity and can be compared only to Flanders." An "immense belt of chestnuts" begins a few leagues away, before Périgueux, and runs up to Limoges, giving the "Limousins" their staple diet. But here you still travel under "horse chestnuts of excellent quality."[1] Swine are allowed to run free in the forest, so they can dig up the truffles among all those curious little streams linking the ponds together. Dom Gerle's mule trots phlegmatically over them: the Babiot, the Farganaud, the Duche, and the Chaulaure. On the far side of the Rizonne, he enters Vanxains. The people will soon be aware that this time the good father has not come to count his tithe.

Ten or twelve thatched roofs on either side of the road. The old humpbacked church, no foundations under it, is flanked by an odd little snow-white excrescence built of new stone: the hermitage which Suzette Labrousse, "the Ribéracian Deborah" as she is known around here,* wanted put up so that her house could touch the house of God "with a direct communicating door to facilitate her entrance into the church in all weathers, night or day."[2] Her parents might be the biggest farmers in the hamlet, but its entire population would never have had enough money to pay for a caprice like that. It was the magnanimous Bishop of Périgueux, Mgr. de Flamarens, who "gave three hundred francs for the initial expenditure."† He was rather pleased to "pin down" that great bawling girl who

---

*Deborah, prophetess but also chieftain of a Hebrew tribe, led the Israelites to victory against the Canaanites; see Judges 5.

†[About $300.] The oratory still exists: leaning against the southwest side of the church, it is used as a sacristy, and nothing in it bears witness to the memory of Suzette Labrousse.

had previously shown a distressing tendency to roam, and might well set his whole placid diocese afire. Better she should play hermits and recluses in Vanxains, whose archpriest proudly exhibits her to visitors. Anyone who fancies a look at her can go there.

It just so happens, however, that Dom Gerle will have to wait a day or two before he can make Suzette's acquaintance, for she has gone to Périgueux, for the third or fourth time, to badger that great lord of a bishop who laughs at her and tries to drown her fire in oceans of unctuousness.

"I am very unhappy indeed to be such a subject of contradiction for many persons. Some of the people I know take me for mad, others for a liar and hypocrite. Only the good people of Vanxains feel any respect at all for me, and even some affection. The thought of my mission never leaves me in peace. At night voices seem to be urging me on: 'Rise up and go!' they tell me, in the midst of the stillness."[3]

Obedient to his nature—and his duty—the bishop tries to play for time by pacifying her.

"You do not believe in the authenticity of my mission, Monseigneur? Give me back the papers I entrusted to you. I shall burn them in your presence."

. . . How is he supposed to tell her that he's already chucked half of them into the fire himself, more or less unread?

"No, no, my daughter, I shall not impose that sacrifice upon you. Your manuscripts are in the hands of learned theologians, gentlemen from Paris. Indeed you will have to abide by their judgment, but they will not make up their minds in such a hurry. But . . . do you *really* believe everything you say?"

"More than my life."

The girl is incurable. The bishop can't keep up the pretense: "I shall certainly not make your case known. People would think I was mad."

He forbids her his door, but how long can you keep Joan of Arc in the waiting room? She periodically descends upon the episcopal portals with a great rustle of angels' wings:

"Monseigneur, I have come to know your answer concerning what is in the manuscript . . ."

In the end all he could think of was to tell her he'd sent it to the pope. So this time she's coming to hear what Pius VI has to say; but Mgr. de Flamarens swallows a large dose of laxative the moment they tell him she's at the city gates. In those blessed days, taking a purge was considered fair grounds for refusing to see callers, and no one could be offended. "Profoundly disappointed, Suzette returned to Vanxains"—where her voices have been looking after her. Divine surprise: she finds Dom Gerle in her parents' sitting room.

They receive him like the Holy Father in person. He spends hours and hours by the fire listening to the Labrousses and Courcelles, the two allied families, tell him the gospel according to their Suzette. They all believe in it with all their hearts, and that's enough to make an impression upon a son of people enough like them to be their brothers, back there in Auvergne—the Gerles and Chalinis, that was his mother's name. Christophe-Antoine Gerle received his simple faith almost as soon as he opened his eyes, in the course of identical evenings on his father's farm near Piom. It wasn't so nice there as here at the Labrousses'. A poorer soil, and a sharp wind that froze his bare feet in their wooden clogs. Did he ever have any idea other than to serve Jesus Christ? He grew up in a transfigured world in which the miraculous and the everyday lived side by side. He learned to read from the Bible. He got his schooling by devouring the Church Fathers and St. Augustine on his own. He never had any desire for a career in the worldly Church. The Carthusian monastery exactly suited his vast need for silence. No chattering could come there to trouble his perpetual dialogue with the Virgin and saints. *Stat Crux dum volvitur orbis,* * that's the motto of his order and of his life. His life: the cell in which, three times each night, he shifts from his bed of planks to his prayer stool, whose Bible stand supports the enormous tome printed in red and black, to recite the three nocturns of matins—alone, but at exactly the same time, to the very second, as all the other monks, each in his own cell; the stove which his rule compels him to stoke so that he will not freeze to death in winter; the little workshop nearby, where he must put in five hours daily; the minute walled garden where he grows medicinal herbs for the infirmary brothers; and, every week, the big collective laughter of the *spaciment* in the forest . . . Few contemplatives lead a more balanced existence than the Carthusians.†

Here he's a long way from all that, as he bends over this woman kneeling in front of him. "Bless me, father." Monk and visionary, the scene played out a thousand times in the mysteries of every religion. Dom Gerle, towering, unfolds like a day of fasting in his white wool robe, so practical—the body moves free as air inside it and one is so comfortably naked under it all summer long. His face is long and high, furrowed by the wrinkles of asceticism, with two enormous child's eyes under a dome of shaven crown. Suzette too is "of a size somewhat taller than the average; she is slender and quick by nature, and her attempts to appear stiff and cool do not always succeed. She is rather a beautiful young woman," but tidal waves of hysteria and the delectations of

*The Cross stands firm at the heart of a changing world.

†In a report on the decadence of the monastic orders which he was instructed to prepare for the Assembly of the Clergy in 1771, Loménie de Brienne observes that the "Order of the Carthusians is assuredly that one which, since its founding, has degenerated least and which still offers the greatest edification."[4]

penitence have imparted "a vague and squinting expression to her deep blue eyes which would otherwise have been perfectly beautiful." "Her hair of a fine chestnut color with amber glints" she has shaved. Her body is ageless in the loose gown of the Périgord peasant woman, with a gray shawl top that makes her look like a nun. She is one too, but of her own order. She chooses her own mortifications, she conducts her orisons as she pleases, she will have none of the convents that are fighting to get her: Notre Dame, St. Benoît, and St. Claire in Périgueux, the Ursulines in Libourne, the Little Sisters of Ribérac or Aubeterre. "I prefer to retreat alone. That is what God wishes of me."[5] She knows so well what God wishes of her! That's what has brought Dom Gerle to Vanxains: he wants to meet a creature imbued with "knowledge of the world and of herself."

For two whole days, she tells herself to him.

"The first words my parents gave me to hear struck me so forcibly that I seem to hear them still . . . They told me that God was present everywhere, that he was the universal benefactor and reward of the good . . . From then on I had but one desire: to see this God . . . The desire became so acute that it soon left me no repose; it was a veritable obsession, a sort of exquisite disease . . ." She often went looking for God at the far end of her parents' meadow, "there where the golden-flowered broom grows, and the pink-belled heather. I lay on my back and stared up at the sky for a long time, because I had been told that God lived beyond the blue . . . When the clouds chased each other across the sky and then were lost behind the huge forest of La Double, I always hoped that he would appear in a rift between them . . ." But God kept playing his eternal game of hide-and-seek with her as with everybody else; she began to enjoy suffering from his absence, and to like the bruises her brothers and sisters gave her when they found her swooning at the foot of a tree and would shake her vigorously, "making her drop down from heaven to earth." "I was nine years old and the desire to climb up into the sky to see God was obsessing me more all the time. Rest had become almost impossible. At last I could bear it no longer and I made up my mind to die. The moment I had taken that resolution, I became calmer. However, for several days I wondered how to die. One morning I heard that a peasant in the neighborhood had poisoned himself by accidentally swallowing a spider hidden in a grape he was biting into. In an instant my way was clear. I began to hunt for spiders and other small poisonous insects. After a few hours I had collected quite a number of them in a little box made from two playing cards, and without the slightest repugnance I was about to eat them when my mother, who was teaching my brothers and sisters their catechism, told them, talking about the fifth commandment, that it was no more permissible to take one's own life than that of another person.

"It was a terrible blow; I hid in the church, I lay down at the foot of the altar and told God how sorry I was that, since he did not want to show himself to those here below, he should also forbid them to die so they could go see him where he was."[6]

Having been deprived of her feast of spiders, she chose slow-motion suicide instead, like Catherine of Siena and so many other girls in her condition. "She saw her body as a foe, which she began to fight in a thousand different ways." She invented a sort of cocktail of soot and ox-gall which she poured over her food and with which "she rinsed her mouth several times a day." She garnished her bed with stones and potsherds. She tried (unsuccessfully) to disfigure herself by applying a mask of quicklime to her face. "She would have given her life for a communion; in the throes of some of her transports, she would have devoured the crucifix itself,"[7] that Christ of Jansenist provenance whose white body screamed on the big black cross over her mother's bed. Sometimes when Suzette looked at it, "the drops of blood painted on the feet" caused her to utter "such cries and sobs that the whole neighborhood heard her"—until the day when Jesus deigns to speak to her at last, in the old church she has herself locked up in one evening. "I was praying, and watching night spread over the chancel. The sacrarium lamp was flickering as though it wanted to go out. I came closer because I could no longer see the door of the tabernacle with the host behind it, and in the host was Jesus. Just then I felt as though carried away by an extraordinary surge of love, and a voice said to me:

" 'Leave the house of your mother and father. Go out into the world, unknown and a beggar, because I want, through a humble girl, to bring down several of the Great of this world and put to rights several evils in my Church.' "

She obeys, but in her own fashion. She drifts into the limited world of Périgord and part of Guyenne, not much farther than Libourne; but was the world that Abraham crossed when he went out from Ur in Chaldea much bigger? Neither unknown nor a beggar, at any rate. People crowd to hear her, to appropriate her. Her parents, assisted by numerous pious persons of the region, never let her go hungry. Ten years of relative wanderings, before returning to incrust herself in the wall of her baptismal church. "At last I was brought back to my beloved Vanxains. There, at least, I would be able to be alone with myself . . ." Precious solitude! Since she no longer goes out to the world, the world will come to her. Here's Dom Gerle, for a start.

TALLEYRAND

29

DECEMBER 1779

Ambition in Every Guise

In the spring of this same year of 1779 another God-crazed woman, the
Norman Catherine Théot, also decides she wants to be free,* although she
takes longer to make up her mind than Suzette. At fifty-five Catherine has had
enough of preaching in the wilderness. The priests she was forever harrying
had stuffed her into the convent of the Miramions, along with the "repentant"
girls.† But what did *she* have to repent of? Listening to the word of God for
thirty years? To hear her tell it, it was the world that needed to repent, and
pretty quickly, and it was the Great, especially those in the Church, who
needed to mend their ways. Otherwise Paris, just like Sodom and Gomorrah
. . . She got on their nerves. Now she's hopped over the wall at the Miramions,
and the tall, "dry and almost diaphanous" woman, "like the ancient Sibyl of
Cumae,"[1] is rousing little crowds on the steps of St. Eustache and Notre Dame.
And when she preaches the new moral order, they don't all laugh at her. A
madwoman of her kind can always become dangerous. In April the police
arrest her on the Rue Geoffroy l'Asnier. A long interrogation, conducted by
commissioner Chenon, convinces the authorities that she's a potential rabble-
rouser. They shut her up for good, in the Salpêtrière.

How many more are there like her, wandering this Christian world in
which Christ seems to be the last thing on anybody's mind? Scores and scores
of John the Baptists, prophets, visionaries, highway hermits, toad-eaters, con-
vulsionaries, and flagellants. You can't put them all in prison, they swarm like
cockroaches. For every one you lock up ten more crawl out of the same hole.

*Catherine Théot meets Dom Gerle after 1789, when she is styling herself "the mother of
God." He believes in her mission, and both are instrumental in manufacturing the cult of
Robespierre, which serves as one pretext for action by the Thermidorians. [The Thermidorians
were a coalition of terrorists, moderates, and everyone else who felt threatened by Robespierre
and decided to strike first, on 9–10 Thermidor Year II (July 27–28, 1794); the ensuing backlash
was directed against both terrorist institutions and Jacobin austerity.—*Trans.*]

†A small Parisian order founded under Louis XIII by Marie Bonneau de Miramion, widow
of a councilor in the Parliament. The "Miramions" ran Ste. Pélagie, and thus they nearly had
Sophie de Monnier as an inmate.

In Rome, for example, how could the papal police arrest Benoît-Joseph Labre, "the vermin of God," whose stench alone sickened the so-pretty, so-cute Cardinal de Bernis, perfumed ambassador of the King of France? Bernis protests: "We have here a sight which edifies some, for all that it scandalizes others . . ."[2]: a beggar who has taken a vow never to wash or cut his hair and who roams through the Coliseum announcing "that an awesome fire will soon sweep everything away, that the abbeys will burn, the priests will be persecuted . . ." The people won't like it if they shut him up. Why couldn't he have stayed in his parents' grocery shop in Artois? True, none of the monasteries would have him, from Boulogne to Rome. But even so, Benoît-Joseph Labre always found shelter among the poor, at every link in the long chain of his faltering pilgrimage. He'll never be forgotten, for instance, by Pierre Vianney, a peasant in Dardilly near Lyons, on whose doorstep he collapses half dead one snowy evening.*

. . . And what about the 256 missions of Abbé Bridaine: "Follow me! I am going to lead you home! . . ." So the docile crowds follow him—to the cemetery.[3] And the soothing sermons of Brother Ambroise, who has just died in Languedoc: "Give your heart to God and remain at peace."[4] And all those Sacred Hearts, displayed on walls, sewed on pillows, slipped into alcoves, viscera streaming blood in the visions of the visitant Sister Marianne Galipaud in Nantes, where local Jansenists are waging war against the *"cordicoles"* by writing graffiti on the walls: why not adore the wounds of Christ, too, while you're at it, his side, his eyes, his feet, his . . . The freethinkers would like nothing better than to complete the list.† In Spain the Capuchin Diego de Cadiz brings whole towns running when he bares his bleeding torso, scored by the nails lining his felt jerkin. Fifty-two persons are picked up on the public thoroughfares of Seville, seriously injured by flagellation after the Good Friday procession in 1779.[5] In his mini-diocese of St. Agata de' Goti near Capua, the ancient Alfonso de Liguori, twisted and tottering, leads the processions with torchlight illumination of a horrific image of a damned soul burning in hell,[6] but the avalanche of infirmities and disgraces hurtling down upon him these days (mainly the persecutions of Pius VI) have not prevented him from abandoning himself to the delights of levitation whenever his Savior

*Jean-Marie Vianney, Pierre's grandson, will be born in this house in 1786, and become the famous Curé d'Ars. [Whose preaching, charity, and austerity drew crowds. Canonized in 1925.—*Trans.*]

†Even in 1740 there were 702 brotherhoods of the Sacred Heart in Europe. In 1780 the official feast day is authorized, but only in Poland, from which Maria Leczinska, a member of the brotherhood, brought powerful support to the French *"cordicoles."* [Devotion to the Sacred Heart of Jesus had its origins in the Middle Ages. It was strongly opposed by the Jansenists, who claimed that the heart of Christ must not be adored independently of the rest of his being.—*Trans.*]

calls.* His nurse, Brother Francesco Antonio, and his confessor, Father Volpicelli, have no end of trouble bringing him back to earth in those moments when he suddenly zooms up and hits the ceiling, to remain there suspended, "motionless between heaven and earth, in a kneeling position, his countenance resplendent." During mass "he mounts into space as lightly as a feather, even though the assistance of two persons is normally required to move him about on the ground."[7]

Introibo ad altare Dei . . .†

Another cleric is preparing to celebrate his first mass a few weeks from now. This one, however, is highly unlikely to start flitting through the air in the course of the ceremony. The only danger for Talleyrand, if he had any gumption left, is that he might take to his heels and begin to run, out of the choir and far from any church. But how can a clubfoot run? *Ad Deum qui laetificat juventutem meam . . .* Talleyrand's God gave nothing but poison to his youth, by allowing his nurse to let him fall off a chest of drawers. Soon no one will be able to believe he was ever capable of crying; yet it really and truly is "in a fit of tears and despair" that one of his riotous chums, young Choiseul-Gouffier, finds him on the Friday of Ember Week in Advent, December 16, 1779, aged twenty-five years and ten months, the day before he is to be ordained a priest for all eternity, "according to the order of Melchisedech," in the chapel of the archbishopric of Rheims.[8] Tears of grief? No, of rage, according to Choiseul-Gouffier, who can't refrain from suggesting that he break it all off now rather than commit his life to a misunderstanding. Talleyrand refuses. He goes on about "his mother, the pain it would cause her, the talk it would provoke: 'No, my friend, it is too late. There is no drawing back now.' "

On Passion Sunday four years earlier the Bishop of Lombez, a La Mothe-Fénelon, gave him fair warning before God and man and in the prescribed liturgical forms before conferring the deaconate upon him in the Church of St. Nicholas du Chardonnet: "Until that hour you are free . . . Once that order has been received, you will no longer be able to break your undertaking, and will forever be committed to the service of God . . . Reflect, while there is yet time. But if you persist in your sacred resolution, then, in the name of the Lord, go forward."[9] A sacred resolution spun of weakness, spinelessness, self-indulgence, and irony. The deaconate enabled him to get out of St. Sulpice and move into a bachelor flat on the Rue de la Harpe, where a flock of pretty girls

---

*Alfonso Maria de Liguori (1696–1787) is beatified and canonized (in 1839) with unusual celerity. In 1871 Pius IX proclaims him a doctor of the Church.

†First words (followed by the Latin phrase in the next paragraph) of Psalm 42, which the Roman Catholic priests used to recite before mounting to the altar: "And I will go in to the altar of God: to God who giveth joy to my youth."

and boon companions quickly gathered around him, thanks to the money his father was sending him for being such a good boy. A fine career as court priest lies open before the flagging footsteps of young Charles-Maurice de Talleyrand-Périgord, known at the moment as Abbé Périgord, that's certainly the only word he has in common with the Carthusian monk and the pious girl who sit talking together these days not far from his ancestors' estate. His family claims to descend from the comtes de Périgord, one of whom, Aldebert, flung the famous "Who made you king?" in the teeth of Hugh Capet. The lineage is difficult to prove, even for the craftiest genealogists. The Comte de Provence expresses his own doubts in the matter, with "The Talleyrands are mistaken in their pretensions by a single letter: they are *du,* not *de* Périgord."[10] There's no doubt about *that,* at any rate [that is, the fact that they are *from* Périgord]: as princes de Chalais, comtes de Grignols, marquis d'Excideuil, and barons de Beauville and de Mareuil, their Périgordine châteaus keep watch over every rabbit hole in the forest of La Double. There, at Chalais, Charles-Maurice enjoyed the only unresentful hours of his life in the château of his grandmother, the one woman who loved him when he was little. If *he* ever wondered what there was "beyond the blue," it can only have been here: "The ways of the Périgordine nobility were like their old châteaus;* there was something grand and stable about them. Little light filtered into them, but what there was came sweetly . . . Chalais was a château dating from that revered and cherished age . . . Next to my grandmother's prie-dieu stood a little chair reserved for me."[11] Chalais was less than five leagues from Vanxains and Montpon, but a universe separated that little chair from Dom Gerle's pallet; and ever since the Abbé de Talleyrand-Périgord was made "promoter of the Assembly of the Clergy of France"—a juicy office in which you could manipulate the levers of both powers, religious and profane, and make a name for yourself while your hands remained clasped in prayer—that rift in the bosom of the one true Church has been steadily widening. "I attentively observed how affairs were conducted within this large body. There was ambition in every guise. Religion, humanity, patriotism, philosophy, each took on a different hue there! . . ." "The intervention of conscience in all these pecuniary complexities has conferred upon the elements of this great affair† a style of eloquence that only the clergy can command . . ." "The five years of ill-humor, silence and reading, which seemed so long and dreary to me at the seminary, were no longer a total loss . . . At the Sorbonne [where he was a day student from 1775 to 1777; here he's thinking of his gilded cage on the Rue de la Harpe] I spent two years occupied with matters far removed from theology, for pleasure takes up a great deal of time in the days of a young

*Written by Talleyrand himself, about his childhood.

†The chief business (or "great affair") of the Assembly of the Clergy was the five-yearly determination of the sum it would "consent" to bestow, or better, allow to be extorted from itself with loud and repeated moans, in taxation—to be paid to the king in the fictitious form of an "unsolicited gift."

bachelor. Ambition also had its moments, and the memory of Cardinal Richelieu, whose handsome mausoleum stood in the Church of the Sorbonne, was
not unedifying in this respect. At that time my only experience of ambition
was of the better kind; I wanted to achieve everything I supposed I might do
well."[12] All the same, better not shake him too hard on his ordination day.
He might disintegrate.

"Go, and bring down several of the Great of this world . . . Go, and put
to rights the evils in my Church . . ." The refrain of Suzette Labrousse's voices
goes straight to Dom Gerle's heart the first time he talks to her. They connect,
those voices, and Suzette's own voice connects, with some fiber in him: the
sensitivity to their century of all children of the light. A certain anger in their
eyes when they descend from heaven to gaze upon the earth. That apocalyptic
wrath running through the notebooks she goes on scribbling in every day.*
There is pathos in them, and total confusion, highlighted by an occasional
robustness of retort worthy of Joan of Arc—or Rabelais: "If my scheme is
successful, it will send some to the other world, some to the antipodes, and
myself to blue blazes . . . If I am not mistaken, we are entering upon an age
when all feeling will be ONE . . . The condition of this plan will be a joyous
event that will make mortals utter unending oohs and aahs . . ." What scheme?
What plan? She doesn't know, of course, she's incapable of describing it. She's
all knotted up in her neuroses and gagged by her inability to express herself.
But what Dom Gerle responds to, more than the words of her message, is its
tone: when she claims that "the mystical intelligences of France have long since
given up interesting themselves in any but earthly concerns, and have become
so powerfully metamorphosed into matter that they now live in their sphere
as shapeless masses,"[13] he's right with her. He understands. He may be the
only one who does, but that's enough to give her the confirmation she's been
waiting for. Dom Gerle is the anti-Talleyrand, or the anti-Sieys. How could
he not understand when Suzette says: "You will strip the old man and reclothe
yourself in the spirit of Jesus Christ. The sight of his image is a block of light
that one might seek in vain within oneself. It will give you tact in the conduct
of your affairs, such as human science will never be able to teach . . . Temporal
cares are a burden to the ministers of the Church. They are like the adorers
of the rich and the Great of the earth . . . They speak the truth, but their actions
lie. Who will be able to believe them, seeing in their deeds what close heed
they pay to the Great?"[14]

Dom Gerle blesses her once more and goes back to his priory, thoughtful
and happy. They'll meet again. He takes her manuscripts with him, and he
doesn't burn them. In return, he leaves her with peace in her heart. A man
of the Church has taken her seriously: "At last! God has deigned to manifest
his will to me through the mouth of a venerable priest. He urged me to set

---

*A fraction of which was published in 1791 by Bishop Pierre Pontard, entitled *Enigmes de
Mlle La Brousse* [sic] *commencées en 1766* [Enigmas of Mlle de La Brousse, begun in 1766].

forth [on September 29, 1779] and announce to the clergy of France, and later to that of the whole world, that the hour for the reformation of the abuses which have crept into the Church of Jesus Christ is at hand. Let the great lords beware! . . . When I was expressing to the Reverend Father Gerle my astonishment that all the other priests had treated me like a madwoman, he answered: 'Remember that the prophets also were judged mad. But the dreadful events they foretold came to pass all the same.' "[15]

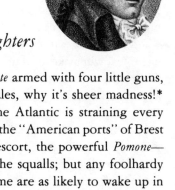

BEAUHARNAIS

30

DECEMBER 1779

Come, and Bring One of Your Daughters

Sailing from the Islands to France on board a *flûte* armed with four little guns, pitching and rolling through the equinoctial gales, why it's sheer madness!* The net of English cruisers stretched along the Atlantic is straining every thread to catch any French craft in the vicinity of the "American ports" of Brest and Rochefort. True, the *Isle-de-France* has an escort, the powerful *Pomone*— a frigate they glimpse now and then through the squalls; but any foolhardy souls trying to return to the Continent in wartime are as likely to wake up in London as in Paris—such as the little court of Marie-Josèphe-Rose Tascher de La Pagerie,† hidden among the flotsam of sugar and indigo, ailing officers and transferred scribes. What is a sixteen-year-old girl doing in this galley?

Getting married. Nothing could be more urgent. We'd sooner brave shipwreck and captivity combined than pass up a Beauharnais, the son of a former governor of the Windward Islands, do you know what that means? For a Creole it means a demigod. Aunt Marie-Euphémie, the one who's been patiently cooking all this up in France for years, has bombarded M. Tascher with threatening missiles: "Alas! Could I but fly and come to fetch you! Come, come, it is your own dear sister who implores you!" Hurricanes, English?

---

*A *flûte* was primarily a cargo ship that also carried passengers, its heavy proportions enabling it to ride low in the water. Colbert had a score of them built, "deep-bellied, four or five hundred tons, designed to be sailed by a small crew."[1] The word comes from the Spanish *fusta* or Italian *fusto*, meaning wood, beam, or cask. Nothing to do with music, much less that particular instrument.

†In 1796, after becoming the widow of Alexandre de Beauharnais and acquiring the pseudonym of "Joséphine," she marries General Bonaparte and, as Empress Joséphine, she succeeds Marie Antoinette on the throne of France from 1804 until her repudiation in December 1809.

Auntie doesn't give two hoots: "Other considerable matches have been offered the [Beauharnais] family. The young man's ardor may cool if you delay
too long."[2]

All right! We're coming! We're on the way! Just hang on, Marie-Euphémie, long enough for us to get there! We had to wait until some transport was
available, and the *Isle-de-France* can't sail any faster than the wind. We left
Fort-Royal on August 29. Call it a month, a month and a half to Brest: the last
weeks Marie-Josèphe-Rose will ever be known as "Yéyette." After her wedding everybody calls her Rose.

Yéyette is in less of a rush than the rest of them, but she doesn't do
anything to hold them back either. She is, and always has been, docility
incarnate. Not out of fear, for her childhood was a pleasant one, but because
it's her nature; nothing has ever happened to her that wasn't nice, passivity is
her lifestyle. She's sailing toward a prince charming who is endowed, according to Aunt Renaudin, "with a pleasant face, a delightful figure, wit, genius
[*sic*]; and he has this priceless asset, that every quality of soul and heart is
united in him."[3]

His priceable assets are even more interesting: Alexandre de Beauharnais
boasts an income of forty thousand livres now, and another twenty-five thousand in "expectations" at his father's death.* More likely to set the father-in-
law's heart going pitty-pat than that of the fiancée. So Marie-Josèphe-Rose
obediently strings along behind Joseph-Gaspard Tascher (pronounced Taché),
a handsome forty-year-old with the self-satisfied air of a man who has made
his career through women: first his legitimate wife, Rose-Claire des Vergers
de Sanois; then his sister, the famous Renaudin, and then his mistresses, picked
up here and there around the Islands, and now his eldest daughter. He's also
conveying Franceward another of his sisters, Rosette—that is, Marie-Françoise, the old maid who'll do duty as a chaperon for Yéyette. Mme Tascher
has stayed behind at Trois-Islets. Well, somebody has to keep the plantation
going, and Rose-Claire cares neither for traveling nor making appearances nor
expressing herself. She will be one of History's silences.† Another living
silence accompanies Yéyette: Euphémie the mulatto, whose semi-existence is
not worth a full name. The island Negroes, like dogs, are only entitled to half
an identity: Euphémie has been chosen this time, but it might equally well have
been Faisan, Manon, Théodule, Appolino, or Dorothée.[5]

Now, let's just run through that again: M. Joseph-Gaspard Tascher de La
Pagerie, flanked by his sister Marie-Françoise and the mulatto Euphémie, is

---

*200,000 new francs in annual income (from plantations in the colonies: good Negro sweat)
and 125,000 "expected," making a total of 325,000 francs [$65,000] a year.

†She was born in 1736 and died at Trois-Islets, Martinique, on July 2, 1807, the year of
Friedland and Tilsit. Napoleon (who never met her) forbids publication of the death of this
"Madame Mère," which would have compelled the court to go into mourning. "All signs of grief
were thus expressly forbidden, not only to the Empress but to her children as well."[4]

taking his daughter Marie-Josèphe-Rose to the bed of the Vicomte Alexandre de Beauharnais, who is no more vicomte than M. Tascher is de La Pagerie. But if you're going to start quibbling, in this century when the title goes to the highest bidder . . .

An alliance between two families from neighboring sources; the Blésois for the Taschers and Sologne for the Beauharnais. But the former have been firmly settled in the Islands for fifty years, whereas the latter were only there on a tour of duty.

The Taschers? Provincial gentry, neither rags nor riches. Small military fortunes made in the king's service. The homestead of this lot is at Blois, where an ancestor, back in the time of Louis XIV, owned a piece of land outside the town called La Pagerie; it's been sold long since, but they thought they might as well keep the name. One son of that Tascher scrambles far enough up in the Church to become one of the ten or twelve almoners of the dauphine, mother of Louis XVI, and extort a few favors out of her for his carload of brothers and sisters. The eldest of the squadron, Gaspard-Joseph—father of Joseph-Gaspard—walks ashore in Martinique one fine morning in the 1730's, scratches together some land here and there, and picks up a wife who, already, is richer than himself, a Boureau de La Chevallerie. Even so, he never manages to break out of a relatively modest condition as holder of a few subaltern jobs at Fort-Royal. They had five children, born in the years around 1740. The two boys (one being Joseph-Gaspard) are able to spend a term in the ranks of the dauphine's page boys, thanks to their priestly uncle Tascher; but they come back again all too soon, and start loafing around in their father's footsteps and sharing his problems. One of the daughters, on the other hand, makes up for them: Marie-Euphémie becomes the mistress of the governor appointed in 1755 to defend the Antilles against the English—François de Beauharnais.

The Beauharnaises? Land and game preserves in Sologne, which they use as a pretext to call themselves marquis, comte, and vicomte. Judicious marriages secure them some plantations in Santo Domingo, which start their fortune snowballing and gild their petty nobility. They're parvenus, however, and a genealogist makes no bones about it: "M. de Beauharnais is not eligible for the honors of Court.* His family is of good Orléans bourgeoisie . . . On April 4, 1667, one of its branches, known as the seigneurs de La Bretesche, was sentenced by M. Machault, intendant of Orléans, to pay a fine of two thousand livres for usurpation of nobility."[6] Hardly more noble than a Beaumarchais, then, and less than a Tascher, but much richer and better placed with the ministers. They've had "somebody in the navy" for a generation.

They reach their apogee with this post as governor of the Windwards; it's François who manages to snag it, a lucky stroke, the first rung on the ladder to real power . . . But no. This curious creature seems to have devoted all his

*In this instance, the right to follow the chase in the king's carriages, for which Alexandre applies in 1786.

energies to a single operation: the permanent conquest of Marie-Euphémie de Tascher, who moves into his home in 1756 as "companion" to his wife—she being one of those mild creatures typical of the marriages of that age, born to keep quiet and bear children. The husband, Beauharnais, looks around for an understanding spouse for his mistress, to consolidate Marie-Euphémie's "position" and enable him to keep her around. This is what brings him in January 1759 to Martinique, where he stays long enough to marry her to somebody named Renaudin—and also long enough for the English to take Guadeloupe, whose four thousand defenders are desperately awaiting the governor and his reinforcements. François de Beauharnais does finally get there—the day after the French surrender. But far from trying to dislodge the shaky English, he sails calmly back to Martinique on a corsair whose highly symbolic name, *Zomby,* is to provide material for many a broadside by the Guadeloupe colonists; because they're apoplectic with rage at their truant governor and would gladly see the King chop off his head like Lally-Tollendal's—is it any less culpable to sacrifice a major island than to lose the trading centers in India? Fifteen years later the people of Guadeloupe are still singing couplets fit to sear the ears of any Beauharnais.

Soyons fidèles aux Bourbons,	[To the Bourbons we'll be true,
Imitons les anciens colons,	Like the colonists of old,
Sans chefs, sans munitions,	With nary a leader, nary a loaf,
Manquant de provisions . . .[7]	And nary a gun our island for
	to hold . . .]

The King's Council deigns to take notice. But all it does is relieve Beauharnais of his duties and abandon him jobless in Martinique, where he has many supporters to defend him against the Guadeloupeans. After all, the English didn't invade Martinique while he was in office—only three years later.* In the interim, the "Marquis" de Beauharnais leaves the island head high, wearing the halo of disgrace. He joins Mme Renaudin, who has preceded him to France on another ship, and leaves behind, in Fort-Royal, a baby too tender to make the trip: Alexandre-François-Marie de Beauharnais,† entrusted to the loving care of the Taschers de La Pagerie. Mme Renaudin is his godmother. You'd think she had cast a spell over them all. During their brief separation the Marquis de Beauharnais dreams only of her: "How much I should have to say, madame, if ever I undertook to inform you how anxious we have been on your account and during your voyage. But you know my feelings for you . . . In France, we shall have so many unkind things to say about this country, madame! . . ."[8]

---

*It capitulates on February 13, 1762. In 1763 both islands are restored to the King of France by the Treaty of Paris.

†Born on May 28, 1760. "Joséphine" is also born in Martinique, on June 23, 1763, nine days after the signature of the treaty that restores the island to France.

Twenty years go by. Now, thanks to the death of little Mme de Beauharnais and the expulsion of the dutiful Renaudin on grounds of attempted poisoning, she reigns absolute over the "marquis's" Parisian town house. She also reigns over the youth of her godson Alexandre, brought over from the Islands when he was five or six. More than a godmother and better than a mother, she is his accomplice and confidante; he's fond of her, he tells her all his escapades. She reigns, by correspondence, over her brother's family, in which she has acquired three nieces. No doubt she's always had this marriage of Infantes in mind, to consolidate her empire. Marie-Euphémie Renaudin wins the battle of her life on October 23, 1777, when François de Beauharnais writes to Joseph-Gaspard Tascher: "My children now* enjoy an income of forty thousand livres each. It is within your power to give me Mademoiselle, your daughter, to share the fortune of my chevalier [whom he occasionally calls "vicomte" as well, why not]. His respect and affection for Mme de Renaudin have caused him ardently to desire a union with one of her nieces." Which one? It would seem natural to choose the eldest, but Alexandre has a different idea: "I own that my son, who is but seventeen and a half, finds a young lady of fifteen too near his own age."[9] If they've got to marry him off like a prince, then the "vicomte" figures he might as well have a proper little doll to play with. He chooses Catherine-Désirée, thirteen years old . . . The poor child dies the same month, of a "malignant fever." Never mind: Joseph-Gaspard offers the third, Marie-Françoise, aged eleven; will she do? He does venture to point out, however, that the eldest "has extremely fine skin, very lovely arms, and a passionate longing to come to Paris . . ." Mme Renaudin jabs her brother in letter after letter; good gracious, what a dolt! "Come, and bring one of your daughters, bring two! Whatever you do will be agreeable to us. We must have one of your children."[10] The "marquis" chimes in: "She whom you judge best suited to my son will be the one we desire"—and, on the forms for publication of the marriage banns at Fort-Royal, he leaves the fiancée's name and date of birth blank.

Marie-Josèphe-Rose wins the toss . . .

A Trois-Islets girl. She has drifted through a green childhood; for her, home was warm and womblike longer than for many another—ten years of tranquillity near the little hamlet which lies close to the sea but turns its back on it, thirty or so straw huts and a wooden church† in the vale of the stream called

*"Now" means "since their mother's death." Alexandre has an older brother, François, born in 1756, who remained in France during their father's West Indies stint. François de Beauharnais becomes an officer, then a—staunchly royalist—member of the Constituent Assembly, then an émigré, and finally a diplomat in the service of Napoleon.

†The church has been restored but stands as it was then, its beams and rafters in the shape

Croc-souris, where Marie-Rose bathes naked like everybody else in the tangle of water and water lilies surrounded by a deluge of mangroves, palms, banana trees, mangoes, and coconut palms. A virgin world, or nearly. Every day the path has to be hacked from the grasp of a greedy double vegetal wall; it leads down to the bay and Fort-Royal, where the boats flap in like exhausted seagulls after their crossing. No beach. The tall rushes grow straight into the sea. Close by, the backs of three green whales float forever: the three islets, Charles, Sixtain, and Tebloux. They're so small you can hardly stand up on them. They gave the village its name. The La Pagerie plantation lies a few hundred yards inland.

The palace of the Taschers: a hundred slaves, twenty mules, three horses, ten cows, and a few sheep live in and around the scattered buildings roughly patched together after the typhoon tore all their roofs off in 1766. The masters retreated to a makeshift camp upstairs above the sugar refinery, and stayed there. Marie-Rose was brought up by Marion, her nice black nurse, over the smell of warm rum and the crackle of breaking sugar canes. Sugar was the alpha and omega of her home, as of every other in the Antilles.* All her notions of economy were reduced to that. How could she understand that her father's real worry, his and everyone else's, was how to get his hands on enough capital to convert his sugar into gold? The Taschers never even had enough to rebuild their farm after the storm.† But once we get our teeth into Beauharnais's forty thousand a year! . . . Joseph-Gaspard's dream lasts the length of an ocean crossing.

The Islands they leave behind them are uneasy. After taking Grenada, Admiral d'Estaing has led his fleet up toward North America to intimidate the English who are in the process of recapturing the South. And what's to stop them, with us here exposed and undefended, from swooping down on our big sugar islands? Just in case, the militia—a few scruffy battalions who haven't got enough guns to go round—are sent out on majestic maneuvers around the forts of Martinique and Guadeloupe.

On the latter island, a Basse-Terre planter named Jacques Coquille, alias Du Gommier,** has just levied and armed at his own expense a company of

---

of an upside-down ship's hull. A plaque near the baptistry commemorates the baptism of Marie-Joséphine [*sic*] Tascher de La Pagerie, Empress of the French.

*Including the governor's: François de Beauharnais's salary, during his term in the Islands, was 60,000 pounds of sugar a year.[11]

†The La Pagerie sugar refinery still exists and has been transformed into a "Joséphine museum."

**Dugommier (History's spelling), as commander-in-chief of the Convention troops sent to recapture Toulouse in 1793, is clever enough to place his trust in artillery captain Buonaparte, and thus becomes the first promoter of his national destiny . . . and Joséphine's.

"fifty volunteers, creole, mulatto and black."[12] In other words, a few whites and half-breeds paid to drive slaves loaned by colonists. Having his little company has knocked years off his age and dragged him out of his premature-retirement blues: Jacques Coquille is forty, almost an old man in the colonies, but he's damned if he's going to go like the rest of them. He's rich, of course, ten times richer than the Taschers; he owns a fair share of the plantations on Guadeloupe. The Coquilles have built up quite a little sugar dynasty there, starting when the two older brothers—Robert-Germain, the prosecuting attorney, and Jacques, our man—married the two daughters of a rich planter from Grande-Terre on the same day. And there are uncles and cousins, too, all those Coquilles you can only tell apart by their nicknames, Coquille Sainte-Croix, Coquille Champ-Fleuri, Coquille Vallon-Court, and the Robert Coquille who is seneschal of Marie-Galante, an hour's sail away.* Jacques has taken the name of his father's allotment in the Gommier woods of Basse-Terre. He is also the proud possessor of a brand-new title conferred under the royal edict of 1769 upon "officers of the Windward Islands after forty years of service."

Jacques's true life is all in that one word: officer. His father's life and his own. Arms and the army. He's a scrapper. Plantation routine is almost as intolerable to him as was that of Père Colin's boarding school in the faubourg Saint-Antoine in Paris, "highly renowned for refined principles of morality and the humanities," where he was sent for his schooling thirty years back. In it he revealed himself to be what he now is in the eyes of the authorities and big planters: "lively, dissipated, loquacious, beloved by his fellows and living with them on terms of great intimacy, restless under the scholastic yoke, unable to apply himself to his lessons, even though, by virtue of his intelligence, he was not at the bottom of his class, answering back to his masters on more than one occasion, telling them to their faces that they were not to force him to do work that caused him nothing but disgust."[13] His most wonderful memory, at fifteen, was when he entered the colonial gentlemen's cadet corps at Rochefort; and his favorite dress was the blue broadcloth coat over the gray-white jerkin with gilt buttons and the hat edged with pure gold braid . . . "At the Rochefort school he distinguished himself by his love of the military life and his fondness for artillery." At twenty came his baptism by fire, when the English, the eternal foe, blockaded the isle of Aix and threatened Rochefort; he was commanding the Fouras battery at the mouth of the Charente. Both sides took a rain check and met again a year later on a Guadeloupe forsaken by M. de Beauharnais, and again on Martinique, where he fought like a tiger before being taken prisoner. And then came peace, discharge—at only twenty-

---

*That one becomes a nonexistent delegate to the Constituent Assembly. A seneschal was a sort of police-court judge.

six!—and a rich, boring marriage, the two don't get along together and keep as far apart as it is possible to do on Guadeloupe. Tedium and monotony in one of the loveliest spots on earth. Is it already time to start pickling himself in rum? The new war resurrects Jacques Coquille. Others' worries are his hopes. Last year he embarked his volunteers on one of d'Estaing's ships and fought off St. Lucia. In a few days he's going to be given command of another battalion, of real volunteers this time—whites. He'll have the Cross of St. Louis "for readiness and ardor displayed in all operations of war." Every morning he watches for English sails from the top of the bluffs. And when they don't show he dreams of going to America to find them.

. . . Marie-Rose Tascher never tells what she suffered or thought during this transition from one world to another. Her father complains, though, and with good reason. Letter from Joseph-Gaspard to Mme Renaudin, on October 1 3: "We are at Brest, where we have just come ashore, terribly wearied from a long and dreadful crossing during which I thought I would die ten times. My life was feared for. My daughter has been nursing me assiduously."[14] The letter doesn't reach the pretty little country house which the "Marquis" de Beauharnais has given Marie-Euphémie—at Noisy-le-Grand, a little to the east of Paris—until October 20. The son-godson-fiancé, Alexandre in short, is in bed there, suffering also, but from a Breton illness contracted in his garrison at Conquet, at the land's end on the Ouessant side, where he spent the summer preparing for the Descent. He's a captain in the Saar regiment. From Conquet he wrote to his godmother: "It is off the English coasts that I should like to forge my way to glory, how glad I should be to send you a letter from Portsmouth or Plymouth one day." Failing Portsmouth, autumn finds him nursing his bronchitis at Noisy, not at all disposed to sit around in the sticks waiting for his fiancée to emerge from the mists.

They don't connect. Two weeks of rain and wind in a gray city, spent in furnished rooms in an overcrowded hotel in the Saint-Louis district at the bedside of an ailing father: that's France's first gift to Yéyette. At last Alexandre turns up, on October 27, on horseback from Morlaix, followed by Mme Renaudin in her carriage. One bit of luck: he's an honest-to-goodness handsome lad, "elegant, very sure of himself, very smart in his white broadcloth uniform with silver-gray lapels and trim."[15] The head recedes somehow, the forehead, or is it the sloping nose, there's something one can't quite catch hold of in his manner, possibly an excess of shyness beneath a carapace of aristocratic hauteur. He's a Beauharnais, and his bearing and cravat alike proclaim how well he knows it. He may outgrow the fatuousness of his years, but he's also got the fatuousness of his class, and will he ever outgrow that?* Yet

*Alexandre de Beauharnais is a representative of the nobility at the Estates General and president of the Constituent Assembly on the day of the king's attempted escape in June 1 7 9 1 ;

something attracts your attention at the back of his eyes, something thoughtful. Unlike so many of his comrades, there's still a glimmer of youth in him. He did well in his humanities studies at the du Plessis collège, the rival of Louis-le-Grand, "the school attended by the children of rich families who would have none of the Jesuits."[16] And his "private tutor," the worthy M. Patricol, took him to learn the German language and customs at the University of Heidelberg before going to tutor for the La Rochefoucaulds at the Château de La Roche-Guyon. The pupil follows the master: Alexandre, virtually adopted by those great liberal aristocrats who return the Court's cold shoulder a hundredfold, completes his education in their midst, inhaling Rousseau, Voltaire, and Diderot after devouring *Werther*. The Duchesse d'Enville de La Rochefoucauld was Turgot's best friend; she brings a breath of fresh air into the little nonconformist hothouse that has found its Eden on those "mountains of Norman chalk" near the loop in the Seine at Vernon. The La Rochefoucaulds are at once proud and annoyed to be descended from Louvois.* La Roche-Guyon "is one of the most singular places I have been at. The chalk rock has been cut perpendicularly, to make room for the château. The kitchen, which is a large one, vast vaults and extensive cellars (magnificently filled, by the way), with various other offices, are all cut out of the rock, with merely fronts of brick; the house is large, containing thirty-eight apartments. The present Duchess has added a handsome saloon of forty-eight feet long, and well proportioned, with four fine tablets of the Gobelins tapestry, also a well-filled library. Here I was shown the inkstand that belonged to the famous Louvois, the minister of Louis XIV, known to be the identical one from which he signed the revocation of the edict of Nantes, and I suppose also the order to Turenne to burn the Palatinate."[17] In this "ducal château where the exquisite pleasures of an opulent, aristocratic, refined life lived on a grand scale are mingled with discussions of the doctrines of equality under the law and equality of color, with benevolence and philanthropy like the latest mode in elegance,"[18] Alexandre de Beauharnais found an anti-Martinique. "Equality of color?" Can he possibly be drifting away from his father, or have broken with him? No; but a little crack has snaked through him, there's a door ajar into another world. Whence his lack of enthusiasm for this forced marriage to the daughter of a small-time slaveholder. But he hasn't yet reached the point of turning up his nose at the income from the land in Santo Domingo. And he belongs to a generation that knows how to marry without joy and without lamentation. What's more, the little parcel of half-baked Creole he finally unwraps is really not too bad. Alexandre has the good grace to reassure his father: "You may find Mlle de La Pagerie less pretty than you hope, but I believe I can assure

---

in that capacity he is "almost a king" for five days.
   *Aggressive, efficient, and bellicose minister of Louis XIV. [*Trans.*]

you that the honesty and sweetness of her character exceed all you may have been told of her."[19] He wanted a child bride? He can relax, he's got one. Light chestnut hair, a dazzling skin. She's already learned how to flutter her eyelashes over a pair of languorous eyes. She has a comical little trumpet-shaped nose and a sway in her walk that looks highly promising to the libertine in him. And if she doesn't deliver what she promises, he can always fall back on the mistresses who've been easing his path for the last three or four years —that Caumont lady who called him "her goat, because of the stray hairs I have on the tip of my chin," or Marie-Laure de Longpré, a married woman eleven years his senior, whom he met in Brittany "in the most wretched place that could ever be seen," that is, Conquet, where she was so utterly bored that they rather skimped the preliminaries. Mme Renaudin has heard all about it, and is counting on hearing about anything else that comes up, in her capacity as matchmaker-procuress: "Who would have thought I should be so happy in Conquet? Yes, I shall not hide it from you: your chevalier [*sic*] has tasted happiness even in these parts. He is loved by a charming woman . . . Her husband . . . has been ordered to spend three weeks elsewhere. I hope with all my heart that nothing will oblige him to return sooner."[20] A few months from now Mme de Longpré will give birth to a child conceived this summer, and will name him Alexandre.

The "vicomte," therefore, isn't feeling too downhearted, and he goes through the matrimonial preparations with a smile, beginning with two weeks in November, which he spends escorting his little party from Brest to Paris by the road, or rather cowpath, of Guingamp and Rennes. Even in Martinique the roads can't be any worse than this: some days the "well-reconditioned cabriolet" purchased in Brest for forty louis* settles up to its axles in mud. Still with a smile, the fiancé pays the exorbitant bill for the trip: three thousand eight hundred livres.† Mme Renaudin takes charge of the trousseau, all the more willingly as it's being bought with the "Marquis" de Beauharnais's money: 20,672 livres.** In addition, she makes her niece a present (keeping use of it for herself during her lifetime) of her little country house at Noisy-le-Grand, "a sort of weekend cottage, where the wedding takes place as though in secret"[21] on December 13, 1779. Yet it isn't far from Paris—just beyond Vincennes and Nogent on the edge of Brie—and the "weekend cottage" stands "in a very pleasant situation on a hill overlooking the left bank of the Marne."[22] Even so, there aren't many people in the little thirteenth-century church‡ where a distant Tascher cousin, "prior of St. Gauburge," utters the blessing that makes Yéyette into "the high and potent Lady Marie-Josèphe-

*4,000 new francs [$800].

†Nearly 18,000 new francs [$3,600]! But that includes the cost of the vehicle.

**Approximately 100,000 new francs [$20,000].

‡Now hideously replastered and restored.

Rose, Vicomtesse de Beauharnais." The people of the Court and the great
nobles know nothing of this marriage of parvenus, which was far more authen-
tically solemnized by the notary on December 10 in the Beauharnais's Parisian
town house.

Final formality: the wedding night. Rose finds what she was expecting.
Alexandre finds a surprise, about which he says nothing at the time: his wife
is not a virgin. Is anybody ever a virgin in the Islands? The Taschers "gave
a dance" during the last carnival for Admiral d'Estaing's hundred and fifty
officers. Among them was one handsome nineteen-year-old lieutenant, Scipion
du Roure. But a certain Tercier, captain in the Martinique regiment, was also
a frequent caller at La Pagerie.* Why try to find out? Does Rose herself know?
Next morning Alexandre de Beauharnais stretches gentility to the point of
silence, and decides not to make a fuss. There are extenuating circumstances:
"She had the prettiest little cunt in the world," her second husband later
says.[23] She teaches the man now marveling over it to compare her private
landscape with that of the "Trois-Islets of Martinique."

31

FEBRUARY 1780

Some Indefinable Presentiments

Roland and Manon Phlipon break up on September 28, 1779. They get
married on February 4, 1780, in the Church of St. Barthélemy de la Cité.
Proof that we must never give up hope about anything. But they reach the altar
as though bloodied by a long premature conjugal quarrel. Marriages are often
ugly. What can be said of this one?

She said yes on May 6, or at least she wrote it, since he was in Amiens
and she in Paris; and their indictment and trial of each other, which they
conduct in the form of a spate of love letters, is drawn out by the rhythm of
the post: two, three days for an answer. On May 9 he is apparently exultant:
"You are mine, you have sworn it; the oath is irrevocable . . . I am seeing to
your home [a house he meant to rent on the Rue du Collège]. Imagine, you

*He becomes a Vendéen general and boasts of this exploit—but during the Empire. [The
Vendée is a region on the west coast of France; during the Revolution the name was given to
royalist counterrevolutionaries from those provinces.—*Trans.*]

will be living in it within the year . . . I should like for everything to be settled between mid-August and mid-September." So it looks as though he's made up his mind to plunge ahead. The wedding this summer. But then why, in the same breath, ask Manon for another yes? "Above all, I should like, on your part, the most inviolable secrecy, and that no friendship whatever should share in it. Do you promise me? Say *yes* [his italics] and I shall be at peace."[1] In other words, we're engaged, but only before God. Not a word to the Cannet sisters (whom he himself is seeing weekly) or to old Phlipon. Roland, on his side, will say nothing to his mother or brothers. What's the point of this clandestinity? They're both legally of age, masters of their acts and possessions, and nothing "bad" has transpired between them, that's for sure! But she is a poor girl, and that's what he's ashamed of. She was expecting this, she had loyally warned him off, and in fact it was one of the reasons for her resistance.

He thinks it essential to wait. For years his people in Villefranche have been pressuring him to marry money; he's the only one of the boys who has not gone into the Church. The sole heir of the Roland de La Platières. He has countered them with inertia. But he hasn't got the guts to tell them straight out that he's marrying the dowerless daughter of a Parisian engraver. So let's wait. What for? For the Holy Spirit to break the news? He hasn't a clue. We'll see. She being no fool, the restriction hurts her. But she plays the game: "You can write me safely as before: I am the one who usually takes in the mail; in the other case [when her father does it], the Amiens stamp would make it seem that it was the sisters writing."

At twenty-five she has to go pussyfooting around as though she were fifteen. And their correspondence degenerates into swamps of molasses. This is the girl who used to write such dense, full letters to her girl friends: you'd think she'd been lobotomized. She becomes hollow, cloying, boring; she modulates into his key. He talks about nothing but himself, so she goes him one better. The yellowed sheaf recording this dismal betrothal forms a volume of three hundred pages, devoted chiefly to the excesses of bile and the colics of Jean-Marie Roland. The war with England, the revolution in America, literature and the arts, their readings—almost totally absent. A lugubrious tête-à-tête.

They go gaga over their plans: "I like to think of myself near you, busy with the duties that will fall to my lot, participating in all your affections and always striving to make them agreeable; going out seldom or else with you, because no place will be so pleasant to me as your house and no presence will equal yours . . . You will enlighten me, I shall think with your ideas, I shall become more worthy and shall love you the better for it, if that is possible" (from her to him, May 11). And from him to her, on the 15: "I did tell you I was dealing with the matter of your home; I have just settled it; I visualize you in it, I see you everywhere . . . But I shall hardly alter it, my friend; that will be your side of things. I have no gift for these matters, and scarcely time to devote to them. It will be the hut of Philemon and Baucis."* Answer: "It matters little whether the dwelling in which I live with you be hut or temple. Wherever we are together, tenderness and honor will have altars and worshippers." In the best style of Rousseau's children. But on his side mixed with complaints from the start.

And what a silly goose she is, with her compulsive yackety-yack! Her barely begun flirtation with Sévelinges, the "old man" from Soissons, is weighing on her conscience. She can't wait to send Roland all the letters she's ever received from him. In return, he sends her a piece of his mind, on May 15: "My jaw dropped and I was completely at a loss. [How could you] not detect such a wavering, weak, inconsistent and false spirit? [How could you] believe him, be duped by him, acknowledge him . . . give him a special place among men?" If she dares to counterattack, reminding him that he himself was rather pushing things the previous winter, he instantly flies into a temper. On June 12: "Good God! my friend,† in what ink have you dipped your own pen? How stiff you are! How you indulge in overdoing things in all directions! . . ."

Thereupon, enter a twenty-year-old apprentice engraver, lovelorn and intense. Not only does he run father Phlipon's print shop, but since Mignonne's death he has also been keeping the house together, doing the shopping, cooking, and heavy cleaning. A nice little man-of-all-work, whose heartwarming zeal comes from the fact that he gazes at Manon with the same eyes that Restif de La Bretonne, another apprentice, turned upon "Mme Parangon," his master-printer's wife, in Auxerre. This time it's the boss's daughter but, as in the case of Restif, she is at once inaccessible and provocative. She treats the boy with exasperating angelicism: "I have found attentive and diligent helpers in our pupils, particularly the oldest, L.F.;** his good heart and devotion to the house became clearly apparent in this circumstance [Mignonne's last illness]. Pressed by work, up at four in the morning to finish it, he nevertheless contrived to find free moments in order to share my burden . . . More eager than ever to have my advice and instruction, he was constantly applying to me. His questions always had to do with manners and morals, and always referred to his own situation . . ." A twenty-five-year-old professor, with such milkwhite skin so skimpily covered: what agony, what ecstasy! He falls sick in turn, poor thing, sick for her: "He distresses me terribly. I sit up with him every night. He is frightfully weak. Nothing seems good to him but what I give him and

---

*Heroes of a Greek mythological fable of lasting love and conjugal fidelity.

†On both sides we find at least six "good Gods" in three months.

**He is never identified except by his initials or phrases such as "the young man," "the apprentice," etc. (The engraving studio on the Place Dauphine employed Phlipon and two apprentices.)

what I want . . . He weeps and frets like a child sometimes; his mind and body both need my care."[2] When will she ever learn? Some kinds of care are enough to kill a man: "L.F. is so grieved sometimes that he loses his rest and his appetite. His manner frightens me. I am very much afraid I have harmed him by nursing him too well."[3] He might have pulled through, though, if the *povero giovane,* as she calls him, hadn't been the first to scent her engagement, with the sixth sense of a thwarted lover. Off he goes, having moods and making scenes of jealousy. Instead of dealing with them on her own she waves this little picture in front of Roland's eyes, and he instantly begins to dramatize: "The jealous person who observed us sticks in my mind more than I would have thought possible, more than I can tell." And yet she's perfectly prepared either to offload this inconvenient wreck or continue exploiting him, even if it means his ultimate ruination: "Obliged to feed and board himself at his own expense, having no more fixed wages, paid only for piecework or by the day, depending on the work, having acquired neither knowledge nor skills, he will of necessity be debt-ridden, at least for a time; there is every reason to fear that anxiety, impatience, his ailing head, and need will turn him into an out-and-out libertine or a soldier [*sic*] within six months." One more dog run down in the gutter of time, like all the other apprentices who haven't pleased their employers well enough to be taken on as partners. This one goes mad with heartbreak. "This morning [June 1] he had a fit of despair from which I feared the most dreadful consequences; I saw the storm coming; I kept a close watch over him and by good fortune stopped him in a moment of rage when he had armed himself with a knife and was about to turn it against himself. I held both his hands for over a quarter of an hour, alternating gentle exhortations and stern rebukes to suit the expressions I saw in his face." " 'I want to master my sorrow,' he told me the day before yesterday [June 4]. 'I mean to look elsewhere, and find enough work to pay for my keep. As soon as I have met that object, I shall not take any more money from here [from Phlipon] and shall go on working here as before, for my food, without anything else. But if you leave,' he added with a resolute and moody look, 'I do not answer for myself . . . Besides, if I must be utterly unhappy, I will not be so for long.' " On June 19, "waves of grief and impatience frequently drive him to resolutions whose effects I can only prevent through sheer cunning and care. His health is failing. He must soon fall ill, or die, or go mad. He is already all three in part"—and Roland, on the other end of the wire, laps it up—Roland who's been fighting for apprentices' rights for so many years from Lodève to Picardy. But this time a *particular* apprentice is involved. It's easy to labor for the happiness of mankind in the abstract, as long as you don't have to lumber yourself with the unhappiness of just one man. And this one really goes too far. By the end of July L.F. has worked himself into such a state that he's talking about setting off for Amiens to stick a knife in Roland's back. She tries to calm

him with floods of good words, but the shorthand version of the melodrama
in her letters only succeeds in throwing Roland into a panic. He takes the
threat quite seriously: "I cannot contemplate the premeditated design of assassination without some feeling of horror, and should find no pleasure in being
dogged by that fear. Could you believe that if business called me to Paris just
now, I should need to endure the fear of this assassination; should I not rather
peremptorily lay the matter before the prosecuting attorney?" In that case the
fate of her rabid young man would be worse than poverty: it would be a cell
in the Bicêtre. Manon puts on the brakes. Maybe she begins to think she's said
too much. On July 22: "We can breathe again, my friend. It will be over. It
is over. I shall be able to tell you, with my august air and my big square phrases,
that your friend can manufacture heroes, but not monsters." She's certain her
good words have averted the crisis. "He is and will remain what he ought
to be; ashamed of his transports, filled with the desire to efface the very memory of them, anxious to gain my respect, unable to bear the thought of
being deprived of it . . . He no longer sees me as anything but another man's
wife, yours. His respect and consideration will be transferred to you; I want
him to love you, to stay with my father after I leave, and be a son and a support to him." Roland gets no thrills, however, from these pleas from a lawyer who has begun warming to her client: "No; a man who has lived an honest
life until the age of twenty-three does not become a scoundrel overnight.
A good nature, which I have observed for eight years to be obedient to the
voice of reason, affected by good examples, and quick to follow them, is not
destroyed in an instant." And later [on September 24], when they're on the
verge of breaking up and wallowing in bitterness, she mentions L.F. once
more, just to rub a little salt in the wound: "Oh my friend, how one loves
at twenty! . . ."

But the "poor young man" is a mere ripple on the surface of the real subject
of their dispute: Phlipon senior. Nothing can be settled until he's been spoken
to; and Roland keeps putting it off, all through May and June. His silence
becomes a sort of provocation. Battle is joined in three windowless cells
between the unconscious minds of three people. There are only two real men
in Manon's life, ones it's a question of living with—her father until now and
Roland henceforward; and in a case like this, a jealous nature is always more
likely to resent the father than a rival suitor. Also, however comfortably
Roland may still be basking in his bachelorhood, Manon can't wait another
minute. She nudges him gently two or three times in May. Would it be all right
for her to begin preparing her father, little by little? On May 31 Roland flares
up: "Sensitive persons are suspicious and mistrustful, my friend. The happiness
of beautiful souls cannot be achieved without a few cruel strokes. But one must
never be unfair, and you already are so to me." What's really getting under

his skin is what he calls her "sensibility," the vibrato that makes her raise the tone a little, whatever she may be talking about. "You depict your walk in the Luxembourg in a most interesting manner. However, your soul became too morbidly exalted. I don't know why, but somber forebodings trouble it all too often . . . I should like to see your soul more at peace, your heart more contented, your pleasures more moderate." It's all very well for him to talk, and in a letter: he's fifty leagues away and he adores his job, whereas she's bored to extinction in the middle of a tunnel. Some pleasures! But what kind of crazy girl is this, who absolutely cannot keep her mouth shut about anything she experiences? She doesn't "hold" herself very well, this Manon Phlipon, in the literal sense of the word—to hold in, to contain: She doesn't obey the law of the constipated, who'd like to see men harnessed like horses. Between a querulous fiancé and an offended father, she can't be as she must be—i.e., totally discreet. Roland gives his side of the story on July 25. "How you fly from one mood to another, both physical and moral! It is one of the things that amazes me most. I confess that I should not know how to abandon myself to extremes so swiftly; especially as you accompany it all with ample dissertations on causes and effects, means and results, the probable and the certain, good and evil, well and ill, fair and ugly, strong and weak, hot and cold, great and small, etc., etc., etc., etc., etc., etc., etc.,* and with phrases, not merely square as you call them, but faceted all round,† circular, pointed, long and short . . ." These texts are known as "Roland's love letters to Manon Phlipon" . . . one would be tempted to call them preliminary evidence in a divorce suit. The poor man's liver can't stand the constant stress. But what's the point of going to treat it for two weeks in the mud baths of Saint-Amand-les-Eaux in Flanders, only to come back to letters from "his dear friend" whose "tone has radically reduced the good disposition [that is, improved health] I was bringing back from my trip? It would not be desirable for me to receive many of that sort. In all likelihood I shall not forget this one for the rest of my life." Roland isn't in love with this girl. He desires her, he's afraid of her, she disconcerts him, so in an attempt to force himself to despise her he concentrates all his venom on Manon's weak point: that father whose failings she was imprudent enough to reveal to him, and even embellish upon. She defends herself as best she can, with dignity: "My family, common and obscure for the most part, carries no stain that spreads as far as myself; my fortune, now reduced to nothing owing to my obligation to help my father, and very narrow at the best of times, but which could become a little something, after all, creates no difficulty for the considerate man who could and would do without it"

---

*This isn't shorthand, it's sound effects: seven etceteras, not one less. A written translation of exasperation. Sounds like a musical crescendo.

†Of the divers aspects or points of view presented by things: "The tone of voice changes the facet of a discourse" (Pascal).

(September 11). These passing sermonettes won't go far toward unknotting Roland! She was alone before he came; now she's doubly alone, for her father obviously isn't going to give her any help.

"Today I was comparing my father as he is now [June 9; letter to Roland —the tactless creature!], gloomy, taciturn, chilling, repellent,* with that father of old, who nearly idolized his daughter . . ." "He seems unable to bear his house, or my presence. He does not eat at home anymore, will not look at me, and tells everybody except me that he wants to be alone and live like a single man" (June 10). She keeps on supplying Roland with ammunition. She realizes it too late—on June 27, when she thinks everything's been fixed up through the good offices of one of those gossipy female cousins people always have up their sleeve for such circumstances, a Mademoiselle Desportes who was instructed to sound out Phlipon senior. "Kiss my letter, tremble for joy; my father is pleased, he esteems you, he cherishes me; we shall all be happy. Peace, salvation, friendship, and joy reign on the face of the earth. If you knew how we embraced, how this poor heart was throbbing with pain, tenderness, fear and delight! Ah, how I wept! My good father loves me so much that he cannot help himself. Nature has strong roots in the hearts of fathers!" Right. Has that done it, is everything OK? All we need now is a letter from Roland to M. Phlipon, the ultimate formality . . . She gets a cold shower, in the caddish vein: "I am delighted with your contentment. And if I put less of the enthusiasm that does honor to your heart into this business which concerns it so nearly, it is because I despaired less than you." Now, with his back to the wall, he tries to shrink still farther away, he goes on beating around the bush. In the normal course of events it would be for him to "ask for her hand" and Phlipon to bestow it. He claims it's the other way around. But has any father ever been known to *offer* his daughter's hand to a man he hardly knows? Now it's Phlipon's turn to shy away. On August 9, however, urged on by his daughter, he takes the plunge. Roland finds his letter standoffish and replies in kind. They start looking for a quarrel. Between two turkey cocks, one quivering young woman. "All I obtain [from my father] is harsh, even humiliating words, added to the eternal refrain that we might have let him into the secret months ago . . ." In August the tension becomes unbearable, every word scalds one or the other. On September 3 she's had enough: "You appear not to be attached to our plans any longer, save out of kindness to me and determination to keep your word." She offers it back to him. Roland, as when faced with a resolution of any sort, panics afresh. "Your father has not answered me [on September 4]. His tone, his statements, his pretexts irritate me. Could I ever have suspected such a flagrant affront? . . . I would not have believed he could be so insensitive, so hard, so cruel, so inconsistent." The

---

*In the sense of "hostile, who repels me."

next day he receives Phlipon's "consent," in the form of an insult: "You have done me the honor, Mr.,* of writing to me: I must have that of replying . . ." He demands that Manon show him the letters she has received from Roland. She refuses. "This, I regret to say, has forced me to tell you that she is free to make full use of her privilege, as a woman who has come of age, to bring this matter to a speedy conclusion."⁴ Roland chokes. With anger? No doubt. But maybe with relief too. His commentary is a release; now his kicks are no longer aimed at Phlipon, but directly at her. What proud girl would stand to hear her father spoken of in such terms? "Seizing upon so false and, I dare say it, so stupid a pretext† reveals a soul that makes me shudder; a man who, dishonoring himself by the ignominy of his character, would commit such an act solely in order to distress someone who would be shamed by his behavior." He adopts the same tone in his reply to "this insensitive, unjust, false, depraved man, incapable of decent response." It's lucky for Manon they're commoners: if they were noble they'd have to slit each other's throats. She feels the partitions of her life closing back in upon her. "I slept three hours [on September 3]. Am I any the better for it? I have only recovered strength enough to suffer more." The wedding? Forget it. Yet she can't, after this, she really can't go on growing old in her father's house. Suicide? She contemplates it long enough to pull up with a start: "From a hiding place near my bed I withdrew, grasped, and threw out of my window a little flask of aqua fortis** which I had procured for another purpose." Roland is unmoved: the ideal egotist, it only makes him moan the more: "Good God, what a state you put your soul in! . . . And I who was relying upon it to calm my own, to soften its harshness, sweeten its bitterness!"

After a long letter in which she puts Roland in his place (on September 11) and tallies the score card of her own errors, she opts for the convent. She exposed herself too readily, she says, but she doesn't regret it: "My attachment and frankness, in portraying myself so openly, showed you the companion who could beautify your days by uniting herself to you . . . It seems I was not steadfast enough for your liking, in the hopes on which I fed, but my experience of misfortune must needs shroud them in some indefinable presentiments . . . I see you fearing, hesitant, ready to repent of your decision; my duty is written in black and terrifying letters but I obey it intrepidly, I release you and immolate myself." As for her father, "he has fewer vices than inconsistencies." Now conscious of having shoved him down Roland's throat, she defends him

---

*Verbatim: "Even the Mr., abridged in that way, is remarkable," acidly observes Roland. [*M.* was the usual abbreviation, although *Mr.* occurs; but in any case the insult lies in abbreviating at all.—*Trans.*]

†As the communication of their correspondence.

**Dilute nitric acid. She would have no trouble getting hold of it, as engravers use it to etch the copper plates called *eaux-fortes.*

—belatedly indeed, but nobly: "Is he different today from what he was, and what I portrayed to you, but a short while ago? How you weight his image! Ah, it is enough that his shortcomings and faults are my torment, and conflict with the ties you forced me to accept; lift your thick black pencil, do not bear down so hard upon his daughter. His conduct is unsettled, he has a narrow, harsh soul and a crabbed mind; five or six of his relatives, who know how ill he has managed his life, have no love for him and little respect; a good many people are not unaware that he has had and may still have a mistress; the public suspects that he is not so rich as it had liked to suppose him: but after all, he is not a marked, dishonored, or contemnèd man, he has done nothing to become such, and is generally looked upon as an honest artist who still plies his trade to increase his resources or provide for his amusements. A thousand others do as he does; a thousand more do so with as little tact and even probity; and those among them who know how to gloss it over with a veneer of good manners or the appearance of a better condition and more considerable remnants of fortune are smiled upon and forgiven."

Phlipon himself writes another letter, on September 23, which might have made everything all right if it hadn't come too late, as in a Molière comedy; in it, moreover, he adopts the tone of some chummy Chrysale* with an abundance of common sense and a flair for repartee: "I frankly acknowledge that my first letter was anything but pleasant . . . But you must acknowledge in return that your reply smacks of insult in more than one place. But let it be said in two words: you forget the one and I shall not remember the other . . . Do with my letter as I do with yours: throw it into the fire. Such letters should be cut to shreds . . . If it is not too late, I give you my consent and approval with complete satisfaction and absolute pleasure. I approve of you with the best of my heart; I should be perfectly easy in my mind about the fate of my child, if this business can be completed." There's even a rather neat little cuff in passing: "If you have seen any qualities in her which can be to your liking, I am the more highly flattered as I believe you to be a connoisseur . . . So now, Monsieur, everything depends upon you, so true it is that a remedy can be found for every ill but death."[5]

The door's still ajar, then, but Roland makes no move to wedge it open. Still in the wash of his first wrath, he breaks off on September 28: "This letter from your father is as thoughtless as the previous one. It proves that one can place little confidence in such a man . . . I believed in happiness, it is a chimera . . . I told you before that I meant to bury myself in my work; that was a plan, now it is a necessity."

*The down-to-earth husband in the *Femmes Savantes,* surrounded by uppish females. [*Trans.*]

She can take no more of these men. On November 6, 1779, she retires, as boarder, to the convent of the congregation of Augustines of Notre Dame, Rue Neuve Saint-Etienne* in the faubourg Saint-Marcel, where she spent a rather pleasant year as a child in 1765. Still in Paris, but already near the fields, lots of gardens, a fountain, and tall trees. There she first met the Cannet sisters, during her little mystical crisis. She hunts for traces of her twelve-year-old girlhood, and finds her dear Sister Sainte-Agathe (who has fortunately been assigned to the boarders, for whom she is a sort of maid-of-all-work); the tender-hearted nun had virtually fallen in love with Manon fifteen years before and would like nothing better than to do it again.† "There exist souls that have no need of cultivation. Nature kneaded hers in sulfur and saltpeter;** the energy thus held in check within her elevated the sensitivity of her heart and vivacity of her mind to a supreme degree . . . With very little help from education, she was superior not only to her companions [the other lay sisters] but to most of the ladies of the choir . . . [During my first stay there] she would secretly try to find out the things I liked best and see that I had them; in the room, it gave her joy to make my bed . . . She embraced me tenderly, and sometimes took me to her cell, where she kept a charming, friendly, sweet canary which she had taught to speak; she secretly gave me a second key to that cell, so that I might go there when she was away . . . I [often] found a little note for me, very tender, and never failed to answer; she kept those answers like precious jewels, and showed them to me later, carefully locked in her oratory. Soon, the only subject of conversation in the convent was Agathe's affection for the little Phlipon,"[6] an affection which survived fifteen years of separation. "My Agathe used to write me tender letters from time to time, whose tones, peculiar to those cooing doves who may not allow themselves to venture beyond friendship, were still further intensified in her by her ardent soul; little boxes, pretty skeins and sweets came with them."[7] There's one person, anyway, who won't fail her. This Christmastide of 1779, the Christmas of the naked heart, Manon Phlipon feels as though Sister Sainte-Agathe is all she has left—like the first milestone on the long road of an old maid's life.[8]

She moves in as though she were going to stay forever. "I could provide some most piquant details of this condition, in which I began to consume the resources of a strong character. I calculated my expenses to a hair, setting

*On the site of the present Rue Rollin, near the Rue Monge.

†Sister Sainte-Agathe was born in 1741 and took the vows in 1758. Born Angélique Boufflers (no relation to the aristocratic family of that name), "the want of a dowry relegated her to a place among the lay sisters."

**This image is a favorite with Manon: we find her using it in reference to Sainte-Lette on p. 103.

something aside for gifts to the people who serve in the house. Potatoes, rice, beans, cooked in a pot with a few grains of salt and a bit of butter, varied my menu and formed my regular fare without requiring a great deal of time.

"I went out twice each week: once to visit my grandparents, and the other time to see my father, look after his laundry, take away what needed mending. The rest of the time, shut in under my roof of snow, as I called it, for I lived on a high floor and it was winter, and not wishing to spend all my days in the company of the other boarders, I devoted myself to study, I fortified my heart against adversity; by seeking to deserve happiness, I avenged myself upon fate that would not give it to me. Every evening, the delicate Agathe came to sit with me for half an hour; the sweet tears of friendship accompanied the effusions of her heart. A turn around the garden, after everyone else had gone in, was my solitary exercise . . . I was not always free from melancholy, but it had its charms; and if I was not quite happy, yet I had within me everything I needed to be so."⁹

But those who always expect the worst are occasionally disappointed. "M. Roland, surprised and pained, continued writing to me as a man who had not ceased to love me, but who had been injured by my father's behavior. He came, after five or six months, and became inflamed upon catching sight of me at the grill"—on January 12, 1780, precisely: after two months, that is, not five or six. Judging from Manon's memory, one might suggest that time lay heavy on the hands of the Augustines' boarder no matter what she says.¹⁰

Their story is, like themselves, riddled with contradictions. Almost the moment they break up, they start writing each other letters reeking of nostalgia. She throws herself into it heart and soul: "I am always burning to receive them, those heartrending letters which I devour and which kill me. I cover them with kisses and tears. Their words drive me to despair, yet I cherish the hand that wrote them no less. I want to believe that mine, dictated by a distracted mind, betrayed me when they caused you sorrow. Ah, my heart was not made to steep yours in bitterness . . ." (December 4). Now he can't take any more, either. Poor Romeo! "Your letters, my friend, found me in a revolution of bile such as I have never known before, for I vomited it up pure, although I had taken nothing to cause this . . . I feel most uncomfortable and, although now purged, my stomach is in a wretched condition; I have got the flux,* can hardly digest, and am very yellowish" (December 10). He drags himself to the Hôtel de Lyon at the bottom of the Rue Saint-Jacques, in other words to the neighborhood of the convent of "his friend"—whom he now sees for the first time since that Yes-and-No stretched out over months of letter writing. Meanwhile, a helpful Benedictine, Pierre, one of Roland's

*Colic.

brothers,* proves to be a master of reconciliation. At last a Roland who doesn't look down his nose at her! He even becomes her ally. He tames Phlipon senior. Manon finds him "a man of intelligence, sweet ways and an amiable nature . . . He preached freedom in his parish as he practiced the evangelical virtues there; a lawyer and doctor to his parishioners, too wise to be a monk,"[11] he undertakes to cure this couple of their congenital idiocy. On January 12 they see each other, really *see* each other at last, on opposite sides of the parlor grill which the nuns impose upon even their boarders.

From Roland the following day: "Triumph in your retirement, my friend! What is this empire you have over me, and into what a state have you cast me!" On January 21 the Benedictine offers to make the "official" motions between them, and between them and Phlipon senior. Roland even achieves simplicity: "Let us not manufacture monsters for the sheer pleasure of doing battle with them . . . My friend, my dear friend! I shall see you on Sunday. Do not give me sorrow; you have had too much of it." Now that everybody's happy, there's no more reason to dawdle. In those days, once a marriage was decided upon it could take place almost immediately. And the approach of Lent was another cause for haste. On the morning after the wedding celebrated in the Phlipons' parish church, the one in which Manon, now Mme Roland at last, was baptized twenty-five years ago, Roland fires off a round of hastily scribbled announcements. "Do not be angry with me for not telling you before. Everything was settled, arranged, and decided in five or six days, and my friends, like my relatives for that matter, knew no more about it . . . My present address is in care of M. Phlipon, Rue de Harlay, near the Palace [of Justice], Paris."

There Manon spends her first night as a woman, in the scene of her hothouse childhood, a few feet away from her father. The notion of a honeymoon hardly existed. And the next day Roland has work to do in Paris, people to see in offices, clerks to badger. "I did not hide from myself the fact that a man less than forty-five years old would not have waited several months to bring me to change my mind, and I openly avow that this very thing had diminished my sentiments to a degree that left no margin for illusion . . . In the end, if marriage was, as I supposed, a severe bond, an association in which it is the woman, as a rule, who contracts to provide the happiness of two individuals, was it not preferable, even so, to employ my faculties, my courage, in this honorable task, rather than to remain in isolation?"[12]

---

*Dom Roland (1732–1789), of the congregation of Cluny, was then prior of a little monastery at Ozay and priest of the nearby village, Longpont, close to Paris.

32

APRIL 1780

The Years I Have Lost

On the first day of 1780 Vergniaud is at his wit's end. He too has had all he can take, and at twenty-six. "I am a burden to myself. I am crippled by a melancholy that deprives me of the use of my faculties. However I try to conceal it from the eyes of those I see, it is always there. I laugh by convulsions [*sic*] and my heart seldom shares the false joy painted upon my face."[1] It is to his brother-in-law and benefactor, François Alluaud, that he's opening this heart withered by a long youth spent in a cul-de-sac. Here's another boy being shunted back and forth between Church and law without much notion how or why.

The cause of his misfortune is lack of money. At this point he's still contemplating the priesthood—like contemplating suicide. One word from his family back in Limoges would be enough to push him over the edge . . . His New Year's letter is an appeal to them to decide for him. He can't bring himself to do it on his own. But if they "do their duty" there will be an Abbé Vergniaud:

> My dear brother [Alluaud],
>
> Here is a new year. I hope it will be a time of happiness for you, for my sister and for all your family. As for me, I have little hope of that [being happy], but I shall at least be comforted to learn that you are. Thoughts of the years I have lost and cannot tell how, always led on by hopes that have never come to aught, run continually through my mind and add much to the cruelty of the situation in which I have been for some time. If I believed the ecclesiastical condition could procure a life I cannot obtain by any other means, I should return to it, and do not think this is inconsistency. I entered it the first time without knowing what I was doing; I abandoned it because I did not care for it, and shall return to it only out of necessity. I am writing to my father today. His advice and yours will determine me. If it were possible to earn my living in some other way, I should prefer that, no doubt, but my way lies before me and all I await is an answer from my father and from you.
>
> *Paris, January 1, 1780.*[2]

Him, a priest? They can't let him do that, he's too handsome, and the girls are so fond of him! None of your sissified good looks: more plebian than aristocratic, with rather heavy features, coarsely carved, but on him they look good. An expression too full of candor to be smug. Of average height, "robust and square in stature," he has "a short, broad nose with proudly flaring nostrils; his rather thick lips firmly outline his mouth."* Later, people will observe "that they were shaped to spout vast streams of words," but that's not why the girls of Paris are eyeing them today. He exudes a healthy sensuality. "His dark glittering eyes seemed to leap out from under prominent brows. His broad, flat forehead had that glow of a mirror in which intelligence is reflected; his brown hair fell in waves when he tossed his head . . . The skin of his face was pock-marked . . . His pallor was that of deep emotions. In repose, no one would have noticed this man in a crowd. He would have been taken for any ordinary man, neither offending nor arresting the gaze."³ Which is exactly what happens to him in the Limoges stagecoach he boards one morning in February 1780, carrying a bundle that weighs not an ounce more than his ten years in Paris, bye-bye, big city; in forty-eight stages the winter road draws a long line of hyphens across half a failed life. What will the other half be? Nobody would bet a plugged nickel on it. But after all, the Alluauds are decent people, even if his father is poor. The family will buck him up a little and try to find some less desperate solution. Back home, it'll all come right.

Thanks to François Alluaud, Vergniaud will just manage to scrape into the law. And in doing so, this Limousin will become a Bordeaux transplant, that is, a Girondin.†

"On the thirty-first day of May one thousand seven hundred and fifty there was baptized in this chursh** Pierre Viturnien son of Pierre Verniau and of Catherine Baubiat his Wife, born that same day‡ on the rue du clocher.

"Godfather, Pierre Viturnien Dassier sometime clerk at the Office of Finance in Limoges and godmother, demoiselle Catherine Baubiat who sign with me Lageneste, parish priest."⁴

Mass must have been a treat at St. Michel des Lions if this cleric was as

---

*According to Lamartine, who made inquiries of his nephew François Alluaud, the son of the one Vergniaud is writing to in 1780. Lamartine also saw the best portrait of Vergniaud as a youth: a medallion by François Dumont, now in the museum of ancient art in Bordeaux.

†Member of the moderate republican party in the French legislative assembly of 1791; they were called Girondins because their leaders were representatives of the département of Gironde, which includes the town of Bordeaux. [*Trans.*]

**Thus the quaint spelling of the "Register for use at baptisms, marriages and funerals in the parish of St. Michel des Lions, Limoges." "Verniau" is only one of the scribe's errors; the entry for February 3, 1750, gives the correct form, Vergniaud, for the marriage of his parents.

‡Or forty years to the day before the beginning of the collapse of the Girondins, on May 31, 1793.

handy with his Latin as he was with the vernacular. The godfather's real name was Pierre-Victurnien (not Viturnien) Dachès (not Dassier). He was the brother of Marie Dachès, the infant's paternal grandmother, and the god-mother was the sister of his maternal grandfather. That weird name of Victur-nien (a Limousin deformation of Victorien?) doesn't stick to Vergniaud, who always insists, contrary to the custom of the time, on being called by his first Christian name, Pierre.

Not a trace of nobility. On his parents' marriage certificate three years earlier, his father was identified as "aged approximately thirty, bourgeois and merchant of this town," and his mother as "daughter of Pierre Baubiat, bourgeois of this town."[5] Both families had been settled in Limoges for several generations, and in the same parish of St. Michel des Lions. Vergniaud was born almost on the doorstep of the old church which tourists of the day described as "half-Gothic, half-Arab [sic], but not finished."[6] The house he was born in* has a ground floor built of stone like all its neighbors, under two stories of "wood daubed with plaster" [half-timbering, in other words] sur-mounted by a steep roof. Embedded in the white and gray block of streets lined with little shops by which his childhood is circumscribed, like that of Manon Phlipon by the Place Dauphine, it, too, neither "offends nor arrests" the gaze. The only difference is that "the streets of Limoges are crooked, narrow, and sloping." But the bourgeois's town which has grown up around the edges of the sleepy old episcopal center is bursting through the ramparts, and Pierre-Victurnien could easily toddle out to "the exterior of the town, planted everywhere with fine rows of ashes affording excellent shade. Indeed, there are several far newer squares [in 1780] outside the walls than within the town; these are large and quite well built."[7]

In theory, little Vergniaud might have swum like a minnow in the stream of fifteen or twenty thousand souls that comprises industrious and wealthy Limoges in the heart of a poor province, with its burghers looking down upon the peasants from very far above. Let them eat chestnuts. We, meanwhile, manufacture "all the commodities of ordinary life: hats, serge, Siamese, woolen goods, etc.," not to mention "porcelain made from the same paste as that of Sèvres,† for the earth of which Sèvres porcelain is formed is brought from a place ten leagues from here."[8] He heard people talking about it all day and every day, like shepherds about sheep or lumberjacks about felling trees. But their talk was cheerless, and here we find another similarity with Manon Phlipon's early years. Vergniaud senior dealt in provisions, especially forage, and supplied the regiments quartered in Limoges, a cavalry roundhouse from

---

*Unrecognizable, it still exists, at 10 Rue du Clocher (formerly no. 23), on the corner of the Rue Gaignolle in the heart of what has come to be known as "Old Limoges."

†The kaolin came from the vicinity of St. Yrieix. "Siamese" was a silk-and-cotton mixture that imitated the cloth presented to Louis XIV by the ambassadors of Siam.

which the king could dispatch horsemen into the Languedoc wastelands to hunt for heretics, or out to catch smugglers on the Spanish border. But the chronic drought of the sixties had gradually brought the "bourgeois and merchant" to the brink of ruin. The intendant of Limousin, a certain Turgot, had done his best to fight famine among the very poor by distributing handouts from the stockpiles, but, true to his noninterventionist principles, he let the market price of grain go sky high. In 1770 it leaped 50 percent. In 1771 "M. Vergniaud was unable to meet his commitments.* He divested himself of the capital at his free disposal, sold his property in the vicinity of Limoges, and retained, as his sole resource, four houses which formed the basis of his wife's fortune. The value of these houses was hardly equal to the amount of his outstanding debts."[9]

It's not pauperdom, but this shrinkage of his estate to the immovable dowry of the demoiselle Baubiat signs the death warrant of a business career and places the childhood of Pierre-Victurnien under the creeping shadow of want. He doesn't take much note of it so long as he's living at home, where he's never allowed to go without anything except possibly laughter. The good Abbé Roby, a Jesuit in disguise, comes to teach him his letters at home and gives him a taste for literature. Now, there was a scholar, a real one—the kind who knows how to make other people love what he loves: the abbé had translated the *Aeneid* into Limousin patois, and recites whole passages from it by the fireside in the evenings. Was it from him that Vergniaud caught the knack of turning speech into song? And at the collège in Limoges he's treated like a little lord, but that doesn't mean much. Then, in Paris, when he's about fifteen, the jaws of money snap shut behind him: the same trap that catches Robespierre, with the difference that Vergniaud's father is still alive, but what good does that do him?

Turgot, still in his Limousin days, gets him a scholarship to the du Plessis collège on the Rue Saint-Jacques, next to Louis-le-Grand where Robespierre, as it happens, is champing at the bit. They're neighbors in misfortune but not likely to rub elbows much: for want of sleeves to cover those elbows, neither ever goes out. Plessis-Sorbonne (where Alexandre de Beauharnais was to come a short time later) is stolid and dingy. Good classical studies. Twenty of the two hundred students are scholarship boys. They're not downtrodden; nor are they helped. Vergniaud emerges in 1775 without leaving a single trace of either reward or punishment in the record books. "No one would notice this man in a crowd . . ." What next? The law, the Church? The same old song. Like Brissot before him . . . and like Sieyes, Vergniaud attends the *petit séminaire* at St. Sulpice for two or three years, then pulls up short before the deaconate. He's not an atheist, but he hasn't a ghost of a vocation. So! So? In 1778, at

*According to a biographical note by François Alluaud junior.

the age of twenty-five, to have no *état?* Unclassifiable, Pierre-Victurnien? They always thought he didn't care what happened to him, but he was only putting up a front to hide his anxiety.

Luckily, he has an older sister who married, early and presumably happily, a Limoges dignitary considerably older than herself, to whom she gives a child a year. Good old François Alluaud, surveyor and engineer of bridges and roadways, treats his young brother-in-law like another son and sends him a louis or two with every post for pocket money; but above all, he gives him a sense that somewhere on earth there's a safe, solid place. He recommends him to another Limousin in Paris, a Monsieur d'Ailly, director of *vingtièmes* [a tax] in the general tax office. The freemasonry of "regional assistance" almost creates family-type obligations. Letter from Vergniaud to his brother-in-law, in November 1778: "M. d'Ailly has given me his word for an office in the Vingtièmes* . . . At this point I have no other wish but to be close to my family. M. d'Ailly was not able to promise me this, but told me he would do what he could."[10] He was escaping from priesthood into clerkdom. On January 3, 1779, a year before the great depression: "I hope I am about to embark upon a less mournful career than has been my lot thus far." But it was a forlorn hope. Vergniaud finds himself on a waiting list, like a nobleman's son waiting for a regiment. The promise is for an inheritance, a seat at a desk when its present incumbent eventually retires or dies. D'Ailly keeps Vergniaud in patience with a cynic's arguments: "I was hoping it would be at the beginning of this month but I shall probably be obliged to wait until the end. M. d'Ailly tells me that no one has died yet but that I should be patient, because this is a month of frost and somebody will assuredly go."[11] January, February, March . . . The Vingtièmes offices must have been well heated. The scribble-bottoms hold out. Spring, summer, fall, and Vergniaud isn't a step closer. Another year lost. He keeps track of the news, but as though he were on Sirius—more in order to have something besides himself to talk about, and without really going into it. "Successful delivery for the Queen, whose health improves steadily . . ."[12] "The Marquis de La Fayette has returned from America. He is said to have brought interesting news . . ."[13] The truth is that he's in no hurry to bury himself in paper work, and he isn't really pushing d'Ailly. He's waiting for something, a sign, a chance. He takes a little turn around a few bourgeois drawing rooms where Turgot's protection has earned him an entry—in particular that of the academician Thomas, a sententious but nice enough "poet," friend of *philosophes* and fashionable pundit. Vergniaud is also a rhymester, but nothing more. And is consequently applauded.

*That is, a job as "supernumerary" in the offices where the general register of this relatively new and as yet approximate tax was kept, amounting to a twentieth of the annual income of all landowners. D'Ailly, who got his job through Turgot, supervised the whole system in Paris; but if Vergniaud could hang on, he might hope for a real job in the Vingtièmes office at Limoges.

A ce bouquet charmant que pour toi l'on a fait
Je vois, gentille Eglé, qu'aujourd'hui c'est ta fête . . .[14]

[From that charming bouquet with which your fingers play,
I see, enchanting Eglé, that your birthday is today . . .]

He's bored out of his mind.

Does he also take a little turn in the tax offices, late in 1779? Is Vergniaud tax
collector for a term? When he calls for help, at any rate, he is one no longer.
Whatever happens, he doesn't let on to his family for several weeks that this
trail has petered out. Maybe he didn't pressure M. d'Ailly hard enough. Maybe
he was taken on and promptly taken off again, for incompetence. Alluaud
doesn't hold it against him, and turns the page to avoid a family crisis. "Vergniaud was unable to overcome the antipathy he quickly felt for this type of
occupation. Through his own fault, he lost an office which M. Dally [*sic*] had
obtained for him, and did not dare admit it to his father for fear of incurring
his displeasure. He invented some subterfuge as an excuse, and soon begged
his pardon for it."[15]

Confession. Recall. Return. Limoges.

"In the month of February 1780, Vergniaud left Paris, where he had lost much
precious time, and returned to his father's home with no *état,* and no idea what
would become of him.

"One morning his brother-in-law surprised him in the act of improvising
a speech. Astonished by the ease of his elocution:

" 'Whyever do you not become a lawyer?'*

" 'I should like nothing better! But how am I to live until I am able to
begin pleading?'

" 'I shall help you.'

"And this answer from his brother-in-law decided his future."[16]

François Alluaud was the deus ex machina at the decisive moment of
Vergniaud's life. *Lawyer:* the catalyst. Everything falls into place, even the
errors and miscalculations. He feels that he was born to plead, destined for it
from his mother's womb. His bags are soon packed.

Lawyer, but where? In Paris where he has drunk the dregs and where you can't
see the sidewalk for law clerks? No; he will begin his career in Bordeaux, the
big city whose weight and influence have long equaled those of Paris in
Limousin eyes. Their alternate capital. Bordeaux is only fifty leagues from

*The dialogue was repeated a hundred times in the family. François Alluaud junior could
say it off by heart during the Revolution.

Limoges. It's the region's door to the sea and trade. The Limousin district, moreover, comes under the Bordeaux Parliament, proudest in France along with Rennes and Paris, and its magistrates livened things up considerably ten years ago at the time of Maupeou.* They're the ones who judge all litigation around here. "Bordeaux was parliament country. Everywhere, the parliaments fed the seeds of resistance, and often created a spirit of contention against royalty. Bordeaux was a city of commerce. Freedom is favorable to commerce, which ultimately acquires a taste for it. Bordeaux was the colonial city, America's big ladder to France . . . And lastly, the soil of Bordeaux was earlier and more fully exposed to the rays of philosophy than was the center of France . . . Bordeaux was the country of Montaigne and Montesquieu, one [of whom] had freely plumbed the depths of religious dogma, and the other those of political institutions. President du Paty had since fomented enthusiasm for the new philosophy."17 It's a good thing for a young man to have a Mecca on his horizon; so Bordeaux takes the place of Paris in Vergniaud's landscape. And du Paty, the very man, President du Paty, the hero of the conflicts of 1770, Louis XV's prisoner at Pierre-en-Scize:†Vergniaud has actually met him, at the Thomases', of course—one of Turgot's gang. Humbly, from a respectful distance, he looked up to this "Roman from Guyenne," a man almost of his own generation, only seven years older and already a legend, the Malesherbes of Bordeaux, this one as lean as the other was broad, with a haggard look caused by overwork, and also, people said, by persecution. You don't forget a pallor like that. Vergniaud managed to capture du Paty's attention, perhaps because of the intensity of his admiration. And du Paty, rehabilitated by the recall of the parliaments, has just obtained—but not without a struggle, for the court has deigned to take an interest in this *philosophe*—an appointment as mortar president.** In this new lease on his twenty-five-year life, it is to du Paty that Vergniaud now runs, as to the Mohammed of his alternate Mecca.

Runs . . . well, sort of. "The Limousin roads have become splendid since M. Turgot was made intendant" and did away with the *corvée*. All along the highroad from Limoges to Périgueux, salaried roadmen "in uniform leather bonnets" are busy repairing the frost-damaged surfaces. But once out of Limousin, it's rocky the whole way. "All the passengers notice the line of demarcation."18 Even for a young man the trip becomes rather an ordeal, and Vergniaud expostulates: "The roads of Périgord are so fine and the coaches so well mounted that it took us thirteen hours, four horses, and a team of oxen to

---

*French chancellor who used strong-arm tactics in 1771 to deprive the overpowerful parliaments, especially that of Paris, of some of their rights. He later fell from power, and died in 1792. [*Trans.*]

†A state prison near Lyons where they also thought of putting Mirabeau.

**The mortar was the fur-lined hat worn by presidents of parliaments in the performance of their duties. The title was one of the highest in the judiciary.

go from Périgueux to Mussidan, that is to say, five stages, and a half . . .* I do not believe, my dear brother [Alluaud], that the roads in hell can be any worse than those in Périgord."[19]

They won't kill him. "After jolts that shook me to the entrails and bruised me everywhere, I finally reached Bordeaux without further mishap" on April 20, 1780. "The grand city of Bordeaux is matched by few others in the world, for commerce and beauty . . . One of the most fertile valleys in Europe; hills covered with what are perhaps the most productive vineyards in the world." He feels the same surge of release and joy as Brissot, five years before, escaping from Chartres to Paris. The springtime of a life meets the springtime of a city. "The entire country is one continuous village, gilded and fortified by a beneficent sun. Anyone who has not looked upon this animated scene has not known the best of France."[20] Of course, it won't all be cake. By May 6 "he has still found no situation with any attorney." He has taken a room in a boardinghouse for fifty livres a month.† But all is not lost as long as he still has du Paty to turn to. *He* won't let him down. And even more important, Vergniaud has gotten his second wind. He knows what he wants and where he's going. "Believe that I shall make every effort to deserve what you are doing for me [to his brother-in-law, of course] and to dispel the bad impression which my previous conduct may have given you of my abilities."[21]

FRANKLIN

33

APRIL 1780

I Did Love Her to Madness MME HELVÉTIUS

Benjamin Franklin will not wed Mme Helvétius. He is just shy of his seventy-fifth birthday, the adorable old satyr! April 1780 brings back to his mouth that bitter tang he thought he was finished with so long ago: the taste of the injured heart. That'll teach him to go playing lovesick adolescent.

But he's always known how to suffer like an epicurean, and you have to look very hard to detect any flaw in his good humor when, on this afternoon as on so many others, the Citizen of Two Worlds entertains his best friends for dinner, from two to six.

*Twenty-one miles.
†250 new francs [$50]!

En politique, il est grand	[In politics he is sublime
A table joyeux et franc	As table mate he is the prime
Tout en fondant un empire	He designs a new empire
Vous le voyez boire et rire	While you watch his glass rise
Grave et badin	higher
Tel est notre Benjamin.	Grave as churchman, merry as sin
	Such is this our Benjamin.]

"It was at one of those dinners, on I forget which birthday of his or anniversary of American liberty," that another master partyboy, Abbé Morellet, composes that ditty to the tune of *Camarades, lampons!*[1]

On ne combattit jamais	[No nobler cause was ever seen
Pour de plus grands intérêts	For any struggle that has been:
Ils veulent l'indépendance	To independence they aspire
Pour boire des vins de France	For of French wines they'd be the
C'est là le fin	buyer
Du projet de Benjamin . . .	And that's what lies beneath the
	skin
	Of this great scheme of Benjamin.]

They sing it over again, all six of them, at dessert after the footmen have been dismissed. The wine is so good, the food so fine at the old gentleman's table; and he knows so well how to season it with some of the wittiest conversation of the age, in his voice with the Boston accent that rolls out the puns like pebbles!

L'Anglais, sans humanité	[The English, quite inhumanly,
Voulait les réduire au thé	Tried to ration them to tea
Au grand chagrin	To the deeply felt chagrin
De leur frère Benjamin.	Of their brother Benjamin.]

The trills and crescendi of the pastoral ballad are executed by the fine voice of Cabanis, the most fashionable physician of the day, supported by the bass tones of the two priestly table companions, Morellet and de La Roche, and echoed by the landlords of the premises, the financier Le Ray de Chaumont and his young wife. Another woman, not so young but fresh and blooming at sixty, beats time with her bejeweled hand; that's "Minette" Helvétius, with the laughing eyes of eternal childhood, the Madonna of these miscreants: "Our Lady of Auteuil." She is very much aware that these fellows are singing for her—and that it's her fault if Franklin falls silent a little too often this evening and forgets to pick up the refrain whenever his shortsighted eyes come to rest on her. A man in love is always such a silly object, but how much sillier when he looks like a big wrinkled egg!

Si vous voyez nos héros	[When you see our heroes brave
Braver l'Anglais et les flots	Both English and the ocean wave
C'est pour faire à l'Amérique	It's only so th' Amerikines
Boire du vin catholique	Can come and drink our Catholic
Vin clair et fin	wines.
Comme l'aime Benjamin,	Wines true and clear but not too thin
	As savored by our Benjamin,]

those wines that sparkle in flagons and flutes, your very good health, my friends! Red and white claret, and some venerable vintages in the lot, champagne and "white sparkling," red Burgundy and sherry, to wash down the two main dishes of flesh and fowl (or big game), followed by "two dishes of entremets, two vegetable dishes and one of pastry, with hors d'oeuvre of butter, pickles, radishes, etc. Two plates of fruit for winter (four in summer), two of preserves, one of cheese, one of biscuits, one of bonbons.[2]

Ce n'est point mon sentiment	[I'd say it was a great disgrace
Qu'on fasse un débarquement	For us t'invade the blessed place.
Que faire de l'Angleterre?	We want England? Never fear!
On n'y boit que de la bière!	For all they ever drink is beer!
Fâcheux destin	And that's a sorry state to land in
Au dire de Benjamin.	According to our dear Benjamin.]

How far away it is here, that war he's accused of having instigated. Almost as far as Paris—a whole league or league and a half, and beginning to exude an unpleasant smell inside its loop of the gray Seine. Here, we're on the "mountain of Passy," with its invigorating air and "hot mineral baths, which Franklin took thrice weekly, and the delightful society which foregathered in the village in spring and summer,"[3] but which assembled on either side of Passy as well, on the two other hills that separate the Bois de Boulogne from the Seine and the Grenelle meadows: Chaillot and Auteuil. All those people "of goodly companie" who want to escape Paris but can't abide Versailles have found refuge here, between Scylla and Charybdis. A conspiracy of the easy life. The merry libertarians have only a few steps to take beyond the tall French windows to find themselves strolling in the gardens of the Hôtel de Valentinois, where Le Ray de Chaumont has loaned his guest a sort of two-story Trianon, "the barnyard" as this part of the outbuildings is still called, although it has now been fully domesticated—a barnyard that would intimidate many a peasant. The lilacs are beginning to open. Franklin will soon be able to resume his daily "air baths," lying stark naked on his big bed and making very little attempt to camouflage himself; he insists they're his only possible remedy for senescence now that gout has made it impossible for him to continue the real baths he used to take from the banks of the Seine shortly after his arrival.[4]

It's been over two years since he pitched his tent here and let the people come to him, not overtaxing his strength by going to them. Turgot and Beaumarchais; Choiseul and Lauraguais; the La Rochefoucaulds; the Broglies and the Noailleses; the Freemasons of the Lodge of the Nine Sisters; the Americans and English in Paris who haven't yet learned to think they are different; the other ambassadors from Congress—Silas Deane and Arthur Lee and John Adams—a perfect persecution of hard work, those three, oh, there's nothing like colleagues for that! Franklin gets along far better with a hundred Frenchmen than with a single one of his countrymen, especially that John Adams, that porcupine who is increasingly coming to take himself for the great white chief of America.* Every time Franklin drinks, Adams gets a hangover. And if ever he catches him in the act of cuddling some pretty female guest, damnation!

And why should Franklin refuse himself that pleasure? "You speak of the kindness of the Frenchwomen toward me. But the French are the politest nation in the world. If they hear that you are fond of mutton, you will get mutton. Somebody apparently put it about that I was fond of ladies. Thereupon everybody began offering me ladies, or the ladies began offering themselves, to be kissed, on the neck, that is. For kissing on the mouth or cheeks is not done here. The former procedure is vulgar, and the latter removes the paint."[5] And so they come, in their upper-class battalions, to condole with him over the vicissitudes of the real battalions lost in the American labyrinth and the vacillations of M. d'Estaing. Not a victory in sight since Saratoga. The South threatened anew. The invasion of England shelved until further notice. The ebb and flow of events, from one continent to another. Anchored at Passy, Franklin keeps his cool, and his patience slowly infiltrates the French.

He lays a hand on Abbé Morellet's arm and waves away the water jug:

" 'When you see your neighbor pouring wine into his glass at table, do not be in such haste to pour water on top of it. In vino veritas, says the sage. Why do you want to drown the truth? Your neighbor probably knows what is good for him better than you do. Perhaps he doesn't care for water. Perhaps he doesn't want someone else to see how little he puts in his glass. Offer water only to children, my friend.' "[6]

The ladies have gone to stir the punch according to the recipe he taught them. Quantities of white rum and a smattering of sugar. Franklin goes on:

*He arrives in February 1780 to push the campaign for French aid.

" 'It is true that God also taught men to turn wine into water. But into what manner of water? Into *eau-de-vie*.* And that was done so that they might perform the miracle of Cana themselves when they needed to, and convert ordinary water into this excellent species of wine known as punch. My Christian brother, be benevolent and beneficent as he was, and do not spoil his good brew.' "

With the help of the punch, the atmosphere waxes sentimental. "Franklin was very fond of Scottish dances. He remembered, he said, the powerful and sweet impressions they had made upon him. He told us how one time, traveling in America, he had found himself beyond the Allegheny Mountains in the dwelling of a Scotsman who lived far from any society after the loss of his fortune, with his wife, who had once been a beautiful woman, and their daughter of fifteen or sixteen; and how one fine evening, sitting in front of their door, the wife had sung the Scottish tune 'Such Merry as We Have Been' in so sweet and touching a manner that he had burst into tears, and that the memory of that moment was as strong in him now, over thirty years later."[7]

Are they really thirty years old, those tears welling in his large eyes tonight when he finishes telling the story? No; they were born two days ago, when "Mme Helvétius spent the day talking a great deal of nonsense with him," according to Morellet who always knows everything. But the real nonsense did not come from her. He asked her to marry him.

He drops in for a neighborly chat, from Passy to Auteuil. He seats himself gingerly, in order not to disturb any of the eighteen angora cats who live in the big blue drawing room and rule the household. Until June they are "sheathed in long fur-lined gowns, presumably to preserve their own fur and protect them from the cold by preventing them from running. When these curious figures leap down from their armchairs, visitors see trains of brocade, dauphine, and satin, lined with the most precious furs, dragging across the floor." Franklin is their accomplice: he undoubtedly loves Mme Helvétius all the more for her cats that come and go in the room "like high court councilors, with the same gravity and the same certainty of their merit."[8] Imperceptibly, by means of oblique parables and a skillful glissando from humor to amour, he tries to persuade her to take on one more large furry pussycat, who would hardly be more trouble to her than Musette, Marquise, or Aza . . . She laughs. She pretends not to catch his meaning. "Mme Helvétius called them all by name . . . Suddenly the door opened and the gentlemen's dinner was brought in on fine plates and served to them all about the room. Breast of chicken or partridge, with a few little bones to gnaw. Then there was a melee, with clawing and spitting and yowling, until each had been satisfied and installed

---

* Literally, water of life, the French for liqueurs. [*Trans.*].

himself with pomp on the lampas-covered* seats, vying with the rest to see which could make the most grease spots."

But Franklin's still waiting for his breast of chicken. Maybe she wants a formal proposal? Down he goes on his knees, all creaky and tottering. He loves her as she is, round and chubby, not very fastidious about her person, crumpled and rumpled and badly powdered, with her overflowing bosom, her dimples and her wrinkles, this woman who for thirty years has entertained every intellect in Europe: the widow of Helvétius. Franklin is proposing to a living institution.

She's fond of him too. But she is sager than the Sage. She shows him, on her mantelpiece, the plaster model of the monument she had made for her husband's tomb: a woman weeping by a mausoleum. Now she stops laughing, Our Lady of Auteuil. Helvétius died nine years ago,† right there in the next room:

" 'There I am, my friend. I am that woman. How could I change?' "⁹

Helvétius, foremost of them all. The one they privately hold in greater esteem than Voltaire and Diderot. The Galileo of philosophy, who was coerced into the monstrous retraction of 1758 in order to save the life of the censor who authorized publication of *De l'Esprit:* "I ardently and very sincerely hope that those who may have had the misfortune to read this book will do me the mercy of refraining from judging me on the fatal impression it has made upon them. I hope they will know that as soon as the licentiousness and danger in it had been brought to my attention, I instantly disclaimed, proscribed, and condemned it and was the first to desire its suppression . . . I did not wish to attack any of the truths of Christianity, which I sincerely profess in the full rigor of its dogmas and morality, and to whose service I take pride in submitting all my thoughts, all my opinions, and all the faculties of my being . . ."¹⁰ *De l'Esprit* was burned even so, on the main staircase of the Parliament, and Helvétius kept quiet for the rest of his days. When you're rich, beloved, and surrounded by friends, it is possible to survive at Auteuil, even with a gag over your mouth . . . "The storm passes and the work remains," Voltaire had written him.¹¹ *Eppure si muove!*** His book is beginning to circulate secretly, passing across Europe from hand to hand—perhaps the most irreligious text of the century . . . Minette, his good woman from Lorraine,

---

*A silk fabric with large motifs worked in relief, much used during the time of Louis XV and Louis XVI as a chair and sofa covering.

†On December 26, 1771, at the age of fifty-six. In his lifetime he published nothing but *De l'Esprit,* which was condemned and burned as atheistic and immoral on February 6, 1759. All the rest of his work is published posthumously.

**"And yet it *does* turn," the words Galileo is alleged to have whispered after his retraction of the earth's rotation. Guy Besse says that Stendhal considered Helvétius "the greatest philosopher of the French."

filled the silence of this man buried alive with her turbulent tenderness.

That's just what's making Franklin so insistent. Has she really given him an answer? Such an intelligent, such a jolly woman, to remain an inconsolable widow forever? Let the dead bury their dead. He doesn't sleep a wink that night. The next morning he sends her the prettiest love letter that could ever be written by a man of seventy-five. He's trying again, under cover of a little allegory:

> Grieved by your determination, so positively pronounced yesterday evening, to remain single for the rest of your life in honor of your beloved husband, I retired home. Falling upon my bed, I fancied myself dead, and found myself in the Elysian fields. I was asked if I desired to see anyone in particular? "Take me to the philosophers." "There are two of them dwelling here, near this garden; they are very good neighbors and great friends of each other." "Who are they?" "Socrates and Helvétius." "I admire them both prodigiously; but take me first to see Helvétius, for I have a little understanding of the French, but not a word of Greek" . . . He received me most courteously . . . "But you ask me nothing of your dear friend Mme Helvétius? And yet she loves you excessively; I was with her but quarter of an hour ago." "Ah!" says he, "you remind me of my former felicity; but if one will be happy here, it must be forgotten. For several years I thought of nothing else; now, at last, I am comforted. I have taken another wife, as much like her as I could find; it is true she is not altogether so beautiful, but she has as much good sense and spirit, and she loves me infinitely; she is constantly studying how to please me . . ." "I perceive," I then said, "that your former friend is more faithful than you, for several good matches have been offered to her and she has refused them all. I confess that I myself did love her to madness, but she used me severely and rejected me utterly, out of honor for you." "I pity you," says he, "for your misfortune, for she is a good and very pleasant woman." . . . At these words the new Mme Helvétius came in, and I instantly recognized her as Mme Franklin, my former American friend. I tried to reclaim her, but she coldly said: "I was your good wife for forty-nine years and four months, almost half a century; be content with that. Here I have formed a new connection which will last for all eternity." Displeased by this rejection from my Eurydice, I determined upon the instant to quit those ungrateful shades and return to this good world, to see the sun and you. Here I am; let us avenge ourselves . . .[12]

It was so well wrought that the next day finds her still undecided. One might well hesitate for less! "Let us avenge ourselves . . ." To avenge themselves together, on unhappiness and even happiness past, on loneliness and imbeciles . . . She's no longer very sure what to do. So she goes to ask her faithful friend Turgot for advice, and that settles Franklin. Advice always cools your hankerings for folly. And besides, it was cheating on her part to consult another former aspirant. She plays them off against each other. A trifle provocative, perhaps, our Dame Helvétius? "M. Turgot has been a friend of hers since his days at the Sorbonne," good-gossip Morellet tells us, or in other words since around 1750, when she was still Mlle de Ligniville and lived with Mme de Graffigny, her aunt . . . "Adoring literature, he secured an introduction to Mme de Graffigny, in whose home many men of letters assembled; but he often left their circle to play shuttlecock, in his cassock, with 'Minette,' who was a tall and lovely girl of twenty-two or three. And I have often wondered that no true passion was born of this intimacy. But whatever the causes for such great reserve, the relationship survived in a tender and enduring friendship between the two."[13]

If Turgot ever loved, it was Minette. But back in those days, Mme de Graffigny had put a stop to their romance:

" 'My poor children, you must have taken leave of your senses! She has nothing, and M. Turgot has nothing too.' "[14]

Two years later Minette had Helvétius, fame, the best salon in Auteuil, and an annual income of three hundred thousand livres.* Turgot went on having nothing and became Turgot. But now he takes his icy revenge. Why, he'll be glad to give her a friendly word of advice. He's fond of Franklin, too, but not fond enough to become his confederate in something like this. He, Turgot, had suffered too much, he's been too miserable since his disgrace, there's nothing left for him now but to die like a stoic; and only four years ago he was shaking France like a puppy with a slipper in his mouth. He's grown thin. He can hardly walk. He's gone all white beneath the twin black vaults of his enormous eyebrows. The look of a man flayed alive by gout. Minette gets a tasty piece of his mind. "Senile babblings! . . . Really, just let me ask, how old are the pair of you?" And for a final thrust, the unparriable argument:

" 'In any event, my good friend, you must suit yourself, but if you take this decision, your entire salon will go.' "

That same evening she gives Franklin a no that means no. "Let us continue as before, my friend . . . I shall come to dinner tomorrow."

The company departs after singing one last verse.

Après notre victoire	[When the victory is ours
Nous leur apprendrons à boire	We'll teach the foe to toast our
A verre plein	powers
A la santé de Benjamin.	By the ton and by the bin:
	Bottoms up to Benjamin!]

He, meanwhile, is still hearing the Scottish lament "Such Merry as We Have

*1.5 million new francs [$300,000]. In his youth Helvétius obtained a position as farmer-general, thanks to his father who was the physician of Queen Marie Leczinska. He shed it at the earliest possible moment, to devote himself to a life of ease.

Been," a little tune that floats through his old age. Ah, this isn't the first time. Just another scar. All that remains of these three days of fever and this dinner party is a story, which Morellet is going to get into the pages of every confidential gazette in Europe: Mme Helvétius has given him the tale of the meeting in the Elysian fields. Grimm publishes it at the end of April. M. Franklin's heartbreak becomes a news item in the history of the Two Worlds. He doesn't mind: such a pretty little heartbreak . . .

LA FAYETTE

34

APRIL 1780

The Wind Is Shifting to the Right Quarter

April 1780. La Fayette's second trip to America. Not exactly the one he was hoping for; still, he's going as an advance guard for France, or at least, since six thousand French soldiers are supposed to be arriving two months after him, that's how he'll present himself. A neat comeback after his disastrous flop in 1777: Bordeaux, Los Pasajès . . . He is now twenty-two.

Last summer while Gilbert sat drearily champing at the bit in Le Havre, Franklin sent his grandson around with a fine dress sword, presented at the behest of Congress. "Thanks to the exquisite artists of France, I see that it is easy to express everything, except the sense we have of your worth, and our obligation to you."[1] It's only a republican pat on the head, but La Fayette takes it as encouragement to try again. If there is to be no Descent, he'll fall back on his first idea: we must send an expeditionary force to relieve Washington. He's been fighting hard for a year now, wielding his pen and his numerous connections. If he can't invade Portsmouth, he'll lay siege to Vergennes instead, backed up by the authority conferred by his firsthand knowledge of the terrain and men.

So General de La Fayette turns lawyer, and he has now won his case. Time and tide come to his aid just when he needs them: England remains invulnerable, India is lost, the score is all tied up in the Antilles. This war for America has to start happening somewhere. What about in America, maybe?

La Fayette's plea, submitted in July 1779, is solid and well documented, and it provides Vergennes with the right kind of arguments to cheer up all the people who're moaning over the great deflation. Momentarily, the minister's calculation coincides with the volunteer's dream, although their motives differ: the former wants to spare London, the latter to save Philadelphia. We hear the novice politician practicing his scales: "You ask me, Monsieur le Comte [from La Fayette to Vergennes], for some ideas respecting an expedition to America . . . Devastated coasts, ruined ports, commerce at a standstill, fortified posts whence these invasions are made [by the English], all seem to call for our assistance both by sea and land."[2] Twenty-six pages ensue, in a fair curving hand whose surface poise masks a mind in effervescence. He can't help day-dreaming now and then, unpacking his old mirages: why not Canada, and Newfoundland, and Florida? Sometimes you'd think he was Beaumarchais: "The idea of a revolution in Canada [sic] is attractive to every good French-man; and if political considerations condemn it, you will admit, Monsieur le Comte, that they run counter to your inclinations." He doesn't push too hard, he knows Vergennes is dead set against the idea. So he swings back to essen-tials, even if it means repeating himself: ". . . I cannot without violating my conscience refrain from reiterating that it is very important for us to send a body of troops to America." He reckons it all down to the smallest detail, how many men (4,300), where they should land, how many ships are needed, what provisions, where ships can anchor: Block Island, to besiege Newport, or Sandy Hook "on the coast of Jersey, in the first days of November, one of the finest months in the whole of independent America. This armament would then seem to threaten New York; and we should find, upon our arrival, pilots for various other points . . ." "November"! "Upon our arrival"! Will he ever stop believing in Santa Claus? The whole of 1779 and the spring of 1780 go by before the expedition sets out, and when it does somebody else is put in command of it. God knows, though, he angled hard enough for the job, almost as hard as the Duc de Broglie. "We shall need officers who know how to put up with frustrations, live frugally and avoid all airs, particularly a sharp and peremptory manner, and are capable of giving up the pleasures, women and literature of Paris for a year. We ought therefore to take few colonels and people of the Court, whose habits are in no wise American." He ingenuously pokes these motes into his brothers' eyes; then, for the beam in his own . . . "Although I have commanded with some success a larger body of troops, and (I frankly confess) feel myself capable of leading them, it is not my intention to urge these claims; but it would be an extravagance to answer for the actions of an unknown person . . ." Oh well, maybe he'd better name names himself since it looks like nobody's going to do it for him. "If I were trusted with this duty [of dealing with the "somewhat difficult" American character] . . . I would pledge my life that all complications would be avoided, and that our troops would be cordially received." And then, hoping he won't be taken literally, he sighs, "I shall be considered too young, I presume, to be given such a command." On that point nobody contradicts him.

All winter long he's been the mosquito in this chariot of state that advances at snail's pace. Maurepas moans that "this young man would be capable of dismantling Versailles to help his Americans."[3] He's in Paris just before Christmas when a son is born to him, whom he promptly names George Washington before returning to his—not unreasonable—siege of Maurepas: "It is important for [the armament] to get there early in the spring; and what could be done with advantage in the month of May will not have the same effect if we postpone its execution. We must count upon a voyage of at least two months. We ought to be ready by the end of February; we ought to write to America in fifteen days; and I wish that in four days I could see the preparations begun in earnest . . ."[4] He prods them into a panic and continues to press his services upon them, not knowing whether it is "My intimate friendship with the General [Washington] or the confidence of the army and of the [American] people . . . or whether it be my *popularity,* to use the English expression . . ." that makes him bold enough to say it, but "Congress elected me out of all the other general officers for an independent command of great importance, in 1778 . . ." and "Few field marshals have led as many men in war, where I have at times been successful . . ."

At the beginning of February he finally drags a decision out of them. They're careful not to put him in charge of the expeditionary corps, if only because of his worship for Washington, but they get rid of him by sending him to make preparations for the landing and act as liaison officer between the French and American forces. At the head of the former Louis XVI puts Rochambeau, an old veteran of the German wars who has the advantage of being out of all the Court intrigues and belonging to no clan, whether of Broglies, Noailleses, Choiseuls, or Polignacs.

Swallowing his disappointment, La Fayette is off like a flash. One year in Europe is enough to make him homesick for America again. Out there, at least, they treat him like a real general. He takes enough money along to equip a division at his own expense: one hundred thousand livres.* His steward is tearing his hair out: the young master has already run through several years' income. They'll have to sell some land. "Monsieur le Marquis, you are purchasing your fame at the cost of your fortune."[5] So sell, my good man, sell . . . La Fayette has no head for money.

Jean-Baptiste Donatien de Vimeur, Comte de Rochambeau, fifty-five years of age, has just lost his father, who died on their estate near Vendôme at the end of a long life blighted by congenital deformity. The news found his son in Paris, where he and a lot of other officers in "the England army" were waiting to find out which way the wind was going to blow them. He had ordered his

*600,000 new francs [$120,000].

coach and horses to return home, untangle the inheritance, and subside into a sort of retirement at Thoré, below Gué-du-Loir, between Montoire and Vendôme.* Fallow fields abounding in game and swarms of monks in the nearby priories for pious gentlemen's Sundays. A cosy little château with a touch of the troglodyte about it, carved out of the soft stone of the slopes just topping the Loir. Exactly the sort of place for mellowing in the sun and living to be a hundred. But he wasn't that eager to start, he didn't feel ready for the shelf. So to him that messenger from the Prince de Montbarrey was like an annunciating angel . . . "The King requires your services, Monsieur le Comte." A general's life is founded on the hope of that visitation. The horses ordered for Vendôme can drive him to Versailles instead. "In a monarchy," d'Estaing has just written to Silas Deane, "the men are like tokens. The sovereign makes them worth whatever he decides."[6] They've hit on exactly the right valuation here; Rochambeau's tarnish is a perfect foil for the glitter of La Fayette, and a perfect match for the color of this war—but it's high-grade tarnish. His style is slightly seventeenth-century, both at war and with his pen, which he prides himself on using well, albeit heavily, as he does all things. One of the army's quiet men. He ought to be able to get along with Washington and yet not let himself be pushed around. His ancestors on his father's side go back to the Crusades, and his mother's family is from the solid landowning bourgeoisie. (Michel Bégon, an uncle on that side, colonizes Martinique and brings back the begonia.) He had one older brother and was dutifully preparing to enter the Church, like any decently disciplined younger son, when the other's death shifted him into the army. It was a close shave, the Bishop of Blois was already calling him "his little vicar-general."

But if ya gotta go, ya gotta go: the good bishop exhorts the young man "to forget everything he had said to him until that day. He had now to serve his fatherland as zealously as he might have served God in the ecclesiastical condition."[7] Being obedient by definition, he applies himself to the task. First he obeys the Maréchal de Belle Isle, in the devastated Bavaria of the forties. "The Danube was frozen so solid that vehicles could cross it" and he catches his death of something or other. "The order to change quarters came just when I was at my worst. Nature, youth, and the force of the fever caused me to sweat on my bed of pain as though I were within the hottest stove."[8] That's how you make a soldier. Even frozen solid, the Hudson won't scare him.

Then the capture of Namur. And the Battle of Laufeld, where he was obeying the Maréchal de Saxe. "Two shots from a biscayen† struck him in the

*Today the village is called Rochambeau-Thoré. The château has remained in the family and affords a lovely stroll along the banks of the Loir, about six miles from Vendôme.

†An enormous long-range gun which the Spaniards first used in the Biscay. It was a sort of small portable cannon. Its projectiles were also beginning to be called "biscayens."

skull and thigh, one entering the head at the corner of the eye and scraping and furrowing the temple bone, and the other, an iron ball large as a pigeon's egg, traversing the thigh from one side to the other without breaking the bone."⁹ A tough hide . . . Louis XV, who is there, confirms it with a glance. And the siege of Maestricht. And the capture of Port Mahon in the Balearics, where he was obeying the Maréchal de Richelieu: the finest day of his life, the Cross of St. Louis at thirty. It's plain as day that this is the man to beat the English. At Klostercamp he commands the Auvergne regiment—and it is his name the Chevalier d'Assas calls out as he dies under the bayonets. For the last seventeen years of peace, Rochambeau has been moping and mooning around like so many others. The wind from America revives him. Modest (relatively), he is (relatively) surprised by this sudden mark of favor. The previous year, however, he was clever but not too clever at beating his superior, the Maréchal de Broglie, on the issue of Guibert's shallow formation at the Vaussieux maneuvers. No courtier, Rochambeau? No; but he always stays on the safe side.

He does know his job. Montbarrey tells him at the beginning of January—a good month before letting La Fayette in on the secret—that "an assistance of four thousand men which the King wishes to send to North America"¹⁰ is going to be entrusted to him. He immediately asks for more. "I accept with the deepest gratitude the mark of confidence with which the King has been pleased to honor me . . . But a body of four thousand men is soon reduced,"* as he knows only too well from the war in Germany when "the troops under my orders were reduced by two-thirds in the three battles of Laufeld, Krevelt and Klostercamp." He demands at least twelve battalions: six thousand men. They are promised. Then, a cavalry detachment. He'll have it. But "how far am I allowed to help the allies [the Americans] with money, bills of exchange, supplies of every kind? People who have nothing need everything." Steady there! "What the King sends with his troops is intended solely for the maintenance of the corps." Oh, by the way: "You will be under the orders of M. le général Vashington [*sic*], commander-in-chief of the troops of Congress . . . The plans and projects for campaigns or special expeditions will be ordered by him" but "the intentions of the King are that the French troops should suffer no dispersion."¹¹ In other words, the help is there but you can't use it. If things go too badly on the mainland, Rochambeau is to retreat to Santo Domingo.

Slowly but surely, orders from offices begin oiling the clogged gears of the convoys. In March six or eight little human streams flow together into Brest, from Lamballe, Quimper, Hennebont, Crozon, Camaret, Landerneau.

*In the sense of men lost.

Good French regiments: the Bourbonnais, the Soissonnais, the Saintonge, then two named after their German colonels, Anhalt and the Royal Deux Ponts (Zweibrücken), most of whose soldiers have been levied in Alsace and will find themselves fighting their neighbors from Hesse who have been sold to the English. It's high noon on "the broken roads of Brittany, which so intimidate the wagoners that they refuse to deliver goods and supplies on fixed dates," whence the delay. It is also high noon in the American war.

On March 6 La Fayette leaves Paris for the second time. What a change! He has just been complimented by the King, encouraged by the Queen. "Etampes, ten o'clock. I pause a moment here, dear heart, to tell you how unhappy I am to leave you . . ." He hadn't spent more than ten days at a stretch with his Adrienne since his return. She subsides into a sorrow tinged with wonderment at the affection in his parting words: "Blois, March 7, at 10 o'clock: My health is good, but I am very sad and I would give the world to see you again for one minute." "This tenth of March 1780: Here I am at Rochefort, since yesterday, my dear heart, and this morning I am going aboard the frigate *Hermione,*" a handsome three-master armed all for him as though he were a prince and commanded by a considerate officer, La Touche-Tréville. "I was infinitely pleased with M. de La Touche . . . The wind is shifting to the right quarter, and I hope we shall have splendid weather."

". . . On board the *Hermione,* this thirteenth March at nine in the evening, it is a cruel moment indeed, and rending, dear heart, in which I begin to write to you. The time has come to weigh anchor" and to weep for six whole pages. "Is it for me, dear heart, who am so happy with you, to make you unhappy by leaving you? Farewell! Farewell . . ." On March 18, peekaboo guess who: "Heavy weather, coupled with the loss of a main yard, has forced us to return to Rochefort . . . This little setback will keep us here until fair weather allows us out again. Once past the equinox, we shall have magnificent winds," but then you also have to leave time for that blessed wind from America to amuse itself bouncing off the outposts of Europe—the same lousy luck every year, it's enough to make you wonder if the New World isn't trying to keep the Old one away. On March 20 they can chance it: "The equinox is past . . . Our frigate is astonishingly handy and smooth. M. de La Touche has given orders to avoid any sails we should meet, and we shall head straight for the nearest American port. I am overwhelmed with kindnesses here, and as the first waves of seasickness have passed, I have great hopes for this second trip . . . I must leave you [this time it's for real]: a dreadful moment. Farewell, and once again farewell; I love you madly."[12]

So: La Fayette leaves Rochefort on March 20. Rochambeau arrives in Brest on the 26th, almost incognito. As yet nobody knows what's actually in store, and opinions remain bemused and disconsolate: "After the colossal effort of the campaign of 1779 everything appears to be disintegrating; at least on the French coasts, the great war is as though over. Ever since Louis XVI's navy let pass the one perfect opportunity to end the war with a bolt of lightning, there seems to be nothing left for it to do in this part of the world. Powerful and numerous squadrons continue to emerge from the port of Brest," which has become the bottleneck through which the war must squeeze before exploding. "But they sail for Gibraltar, the United States, the Antilles, Hindustan. No longer even to conquer the approaches to London."[13] Since only a handful of the initiated know where these convoys are really bound, it's all a complete puzzle for France, and even for the court.

But anyhow, Rochambeau is in Brest. His appearance inspires confidence: a tall, very French-looking figure, very much "one of us" with his long aquiline nose, neat rolls of white hair, and the scar on his temple from the Laufeld bullets that labels him a warrior. The lofty stature and slow gait of people who have their feet firmly on the ground. The reassuring speech of those who don't have too many ideas, but a good memory and consistency. And he's going to need it around here, in the sort of organized bedlam that is highly symbolic of the King at twenty-five. On the army side all's well. Everything has been provided for, down to the last cartridge pouch. But on the navy side something's gone haywire. What's the good of massing your regiments if you've got nothing to embark them on? The Prince de Montbarrey has written out most detailed instructions for Tarlé, the quartermaster general of Rochambeau's troops: he is to see that "the goods and supplies for the King are carefully packed and distributed among the vessels intended to transport them . . ." The hospital ship, for instance, that's being sent over from Saint-Malo: "a considerable number of sick and injured must be expected." They have collected 10,000 shirts, 10,371 pairs of boots, 1,200 hooded capes, 4,000 blankets, 1,210 tents, 1,000 stewpans, 1,000 mess tins, 1,000 canteens, 1,000 billhooks, 1,000 spades and shovels, 1,000 picks, 1,050 axes.[14] But where are the ships to carry it all? Nowhere and everywhere: at l'Orient, at Saint-Malo, at Rochefort, at Bordeaux, even at Le Havre. The Brest roads are practically empty. The preparations for this expedition have apparently been dreamed up by a hemiplegic: everything's ready except the boats, to which sailing orders were issued much too late. "The result," Rochambeau writes to Montbarrey, "is that the utmost capability of the port of Brest is to embark five thousand men* for departure on April 8, wind and the court of London permitting . . . Reckoning on a third fewer troops, I have proportionally reduced the artillery, food, hospital provisions, and articles of replacement . . ." A considerable handicap for an expeditionary force that expects to land on

---

*In all, "5,034 officers, under-officers, corporals and men, including 295 officers and 13 gentlemen cadets."

war-torn soil and was originally intended, on La Fayette's advice, to carry supplies for six months.

Instead, they take on two and a half months' worth of flour, salt beef, bacon, rice, salt, and oil.

The sailor chosen to lead this little armada is a contemporary of Rochambeau, another veteran who's been hanging around for twenty years: the Chevalier de Ternay d'Arsac. For a time he was governor of Ile de France.* In the other war, he forced his way through the English who were penning up his ships in the Vilaine. He has recently commanded in the Antilles—but under d'Estaing—and in the Channel—but under d'Orvilliers. At last his moment has come. He ought to be jubilant. He's groaning: "Have the difficulties of such a transport really been weighed? Is it absolutely essential for the expedition in view? War in the New World is not waged with this vast paraphernalia I am dragging behind me."[15] Why, would he rather carry the men over naked? And to boost the squadron leader's morale another notch, here comes bad weather: eight consecutive days of rain at the beginning of April, pounding down on the thirty-two transport ships which have finally been rounded up,† the *Fantasque, Saumon, Écureuil, Aventure, Père-de-famille, Vénus, Aimable-Marie,* and so forth. They're still waiting for three *flûtes* from l'Orient. On April 21 four regiments are embarked: the Bourbonnais, Soissonnais, Saintonge, and Royal Deux Ponts; the rest will catch up when they can. Plus the resurrected "Lauzun legion"—five or six hundred Germans; plus, by way of artillery, the second battalion of the Auxonne regiment, five hundred men with both campaign (light) and siege (heavier) equipment. Sweating blood and tears, the convicts from the Brest jail are requisitioned to help them load their fifty-odd pieces of the finest cannonry in the world, cast from the designs of M. de Gribeauval, who has just modernized French artillery. Plus one detachment of twenty-six laborers and sixteen sappers. They've even got a provost marshalry—that is, a military police court with its lieutenant marshal, crown prosecuting attorney, registrar, and two *caporal-schlagueurs* who administer the floggings.

By April 17 everybody is stowed aboard. Not too crowded; according to the rule, every soldier is allotted two barrels' worth of space. Rochambeau's ready. "If the weather clears, I shall sleep on board the *Duc-de-Bourgogne* [a beautiful eighty-gun ship with a copper-sheathed hull, a recent innovation which was supposed to delay deterioration] tomorrow at the latest, in order to take advantage, under the orders of M. le Chevalier de Ternay, of the first north wind." Always the north; on this outer tip of Europe the wind never blows from the east; you've got to catch the "wind from England" and let it blow you down to the Azores or beyond, where you can pick up the trade

*Mauritius.
†With a total cubage of 12,800 tons.

winds that will finally carry the ships back west-northwest . . . "If the weather clears."

They're not going with empty pockets. Quartermaster general Tarlé has loaded 2,625,000 livres on to various ships,* but in Spanish piasters: nobody has any faith in those paper livres the Americans are issuing, whereas the piaster is legal tender everywhere out there, and especially in the Islands.

All right, are we ready? Can we go? A great stir and hubbub down the two long shop-lined quays and inside the prison buildings. The sails play hide-and-seek with the sun. Because it brings the north wind with it, they race up the yards the moment it peeks out between squalls. April 23. Europe's most beautiful roads are in labor: the transports move forward to anchor at the entrance, where their pilots have to maneuver with precision to get through that devilish passage whose rocks have gutted so many hulls. Left within the vast red-banked circle—you'd think it was a lake—are ten or so ships of the line and frigates grouped around the *Duc-de-Bourgogne,* hung with multicolored bunting: the signals everyone is watching. It's go! No, stop! Two transports come lurching back: they've collided. The *Comtesse de Noailles* has to be repaired—a bad omen for a vessel bearing the name of La Fayette's in-laws. Too bad, we'll go without her. No, no! Now the wind's veered around to the west. "Fortunately, it is also raining on Portsmouth!" Rochambeau writes. Everybody's thinking it, but nobody says it: if the English fleet, far superior in numbers, were to drop in for a chat just when we're trying to get away, it could make a pretty mess of us. Sorry, your aid has been forcibly canceled . . .

They sit back to await God's gracious pleasure again. But "the regiments are wearied by this long delay on board. There are twelve or fifteen down sick in each; fifty in the Bourbonnais alone." Not scurvy again, like last year?

---

*Or 13 million new francs [$2.6 million]. The total expenditure budgeted by Necker for Rochambeau's corps for one year was 6,336,000 livres (32 million new francs [$6.4 million]), divided into *ordinary* expenses (the pay of the six regiments—1,980,000 livres) and *extraordinary* expenses (to defray the cost of the expedition—4,356,000 livres).

35

"St. Louis et Philadelphie"

La Fayette's next ordeal is a holiday month in mid-ocean, and the loneliness of long-distance voyages: La Touche-Tréville having been told "to avoid all sails," his passenger doesn't even have to bother about writing to his dear heart. He is surrounded by silence. He has plenty of time to peruse the twenty pages of meticulous instructions that Vergennes has ground out for him:

"M. le Marquis de La Fayette, in proceeding to America, will hasten to join General Washington, to whom he will announce under the bond of secrecy that the King, who desires to give the United States a new proof of his affection and of his interest in their welfare, has decided to send out to them early in the spring a reinforcement of six ships of the line and six thousand men of regular infantry . . ."[1] This time La Fayette's is no small mission: when the French squadron is sighted off the coast, he's the one who'll give the disembarkation order via "some of the French officers who are attached to him, each of whom shall bear a letter from him which shall assure the commander of the French fleet that he may safely enter the port . . . If no French officer shall appear with a letter from M. le Marquis de La Fayette to give information as to the best course by which to approach the shore and as to the possibility of disembarking, then the fleet will [bear away from Rhode Island, the first choice for a landing, and] put into Boston with its convoy, and await orders there from General Washington . . . The watchword shall be *St. Louis et Philadelphie.*"

. . . But it will be *Marie et Boston* "if the winds should drive the fleet southward, [and the ships would] then endeavor to find the capes of Virginia." So Vergennes, with that infinite capacity for taking pains which is his finest quality, has thought of everything. The ideal? To capture New York, "the central point of the British, and arsenal of the thunder and lightning with which they imperil America." If Washington prefers, however, he's free to use his reinforcements in the South as well, which has now been partly reoccupied by the English—Georgetown and Charlestown are threatened, Savannah is lost—although they didn't have much trouble taking that city, for Georgia is rife with Tories who simply opened their doors. D'Estaing barked his shins badly on Savannah, or rather his thighs: both his legs were shattered by shells while he was vainly trying to storm the ramparts at the head of his troops. He failed to repeat his Grenada exploit,* and the Americans decidedly do not cherish his memory: his record so far, on their side of the water, is one defeat a year, and they couldn't care less about Grenada. In 1778 he let them down in the North, and in 1779 he got himself beaten outside a state capital. That winter he went back to Versailles a doubly broken man, both body and spirit in tatters. "M. d'Estaing, armed with his crutches of glory, has left Brest to travel by short stages to Versailles . . . The good Bretons covered his carriage with laurel wreaths," unaware that they were also adorning a hearse, "but the officers of the navy, who fear so stern a leader," and above all could never stomach the landlubber in him, "paid him very little homage. The King sent his litter-bearers out to meet the great man. As he has openly declared himself the antagonist of the minister of his department,† no one can predict what effect his appearance will produce."[2] It could have been worse: Versailles had a shortage of conquering heroes to exhibit, and since there was nothing else to celebrate the court made a great to-do over the capture of Grenada. But the victory was as lame as the victor, and the glow lasted only long enough for a turn through the galleries and one king's mass. The backlash of opinion stung d'Estaing like a rifle's recoil. He went home to convalesce: in Auvergne, at least, the fireworks were sincere. At Versailles, "for want of a tribunal, the drawing rooms became our battlefields," observes young Ségur, who has just distinguished himself on those same battlefields, "so that although the government fully enjoyed authority of action, we contrived to possess ourselves of authority of opinion."[3] An authority most useful to La Fayette, for the little clique from the Epée de Bois is now ensconced at Trianon.** They're the ones he has to thank for "this magnificent wind" that is pushing him around the American billiard table, ricocheting off d'Estaing's crestfallen return and the disaster of d'Orvilliers. But on this point at least Gilbert has lost his illusions: if he fails too he knows perfectly well what kind of reception he can expect when he gets back.

April 4. Fersen reaches Brest, where he is attached to Rochambeau's staff. At last something serious! A chance to go to a real war. "Here I am, my dear

---

*Shortly after that operation d'Estaing left the Islands with 3,000 men and tried to take Savannah by surprise, in September 1779.

†Sartines, transferred from police to navy. As we recall, he inherited a totally dilapidated fleet and was doing his best to build it up again, but only by fits and starts. It was easy for squadron leaders to blame him for everything that went wrong in the navy.

**A group of young noblemen who used to meet at the cabaret called the Epée de Bois, almost all of whom now enjoy the Queen's favor.

friend [to his sister], having reached the first stage of my destination. I left Paris on March 23, but bad roads and poor horses forced me to spend six days on a journey otherwise completed in three or four. I am perfectly delighted to think that we are going to leave, and that I am going to war and shall accomplish something. Everyone here treats me beautifully; the general [Rochambeau], who knows my father very well, is extremely kind, and we are six aides de camp with him. Our days are filled with activity; only the evenings are a little long. Society is not very gay in Brest. But soon we shall have the resource of the spectacle that is about to begin. There are many young men from Paris and the Court here, serving as colonels in the army or aides de camp; I am on excellent terms with them all, they appear to want to be my friends, and we often sup together."[4]

Of course they're there, or most of them anyway, Marie Antoinette's playmates. The drawing rooms' branch office. "The major portion of the recent military promotions were made under the auspices of the Queen's protection.* On this occasion all the Polignacs played a great part, less for themselves than on behalf of their friends, but the latter obtained a great deal more than they could reasonably have desired . . . The King indulgently fell in with all the Queen's wishes; he himself drew up the lists, which were revised several times as a result of the intrigues of candidates who succeeded in having them changed."[5] So here they are, at the rendezvous that has finally come off —Lauzun and the Dillon brothers, and Damas, and Noailles, and Charlus (son of the Maréchal de Castries), and Montmorency. Ségur's coming later. They're pouring in. Have they changed? Why should they? "The Comte Arthur de Dillon, lieutenant colonel of the Lauzun legion, disappeared for several days. They searched everywhere for him. He finally returned from Nantes with two sword wounds," anybody's guess who gave them to him! His cousin maybe, or his colonel . . . When it's raining, you pass the time however you can. Rochambeau, who knows their tricks of old, shrugs his shoulders and calmly notifies the minister:

"I have now ordered him to be placed under arrest on board his ship, to recover from his injuries and as punishment for his disobedience."[6]

On the outskirts of this agitated little coterie, Rochambeau singles out a few officers with a future and carefully attaches them to himself. There is "the Comte Charles de Lameth," he writes in a report to Montbarrey, "supernumerary captain in the La Rochefoucauld Dragoons,† a very pretty specimen

*This is from Mercy-Argenteau to Maria Theresa, on March 18, 1780.

†This is the oldest of the Lameths. He will play an important part in the Constituent Assembly. His brothers Alexandre, Théodore, and Augustin will also take part in the American war. The combined favor of the Broglies, to whom he is related, and the La Rochefoucaulds, whom he frequents, has earned Charles a place on the waiting list of captains of this regiment pending availability of an active post.

[*sic*], intelligent, with a head for detail," and "Sieur Mathieu Dumas, second lieutenant in the Médoc Infantry regiment,* a fine draftsman who sees things with a military eye and can speak and write English." Then he shifts from Dumas to Fersen, from the commoner and under-officer to the Swedish aristocrat, as though sensing that his little expedition embraces two worlds: "And lastly, the Comte de Fersen, Swedish, a supernumerary colonel in the service of France,† speaks English well and is highly recommended by the ambassador of Sweden."⁷ And, it goes without saying, by the Queen.

But no more than the rest: he's just another of her intimates, and there has been little change in the situation since the Comte de Creutz notified the King of Sweden last year of Marie Antoinette's "leaning" for Fersen. She's still leaning, but rather in the manner of the Tower of Pisa—it's a stable inclination. The initiated whisper about it, as they did before about Coigny, Besenval, Lauzun, or Artois. "There is talk of meetings and protracted conversations during balls at the Opéra, of looks being exchanged when no conversation is possible during intimate evenings at Trianon; the Queen has been seen at the piano, I am assured, singing impassioned couplets from the opera of *Dido:*

Ah! que je fus bien inspirée	[Ah, how well inspired I was
Quand je vous reçus dans ma	To receive you at my Court . . .]
Cour . . .	

"At this point her eyes sought out those of Fersen, and she could hardly dissemble her emotion."⁸

But that story's been going around for a year now, it gets dragged out at every one of these gentlemen's departures, real or feigned, for the Americas. She's never learned the art of hiding her infatuations, and people are beginning to know her by now, after interpreting her every sigh for the last ten years. It's precisely because this behavior is so habitual with her, and is now known not to mean very much, that Fersen is no longer taken any more seriously than the rest.

He's been careful, too. No smugness. Does he even realize what's happened to him? Up to and including this departure, apparently not. He's got other women on his mind. In 1778, before his return to France, his chief preoccupation was a projected marriage with a young English

---

*Mathieu Dumas was born in 1753 into a family of minor magistrates from Montpellier. At fifteen he enters the army technicians' corps, which later becomes the engineer corps. He is a member of the Constituent Assembly, and one of the commissioners ordered to bring Louis XVI back from Varennes after the escape attempt so badly botched by Fersen.

†That is, on the waiting list of colonels to be given a French regiment when one becomes available.

heiress, Miss Leyel, tolerable to look at and loaded with East India Company millions. He went all the way from Stockholm to London, for nothing: "The girl assured me that she did not want to leave her parents and would not change her mind . . . I insisted, however, I said everything the most impassioned lover can say, but in vain." He's still smarting, but the wound is no deeper than his pride. "Since this affair is broken off, let us first follow the military objective. I am young, I still have much to learn . . . My idea would be [this was in November 1778] to let matters take their natural course. If she loves me and continues to love me, there will always be an opportunity to take it up again, and I believe that in four or five, even six years, it will be time enough to go into the matter seriously. In the meanwhile, I might perhaps go on some campaign. Mr. Leyel senior is old and ill. If he died, there would be no further obstacle from that quarter and all his property would come to me immediately . . ."9 Not what you'd call a great romantic, the subject of the Leaning. He picks up whatever comes his way, never going overboard, never getting hurt. For two winters, between "campaigns," he pays a rather distant court to a well-preserved widow, Baroness Korff,* and, closer at hand, to another of the queen's friends, the Comtesse de Fitz-James. He gets his best evenings, however, from Julie, a chambermaid in the Swedish embassy. In Brest he's all full of "a pretty, slightly red-haired countess" whom he met somewhere in Sweden and who writes to him intermittently. She's the beloved. The confidante is Sophie, the little sister from whom he hides nothing: "You mischievously ask how I have discovered that Mme Homberg, whom I thought red-haired on first inspection, is no such thing. The explanation is that at that time I had only seen her once, in passing; but she is a darkish blonde who used to apply a quantity of red powder. Since she has ceased to use it, she has ceased to be red-haired."10

April 27. Like everybody else, Fersen is waiting for the great wind that will blow them all away. He's on board the *Jason,* sixty-four guns, "in the Brest roads." He's dying of impatience. "We are still on board and forbidden to go ashore, except on business. You feel that everyone has some [business], or manufactures some. I have, quite often. I like being ashore, and staying on board a ship is dreadful. However, I am in good company and with people I know . . . The wind is still contrary, and it is not known when we shall be able to leave, to our great despair . . . Farewell, my best friend. From a brother who adores you."

That same day, on the other side of the ocean, the *Hermione* comes

---

*Whose passport is used for the "flight to Varennes" twelve years later. Of Swedish origin, she is the widow of a Russian minister in Paris.

within sight of Boston. La Fayette forges the first link in his chain by writing Washington that "he had an announcement of the greatest importance which he had been directed to make to him personally" and begging him, if he should be north of Philadelphia when the letter came to hand, to await his arrival—for he has no idea where headquarters are now or what's happening with the war. The letter does not reach the commanding general until May 7, at Morristown, about level with New York but to the southwest, and well within the area he's just managing to hang on to. But on April 28 the Bostonians give La Fayette a welcome that makes up for everything. What an improvement over the cold shower he got in Philadelphia three years ago! "The reception which all the people were good enough to give me quite beggars description . . . My return was known through the men who went to find pilots. This afternoon I went ashore, among a huge crowd," into that "ancestor of all other American cities, which is exactly like some large old town in England."[11] The joy, the surprise, the first whiff of the mob like the discovery of some incomparable aphrodisiac. A whole town flings itself upon the neck of the man who still goes unnoticed in France. *They* believe in him, anyway. "I was welcomed with cannon salutes and ringings of every bell, with music marching before us and the hurrahs of all the people around. Thus I was conducted to the house which the council and representatives' assembly of Boston had prepared for me. There were delegations of these bodies to welcome me; I asked permission to present my respects to the two Chambers,* which were meeting for that purpose, and I tried to resurrect my English during the hour I remained there. In the evening, the people gathered outside my door and made a great bonfire with much cheering, which went on until past midnight."[12]

On May 1 he sets out for Morristown at full gallop. He thinks Rochambeau has already left and might be halfway across. There's not a minute to lose, in preparation for the disembarkation.

Meanwhile, that very day, the "contrary wind" over Brest finally subsides, and the rain is no worse than a Brittany caress. On May 2, 1780, the squadron weighs anchor at five in the morning, "with a light northerly breeze which it is hoped will freshen." "At sea, on board the *Duc-de-Bourgogne,* May 3," Rochambeau sends off his last letter to that France whose fortunes have been entrusted to him: "We had the finest departure possible and are sailing under the best northeasterly wind, without incident, and crossing the gulf [of Gasgogne] with the weather all we could hope for."[13]

The great moment at last! After so long, nobody believed it would ever

_____
*Of the state of Massachusetts.

happen. Fewer than five thousand men in the end, but even so it's one whole wall of the Old World making tracks for the New. The men who couldn't squeeze in are like to commit suicide. "The departure of the Chevalier de Ternay* will make me shed tears of blood," writes one.[14] Some keep trying to gatecrash even after the party's over. Those two brothers, for instance, Louis-Alexandre and Charles-Louis Berthier, one almost an old man and the other almost a kid, twelve years between them—they're the sons of the governor of the ministry buildings in Paris. The elder has already had a fine career: as survey engineer of the king's camps and armies and captain of infantry in the Soissonnais regiment, he's worked hard for his twenty-seven years.† And the younger one has gotten a place as supernumerary captain of dragoons, which means he'll be an officer in a few months. What do they think they're doing, on May 3, two wild-eyed fellows in canvas jackets and trousers, gesticulating on the deck of the rearguard cutter** that's following the majestic *Duc-de-Bourgogne* like a seagull? Rochambeau is terribly sorry, but it's no go. That's what he's there for. His letter to Montbarrey returns on the cutter: "Messieurs Berthier gave us your letters and those from M. de Sartines the moment we were past the estuary current. They offered to come with us as simple seamen." But there's not enough room for a cabin boy. "M. le Chevalier de Ternay was unable to assign them a place on his ship, or any other in his fleet . . . The poor young men are both deserving and in despair, but the chevalier really has nowhere to put them."[15] To the end of the line, Berthiers, like everybody else! Fame will wait.‡

Another pair of rejects, but these two already famous, sit gnawing their nails while the gyrating court eddies around them: Philippe de Chartres, who is decidedly being kept in the freezer, far from any responsibility; and John Paul Jones, who's made enemies among the authorities everywhere. He's won victory after victory, though, including one moonlight caper near Hull when he faced a genuine little English fleet. But people dread his hot temper and repartee. He has recently been gagged with praise at Versailles, giving the Comte de Provence an opportunity to dissociate himself, in passing, from all this American nonsense which, to his mind, bodes no good.

" 'Here is high honor for Mandrin,' he said in reference to Paul Jones's reception at Court. 'All we need now is to raise temples to Cartouche-Washington.' "††[16]

*Who's commanding the squadron, we recall.

†General of the Revolution, Louis-Alexandre Berthier becomes "Napoleon's right arm"; he is subsequently Maréchal d'Empire and Prince de Wagram and Neufchâtel, marries a Bavarian princess, and commits suicide at Bamberg during the Hundred Days. The younger brother also fights in the wars of the Revolution and Empire and becomes a general.

**These small single-masted warships are just beginning to be called *cotres*.

‡Along with a few other officers, the Berthier brothers eventually join the American army on September 30, 1780.

††Mandrin and Cartouche were notorious outlaws. [*Trans.*]

36

MAY 1780

Charlatans Among the Scientists

The *Journal de Paris* of April 6, 1780, invites the Parisians to savor something new in the way of edification:

> M. Fillassier,* member of several Academies, proposes to give some courses of experiments on the nature of fire, based on the discoveries of M. Marat, doctor of medicine.
>
> The beauty and novelty they offer, by making visible a being† that plays so great a part in nature, would in themselves suffice to arouse curiosity; but they have a greater aim, that of extending the knowledge of the human mind.
>
> Each course will be composed of eight lessons, during which the divers experiments needful to establish the new theory of fire will be conducted . . . The first course will open on the 18th of this month; they will be held in the main hall of the Hôtel d'Aligre, Rue Saint-Honoré, near the Croix du Trahoir. As most of M. Marat's experiments require the presence of the sun, two courses will commence simultaneously, so as to take advantage of the fair weather, the first from one to two in the afternoon and the second from four to five. [The public was invited to sign up for this] interesting course at the shop of the son of M. Jombert the elder, bookseller to the King,** Rue Dauphine, where the author's great work on fire is also to be found.[1]

Now what—is he trying to compete with Lavoisier? "Philosopher, physicist" . . . why not "aerial traveler"? There's a touch of the Cyrano in the Marat of this period. He'll be thirty-seven next month. He's still physician to the Comte d'Artois's life guards, he still looks after his clientele of pretty society ladies, and he's still discreetly writing vengeful diatribes against the society that feeds him. But he is also deepening the furrow he traced with his treatises on diseases of the eyes and his book on the nature of man. Now he's the author of *Découvertes de M. Marat sur le feu, l'électricité et la lumière, constituées par une suite d'expériences nouvelles* [M. Marat's discoveries on fire, electricity and light, derived from a sequence of new experiments]; this is the book, published in 1779, that can be purchased on the Rue Dauphine, and the book Jean-Paul

---

*Abbé Fillassier was Marat's "pupil and preparer" and, on the side, did his secretarial work.
†An "element": fire.
**Meaning that this bookstore had managed to sell at least one book to the court.

Marat is going to present, complete with audiovisual aids, to the new end-of-the-century public—all those intellectual sluggards who, since the demon of curiosity first skipped across enlightened Europe, have begun aching to know the who, how, and why of things. You can't find a corner to hide in among all the "Lycées," "Musées," "Private Courses," and "Experimentations" blossoming in the Jardin du Roi and spreading over both banks of the Seine. Eight hours of this weird brown bird who claims to dissect the Paris sun: they come flocking to him, and to others. But what a curious fellow! He starts with fire, then moves on to man. Or maybe the soul. Does he know himself? He's searching, searching like all self-taught men who are incapable of putting up intellectual partitions. He embraces optics, physics, and chemistry, and seasons the whole with a pinch of metaphysics. The people crowding into the Hôtel d'Aligre during the next six months will gawp at a lopsided contraption he's erected there, known as M. Marat's "solar microscope." With it he proposes to catch the sun's fire, father of all other fires, and use it to ignite ordinary objects, thus rendering visible "the igneous fluid, the electrical substance, air itself . . ."[2] with a sneaking hope that the soul might also be spied leaping out of a spark, and why not the Supreme Being as well? Rousseau believed in God, so Marat does too. The atheism of a Diderot or Condorcet exasperates him, maybe because it humiliates him—or because he envies it, who knows. For the time being he's quite content to combat the diabolical theories of another of those godless men, Lavoisier, by joining forces with those who won't accept his denial of phlogiston, discovery of oxygen, and eviction of fire from its place as a fundamental element alongside air, earth, and water. Marat is defending the honor of fire, but with the pettishness that sometimes stems from lack of conviction. Here we see the domesticated Marat of 1780, although he's already been censured: not only was his *Plan de législation criminelle* refused a prize by the "Société Economique de Berne," but Miromesnil* ordered that the copies printed in Neuchâtel be seized en route and had all the "subversive passages" torn out—and that meant a lot of passages, all the ones defending the guilty poor against the "right-minded," condemning torture and capital punishment, and intimating that crime was a product of a society founded on class and privilege. "The right to own property follows the right to life . . . Nothing superfluous could belong to us *by right* when others do not have even the necessities."[3] In this Marat is only saying what the Church Fathers said before him, but they have now been silent on the subject for a thousand years and this son of a Sardo-Swiss "language master"† is not about to be

*Lord Chancellor since the accession of Louis XVI.

†Jean Mara, "language master" but also "painter-draftsman," born in Cagliari in Sardinia, was in fact a subject of Frederick II, since he settled in Boudry (where his son Jean-Paul was born) in 1747, and Boudry was in the principality of Neuchâtel, a Prussian enclave among the Swiss cantons. Jean Mara dies in 1783, leaving an estate of 638 florins: less than 5,000 new francs [$1,000].

allowed to take over from them. Many before him, beginning with Helvétius, have undergone the ordeal of the gag. Marat can't resign himself to it. The silence these people are trying to impose on him is taking away his appetite. Nevertheless, he goes on as though that half of himself were in parentheses, and pretends to become a scholar. He transforms part of his handsome apartment on the Rue de Bourgogne into a dissecting room. The nearby Hôtel-Dieu provides a steady supply of cadavers, but he needs live animals too: "I have made an arrangement with a local butcher who supplies me with ewes, calves, swine and even bullocks if I need them. As he takes it all back, I pay only for any damage done to his meat."[4] The enormous stables of the Palais des Bourbons, just next door, house his livestock while he's torturing it. So he's a vivisector too, along with everything else, but only in passing. In 1780, however, top priority goes to physics research: "There is much talk of a new Newton, the son of M. Marat of Geneva [*sic*]. This physician has invented a novel means of seeing into the secrets of nature. At first he had the entire Academy against him," writes a native of Geneva passing through Paris, "but he contrived to coerce it into witnessing his discoveries, and, what is more, endorsing them."[5]

Not so: this is a mistake, or a Marat-manufactured exaggeration, as May is soon to prove. The Academy—of Sciences, in this instance—is well and truly "entirely against him." And it's not changing its mind. On the contrary: when he challenges it and tries to "coerce" approval out of it, it shies away with a loud snort and shatters Marat's dream—another one.

At first, though, it looked as if all would be well. Crowds come, the initiated show interest, a few opinion-makers smile benignly. Marat wants Franklin, and gets him; and in Paris this year, what Franklin says goes. He is one of the first to accept the personal invitation extended with due formality. All his carriage has to do is trot along the right bank of the Seine, down from Chaillot and along the Rue Saint-Honoré, to reach the Croix du Trahoir, that knot in the tangle of old streets that converge around the Pont Neuf, near the grain market. The coach stops at the fountain surmounted by a cross, "which supplies water from Arceuil" and has just been rebuilt "according to the drawings and under the direction of the late M. Soufflot, who was obliged to form [*sic*] a dwelling in this place in order to accommodate the Judges at executions."[6] They've been held on the Place du Trahoir "since time immemorial, whenever the Place de la Grève is encumbered or when the misdeeds were committed in this district," where numerous thieves have their appointments with the tradespeople. "It is for this reason that a cross was put up, so that the condemned might have it before their eyes and derive consolation from it in their last moments. Many authors have tried to trace the origin of the name Trahoir. Some derive it from *trahere*, 'tirer' [pull or draw, as water], and others from 'trier' [sort or grade], because this crossroads was formerly a marketplace where livestock was sorted for purchasers."

So Franklin comes along to sort the wheat from the chaff in the market-place of his special expertise, that is, the sciences; and he cloaks his judgment in the courtesy of silence, a practice which has now become second nature to him. Stumbling over the round paving stones, he enters the hall of the Hôtel d'Aligre and is led to a chair in the first row, facing the platform where Marat is making passes like a sorcerer and exposing a heated metallic ball to the lens of his solar microscope. "Observing the cloth on which its shadow is outlined, one sees an undulating sphere of perceptible vapors around the ball."[7] But Franklin, who can never live through even the gravest hour without a little diversion, points out that there is a second sphere in the room. Try it, my friends. Ineffable moment: "M. Franklin having exposed his bald pate to the lens of the solar microscope, we perceived it ringed with undulating vapors ending in twisted points; they resembled the sort of flame which painters have made the attribute of Genius." If Michelangelo had happened to be there, Franklin might have modeled for an answer to his Moses. Will Marat now be tempted to isolate the substance of genius, like some variant of phlogiston? A few days later the joke's over.

The first round with Lavoisier has already been fought. He is the most famous, if nothing else, of the academicians against whom Marat is waging his avant-garde campaign, and therefore Marat expects more from him even though he poohpoohs his theories. And will be all the more hurt as a result. He had sought "the approval of the Academy of Sciences" so that he could show other European scholars a sort of manufacturer's guarantee that the experimenter was free from any taint of amateurism. But the academicians appointed to observe his course apparently turned up without warning one cloudy after-noon when nothing was working. They did it on purpose, of course—accord-ing to Marat, who receives them "with very little consideration,* and appears to have behaved with arrogance, especially toward Lavoisier, saying that he did not particularly care whether the scientist came to see his experiments."[8] Whence the academicians' reservations about him. They keep putting off their decision—let him wait, the porcupine. Meanwhile, a funny little bell begins to tinkle in his head concerning *"the coryphaeus of charlatans, Sieur Lavoisier, son of a skinflint,† apprentive [sic] chemist, pupil of the Genevan speculator* [that is, Necker], *administrator of the Discount Counter, secretary to the King, member of the Academy of Sciences."*[9]

Lavoisier, however, does not personify the whole Academy, whereas

*Quoted in Gérard Walter's *Marat*.

†Coryphaeus is used figuratively here to mean the leader of a sect. The "skinflint" is Lavoisier's father, who was an attorney. Like Beaumarchais, Lavoisier had obtained the honorary title of secretary to the king.

Condorcet, having become its perpetual secretary in 1773 at the age of thirty, does. So it's to him that Marat keeps sending increasingly irate letters in April 1780, trying to force the Academy to inform him "of its determination with respect to his experiments." But Condorcet is in no hurry. Is it negligence? Irritation? In any event, this business has so little importance in his eyes . . . His work as perpetual secretary accounts for only an infinitesimal part of the frenzied activity into which this desperate bachelor* is plunging ever more deeply now that his romantic friendship with Julie de Lespinasse has contracted such a bad case of the staggers. He takes very seriously his duties as inspector of the mint—a job Turgot got for him—and is concocting a scheme to unify and simplify the system of weights and measures. He is also working at a monumental literary series, the *Eloges* of sixty-one scholars who have been members or correspondents of the Academy of Sciences since its foundation. He wants to make it a sort of biographical history of modern sciences, "their *history* rather than their eulogy, for we owe to the dead only what is useful to the living: truth and justice." And even that's not enough: the bulk of his cerebration is being expended on an attempted marriage of mathematics and politics. Ah, if only it were possible! To reduce Machiavelli and Caliban to an equation . . . He's just written an *Essai sur la probabilité des décisions rendues à la pluralité des voix* [Essay on the probability of decisions taken by plurality of votes], but this is only the first installment of the *Mathématique sociale* which he hopes to make his life's work. So Marat's antics, coming on top of all that . . . Besides, the Academy is besieged by a swarm of inventor-mosquitoes who are all claiming to make the world over every morning. And so the flyswatter notification of May 10 that flattens poor Marat must have seemed the merest brush of the fingertips to Condorcet, when he scribbled his name at the bottom of it so it could be sent out with the perpetual secretary's visa.† "As these experiments are very numerous, and we have therefore not been able to verify them all with the necessary exactitude; as, moreover, they do not appear to us to prove what their author imagines them to demonstrate, and are, on the whole, contrary to the best-established facts of optics, we believe it would be pointless to enter into more detail with a view to making them known, not considering them to be such as the Academy could approve or endorse."[10]

"Contrary to the best-established facts" . . . of optics, of physics, of criminal law: exactly the accusation Marat was waiting for. He asked for it. *"I dare flatter myself that I did not miss my target, judging from the ignoble persecution*

---

*The chief cause of his despair being his rejection by young Adrienne de Meulan, whom he loved in the early seventies "to the point of wanting to do away with himself." We will meet him again at greater leisure when he marries in 1786.

†The notification is written and signed by the three "commissioners" delegated by the Academy to investigate Marat: Le Roy, Cousin, and Sage. No mention of Lavoisier, who was a spectator but not a consultant expert.

which the Royal Academy of Sciences has unceasingly inflicted upon me, * once it had made certain that my discoveries relating to light overturned its work of a century . . . As the d'Alemberts, Caritats [Condorcet], Lerois [sic], Meuniers, Laplaces, Monges, Cousins, Lavoisiers and the charlatans among the scientists wished to stand alone on the pedestal, and as they held the trumpets of renown in their hands, they succeeded, can you believe it, in having my discoveries belittled throughout Europe?"*[11]

There's something wrong here: Marat is roaring at an outrage which, he swears, will keep him from outdistancing Newton; while Condorcet is calmly writing, somewhere in a letter to d'Alembert, "I would (sometimes) reproach the academies for being too lenient. M. Marat is a case in point. The Academy's only error was to have seemed at first to condone experiments put forward as being new, but which in fact were known, the only new thing about them being the systematic jargon in which their author clothed them. Academies have two indisputable uses: the first is to act as a barrier, unswervingly opposed to every form of charlatanism, and it is for this that so many people complain of them; the second is to ensure the use of proper scientific methods."[12]

Who is the charlatan of whom? Marat, anyway, isn't retracting a single word: *"This sort of charlatan is always in our midst, fluttering in fashionable circles . . . fattened by the government and devouring, in idleness and pleasure, the substance of unfortunate craftsmen and poor laborers . . . calling oneself a scientist does not entitle one to extort favors from princes, or rather pennies from the poor."*[13]

There's a difference, however: Marat's bellowing does no more damage to Condorcet than the buzz of a bumblebee. But the verdict of the Academy tosses Marat back into the mob of tightrope-walkers and quacks. He won't be accredited. His experiments in the spring of 1780 lead to nothing constructive. He has banged his head against the wall of another dead-end alley. It hurts. He cries ouch. Bad taste.

And yet . . . "Love of the good and of glory are the only constant passions he knew. These passions become those of all enlightened men, and that is why there is such a powerful league against them; their enemies are all the people who are driven by petty, individual passions . . ." Is this some text on Marat? Or by Marat? Hardly: it's Condorcet who wrote these lines, to Turgot, about Voltaire.[14] And that same Condorcet has just quarreled with Maurepas, after refusing to eulogize the old mentor's finally deceased cousin, La Vrillière, at the Academy. He's also preparing "a clear, moderate work, well supplied with authorities, that would contain an account of all the assassinations, massacres, seditions, wars, ordeals, poisonings, ignominies and scandals which have formed the history of the Catholic clergy for the past 1,774 years."† At war

*This text was written thirteen years later, just before his death.

†The scheme was presented to Turgot in these terms in 1774, but Condorcet is still working on it in 1780. It becomes his *Almanach anti-superstitieux.*[15]

with the priests; and at war with the privileged, too. It's not Marat who just wrote, "I fear this Necker will starve us all with his determination to advance his projects without convulsions.* It is a sorry thing that twenty million men should be tossed about at the mercy of madmen, imbeciles and scoundrels."[16] Another sentence by Condorcet. Between these two men—the first of whom, Condorcet, ignores the second from the height of his position as a man who has "arrived," and the second, Marat, has just conceived an undying hatred for the first—the agreement in their disagreement is complete, even to their political (although not their social) indignation. Unwittingly, they contemplate the society of their day through the same pair of eyes.

And they are also united in their hostility toward Lavoisier, the farmer-general and enemy of Turgot, vehemently denounced to him shortly before his disgrace, by Condorcet.

Yet Lavoisier himself has just written, at Mme Necker's request and for her husband's perusal, an appalling report on the Conciergerie of the Palace of Justice† and the management of Parisian prisons, "filled with filth, vermin, corruption," to which he appends a catalog of measures "to remedy a tableau so afflicting for mankind."[17]

Marat, Condorcet, Lavoisier . . . 1780 is Year I of the great misunderstanding.

BRISSOT

37

MAY 1780

On the Eve of All That Is About to Pass

Marat has not been entirely forsaken, however. His persecution, or at least obstruction, by the Academy attracts the sympathy of the little world of the marginals. One of them has just held out a helping hand: Jacques-Pierre Brissot. This is the beginning of their friendship. We find them companions in wrath.

What triggered off the meeting? Hard to make out. Perhaps Marivetz, a

---

*To carry out a nonviolent revolution, in other words.

†From which Lavoisier will set out for the guillotine, along with twenty-seven other farmers-general, on May 8, 1794. In the interim, Necker's first fall will prevent this report from having any effect. Until 1789 the city prisons remain unspeakable sewers.

second lieutenant in Artois's guards, took Brissot to see Marat.[1] But Brissot had wanted to meet him anyway, precisely because of the little ripple his "experiments" have stirred up in parascientific circles. Because in 1780, for want of anything better, Brissot is also thinking of turning physicist. Life has made him, like Marat, into a sort of animal with neither herd nor lair, living nose to the wind. But both have so much on their minds, and so much to say! The first cause of their provisional alliance is a confluence of fates.

They meet several times a month at Antoine Fourcroy's chemistry course. Now there's a man who appears to be succeeding where they have both come to grief. Battered by wind and tide, opposed by all the VIPs, Fourcroy is nevertheless conquering the Parisians. Brissot would gladly take him for a model: *"The ease with which young Fourcroy* expounded the strange phenomena of the decomposition of bodies fired my enthusiasm for chemistry. I absorbed him* [*that is, I attended his lectures*] *with obstinate fervor . . . He had begun to acquire his excellent reputation despite the pettiness and jealousy of the medical faculty, which nearly put an end to his work by refusing the qualifications which he was compelled to buy. His courses drew crowds. In the place of Marat's difficulties of expression, hesitations and incoherencies, and of all the bitterness he put into his lessons,*† *Fourcroy had only clarity, elegance, and ease. His voice was pure and pleasant, as was his language; he brought science within the grasp of everyone."*[2] A true popularizer, exactly what "the personage of some forty years" whom Brissot encounters in front of Fourcroy's platform is longing to be—that Jean-Paul Marat, "small, square-shouldered, with a yellowish complexion,"[3] whom the other man finds "fashioned like a monkey, hardly made to please," but who appeals to him nonetheless because he is so "indefatigable at work, and skillful in the art of performing experiments." Didn't Brissot hear "Franklin pay homage to him one day? He was delighted with his experiments on light. I cannot say as much for those on fire or electricity . . ." "Curiosity and the desire to learn had caused me to seek him out; and the desire to be of use to him, as he appeared to be oppressed, caused me to keep up the acquaintance . . . Insensitive to the pleasures of the table or the embellishments of life, he devoted all his resources to his physics experiments, and occupied his days and nights rehearsing them; he would have contented himself with bread and water for the pleasure of humiliating the Academy of Sciences."[4] Marat, on his side, is favorably inclined toward this gaunt young man with the wide-open eyes turned everywhere, on everything. He knows that Brissot dabbles in journalism and politics, and has already been

---

*Antoine Fourcroy was born in 1755. We'll meet him again at the Convention. The boldness of his ideas and brilliance of his speech alienated the authorities on the medical faculty, who blocked his access to normal channels of competitions and fellowships. A collection taken up by his friends has enabled him to buy his doctor's diploma, and, like Marat, he has opened a course and charges admission.

†This was written by Brissot twelve years later, after their quarrel.

labeled a troublemaker. "This was a qualification (in my eyes), and set him apart from the mob of the ignorant."[5] Why do they have to work so hard finding reasons for their friendship? In May 1780 they simply take a fancy to travel a stretch of the road together.

Brissot is sick of twists and turns. The six years he has just been through since leaving Chartres are like a path traced by a man in a maze.

A few landmarks: Paris, the year of his twentieth birthday and the old king's death. He conscientiously writes out documents in proper legal form near the Temple, in the office of attorney Nolleau, whose "shaft horse,"* or chief clerk, he joylessly becomes. Anything is better than Chartres and the family, sure, but still he was hoping for a little more than this from the big city. Nolleau dies. His brother-in-law Aucante succeeds him and treats Jacques-Pierre with equal benevolence. "He left me all possible latitude for my own work (my private study) and treated me as a friend. He had guessed my thoughts. One day [in 1776] he said to me, 'Even if you remained here forever, you would learn no more. Devote yourself to literature or to the bar, but leave off pettifogging.' "[6]

When you haven't got a red cent, it's all very well to talk. But that signal was what Brissot was waiting for. He dives into the dubious waters of literary salons, vaguely piloted by a childhood friend named Guillard. "I had to live. My mother, to whom I turned, secretly gave me what little help she could for three or four months, but my needs were becoming pressing. I conceived the idea that some small leaflets on subjects people were then preoccupied by might earn some money for me." So he knocks off a few rather nasty little pieces, including a vaguely porn and too specifically tattling *Pot-Pourri*. Police commissioner Le Noir frowns. Brissot is threatened with a *lettre de cachet*. He runs to Chartres long enough to have a "malady of weakness" which his mother treats with quinine; then a fresh departure, as soon as he's on his feet again, back to Paris and poverty. Driven to expedients, he flounders into a dismal business of bills of exchange meant to cover the purchase of some jewels by a German adventurer . . . His lowest ebb. He's neither old enough (still a minor) nor rich enough to sign such bills. Commissioner Le Noir decides he's too small to keep and throws him back—but he's marked.

He gets bailed out of this scrape by Swinton, a big fat John Bull-type Englishman who runs the *Courrier de l'Europe* in London—circulation one million, the cheap rag of the day. Nothing but gossip and scandal, although a certain liberal tinge gives it the striking force of opposition. A pen-pusher was needed to look after the French edition at Boulogne, since the war was

---

Limonier: the strongest horse in a team, the one counted on to set the others in motion. A slang expression.

preventing the paper from being distributed on the Continent. Why not little Brissot? Well, yes, why not? "Bayle, I told myself, was a tutor; Postel was a collège drudge,* and Rousseau a marquis's footman; so I can be a gazeteer. If we honor the craft, it will not dishonor us. Rather than scandal and gossip, we shall talk of constitutions and the public interest . . ."

So that's how you end up working for the lowest-grade muck-merchants in Boulogne in 1778, grinding out the details of actresses' love lives in the *Variétés* column. A pen drudge. As for changing the face of the world . . . The discovery of the sea saves Brissot from the ultimate despair of self-loathing. To a child of inland Beauce and a Parisian adolescent, being suddenly flung on the shore of the Channel is either passion or panic, wonderment or terror. In his case the sea is illumination, it awakens the romantic in Brissot. "With what delight I would go to gaze at it during my solitary walks near the ruins of the Tower of Odre that carried my imagination back to those remote days of the titanic Romans. I went there every evening, and each time the sight was new to me! How insipid and trivial the Tuileries and Palais Royal seemed by comparison with this imposing prospect! . . . Nature expands the soul, society shrinks it. Show me men, palaces, houses, and I cease to be anything but a mere mortal, small, full of passions, dissatisfied with myself. Set me in front of the Alps, their torrents, their snowy peaks, and I positively leave the earth, I soar far beyond my body, I become myself." His favorite author is Shakespeare— another sea, as disconcerting as the real one, and this preference alone sets him apart from most of the educated people of his time.† He reads him in English during his long spells of tedium in Chartres, where the well-stocked library of Dom Mullet, a lapsed Benedictine, gave him refuge and enabled him to learn English, Spanish, and Italian. "I love those whistling winds that drive before the storm, those tossing trees, that thunder crashing and muttering, and those torrents of rain flooding down. My heart shudders, suffering, battered, torn; yet that agitation is sweet to it, for it cannot tear itself away. There is a dreadful charm for me in that moment, a pleasure I feel more strongly than I know how to express: no doubt that is the impression produced by Shakespeare and the playwrights who imitated him . . . This is not a want of taste on my part, it is a need of the soul."

So being stuck out there isn't a complete waste of time. His romanticism serves him, like so many others, as a sort of consolation prize for a kidnapped

*Pierre Bayle, author of the *Dictionnaire historique et critique,* was the father of modern criticism. Less famous, Guillaume Postel was an orientalist of renown in the sixteenth century.

†Nevertheless, the passage just quoted is so orthodox in its Rousseauism as to be almost conformist. He had never seen the Alps . . . The French "intelligentsia" of the day rather looked down on Shakespeare: Voltaire didn't like him, but Diderot defended him. He could only be apprehended in the original, for French translations of that time softened and emasculated him beyond endurance.

adolescence, but it also proves that he hasn't given up the fight. His style is growing more confident. He delves more deeply into his desires. He bides his time in Boulogne as well as and better than in many other places, preferably staying close to the port in the lower part of town beneath the crown of high-perched ramparts, in that section where the "new district" and docks ramble off into the sand on either side of the mouth of the Liane. He loves the very odor of the tar drying on the caulker's keels; on the Rue du Cul-Salé, in the course of huge, already quite Flemish feasts, he becomes the caterer's son again. "There, my dangerous facility made me eager to follow wherever anyone chose to lead, into long, noisy meals, games of cards—which I have always detested—and frivolous and puerile conversations. Boulogne, or at least the lower town, was populated by well-to-do, comfortable tradesmen accustomed to good eating, and to inviting one another turn and turnabout. I shall always remember with gratitude the esteem and friendliness shown me by the Cavilliers, Casin, and Coilliot households, etc.,"* but most of all by that of Mme Dupont, a widow who, making the most of the war like everybody else in Boulogne, shrewdly manages the export business built up by her husband. She has three pretty daughters to tempt a single man, two of whom have been gifted with Franco-English names: Lucy, Nancy, and Félicité. Jacques-Pierre rather fancies the last, but Félicité is "promised" to somebody else. So he sips here and there, absentmindedly, for women are well down on his list of priorities. Poring over the gazettes, for example, he learns that the Société Economique de Berne is holding a competition for texts on criminal law.† Two years before his meeting with Jean-Paul, Jacques-Pierre also tries his luck—in vain—with a *Théorie des lois criminelles* that borrows a good deal from Linguet and scares the stolid Swiss stiff. So what? Even without that, he's Marat's half brother already: the one aim in both their lives is to bring down the established order. "Still too young [Brissot's testimony], and in too great a hurry to publish my ideas, I yielded to my impatience to undertake a major work and distinguish myself by striking out at the political tyranny which had always revolted me. From that time forward, I swore to devote my life to its destruction. Religious tyranny was surrendering to the blows of the Voltaires, Rousseaus, and Diderots; I wanted to attack political tyranny, to shatter the idol of government which, under the mask of monarchy, was practicing pure despotism."

He strikes another blow for nothing by making a trip to London—yes, yes, we know there's a war on—to see whether he could invent some means

---

*Sainte-Beuve is born in Boulogne, and is related to the Cavilliers family. In 1835 he writes that he "never heard a single word spoken against Brissot's unflagging integrity during those maligned years, and his poverty was at all times without vice."⁷

†Marat found the subject inspiring enough to use it as the basis for his *Plan de législation criminelle.*

of transforming the *Courrier de l'Europe* into an anti-royalist explosive on the English king's home ground. Funny, phony war! The trip itself, at least, is impeccably lawful, thanks to "Monsieur Minet's boats," which imperturbably advertise their services in that same *Courrier de l'Europe:* "The Sieur Mariée of Dover has the honor to inform the public that four ships, known as Bye-boats, belonging to M. Minet . . . have received permission from the courts of London and Versailles to ply between Dover and Calais, and regularly to carry passengers who need have no fear of being molested by ships of war."[8] It costs you half a guinea, or twelve French livres.* Was there an extra charge for watching battles from the Bye-boat bridge? In any event, Brissot draws a blank in London. "Everything Swinton told me was a lie."

1779. Paris, but worse than before. Hunger. SOS to the family. Reply from the father, Guillaume Brissot: "Your mother is still in her previous condition [of increasing mental derangement] . . . Your sincere and lasting return to God might perhaps afford her some relief, and that is where you should begin." Jacques-Pierre hits bottom. He sells his pen wherever he can; he even, oh, rage and fury! writes articles for an ecclesiastical dictionary of France. He is about to die of dis-ease. Mentelle saves his life.

Edme Mentelle—a crossroads man, or living link if you prefer.† Born and bred to hold out a helping hand, a shoulder to lean on in time of need. He knows Mme Dupont, the friendly widow from Boulogne. She sends Brissot to him. He's an instructor at the military academy, and "geographer to the King," for whom he has just built an enormous double-walled globe by means of which earthlings can at last discover the world as it really is: political on top, physical underneath. These days, everyone's playing Bougainville.** Mentelle has just published seven octavo volumes on "Spain, Portugal, Italy and European Turkey." At the moment, he's well known and well paid. But when he was "young, he had been without support, like myself [writes Brissot]. My position, so similar to his, touched him, and he treated me as a brother. His wife's gifted playing on the harpsichord attracted all the most skillful musicians to her home, just as the excellent nature of her husband brought the most celebrated men of letters." Mentelle is now fifty, with a heartwarming phiz built around a large, burgeoning bottle-nose; he's a human sun. He knows Mme Roland, her husband, their friends, and Dupont de Nemours, and Fourcroy, and Laplace, and Lavoisier, and a hundred more . . . That rescues

---

*About 60 new francs [$12]. According to Brissot, this was an intermittent communication, and it ceased in 1779. "I left Calais by the last packet for Dover."

†He is the witness and friend of the last hours of Brissot and Mme Roland.

**That is, explorer. Louis-Antoine, Comte de Bougainville (born in Paris in 1729), was a lawyer, diplomat, and famous explorer whose travels through the Pacific were reported in 1771 in his *Voyage autour du monde.* We encounter him at the Battle of the Chesapeake. [*Trans.*]

Brissot once again. He's liked, he's understood, and he's given interesting work to do.

Another stroke of luck: Guillaume departs this life. Jacques-Pierre whips over to Chartres long enough to bury his father and sever the last strands of umbilical cord tying him to a mother, now mad as a hatter, and a flock of bigoted brothers and sisters. "What can be the bonds that bind us to such individuals? Only two remain: pity and gratitude." The caterer had been careful to pare his miscreant son's share of the inheritance down to the bone, but couldn't stop him from getting his hands on the first real money of his life. "I had four thousand francs!* For me it was a treasure. I thought it would last forever." Why doesn't he use it to give himself an "estate" and quit floating around in a vacuum of classlessness? Become a lawyer, for instance, without cracking a lawbook. If you've got money, nothing could be simpler. At Rheims you can purchase this "grotesque harness"⁹ in a week. "My trip to that city convinced me how degraded its University had become . . . Everything was sold there, theses, degrees, and arguments. I blushed for the doctors examining me . . . for they questioned, or feigned to question, me very seriously on the issue of whether eunuchs could marry. After paying five or six hundred livres for this farce, I returned to Paris and presented myself at Parliament," making even greater haste now because at Mentelle's house he finds Félicité Dupont, released from her previous engagement. They love each other. Brissot thinks he's home safe—a lawyer, a married man . . .

Parliament slams the door in his face. His purchased degree is no help to him when he has to face the burly body of the Order of Paris,† which is ruled by stuffed shirts like Gerbier and violently rejects any applicant who's ever been within miles of Linguet. "Before being called to the bar one had to serve a four-year apprenticeship. This novitiate was called a pupillage. The bondage did not end there. The venerable elders [whom Brissot also calls the "matadors of the Order"] even claimed the right to put their pupils' ideas in chains . . . As soon as I had attended two or three of their lectures, finding myself back on the school bench and under the master's rod, I determined to give up the Palace [of Justice]."

Brissot is a lawyer who will never plead a case. His life continues to be dammed up on all sides, like that of Marat. This is the year of their meeting. Jacques-Pierre has the same paranoid reflexes as Jean-Paul. "In the eyes of my inquisitors I was guilty of an abomination: I had just published my *Théorie des lois criminelles!* I, a neophyte, daring to censure the jurisconsults! . . . Daring to trample underfoot the old laws that murdered

---

*20,000 new francs [$4,000]. His law degree will cost him about 3,000 [$600]. Roland and Danton both acquire their degrees in the same way and also at Rheims.

†Equivalent of the bar association. [*Trans.*]

the innocent! I had to be proscribed, and I soon was."*

Who is the more aggressive of the two? For the moment it's Brissot, beyond any doubt. "I was caviling, caustic, intolerant, and violent in argument, and I claimed that this was philosophy . . . I was looked upon as a dangerous savage." One fine morning at Mentelle's he goes for Laplace, one of the lords of geometry†—because Laplace was making fun of Marat. Brissot knocks him flat with, "Monsieur, you are like those theologians of the sixteenth century who thought they were accumulating reasons when all they were accumulating was words."10

He even dares to attack "the high priest d'Alembert." He tears the Academy to shreds on the occasion of La Harpe's admission: "It was all long, cold, dogmatic and soporific; it was also mightily bombastic and out of place. There was something of the fairground quack, touting his drugs in the market square, about these little great men swinging their censers and singing praises to kings, queens, ministers, the dead, the living and themselves . . . I was pained to observe [at Mentelle's] how men of letters and academicians hated one another and were forever at one another's throats. The dryness of their souls revolted me no less than their haughtiness and arrogance . . . The geometricians took sides in obedience to the tastes of the noblemen who tossed them crumbs from their tables."

Brissot, Marat, Linguet . . . A sort of league of the flayed-alive is beginning to form, with anti-academism as the nucleus of its creeds.

" 'How old are you?' Linguet asked Brissot the other day, in London.

" 'Twenty-six.'

" 'Blessed mortal! Twenty-six! And on the eve of all that is about to pass . . .' "11

As for Marat, he's got an idea about Brissot, a sort of scheme for an association through which they will express their joint aspirations—showing that he did consider the young man more socially competent than himself. "Full of desire to see him prosper, I [Brissot] was continually bringing new acquaintances to him to witness his experiments . . . However, he realized the difficulty he had in expressing and governing himself in a discussion. He was looking for an educated man who had the gift of speech and could expound his theories for him. On several occasions he suggested that I should act as his deputy."

Brissot very nearly accepts. All year long he wavers on the verge of a lasting commitment to Marat. But "my inner sense drove me away from him,

---

*They also reproached him with those unfortunate bills of exchange from 1776, a subject he never cared to dwell upon.

†Pierre-Simon de Laplace, born in 1749, is a high dignitary of the Empire and Restoration. A student and disciple of d'Alembert, he was professor of mathematics in a military academy at the age of nineteen.

rather than bringing me closer." He can't quite find the energy to sign a binding contract.

There's already one corpse between them: Voltaire's. Marat execrates him. Brissot loves him. He also loves Rousseau, and begs to be allowed a heart and mind large enough to contain this double allegiance. "I loved philosophy too dearly to make a profession of fighting it. At bottom, I was too attached to the cause of the Encyclopedists to join forces with their sworn enemies." There lies the germ of discord, curled up at the core of their new friendship and alliance.

So Brissot decides to help Marat, but on his own terms and as the occasion arises. No formal structure in their union. And he begins writing his treatise on *La Recherche de la Vérité et les moyens d'y parvenir* [The search for truth and the means of finding it]. "None of my works ever gave me sweeter satisfaction," because in it he sees himself as he has become: proud of himself at last, as sure of his pen as a surgeon of his scalpel, Jacques-Pierre Brissot, a free man. Félicité is his. He'll marry her when he can.

DUPONT DE NEMOURS

38

MAY 1780

Persevere on Your Knees

Victor de Mirabeau died on October 8, 1778, aged five. "Sophie-Gabriel [*sic*], daughter of the lady Marie-Thérèse-Sophie Richard de Ruffey, wife of Messire Claude-François de Monnier, departed this life aged two years and sixteen days in the year of Our Lord one thousand seven hundred eighty, on Tuesday the twenty-third of May, in the home of Jacques Quillet where she had been put to nurse, in the parish of Notre Dame de Deuil of the diocese of Paris."[1]

Between the death of his son and that of his daughter—whom he will never have known—Mirabeau has spent 590 days in the prison of Vincennes for having loved a married woman. And it's not over yet. But a change is slowly taking place inside him in the course of his long voyage around the four walls of his cell. This period of his life might be called "Chronicle of a Man Being Brought to His Knees."

Since the death of the heir to the family name his father has changed targets. It's no longer Gabriel's life he wants, it's his capitulation. His marriage has got to be patched up again, at least long enough for one coupling. He must be permanently returned to the paternal fold and made to declare war on his mother and sister, if only as a public demonstration of his surrender. This is the big year for the Friend of Man, who has obtained a sort of blank checkbook from Maurepas on the prisons of the Church: no less than four *lettres de cachet* to lock up the marquise in a convent, and another two for Louise de Cabris. His son is in his power for keeps. Mirabeau senior must be as close to happiness as his neuroses will ever let him come. He gloats over his victories as he tells his brother (the bailli) about a conversation he's just had with somebody or other:

> "Is your trial against madame la marquise over now?"
> "I won."*
> "And where is she?"
> "In a convent."
> "And your son, where is he?"
> "In a convent [he means Vincennes!]."
> "And madame your daughter in Provence?"
> "In a convent."
> "Have you undertaken to fill all the convents?"
> "Yes, sir, and if you were my son you would have been in one long ago
> . . . I know that, to listen to some people, I am the Nero of the century. But what
> do I care for that? If I were sensitive to the touch, I should have been dead long
> since. The public is no judge of mine."[2]

"It is certain that, so long as my grandson lived, I should have firmly held [the ministers] to their promises, to keep the father shut away and even to lose all trace of him . . ." But there it is. The point now is to make him procreate legitimately again; and even the marquis can't quite envisage dragging Emilie to a prison cell at Vincennes for the purpose. Moreover, he has observed an unwonted lack of enthusiastic support in his own circle on the subject of his son's martyrdom, which inclines him to suspect that the good old days of Louis XIV may be dead and gone. Ah, where are the bastilles of yesteryear, in which nothing and no one could prevent Fouquet from being forced to die? "That breed of cold-blooded toads in Paris who pass for friends are spent and spineless."[3]

The task is challenging but feasible, and clearly delimited: Gabriel will have to be released, but only on condition that his spirit is broken first: "If there be one means of taming that vindictive, empty and vicious head, it is humiliation . . . There could be none deeper for him than to kneel to his wife,

*He's counting his chickens. The "criminal" case was won, if you like, when he obtained authorization for her internment. But the civil proceedings are still pending, and a huge fortune depends upon the outcome.

to implore her, to confess his wrongs to her; he must be brought to it. As yet he has come a very little way, but patience! Else let him die, I care not, it must be that or nothing . . . That man [he's still talking about his own son] is nothing but through his pride. Take that away, and he is no more than a burst soap bubble." The first phase of treatment is already well advanced: month after month "in a place where one's sole company, among lugubrious Gothic vaults, is the nocturnal screaming from the cellars and other such neighbors. It is a medicine that cannot fail to renew a mind. The man must have unhappiness." The marquis is quite certain that his son will thank him for it once he's tamed, and if he survives—and yet he's got an odd little premonition, for all his clear conscience: "The century of people of his sort is fast drawing nigh, for there is no woman's womb today that does not carry an Artevelde or a Masaniello."*

The process envisaged: (A) a letter from the captive to his wife, confessing his wrongs and requesting resumption of conjugal relations; (B) a letter from Emilie to Mirabeau senior, granting her forgiveness and "interceding" with him to have mercy on his son; (C) a second letter from Gabriel, announcing his unwavering intention to return to the straight and narrow, and begging conditional release under the supervision of his father, invested by the king with discretionary powers to have him jugged again at the first sign of insubordination. In return, he would be transferred from a state prison to conditional semi-freedom in his family.

One small detail: Sophie. And their little girl. What about them? Gabriel will just have to sort that out for himself. Why did he have to clutter up his life with females? The Marquise de Monnier is sequestered at Gien; let her be forgotten there.

But you can't operate without a surgeon; and it would not be consistent with the marquis's dignity to act in person. Besides, for the past twelve years (since Gabriel's first incarceration in the Fortress of Ré) his attitude has never wavered: as far as he's concerned, so long as his son remains in prison he is dead. He never answers letters. But the Friend of Man has a perfect go-between at his beck and call—little Dupont, from Nemours,† his full-time toady. The marquis sees him as a man of "wit and talent," although he criticizes him for being "all of a piece, romantically minded, and, moreover, eternally preoccupied with himself and his role in things."4 Even so, Dupont seems the ideal man for the mission now entrusted to him.

---

*Artevelde: fourteenth-century Flemish revolutionary. Masaniello: Neapolitan revolutionary of the seventeenth century. The power of both was too ephemeral for any of their ideas to become realities, and both were killed. Their stories were told by their conquerors.

†The French is Dupont, de [from] Nemours; the author points out that the comma is no mistake: at this stage Dupont de Nemours is still just plain M. Dupont, or du Pont, depending on how he signs his name (which is as common in France as Jones is in England). [*Trans.*]

On May 8, 1779, after twenty-three months in solitary, with his wardens or the censors as his only visitors, Mirabeau sees the face of a friend, or so he supposes, at the door of his room. A face from his youth. He clasps Dupont to his heart.

The angler feels a nibble, the big catch tests the bait; they begin to play each other in a dialogue of parrying and patience, interrupted by tactical pauses, which is still going on a year later. Their first conversation is a superficially affectionate heart-to-heart, each taking the other's measure for four long hours, and finding unjustifiable grounds for optimism. "He's ripe," thinks Dupont, "I'll make short work of him." Gabriel, meanwhile: "As big a fool as ever. I'll make him think whatever I like." Physically, Pierre-Samuel Dupont is unaltered. The disgrace of his beloved Turgot flowed over him like water off a duck's back. Besides, he's still connected with the treasury office although at a distance, working for Necker in the inspectorate of manufactures and trade. What else? He's planting "artificial prairies" in the Gâtinais. He's happy, has no problems with his wife and children. A profound self-satisfaction is beginning to give shape to the weak features surrounding his broken nose. He was thirty at Christmas 1779. But "although hot-tempered and even impetuous, he was never youthful . . . He looks no more than thirty. At first sight, everyone takes him to be younger than me."[5]

Whereas Gabriel-Honoré de Riqueti, Comte de Mirabeau, is Dupont's senior by six months and looks like an old man. His worn-out eyes bulge from his head, he's bloated and fish-belly white, he pisses mud, he's inhabited by an army of itinerant aches and pains. "For over a year I have been barefoot in my shoes; for six months my breeches have been letting show things which it is pointless to display, there being no women here."[6] He knows perfectly well that his one hope for a new lease on life hangs on the negotiations which are now beginning. And what does Dupont risk, in case of failure? Mild irritation.

Mirabeau is soon undeceived. Already in July 1779, "my opinion shows me Dupont conniving with my father and finding excuses to procrastinate, but really doing so in obedience to my father's views and methods."[7] All the more reason to play it close to the chest. Gabriel doesn't object to the idea of writing to his wife, he even copies out a draft supplied by Dupont, who volunteers to go to Provence, fetch back Emilie's answer, and have a little chat with Sophie on his way over the Loire, if that would be any help. He buzzes around everywhere, sticks his nose into everything. Mirabeau lets him, having firmly made up his mind from the outset that he would not be trapped into betraying his private freedom, which he still identifies with his love for Sophie.

Once again Emilie adds fuel to his skepticism by her chilling reply: "I feel most vividly, Monsieur, the horror of your position, but you have put me in the case of being unable to join forces with you . . . I am therefore compelled merely to desire that your father will do as you wish him to do; and although I cannot cooperate in your happiness, I should be delighted to learn that you had found it." There's one, anyway, who hasn't signed on with the old man, and it's almost a relief to Gabriel. "It is a source of secret satisfaction to me to see how many grounds I have for holding that base and gangrened soul in contempt."[8] But his temper begins to fray in the company of the deliberately apathetic Dupont and his sticky-sweet way of forever siding with his father. There's something positively clerical in his attitude: "I complain of his want of good faith, of the wrapping of policy that shrouds his friendship, of the decision he appears to have taken to blame me for everything." Mirabeau is beating his head against a rubber wall. Dupont bends but never breaks. A one-way-only friendship. "He was meek as a lamb, and always is when he speaks . . . I can't bear any more of it, and I challenged him with the most awful of my father's wrongs against my mother and myself: 'How can you qualify the action of a father who tells all Paris that his son has slept with his wife,* and who says it without believing it? Which of us began this war? How can it be ended?'[9] He responded with his usual generalities: how I could not come off with honor without the consent of my father," to whom he now has to come crawling, especially as Emilie's defection leaves the marquis holding all the trump cards. "We parted good friends" on August 7—but not for long. Autumn and winter find them quarreling again like ragpickers. Mirabeau is floundering in a tightening net. The dialogue of deaf-mutes drags on for ten months:

"Your father may have been severe . . . But when was he ever unjust?"

"His conduct toward me has nothing to do with severity. It is an attack upon nature, justice and law . . . When was my father unjust? Since the day I was born."

"Your father does you the kindness to believe you mad. That is the most charitable opinion of you he can hold."

"If my father does me a kindness to believe me mad, then he ought to study his duty toward a madman, and that duty is not to kill me."

A casuist can always be driven over the edge. Dupont explodes:

"I shall say like your father that you tend toward madness, that you have been mad; because I wish neither to say nor to believe that you have been depraved and unnatural."

"If you can excuse my past conduct only by saying that I am mad, or depraved or unnatural, please stay out of my affairs—for I warn you that I am not mad."

"You must be blamed, my dear count, and maltreated, and bitterly chastised.

---

*Meaning, "that I slept with my own mother." This rumor of incest has been pursuing Gabriel ever since his departure from Bignon, and probably did arise from some verbal or written exaggeration of the marquis.

Only consider that all who have had to do with you, all whom you have loved or who have loved you, have gained nothing but misery for their trouble."

"No, my dear Dupont, misfortune must not be bitterly chastised. It must be respected. Above all, you must not judge a man without enough knowledge to do so. I deserve to hear the truth; but you do not act in good faith with me. You are not even charitable. You have seen and heard me, well determined in advance to blame me for everything."[10]

They lose their tempers but don't break off. They see each other again, make up, and start bickering all over; they become necessary to each other, in a bond of mutual cruelty. Dupont isn't man enough to dissimulate to the end. He confesses: "My desire and my plan are to see you resigned, touched, softened, abandoning all thought of justification or recrimination, having denied yourself all right to them if indeed you ever had any, abjuring all spirit of contention and war, crying for mercy and no other thing from the father whom you have offended."[11] That's Dupont, who broke with *his* father at twenty! He's probably never forgiven himself. He becomes more and more personally committed to the disciplining of Mirabeau, as though his whole view of the world and life depended on paternal primacy. In the end, he's so anxious that one might think they'd switched roles—he's the real prisoner, of structures he can't conceive being challenged with impunity. For himself too, for his own moral security and that of the millions of little Duponts on whose behalf he is bearding this wild animal in its cage, Mirabeau *must* knuckle under. Order or death.

> I showed him quite plainly that I was not fooled by him. He was trying to prove to me that under no circumstances should I desire my freedom other than through my father. I told him that I was not at all of his opinion.
> "You will do me," said he, "an irreparable wrong."
> "What wrong?"
> "That of giving the lie to my assertions."
> "Ought I to allow myself to be killed by my father rather than escape his blows?"
> "Yes."
> "Much good may you derive from that sentiment! I, personally, mean not to put my own neck in the noose."
> Thereupon he became very flustered and looked extremely gloomy.[12]

And when Mirabeau finally begins to sag, from need or grief, or simply because time is passing and he's exhausted and desperately wants to live a few months more, his hangman of a friend issues a few ineffable words of consolation: "The one law of our deplorable condition is *Woe unto the conquered.* We must be grateful to the stronger when they do not abuse our gratitude . . . You are a prisoner of war, a war you ought not to have begun, one you cannot choose but repent of . . . Should your approaches [to your father] prove unfruitful, my friend, you must renew them, vary the form and persevere as to the substance, but persevere on your knees."13

Gabriel's coming to it, but not without lamentations. He's a heretic by temperament; you can ask anything of him, except silence.

"I cannot accustom myself, my dear Dupont, to seeing you maintain that everyone else is in the right against me, when right is so patently on my side."14

"Du Con de Nemours"* treats himself to the last word:

"Even when both sides are equally wrong, the public and people in high positions always side with the fathers against the children, and they are right."

MIRABEAU

39

MAY 1780

To Stiffen Every Prick in the Universe

And what's Sophie de Monnier doing all this time? Well, she's been given a front-row seat at her own strangulation. The correspondence between the prisoner of Vincennes and the recluse of Gien allows her to savor every bitter drop of the transformation as it falls.

They've been permitted to write to each other since September 1777, when she was first shut away, pregnant, in the home of the demoiselle Douai. Le Noir† was delighted; he saw "these authorizations to correspond as a great help in calming the fermentation of minds heated by solitude and captivity."1 Clever man, this top French jailer. He exploits his safety valves to the utmost. So many prisoners were being asphyxiated because they didn't know how to write! . . . At least these two will be able to let off steam, and they don't miss a single opportunity. Floods of ink pour out every week, over and over again, enveloping their health, their memories, their dreams, what they read, what they think. The tone is often a trifle annoying, like that of people talking too loudly in a room with no windows. But that's not their fault: they know all

---

*Untranslatable pun on *pont* (bridge) and *con* (ass—*not* the quadruped). The author comments, "Not a misprint. Dupont's last word should be compared with that of Malesherbes, diametrically opposed, on the subject of quarrels between fathers and sons." (See Volume I, p. 311.) [*Trans.*]

†Reminder: the Paris Police commissioner, enemy of Turgot and Mirabeau senior, and thus inclined to look upon Mirabeau *fils* with a benevolent eye.

their letters are read by Boucher, the chief clerk of secrecy and Le Noir's right-hand man, and also by Le Noir and others, at court or in ministry offices. So they act out a sort of parade of love in the Rousseau manner. But it is embroidered on a canvas of profound tenderness that endures until the very end. Some outcries, such as this from Gabriel to Sophie (not dated, but written in July 1779), cannot be faked: "You do not give me one instant of peace. You are with me at night, you follow me the whole day through, you keep me from my studies; I no longer have mind or memory, or feeling or sensation or faculties, save through you . . . I live, I breathe, I suffer, I rejoice, in you. Ah, Sophie, you love me. I believe it, yes, I believe it; but I deserve your affection, for mine has no limit nor expression. Perhaps you would sense it more clearly in my eyes, in my silence, in my sighs, than in my letters. I am mightily displeased with these letters! But how can I help it; love slays the spirit, it dampens the verve. How is one to string words together when one cannot shake off the delirium of passion; and how can one write without stringing words together?"[2]

And desire? The written word is Gabriel's one erotic outlet, and they certainly don't want the censors slobbering over their transports, so for one whole year they try to make love by scribbling in the margins or between the lines with lemon juice that darkens when the paper is held over a flame. This little ploy is discovered in March 1779, but Le Noir's henchmen aren't particularly startled—they've heard worse in the supervised whorehouses. For form's sake, however, they have to put a stop to it, and the sympathetic ink disappears from the margins. But Sophie and Mirabeau have managed to make a few friends in Gien and Vincennes, interested or otherwise, and a parallel correspondence is set up through them.* Here we do not see Sophie at her best: a respite from sexual activity is actually one of the things that makes life bearable for her at the convent of the Poor Clares. But her courage never fails her, not even in this field—as, for example, when she bravely draws an erect phallus from memory, beneath the motto, "I suck you," like those chivalric pennons surmounting certain coats of arms.[3] Gabriel even has to beg her to be a little more circumspect: after all, if letters like that were ever intercepted . . . At the beginning of March 1780, he sends her a coded alphabet for use when composing compromising passages, erotic or political—it's a question of freedom in either case. Thereafter, Sophie's letters begin to look like a bouillabaisse of words, numbers, and hieroglyphs. Mirabeau spends hours and hours laboriously deciphering and reveling in them. Time suspended . . .

*M. Paul Cottin, the otherwise ingenious and diligent historian of this correspondence, writes (in 1903, it is true, when the row of dots was still the rule among historians): "Most of the letters which Sophie received from the count by this means have been destroyed, with the best of intentions, by M. Lucas de Montigny, Mirabeau's adopted son, owing to the indecent language in them."

Another subject abundantly treated, and one that doesn't require secrecy, is their daughter, that little bit of confiscated human flesh, Gabriel-Sophie, as they call her, self-consciously marrying the two genders of their names. She's been taken from both of them. Sophie implores every echo to restore the child to her at Gien, where some of the boarders have been allowed to keep their babies. Yes, but those are widows, madam, or young unmarried mothers whose sincere repentance has been endorsed by their parents. Where would we be if deliberately adulterous women were allowed to do as they pleased? She's perfectly happy, your Gabriel-Sophie, she has everything she needs. The demoiselle Douai, who knows all the right people, has put her out to nurse with someone named Jacques Quillet, a stonemason at La Barre, near Deuil, on the edge of the forest of Montmorency. It's due north of Paris in the country, lots of fresh air; for centuries the few thousand inhabitants of Deuil have been purveyors of rotgut to the monks of St. Denis. As the crow flies, Mirabeau's not so far away from the little girl, and his jailors' indulgence enables him to keep a closer watch on her than Sophie can, by means of vicarious visits. De Bruguières, their darling policeman and friendly neighborhood stool pigeon, the one who brought them back from Holland, is their agent here. He makes two or three trips out to Deuil to check on Mother Quillet, so that the sinner and his partner in sin can share the latest news about the fruit of their sin, a child whom their honor places far above all church-blessed babes. But Gabriel and Sophie are neither Henri IV nor Louis XIV, nor Gabrielle d'Estrées nor La Montespan; and the legitimizing of bastards, that fugitive honesty available only to sovereigns, was stricken from the official code of conduct by Louis XV—who would have had to legitimize too many.

Mirabeau had forebodings way back in July 1778: "I am anxious about your daughter. As yet it is a vague and not very rational anxiety . . . In any case, my Sophie, remember that you were a lover first, before becoming a mother. You owe more to me than to your daughter. It is for me that you must live, love life, and take care of your health . . . One of the ancients wrote these touching words: *The funerals of children are always premature when there is a mother to attend them . . .* Our daughter, I dare to hope, will make a third at our union, but do not take to believing her immortal, or that her childhood will be traversed without mishap . . . Let love be your shield against devouring anxieties, and if need be, alas, your antidote to a cruel pain."[4] Had he heard that the child was sickly or ill cared-for? It seems not. But he shared Rousseau's prejudice against the farming out of children in any form. "Procure yourself a book by M. Fourcroy,* entitled *Les enfants élevés dans l'ordre de la nature* [Children brought up in the order of nature] . . . You will see whether my advice to you was so scatterbrained, and whether I have given serious thought

---

*Proof that Fourcroy was the "in" popularizer.

to the physical education of children. You will see, and sigh to see, how dangerous is the recourse to substitute nurses."

A year later—although his son has died in the interval—such somber thoughts are far from his mind. "Imagine that, upon seeing my man enter the room, [de Bruguières, that is] this little demon (I am speaking of my daughter) fell to scrutinizing him earnestly with two enormous eyes; that, after doing so, she made it her entire passion to become intimate with him; but that, while she was upon his knees, and observing her milk sister, Mlle Thérèse, take a chair, she hopped down and ran over to Thérèse, slapped her, took away the chair and placed it where she wanted it . . . For the rest, she was very well kept, extremely clean, extremely chubby and white as a lily. Her clothes were removed. The little wanton performed her toilette in the presence of a man. She hasn't a pimple on her body, not one spot from bite or sting on her underclothes. In a word, she's in perfect health."[5]

In September 1779 "the little one is in very good health, has an extremely sound constitution, the loveliest complexion imaginable and is quite sturdy. She is just getting over a looseness* as a result of what the nurse calls the chicken pox but it is only a rash, the germ, or symptom of the germ, of teething. She has but sixteen of them. The gums are swollen and she will soon have more . . . She is very pretty, so she does not take after me in that, but we have other features in common: she is turbulent, wicked, and as noisy as ten legions of devils, she stamps her feet, cries and storms, I believe she even swears and drinks wine, and drinks it so eagerly that her goblet had to be taken away from her, for she had already gulped down the half of it; she is forever saying *I want, I want, I want.*"[6]

So in the spring of 1780 the little girl is giving her mother no cause for concern—grief, yes, but that's something she has in perpetuity. Her real source of anxiety is her other child, that big irresponsible baby about whom she has been so quick to understand that he's trying to find reasons for giving in to THEM. All right, he'll get more than he's asking for—because of her spirit of sacrifice, or her dignity, or her masochism, as it will later be known. Sophie de Monnier is forever stretching out her hands to Mirabeau, but her hands are open. She's not a clutcher, she gives with her whole heart, and she pretends to believe in the scheme he has concocted after Emilie's refusal: Gabriel will place himself wholly in his father's power, shamelessly reversing the family alliances, and will help the Friend of Man demolish the Marquise de Mirabeau and Louise de Cabris; the new alliance will then be turned against the Marignanes. United with his father, and for once supported by him—financially too —he will sue Emilie and, because she refuses to resume marital relations with him, he will win his suit and obtain an advantageous settlement. Don't mention

*Colic.

divorce: in 1780 this hypothesis, in the most Christian kingdom of France, seems about as farfetched and utopian as the founding of a republic. But once rehabilitated and legally separated from my legal spouse, I shall enlist in the first army I see, French or not, I shall become a colonel, general, political adviser, Sophie will join me with our daughter, we shall live together better than if we were married, flouting the frowns of every bigot in the world, in our little hut on the riverbank, naked in the shade of the willow . . .

In a thin little voice Sophie keeps saying yes, yes, of course, that's just how it will be. What do I have to do? She signs everything they ask her to. She even writes a letter to the marquis, so noble that it leaves him gasping. Good God, if only his accursed son had met that young woman before they were both married; but what's done is done . . . And that other bonehead has to put in his oar—the winebag, Boniface de Mirabeau, that degenerate younger brother who succeeds, by virtue of his father's favor, in perpetrating all the atrocities attributed to his elder and gaining fame and fortune from them, the "chevalier" as they call him. He turns up at Bignon around mid-September 1779 after one of his habitual binges, but this one has gone on so long that he has to think up some new way to pass it off. Excellent opportunity to indulge his old-maid predilections by capitalizing on Gabriel's plight. He tells how he's been to see Sophie at Gien, how he sneaked into the Poor Clares disguised as a nun, how Sophie took him in, how she gave him the key to their letter-writing code, how she was extremely kind to him, so kind that if he had wanted to . . . The bastard! Sophie just stares. "The Chevalier de Mirabeau is apparently an odious monster who is seeking to compromise me . . . I have not written to him, have received nothing from him. I have not seen him; he never came to Gien. It is all a tale spun by him for the mere pleasure of it . . . To prove that he is lying, let him be asked to describe my appearance!"[7] The chevalier will never be punished for such a trifle. He'll be allowed to set out for the Americas, sailing with the little naval division of M. de Guichen, which is going out to reinforce the Islands garrisons even before Rochambeau himself leaves. His brother shrugs: "He will be good for very precisely nothing out there, save to get himself killed a little sooner by the Negresses rather than by the whores of France; whilst I [if I went] should be an intrepid soldier and a useful officer."[8] America, lurking in the far background of his ordeal. So much is happening, and so much more is about to happen there, and all without him, it's too stupid. "Alas, were we in Boston now, you [Sophie] would be very nearly at peace, and I would be useful and esteemed, my daughter would be American, that is, born among the most respectable nation of people on earth. By now she would have a brother, who would become a little hero, and I doubt that France would ever see me again."[9] Then there's politics, like a second America on his horizon, even in his letters to Sophie, although she's a bit vague on the subject. Their personal condition, he tells her, will change only when the condition of all changes. Is there any other way out of this mess except to blow up Europe? Subversion becomes the air vent in his cell. Never before has he come so close to an awareness of the real world—oh yes, he's begging for release as an act of charity, but that doesn't touch Mirabeau-powder-keg: "Every day princes hear their benevolence vaunted even beyond the confines of the country on which their despotism has imposed falsehood and silence. While they devastate immense regions over which their sole rights are the promptings of the most unbridled ambition ever known to man, they believe, and may do so in good faith, thanks to our infamous flattery, that they have paid their debt to mankind by performing one or two good deeds which cost them no more than the wish, which affect two or three individuals at most, and which cause their courtiers to cry out in admiration and excite fools to delirium. Will we betray the truth forever, for the sake of those very same persons whom we have no smallest cause to flatter? Will we unendingly conspire against our own peace of mind and that of our fellows? When the blaze of the crown gives them publicity, we sanctify actions which the most commonplace being, the basest soul, would blush to consider, and, like cravens, we keep silent! . . . Nay, more: for the most part, we make ourselves hoarse singing hymns to deeds that would set human tribunals up in arms against anyone other than the princes."[10]

This diatribe is not an extract from some manuscript. It occurs in a letter to Sophie. True, their correspondence is more than billing and cooing at the worst of times, but is he writing only to her? One is tempted to say he's looking for an audience. Or a way out. "I was born a gentleman in a land of the enslaved, that is, I was born the slave of slaves. But I know there are paths eternally and infallibly leading on to liberty."[11] For him, they are paths of words.

. . . Even if he sometimes loses his way in their meanders, straying into despair and provocation. Week after week Sophie observes the slow entombment of a great spirit in the mire of mythomania; he's predisposed that way anyway, but here it becomes his best defense against the sheer hideousness of existence. At the beginning of 1780 he is finally allowed to take some exercise, to slow the course of his physical deterioration. He's granted "the freedom of the galleries," meaning that he can walk around the circular gallery inside the tower walls. Vincennes is two distinct worlds: the tower, which is a prison, and the château, which is a sort of superior retirement home, its apartments fought over by ruined aristocrats. A Louvre with no artists. It is there that Canon Bimont, Manon Roland's "little uncle," is living out his autumn years. From tower to château, six hundred yards and ten centuries. "The Château de Vincennes* is a little like a small provincial town. Its inhabitants are divided

*According to a 1777 description by Rougemont, prison governor and Mirabeau's *bête noire*.

into societies and coteries in which passions of every description form the dominant spirit, and it is that spirit, generally republican [*sic*], which leads them to desire whatever can procure them the most absolute independence . . . From all the foregoing there results a sort of confederation among the inhabitants, respecting to the princes [of the blood, and particularly the Condés], who are brought daily to the château by the races and their hunts,"[12] and several of whose womenfolk are housed here—not only the dowagers, but daughters, nieces, and companions as well. As soon as they spy the man with the big head whose reputation has filtered through the walls, they crowd to the windows and offer him his first sight of a female face in over two years. "A passable Provençal woman and two extremely handsome lawyer's daughters" is the briefing he gets from his guards, although in his present condition he'd have found the Gorgon sexy. Another "very comely person casts sweet glances at him for half an hour"; it's possible. And what about the wicked governor's sister-in-law, "a very brown brunette"? Well, we'll give him the benefit of the doubt, and even credit the encounters he claims to have with Rougemont's own wife, which now become more frequent; after all, she's thirty years younger than her husband—so here is Gabriel back in his Pontarlier days.[13] Also plausible are his opportunities for voyeurism from a post in the gallery "from which one may readily look into some of the rooms in the King's pavilion, in particular the apartments of Mme de Sparre. One could see very clearly into the lady's dressing room; she had had the sill lowered to chair height." Shared thrills: seeing and knowing one is seen. Flirting with a prisoner, how delicious. "This indiscreet observing captured Mirabeau's fancy. He sang delightfully, accompanying himself on all manner of instruments which M. Le Noir had given him or permitted him to use. He also had a very fine spyglass."[14]

. . . But from there to his claims that the noble friends of these ladies also took an interest in him when they visited Vincennes! . . . Madame de Genlis, the Princesse de Guémenée, the Princesse de Lamballe . . . No? Why, of course! Mirabeau nimbly takes the plunge: why shouldn't they be having themselves conducted to his chamber? He boasts that during his term in prison he manages to cuckold the ducs de Chartres, Vaudreuil, and Lauzun. He tells Sophie all about it, or lets her guess, by mixing together truth, possibility, falsehood, and allusions to his past, reverting to the lies he used to tell ten years ago and embellishing them with the fantasies of an unchained imagination. The feebleness of a child's inventions in the service of a decadent's eroticism. Does Sophie believe him? She pretends to. "Take every one that wants to come, so long as I keep your heart." That kind of gift doesn't cost her too much; and she lulls his delirium by wrapping it in broadmindedness.

Another swamp for him to sink into: pornography. Beginning in February
1780, "I am working at an utterly mad book entitled *My Conversion*. The first
paragraph will give you an idea of the subject:

" '*Until this moment, my friend, I have been a useless fellow; I have toured the
beauties and played hard-to-please. But now virtue has re-entered my heart. I shall fuck
no more,* * *save for money. I shall advertise myself the certified stud of ladies past their
change of life and I shall teach them to play assholes at so much a month . . .*'

"The idea is quite mad but the details are charming, and I shall read it
out to you one day, at the risk of having my eyes torn out . . . It is a good
caricature, and a truly moral book."[15]

What it really is, is a thin, over-salted stew on the misadventures of a
gigolo. The preface, in the form of a letter from Satan, seems mildly promising, if only by virtue of the scope of its ambition: "May this reading stiffen
every prick in the universe." No chance. From the opening page, Mirabeau's
originality goes down for the count, when he describes his hero's defloration
by "a big momma no more than six months short of the end of her forties"
. . . An old woman, for those times. "Faugh! It will not harden . . . I grow
sad. My problems pour into my mind: the insatiable creditors . . . But ah, my
friend, behold the ass of my fat lass, see how it bounds! Her chest whistles,
her neck contracts, her cunt discharges, she has become a living fury, she tries
to drag me with her . . . Hey, hey, gently there! The pain pours through me;
I weep. The gold appears . . . Gold! God Almighty! I harden and fuck her."[16]
And off he goes for two hundred pages of dreary screwing, with the coins
clinking louder and louder to the flaccid heaving of his turkey hens. Enough
to unstiffen every prick in the universe. Mirabeau is neither Restif nor Sade.
Another washout. But it is impossible to spend two or three months writing
on a subject of one's own choosing without betraying a state of heart. *My
Conversion* is the story of Mirabeau's conversion to gold. Its composition, in
the spring of 1780, seals his allegiance to those who dispense manna. Eroticism
ceases to be a source of freedom for him and becomes a cynically affirmed
breadwinner. Facet by facet his ego is tarnishing. Even the thought of Sophie
is no longer a pollution-proof refuge: he doesn't admit it to himself, but he's
already given up the idea of living with her again. That same spring, Dupont
can triumphantly bear the glad tidings to the Friend of Man. One pure spot
remains: politics, where he now attains to supreme lucidity. The only area in
which he resists alienation—for the moment.

Even his daughter becomes a pretext for tawdry fantasy. "I have my plan

---

*The text is faithfully reproduced; after two pages of preface, this actually is the opening
paragraph.

for that child . . . I shall tell you the most secret and cherished part, which can only become a reality on the assumption that I shall soon leave this place, and which I can confide to no one but you."[17] The plan is destroyed by his censors or heirs, but it's easy enough to reconstruct: a utopia of incest. Not only their children, but their "grandchildren and their children after them must proceed in direct line, so as to avoid all admixture of foreign blood and preserve an eternally young Sophie for him and a Gabriel for her."[18] A challenging program for a man who claims to be on his deathbed. Sophie even acquiesces to that without a murmur, which is proof positive that she has become certain of the worst. He can erect whatever he pleases—in his dreams. She lets him run on.

But Mirabeau is not given the opportunity to cultivate a nursery of mini-Mirabeaus. On May 28, 1780, he begins a long letter to Sophie, full of the futile words one utters in such circumstances: "My friend, the moment has come to prove the strength and extent of your love for me . . . Our child is no more! But me you have still!"[19] This is no longer entirely true. She musters the courage to thank him for giving her the news before the convent sisters do, and for consoling her so abundantly. But although their mutual sufferings may be genuine, their expression doesn't ring true.

The child's "teeth were coming through." On May 23, at her foster mother's, she fell victim to a fatal convulsion, or rather, as people said in those days, to one of "those illnesses that are generally acknowledged to be spasmodic, such as epilepsy, hypochondria, hysteria, convulsive asthma, palpitations of the heart, the hiccough, opisthotonos and emprosthotonos [two conditions associated with tetanus], incubus, priapism, a few forms of colic, and particularly that commonly called *lead* or *painter's* colic, the sardonic rictus, eclampsia or children's epilepsy, *hieranosos, chorea sancti vitii, beriberi,* the cough, the sneezes, yawns . . ."[20] God had a wide range of punishments to choose from.

Sophie is broken, like a prisoner drawn and quartered and flung aside. From this time on her letters have a haggard ring. Gabriel writes to his sister, Caroline du Saillant: "It is good for a man to be ground to a pulp, and Bacon was right to compare him to an aromatic herb. But if he is ground too fine, all the perfume is pressed out of him and nothing remains."[21]

This is his state of mind on June 28, 1780, when he meets, for the first time, his distant cousin and companion in misfortune Donatien-Aldonse de Sade,[22] who has also been driven beyond endurance. He's been shut up in the tower for three years,* it's driving him stark raving mad. Like Mirabeau, he was also

---

*Except for two months of ephemeral escape toward La Coste, in the summer of 1778.

let off the leash for an occasional walk around the gallery, and took advantage of it to thrash a warden who was annoying him. So no more walks, says M. de Rougemont.

Now confined to his cell, he spends his time howling like a wolf. His voice fills three stories of the tower, calling upon all the other prisoners—who couldn't care less—to witness the perfidy of his mother-in-law and the inhumanity of the ministers.

"It is the Marquis de Sade, cavalry colonel, who is being subjected to such abominable treatment! Deprived of air and light! Rally round, my friends! It is in the interests of all!"

Prison silence is his answer, the unique silence of those coffins of revolt —as if there were anything new about a prisoner bellowing for justice! . . . Instead of the responses this agitator yearns for, all he hears are the tranquil footsteps of a more fortunate inmate strolling beneath his window. Sade climbs a stepladder and peers between the bars. Is he really unaware of the identity of the big-headed man with the eruptive hair whom he greets with insults because he's one of the governor's pets, a man allowed to do what he can't? Or is this his indirect way of settling accounts with the image of Mirabeau he has held for years?

"It's all your fault, you bastard, that I am not allowed to walk out! You governor's catamite, why don't you go kiss his ass instead of jeering at me!"

At first Mirabeau doesn't answer. He lets his temper rise. *He* knows who his insulter is, and he feels contempt for him, more because of his reputation than for any real misdeeds. Sade raises the ante:

"Come on, you confounded bugger, answer! Tell me your name if you dare, so that I may cut off your ears once I am out!"

"My name is that of a man of honor, who has never dissected or poisoned a woman! And I shall gladly write that name on your shoulders with my sword if you aren't broken on the wheel before then!"

And Gabriel walks on. The skirmish between two of the most extraordinary men of the century has lasted no longer than an exchange of paw swipes between a pair of tigers in their cages in the king's menagerie.

40

We Are Now, Sir, Under Your Command

From Washington to La Fayette, on May 8, 1780: "I most sincerely congratu-
late you upon your safe arrival in America, and shall embrace you with all the
warmth of an affectionate friend, when you come to head-quarters, where a
bed is prepared for you."[1] This highly symbolic yet sincere embrace takes
place on the morning of May 10, at camp in Morristown. On leaving Boston,
La Fayette falls back into the rhythm of his long-distance gallops: almost one
hundred leagues in two days without pulling off his boots, accompanied by two
or three companions, pistols cocked and naps snatched while the horses are
being changed: there's a strong smell of Tory around here, you scurry from
one free base to another without knowing whether these friendly folks who
bow so politely aren't going to turn around and take you prisoner. An America
as rotten as its spring weather, is it May or March? You'd think you were in
Canada.

No time to be cold. Too much to do. We're the vanguard of France, she's
right behind us, hang on, friends! They make a wide arc to get from Boston
to Morristown without going near New York, where the English spider lurks
in the center of her web. They cross the Hudson at West Point. They weave
in and out among the ponds and streams of this mountain region where men
are lost like lice in the cotton wool of the big forest. Hiding in ambush like
the Indians of yore, the Americans peep over the mountain's shoulder to spy
on the English. The two sides are only ten leagues apart. Battle is only a day's
march away.

At the end of the dusty trail he finally discovers some rebel forces that
look solid and "make a good appearance." Washington's light infantry is
"better clothed than the rest of the army," which isn't saying much, the rest
being more or less totally unclothed. Shouts of recognition run along the chain
of sentries as the young man, slender under the plump curls of his powdered
hair, dressed in his blue, white, and gold general's uniform, gracefully salutes
these last-ditch soldiers. There they stand, hatchet-faced in their grayish uniforms, each with a sort of boiled leather helmet on his head, armed any-old-

how with espontoons* and assorted guns . . . The irreducible nucleus of the New World. No money, almost no ammunition, honor to spare, and, here at least, decent discipline. La Fayette can break into a trot between two rows of huts, so quaint with their chimneys built on the outside to conceal the entrance and keep the heat in. At the end of the soldiers' camp stands the little encampment of the supreme command: a small clearing with a circle of wagons, the tallest hut of all, and the tallest man moving forward majestically, as he does everything else. La Fayette slithers off his horse and into the general's arms.[2] He prepared his little speech long in advance:

"When putting an end to my furlough, I have been able again to join my colors, under which I may hope for opportunities of indulging the ardent zeal, the unbounded gratitude and, I might say, the patriotic love by which I am forever Bound to America."[3]

You'd think they were posing for History's camera. But the pretty picture is promptly laid aside, to be admired later on if God will. Washington is starved for news. Just what is his little marquis bringing him, with his air of a godfather at a baptism? He orders a fresh horse, trained by his own hands, with a soft mouth and quick reflexes, and takes La Fayette far from the confinement of the hut and over the still snow-spotted fields for a long heart-to-heart ride, where they can talk with only the wind to hear them. Gilbert does his best to keep up the fast pace of his adoptive father, the best horseman in Virginia for twenty years, "leaping the highest fences, and going extremely quick, without standing upon his stirrups, bearing on the bridle, or letting his horse run wild."[4] For four years now he's been struggling to train the thirteen states to perform the same way, but even such horsemanship as his has been unable to prevent the rambunctious American team from pulling in seven directions at once. "I see one head gradually changing into thirteen. I see one army branching into thirteen, which, instead of looking up to Congress as the supreme controlling power of the United States, are considering themselves as dependent on their respective States."[5] La Fayette supposes that his announcement of the arrival of six thousand French soldiers will make the general's cup run over, but Washington's joy does not exceed the demands of good manners: he was expecting three times that number, and most of all, a bigger naval force. How can he take New York without blocking the mouth of the Hudson? The King of France is trying to overwhelm him with a pittance. The state governors and congresses will use the paucity of the French aid as a pretext for refusing to lift a finger.

La Fayette prattles on, rebuilding both worlds; he captures New York, snatches Canada in passing, delivers Charleston, signs a peace treaty in London . . . While Washington, behind his eternal mournful smile, is

*A sort of half-pike, a compromise between a lance and a sword.

thinking: ". . . it will be impossible for us to undertake the intended co-operation with any reasonable prospect of success. Unless the States should make extraordinary and effectual efforts now, the succor designed for our benefit will prove a serious misfortune . . .* Drained and weakened as we already are, the exertions we shall make, though they may be too imperfect to secure success, will at any rate be such as to leave us in a state of relaxation and debility, from which it will be difficult if not impracticable to recover."[6]

In other words, everything's just dandy.

Oh well, we'll have to make believe. Conferences in the big hut from May 11 to 13, trying to work out a plan for a combined attack upon New York; La Fayette will carry it to the French as soon as they get here. Washington's officers are so used to their general's pessimism, it has become so much a part of their everyday setting along with the snow and mud, that it hardly affects them anymore. They grimly set to work. Among the general officers present on those days Gilbert notices one eagle-nosed little fellow snorting fire in spite of a game leg torn up by an English shell: Benedict Arnold, one of the victors at Saratoga, whose zest and dash make up for the defeatism of the rest.

La Fayette is soon able to see how the forces balance out. "The English and German troops, divided between New York and the outlying areas, do not exceed ten thousand men. To these regular troops can be added a few militia and refugees and, assuming they were to unload the seamen from their ships, these three bodies of troops might come up to around five thousand men. We accordingly think that the enemy army ought to be evaluated at fifteen thousand."[7] But there are another twelve thousand English in the Carolinas, those who have just gotten even with us for Saratoga by capturing General Lincoln's five thousand men in the pretty city of Charleston where La Fayette spent his first days on American soil. His lovely memory is all spoiled. And what have we got to face the English with? Fewer than seven thousand rebels in arms, and we haven't got them for long. "An army that is reduced to nothing, that wants provisions, that has not one of the necessary means to make war, such is the situation wherein I found our troops, and however prepared I could have been to this unhappy sight by our past distresses, I confess I had no idea of such an extremity."[8] He had forgotten that that was America. The soufflé of his enthusiasm collapses in the frosty wind of Morris-town. So all that remains is to fight, with a clear head and virtually empty hands, as in the days of Brandywine.

However, every time La Fayette finds himself with his back to the wall he quits blathering. All right, let's count again: seven thousand rebels, plus six

*Extract from a letter Washington writes to Congress after his first talk with La Fayette. The military expenditure of the United States had fallen from $24 million in 1777 to $3 million in 1780, and they are counting on gold from France to make up the difference.

thousand French, against fifteen thousand English . . . Zounds! And at that
we'll have to hurry before the ones in the Carolinas, released by their victory,
have time to come up and reinforce the garrison in New York.* Oh, well, who
wants to fight from a position of strength every time . . . For two months La
Fayette engages in a sort of dance of doggedness, Morristown to Philadelphia
to Newport, shaking people up, haranguing congresses and governors for
money, setting up his network of messengers and pilots in anticipation of
Rochambeau, whose arrival is expected any day. They hoped he'd get here by
May 31, then June 15, then June 30 . . . Has he been shipwrecked? And it
would be some help if we knew where he was going to turn up! Please God
he doesn't head for "the Virginia Capes" and fall into the trap there! And
don't let him hang around just north of there either, near the Delaware, where
he'd only be wasting time! It's at Newport and nowhere else that Rochambeau
can be useful, and then only if he gets there PDQ.

When, on July 10, the French sails are finally sighted off Newport, a third
of the fighting season is already gone. La Fayette is at headquarters. He sets
out at once. Louis XVI's envoy to Washington becomes Washington's envoy
to Rochambeau.

Letter from Rochambeau, dated July 11, "at sea off the Island of Rhode,† on
board the *Duc-de-Bourgogne:* We are now, sir, under your command."⁹ The
phrase is noble, but so far it's only a phrase.

At least give him time to put down his suitcase. Everything incites him
to disembark with the greatest prudence: his own personality, the strong
position of the English only fifty leagues away in New York, and the potent
menace of their phantom fleet scouring the four corners of the Atlantic: the
sails of Damocles.

A few cables** away on the *Provence,* whose two topmasts have been
fractured by a storm, Lauzun is about to embark on his thirty-sixth life.‡
Feeling despondent and sentimental. Before leaving for Brest he "bade farewell to Mme de Coigny, at the Tuileries . . . Since that day I have seen how
far I could love her. Ten times I was at the point of telling her so, just as I
was about to part from her forever, perhaps . . . I cared little for life; she might
have made it so dear to me. And yet I dared not. What one thinks most deeply
is often what one has most difficulty saying."¹⁰ The ocean has blown that off

---

*Which is done a month later. Still, La Fayette's evaluation of forces is colored by his visceral
need to exaggerate. General Clinton, the victor at Charleston, brings only four thousand men into
New York on July 17.

†Rhode Island. He is writing to Washington, of course.

**A cable's length is one-tenth of a nautical mile or 720 feet in U.S. Navy, 608 feet in British
Navy. [*Trans.*]

‡Readers are reminded that Lauzun becomes the Biron of the revolutionary armies.

him. Less preoccupied than when he was commanding the Senegambia expedition, he has plenty of time now to take a cool look at the navy, that kingdom within a kingdom. The officers? "They form a body that exudes nothing but jealousy and insubordination, wherein anything that did not begin life as a cadet is loathed and scorned, and every individual officer has prejudices which could be removed only by discharging the lot of them and starting afresh."[11] Are you implying, Monsieur le Duc, that there'd have to be a revolution? The flabbergasted Lauzun has heard two or three of these sea sloths come within an ace of fighting a duel because one of them insisted that the Tiber ran through Constantinople, and another looked at a map and called the Black Sea the Mediterranean.

And the men? Lauzun alone, or almost, among the gentlemen on board, lets his gaze fall a little lower than the end of his nose—upon the condition of the soldiers and seamen, whom it was considered chic to ignore. He has the clearest head of any in his caste, and not for the first time. "Confined six or seven hundred to a ship, they can scarcely move. To drink, they have water so ancient it has turned red. They are devoured by lice, bedbugs and fleas. All these wretched, ill-clothed seamen assemble in the middle of the poop, sit down on the boards and, in troughs like those used for horses, are served, five mornings a week, rock-hard biscuit, sometimes inedible, with a little wine; at noon, more or less the same frugal repast, except that a bit of salt meat is added to the biscuit; and at five o'clock, a soup made one day with beans and the next with pickled cabbage. It would be preferable to give them these vegetables separately* but this is not the custom on shipboard, and besides it would inconvenience the officers; hence, they prefer not to pay any heed."

What they prefer, when the sea is calm, is to go visiting from ship to ship, or draw as close as they can to the *Provence* whenever Lauzun orders the musicians in his legion to give a concert, and fife, bugle, and drum wreathe these rotting, floating prisons-of-war in garlands of grace notes. "In the evening of June 18 the weather was calm and fair, and music charmed the fleet."

Any other entertainment? "On June 11, a small ship laden with cod, herring, oil, and biscuit was seized. This was a great event for the entire squadron. Every warship was permitted to send for its share of the booty; there was an abominable pillage. Men were fighting with drawn swords. At the height of the affray, one sailor fell overboard. He did not know how to swim."

On June 20, a serious alarm: six English warships sighted off the Bermudas. The decks are cleared and Lauzun is edified by the discourse of the Leaguer brother, a Capuchin friar serving on board the *Provence*: "You have an excellent captain; he has given proof of courage and talent. Perform an act of contrition, God will pardon all your sins, and no quarter to the enemy!"

*That is, not cooked in the soup.

. . . But the enemy slips away in the night, and the officers bawl and snarl because the Chevalier de Ternay refuses to go after them. He has explicit orders not to deviate from his course for America by so much as a single hour. While he was capturing six ships he might well find twenty or thirty more haring up behind him, that famous fleet of Admiral Graves which has put out of Plymouth to look for him. So, willy-nilly, Ternay joins d'Estaing and d'Orvilliers on the roster of wet-hen admirals that was being pinned up on all the wardroom walls in those days. It makes him even more lugubrious than before, if that were possible, an old man full of death whose depression permeates the entire fleet. Here, too, morale is high: "Never had a more unenterprising admiral been seen. He spoke to no one, and in the end his gloom was transmitted to the officers. They are all infested with melancholy and boredom; several have become ill," even though *they* are fed relatively decently. And now the men are beginning to succumb to that eternal passion of seafarers, yes, it's our old pal scurvy, where've you been all this time! Two hundred and fifty down with it on board the *Provence,* as many again on the *Conquérant* and *Jason,* more on the *Duc-de-Bourgogne* . . . One might almost make a scientific prediction of their numbers by solving the equation (undernourishment) + (vermin) + (damp) + (lack of hygiene) + (lack of exercise). Is the Descent upon America going to be another Descent upon England? All the more reason to make haste. After two months the seawater changes taste, the sky darkens, birds, algae . . . The sweetness of nearing land, even if land means nothing but a grave. Grand council of captains to decide where to go first to look for their disembarkation signals. Soon the coast of America will fan out in front of them. You always come at it from the south, because of the prevailing winds; but we know Charleston's threatened, even if we don't know it has fallen. What about the middle of the fan, up around one of the two great wind-shelter bays, the Chesapeake near Baltimore, or the Delaware near Philadelphia? But to do what? Parade? No, no, we've got to go right up north and settle in the hollow of that crook in the sea formed by the jut of Connecticut and Rhode Island. With a good east wind, that'll put us a day from New York. "Rhode Island is in our possession," La Fayette has written to Rochambeau a dozen times, and informed him by a fleet of messengers. "You can put in with safety there, you will be awaited by letters, signals and pilots according to my instructions." Another south-facing bay, but smaller and rounder than the other two, where the Island of Rhode looks like a tongue detached from the mouth and left floating in it. Above the tongue is the mouth of Narragansett Bay and the fishing ports with those soothing names: Providence, Peace Dale. Stuck like a fly on the tip of the tongue, the port that was new two centuries ago, at the same time as the Pont Neuf in Paris: Newport, comfortably protected from storms and surprise, with "a superb roadstead, very safe against winds, and eight leagues from a navigable stream."[12] Ever since d'Estaing's misadventure the French sailors have been in holy terror of Boston, with its hostile crowds and brawls. In Newport we'll be at home, almost in the position of an occupying force.

That's just what the inhabitants are afraid of, and they remain poker-faced. The temperature at welcoming time is well below freezing. Rochambeau and his general staff come steaming ashore toward the little Jerusalem of their crusade and proceed through the two streets which constitute the town—two totally deserted streets, lined by the closed shutters of the pretty white "farms." The rare Americans they encounter eschew all effusion and send the new arrivals packing to board in the dingiest tavern in Newport. The commander of the French army spends his first night in America in the same conditions as La Fayette in Philadelphia three years earlier. Not exactly forging ahead, the grand alliance.

The next day brings a mild thaw. A deputation of starchy fellows dressed in black as though for a funeral come to pay their respects at arm's length. The governor of Rhode Island is among them, the judges, and the big merchants. You feel that some of them are still Tories at heart; but since everybody knows that the northern provinces are peopled by icicles, the general decides to ascribe their coldness to an ethnic predisposition.[13] They aren't much more demonstrative at Vendôme, after all, and Rochambeau has been handling that bunch for thirty years. So he harangues these Newport gentlemen in the tones he would use to dignitaries on the banks of the Loir, and he gives a good performance, winning them over with his aristocratic bonhomie. Some fear the newcomers will be too many—our fields, our fowl, our girls!—and others are appalled because they are so few—all they'll ever succeed in doing is bringing down the wrath of God upon our heads. To the latter Rochambeau blandly declares that his little troop is only the vanguard; to the former he swears that he will hang the first marauder high and short. Then they shuffle out again, but that afternoon little groups begin collecting outside the meetinghouse and that's a good sign; the shutters open, the tavernkeeper pours out his best home-grown wine. At nightfall the church bell tolls, that single sad, sweet ding-dong of the Protestant bell which the French always mistake for a death-knell. This is the invitation to the timid little reception the Newport Whigs have finally brought themselves to offer their guests, like a poor wench in rags saying "maybe." "Glasses of suet" are lit at the four corners of the wooden steeple, a few firecrackers are set off, and bonfires flicker in the squares. A dozen skyrockets fly away to smother in the sea mist beyond the quays. A wee salt celebration. It's enough to make the French take heart, however, and decide to disembark the following day. They promise the governor to camp outside the town, just nearby, so as to cause the least possible trouble. It's true that the couple of thousand scurvy and dysentery patients dumped in the Newport hospital raise the town's population by a third; those least badly off are laid under canvas in the open street. Look at all these sick people who've come to help us!

The disembarkation proceeds from July 13 to 20. On the 21st, panic at headquarters: the lookouts have spied twenty-one English ships: Admiral Graves's fleet, reinforced by the ships back from Virginia. Ternay was right to keep a move on. But here are his ten ships, and Rochambeau's men, trapped before they've had time to sit down.

Threaten New York, my grandmother! We're up the creek with no paddle.

LA FAYETTE

41

SEPTEMBER 1780

The French Blockaded at Rhode Island

La Fayette reaches Newport on July 25, 1780. A cascade of bilateral disappointment. He was counting on at least six thousand French; he finds fewer than four thousand on their feet. Rochambeau was expecting Washington in person; all he sees is La Fayette, of whom he is doubly mistrustful: he's too impulsive, and too much on the side of the Americans. La Fayette comes dashing up to implore Rochambeau to attack New York at once; Rochambeau, meanwhile, is calling for help from these people he's supposed to be rescuing. All he can think of is digging into Rhode Island so he can fend off an assault by the English who are sailing around under his nose and whose attack he wakes up anticipating every morning. He's very much afraid he'll collapse at the first blow. He openly asks Washington for help. La Fayette turns scarlet: "We could not speak of our grand operations, and they are wholly taken in their expectations of attack by the enemy . . . Nothing as yet (the [enemy] ships of war excepted) has come in sight; but the French generals who have not the smallest doubt about their coming are hurrying their preparations of defense."[1] That's his first view of the saviors' camp: a building site. Batteries are set up on headlands, roads are cut through the island, the fortifications which the English built ten years ago are reinforced. Dust and heat float over the organized agitation of every able-bodied man gouging away at the earth with the butt of his gun for want of a shovel. Rochambeau strides about hollow with anguish and outwardly impassive; he supervises everything and mobilizes everybody, ably seconded by Lauzun, who regains his true stature when he has any intelligent activity to engage in. He has been put in "command of the coast and everything within range of the points at which it was possible to disembark."[2] Just let his darling English show their faces, he'll know how to greet them.

But La Fayette is tearing his hair. What an absurdity, these two topsy-turvy worlds! Have the French come all the way across the ocean just to get themselves besieged and maybe captured? "The number of sick is such that by the report given before me to Count de Rochambeau, it appears they will have but three thousand six hundred men fit for duty if they are attacked within the next few days."[3] Washington, here we are—Help! "Count de Rochambeau asked me so often if you would not send a body of Continental troops to their relief; if, in the course of twelve days from this they could not be arrived or that I knew he wanted me to write to you about it, and at length he told me he did not want it . . . ."

Washington gets this letter on the 30th, in the midst of his preparations for battle. He shrugs, and mutters between his teeth. Those damnfool Frenchmen don't need to draw him a picture, he saw it all as soon as he heard the English had sailed for Newport. And, being a strategist, reacted instantly. Send a detachment to Rochambeau, as if he had more men than he needed himself? No fear. But we can try to help him out with local militia levied on the spot. As for Washington's army—the last bucket of water of which not one drop can be wasted—he sends it off to play chess on a six-state board. That's all he can do, but it's a lot: march on New York to put a scare into the main body of the English. If they panic, they'll recall the men they've sent up toward Newport—provided the French can hold out.

And so goes the end of July; it looks as if they're headed for subterranean skirmishes. On August 1, having marched northeast at a smart pace, Washington is at Peekskill on the Hudson, fifteen leagues north of New York. Now that he's emerged from the mountains, the English might just think he's about to swoop down on them like a ravenous beast, which he hasn't the remotest intention of doing, of course, but he hardly even needs to pretend.

On July 27 Sir Henry Clinton has six thousand men loaded on board his transport ships; why doesn't he just hurl them at Rhode Island, the French haven't finished digging in and would have to fight two against three? Even if a thousand English die, the rest will get through and demolish Louis XVI's expeditionary force, a world victory, a war won . . . Rochambeau is absolutely right to squat down and start scratching.

But all for naught. Clinton does disembark, on July 31—back home again, near New York! And proceeds to release his six thousand groggy Germans and English, who have long since given up trying to figure out what goes on in their chiefs' brains. Now their general has lowered his arm without firing or receiving a shot.

That day, England lets slip her great chance. Clinton will blame it on Admiral Arbuthnot, who has taken command of the enlarged fleet. Arbuthnot will incriminate Clinton. The pair of them, like Rochambeau and Ternay in the opposing camp, form one bicephalous command, half on land and half on the water, whose heads have been bickering nonstop for a month. Clinton hasn't copped out with the jitters, but when he gets his horse to the foot of the wall he thinks it looks too high. He imagines the French are more numerous, better defended, and more resolute than they are. Washington's march on New York has produced the desired effect. Sacrifice New York for Newport? Heaven forbid!

The opposing leaders all belong to the same family: d'Estaing and Byron, d'Orvilliers and Arbuthnot, Clinton and Rochambeau—they're brothers when it comes to chickening out. It's not the actual battle that scares them, it's the thought of attacking. Conservatism, like creeping obesity, has mounted into the very top loft of the armies, and is positively stifling this war.

Whatever the reasons, conflict is adjourned. The summer is written off. Each side goes on decorating its foxholes, Rochambeau at Newport, Clinton in New York, Washington on the Hudson, and farther down, in Carolina, a certain Lord Cornwallis, commander of the English in the South, now being reconquered. Provisionally, La Fayette resumes his military role. "I have a charming command composed of about two thousand men of the light infantry . . . led by two brigadiers serving under me. [I also have] one hundred riflemen, a species of half-wild huntsmen, and a legion of three hundred men, half infantry and half cavalry. These two thousand four hundred men form a scouting party, always at the fore and independent of the great army,"[4] which "great army" counts fewer than eight thousand men. So now we have La Fayette commanding one-fifth of the armed forces of America, "colonel-general of light troops"—the vanished dream of the Duc de Chartres. He continues to ruin himself fitting out his men at his own expense, with cockades for the soldiers, swords for the officers, flags for the battalions, and long black and white plumes. He's got his toy.

But what's the point of it, if he has to keep all his tin soldiers in their box? On August 9 he's sending a tome of a letter to Rochambeau and Ternay, in which he takes himself a shade too much for a war lord and, ostensibly summarizing their exchanges, starts nagging at them again to attack New York, or more precisely the Fort of Brooklyn,* for "I told you that the

---

*The fort protected the western tip of Long Island, facing the tongue of Manhattan (often called "New York Island"), which in those days contained the whole of the city of New York. For the French, an attack on Brooklyn meant disembarking on "the long Island."

American troops would take charge of New York, and that the fort of Brooklyn, where you could operate in concert with a division of our army, is simply an earthwork of four bastions, with a ditch and a shed, containing from a thousand to fifteen hundred men," in other words, it's a cinch. "I represented to you that Long Island is a fertile country where . . . we were sure to be joined . . . by the militia of the island . . . In view of these circumstances it is my personal opinion that the action should be begun . . . before we obtain the naval superiority." As for the risk of abandoning our brand-new base on Rhode Island, "if the English should make the mistake of seizing it, a superior fleet, assisted from the Continent, would be able to retake it at any time." La Fayette is definitely not one of your run-for-cover-and-stay-down men. He wins all his battles before they're fought with a few flicks of his finger, which makes it all the easier for him to prod the others. "I had the honor of saying to you, in conclusion, Sirs, that, in order to operate against New York, it would be necessary to begin at latest toward the first days of September . . . I assure you, Sirs, as an individual and in my own name, that it is important for us to act during the present campaign, and that all the troops whom you may expect from France next year, as well as all the plans with which you may flatter yourselves, will not repair the fatal consequences of our inaction now."[5]

Rochambeau is already annoyed at Washington's tardiness in coming to meet him, and furious at his humiliating position of being blockaded by the English fleet. He takes the bait, and gives our whippersnapper a piece of his Seven-Years'-War-experienced mind: "I confine myself to waiting for the final orders of our general [Washington] and I beg of him as a favor to appoint a rendezvous . . . We should accomplish more in a quarter of an hour [of talk] than in a multitude of dispatches . . . While the French fleet is guarded here by a superior and concentrated naval force, *your** coasts of America are undisturbed, *your* privateers make valuable captures, and *your* merchant marine is entirely free. It seems to me that under such comfortable circumstances it ought not to be difficult to wait for the increase of both naval and land forces which the King assured me he intended to send."[6]

La Fayette sees that he's gone too far and shifts back to low gear, but reluctantly: "I cannot help being pained when I see you give to my letter so unfavorable an interpretation and one that I never dreamed of . . . I will admit to you, in confidence, that it hurts my feelings, in the midst of a foreign country, to see the French blockaded at Rhode Island; and the mortification that I feel makes me anxious for active operations . . . If I have offended you, I ask your pardon for two reasons: first, because I am earnestly attached to

---

*The italics for these acid possessives are mine; coming from the pen of Rochambeau, they make La Fayette an American citizen.

you; and second, because my purpose is to do everything here that I can to please you."[7]

Okay, okay, that'll do, Rochambeau decides to make up on August 27: "It is always right, my dear Marquis, to believe that the French are invincible, but I shall confide to you a great secret, after an experience of forty years: there are no troops so easily beaten when once they have lost confidence in their leaders . . . Of the fifteen thousand men, or thereabout, who, under me, have been either killed or wounded in the different ranks and in the most sanguinary engagements, I have not to reproach myself with having caused the death of a single man for my own personal advantage." It's a stern lesson; will that hothead kid get the message? However, enough said, now let's have a French-style embrace: "I decided immediately that the fire of your heart and mind had somewhat warped the sobriety of your judgment. Preserve this latter quality in the council, and keep all of the former for the moment of execution. This is still *le vieux père* Rochambeau talking to his dear son La Fayette, whom he loves, and whom he will continue to love and esteem until his last breath."[8] Provided he keeps out of my way hereafter.

This little spat goes unnoticed by the staff officers, who have plenty of work to do organizing themselves, morosely enough, in this lost hole while they wait for hell to freeze over. "You know the French," Fersen writes to his father, "and what are called the people of the Court, well enough to imagine the despair of all our young men of that class who find themselves compelled to spend their winter quietly in Newport, far from their mistresses and pleasures in Paris; without suppers, without theater or opera, without balls, they are beside themselves with misery . . . We had most excessive heat here in August, worse than any I ever knew in Italy." He himself, a Swede whose soul has been tempered by tedium in Stockholm, is in better spirits. "There is little society in Newport; five or six houses which entertain. I have been in only two of them, where I go of an evening to divert myself and speak English. In one, that of Mme Hunter, there is a daughter of eighteen, pretty, pleasant and gay, a very good musician. I go there every evening, I am very fond of her, but there is nothing in it."[9] He can appreciate these people, they remind him of the little gentry of Dalecarlia: "The Americans [the well-off ones, that is—the only kind he associates with] make do with a minimum which in other countries would be found only among people of inferior condition. Their dress is simple but of good quality, and their manners have not yet been spoiled by the opulence of the Europeans." But why does that bitch politics have to meddle with everything? "It is a country that will be extremely happy if it can enjoy a long peace and if the two parties dividing it at present do not bring it to suffer the fate of Poland and so many other republics. These two parties are known as Whigs and Tories; the former is wholly in favor of liberty and independence. It is made up of people of the lowest extraction who own no property at all, and most of the people living in the country belong to it. The Tories are for the English, or, to be more exact, for peace, without caring too greatly whether they are free or subjects; these are the people of a more distinguished class, the only ones who have any fortune in the country." Not too hard to see where his affections lie. You can't beat a good enlightened despot like Gustavus III.

No danger that Fersen will stray La Fayette-like into that mobbish "republic" whose very name makes his pen squeak. He feels right at home in the camp of a monarchy, where Rochambeau has imposed a reassuring order. "The most exact discipline is enforced; nothing is taken from the inhabitants without their consent and they are paid in cash; there has not yet been a single complaint against the troops. This discipline is admirable. The inhabitants are all amazed at it, accustomed as they are to the plundering of the English and their own troops." There, at least, La Fayette has found one thing to be proud of in his relations with Washington: "the French discipline is such, that chiken [*sic*] and pigs walk between the tents without being disturbed, and that there is in the camp a cornfield, from which not one leaf has been touched. The Tories don't know what to say to it."[10] Under the threat of the *caporal-schlagueur* and the shadow of the gallows promised to all marauders, three thousand poor numbskulls are starving to death without a murmur; that's the army. For want of the fifty tons of supplies left behind at Brest and awaited every morning like manna by the Hebrews, the men have been put on short rations of flour, meat, and spirits, as though Rhode Island were just a slightly bigger ship about to be engulfed by the sea. Fersen himself has money problems, and that's saying a lot! "Everything here is extremely expensive, twice as much as in Europe. Horses are appallingly dear, fifty louis is the common price for a good horse, and nine livres to shoe it. Every shirt costs twelve sols to have laundered.* My servants could not live on their wages if I had not come to an understanding with the supply-masters to give them bread and meat at the soldier's price."[11] Fortunately, being a staff officer gives an aide-de-camp financial credit beyond the dreams of the simple soldier: "If you will be so good, my dear father, as to take steps to have money sent to me; the order should go to M. Tourton† to have a letter of credit for me conveyed from M. de Sérilly, general treasurer of the land, to the treasurer of our army."[12]

---

*For the horse, 5,000 new francs [$1,000]; 45 [$9] to shoe it, and 3 [60 cents] to wash the shirt. Fersen mentions the "soldiers' price": the troops received 15 sous, or about 4 new francs [80 cents], daily to live on, and paid less than officers.

†Chief banker of the Swedes in France. Sérilly should be read as "general treasurer of the land army."

BENEDICT ARNOLD

42

OCTOBER 1780

But for the Honesty of Certain Countrymen . . .

Numbness soon sets in, and they slip back into the old habits: "On September 8 there was a private fight between M. Dillon and the Vicomte de Noailles over some triviality. The latter was injured."[1] Are they going to start cutting each other's throats? Rochambeau feels a need to do something, anything, before winter sets in. If there aren't going to be any battles, let's at least have that summit meeting we've been awaiting so long. At last, Washington proposes September 20, in a town in Connecticut halfway between Rhode Island and the Hudson: Hartford. You'd think the place was chosen by protocol, and it more or less is. The delegations are also selected as though they were staffing embassies. Washington announces that he will bring La Fayette, General Knox, who commands his artillery, and some engineers; so Rochambeau, in addition to the inevitable Admiral de Ternay, picks Fersen and Mathieu Dumas, whose knowledge of fortifications and fluency in English have already rendered him indispensable and gotten him promoted to the rank of "chief engineer."

This little band, delighted to be moving at last, sets out on September 18 into what Fersen calls "the most beautiful country on earth"—"well cultivated, delightful views, the people are comfortable but without luxuries or opulence"[2]—that broad strip of good land bordering the sea between Narragansett Bay and the Connecticut River. Men have been tilling and taming it since the beginning of English time, a century and a half ago. But if you stray too far from the sea, the America of the pioneers takes over again. First come swamps, then increasingly wicked hills, and the road becomes so rough that the coach hired back in civilization is slowed to a snail's pace, and finally breaks down.

An axle goes at nightfall. Five or six bemedaled gentlemen in the splendid uniforms donned for their summit talk find themselves lost in the wilderness. Fersen and Mathieu Dumas, the only ones on horseback, set off to reconnoiter and finally unearth a blacksmith after miles of riding blind through the countryside. They charge up and offer to empty their purses, but in vain. The man is like some sort of bear, and he's also sick, in bed with a fever. You can go to hell.

"You won't make me get up this night, not if you fill your hat with guineas and give it to me!"[3]

And tomorrow Washington will be at the rendezvous. French courtesy be found wanting? Never! Rochambeau, dragging a shaky Ternay, comes in person to beard the bear, and plays a card he's seldom had out of the deck in Europe: elementary democracy. When in Rome . . . With Dumas interpreting, he tells the lout what's up. Is the supreme conference to fail because of him? The hovel stinks, there are hens setting on the table. The bear opens one eye:

"You're no liars. I can see that from your faces. It's been announced in the Hartford paper that Washington is coming. They've even got out the lanterns. Is it a public service you're wanting of me? Then why the devil were your men trying to give me gold? Smith's word, you'll have your coach by six tomorrow morning."

America is also that.

The next day she welcomes a France which is somewhat rumpled from having slept in its coach but still eminently presentable. This isn't the first time Rochambeau's had to rough it, and his grandeur is finally a match for Washington's. La Fayette would hardly count between the two of them if they didn't need him to interpret. First, let's get the cordialities out of the way. A general heat wave spreads around the stout inn table hewn from a single trunk and laden with a profusion of cakes, punch bowls, and jugs of a cider almost as lethal as the punch. The sun of a September that is always glorious in these parts gives life to the white walls of the sempiternal little houses and glances off the sails of the fishing boats strung along the wooden quay and the flag flying in honor of the two great chiefs. Curious country, that can offer its visitors a port in the middle of a forest, after leagues of backbreaking roads! A river port, true, but the Connecticut at Hartford is wider than the Loire at Nantes.

Fersen finds Washington enchanting. "M. de Rochambeau sent me ahead to announce his arrival, and I had time to observe this illustrious, not to say unique, man of our century.* His comely and majestic face, at the same time mild and dignified, perfectly matches his moral qualities. He has the air of a hero. He is very cold, speaks little, but is courteous and proper. His physiognomy is marked by sadness that does not ill become him, and indeed renders

---

*This is the same Fersen who, a few days before, wrote the bittersweet comments we have just read on the subject of the "republic" and the "Whigs." But the European élite were already beginning, partly under La Fayette's influence, to see Washington as the exceptional man, the man of destiny, and to remove him from his political context—they were looking for a king for the new republic.

him all the more interesting . . . In addition, he had an escort of twenty-two dragoons, which was necessary, for he was riding through enemy country."[4]

"The repast was in the English fashion, consisting of eight or ten large dishes of butcher's meat and poultry, with vegetables of several sorts, followed by a second course of pastry, comprised under the denominations of pies and puddings. After this the cloth was taken off, and apples and a great quantity of nuts were served, which General Washington usually continues eating for two hours, toasting and conversing all the time. These nuts are small and dry, and have so hard a shell [hickory nuts] that they can only be broken by the hammer; they are served half open, and the company are never done picking and eating them . . . There was more solemnity in the toasts at dinner: there were several ceremonious ones [to the king, the queen, the princes, Congress, etc.]; others were suggested by the General . . . After supper the guests are generally desired to give a *sentiment;* that is to say, a lady to whom they are attached by some sentiment, either of love or friendship, or perhaps from preference only."[5]

In an atmosphere like this, who could want to disagree; and an understanding is speedily reached—as to the vital necessity for both sides to do nothing. They were sure of it beforehand, but it's always nice to hear the other fellow say so. With our present strength, any offensive operation would be suicidal. So we'll settle down and pass the winter as best we can, while Washington on one side and La Fayette and Rochambeau on the other redouble their efforts to shake the resources they'll need for next spring out of the pockets of America and France. A report is painstakingly drawn up in the form of a two-column dialogue, with the French proposals running down the left side and those of the Americans on the right. In Article 7, Washington sums up his position and makes very few bones about it:

> 7th. The situation of America makes it absolutely necessary that the allies should give it their vigorous support, and that His Most Christian Majesty should add to our many other obligations and to the many other proofs of his generous interest, that of assisting the United States of America by sending them more ships, more men, and more money.

So Rochambeau's expedition is just an appetizer, and the main course is up to the King of France. For the moment, everybody is only too happy to have survived the summer without catastrophe. They part the best of friends.

The return trip, like a film run backwards. Is it bewitched? The coach begins to whimper near the den of that bear of a blacksmith, and the same axle gives up the ghost at the same time and in the same place, as though it had been wound up to do it. In a better mood because in less of a hurry, they march off arm in arm to find old Smith, still shivering with his fever but delighted to see them once more:

"I see you want to make me work the night again . . . All right, you're good folks. You'll have your wagon tomorrow . . ."

He pulls himself up, clambers out of bed, "and goes off to his forge exactly as mother nature made him; he was so hairy that one would have thought him furred [*sic*]." But he's got something on his mind:

"Tell me, gentlemen, I don't mean to pry into your secrets, but were you pleased with our Washington?"

A chorus of praise. But he has another question:

"And what about him? Was he pleased with you?"

Even leather-hided Rochambeau is overcome. He actually contradicts Fersen's analysis. "His [Smith's] patriotism was satisfied, and he kept his word to us. I do not claim to give it out that every American is like this good wheelwright; but all the farmers in the interior, and nearly all the landowners of Connecticut, have such a public spirit that many another might take it as a model."[6] He does say "nearly all."

The French staff is back in Newport on September 23, feeling relatively cheerful. That same day, Washington and La Fayette are in the gravest danger, and the whole applecart just misses being overturned.

They're inspecting the banks of the Hudson together, to make sure that General Arnold has still got the river locked up tight less than twenty leagues north of New York, and is guarding the passageway between the northern and central states.

"Come have lunch with me at West Point, at Arnold's," Washington suggests to La Fayette.

What better way to shake off your worries than one of those brisk rides he so adores? Off goes the little band of aides-de-camp, escorts, and generals, trotting up the Hudson. The September rains have raised the water level, the wind is lashing at the willows and poplars, still green; here we are at Fishkill, where La Fayette was so sick almost two years ago. Things are looking better now, eh? He's just had a choice part to play interceding between the two worlds, he's got two thousand men to command. Live and learn, beautiful morning. There are some fine new redoubts at West Point, at the very edge of the war: the outposts cannonade each other two or three times a day, and La Fayette is looking forward to meeting General Arnold again—now there's a real go-getter, the kind of hero he'd like to see more of. His wife will receive us at Robinson House, and the young and pretty Mrs. Arnold is renowned for her cooking. Gilbert's mouth begins to water at the memory of those melting eyes that smiled at him before.

La Fayette and Washington linger behind with a few officers.

"Go ahead and start dinner at the Arnolds' American-fashion, don't wait for us," Washington tells the others.

He too has a weakness for the robber-baron ways of Benedict Arnold, a throwback to the clan chieftains of the good old days. His soldiering temperament was aroused late in life, by the Independence; he was a Canadian eagle, a ravisher of innkeepers' daughters, a plunderer, a pirate. Washington has often had to overlook his bucks and bolts, and it was against the commander's will that Congress indicted Arnold before a council of war seven months ago for embezzlement and abuse of authority. He was acquitted, but the man with the game leg is still feeling the sting.

When Washington reaches Robinson House, he finds the aides de camp looking bewildered.

"Is the feast already over?"

"Arnold is in some difficulty, sir. We had hardly started on the punch when somebody brought him a message. They had just arrested one of those English spies who often come upriver in rowboats. The general seemed greatly upset. He called for a horse and asked us to tell you that he was going to West Point and would be back in an hour."

"And Mrs. Arnold?"

"She is in bed."

"At four in the afternoon?"

"She's not well."*

Washington is unruffled. In wartime you can never count on anything. He suggests that La Fayette and he push on a little farther, to West Point itself, where they inspect the works. All in order. But when they return at nightfall, still no Arnold. No more Arnold ever again. The hero has gone over to the other side.

A dismayed group gathers around a handsome young fellow in civilian clothes, proud and poignant, with the pallor of a man condemned—Major André, adjutant general of the English army, knows well enough that any spy caught in the act must be sentenced to death. But what was General Clinton's right arm doing there anyway, prowling along the Hudson under Arnold's very windows? Are the English so short of spies that they have to send out their best officers to do their dirty work?

" 'It was no dirty work, sir. His object was nothing less than to kidnap you. Read the papers that man has on him, which the countrymen who stopped him seized when he tried to swallow them' ":

"A copy of a very important council of war, a statement of the strength of the garrison and of the works, and certain observations upon the methods

---

*The episode is described in great detail in the letter La Fayette wrote the following day to the Chevalier de La Luzerne, the king's ambassador to the United States.

of attack and defense, all in General Arnold's handwriting."[7] Worse: the general was to intern his guests in "the house of the Chevalier Smith," a local dignitary, not far from the fortifications and close to the river. "The plan [of the English] was to come up [the Hudson] suddenly before West Point and to present all the appearance of an attack. Arnold intended to say that he had been surprised by a superior force"; after retreating to his redoubts, he would have let Washington, La Fayette, and the rest be captured while he stood by wringing his hands. "And but for the chance of our arrival . . . but for a slight cannonade of no consequence which attracted the attention of people along the road Major André had naturally taken and obliged him to proceed in disguise, and, finally, but for the accidental presence and the honesty of certain countrymen [the ones who arrested him], it would not have been possible to escape the disaster which threatened us, and Arnold would perhaps have betrayed us again afterward"—why not, once he became supreme commander of the American forces, for he was one of the three or four candidates best placed to take over from Washington. But he can't stand to play second fiddle. Benedict Arnold is a man who needs action. This slow-motion war is stifling him. When he left the English side five years ago and turned coat the first time, it was because he wanted a fight; and London cried treason then as shrilly as it'll be cried now in Philadelphia: in a civil war you're always a traitor to half the people fighting it. At first he intrigued to get top billing with Congress, but it's too late for that now; won or lost, this is Washington's war, the man is being turned into an institution. Switching back to the English in time to give them two or three decisive victories could put Arnold in the driver's seat there instead of Clinton the inconsistent. That, added to the allure of profit—for his path was paved with gold—the pressure of the wind, which was blowing against the Rebels, and a corresponding revival of Tory feeling . . . Arnold made his choice.

And maybe, on top of everything else, there was an opportunity for a repudiation that could be made to look unintentional? "The unhappy Mrs. Arnold," claims La Fayette, "did not know a word of this conspiracy; her husband told her before going away that he was flying, never to come back, and he left her lying unconscious. When she came to herself, she fell into frightful convulsions, and completely lost her reason." She recovered it the next day sufficiently to summon an instantly quivering Gilbert to her bedside. ". . . I am upon very good terms with her,* [so] she sent for me to go up to her chamber. General Washington and every one else here sympathize warmly with this estimable woman, whose face and whose youthfulness make her so interesting. She is going to Philadelphia . . . It would be exceedingly painful to General Washington if she were not treated with the greatest kindness

---

*That's quick work—they've met three or four times at most.

... As for myself, you know that I have always been fond of her, and at this moment she interests me intensely. We are certain that she knew nothing of the plot."

But there's somebody else within reach of La Fayette's influence, and his plight is far worse than Mrs. Arnold's: Major André was doing no more than his duty by obeying his superiors, and he is threatened with an infamous death. He's the same age as Gilbert, he has the same impetuous outgoing nature; he might almost be La Fayette's English double. "Promise of distinction in the British army." But no Newfoundlands or St. Bernards for him. "We are now examining Mr. Smith [suspected of being an accomplice] whilst we are waiting for the adjutant general. I hope both of them will be hanged, but especially the latter, who is a man of influence in the English army and whose very distinguished social rank will act as a warning to spies of less degree." And yet the wolf now howling so loudly for the kill went to London, paid his court to King George, and toured the enemy ports two weeks before leaving to fight the English. And his friend Lauzun, of "very distinguished social rank" if ever anyone was, made his preparations for the Senegambia expedition in the drawing rooms of the London smart set, before sailing up to Saint-Louis under cover of an English flag. That never occurs to La Fayette. In this matter his sense of fair play, even his class loyalty, bow down before the one unpardonable sin, both in war and in life: *flagrante delicto.* André was caught in the act; let the bungler be hanged.

You can count on Washington for that. He takes his time, methodically dealing with first things first: posts to be double-guarded, garrisons to be alerted, investigations to be ordered—for who knows how far the conspiracy has gone? The tall man is matchless in a situation like this: not one muscle twitched when they showed him the papers taken from André. If you spend your whole life expecting the worst, let it at least be some use to you when the worst finally happens. He doesn't turn a hair. He does his job quickly and well and, by his manner of meeting the crisis, reassures his army without uttering a word. But once that's done, just shut the door, my boy, this is between you and me. The court-martial is summoned for September 29: six major generals and eight brigadiers, including the marquis de La Fayette, have to decide, according to the laws and usage of war, whether or not Major André was arrested in civilian dress on the morning of Saturday 23rd of September about ten o'clock at Tarrytown, on his way to New York, by the countrymen Paulding, Williams, and Van Wert, and therefore within the American lines, while seeking, with the plans of the treacherous general Benedict Arnold on his person, to join the enemy sloop of war *Vulture* which was waiting for him but had been obliged to change her moorings, being too close to an American battery on the shore, which had promptly opened fire.[8] Cold, calm, and desperate, André challenges only one point: his designation as a spy, which he considers defamatory. General Clinton writes, as from one supreme commander to another, asking Washington to spare him and taking full responsibility upon himself. Washington plays deaf. At the council of war not one voice is raised to defend the accused, who is sentenced to be hanged.

He has two days to live, just long enough to have his sentence confirmed by Washington, who has returned to headquarters. He takes advantage of them to write and ask if he cannot at least be shot:

> Sir,
> Buoyed above the terror of death, by the consciousness of a life devoted to honorable pursuits, and stained with no action that can give me remorse, I trust that the request I make to your Excellency, at this serious period, and which is to soften my last moments, will not be rejected.
>
> Sympathy towards a soldier will surely induce your Excellency, and a military tribunal, to adapt the mode of my death to the feelings of a man of honor.
>
> Let me hope, Sir, that if aught in my character impresses you with esteem towards me, if aught in my misfortunes marks me as the victim of policy and not of resentment, I shall experience the operation of these feelings in your breast, by being informed that I am not to die on a gibbet."[9]

The general has already ordered that gibbet erected within view of the troops at West Point. To be sure, he could still lift a finger, that would be enough. But who do you take George Washington for? Major André is hanged at noon on October 2.

The funeral oration for the unfortunate man, by Washington: "André has met his fate, and with that fortitude, which was to be expected from an accomplished man and gallant officer." As for Arnold: "He wants feeling."[10]

The same, for the same, by Fersen: "They say Major André has been hanged; it is a pity. He's a young man of twenty-four who has [*sic*] much talent."[11]

The same, for the same, by La Fayette, in a letter to his dear heart, written just after signing the death warrant: "He was an interesting man, the confidant and friend of General Clinton; he conducted himself in a manner so frank, so noble, and so delicate, that I cannot help feeling for him with infinite sorrow."[12]

43

NOVEMBER 1780

Work, and Some Bread

"A hapless guest at the feast of life," Nicolas-Joseph-Florent Gilbert arrived hungry, and nobody gave him anything to eat. He knew every kind of hunger: for food, for love, for fame. He was hungry for life. That's what he's dying of, in November 1780. "What had contented my heart, do you know? / Glory: but glory spurns the call of woe."[1]

Who is that half-naked young man waving his arms as he runs raving along the Marne in the middle of the night of October 23–24, 1780? An escapee from the little twelve-bed loony-bin walled in by its vines back there on the Charenton hill?* He must be on his way back, then, since he's coming from the Conflans quarries and going up the bank of the Marne toward the famous Charenton bridge, the first one you meet on your way out of Paris; whoever holds it can block off the entire southeastern part of town, as Etienne Marcel,† Henri IV, and Condé have all learned. But there's nothing martial about this madman; he couldn't care less about other people's wars, he's too taken up with his own. Cries for help, insults howled at the moon, retchings as though he was choking, why does he keep putting his hands up to his throat? Now he's in the old part of Charenton, a handful of hunchbacked buildings huddled in a ring for the last thousand years around the end of the bridge.** He heads straight for the presbytery and thunders on the door, shouting for the priest as though the flames were scorching him. There's a fire, all right, the fire of hell to flee from. A servingwoman in cap and nightshirt puts her nose through the door. She has no trouble identifying this little fancy-pants with the pock-marked face, this distillate of bitterness:

"Monsieur Gilbert! Goodness, what a state you're in!"

"Go wake up the priest, quick! Hurry! I must have the last rites. I'm dying."

*It is only after the Revolution that this minuscule hospital, founded by a charity bequest in 1642, begins to grow into the most famous mental home in France.

†Etienne Marcel, fourteenth-century middle-class liberalizing reformer, provost of Paris. [Trans.]

**Of course nothing of them remains today.

The priest of Charenton-le-Pont doesn't like to be dragged out of bed, and even less in such circumstances. But he really can't refuse that poor Florent Gilbert, such a Christian man of letters, they don't grow on trees in these blasphemous times. Why, the archbishop himself has given him a lodging and money, so you see what I mean. The overwrought man must be reasoned with, no, no, Monsieur Gilbert, you're not dying, what is this nonsense, you've just got a fever, you're all flushed, you who are always so pale. Of course, we know you haven't been quite well since you fell off that horse last spring near the Parnasse hill, and your poor head was bleeding so hard, but you didn't die of it, why, here you are, and they didn't even trepan you, only put you on a diet, they had to do it, that's what has brought you to such a pitiful condition, three months without food, and then the leeches on top of it . . . But that's no reason for leaving Monseigneur's house like that, where you're so well looked after, in the middle of the night and in really not very presentable attire . . . What's that? What are you saying? You've swallowed the key, do calm yourself, Monsieur Gilbert, you've taken leave of your senses. Is your throat so sore as all that, you keep holding it with your hand? The last rites, certainly not. I only give them to people who really are dying. Oh, dear, there he goes streaking away like a rabbit and hurling insults. But wherever are you running at this time of night?

To the archbishop; Gilbert doesn't have far to go to find him at Conflans, where the bishops of Paris have their country residence, a little palace on the hillside.* There lies Mgr. Christophe de Beaumont, in perpetuity you might say, since he doesn't seem able to make up his mind to die after burying the late king. Sometimes he is carried out in a chair onto the terrace overlooking the confluence of the Seine and the Marne; three times a year he is transported to Paris to preside over the great religious holidays; the rest of the time he's here, on the second floor, preserved in canonical fat. Gilbert lives in one of the outbuildings, but now he goes to the portico of the château and sets up a great agitation among the torchbearing footmen. They don't dare use force to keep him out, he knows his way, and he erupts, screaming, into the chamber enclosing a small livid, gurgling object wrapped in layers of wool—His Grace: Christophe de Beaumont, Archbishop of Paris.

"The last rites! The last rites, Monseigneur! The priest refused to give them to me, he's in league with my enemies! They want me to die without the last rites! The key is choking me! The key . . ."

He rolls on the floor.[2] Three flunkeys leap on him, tie him up, and bundle him into a coach that enters Paris an hour later by the Vincennes barrier and conducts him to the foot of Notre Dame, to the hospital which Beaumont

*Which they abandon after it is sacked during the riots of February 1831.

designates, in a few mumbled orders, as the end of his road: the overcrowded Hôtel-Dieu. It's constantly refusing patients, except when they're sent by the bishops of Paris who have three wards permanently at their disposal. And here Gilbert really does die; but he has twenty days of agony to go.

That's more than enough time in which to mull over thirty years of a dog's life. He has fought his best in the cause of a good Lord who never made it easy for him. Grimm tosses off a pauper's obituary, ten skimpy lines in the *Correspondance littéraire:*

> Born at Fontenoy-le-Château, near Nancy, of poor but honest parents, he was drawn to the capital by his taste for literature. Finding no other means of subsistence there but the bread of M. the archbishop and Master Fréron's wine,* he considered himself obliged, out of gratitude no doubt, to devote every ounce of genius and malevolence he could muster to the destruction of the *philosophes;* it must be said to his credit that no one has written verses of a more original or virulent stamp against them . . . For some months he had been afflicted with the vapors, which quite deranged his reason in the end. Like Jean-Jacques, he became convinced that the *philosophes* had aroused the entire universe against him . . . The last lines we have seen by M. Gilbert are a translation of a psalm† in which the following poignant verse may be remarked:
>
> > Au banquet de la vie, infortuné convive,
> > J'apparus un jour, et je meurs;
> > Je meurs, et sur ma tombe, ou lentement j'arrive,
> > Nul ne viendra verser des pleurs.[3]
>
> > [One day I appeared, a hapless guest
> > At the feast of life, and now I die;
> > And by that tomb to which I'll soon draw nigh
> > No tears will flow on any human breast.]

"And now I die . . . and now I die . . ." This is not dementia. Gilbert raves from very sanity, when he comes to look back over the mess. His first misfortune—or his first mistake, it's all the same, who knows what he's doing at fifteen—was to have left Fontenoy-le-Château, in its little sunken vale among the pines in the marches of Lorraine, the banks of the Coney leading to the Saône, and the sharp, piercing forest around Epinal . . . "Thus, I strayed, with no money or counsel of sage / In folly forsaking my placid village / And the fields where my father lived out his old age," a farming and seed-trading father who was sufficiently well-off to be named mayor of his village, and who planted a walnut tree in the orchard

---

*A talented Roman Catholic polemicist, Fréron is the father of the future member of the Convention who helps to bring down Robespierre and directs an anti-Jacobin newspaper.

†No; an original poem, vaguely reminiscent [in French] of the style of the psalmists.

the day Florent was born.* His mother dies when he is nine, his brothers don't like him, his father doesn't understand him. Gilbert *père* wants to turn him into a lawyer when he finishes school at Dôle, but the lad says he wants to be a poet. A *what?* It's enough to give you a heart attack. Suspicions about his sanity have undoubtedly pursued him ever since that quarrel on the tenant farm of the hamlet of the Molières:

" '*Let me paint!*'† 'You pain a father sore! / Trust me, son, think that I am poor; / Forget so mad a longing! Your mother is no more, / And you will lose me soon; who then, / By my white head, will help you to the shore?' / '*Let me paint!*' 'Oh, go then where you will; / I wash my hands of you, for good or ill.' "

A starveling. The growing ulcer of debt in the pit of his anguish, from the age of twenty on. "I acknowledge that my late father** owes the Sieur Desoye, attorney of Dôle, the sum of fifty-eight livres and six sols for the balance of my board and lodging in his home for six and one-half months, at the rate of twelve livres a month . . . At Dôle, June 19, 1770."4 "Talent sinks and dies when it has no wings of gold." Gilbert sank toward Paris, via Nancy and . . . Lyons. "As he had gone to Lyons with poems, he entered Paris with a few more elaborate productions. Unknown, with no resources, and deeply religious, he possessed every conceivable qualification for failure."5 Three nights sleeping on the Pont Neuf, next to the guards. His religious faith doesn't prevent him from turning to the *philosophes* first, and it is tempered steel-hard by their disdain; his will be a Christianity of resentment. D'Alembert shows him the door: "What had I of them? Gifts? No; rejection and shame. / 'Work,' so you told me; 'you have gifts to win your fame.' / Barbarians! Work? What but work was I asking, / Prostrate at your feet, my hunger unmasking? / Of my outcries work, and some bread, were all the aim." He finds them, meagerly, in the opposing camp, with old Fréron who gives him a job on his *Année littéraire* for a pittance, feeding him as though he were training a police dog. And with Baculard d'Arnaud, "who had the signal honor of being proclaimed for one minute the rival of Voltaire" and being demolished by Beaumarchais; a towering old man "with a lachrymose face, cadaverous complexion, dim blue eyes, nose pointing skyward, who sighed incessantly; as he was deeply offended by his wrinkles, he gathered them all up at the crown of his head and, as a woman does with her chignon, tied a

---

*December 15, 1750. In 1858 a biographer of Gilbert, J. Salmon, deposited the poet's account book in the Bibliothèque nationale and, along with it, a few leaves from the tree, which was then over a century old.

†The italics are Gilbert's own, both times; the dialogue is reconstructed by him in his ode *Le Poète malheureux, ou le génie aux prises avec la fortune* [The poet thwarted, or the struggle between genius and fortune].

**Who dies in 1768.

ribbon around them." How are you supposed not to become neurotic when you're delivered hogtied and bound to friends like these? As the inventor of "literary sensibility," Baculard d'Arnaud deals mainly in exclamation points and moist sighs. "His tearful humidity soaks through the stoutest binding."[6] Gilbert sheds few tears; he bites. He believes himself a poet, but fundamentally he is a polemicist.* "I want . . . To flay those great men of a day with stinging verse," something like a Marat or Brissot of the Alexandrine, and with the same anti-academic fury. How he gave it to them! Take that, priests of the court! "Milord puts on trial the God that fattens him, / Calls devoutness fanatical, rends it limb from limb, / And gives lessons in atheism, as though it were a whim." And that, you "icy d'Alembert, who to Parnassus lays first claim, / And thinks himself a great man, with one preface to his name."† And that, *Vol-à-terre* (Voltaire), *Anti-chaleur* (La Harpe), *Obscuro-du-fatras* (Diderot)! They give him tit for tat: "Poor fool! Misguided, you suppose that by your feeble rage / You can bring down our best authors to your own crass stage? / O'erleap the nasty dungheap where with both hands you seize / The filth you fling upon your abhorrèd enemies."[7] "Scribbling scum!" "Young jingle-maker, who looks upon the turning of a rhyme as the supreme achievement of the human spirit . . ." He scratches himself raw on the briars of these insults, both given and received. And no woman to soothe the sting, he flees them, the Lady in his life is the wallflower of the century: religious poetry; and he wears himself out trying to pour the lava of the prophets into the neatly tied cadences of periphrasis. Working absolutely against his own grain. The only way you can make a living from the pen these days is as flashing skeptic or servile religious pedant. He's religious, yes, but also talented, and thus suspect to both sides, and condemned to survive on day-to-day handouts. Bigoted philanthropists never give too much at a time: charity is a bad investment if your protégé turns sour on you.

In 1776 some friends almost pull him through. They get sister Thérèse de Saint-Augustin, the most influential nun in the kingdom, to take an interest in him. She is no less a person than Madame Louise, the daughter of Louis XV, who has installed the headquarters of her reign of terror in the Carmel of St. Denis, from which she exhorts the Church of France to fight on to the finish. This right-minded poet is brought to her notice; with one word she could dub him a knight of the good cause and save him from misery forever by means of a pension from her nephew. Not so fast! Madame Louise wants gilt-edge security: "With regard to the Sieur Gilbert, I know with certainty that he is gifted, that he has come out in favor of Religion, that people who love

*Ten years later he would have equaled André Chénier, and undoubtedly would have been in the same camp.

†Meaning the preface to the *Encyclopédie,* which indeed does remain d'Alembert's most valid work.

Religion wish him well, that the *philosophes* are striving to win him over, and that the temptation is all the more to be feared as he has no fortune . . . I ask you* only to verify your information with the greatest care, for the enemies one makes in the defense of Religion possess an infinity of hidden resources, even among those who love and would protect her.''8 So Gilbert can wait for his pension. His inspiration must row against the current of his instruments too. He spends a whole year scratching paper, translating German religious poetry.† Fine, except that he doesn't know any German. Never mind that: he gets a literal translation made by somebody else and puts it into French verse; that's the sort of boiled and reboiled porridge he has to flounder around in, and every time he awkwardly strikes out in search of his own style and voice, everybody laughs at him: "My friend, you are very young; what have you brought me here? *Héroïdes?* . . . The season for them is long past. In any event, poets are hardly being read these days.''9 And then that parasitic shuffling back and forth between Nancy and Paris, like a humiliated schoolboy being hustled from one class to another. In Nancy "François de Neufchâteau often criticized him, and he did not take kindly to it. Perhaps his pride was ruffled by the forthrightness or severity of François's remarks;** that is possible. Gilbert was proud and pretentious, even in his poverty; this cost him the protection of his friends.''10 And then, why does he have to frighten them so when he declaims? "His voice grew hoarse, his muscles tensed, his veins swelled, he rolled haggard eyes, everything in him struck terror." François used this as a pretext for a *Discours sur la manière de lire les vers* [Discourse on the proper way to read verse] that sends the Lorraine drawing rooms into howls of hilarity: "Heedful not to ape, in his demented dance, / The rolling eyes, the writhings and contortions of his stance / We shun this rabid lover of his own perform- ance . . .'' Can any circle be more vicious than the scribblers'? Gilbert's hide is too thin, their teeth have flayed him.

He thought he was beginning to see the end of the tunnel. In 1779, at last! a steady job on the *Gazette de France,* a sort of fictitious salary granted at the king's behest. Help from the archbishop. A soft job as tutor for the Webbs, a rich Irish family living in Paris. Too late, it's all too late. "And now I die; / And by that tomb to which I'll soon draw nigh / No tears will flow on any human breast." The fall from the horse only hastens the process: Gilbert had already stopped eating, no longer slept. A man cornered, at the end of an impasse. He writes his final ode in the little house at Conflans, the right

---

*The letter, to Amelot, minister of the King's Household, is dated October 5, 1776.

†*The Death of Abel,* by Gessner, an emulator of Klopstock: religious poetry was having a great revival on the far side of the Rhine.

**He was the same age as Gilbert, but life had given him everything she withheld from the other man.

cadence at last, the right words, a suddenly pacified tone that will stand the test of time. "Justice and pity I'll awaken for thee / In the incorruptible that is to be." With his last poem he becomes a great poet. Also too late, Florent Gilbert. Why? What an absurdity! Maybe that was what he meant to show when he swallowed the key, the big stout key to the box he kept his papers in. At the moment, that is what he's dying of; he keeps telling them, shouting to them, he's been telling them for two weeks, but nobody will believe him. If you had to believe what every crazy person says . . . The hapless guest has swallowed the key to the secret, he's choking on it, with his hands at his throat and the ultimate question burning through his chest and the whole of his insides on the rack. The Hôtel-Dieu stinks. I've swallowed my key, I tell you. A beautiful white room for his eyes' last gaze, rebuilt in too much of a hurry after the big fire, but the walls already smell of corpses. Two thousand five hundred patients in one thousand two hundred nineteen beds. Gilbert's got nothing to complain about; he's alone in his, thanks to the archbishop. But why won't you please open me up and take away this key that's choking me? Herb tea, whey, and violet syrup are his sole medication.* Sister Sainte-Clothilde, Simon the nurse, François the apothecary are death's only faces, and death keeps him waiting until November 12.

"What would seem almost incredible, had the fact not been certified by the surgeons of the Hôtel-Dieu, is that after having well and truly swallowed a large key, he should nonetheless have lived for fifteen days. After medicine restored him to his senses he often spoke of this key, but what he said was taken as a remnant of his madness. It was only after his death that, upon opening his body, the truth of so singular a phenomenon was discovered. The key was found caught by one edge of the bit on the membranes of the esophagus near the upper orifice of the stomach."[11]

*Which costs his heirs—his brothers—62 livres and 9 sols: 315 new francs [$63].

44

NOVEMBER 1780

Passing from One Room to the Next

A great bustle of courtiers, guards, and laborers in the choir of the Capuchin church of Vienna, right in the center of town near the imperial palace. The most envied Capuchins in the empire—those who guard the sovereigns' tombs—stand in three rows along the stalls on either side, and these hundreds of living statues in front of the baroque stone ones create a funereal setting worthy of a Borgia. Who is being interred?

The empress; but alive. Strange scene. A few slabs are raised and a complicated system of ropes and pulleys installed, so that Maria Theresa's sedan chair can be lowered straight down into the crypt containing the mortal remains of the sixty-four emperors, princes, archdukes, and archduchesses buried there since Emperor Matthew. She's become increasingly unwilling to undertake the endless perambulation down the gloomy corridors and past all those horizontal hosts; they delay her weekly rendezvous, and she can't wait to get to the tomb of her beloved Francis, whose marble effigy is so well-muscled that it brings back throbbing memories. Sixteen children . . . Maria Theresa has carefully designed every detail of her own tomb, already yawning next to his. On the day of the resurrection of the flesh their dust will leap together in a single bound.

The dark, stout little lady, stately and self-contained, disappears through the floor of the church as though sucked down by her ancestors. Bent double, her entourage are bowing as she descends, when a sudden loud crack brings them upright with a jolt. One of the chair's bars has broken; there's the empress dangling at the end of three ropes midway between choir and crypt, where arms reach up to gather her in. She doesn't budge. Never once, in her entire life, has she lost her sang-froid.

"It's Francis calling me to him," is all she says.[1]

She's right. She's only sixty-three but she doesn't want to live any longer. Sorrow has worn her out, or rather the daily chafing inflicted upon her by people who refuse to behave as they ought. The incompatibility between herself and her era is personified by her son, whom everyone, beginning with himself, is waiting to see reign alone. Maria Theresa is *de trop*. She will make her exit like a lady. Good manners consist in knowing when to go.

Her cheeks have veered from pink to waxen yellow, she can hardly walk, she's tormented by an unquenchable thirst and drinks jug after jug of iced lemonade even in winter; worst of all, she can't breathe, even with all the windows open. She is oppressed by the asthma of acute anxiety, it's as though her nostrils were clamped shut against the stench of a rotting epoch. "Evil and personal interest alone rule society."

Why linger on in an uncorseted world? "The empty halls at Versailles, despite the recent stipulation of particular days on which people might pay their court to the sovereigns, is fresh proof that it is always an error to abolish etiquette from a great court. I see the effects of it here all too plainly: everything sinks into immobility and no one is content."[2] "I am distressed by the anglomania which continues to grow here."[3] She derives some small comfort from the fact that in May London is shaken by violent uprisings:* "Behold [the results of] that much vaunted liberty and that incomparable legislation! Without religion, without morality, nothing hangs together."[4] But there's something even worse than England, and that is her bastard daughter America; whenever Marie Antoinette wants to cheer up her mother she says all the nasty things she can about it. "The capture of Charleston is most vexatious, on account of the facilities and conceit it will afford the English; and perhaps even more because of the wretched defense put up by the Americans; nothing can be expected from such hopeless troops."[5] One feels the Hapsburgs, both mother and daughter, as exasperated by these English quarrels as if there were sailors brawling beneath their windows.

But the good old Christian Europe, that Holy Roman Germanic Empire whose rock she has stubbornly insisted upon being for the past forty years, is starting to crack. As Maria Theresa's influence begins to wane, that of the two great miscreants waxes apace: one is her eternal enemy, cloven-hoofed Frederick, friend of Voltaire; and the other is that bitch of the North, that Catherine so copiously reviled and so hugely envied for helping herself to every handsome man in her retinue. And another source of affliction: Joseph has taken it into his head to pay court to Catherine. "This winter, in jest, the Emperor allowed me to glimpse his desire to have an interview with the empress of Russia on the occasion of her voyage to Mohilev, and intimated that he would try to be in Bukowina at the same time.† You can well imagine how little

---

*The causes are social, but there are religious motivations as well, directed against the "papists." We shall learn more of "Black Wednesday" in connection with Pitt.

†This is Mogilev (modern spelling), on the Dniestr in southwest Russia, the other one is on the Dnieper. Joseph II's presence in Bucovina (modern spelling), an Austrian province in the Carpathians, made it possible to arrange an unofficial visit as between neighbors. Here Maria

delight I took in such a project, owing to the aversion and loathing which a character such as that of the empress of Russia invariably inspires in me."[6] Joseph wasn't about to miss this opportunity to annoy his mother, but also, above and beyond their private quarrel, he wanted to meet his ideal image of an enlightened despot; at last a sovereign who's reshaping the planet, doing things, finally acting! They meet on June 4 and play cat-and-mouse in a palace conjured out of the mud by magic expressly for their interview, amidst wretched hovels and a terrorized populace: Mohilev was torn from Poland only eight years ago. They spend two days dreaming about how they will divide up the world they don't yet possess. Turkey's about to fall apart. We'll carry out an enlightened crusade there together. Catherine has just had her second grandson, born a month ago and christened Constantine; with that she signs her ambition. A new Byzantium! Constantine will reign over a resuscitated Greek empire under Russian enfeoffment. But what about Joseph, then? Well, let him reunify Italy! Let him claim the Papal States, the "sacred heritage of emperors."[7] After all, it was they who presented them to the popes in the first place. Catherine gives Joseph the old Rome and keeps the new one for herself; numerous toasts are drunk to grand designs in the fumes and fog of the future. A certain intimation of change is a component in the greatness of them both. They sense that Europe is tottering; why shouldn't they be the ones to push it over the brink? Maria Theresa's shock, at her son's return: "Everything we have built in the last forty years will be lost, in Hungary and elsewhere!"[8] Unlike these two birds of prey, *she* worries about the barnyard fowl. "I know that a long-standing prejudice prevails in you [to Marie Antoinette, on August 2] against the prepotency [*sic*] of our House and its spirit of aggrandizement. For the latter, I may answer for it that no such thing exists [in her mind, maybe; but what about Joseph's?] . . . And with regard to the prepotency of our House, that has utterly ceased to be, and there is too little thought of the general welfare."[9]

She gets no comfort from that child queen, however—the last of her brood, whose court she sees through an ever-darkening glass, thanks to the reports of her sneak informer Mercy-the-Moaner. "I would hope [on January 31] for greater circumspection in my daughter's relations with her favorites, so that she will not become involved in improper actions through their greedy and self-seeking ends. I am shocked at the pretensions of the Polignacs and the vivacity with which Maurepas supports them."[10] Wasted words: in March Marie Antoinette easily twists a dowry of eight hundred thousand livres out of Louis XVI for a little sister of Yolande de Polignac, a duchy for her husband, and an annuity of thirty thousand livres for her lover Vaudreuil.* "I

Theresa is opening her mind to Mercy.

*400,000 new francs [$80,000] for the dowry; 150,000 [$30,000] for the annual pension.

must warn you [from Maria Theresa to Marie Antoinette] that this is causing a very great sensation of an undesirable nature in the public and abroad . . . By comparison, such excessively generous gestures make others feel more unfortunate and encumbered. I have been unable to pass over these anecdotes in silence; they reflect too closely upon your glory and through them, owing to your good heart, you indulge the greed of these alleged friends. If I did not warn you, who else would dare to?"[11] She needn't have bothered. Nowadays Marie Antoinette answers back: "I am too accustomed to the inventions and exaggerations of this country to be surprised at what has been said about Mme de Polignac. It is quite a matter of course that the King should contribute to the dowry of persons of the Court and high blood who are not rich."[12] She's on her own now, the umbilical cord is cut for good. In June, "the Court [of France] spent a week at the Château de la Muette. The confinement of the Comtesse Jules de Polignac was the object of the stay and had determined its date. The Queen, finding herself within reach of her favorite [Mercy no longer minces words], went to see her regularly every day . . . During this period, the King called upon the Duchesse de Polignac. Hers is the only private dwelling in Paris which the monarch has entered since his accession, and such a high mark of distinction has caused a sensation with the public almost greater than all those material favors accorded to the favorite."[13] The empress's most recent source of chagrin, and it's a big one, is that the queen and her company took to acting plays by contemporary authors last summer, on the stage of a gold and marble candy-box theater at Trianon, while the corpses of real actors are still being thrown into open graves. "I should like to see copies of the texts performed at Trianon, with the names of those who have taken each part and especially those played by my daughter."[14] What's the use?

It'll only upset her even more. Marie Antoinette will have done her bit to help Joseph and his century disgust the old lady with life. "I cannot consent that the Queen should sleep at Trianon without the King," as she did during part of August. If they start carrying on like that, how will there ever be a chance of a dauphin? And there is no salvation outside the dauphin. "As regards my daughter's pregnancy I wait for Providence to provide fulfillment of my hopes and those of France. It seems to me that my daughter is being given too many drugs, and all these different sorts of milk and purges administered to her are excessive in my view."[15] But the alternatives she suggests make one wonder: "Lassone is apparently right to give you iron, which worked miracles for the Queen of Naples,* and a bloodletting would do you no harm. I could always be certain of getting pregnant when I had myself bled."[16] Maria Theresa has worked herself up to such a pitch of mental anguish

---

*She is referring to "Mars balls," which were then all the rage: a powder obtained by passing successive decoctions of vulnerary plants over steel filings. It was given in the form of pills.

that the thought of her daughter actually becoming pregnant is also a torment: "I can no longer hide from you the anxiety which I originally felt on the subject of the fearful accident that befell my daughter at the moment of her delivery,* an anxiety which is constantly recurring. Could not this incident have been the product of an attempt upon her life, verily the blackest form of mischief [on whose part? Provence? Orléans? . . .], but not wholly inconceivable in a nation that harbors many scoundrels?"[17]

November 3. Joseph II "is wholly engrossed in a plan to go to the [Austrian] Netherlands early in March and to spend the entire summer away [from Vienna]. It [his wanderlust] grows worse every year, and adds to my pain and worry, at an age when I might rather see help and comfort, but one after another I am losing all my loved ones; I am utterly cast down."[18] However, the time for your long vacation is at hand, Majesty, you'd better start packing your bags. She sounds the alarm in the same letter: "For four weeks I have been much troubled with a rheumatism in my right arm, which is the reason why this is even less well written than usual." One last complaint, just to make sure that the cause of the evil is clearly identified—Joseph II and his schemes for reform in Belgium: "While I live I shall let nothing be touched in the government of the Low Countries; but I cannot believe that will be very long. My sorrows of every description are too great, and grow greater every day, and I have no help or comfort; at my age such a thing becomes unbearable, and my health is failing at a great rate."[19] Those are her last words to her old servant Mercy.

On November 8 she returns from the country with death in her face, and buries herself prematurely in the Hofburg, that tomb of a palace. Her breathing is so raucous that it keeps the servants awake nights. She herself has virtually given up trying to rest. "May God soon choose to put an end to my sufferings, otherwise I do not know how I shall endure them."[20] She needn't worry: whenever she can rise above triviality, she knows how to put up a good fight.

A cough and a rising fever. The solemn ballet of physicians and priests. The diagnosis is "a hardening of the lungs."† She feels herself "becoming like stone on the inside." She complains of a fire in her chest and orders all the windows opened wide in the winter fog. On November 24 she abandons her bed, where her catarrh was suffocating her. She'll die upright. That evening her chief physician, Störck, keeps the promise she long since extorted from him: the truth. She isn't afraid to die, but to die without confession, yes.

On the morning of the 25th she confides the petty sins of the end of a

*Marie Antoinette lost consciousness for a few minutes.
†Presumably a pulmonary edema.

great life to the most reverend Ignace Müller, abbot of the Benedictines of St. Dorothy. And whatever else they may be, her sins are not the ones imputed to despots who die convinced of the goodness of their public deeds. Who among them ever counted how many men he had hanged? Here she is, calm and kindly to her friends. She turns her death into a drawing-room reception, discreetly talking of other things. One of her readers bursts into tears.

" 'Withdraw, my good friend. Go weep outside. Do not come back until you can do your work properly.' "

The apostolic nuncio brings her the viaticum in the evening of the 26th and finds her kneeling on a prayer stool with her eternal black mantilla draped over her head, as though this were an ordinary mass. Joseph has gotten back just in time from the maneuvers he was commanding in Bohemia, and is skulking in a corner of the room, condemned to interrupt his globe-trotting for a few hours. He's never seen his mother choking for breath. He's appalled. She's been going through *that* every night for months? The old young man is suddenly shaken by strange spasms, oh, how amusing, Joseph II is crying! Nobody could ever have believed it—and nobody does believe it—but his sisters actually see him, and they hear Maria Theresa say:

" 'Don't cry! . . . Don't cry, for I would lose my strength of soul as well.' "

She uses the familiar second person to him, in French. The Empress of Germany dies in the language of Louis XVI. "At first she spoke German to her daughters, but as she grew weaker it was in French, the language of the Court, that she uttered her last words, which were addressed to Joseph." So is she going to forgive him? She pretends to, as best she can, in a supreme gesture of coquetry—in this instance, forgiveness is the highest form of revenge.

She almost passes away during the night, and receives extreme unction at dawn on the 28th. She wears a white cap, as though mourning meant more light instead of less, and a brown dressing gown "which she kept on until the last minute." During the ritual the onlookers catch fleeting glimpses of pale, clean flesh; she knows how to behave, and will not inflict any nasty odors or droolings on them. When she's had enough of her daughters she packs them off, duly blessed:

" 'Go! It pains me too much to look at you.' "

She remains alone with her son. "During the last afternoon she spoke about every manner of thing with the Emperor, in French." It's raining cats and dogs outside. "I'm not having very good weather for my trip." She dictates two last letters to him: not for her children, she's finished with that clamoring brood for good. One is for Kaunitz, the only man in her life after Francis; ah, if only the good Lord were less strict, she could have, with all her heart . . . Kaunitz meanwhile is barricaded in his rooms, he can't bear the sight of illness, she loves his very absence. The other letter? To Prince Esterhazy,

Chancellor of Hungary, and through him, to those Magyar nobles to whom she owes her ascension. How beautiful she was forty years ago, with her long hair streaming in the wind, the horsewoman from Presburg standing in her stirrup at the top of a hill built just so that she could canter up it after the coronation! The other peoples of the empire did not want a woman to succeed Charles VI, there was rebellion everywhere, muttering, apathy—and Frederick II swooping down upon them, Silesia invaded, everything going to hell . . . A roar of applause: the Hungarians love her. Standing there on her black horse with the crown of St. Stephen on her head, she draws her sword according to the ritual and salutes each of the cardinal points in turn. She will keep the faith. That day Maria Theresa existed. The empire too.

In the evening of November 29, 1780, she rises unsteadily from her armchair. Haggard, her hands outstretched like a blind woman.

" 'Where are you going, madam?' "

" 'I'm afraid of falling asleep. I don't want to be taken by surprise. I want to see death come. It is as though I were passing from one room to the next.' "

" 'You are not feeling well.' "

" 'Well enough to die.' "

Refusing all offers of assistance, she walks alone to her chaise longue, where she is seized with violent trembling. Her last words are for her doctor, and against Joseph:

" 'Light the mortuary candle and close my eyes, for that would be too much to ask of the Emperor.' "

Joseph II is one of the first to leave, his eyes now dry for all eternity. "Nobody ever called me *father;* no one calls me *husband* anymore; no one will ever say *son* to me again . . ."[21]

NECKER

45

JANUARY 1781

A Pure Appeal to the People

One person, however, still uses terms of endearment when she speaks to Joseph. "Oh my brother, oh my friend!" Marie Antoinette writes him on December 10 after receiving the news, "I dissolve in tears as I write you . . . Now you are all I have left in a country [Austria] that is and will always remain dear to me! . . . Farewell! I can no longer see what I write. Remember: we are your friends, your allies; love me."[1] But how to make that king-husband of hers share her emotion when contempt for him is now firmly anchored in her? On December 6 Joseph writes Louis XVI a long, relatively warm letter full of overtures for active friendship, a ball to be caught and tossed back at the beginning of a reign, when every gesture may settle the fate of a quarter of a century. Louis XVI replies with twenty lines of pap, no heart, no muscle. It's enough to make the queen weep with frustration: "I send you the King's letter, my dear brother. I hope that in every circumstance, as in this one, you will see nothing but the good disposition of his character, and not pause over matters of style. Yours, my dear brother, was admirable."[2] But the weather's wrong for grieving at Versailles, where the court, absentmindedly donning full mourning, is in such a hum over the current ministerial reshuffle that Marie Antoinette is brought back to politics in the same letter: "M. de Montbarrey has been dismissed, but out of consideration for M. de Maurepas, who is of the family, he has been allowed to hand in his resignation. It was high time, for through his personal conduct and the pillage he had tolerated, to say the least, in his department [of war], he has lost all esteem and rendered himself incapable of any good. The King has not yet named anyone for his place. I believe it will be M. de Ségur, a respected and admired lieutenant general,"* but his prime qualification in the queen's eyes is that he is the father of one of her little playmates. In the navy, Sartines has already been replaced by Castries. Something's stirring at court for the first time since Turgot's fall.

What's stirring is that they have to find scapegoats for all the things that have gone wrong in the last five years: the failure of the Descent upon England, the paucity of Rochambeau's resources. Sartines and Montbarrey are close by and can be given the boot, although the real causes of the debility of France are the king, who is untouchable, and Maurepas, who is ravaged by gout and whose demise is expected with every attack, so he's being left to decline in peace. Two men are on the way up: Vergennes and Necker, and are antagonists simply because there are two of them. For the moment Necker's in the lead: he holds the purse strings, and the drawing rooms are for him. He has another backer, in return for certain services rendered twenty years earlier, in the person of Choiseul, who has not completely abandoned hope. And backing Choiseul, by fits and starts, is the queen; and therefore the queen, by fits and starts, is backing Necker. "The Austrian party" is on its feet again, and scores two hits with the appointments of Castries and Ségur.

But Jacques Necker is the man of the hour. He has maneuvered judiciously and been clever enough to fall in with the rhythm of Louis XVI: after four years of preparation in the shadows, it takes him four months to change

*Term corresponding to the present-day full general.

two ministers. In January 1781, having secured support in the Council (access to which is forbidden him by his religion), he thinks he can step up the pace and drops a bomb with the publication of his *Compte rendu au roi* [*Account Rendered to the King*]. An unprecedented event. For the first time in history the financial state of an absolute monarchy is brought before the eyes of all.* The king's secret is violated at its most sensitive point: the pocketbook. The shock waves eddying out from Versailles are going to engulf all France: stupor among the courtiers, terror among the rich, enthusiasm in the bourgeoisie; and some interest is aroused even in the fringes of the lower strata bordering upon informed circles—money is the surest common denominator in public opinion. Necker is making his bid, who can doubt it: a "principal minister" is rising over the horizon of France to step into Maurepas's shoes, and playing popularity as his trump card. A foreigner? A Protestant? What of it: we've already had Sully, Mazarin, and Law. But—who is this Jacques Necker?

He's one of those men who think they still haven't accomplished anything when they've already succeeded at everything. He's forty-eight years old. He was born in Geneva, that free town on the edge of the Swiss cantons where politics runs in the blood. Little Jacques heard his nurses talking about government the way other people talk about the weather. So is he Swiss? If you like. In fact he's nothing, he's anything, he's the foreigner *par excellence,* and some people make no bones about telling him so. If you go back to Henry VIII, you'll find Irish Neckers. Then you lose them. You find them again in Pomerania, already confirmed Protestants, clergymen. That makes them German. But it was a king of England, at the beginning of the reign of Louis XV, who encouraged Charles Frederick Necker, the father of our man, to found a French school for young Englishmen in Geneva . . . At this level of cosmopolitanism, you might as well go the whole hog: Charles Frederick marries a Frenchwoman, a demoiselle Gautier. Jacques Necker, in short, is Germano-Franco-Genevois. His father's estate, where he is born on September 30, 1732, is called "La Germanie." But the father is already a good burgher of Geneva and takes the local quarrels so much to heart that it stops (his heart) in the thick of an election riot in St. Peter's church in 1762. By that time his son is already swimming like a fish in the currents of the Paris stock exchange, making a fortune, and becoming almost a Frenchman.

No question of a childhood, he hasn't got time. "In his games with his playmates he was always painstakingly organizing miniatures of the countries he learned about in his readings, so that he could outline laws for them."[3] Several such anecdotes are now making the rounds, like the flight to Jerusalem

*It is already a long-standing custom in England, and Necker doesn't fail to mention the fact in his text, taking it as a model. But the English pride themselves on being a parliamentary monarchy.

of the infant Jesus. In Geneva "the highest praise a child could earn was to be called steady. Being steady meant working like an elderly papa or standing up stiff as an alderman."[4] From that point of view, Jacques far surpasses any parent's wildest dreams. At sixteen, stiffened for life and in no danger of being corrupted by the big city, he sets out for Paris "to make himself an independent situation in trade."[5] He takes to the bank like a monk to the monastery.

To the Protestant bank, the kingdom beneath kingdoms, an international league of financiers on the crest of the wave, where nobody could care less whether he believes in predestination. In 1760 Geneva becomes the most important clearinghouse for European capital; British and French investments, of course, but loans to the King of Sardinia too, and to Austria and Denmark. The "Genevan network of international commerce"[6] is beginning to depart from so-called "pure" speculation and move increasingly into active participation in business, inaugurating the process that subsequently becomes basic to big money. The life of Jacques Necker coincides with this trend and personifies it: a transfusion of gold and silver traveling over the threads of a spider's web spun out from the Protestant diaspora into all profitable activities. The Geneva bankers control trade in timepieces, in exports from Marseilles, in the southern French textile industry, and in the sugar plantations of Cadiz and the Americas. "Beginning in 1763, an analysis of bankruptcies shows the importance to banking of trade with the colonies, speculation in shipping, coffee, sugar, indigo, slaves, piasters."[7] When, at the age of twenty, Necker becomes, by virtue of his capacity for hard work and his intuition, probity, and punctuality, the trusted henchman of the Parisian banker Isaac Vernet, "banking, merchant trading, shipping speculation, and currency exchange are united in professional practice and on an international scale."

That last item is the throw of the dice that makes him a millionaire. His foes hold it against him, as the original sin underlying a fortune for which he is never forgiven. In 1762 Necker learns, as usual through the network of Protestant men of affairs, of certain secret articles in the preliminary peace treaty between France and England. He buys up vast quantities of Canadian securities issued by the French government, which are going for an 80-percent loss on the stock exchange. He then sends them to London, where one of Vernet's correspondents, bearing false letters from Canadians, has himself reimbursed by the English at full price, under the terms of the treaty.[8] Who, me? Never heard of it. From that moment on, the Banque Vernet *is* Necker. When Vernet retires, Necker becomes the partner of Thélusson, the nephew and heir to the bank. When Thélusson goes to London in 1765, the Thélusson-Necker tandem, left wholly in the latter's hands, "administers the deposit and current accounts of some three hundred fifty foreign clients, most of whom are involved in the loans floated by the French monarchy"—the last resort of a royal treasury perpetually in the red. Necker becomes the banker of the king's creditors. He deals as an equal, first with Choiseul, then with Terray; he bails out the French budget on two or three occasions, and lends money to almost all the top people at court. In 1772 he can pretend to "retire" with a capital of 7.5 million;* he's got the whole shebang under his thumb. He then begins his second life, keeping one finger in the Thélusson pie through his brother Louis, who takes over from him as director.

There are also two or three pamphlets published at the right moment, including *In Praise of Colbert* (1772), which give a clue to the scope of his ambitions. Then there's the installation of Mme Necker's salon at Saint-Ouen, neatly bridging the gap left by such defunct or outmoded socialites as Lespinasse, Geoffrin, du Deffand. And then, when Turgot is tottering, Necker gives him a firm shove from behind by disclaiming any allegiance to "ideologists" . . . One after the other, Necker manipulates the two factors in a great political career that are so often opposed: the opinion of the intellectuals and favor at court. His supreme ruse was to content himself, in November 1776, with a back-row seat as a means of gaining entry to the general accounts office†: the job without the title. Louis XVI isn't ready to allow a heretic on his Council—not yet. But Jacques Necker knows how to wait. He has worked steadily, efficiently, smoothly. Suddenly, today, by a sort of process of osmosis, everybody is noticing his singularly overpowering presence. "What is Necker going to do? . . . What does Necker think about it?" The question has become a conditioned reflex in anyone trying to take any initiative in France. Everybody's also noticing that the king's finances have assumed a different aspect —his. They used to be matters for super-aristocrats, dealt with by a sort of steward. They're becoming capital, in good or bad condition, managed by a specialist. On the inside, the accounts office is beginning to look like a bank: the Trojan horse of the bourgeoisie.

The mere sight of his handsome Teutonic features inspires confidence. A heavy, massive body, big feet and big hands, beautiful, slow-moving eyes. Is the chin thickening, the jowl starting to swell? Signs of good health. How could you not lend money to a man like that? He tranquilly radiates self-worship: all the more reason to trust him. With every syllable he utters you'd think he was going to lay an egg. His champions consider that his slowness, and a certain apathy, are rare good qualities. True, "one of the most striking features of his character was the prodigious difficulty he always had in coming to any final decision . . . His mind was so attuned to considering every side of a matter with such exactitude and thoughtfulness that even in the most urgent circumstances he was troubled by the impossibility of reaching any conclusion at all, and could only be brought by force, so to speak, to want what he wanted." But that makes him all the more ideal a companion for Louis XVI. "He was known to sit more than quarter of an hour in his coach, time and time

---

*37 million new francs [$7.4 million].

†Also known as the Office of the Comptroller. [*Trans.*]

again, before deciding which house he would be driven to first."⁹ What of it: "His wife teased him for his clumsiness and taciturnity, but always in such a way as to show to his advantage."¹⁰

His policy is not to have one. No plans, no projects, no designs. That's not what bankers are for, and it's in this sense that he is the opposite of Turgot. He let the guilds be revived and the *corvée* be restored on the main roads, more out of lethargy than as a matter of principle.* He taxed the price of grain again, since it was on that point that he had come out against Turgot. He used the softest of kid gloves when tampering with the network of privileges of the King's Household, so as to alienate neither the queen nor the princes. Year after year he has plugged the leaking treasury with loans and lotteries, a process that works very well in the short run when confidence reigns—and there he stands to inspire it—and when circumstances do not necessitate any extraordinary expenditure.

But that's where the shoe is now pinching, and that is what has finally driven him out into the open: the war. He wanted it no more than Turgot; no minister of finance ever wants a war. But he was shrewd enough to put up with it, while doing his utmost to restrain extra spending. Whence the latent conflict between him and the "extravagant" ministers of navy and war, Sartines and Montbarrey, whose lack of funds was their best defense against the shrill complaints which the west wind kept flinging in their faces. How far did Necker drive them to exasperation and unpopularity on purpose, in order to set up safe friends of his own in their places and thus build the nucleus of "his" government under the king's very nose? Such a degree of machiavellism seems hard to credit in him, but he's not at all displeased to see it imputed to himself.

This autumn, in any event, he has managed to act. He emerged from his silence and challenged Sartines, in front of the king and Maurepas, on the subject of overspending. It was a banker's anger: 26 million of debt for the navy isn't exactly chickenfeed—and only 16 confessed!† Has Sartines had his fingers in the till? He's not above it, but he's also been trying his best to renovate that navy on which all else depended. With a sigh, the king relinquishes his lively gossip. A big sigh—exit Sartines. Beaumarchais is sorely grieved. To replace him, Maurepas will have none of the Marquis de Castries despite his incontestable assets: a nasty temper, handsome military career, and immense fortune. He's governor of Languedoc, acquired as a family heirloom from an older brother to whom Louis XV gave the post at the age of three

*The abolition of these had been among Turgot's basic reforms.

†130 million new francs [$26 million]. The size of the budget of the navy, France's sole "striking force," is comparable only to the expenditure of modern-day great powers on armament and nuclear energy. To put the figure into some perspective, 31 million was budgeted for "ordinary" expenses, 25 million for the King's Household—and 800,000 for hospitals (these are 1780 francs, of course).

and a half.* But the moribund old Mentor means to hold out to the bitter end, and any "Choiseulist" is anathema to him. However, egged on by Marie Antoinette, Necker boldly advises Louis XVI to take Castries anyway . . . on the grounds that Maurepas wants him! Louis XVI signs without reading the fine print, and Maurepas nearly dies of rage, but too late.[11] At that point people realize that the limpid Genevan is as good a cheat as the next man, and they begin to endow him with political stature. Using more or less the same tactics, he obtains approval for the Maréchal de Ségur two months later, although this time the queen has to produce a fit of nerves to tip the scales.[12] Now she can make ministers with a wave of her fan. Her shy and retiring days are definitely over. It looks as though they're also over for Jacques Necker, who appears on the threshold of the new year as Marie Antoinette's man. He leans on the pedal again, but a shade too soon, a touch too heavily. He's going like a steam roller. The risks are high. Once he's in motion, you wonder if he'll ever be able to put on the brakes.

"People are talking of nothing but M. Necker's *Account Rendered to the King,*" announces Métra's *Correspondance.*[13] "The Panckoucke bookshop will make a great deal of money from the sale of this pamphlet. It is being printed night and day" in the print shop of the king's cabinet, which has fallen under Panckoucke's control along with some thirty other small book and pamphlet factories in Paris and Versailles, Strasbourg, Lille, and Tours. Less and less a bookseller and more and more a publisher, Charles-Joseph Panckoucke is rubbing his hands over this latest stroke: at least thirty thousand copies, selling for an écu† apiece. Necker has given up his own rights to any money by adopting the bashful pretense of publishing "by order of the King," as an official act. Panckoucke signs a contract with the accounts office and pays it a lump sum "for the work of M. Necker."

The two men were born to be brothers. With his tall, strapping Flemish silhouette, Panckoucke even looks like Necker; but as everybody knows, the people of Lille are the Provençals of the north, and this one is no exception: he has been hustling and bustling nonstop ever since he came to seek his fortune in Paris at the age of twenty-eight. That was in 1764, and here he is, already emperor of the book trade. He comes by it naturally. His father was the biggest bookseller in Lille, and wrote his own compilations for the pleasure of publishing them himself, situated as he was "between Paris, where the most-read books in Europe were made, and Holland, where the greatest trade in them was done."[14] In Paris they think, in The Hague they sell. All the better for this flittermouse of the pen, the "bookseller" trying to combine three

---

*And who died at the age of eighteen, during the Seven Years' War.

†A silver coin worth between 3 and 5 francs of those days, which means that the *Account Rendered* cost about 20 new francs [$4].

vocations: writer, manufacturer, and salesman. Charles-Joseph was "destined, by his studies and his talent for mathematics, for a professor's chair or a post in the army engineers" when his father suddenly died. Blessed release, for the son had no flair for either teaching or the military life. "At the moment this thunderbolt struck, with his mother and his brothers and sisters to think of, he could entertain no other calling than that of head of his family and director of trade in his firm," and he decides to move closer to the source. He leaves the shop to his mother in Lille and "with his capital invested in nothing but probity and native wit, both of which were imprinted upon superb features [*sic*], he went to Paris, taking two sisters to run his household, and settled in the most literary district, which in those days was also the most magnificent one, near the Comédie Française and the Procope café, the meeting place of all talent and every form of brilliance, the center of that faubourg Saint-Germain in which the finest libraries formed part of the opulent display of all the higher aristocrats, and were a genuine need for those nobles who thought like the La Rochefoucaulds and d'Envilles."*

"Of M. Panckoucke's two sisters, both extremely young when they first came to Paris, only the younger was pretty." He perspicaciously marries her to Antoine Suard, one of the rising young authors in right-minded circles, who can do him enormous favors because Malesherbes has appointed him censor to the king's bookseller, and a brother-in-law like that can remove Panckoucke's "tradesman" stigma. He becomes a man of letters. "His houses in Paris and Boulogne [another multidirectional antenna, this one pointed at England; one of the things it picks up is Brissot] brought together, like those of Helvétius and the Baron d'Holbach, the cream of literary people, artists and scholars. He printed not only the works of others but also some which were his own," mainly in the *Mercure*, which he bails out of a tight spot and revives. He also takes over the *Encyclopédie* from Lebreton and publishes the supplements to it; above all, he undertakes the parallel publication of a sort of poor man's, or rather lower middle-class man's encyclopedia, the *Encyclopédie méthodique*, flooding France in sixty volumes. He takes anything, publishes anything—newspapers, broadsheets, pamphlets, dictionaries, folio, 8vo, 16mo, Voltaire, Linguet, La Harpe, and Rousseau. He's up to volume thirty-three of Buffon. And now Necker . . .

Publisher and financier: the ideal team to draw the new chariot of the times. The sign of their alliance: the *Account Rendered*.

Ten years later Rabaut-Saint-Etienne† writes that "the *Account Rendered* had the effect of a sudden beam of light piercing the darkness. Enthusiasm was

---

*This piece of hyperbole, typical of the style of biographers of the day, is by Garat, in his *Vie de M. Suard.*

†A Protestant pastor at Nîmes in 1780, one of the more striking figures of the Convention. Allied to the Girondists, he dies with them.

universal. This book was touched by every hand. It was read in villages and hamlets."[15] An exaggeration, but one that proves the impact of the event on the semi-clandestine Protestant communities in which outlawed preachers inform their flocks of the undreamed-of daring of one of their brethren. It is a fact that a tremor runs through public opinion from the deserts of Languedoc to Versailles. Necker is arousing a slumbering France. Grimm is beside himself: "The sensation caused by this work is, I do believe, unprecedented." And Ségur (the son): "There was a copy in every priest's pocket and on every lady's dressing table." "The Archbishop of Aix [according to Mme Necker] says there is intelligence in the very numbers in the *Account Rendered.*" Owing to its blue cover, the standard binding on all products of the royal printers, the book soon acquires a nickname: it becomes "the little blue book" brandished "in cafés, salons, at Versailles, and in the Palais Royal." Anyone unable to quote passages from it by heart is banished to Boeotia.

It is clear, easy to understand—good popularization, aimed at the layman. An "open letter" to Louis XVI that treats him like a person who doesn't understand much about figures. The author explains the mechanics of his finances patiently and kindly, but in tones so lofty that they float past the sovereign's shoulder and address themselves to the general assembly. You could almost believe you were hearing a national budget being presented to a parliament by a secretary of state in a democracy.

"Little blue book" . . . well, sort of—if you compare it with the mammoth tomes of the *Encyclopédie* and other folios so hefty that you have to have a footman to manipulate them under the reader's gaze. But the *Account Rendered* is a respectable size: 116 square octavo pages, a sort of notebook, but still a long way from your modern Penguin.[16] The admirable typography of the day makes it a work of art by the very rhythm of its basic typeface—Garamond 6 point—and its stately italic headings. Bonus features: two cool-hued maps of France—one of farms and the other of salt-bonding sites—and a large folding table that summarizes the whole event: the budget of France for 1780 at a glance. The "moneys paid out by the Royal Treasury" stand across from the "income received by the Royal Treasury." One enormous subtraction winds up the whole:

Income amounts to:	264,154,000 livres
Outgoings to:	253,954,000 livres
Income exceeds expenditure by:	10,200,000 livres.

A credit balance of 10 million* after three years of war! It would be enough to make the Chancellor of the Exchequer and the great financiers of every country on earth turn mint-green with envy—if it were true.

The body of the book annotates the headings on the table in Necker's

---

*Rough approximations in new francs: Income: 1 billion 320 million [$264 million]; expenditure: 1 billion 270 million [$254 million]; excess: 50 million [$10 million].

ponderous style—written in the second person because he's talking to the king, but always for the benefit of the first person, the writer himself—from start: "Sire, having devoted all my time and strength to Your Majesty's service . . ." (page 1) to finish: "Lastly, and this I confess as well, I have proudly relied upon that public opinion which the wicked vainly seek to arrest or lacerate [*sic*] but which, despite all their efforts, justice and truth compel in their wake" (page 104). In the meantime, Jacques Necker can hardly be said to retire behind his figures, and at every opportunity he is lavish with the kind of praise one customarily bestows on oneself failing a handout from any other source.

As it stands, it's a fascinating piece of reading, the first attempt at a financial anatomy of France:

"My successor will have a less arduous task because I have formed what never existed before—that is to say, complete tables, substantiated by the elements necessary for a ready understanding of all the details of the financial situation." We learn at the outset that Necker has made good a deficit, confessed by Clugny,* "of twenty-four million of income under the heading ordinary expenses." Thereafter we were sailing straight for the golden age when bam! "The year 1777 was a year of war for the Royal Treasury"— although the war hadn't actually been declared yet, the navy had to be rebuilt. So it was necessary to cut and prune, scrape around, tighten up. First blow against "the favors, largesses, and extravagant festivities . . . Your Majesty supported my resistance to all the multiple demands for gratifications, indemnities, exchanges, concessions, and other sources of drain upon the Royal Treasury which a long period of laxity had introduced . . . Your Majesty has not come to the end of the economies and improvements of various sorts which Your Majesty may wish to effect, and several of which have already been prepared in my department." The temporary panacea: borrowing. "Your Majesty has hitherto borrowed at no more than 9 percent . . . But I believe, Sire, that circumstances demand of Your Wisdom that the terms of the forthcoming loan be more favorable to the lenders," in other words to the clients of the Thélusson bank who will owe full credit for their profits to Necker. At times, the *Account Rendered* sounds like a prospectus for a stock issue.

He goes further, enumerating the simplifications already carried out or about to be introduced, in the levying of taxes and commitment of expenditure: a cut in the number of chief collectors and a leveling off of farm contracts —measures which, without upsetting the antiquated machinery of the Treasury, go some way toward tidying it up. Here and there we find a line portending a change in the heavens—gold is dethroned, for example: "The richest financiers and the most adroit bankers can no more increase the imports of gold and silver into France than reduce them; and in this respect they have

*Who fleetingly succeeded Turgot in 1776.

less effect than the smallest manufacturer of Lodève or Louviers who succeeds, through hard work, in increasing the kingdom's trade abroad by so much as one bale of cloth." We learn in passing that the total amount of tax levied annually "on the people, accruing both to Your Majesty and the towns, hospitals and communities, is nearly five hundred million,"* of which the French state *per se* receives only the smaller half, the rest going to a mafia of seigneuries or local authorities at the whim or mercy of tradition: total exemption in one place, another overtaxed to the point of paralysis, France played like a lottery over the course of the centuries.

On page 62 Necker drops his mask and becomes Necker, when he proposes to "fix permanently the rate for each taxpayer paying the Vingtièmes . . .† Because any exception, any favor, sooner or later becomes an injustice to society." On page 64 he protests against the arbitrary collection of the *taille,* to which various parts of the country are subjected haphazardly in addition to the *vingtième.* He begins whistling another little reformatory tune on page 65: "After having thus determined the Taille and the Capitation [head tax], there will remain one great good to be done one day, which will be the work of Justice and Virtue [the capitals are his, in this invocation of Enlightened Despotism]: an effort must be made to apportion taxation more equitably among the provinces . . . For how can the justice of the distribution of taxes be made perceptible so long as the amount of the tax remains arbitrary or unsettled? . . . I do not believe it can be said too often: either great schemes must be given up, or they must be prepared by simple and open means. Men, and taxpayers especially, have so often been deceived that nothing but a long period of forthrightness and sincerity will overcome their misgivings." Sounds as though he's warming up and becoming more self-confident; now he shifts from correct methods—where he's still a mere common-sense technician—to just causes—where he's already a party leader. On page 70 we find him echoing Turgot: "It is to be hoped that some means of abolishing the Corvée will be encouraged.** Ultimately, this question is but a debate between poor and rich, for it is easy to perceive at a glance what advantage there is for the poor in the abolition of the Corvée. . . . There is no doubt that the Corvée is patently contrary to the interests of this class of your subjects toward whom Your Majesty's bountiful hand should ever be outstretched, in order to temper, insofar as possible, the imperious yoke of property and riches."

What's all this about a yoke? A man of wealth denouncing the wealthy? That little tune of Necker's, that calculated confession, will be enough to set

*2.5 billion new francs [$500 million].

†An annual tax, we recall, equal to one-twentieth of income from property.

**A personal tax, in the form of labor, imposed upon the peasantry, who were required to spend one or more weeks each year mending roads. Turgot had tried to replace it by a money tax, amounting to a few sous per head.

him apart from the rest of his class in the eyes of the poor wretches who learn, through the voices of admiring readers, that he exists and what he is demanding. Those little sentences in his *Account Rendered,* timid though they may be, define him as a righter of wrongs marching up to the king and telling him off. Sometimes it takes so few words to sweep away the lie of apparent permanence! Necker has just built his own monument. Vergennes, as spokesman for the horrified Haves and potential prime minister thwarted by the Genevan's rise, is preparing a smashing retort in the form of a Memorandum to the King: "This *Account Rendered,* in the final analysis, is a pure appeal to the people, and its pernicious effects upon this monarchy cannot as yet be either felt or foreseen."[17]

MESMER

46

MARCH 1781

Contrary to Everything We Have Been Taught

On March 29, 1781, Doctor Franz Anton Mesmer writes the Queen of France a long letter that might well land him in the Bastille. A foreigner, jeered at and called a quack by the academies, and he treats himself to the luxury of insolence! Here's a man who's never heard of fear or servility, and if he's going to burn his bridges he might as well do it in style . . . Another one trying to teach royalty a lesson:

> Madame,
>   . . . I abandon all hope of reaching an agreement with the French government . . .
>   . . . Madame, I seek a government which is able to perceive that a truth capable of working great changes, by virtue of its effect upon the physical part in humans, cannot be allowed to come upon the world unattended . . . The conditions offered to me in Your Majesty's name having failed to meet these views, the austerity of my principles imperatively forbade me to accept them.
>   In a cause of first concern to mankind, money must be but a secondary consideration. In Your Majesty's eyes, four or five hundred thousand francs more or less,* rightly employed, are nothing. The welfare of the people is all. My discovery must be received and myself recompensed with a munificence worthy of the greatness of the Monarch to whom I shall attach myself.[1]

*2 or 2.5 million new francs [$400,000 or $500,000].

A modest chap, apparently, and easygoing too.

From his library, "the sole possessor of the most precious truth for the human race" can hear the hum of the little Parisian plebiscite that reassures him: a line of coaches outside his door on the Rue Coquillière, on the right bank near St. Eustache and the Rue Plâtrière, where Rousseau spent his last years. A line of patients in the waiting room of the apartment he has rented in what used to be the residence of Claude de Bullion, superintendent of finance under Louis XIII.

Now and then Franz Anton pauses in his diatribe to check and see that everything is going smoothly and his patients are submissively treating themselves in accordance with his instructions, under the supervision of his faithful Antoine, the "valet–layer-on-of-hands." Darkness and music reign in the string of rooms with shuttered windows. Beyond the anteroom, "decorated like a dining room, several persons move about. One may see an open piano-forte and two or three guitars. In the main drawing room people converse in extremely hushed tones. A few persons, some ill and others believing themselves so, are making ready to enter the bucket room"[2]—buckets it should be, since there are four of them, containing bottles immersed in "magnetized" water—that is, water over which Mesmer has made passes—but also in a mixture of iron filings, crushed glass, and sulfur, the smell of which pervades the room and inspires thoughts of the devil in the credulous. The "large round containers, some eighteen inches high and made of heavy oak, are hermetically closed. The patients communicate with the bucket either by means of angle-iron bars entering it through holes in the cover and allowing free play, or by means of ropes tied to a large central bar of iron." Circling around the buckets are a score of well-dressed men and women, the migraine-ridden, the hysterical, the constipated, and the curious, all groping in search of their cure. "Some point an iron bar in the direction of the obstruction, or some other part of the body they believe to be affected. There are men bent double, women in trances; some utter cries at regular intervals, others are lost in slumber, and still others are laughing convulsively." A door leads to the "quilted room" where anyone throwing a fit is deposited. "The music, violent or poignant, varies with the intensity of the attack"—and "in the distance a voice with an aerial tone sings an Italian arietta, accompanied by the guitar." Mesmer, the high priest of the temple, paces solemnly back and forth "with calculated slowness" in his fine lilac silk costume, not uttering a word. His very aspect soothes his faithful flock. Forty-seven years old, the dignity of a phlegmatic wrestler, a broad, swelling brow, forceful features, blue eyes you don't forget, a stubborn jaw. "When he enters a room, every eye turns upon him." A sort of Roman Teuton.

Such is Franz Anton Mesmer, the inventor—or so he thinks—of animal magnetism, which doesn't exist, and—although he has no inkling of it

—of psychosomatic medicine, which will, but not until more than a century has passed. A patient of Mesmer's is never a stranger to him. He tries to find out and records on file cards the circle to which his client belongs, the history of his childhood and parents. "The moral treatment is then adapted to his tastes, his family life, his social condition. He knows by experience how important it is to understand why a lady has fallen into a decline and is suffering from the vapors, why this lord or that financier flees human society, why a scholar abandons his research." Medicine has just punched a second hole in the congealed lava of classical practice which ground Molière and so many others into sausage meat: first inoculation, now "magnetism." This is one revolution that goes entirely unnoticed although it will change the face of the earth. "Mesmer is prodigiously interesting from the threefold viewpoints of history, the history of medicine, and psychiatry."* But at the moment he's flailing about in the dead-end alley of the pioneer between a handful of cumbersome zealots and the great mass of his detractors.

Between Mme de Lamballe and the Comte de Maurepas.

Marie-Thérèse de Savoie-Carignan, Princesse de Lamballe, casually drops in one winter day to ask Mesmer to heal her or divert her, it's the same thing. The richest woman in France is afflicted with incurable boredom. The mere effort of existing leaves her prostrate. Ever since the queen decided she liked Yolande de Polignac better, the Princesse de Lamballe has avoided Versailles insofar as her golden sinecure as chief lady-in-waiting will allow her. She holds her own court at Rambouillet, whither her father-in-law Penthièvre has retired. There she can be mini-queen of a hundred guests over whom she lets stray the benevolent gaze of her large, vacant blue eyes, amiable to the point of idiocy, always agreeing with everything, yes it is, yes, indeed, lovely weather for this time of year. No lovers: too tiring. Only her woman-servants know the knee-length fall of blond tresses that are her substitute for beauty. Sweetly plaintive, she loves to be pitied, and has just (on February 20) let herself be led by her friends to the presidency of the "Scottish Mother Lodge of Adoption," one of the inner sanctums of socialite Freemasonry. They're no worse than any other divertissement, these aproned-and-bonneted gesticulations of great ladies playing high priestess around M. Robineau de Beaunoir, author of the "Masonic chant to the most serene sister de Lamballe, Grand Mistress":

---

*According to Professor Levy-Valensi, in his preface to Jean Vinchon's *Mesmer et son secret* (Paris, Legrand, 1936).

Amour, ne cherche plus ta mère	[Love, seek thy mother no more;
Vénus abandonne Cythère	Venus is gone from Cytherea's
Pour présider à nos travaux	door
On est toujours grand maîtresse	To preside over our labors here;
Quand on règne sur tous les	Grand Mistress ever is she
coeurs.[3]	Who over all hearts the sovereign
	can be.]

To the archduchess, vicereine of Belgium, who is terrified to learn that Freemasonry is lapping at the foot of the throne, Marie Antoinette has just written: "I believe, my dear sister, that you worry far too much about Freemasonry, as far as France is concerned. It is by no means so important here as it may be in other parts of Europe, for the simple reason that everyone belongs to it . . . It is now nothing but a society of beneficence and pleasure-making; there is a great deal of eating, talk, and singing . . . It is in no way an association of avowed atheists, for God is on everyone's lips there; they do a great deal of charity . . . The Princesse de Lamballe told me all the pretty things that were said to her, but there were even more glasses emptied than verses sung. Two girls are shortly to be given dowries"[4] . . . and a new use will be found for the Penthièvre gold mine.

But none of this prevents Louise de Lamballe from swooning in her daily pythian trance, as they will later come to be called,* which rather tends to monopolize attention. Hysteria is her compensation for an empty head. Mme de Genlis has seen her, "in Holland, swoon in Mr. Hope's consulting room after casting her eyes upon a little Flemish painting portraying a woman selling lobsters . . . Without changing color, she closed her eyes and remained motionless more than half an hour before waking the moment her surgeon called for a basin of hot water and lancet in order to bleed her."[5]

Mesmer, it goes without saying, is also a Mason, a member of the Vienna "Truth and Union" Lodge. So it was only natural for his brothers and sisters to form a procession and lead their sister-mother-mistress of the Scottish Rite to his door. This type of patient is his specialty, he cures them by the carload. He welcomes Mme de Lamballe like any other, with his habitual affectation of courteous brusqueness. An instant convert: no more vapors for three weeks. That alone is almost enough to make Mesmer this season's god. What he's been vainly trying to get the Paris doctors to admit for the past three years, a little blond advocate seems likely to shove down the Court's throat in a few words. Patiently, passionately, Franz Anton tries to make her understand that he is the Newton of medicine.

---

*"Said of a nonorganic disturbance caused by suggestion and curable by it" (*Dictionnaire Robert* [Twentieth-century]).

I have discovered the sixth sense. I, son of the gamekeeper of the Archbishop of Constance, I have understood the basic principle of all healing: "Nature offers a universal means of curing and protecting men."[6] It is animal magnetism. There is a vital fluid in which all nervous systems bathe and it is I, I, Franz Anton Mesmer, who am about to touch and will shortly isolate it. Newton discovered gravity. Volta is about to discover electricity and Lavoisier oxygen. I, I master the sources of life, "that ebb and flow subject to mechanical laws which have hitherto been unknown," that tide of being and beings which encompasses stars, earth, and human bodies. I connect the motions of the planets to the fingertips of this poor swooning girl through the mediation of my eyes, the touch of my hands, "magnetized" water, the iron conductor. "This principle can cure nervous ailments directly, and all others indirectly . . . By means of a new theory of diseases, I shall demonstrate the universal utility of the principle with which I combat them . . . This doctrine will at last enable the physician to judge correctly the degree of health of each individual and guard him against the afflictions to which he may be liable. In this way the art of healing will reach its ultimate perfection." What is so surprising in my treating kings and queens as equals? Did not Plato equate enthusiasm with magnetism? I, a modern Plato, started from observations of the magnet and iron filings to arrive at the magnetization of living beings and understand the mechanism of all inspiration. A visionary? No. I have no kinship with those adversaries of science who cause tables to rotate and pretend to raise the dead or reincarnate Moses. The name of God is found in my notebooks only in the margins, as a measure of courtesy or a precaution. "I hope that my theory will hereafter preclude those interpretations which gave rise to and nourished superstition and fanaticism." I go even further; by "opening up a simple and straight path to the truth . . . I have in great measure disengaged Nature from the illusions of metaphysics." With me the mystics had better be on their guard, for "the miraculous apparitions, ecstasies, and inexplicable visions which are the source of so much error and absurd belief" are nothing but "magnetic attacks. One feels how greatly the very obscurity which has shrouded such phenomena, when combined with the ignorance of the multitude, must have fostered the growth of the religious and political prejudices of all peoples."

. . . Did he write "political prejudices"? He did. The Comte de Maurepas, that little bunch of bones in a large golden gown, all twisted and warped in his easy chair, opens one round eye to stare at the tall solemn man who is pretending to overthrow medical dogma without reference to religious dogma. A charlatan, say the gentlemen of the Faculté—except, it is true, for Jussieu, but Jussieu doesn't pull much weight alongside Vicq d'Azyr and Leroy and Daubenton and Desperrières and Abbé Tessier.* "This system is contrary to everything we have been taught." A funny kind of charlatan, who believes in neither god nor devil! A materialist treating the spiritual. "Everything can be explained," he claims, "by mechanical laws found in Nature, and all effects derive from modifications of matter and motion." Next thing, he'll be meddling in politics . . .

It was no go all the way during that decisive interview with Maurepas on which his whole future hung. Mme de Lamballe and other great names set it up for him; the queen herself intimated that she was interested in the man. She wrote to Joseph II: "You are most kind to let me importune you so about Mesmer"[7]—but her brother informs her that the pretentious miscreant is no longer tolerated in Vienna and she would do well to tell him to go peddle his wares somewhere else. It was precisely because Mesmer was a subject of universal contempt in Austria and had just quarreled openly with Störck, Maria Theresa's physician, that he came to try his luck in Paris. But Louis XVI doesn't want to see him. And Mesmer is asking for the moon, or almost: a substantial pension, a château at Créteil to treat his choice patients, rich or poor; and above all, he wants official approval of his methods, accreditation to all Europe.

A ticklish case. Like every other tangle, it was passed on to Maurepas. That's all the Mentor is good for these days; this eternally agonizing elder statesman is treated like a royal garbage disposal. Skeptical, desperate, embittered, godless, and cheerless, he might at least have appreciated Mesmer's practical side. But Mesmer is motivated by the religion of man. He wants to save the whole human race with his science; but can he cure Maurepas's gout? There was no hope. For two hours two irreconcilable worlds confront each other, the healer and the minister of state, utopia and pusillanimity. Maurepas no longer has the strength to laugh, but he can still grit his teeth. And then he gets it all backwards, turning an affair of state into a question of money. Just another beggar . . .

"The King grants you a life pension of twenty thousand livres and will pay a rent of ten thousand francs for your house.† But all further favors remain conditional upon the subsequent recognition of the value of your discoveries . . ."

By whom? Mesmer flies into a rage. Like Marat, like Brissot, like Linguet, like Beaumarchais, like all whose future is blocked by prejudice. What a century of mummies! How is one supposed to change the world in this cemetery of ideas?

---

*All members of the "commission" appointed by the Royal Medical Society to condemn Mesmer without inspecting his work.

†Or a total of 150,000 new francs [$30,000] a year, leaving Mesmer free to charge his patients for treatment.

I am already accustomed to the impression I make upon them. Accusations of vanity, self-importance, obstinacy, feigned disinterest have come to my ears from all sides . . . The offer which you make me appears to err by setting out my pecuniary interest, and not the importance of my discovery, as the main objective. The question absolutely must be seen the other way around, since without my discovery my self would be nothing . . . If people do not believe in my discovery, they are clearly doing a great wrong to offer me thirty thousand livres of income for it . . . I cannot conceive that the Nation's most enlightened minds are so subservient to the scholars that they fear to incur their displeasure on my account . . . Does it matter what the medical Faculté feels, if it feels no concern for the fate of mankind? I can undertake to enter into no agreement with you unless the French government first gives official acknowledgment of the value of my discovery.[8]

Mesmer carries on in that tone until he's hoarse. Maurepas curls up to wait for the storm to blow over. "No harsh expression issued from his mouth. Calmly, gently, his voice quietly expressed his objections, and his ear attentively listened to mine" . . . But his mind is made up. This is a madman he's dealing with, that is, a man who refuses money on principle. "Believe"? "Discover"? What could they mean to this dotard who is as universally blasé as the rest of his world? He makes a little gesture with his hand. Take it or leave it. Mesmer leaves it. To close the account, he writes to the queen:

"Madame, anyone who has an eye to the judgment of Nations and posterity will bear so cruel a reverse without pride, but courageously. For he will know that there are many circumstances in which kings must guide the opinion of the people, but there are an even greater number in which public opinion irresistibly dominates that of kings. Today, Madame, Your Brother feels nothing but contempt for me. Well, once public opinion has decided, he will render justice to me."[9]

It's lucky for Mesmer that Mme de Lamballe is a patient of his. Many another has been sent to prison for less. Then, having said his piece and set his heart at ease, he calmly puts his affairs in order, prescribes treatments for his patients, and heads for Spa, the Belgian watering hole then in fashion, where a minute republic of the ailing lives suspended between empires. There he will find the peace and quiet he periodically requires. Only "the country-side, the forest, and the most secluded and lonely places have any attraction for me . . . Whenever we have an idea, we instantly and without reflection translate it into the language most familiar to us. The bizarre notion of freeing myself from this servitude has recently occurred to me"—his quest for freedom goes to those lengths. But at Spa he will be able, as he has done before, "to think for three months without language,"[10] and it will be easier there than in Paris for him to return to that fourth and all-encompassing dimension of his life—music. "There is music in the inn on rainy days, when the stream running through the town rises and overflows like a mountain torrent."[11] And when Mesmer returns from his long liberating walks ("fortunately my words, lost in the silence of the woods, have only the trees to witness their vehemence; I must certainly look like a man possessed"), he finds in his room the "harmonica" from which he is never parted and which he has ordered to be played to him when he is dying: five drinking glasses side by side, filled with eau-de-vie, wine, plain water, and oil. "The musician formed his sounds by rubbing his finger around the rim of the glasses." Probing far beyond his panacea to heal all physical ailments, Franz Anton seeks the secret of universal harmony in the Masonic murmur beginning to rise ten or twenty thousand voices strong between Danube and Seine, tuning up for the cantata of mankind. His real life, his true friends, are there. "The great question I am working on is neither individual nor national; it is universal. It is to the whole of mankind, and not only to Paris, France or Germany, that I must give an account of my efforts. It is to all the peoples of the world that I must speak."

On March 10, 1781, twenty days before Mesmer's outburst in Paris, Mozart reaches Vienna, where he hasn't set foot since 1773. At last, in Munich, he has just had his first adult success: the first performance of *Idomeneo*. Nevertheless, he's restless, anxious, ill at ease in his role as "musical servant" of the Prince-Archbishop of Salzburg. Where does he go? To whom does he turn for comfort and human warmth? To the brother and nephews of Anton Mesmer,* who still live between the Landstrasse and the Danube in the huge house hidden among the foliage of its ample grounds filled with shrubbery, a pond, and a belvedere, where Franz Anton used to entertain and encourage him. And it was there, in the little theater-on-the-lawn built by Mesmer where Haydn and Gluck came to present their works, that the first original opera of the youth who didn't want to be a child anymore was performed—*Bastien und Bastienne*. "Oh, I am assuredly going to thumb my nose at the archbishop! What a joy that must be! . . . and most politely, too . . ."[12] Those are among Mozart's first words in Vienna, written on April 4, a few days after his old friend Franz Anton most politely thumbed his nose at the Queen of France.

---

*Who was already separated from but on good terms with his wife, the young widow of an Aulic (imperial German) councilor, to whom he owed his considerable fortune.

47

In the Course of Ages . . .

On February 20, 1781, from his New Windsor headquarters, still within reach of New York, Washington writes the fateful letter to La Fayette:

> Sir, I have ordered a detachment to be made at this post, to rendezvous at Peekskill on the 19th instant, which, together with another to be formed at Morristown from the Jersey troops, will amount to about twelve hundred rank and file. The destination of this detachment is to act against the corps of the enemy now in Virginia . . . You will take command of this detachment.[1]

With this order the tide in the American war begins to turn, on a north-south axis. Washington is going to try something new: in the North progress is completely blocked as long as no serious move can be made against New York; in Virginia, on the other hand, things are happening, and the traitor Arnold is there attempting a risky maneuver intended to exploit the English gains in the South. There and only there can we try to tip the scales. And it's also in Virginia that we can make best use of this frisky little general who's more American than the Americans. La Fayette still has faith. But he's one of the last.

He's been waiting for six months now, like a sailor's wife on a widow's walk, for the reinforcements which Rochambeau's son went to beg from Vergennes after the Hartford interview. What in God's name are they doing back in Brest? What's happened to the soldiers Rochambeau had to leave behind because there weren't enough ships? It's to him that Congress keeps turning, and even ordinary people: isn't he France? Hasn't he promised everything—too much—in her name? Poor Gilbert's been lumbered with the part of Sister Anne. M. de La Fayette, do you see them coming? Gilbert, Brother Gilbert, is there any sign? . . .*

"Good God! The promised fleet really must get here soon!† Without

---

*In the tale of Bluebeard (by Perrault), his last wife keeps crying out to her sister posted on the parapet, as she begs for time from her homicidal husband, "Anne, Sister Anne, do you see them coming? Anne, Sister Anne, is there any sign?"[*Trans.*]

†Letter from La Fayette to Mme de Tessé, October 4, 1780.

ships, all we can count on is blows . . . This is as monotonous as a war in Europe [of which his only experience was the months spent stagnating in Le Havre]. Meanwhile, we are of a frugality, a poverty, a nudity which I hope will be charged to our account in the next world, and relieve us of the need to go to Purgatory."[2] That's the tune in the autumn; and a ghastly winter has done nothing but raise the pitch. Everything is black because France is letting us down. You can count on the fingers of one hand the people who still seriously maintain that we will win this war.

Fersen, for instance, got the picture some time ago. He has heard that in the Carolinas, "the militia under General Gates all went over to the English from the very start of the action. If that is true, how can we rely upon such men, and must not a brave man consider himself to be pitied if he is put in command of them?"[3] And as for Rochambeau's camp in Newport, what a spectacle! "We vegetate, within range of the enemy's fire, in the most sinister and horrible idleness and inactivity, and because of our small numbers we are compelled to play the exhausting part of the defenders; we are no use at all to our allies; we cannot get off our island without exposing our fleet to capture or destruction; our fleet cannot go out without delivering us into the hands of our enemies who, with superior numbers in ships and men, would not fail to attack and cut off our retreat upon the mainland . . . Far from being useful to the Americans, we are a burden to them; we are not reinforcing their army, for we are a twelve days' march from it, separated by estuaries which cannot be crossed in winter when they are filled with ice floes. They are having to pay for us, too, as by increasing consumption we are making supplies more scarce, and by paying coin we cause their paper money to fall, and in so doing we make it impossible for Washington's army to obtain supplies with ease, because the people will not sell for paper"[4]—for those paper dollars now undergoing their first devaluation ever. In this instance, a total collapse. From this point of view, Fersen is quite clear about "the reasons militating against the raising of an army that can be levied and maintained with money alone," that money which (but he's judging only by the natives of Rhode Island) is the "*primum mobile* of all their acts, they think of nothing but how to get it; each man is for himself, nobody for the public weal. The coastal inhabitants, even the best Whigs among them, bring every manner of supplies to the English fleet, because they are well paid; but they fleece us unmercifully, the price of everything is exorbitant, and in every agreement we have made with them, they have treated us more as enemies than as friends. Their cupidity is unequaled, money is their God; virtue, honor, all that is nothing to them, when measured against that precious silver metal."[5] Count Fersen himself, however, is not wholly above such vulgar considerations: "I am most pleased, my dear father, that you approve of the arrangement I have made for obtaining money . . . The letter of credit which M. Tourton gave me was for twelve thousand livres . . . This sum, although large, cannot suffice for all my needs in America,"⁶ including clothes and food for his valet and two grooms.*

The situation really is looking hopeless. Admiral de Ternay actually dies of despair on December 15, but not before warning Vergennes: "The fate of North America is yet very uncertain, and the revolution is not so far advanced as has been believed in Europe."⁷

La Fayette, meanwhile, is cultivating that infuriating kind of optimism that either moves mountains or brings them crashing down on your head. At the end of October he even tries to move Washington by suggesting that the Americans attempt a suicide operation against Staten Island. He plaintively writes to his beloved general: "The French court have often complained to me of the inactivity of the American army, who, before the alliance, had distinguished themselves by their spirit of enterprise. They have often told me, 'Your friends leave us now to fight their battles, and do no more risk themselves.' "⁸

Washington sweeps away the insinuation with a backstroke of the pen. He has put a freeze on the war because there was nothing else he could do: with no money, and therefore no men, no ammunition, no equipment, no naval supremacy, all he can expend is hope. "It is impossible, my dear Marquis, to desire more ardently than I do to terminate the campaign [of 1780] by some happy stroke; but we must consult our means rather than our wishes."⁹ La Fayette goes burbling on undeterred. How about if we called on the troops in the Spanish colonies for help? What if those slumbering allies woke up long enough to attack Jamaica, at least? Why shouldn't I write to them, in the name of Rochambeau and Washington? Another cold shower from the latter: "You must be convinced, from what passed at the interview at Hartford, that my command of the French troops at Rhode Island stands upon a very limited scale, and that it would be impolitic and fruitless of me to propose any measure of co-operation to a third power without their concurrence."¹⁰

But La Fayette keeps lashing out, even to the detriment of the good cause —as with Vergennes, to whom, upon moving into winter quarters, he sends an account so grim—for once—that it adds fuel to the pessimists' fire. It's a pretty good sketch of a last ditch:

> Without maritime superiority, Monsieur le Comte, there will be no certain operation in America . . . The second division [promised and vanished] gives us as much anxiety as its delay causes us impatience and creates doubt in the minds of the Americans . . . The Congress has no money and little power. Our troops are in want of food, of pay, and of clothing. By the 1st of January the [American] army will not amount to six thousand men . . . [but] the Continental troops that

*60,000 new francs [$12,000].

we still have are equal in every respect to those of the enemy, and they have a patience in their misery which is unknown in European armies . . . The great obstacle, Monsieur le Comte, is the lack of money . . . A sum of money, in specie, intended exclusively for the American army, would remove three-quarters of our troubles, and . . . is absolutely necessary for our clothing next year . . . We ought during the course of this winter to receive, independently of what may already have been shipped, fifteen thousand complete uniforms, with underclothing and blankets; and, provided that fifteen thousand muskets arrive, we shall require a large additional quantity of powder. [To conclude:] In the present condition of affairs in America, and in view of its present attitude, it is essential to the interest, as well as to the honor, of France, that our flag should rule over these seas, that the campaign should be decisive, and that it should begin with the coming spring.[11]

Now our young general is trying his hand at the language of statesmanship —but the man behind the desk on which one rubber stamp could still save everything is not La Fayette, it's 'Fraidy-cat Vergennes.

And the great storms of winter roll on and over all, viciously uprooting the last of La Fayette's illusions: the Pennsylvania troops revolt at Morristown, it's rebellion within the Revolution, insurrection among the Insurgents. On January 1 the despairing men massacre a few officers, put themselves in the hands of their sergeants, and follow an English deserter, Williams, to Philadelphia—that's all we needed! Congress caught between two fires, the mutineers and the English. What an opportunity for the latter, if only they could react quickly enough! But thanks be to God, they go on digesting their Christmas puddings while the American leaders are being insulted and mauled by their own men, one after the other: Colonel Laurens, St. Clair, Knox, Wayne, La Fayette himself, a nightmare of snow, snatches of French lost in torrents of English oaths, they want bread, clothing, and coins, not speeches, not promises.

Washington has to step in and outface them. Out-doubleface them, in fact, with a pearly smile on one side and an iron mask on the other. He makes a few concessions to the Pennsylvania guys, here's all the cash we can give you, have a promotion, have a furlough, have two! But the New Jersey men who were about to follow suit are made to pay for everybody else. Washington pitches into them with a thousand crack troops while he negotiates with the other bunch. "You are surrounded. Unconditional surrender. Hand over your leaders. You have two hours to think it over." On January 15 the rebels are put down, but only just. A dozen of them are shot in the name of freedom and the fatherland. Face is saved, but news of the uprising makes the rounds at Versailles, and Vergennes, wearing a funereal expression that makes his views all too plain, is not the last to carry the tale.

Versailles—where the desperate mission of the Vicomte de Rochambeau, whom La Pérouse has miraculously conveyed through the English blockade from Boston to Brest, is turned into a song, of course:

Le Roi demande à Rochambeau: [The King to Rochambeau bends
"Qu'apportez-vous donc de   an ear:
    nouveau?"   "Quick; what's the news? Do tell!"
—"Sire, lui dit-il à l'oreille,   "Sire," whispers he, "you'll be
Mon père se porte à merveille."[12]   pleased to hear
                                           That my father's uncommonly
                                               well."]

As a change from the mourning imposed upon them by Maria Theresa's death, they begin tearing the scapegoat to shreds. Everybody's bored to tears by this war, it's like a play that never ends. Curtain! Curtain! Five months of silence is their answer to America's calls for help. They're thinking about it. So Congress sends yet another messenger, but this one really is their last hope: Colonel Laurens. He sets out for France on February 13 on board the *Alliance* (the same frigate that brought La Fayette two years earlier) to put not only Vergennes but Necker as well against the wall—that Necker to whom La Fayette has just written "that he must be persuaded of the necessity to send money to the Americans."[13] How can the Rebels guess that Laurens is going to land plumb in the middle of Necker's dying-swan dance? Vergennes is furious at the intrusion. "The King is obliged to take recourse to retrenchments and to loans for his own service: he was justified in expecting that the United States would at least provide for the expenses of their army . . . We wish, therefore, that they had not sent Mr. Laurens to us," a boor, a hothead who stomps through the Hall of Mirrors like a man at war whose country is dying. He shouts. He demands. Vergennes finally bestirs himself, but only to put him in his place. "We flatter ourselves especially that Congress will not only share, but will severely condemn, the dissatisfaction expressed by Mr. Laurens, and that it will endeavor to influence that officer, who is imperfectly acquainted with our customs and with the consideration due to ministers of a great Power; he has presented several demands not only with an importunate insistence, but even with threats. He demanded that the King should furnish the Americans with arms, clothing, and munitions to an amount exceeding eight millions of livres, and that he should lend them, or at least obtain for them, twenty-five millions more . . .* I know that he has made the most

*In new francs, 40 million [$8 million] in supplies, and an additional loan of 125 million [$25 million]. Necker and Vergennes—in agreement for the last time—give the equivalent of 70 million [$14 million], a good half of it indirectly, in the form of security for a Dutch loan to the USA.

indiscreet complaints because he was unable to obtain everything that he asked."[14]

Franklin has to intervene. Has he crossed the Atlantic only to chat a few years away in drawing rooms? The Sage raises his voice, one of the few voices capable of moving the Court of France to rise to the occasion—because of its vibrato, yes, but also because of the range of its echo. Whatever Franklin says to Vergennes is heard clear to Nantes and Bordeaux. No one knows better how to shift from pathos to the threat of the British dragon without even changing key. Woe betide you Frenchmen if you don't get the message!

> I am grown old. I feel myself much enfeebled by my late long illness, and it is probable I shall not long have any more concern in these affairs. I therefore take this occasion to express my opinion to Your Excellency that the present conjuncture is critical; that there is some danger lest the Congress should lose its influence over the people if it is found unable to procure the aids that are wanted, and that the whole system of the new government in America may thereby be shaken. That if the English are suffered once to recover that country, such an opportunity of effectual separation as the present may not occur again in the course of ages; and that possession of those fertile and extensive regions and that vast seacoast will afford them so broad a basis for future greatness, by the rapid growth of their commerce and breed of seamen and soldiers, as will enable them to become the *terror of Europe,* and to exercise with impunity that insolence which is so natural to their nation, and which will increase enormously with the increase of their power.[15]

Over Vergenne's head, Franklin is talking to Louis XVI. America has spoken. Do you read me, France?

Who's going to win? Vergennes and Necker or Laurens and Franklin? La Fayette, meanwhile, is off at full gallop once again, this time under torrential spring rains, toward a tiny dot at the back of beyond—they call it Head of Elk, [now Elkton] at the top of Chesapeake Bay. And who's going to win in Virginia? Arnold and Cornwallis or La Fayette and Steuben? In March 1781 La Fayette is the only man in the freedom camp who's on his feet and moving, trying to do something. He rushes around, he eats it up. At Pompton the roads are so sodden that the horses founder. He ploughs ahead on foot, through a morass of weeds and water; the Delaware in spate has transformed the New Jersey flatlands into soup, but this little redheaded devil is so happy to be on the move that he'd have his boys walking on the water, despite the squalls of mutiny buffeting them. His boys: ten companies from the Massachusetts Line, five from Connecticut, one from Rhode Island, and two from New Hampshire, carrying five more from New Jersey who are still raw and unreliable. The whole commanded by officers who are half French, half American, La Fayette's cronies, everybody's pals; they communicate in sign language when words fail them. They're chasing the traitor of West Point and they mean to punish him good and proper: "You are to do no act whatever with Arnold that directly or by implication may screen him from the punishment due to his treason and desertion, which, if he should fall into your hands, you will execute in the most summary way."[16] Punish and liberate, the clean war.

First of all, he's got to reach Head of Elk at top speed, where French convoy ships are supposed to be waiting to save his twelve hundred men the exhausting and arduous trek on foot down the west side of Chesapeake Bay, a detour of almost a hundred leagues, littered with obstacles. They'll glide gently and swiftly down in ships instead, to the mouth of the bay where they'll be able to dive straight into Virginia and find out which way the winds of war are blowing. "When you arrive at your destination, you must act as your own judgment and the circumstances shall direct. You will open a correspondence with Baron Steuben . . ."—a Frenchman and a Prussian, like a pair of thieves in a ditch, to drive the English out of the country claimed for the Virgin Queen . . . Elizabeth will be turning in her grave. From La Fayette to Steuben on February 24: "The troops are marching through Rains and Bad Roads, but with such expedition as will accelerate our junction sooner than I expected . . . Adieu, my dear Baron. I am Happy to be employed with you on an expedition where I Hope to avail myself of your experience and of your Advice . . ."[17] failing those of Kalb, who bravely ended his career as a *reître* by getting himself killed at Camden last summer.*

March 3. La Fayette camps at Head of Elk with "his dirty little army"— ever and always with one hand clapped over his eyes peering out at the horizon: no convoy in sight. Once again the French fail him, those of Newport like those of Brest. Chevalier Destouches, a provisional "admiral" replacing Ternay, is indeed preparing for a six- or eight-ship tour down to the Chesapeake, but hasn't the slightest intention of letting himself get sucked inside it, and still less of sending troopships all the way to the north end of it just to please that little pipsqueak. Rochambeau approves. One or two messages make it clear to La Fayette that he's the man every officer in the French expeditionary corps is gunning for. So he wanted to be an American, did he? Well, he can just be one! Washington warns him: "The Chevalier [Destouches] seems to make a difficulty, which I do not comprehend, about protecting the passage of your detachment down the Bay; but, as it is entirely without foundation, I take it for granted it will cease on his arrival."[18] Take it for granted my foot! He's already making arrangements on the Virginia end, with the help of his itinerant governor Jefferson, to assist and equip La Fayette by land if the boats don't show. What this is, on Rochambeau's side, is a nonviolent mutiny of

---

*On August 16 in a battle waged by General Gates, whose defeat opened North Carolina to Cornwallis. Gates was then replaced by Greene.

higher officers. They're all older than La Fayette and can't bear the thought of serving under such a child. Him a major general? On parade, maybe. But in the field . . . The Baron de Vioménil, embarked with a few infantrymen on Destouches's ships, is waving instructions signed Rochambeau authorizing him, "if the welfare of the service so required,"[19] to deal directly with the militia of Virginia before La Fayette gets there—in case the marquis should be detained. "Detaining" him will be easy enough: all we have to do is not go get him.

La Fayette seems to have grown up at last, he's no longer dumfounded at finding himself hated and left to fend for himself, and he doesn't waste time feeling indignant. American? So be it then, all the way. He unearths a little fleetlet of small craft armed with cannons stuck on with chewing gum, not enough to go all the way down the Chesapeake but enough to flea-hop into the middle of it. He unloads his men at Annapolis and settles them there, then goes off to reconnoiter in a little sailboat, almost alone. He does have one loyal companion, though, the young Comte de Charlus, who could be useful since he's the son of the new minister of the navy, the Marquis de Castries;* he'd be the ideal man to talk to Destouches if La Fayette can manage to connect with him, somewhere between Yorktown and Cape Charles on the edge of the high sea . . .

He doesn't manage. On March 16 Destouches's eight ships meet eight of Admiral Arbuthnot's fleet, which has been guarding the passage. A lively cannonade. Two hundred dead. A sham; both sides say they've won, but it's Destouches who withdraws and takes his fleet back to Newport. The English remain masters of the Chesapeake from the sea. The Americans, now reinforced by La Fayette's men, are holding the shoreline, but for how long? From New York General Clinton will be able to send reinforcements to Benedict Arnold and Cornwallis by sea, and they can then come up out of Carolina and invade Virginia, driving back Baron Steuben's inferior forces and circumventing Greene's army, which is curled up like a hedgehog. It looks like a nasty spring. After the South, are the Middle United States about to fall like an overripe peach?

*Under the Restoration the Comte de Charlus becomes the first Duc de Castries.

48

MAY 1781

Now or Never

From Washington to Colonel Laurens, on April 9, 1781:

> If France delays a timely and powerful aid in the critical posture of our affairs, it will avail us nothing should she attempt it hereafter. We are at this hour suspended in the balance; not from choice, but from hard and absolute necessity; and you may rely on it as a fact, that we cannot transport the provisions from the States in which they are assessed to the army, because we cannot pay the teamsters, who will no longer work for certificates. It is equally certain that our troops are approaching fast to nakedness, and that we have nothing to clothe them with; that our hospitals are without medicines and our sick without nutriment . . . our public works are at a stand, and the artificers disbanding. But why need I run into detail, when it may be declared in a word, that we are at the end of our tether, and that now or never our deliverance must come?[1]

Vergennes is unmoved by such considerations. Whenever large sums of money are involved, this diplomat adopts the attitude of an estate manager: "Congress relies too much upon France for subsidies to maintain their army. They must absolutely refrain from such exorbitant demands . . . The last campaign has cost us more than one hundred fifty millions of extraordinary expenses,* and what we are now about to furnish will surpass that amount"—but Franklin has finally spoken, the courtiers are unanimous, and although the news of that strange spring showed an exhausted America out there, it also disclosed an anemic England nearby, on the verge of revolution. Just one tiny shove, Monsieur le Comte! "It has been owing, in great part . . . to the confidence we put in the veracity of Dr. Franklin that we have determined to relieve the pecuniary embarrassments in which he has been placed by Con-

---

*This conflicts with the figures in the *Account Rendered.* If you add together the amounts it gives under the headings "extraordinary, for wars," that is, for the king's own military establishment, the artillery, engineering, navy, colonies, and foreign affairs (which might be a cover for funds to the Rebels), you get a total of 119,806,000 livres (600 million new francs [$120 million], more or less), all of which was obviously not spent on America. Who is right, Vergennes or Necker? The former, no doubt, for the missing 30 million just cover the budget deficit which Necker has kept hidden from the public.

gress."[2] Six million in instant alms, like a gasp of fresh air. But the reinforcements? Ah, no! We're paying the Americans to get *themselves* killed, we're not going to send one more of our own men to be killed for them, at least not the few we have left. Vergennes drives Rochambeau, who's crying for ten thousand, to distraction: "For New York cannot be taken with thirty thousand men if it is defended by fifteen thousand, as we are told it is."* What does he know about it? Is Vergennes trying to turn strategist now? He's turned Munchausen, at any event, with the mind-blowing reasoning he has just persuaded Louis XVI to swallow: "If we should transport a reinforcement of ten thousand men to the American continent, the English would shortly send an equal number; which would make that country the real theater of the war, without hastening the end, and would but add infinitely to its exhaustion and to the sum of its calamities . . . Considering all this, sir, it was decided that we could not properly agree to the plan of the Comte de Rochambeau, even if we were in a situation to carry it out. The King has therefore concluded not only to refuse this request, but to abandon the expedition of the second division of troops, which was to have been sent out last year, but which has been detained in one of our ports by the presence of an English squadron superior to our own. He is convinced, sir, that the more troops we have in North America, the more difficult it will be to maintain them, and the less useful they will be, and the less able to render effective service."[4] If we accept this hypothesis, maybe all we need is for the French to withdraw entirely, to make the English do the same? Interesting idea: peace through dissolution. Rochambeau isn't too happy with it. He doesn't exactly jump for joy when he gets the news, but he doesn't tear his hair out either. He's seen worse. "My son has returned to this country quite alone, indeed, but whatever may happen, the King must be served in the manner which he directs."[5]

Is this the end? France sending almost no money and no troops at all . . . Is America going to be lost? Not yet. Franklin and Laurens have at least obtained satisfaction on the third item in their appeal: naval assistance, the one that can still change everything. Oh, it isn't quite what they've been hoping for in Newport; parsimoniously, cautiously, provision is made for naval reinforcements which might possibly be able to assist Washington on condition that . . . assuming . . . in the eventuality of . . . but very definitely only to further what is the real issue of this war in the eyes of the French governing classes, obsessed by their sugar plantations: possession of the Antilles. Vergennes announces the decision as though it hurt him. "M. le Comte de Grasse, who commands our fleet in the Antilles, has been ordered to conduct, sometime toward the approach of next winter, a part of his fleet to the coast of North

*He got the figure from La Fayette in May 1780. It was correct. "The effective strength of the English army" for September 1, 1780, records 16,701 men in New York, including 5,932 British, 8,629 Germans and 2,140 royalist Americans.[3]

America, or to detach a portion of it to sweep the coast and to cooperate in any undertaking which may be projected by the French and American generals . . . The number of ships to be sent to the north will depend upon the need which the Spaniards have of our assistance, and can be determined only when M. de Grasse shall have reached Santo Domingo, after having distributed the supplies to the Antilles, and after he shall have conferred with the Spanish commanders."[6] First priority, thus, goes to the protection and expansion of Franco-Spanish dominion in the Islands. If there's any time left over for a little caper up to New York or the Chesapeake, de Grasse can think about it. In any event, the Americans won't be able to burst into cheers right away, for they're not to know anything about the plan. In view of the great danger which would be sure to follow its disclosure to the enemy, "it will be necessary that the intention of the King to send to the north a part of his fleet in the Antilles, and the time at which it will proceed thither, shall remain veiled in the most profound secrecy." Vergennes extends the restriction to Washington himself and urges his ambassador, La Luzerne, to be on his guard against loudmouthed republicans: "There is so little secrecy in Congress that we shall be obliged to conceal from it the secrets of the plans by which we intend to benefit its cause . . . You will understand, sir, how far you may disclose this secret to General Washington. He is said to be very discreet and exceedingly reserved; but whether he will be able to be reserved in his relations with Congress is a question you must decide." Such was Versailles's view of the alliance.

Anyway, it's better than nothing. And Admiral de Grasse will soon be setting out for the Islands, taking a score of warships with him from Brest. Enough to shift the fragile balance of power in the West Indies. From Vergennes to Rochambeau: "He has twenty ships, he will find ten at the Islands, and you have eight more to give him. So that, as he is master of his own movements, with the authority to unite or to separate his forces, I trust he may control the American coasts for some time to come, and that he may cooperate with you if you are projecting any enterprise in the North."[7]

De Grasse "master of his own movements," Rochambeau left free to project "any enterprise" . . . Having put an ocean between himself and the two men in charge, and having giving them full freedom of initiative, Vergennes can wash his hands of the latest American episode and move on to more serious matters. Here, the queen is pregnant again, Necker's at bay, and they're moving in for the kill.

March 14. La Fayette and Charlus reach Yorktown in their little dinghy. The heart of Virginia and its almost tropical spring, moody and capricious. Swamps, mosquitoes, bulrushes, corn, and tobacco. In the early days, the town of York was a hamlet of rough log cabins flanked by a few official buildings. The logs became polished planks, the buildings clothed themselves in brick, and the town filled out along the banks of the York a little way from where it weds the sea. This is the entrance to the Chesapeake, and La Fayette, who hasn't heard about Destouches's fight and retreat, is still hoping, on the off chance, for reinforcements from Newport, but begins making plans to do without them if need be. ". . . Baron de Steuben had been very active in making preparations, and, agreeably to what he tells me, we shall have five thousand militia ready to operate. This, with the Continental detachment, is equal to the business, and we might very well do without any land force from Newport,"[8] who are "too green", according to him, and only "good for camp followers" . . . In America the French appear to be playing a game of blind-man's buff and getting their biggest kicks when its loser wins.

La Fayette starts scuttling around this dueling ground of the first English conquest in which every place name alludes to some prince or town of the reign of Elizabeth. He's racing against the clock and his own doubts, on a tongue of land cut out by the York (to the north) and James (to the south), both flowing west–east and losing themselves in the Chesapeake. Opposite Yorktown the pioneers planted its twin town of Gloucester on the north bank of the York.* In the middle of the little peninsula is the town of Williamsburg, and there are a Plymouth and a Portsmouth not far away. For once, in this little tufted space of land and water, the distances are on an English scale. Yorktown is only three leagues from Williamsburg—which La Fayette throws into a tizzy on March 17, clamoring "in default of horses, for oxen to draw the cannon" . . . which are still stalled in Annapolis (Queen Anne's town)—and fifteen leagues from Portsmouth, where he is finally compelled to admit that the fleet he sees lying at anchor between the capes, like a row of corks bobbing at the entrance to the vast Chesapeake,† belongs to Arbuthnot and not Destouches. "Nothing could equal my surprise in hearing that the fleet certainly belonged to the enemy."[9]

He goes back to Williamsburg. Now what? He can stop playing Sister Anne, anyway. And he can stop being this general without an army whose solitude is beginning to demoralize the Virginia militia. He continues back up to Annapolis to pick up his twelve hundred men and await orders from Washington. The distances begin to be American again: sixty leagues from Williamsburg to Annapolis, eight days on horseback, although by a round-about route: "I confess [to Washington] I could not resist the ardent desire I had of seeing your relations, and above all your mother, at Fredericksburg.

---

*Today the towns, joined by a bridge, have remained on a human scale, unlike their burgeoning neighbors Washington, Richmond, and Norfolk.

†The importance of the sea and land operations in this area, and the value of points like Yorktown, can only be grasped by consulting a map and realizing that Chesapeake Bay is a sort of inland sea in the form of a large inverted bottle, running north–south, with the neck opening out into the Atlantic.

For that purpose I went some miles out of my way; and, in order to conciliate my private happiness to duties of a public nature, I recovered, by riding in the night, those few hours which I had consecrated to my satisfaction. I also had the pleasure of seeing Mount Vernon,"[10] the Washington family's large homestead with its acid green lawns beneath great oaks on the banks of the Potomac sparkling "like molten silver," and the white house all on two floors under its little dome, a model of the "Virginia style" lost among fields stretching out to the horizon. But the war has been there too: all the slaves are carrying arms, the steward is at his wits' end. The English actually dared to come up the Potomac the other day and raid the holy of holies.* The steward gave them all the livestock they asked for and earned a scathing long-distance reproof from Washington: "It would have been a less painful circumstance to me to have heard, that in consequence of your noncompliance with their request, they had burnt my house and laid the plantation in ruins . . . I have no doubt of the enemy's intention to prosecute the plundering plan they have begun; and unless a stop can be put to it, by the arrival of a superior naval force, I have as little doubt of its ending in the loss of all my negroes, and in the destruction of my houses; but I am prepared for the event."[11] Under the circumstances, the Washington ladies have withdrawn to Fredericksburg, where the militia are guarding the general's redoubtable dowager of a mother —one look at her and you begin to understand the waves of melancholy that emanate from her son—and the wife, "a little stout, but fresh and comely of face."[12]

April 4. La Fayette rejoins his detachment, crouching in Annapolis under the threat of two English twenty-gun corvettes. Do we set out by land? That means leaving the equipment and artillery behind. Oh, come on, let's *do* something, for God's sake! They pile themselves pell-mell, men and arms together, onto two sixty-ton sloops lying in the harbor, and head for the English ships spouting all the fire they can muster. The English think we're going south and hurry away to seek reinforcements, while we turn due north and race back to the top of the bay we set out from so jauntily a month ago. On April 8, re-bivouac at Head of Elk. Not a man lost. But the time?

At dawn on March 22, Admiral de Grasse's fleet sails out of the Brest roads, saluted by the Marquis de Castries, who comes, as his first official act after taking up his duties, to inspect what Sartines has managed to put together before handing over to him: in the end it amounts to thirty-eight combat ships (five of which will leave de Grasse in the Azores and try their luck under Suffren in the Indies) and, more important than them, nearly a hundred troop transports and supply ships destined for the Islands. The grand parade of the

---

*Mount Vernon is on the south bank of the Potomac. Almost directly opposite, on the other bank and farther north, lies the already good-sized town that becomes absorbed into the city of Washington.

Occident is led by Bougainville's "blue squadron." Many of the people massed on the château towers in garrison and arsenal assume the fleet is heading straight for the United States; it seems to them that France has finally made up her mind.[13] But when is La Fayette going to hear about it?

North or South? The old temptation of New York. We know Washington's still hankering for it. The bulk of his army has remained in the vicinity, La Fayette can bring his men back from Head of Elk in a few forced marches, and last year's treadmill will start turning again: the Hudson, Newport, Boston . . . If that's what happens, it'll make Gilbert's little lap around the South look like one hump by an inchworm.

But Washington decides that too much is enough. He sends the ball back south. Letter of April 6, to La Fayette: " . . . the general officers . . . are unanimously of opinion, that the detachment under your command should proceed and join the southern army,"[14] that is Greene's, lost in the Carolinas and almost cut off by the English advance in the center. That's just the point: on his way down La Fayette is supposed to do them all the damage he can, and even try to put them out of action. No naval protection in sight, and no reinforcements? Sorry about that. "You will be guided by your own judgment, and by the roads on which you will be most likely to find subsistence for the troops and horses . . . You will now take with you the light artillery and smallest mortars, with their stores and the musket cartridges. But let these follow under a proper escort, rather than impede the march of the detachment, which ought to move as expeditiously as possible without injury to them." Was it action he was wanting? Help yourself, take plenty. He's not likely to imagine he's still in Europe now. He's got it, his American war—that sensation, or that illusion, of being the grain of sand that strips the gears of worlds. La Fayette, one-man expedition into the future: he's been dreaming of this instant ever since the luncheon party at Metz.

On April 13 he's at Bald Friar ferry, crossing the Susquehanna. The equinoctial gales are still lingering in this Maryland baptized in honor of the Virgin Mary by immigrant Catholics led by Lord Baltimore. "The wind was blowing so hard at the ferry that, although he had [sent] his men over, it was impossible to cross with the wagons and provisions."[15] And this blast isn't the worst one: the ill wind blowing through the minds of his soldiers from Boston and Newport is far more dangerous. They're furious at being sent down to swelter in the Carolinas and Georgia. Why, it's like asking Norwegians to go conquer Naples. "Dissatisfaction and desertion being two greater evils than any other we have to fear, I am anxious to have rivers, other countries, and every kind of barrier to stop the inclination of the men to return home . . . Whatever sense of duty, ties of affection, and severity of discipline may operate, shall be employed most earnestly by me . . . I wish we might come near the enemy, which is the only means of putting a stop to that spirit of desertion . . .

"While I was writing this [to Washington], accounts have been brought to me that a great desertion had taken place last night. Nine of the Rhode Island company—and the best men they had, who have made many campaigns and never were suspected; these men say they like better Hundred lashes [*sic*] than a journey to the Southward. As long as they had an expedition in view, they were very well satisfied. But the idea of remaining in the Southern States appears to them intolerable, and they are amazingly averse to the people and climate!"[16] La Fayette seems to have a very short memory of the delights of the murderous southern forest, the death marches along trails of sand, the night sweat, the malaria . . . He has a gift for forgetting. When will he ever realize that each soldier here is fighting for his *own* church steeple, his *own* field? That's the very heart's blood of this revolution. Him and his grand ideas! He makes them want to laugh. Endearing young lord, come over from Europe to explain America to the Americans! He herds them into a square on the west bank of the Susquehanna, just the other side of the yellow waters swollen by the spring thaws. Sitting erect on his horse, his hair for once streaming loose in the wind, he strains his falsetto with so much sincerity and tactlessness that nobody dares defy him to his face. The men hear snatches of his succulent English: liberty, victory, United States, God . . . The voice and the words don't carry, but the gesture does: a kind of warmth, something genuine, and above all that appeal to honor, the supreme ruse of all good officers: "Anyone who wishes to leave may go. I shall force no one to remain. Soldiers desiring to return need but apply to me for a pass, and I shall send them back to their winter quarters." Before offering them their chance to go back, however, he's taken the precaution of putting the Susquehanna between them and those winter quarters. Nobody budges. Oh, we can stick it as far as Baltimore anyway, General. That isn't really the South. And Corporal Dullivan, who tripped over a stone and injured his leg, refuses to take a leave like the rest and hires a cart so he can follow the train.

A pause in Baltimore, midway between Head of Elk and Mount Vernon. A pretty port town on the Chesapeake, all fine brick houses, gayer than those in Philadelphia. The ladies were preparing to hold a ball for the officers: La Fayette requisitions them for a patriotic sweatshop. If the truth be told, mesdames, we lack everything, or almost everything essential to the fitting out of a soldier . . . So the ladies and misses set to work sewing "overalls, hunting shirts, hats, and blouses" from the linen and wool that seems to have been spun out of the paving stones but actually comes from the Baltimore warehouses —not as free gifts, the merchants haven't gone completely off their rockers— but loaned, to the tune of two thousand guineas,* on La Fayette's signature.

*The guinea was a coin minted in England from gold found on the coasts of Guinea under Charles II. It was worth more than the louis—26 of the francs of that day. So at this point La Fayette

"I became security and promised it would be returned with the interests in two years' time."[17] He's taking a big risk, but so are the cloth merchants.

On April 19 La Fayette rides off southwards at the head of a troop of brand-new men, every one in a shirt, trousers, and pair of shoes suitable for the hot climate. This time there is no grumbling. At the same moment, a hundred leagues below him, Cornwallis's army leaves Wilmington, North Carolina, to join forces with Benedict Arnold, whose two thousand men have already entered Portsmouth; they intend to march up the James River, over the same terrain where La Fayette sat waiting for the French to turn up a month ago. The local militia, badly armed and punchy, fall back. This time, all Virginia's got to count on is La Fayette.

He understands. He's hit his stride, he feels at home in his part. If nothing else, he's determined to save the two towns that bar the main passageway from South to Center: Fredericksburg and Richmond. He leaves his tents and even the small artillery "under a guard, and with orders to follow as fast as possible, while the rest of the detachment [a thousand men], by forced marches, and with impressed wagons and horses, will hasten to Fredericksburg or Richmond ... This rapid mode of traveling, added to my other precautions, will, I hope, keep up our spirits and good humor,"[18] even if this head-over-heels tumble from north to south is one of the worst journeys that could ever be imposed on a body of soldiers. They have to scramble over every waterway in Virginia, all of which flow east–west and empty into the Chesapeake, so that their march becomes a game of leapfrog in which the frogs have Indian names: the Patapsco just outside Baltimore, "where the empire of the snows comes to an end," and the Patuxent before the Potomac, and the Rappahannock at Fredericksburg. No bridges, except in the big towns. It's luck if we find a ford, even if we go in up to our ears; but in the high-water season they usually have to improvise rafts, requisition ferrymen, straddle tree trunks and planks lashed together—not quite like crossing the Meuse or the Rhine. A pioneers' march. On April 25 they're cheered at Fredericksburg, about to be evacuated. "Our men are in high spirits. Their honor having been interested in this affair, they have made a point to come with us; and murmurs, as well as desertion, are entirely out of fashion."[19] There's calamity in the air, though: La Fayette encounters the terrified eyes, the ambiguous greetings, and the closed shutters of the Philadelphia of his early days in America. All the sights that inoculated him against the hazards of war. But one thing has changed: here, *he* is the little Washington, the man on whom everything depends—and the last Whigs kiss his boots as he passes, imploring him not to abandon them, imploring *him*

---

is borrowing the equivalent of about 250,000 modern francs [$50,000]. He was hoping the sum would be counted as part of France's total aid to the United States, and it is.

. . . because what's happened to Thomas Jefferson, the elected governor of Virginia, the man of the Declaration of Independence? La Fayette can't find him even in Richmond, the state capital, the town that ties the knot between the hills and the alluvial plain, which he and his men reach on April 29. And just in the nick of time: Arnold's troops have been sighted two leagues away, and here as in Fredericksburg all the prosperous folks have cleared out, the streets are deserted. His objective is no longer to reach Greene in Carolina and join forces with him. It is, with one thousand men, to save Virginia if it means being killed where he stands.

TURGOT

49

MARCH 1781

A Universal Doctrine

What a lot is about to happen, in France and the rest of the world, while La Fayette, in Virginia, races down his little offshoot of the main road! The spring of 1781 is one of those moments when everything starts moving at once: the scenery whizzes up into the flies, we rub our eyes as a whole new cast comes on stage. New actors give the play a new tone. The sky clouds over. What's that rumbling noise in the background? Thunder or cannon? The historian who barks his shins on those few weeks sticking out of the corner of his card index won't forget them in a hurry. He wasn't expecting them, they're not in any chronology of great dates; but it is with them that the great dates begin.

In March 1781 the publication in France of a new and completely revised edition of the *Histoire des Deux Indes* bursts like an incendiary bomb. Its official author, Abbé Raynal, will be proscribed. Diderot, its unofficial author, has a quarrel with Grimm and begins to see red. Living semi-clandestinely, he becomes a prophet of decolonization and the bloody revolution. Then Louis-Sébastien Mercier publishes *Le Tableau de Paris,* as though to hurl the whole town into the flames. This all makes the defenders of the condemned but established order very angry, and they clamp down. Louis XVI opts for repression and a nobiliary backlash: he dismisses Necker two days before Raynal is sentenced.

Is this just a tempest in a French porcelain teacup? On the Peruvian plateaus, meanwhile, a great Indian uprising is crushed, providing the bloodiest possible illustrations for the pages of the carpet-slippered *philosophes*. Tupac Amaru is executed on the very day of Necker's fall. What is the link between them? The same sun shone on both that morning. The men of those days knew nothing of the simultaneity of events by which modern-day Europe and America, with their 3 billion voices debating reform versus revolution, have become increasingly preoccupied.

As a curtain raiser, Turgot dies quietly at ten in the evening of March 18, 1781. No one, even among his most loyal followers, was hoping for his return to power. His real demise took place on May 12, 1776, and he has been stoically surviving himself ever since, his gout and grief keeping each other alive. He went to sittings of the Académie des Inscriptions et Belles-lettres; why not? He chiseled out translations of Latin verse. He lived with the La Rochefoucaulds at La Roche-Guyon as though at his own home, and let them malign his persecutors without much help from him. Why bother? No indignation, not even Condorcet's, could match his own bitterness at having been in a position to act and not having acted. He called on Franklin now and then, in Passy.* When he had to give up going about, even on crutches, he bought the Hôtel de Viarmes in the Rue Bourbon Saint-Germain,† selling off his family property to do it. He observed things from very far, from Sirius, now and then lashing out like a solitary old tomcat curled in a ball: "There is M. Necker, as radiant with glory now as he was bloated with it before . . . That man is and ever will be odious to my eyes."[1] He kept score between Maurepas and Necker. "M. de Maurepas is said to be powerfully weary of M. Necker and his projects. M. Necker is reputed to be yet more weary of M. de Maurepas . . . I quite fear that these two Gentlemen, in their efforts to anchor themselves still more deeply [in the queen's favor], may one day afflict M. le Duc de Guines upon us." Thinking of America was refreshing. Change could only come from outside that France whose fabric was so rigidly conservative that even he had been unable to unstarch it. "The American people might become a model for all others, so long as they never come to resemble our old Europe, a heap of divided powers quarreling over territory or trade profits, and continually cementing the enslavement of their peoples with their own blood." He wrote this to Richard Price, one of a group of English liberals who were standing fast, holding out against King George. But the letter was carried *via* Holland: Le Noir read his mail. "Keep my confidences to yourself, my friend, and do not answer them, for my letters are opened and I should be thought too much a friend of liberty by half to be a minister—even a minister in disgrace."[2]

---

*Where he advised Mme Helvétius against marrying him.
†Today 121 Rue de Lille, near the Palais Bourbon. He dies there.

Who is this cross-Channel friend, the friend never met in person, the man to whom everything, therefore, can be told? In those days letters were like bridges between the explorers of the future exiled in the present. The Reverend Richard Price received Turgot's in his vicarage at Newington Green, a "small residential part of a quiet town on the outskirts of London where numerous dissenters lived."[3] These happen to be "Unitarians," one of the thousand and one little flocks which the Anglicans are prepared to leave in the fold as long as they grow no fatter. They browse unaggressively within the walled garden of their faith in a single God, Father of all things and Supreme Being. Whence the name Unitarian. To them Christ is a human, just a little better than the rest of us, and he may be the "son of God" but so are they, and equally. That's what their good pastor Richard Price has been telling them every Sunday for the best part of twenty-three years in the small pink church built with a donation from a converted City banker*—but as time goes by, he's been talking less and less about God, and more and more about men.

. . . Their timid, stocky little pastor, an emigrant from Wales, where his redoubtable father, also a pastor, so tortured him with punishments and prohibitions that Richard came to prize tolerance above all other things. He married a gentle young woman of the Anglican faith, who is now dying of tuberculosis, unconverted and undemanding, at the end of a quiet and loving marriage. Price leaves her bedside only to take long walks through the fields, where he frees snared larks but leaves coins in their place for the bird-catchers. Just the other day, engrossed in his perpetual internal discourse, he absentmindedly walked past a cockchafer lying on the path with its legs waving in the air. He smote his brow and turned back to help the creature out of its predicament before returning home to look after the blind old horse he will keep in his stable until it dies. Good people of every persuasion love to see him coming in the distance, all in black, with a stick in his hand, his keen eyes seeking out theirs:

"There's Dr. Price! Make way for Dr. Price! . . . *Friend to freedom* . . . *Brother of man. . .*"†

What they love best in him, though, is his ability to listen to them for hours without saying a word. Their works and days become the subject matter of his letters to the four corners of the earth and of his Sunday sermons, in which, week by week, he edges a little further from idealism and a little closer

---

*It still exists, swallowed up by the Greater London conurbation. Price preached there from 1758 to 1786, before continuing his ministry in Hackney. Along with Priestley, Paine, Cloots, etc., he becomes one of the "citizens of the world" upon whom the Convention bestows honorary French citizenship.

†A plaque bearing these words was put up in memory of Richard Price inside the Newington Green church shortly after his death.

to realism without losing any of his influence. His two best friends are the chemist Priestley and the economist Adam Smith. Neither of them believes very much in God. He sees them at the annual meetings of the Whig Club, also known as "The Friends of Freedom," which Franklin used to visit too before he was banished. Without either being aware of it or wanting to do so, they are transforming their association into a minute congregation "for the free examination of all things from the viewpoint of reason, combined with an inflexible desire for social progress based on the strength of the middle and even laboring classes."4 There's no great rush to sign up. An ocean of reproof submerges any who dare to plead in favor of the Insurgents. All three main religious currents in England support the opinions of the majority of their violently colonialist flocks: the Anglicans are loyal to the king; the Methodists preach obedience, always and ever, to anybody about anything; even the Presbyterians want to be right and have their American brothers be wrong. Several members of Parliament are courageously raising their voices in the Commons: Burke, Fox, Sheridan. But "publication in full of parliamentary debates remains prohibited, with the result that their great speeches are effectively censored for public consumption."5 And not one line by the Scotsman Adam Smith has prevented Scottish soldiers from setting fire to plantations in the Carolinas.* "It is not so easy to make oneself heard by an entire nation from the pulpit of a parish of sixty souls." It is nevertheless the welfare of those 8 million deaf† that increasingly occupies Richard Price's days, which are spent devising "a national system of retirement pensions applicable to the entire population"—nothing less than the initial English outline for a social security scheme. It's been eight years since the House of Lords rejected the first bill he got his friends to place on the agenda. He's on his fourth now. He'll keep going. Here and there a few keen ears are beginning to catch the sound of the voice of the little pastor from Newington Green, and greet it as one of the few tangible comforts in a comatose age. Condorcet, for example: "At last a universal doctrine was seen to be developing that was to deal a death blow to the already unsteady structure of prejudice: it was that of the limitless perfectibility of the human race, a doctrine of which Turgot, Price, and Priestley were the first apostles."**

---

*Part of the reinforcements that Lord North sends to Clinton and Cornwallis are composed of Scotsmen "rounded up" in Edinburgh and Glasgow, which suffered from endemic unemployment.

†Probable population of the British Isles, not including Ireland, in 1780. Price, who was fascinated by the newborn science of demography, wrongly estimated it at only 5 million.

**Condorcet writes these lines a few days before his death, in 1793, in the "Ninth Age" of his *Esquisse d'un tableau historique des progrès de l'esprit humain* [Outline for a historical table of the progress of the human mind].

Anne-Robert-Jacques Turgot, the first-named apostle, is also first to abandon that thankless race—perfectible no doubt, but for the moment highly intractable as well. He's done what he could. Farewell, Price! Farewell, Adam Smith! To the last, Turgot kept up his correspondence with Smith too, in Edinburgh where he is playing the unrewarding part of customs director: a sinecure. Turgot was fond of the red-haired Scotsman, all passion beneath his Caledonian chill, who once came to discuss his *Theory of Moral Sentiments* with him and Abbé Morellet. "He spoke our language very badly, but M. Turgot, who loved metaphysics, greatly admired his talent. We saw him several times. He was introduced at the Helvétiuses'. We spoke of commercial theory, banking, public credit, and various points in the great work he was then engaged upon"[6]: the *Inquiry into the Nature and Causes of the Wealth of Nations,* which came out in London a few days before Turgot's fall in Paris and whose two thousand-and-somethingth final page urged on the English to the only action of any real use to a people, that is, an awakening: "The rulers of Great Britain have, for more than a century past, amused the people with the imagination that they possessed a great empire on the west side of the Atlantic. This empire, however, has hitherto existed in imagination only. It has hitherto been, not an empire, but the project of an empire; not a gold mine, but the project of a gold mine . . . It is surely now time that our rulers should either realise this golden dream, in which they have been indulging themselves, perhaps, as well as the people, or that they should awake from it themselves, and endeavour to awaken the people."[7] Adam Smith, Price, Turgot: a little club of awakeners, a miscroscopic fraternity of clearsighted men. What great things they might have done! But they couldn't. So they said them.

Turgot's last letter to Condorcet: "I think as you do that, all in all, there is more good than evil in life."[8] He hasn't been out of bed since Christmas. His sister and brothers are God knows where. He never had much family feeling, except for the family that grew up about him in the course of time, the real one. The Duchesse d'Enville and Mme Helvétius are his nurses. Condorcet sits by his side chewing his nails. Still young himself, must he be condemned to watch everyone he cares about dying around him? First Julie, now Turgot . . . Dupont whirls in between two visits to Mirabeau. Turgot dictates to him a translation of a Horatian ode on equality in the face of death:

Un même torrent nous entraîne,	[A single flood sweeps us along,
Le même gouffre nous attend.	The same abyss awaits us all.
Nos noms, jetés confusément	Our names, tossed in confusedly,
S'agitent dans l'urne . . .[9]	Swirl about in the urn . . .]

Tronchin is called in on February 25, as he was for Voltaire; this Calvinist seems destined to witness the death agonies of miscreants. His patient is yellow, has stopped eating. Gout prepares him, but it's a "bilious fever" that carries him off. Hardened by ten years of torment, it never occurs to him to complain. Only, a great shudder runs through him now and then, a tic, a habit, the bite of the beast. "His soul contemplates with equanimity—at least that is the impression he contrives to give Condorcet—the approach of the moment when, following the eternal laws of nature, it is to go and occupy, in a different order, the place which those laws had marked out for it."[10]

Does he, with infinite tact, pretend to drop off to sleep on that evening of March 18, despite his gasping and the rattle in his throat? It's too much for Dupont, who persuades the ladies to leave:

"He's asleep, you can see for yourselves! Come! 'The ordeal is too painful.' "[11]

When they re-enter the room Turgot has died alone, more or less as he lived. Dupont is dumfounded: "He had not thought the end so near, and had not called the priests" whom the dying man had no wish to see.

"Three or four dozen small stones were found in his liver, and people did not fail to observe that if he had had them in his heart instead, he would have been better fitted to be a minister."[12]

But he was one of those who are never dead enough. The sister and brothers emerge on cue for their inheritance, and shudder at the sight of a little box capable of blowing the country to kingdom come. It contains Turgot's secret papers, and in particular, copies of letters written to Louis XVI in the last days of his ministry. What should be done with them? Malesherbes, the other great disgrace of the day, strikes the family as the perfect person to go through them and burn or keep the right ones. He censored France for thirty years, surely he can censor Turgot. The papers are sent to him in his little family home, where he is living in a retirement as placid as Turgot's was painful.

No, Malesherbes hadn't made it all up. He does his work quickly and thoroughly, in eighteen days. To a man who has seen many perilous words, few ever seemed more so than those of the final remonstration: "Never forget, Sire, that it was weakness which brought Charles I's head to the block . . ."* The man was out of his mind! Where would he have taken us? "I hope that the letters written to the King will be buried in the deepest oblivion. If this were not to be the case, it will not be through any fault of M. Turgot or of his family. But they must not be able to reproach themselves for having any hand in it by keeping his papers. I even urge M. le Marquis de Turgot [the younger brother] not to read them himself . . . At present, I should prefer never to have read them,

---

*The text is destroyed by the family, but mercifully exists, almost complete, in the form of a copy that Turgot sent to Abbé de Véri, who recopied it into his diary.

so greatly do I fear that if the secrets of the King's minister be one day di-
vulged, I shall be held to account . . . It is a mark of respect owing to the King
to burn them, if that be possible, in the presence of a person who can assure
him of the deed.''[13]

Thy will be done, before April is out. What's happened to Malesherbes's
courage? He was off by quarter of a century. It's no longer possible to keep
people from all knowledge of what goes on in the world. There are too many
tales, too many books, everywhere. The ashes of Turgot's papers have hardly
been ground underfoot when the brick hurled by Abbé Raynal and Diderot
comes crashing through the windows.

RAYNAL

50

MAY 1781

Abbé of the New World

"Young prince: you* who have succeeded in preserving your horror of vice
and dissolution, even in the heart of the most dissolute Court and although
taught by the most inept of masters:† deign to hear me out with indulgence
. . . The highest tribute I can pay to your character is the fearlessness with
which I shall tell you truths your predecessor never heard in the mouths of
his sycophants, nor will you ever hear them in those of yours.''[1]

Somebody must have herded cows with Louis XVI in his youth to be able
to say *tu* to the king? Apparently Abbé Raynal did, for it is he who signs the
monumental new edition of his *Histoire des Deux Indes* in 1781, although Denis
Diderot is the real author of this open letter to the king, slipped into the pages
of Book IV and looking totally out of place between a passage on the French
East India Company and another on the attempted colonizations of Denmark,
Austria, and Sweden. This sudden detour snatches the reader out of a long,
dense thicket and dumps him down in the middle of a clearing. Apropos of
the Indies, let's talk about France. Really, Malesherbes needn't have gone to
all that trouble to burn Turgot's words of advice. Diderot now picks up the

---

*In French, the second person singular is used throughout; it was *never* used to royalty, under
any circumstances. [*Trans.*].

†The court is that of Louis XV; the "most inept of masters" is the Duc de La Vauguyon, tutor
to Louis XVI before his accession.

broken pen and outwrites Turgot by furlongs, and this time in the open: "Ah, if only, as I speak, two tears should steal from your eyes, we are saved . . ." Two tears from those inscrutable eyes, the pale blue of the void now becoming known as "the color of the king's eyes" on ribbons and curtains. Will they be enough to wrench France free of its implacable process of self-colonization? "Cast your gaze upon the capital of your empire, and you will find two classes of citizens. The one, glutted with riches, displays an opulence which offends those it does not corrupt; the other, mired in destitution, worsens its condition by wearing a mask of prosperity which it does not possess: for such is the power of gold (when it is become the god of a nation, stands in the stead of all talent, and takes the place of every virtue) that one must either have wealth or feign to have it." It takes fewer words to paint France's portrait than that of Bengal. "Fix your gaze upon the provinces, in which industry of every description is dying out. You will see them bowing under the yoke of taxation and the harassments of the agent's swarm of satellites,* as varied as they are cruel . . . Then let it fall upon the countryside, and contemplate dry-eyed, if you are able, the man who makes our wealth condemned to die in penury, the hapless laborer who can scarce command, from the fields he has cultivated, straw enough to thatch his hut and stuff his bed . . ." Turgot may be dead, but Necker's not far off. You'd think he was prompting in the wings. However, it was last year that Diderot wrote this diatribe—along with the other texts scattered through Raynal's book—that resembles a dramatized amplification of the recently published *Account Rendered.* But it's easy to exchange manuscripts and compare notes in Mme Necker's drawing room at Saint-Ouen. Diderot has caught the minister's cautious suggestions in midair and used them to ply his writer's craft, which consists, first and foremost, in calling a spade a spade: "Ask yourself whether your intention is to perpetuate the senseless profusion of your palace, to keep that multitude of greater and lesser retainers who are devouring you," and so forth and so on, help yourself and have some more, he gets them all in, the trips, the festivities, the châteaus, the towering hair-dos, "the fodder for your horses whose equivalent would feed several thousands of your subjects who are dying of starvation and poverty." What a drubbing! Diderot-Marat.

The court and Vergennes's supporters call it a calculated maneuver, Necker leading a political offensive while remaining himself incognito as the *philosophes* advance in the open. The latter work on the public, the former on the king. In reality, however, it's a coincidence and not a conspiracy, although the suspicious-minded can be excused. On January 14, in the month of the *Account*

*"The swarm of agents of the tax collector" that is, or, to be more exact, the local forces of law and order which the farmer-general (the "agent") could call out to enforce payment of taxes.

Rendered, the *Correspondance secrète* announces that "The entrance into France of the *Histoire philosophique des Deux Indes*, which Abbé Raynal has had printed in Geneva, has been most strictly forbidden.* So much the better for the booksellers, who will sell copies at exorbitant prices, and no amateur will forgo the purchase on that account."[2]

Raynal may conceivably have been counting on this black market to relaunch his book, which wasn't selling too well. It was already in the library of every *"honnête homme,"* so it would be quite a clever trick to get "well-informed circles" to buy it a second time! However, it is not the greasy features of a speculator we see gazing out from the frontispiece of this fourth edition, fattened by Diderot's fiery pages. Whozzat? This fierce creature with the powerful torso and hawk's head crowned by some compromise between a handkerchief and a turban.† A highwayman? A buccaneer from the Antilles? Far from it. He's the Abbé Raynal himself, or at least the image of himself which he has asked the engraver to present to his readers.

Not exactly a typical specimen, apart from the ruddy complexion he shares with so many Rouergats. Those born and brought up at La Panouse, near the source of the Aveyron, almost at the foot of the Château de Séverac, do not turn out Caspar Milquetoasts. When Guillaume-Thomas, son of the prosecuting attorney of Saint-Geniez, came away from the stinging air that had weathered his features, he brought with him "that devilish accent" that gave his congregations the giggles in the days when he used to preach at St. Sulpice as though he had a bushel of pebbles in his throat. Days long gone now. The Raynal of 1780 is about as much of an abbé as Voltaire or Rousseau, except that he's still wearing—because it's only decent and, after all, you're *sacerdos in aeternum*—"a brown gown, a coat, black breeches, and hose and buckle shoes" and "a round wig and a flat-topped hat with three sharp corners, that seemed by its clerical form to be saying to him, 'When you were a priest!' ... an expression that recurred continually in his conversation, almost involuntarily, as a sign of some tic or second self ... A gold-pommeled cane completed his attire, which was in every particular the same as that of Abbé Morellet and the other *philosophe*-abbés."[3] A crow doesn't have much choice of dress. No priest of that era, whatever his background, ever came into the Church of his own free will—the decision was made for him before he was twelve, and the notion of the late-flowering vocation applies only to a few monks. But to be

---

*Its complete title is *Histoire philosophique et politique des établissements et du commerce des Européens dans les Deux Indes* [Philosophical and political history of the settlements and commerce of the Europeans in the Two Indies]. A curriculum in itself. "Philosophical" means that the book asks the question have we any right to be there? And "Two Indies" means that the book's subject encompasses the whole planet.

†In 1793 and 1794 a number of prints of *L'Ami du Peuple* [*The Friend of the People*] are based on this portrait.

a priest is to have an estate, and Raynal makes the most of it from Pézenas to Paris, taking in the collèges of Clermont and Toulouse on the way, as student, Jesuit, preacher, professor; so far, that's all the ground his body has covered, while his phenomenally curious mind has been scampering about the five continents in books and conversations. Erudition has made up for the rest, although in his case erudition is like a waterfall or an overflow valve. He learns only to teach, that's why he's fond of preaching, "subjugating his listeners, he so inflamed the lectern with his heated and ardent delivery."[4] When he didn't have a ready-made quotation to polish off one of his periods he manufactured one to order, just to pin back his professors' ears:

"I am distressed, father, to hear that the passage I quoted is not in St. Augustine; but if it is not, it ought to be."

Chaste? Not unduly—average, no scandal. Poor? Less and less; starting from nothing, with no baggage but the chestnuts of Séverac, he began by knocking off cut-rate masses* and went on to traffic in Protestant burials: sixty livres for an "honorable" entombment.† Then he sold sermons, which guaranteed eloquence in their purchasers. Then he got himself a job as secretary to a member of the Parliament, then as a compiler, then as the secret author of a *Histoire du stathoudérat* which condemned the House of Orange, and a *Histoire du Parlement d'Angleterre* which condemned the House of Hanover: that puts him in good odor with the *philosophes* and gets him money from Choiseul, release from parish work, and an introduction to the *Mercure* and the salons of Helvétius, Grimm, d'Holbach. At first they find him entertaining. Then, by dint "of having an opinion upon every subject, talking more loudly of warfare than the Duc de Broglie and teaching Mme de Genlis how to play the harp,"[5] he becomes something of a menace, but he always knows when to stop: "He talked prodigiously, but always ceased when he saw that attention was flagging."[6]

He met Diderot somewhere along there, years ago, by a fireside corner. They found that they were brothers in universal curiosity, two sons of the people bursting with ideas, who had strayed into the aristocratic salons where they were employed as a combination professor and clown. They resemble each other, with their rather imposing demeanor and that breadth of back that splits seams and stretches cravats. Twins of 1713—almost as old as the reign of Louis XV that put the slump in their shoulders and the bile in their blood.

Diderot sees himself in Raynal: "I know, in truth"—this is Denis confess-

---

*One, for which Abbé Prévost received one franc, was passed from priest to priest until it was bought by Raynal, who actually said the mass, for eight sous.

†In the Roman Catholic cemetery, the only authorized cemetery in Paris, where the corpses of clandestine Protestants were thrown with the rubbish. All he had to do was fill in a false certificate of "proper death" and the deceased was buried according to the laws of the Church, which avoided trouble for his family. Sixty livres were equal to about 300 new francs [$60].

ing—"quite a large number of things, but there is almost no man who does not know his own thing far better than I. This mediocrity in every subject is the consequence of a boundless curiosity and so modest a fortune that it was never possible for me to devote myself wholly to a single branch of human learning."[7] He's got his fingers into every pie and, somewhere in the sixties, encounters Raynal's hand groping under the same crust, the former as rubbish collector of the universe for his *Encyclopédie,* the latter flitting from flower to flower for his *Histoire des Deux Indes,* which is nothing more than an encyclopedia of the relations between Europe and the rest of the world. Then, ten years ago, came resounding success. The book to end all books. The abbé spent fifteen years on it, dipping here and there in a hundred different sources and making scores of literary slaves sweat for the salvation of the Negroes. Amsterdam 1770, the first edition the thunderbolt. Europe's nose rubbed in its own filth. A whole world, accustomed for centuries to be right everywhere and at all times, suddenly stripped bare and daubed with blood and clay—that's what we have done, and what we're still doing. The Indians massacred by the Spaniards and Portuguese. The Negroes deported by the French and English. With a shiver of excitement, Christian Europe rushes to inspect its naked face in the mirror: "This work has found many readers.* To political men it offers views and speculations concerning all the world's governments; to tradespeople, calculations and facts; to philosophers, principles of tolerance and the most resolute hatred of tyranny and superstition; to women, pleasant passages in the romanesque vein."[8] After Raynal, people can't look at each other the way they used to. The silk stocking of your life has got a run in it. You know. And at the very first meeting between Manon Phlipon and Jean-Marie Roland,† "we argued about the Abbé Raynal."

But, good God, what a hodgepodge! "He tells about everything on earth,** how conquests are made, and invasions, errors, settlements, bankruptcies, fortunes, etc., he relates the natural and social history of every nation, he talks commerce, navigation, tea, coffee, porcelain, mines, salt, spices; Portuguese, English, Germans, Danes, Spaniards, Arabs, caravans, Persians, Indians, Louis XVI and the King of Prussia . . . rice and naked dancing women, camels, gingham‡ and muslin; and millions and millions of livres, pounds, rupees, and cowries, iron cables and Circassian women, Law and the Mississippi; he attacks every government and every religion!"[9] Everything man knew about men agglomerated into a baroque cathedral.

*According to La Harpe, in 1772.

†On January 11, 1776, at five in the afternoon.

**According to Horace Walpole, after reading the first edition, which was circulating in England almost as soon as in France.

‡White Indian cotton, it was then; the name comes from Gangam, a Hindu town, and not Guingamp in Brittany as people thought at the time.

So is this Abbé Raynal a firebrand? If so, he's well disguised. As soon as he gets his hands on some money, "he began giving superb luncheons where it became a fashion for the prettiest women to come and take coffee, tea, cocoa and spirits from the Islands with their historian . . . They found themselves in an assembly of diplomats, Italian princes, and German barons at which the petulant old man, gabbling away at the top of his Gascon lungs, playing the gallant in spite of his face and kissing the ladies' fair arms, provided an inexhaustible store of anecdotes, little tales, and compliments."[10] It is whispered that no one is better placed to tell you which slave-trading enterprises you can invest in at 100 percent.* He continues to associate with aristocrats and financiers, the bulk of whose fortunes come from plantations on Santo Domingo or Martinique. Some of them have actually supplied his most reliable information. Also, therein lies the explanation of what has kept Raynal going for twenty years: "An enlightened fraction of the bourgeoisie, which is henceforth involved in the conduct of affairs, can offer alternate solutions to the most important problems,"[11] including those of the colonies—provided the prevailing ossified and conservative methods are abandoned. This enlightened fraction has put its words in Raynal's mouth, so he can jar the clan of obtuse intendants and possessors of the divine right with the brickbat of his huge political manifesto, "far more reformist than revolutionary." Among his colleagues are two academicians, Thomas and Saint-Lambert, and two ministers, one of yesteryear and one of today: Choiseul and Necker[12]—not exactly terrorists. If only Raynal's work can bring about a shift in their direction, all will be well. Just shove over a bit, will you, so we can have a seat . . . The imbecilic and vicious planter will be replaced by the kindly planter, slavery will become an economy of human liberation—but we'll keep our hold on its lifeline. A calculated shake-up. We'll denounce our predecessors' crimes, and take advantage of the situation they've created.

But it doesn't work. Or at least not yet. The shake-up gets drowned by the waves from the parliaments affair and the late king's death. Raynal is almost annoyed at not finding himself in prison. A second edition, revised and supplemented, comes out in 1774 and sells like hotcakes, but in the manner of *La Nouvelle Héloïse.* The eagle is being taken to the taxidermist. His book is becoming a library classic, whereas he and his friends built it to be a battering ram.

. . . Well, what if we go a little further? Add some more gunpowder. These people are so hard to wake up. They don't bat an eyelid when we tell them about Negroes. What if we tell them about themselves? It is with this

*This rumor, spread by Sébastien Mercier in particular, was on everyone's lips. But I have not been able to find any document showing proof that Raynal was involved in the slave trade.

in mind that the "abbé of the New World"* goes to call on Diderot in 1779 and offers him the new lease on life he was beginning to despair of. Does he want to rewrite the next edition in sulfuric acid? They're giving him an opportunity to change his quill into the fer-de-lance of the Enlightenment.

Diderot, the gagged giant. Reduced to a silence almost as total as Helvétius. To anonymity, rather. Voltaire's triumph gave him a headache, and he's already got indigestion from the brass-band flourishes heralding the imminent publication of Jean-Jacques's *Confessions*.† What about *him?* One foot in the grave, and still so much to say! Ever since they chucked him into Vincennes in 1749 and extorted a promise from him never to publish any more "dangerous works," he has poured all his vast energy into the *Encyclopédie*, which isn't bad for a start, but what about his own work? His own vision of the world and life? They allow him to publish rhapsodies on artists' salons and pouts to entertain princes in Grimm's *Correspondance*. He's holding *Jacques le Fataliste, Le Neveu de Rameau, Est-il bon, est-il méchant?*, and *La Religieuse*** in reserve. That'll give 'em a turn. But when? At his funeral?

He can no longer pretend that Catherine II will let him make another *Encyclopédie*, one that will hang together. Why has "the great project" aborted? Did the autocrat have second thoughts? Did the courtiers in St. Petersburg object? Diderot himself hasn't pushed it too hard: as the years go by he feels increasingly ashamed of having paid court to the empress, and the time gap has enabled him to see Russia in its true colors. These days his letters to his great friend contain nothing but trivialities but he goes on writing them all the same, out of courtesy and because it's useful to keep her on the line so he can put the touch on her in an emergency without blushing.‡ But Diderot has been enduring the agony of a man who has something important to get off his chest and can't. Even if he is allowed to publish his novels or plays, he has censored himself so thoroughly that they will be no more than a muted moan. He leaps at Raynal's offer like a pack of famished lions at the early Christians. Can I really write *everything* I think? Everything, answers the other man a trifle irresponsibly—he imagines he's hir-

---

*Expression used by Diderot to his daughter.

†From the viewpoint of the 1970's, Diderot is the most "modern" of the three greats. The tragedies of the first and lengthy discourses of the second make heavy reading today (I'm not speaking of their correspondence), but *Le Neveu de Rameau* and *Jacques le Fataliste* don't show a wrinkle.

**To Meister, Grimm's assistant on the *Correspondance littéraire*, on September 27, 1780: "It is something I wrote at the whim of my pen . . . A counterpoint to *Jacques le Fataliste*. It is full of heartrending scenes . . . I call it *La Religieuse*, and I do not think a more terrifying satire of convent life has ever been written.'[13]

‡For example, for 2,000 rubles in June 1779, to help his son-in-law buy the Duc de Bouillon's forges. That amounted to about 10,000 livres, or 50,000 new francs [$10,000].[14]

ing a tame old beast with a couple of worn stumps in his jaws.

Who roars down the circus tent. And shakes his mane all the harder because he's really a lion baboon, who personally has not the faintest desire to go back to jail, and Raynal's name will be the only one on the book. All the persecution will be for him, which is fine, since he seems to be pursuing it like some hot new investment. For Diderot this is the big unloading. "All his thoughts, his entire life's work are concentrated in Raynal as by a lens . . . The great work he has always dreamed of and thinks he never wrote appears at last, behind another man's mask, and it constitutes the revolutionary testament of the eighteenth century."[15]

DIDEROT

51

MAY 1781

These Great Revolutions of Freedom

The Raynal-Diderot bomb doesn't burst until the spring of 1781, but Diderot's new lease on life dates from the moment he sets to work, with all the ardor of youth, in May 1779. The hot weather comes early that year. Even high on the Sèvres hills, the parched earth won't let the flowers through. Beneath a precocious sun sits an old man, free to burn at last—that is, free to write what he wants to write. It keeps him awake nights. "My day, which commonly begins between four and five in the morning, is all of a piece. If the good abbé keeps it up [keeps adding new passages], I cannot think when we shall be rid of each other; the design of his tapestry spreads at one end of the loom and shrinks at the other, from which it follows that with me doing as fast as he is undoing, I have become like Hohoye the messenger boy* who never stops running but always stands still . . . I have not yet set foot in Paris since I left . . ."

His one relaxation: the visits of his cherished daughter, accompanied by her husband, Caroillon de Vandeul, and their gaggle of offspring. His heart sinks every time she goes back to Paris and leaves him to the company of his grumpy spouse, the woman who is nothing to him anymore. "Your mother's health is quite good. On Sunday she takes the air in the garden; on working

*Character in a children's game who pretends to run but never moves and shouts like a postilion.

days she takes it at the window." At last the rains come: "Your absence saddened the town but embellished the countryside, especially when the skies dissolved into water and the prairie nearly vanished between the two arms of the Seine below our terrace . . . At night, I seemed to hear the leaves on the trees shudder from the battering of the raindrops,"[1] just as his whole bulky carcass is shuddering from the battering of the flood of his ideas. The adventure of the mind unleashed once again. This one man, all alone between Paris and Versailles, trying to write a progress report on the human race with the aid of a few milestones placed by Thomas Raynal. Where have we gotten to now? Hmm; could be prettier. All the more reason to sing out loud and clear.

For Diderot, that springtime lasts over a year. In January 1780, "I am ill, and compelled, in spite of my indisposition,* to work almost night and day at one devil of a task that will brook no delay"[2]: giving Europe a jolt. He never stops for breath until sometime around August, when the *Histoire des Deux Indes,* "radicalized" by him,† goes off to the printer in Geneva. He's done all he can. Reader, your turn now.

"Freedom is the right to dispose of oneself."[3]

Yet we have robbed and are at this moment robbing the slaves of that right. "Misfortunes, even imaginary ones, bring tears to our eyes in the silence of our reading rooms, and especially in the theater. Only the fatal destiny of the hapless Negroes leaves us indifferent. They are tyrannized, mutilated, burned, stabbed to death; and we hear it said coldly and without emotion. The torments of a people to whom we owe our pleasures never penetrate to our hearts." And don't try to make me swallow that old argument for fools, "that's the way it's always been." Here's your answer: "But what care I how other peoples have behaved in other ages? Is it to the customs of the times or to one's conscience, that one must appeal? Is it interest, blindness, barbarousness, or reason and justice that must be heard? If the universality of a practice were proof of its innocence, there would be no more need to seek excuses for usurpations, conquests, and oppressions of every sort."

The foundation of all revolutionary thought lies in this idea that *now* is what matters, and don't try to tell us about anything else. And as one scans the images of that now, the temperature begins to rise. And keeps on rising until it reaches that irrepressible indignation at injustice, the burst blood vessel of Revolution, the wrath of love. "I may not kill my slave, but I may shed his blood, drop by drop, under the lash of an executioner; I may force him to the

---

*A sort of asthma or cardiac fatigue that made it hard for him to climb stairs. His daughter dates the real decline of his health from this time. "My father sometimes worked fourteen hours at a stretch."

†Yves Benot's expression.

ground with pain, hard labor, privation; I may attack on every side and silently
undermine the principles and mainsprings of his life; I may stifle by slow
torture the miserable germ which the Negress bears in her womb. One might
think the law protects the slave against sudden death only in order that my
cruelty may have free rein to kill him every day. In truth, the right to slavery
is the right to commit every sort of crime. Crimes against property: you do not
let your slave own his own body; crimes against security: you may immolate
him according to your whim; crimes that cause modesty to shudder . . . My
blood rises at these horrible images. I hate, I flee this human race composed
of victims and executioners; and if it is not to become better, may it annihilate
itself!''

In the end, it's not just the executioners who have to be dealt with—
they're only doing their jobs. But who can fathom the stupidity of their
victims? Obedience becomes the greatest sin of all: "The subject of a despot
is in a condition no less unnatural than the slave. Whatever contributes to
maintain him in it is an attack upon his person. Every hand that attaches him
to the tyranny of one man is an enemy hand. Shall I tell you who are the
authors and accomplices of this violence? They are the people closest to him.
His mother, who gives him his first lessons in obedience; his neighbor, who
sets him an example of it; his superiors, who coerce him into it; his peers,
whose opinion drags him to it. Each and every one is a minister and instrument
of tyranny . . . Which do you find more incomprehensible, the ferocity of the
sleeping nabob or the ignominy of the man who dares not wake him?''

The chief agent in this universal submission: religion. Let's not get off the
subject by talking about other peoples' religions—ours is the one that matters.
Is this book going to be signed by an abbé? Oh, sweet revenge. Here we go:
"In all places religion has been an invention of cunning and politic men who,
not finding in themselves the means to govern their fellow creatures as they
desired, looked up to the sky for the strength they lacked, and brought terror
down from it. Their daydreams were widely accepted in all their absurdity. It
was only by virtue of the progress of civilization and enlightenment that people
made bold to question them, and began to blush at the beliefs they held." But
the harm's been done, we're in the power of the priests. "To explain the
enigma of his existence, his happiness and his unhappiness, [man] devised
various systems, all equally absurd. He peopled the universe with good and
malicious intelligences; and such was the origin of polytheism, the most ancient and widespread of religions. Polytheism gave birth to Manicheanism,
whose vestiges will be with us eternally, whatever progress reason may make.
Simplified, Manicheanism engendered deism; and out of the midst of these
divers opinions arose a class of men to act as mediators between heaven and
earth.''

No progress is possible, thus, without materialism. We're light-years away from the Savoyard vicar who never set foot outside his valley. "Voyages upon the seas have weakened national arrogance, given rise to civil and religious tolerance, restored the bond of the universal brotherhood of man founded upon identity of needs, pains, pleasures . . ." But watch out! Greed for gold is taking us out of the frying pan into the fire. At the stage the colonizer has now reached, insurrection becomes the only possible ethics of salvation: "Flee, you unfortunate Hottentots, flee! Bury yourselves in the depths of your forests. The wild animals that dwell there are less to be dreaded than the monsters under whose empire you are about to fall. The tiger may rend your flesh; but he will only take your life. The other will ravish you of innocence and freedom. Or, if you have the heart for it, seize your hatchets, draw your bows, send down a rain of your poisoned darts upon these strangers. Leave not a single one alive to carry the tale of their disaster back to their citizens!"

By the time we get to the final pages we're a long way from the Hottentots. "These horrors revolt us, but have we the right to refuse them, we who boast of some degree of philosophy and a milder form of government, and who nonetheless live in an empire in which the wretched country-dweller is thrown into irons if he dares to mow his meadow or cross his field when the partridges are mating or setting; in which he has no choice but to let the rabbits gnaw the shoots from his vine, and the does, stags, and boars lay waste to his crop; and in which the law would send him to the galleys if he were rash enough to strike at these voracious animals with a whip or stick?" I'm talking about us now. About me, who went slavering off to Russia seven years back to hurl myself at the feet of an enlightened despot. Diderot has digested his trip. It's taken him a while to chew all his cuds, but it's never too late to repent "between the stirrup and the ground." Don't talk to me about enlightened despots anymore, not even—especially not—when they're good. Good is not done to people in spite of themselves, and apathy is the worst slavery of all.

> Nations sometimes attempt to deliver themselves from the oppression of force, but never from a slavery into which they have been led gently, by degrees . . .* You will hear it said that the happiest government would be that of a just, firm, enlightened despot. What extravagant madness! And what if the will of this absolute master should chance to conflict with the will of his subjects? Then, with all his justice and all his enlightenment, would he not be wrong to despoil them of their rights, were it for their own benefit? Is it ever permissible for a man, whoever he be, to treat his constituents as a herd of cattle? Cattle may be compelled to leave poor pastures and go into a richer meadow; but would it not be tyranny to employ the same violence in a society of men? If they say:
>
> "We are content here"; even if they say, "True, we are not well off but we want to stay," then one must labor to enlighten them, undeceive them, bring them to a sounder understanding by means of persuasion, never force. The best of

*Almost word for word one of Marat's maxims in *The Chains of Slavery*.

princes, had he done good against the common will, would be a criminal for the sole reason that he was not within his rights in doing so.

With that the philosophy of absolute democracy is founded, as though in an aside, by the last great thinker of the century. "Peoples, do not, therefore, permit your so-called masters even to do good, if it be against your general will."

And this appeal is launched on the soil of France between January and March 1781: "In every well-ordered society there must be no subject that cannot be freely debated. The more serious and difficult the matter, the more important it is to discuss it." There's only one common denominator: happiness. "Thunder and threaten on every side as long as you please, let gape the prison cells before our eyes and the hells beneath our feet: but you will not stifle in me the wish to be happy. *I want to be happy* is the first article of a code older than any legislation, than any religious system."*

And it's not enough to be on our guard against despots and priests; we also have to keep an eye on the family: "Who among us has ever thought to protect his posterity from paternal and maternal seduction?" Freedom—listen to it, Dad, Mom, Sweetheart, Reverend Father, Monsignor, Sire—freedom is the right to dispose of oneself.

"So it is that disorder reigns, through the childishness of sovereigns, the ineptitude or conceit of ministers, and the patience of victims . . . In consequence, we see the man of genius reduced to silence or strangled, and a nation tethered by the barbarity of its religion, its laws, its customs and its government." If that's so, then what's the use of protesting? Is the author so eager for the prison cell or the hangman's rope? Is Socrates addicted to hemlock? But Socrates can't keep still, he has no choice. "Prohibition [to write] merely irritates and instills a feeling of rebelliousness in the soul, and a libelous tone in books . . . The question may be reduced to these two terms: is it better for a people to remain eternally in a stupor, or to be turbulent upon occasion?"

On goldsmith Belle's terrace just above Seguin Island,† Denis Diderot has heard a very different note in the wind from America—a note different from the one that's ringing in La Fayette's ears: "When we hear the sound of breaking chains, it seems to us our own may become lighter . . . These great revolutions of freedom are lessons to despots. They warn them not to rely upon too lengthy a patience among peoples, and eternal impunity . . . If peoples are happy under the form of their government, they will keep it. If they are unhappy, it is neither your opinions nor mine that will convince them

---

*These two sentences occur in a chapter entitled "Notwithstanding the prohibition of the grand mufti, coffee continued to be drunk in Constantinople."

†Where the Renault factories are today.

to alter it, but the impossibility for them to suffer more or longer; there will be a salutary movement, which the oppressor will call *revolt,* although it is no more than the legitimate exercise of an inalienable and natural right of a man who is being oppressed, and indeed of a man who is not being oppressed."

A day will come when words will give way to deeds. History will not always be written with a pen. We are in 1781: listen to the rising mutter.

Sooner or later, justice must be done. If it were not so, I should turn to the populace. I should say to it:

"Peoples, you whose roars have so often caused your masters to quake, what do you wait for? For what moment are you saving your torches and the stones that pave the streets? Tear them up! . . . Legislations tending toward liberty are troubled, swift, violent. The movement is a fever, more or less acute but always convulsive. Everything presages sedition, murder. Everything is edging toward a general dissolution; and if the people be not doomed to the ultimate misfortune,* it is in blood that their felicity will be reborn.

"Therefore, conclude with me:

"That there is no form of government whose prerogative it is to be immutable.

"No political authority, created yesterday or a thousand years ago, that cannot be repealed in ten years or tomorrow.

"No power, be it ever so respectable, ever so sacred, that is authorized to consider the State as its property.

"Whoever thinks otherwise is a slave. He is an idolator of the work of his own hands.

"Whoever thinks otherwise is a madman, vowing himself to eternal misery and his family as well, his children and his children's children, by granting his elders the right to contract for him before he was, and taking to himself the right to contract for his nephews who are not yet.

"Every authority in this world began either in the consent of its subjects or in the master's force. In either case it can end legitimately. Nothing prescribes for tyranny and against liberty."

*Annihilation.

52

Three Hundred Years of Tears

It all began on November 4, 1780. For Tupac Amaru* it all ends on May 18, 1781. He never read Diderot and was unaware of his existence. But the torrent of this bloodshed overflows into the margins of Raynal's book, where it would be called a "Philosophical and political history of the great revolt of the South American Indians" . . . A scarlet chapter, one it takes Europe centuries to decipher.

November 4, 1780. The feast of San Carlos, the feast of the King of Madrid, is being celebrated all over the world, throughout the length and breadth of that empire on which the sun never sets. So there's a banquet in the priest's house in Virgen Morena (Black Virgin), as well as in the Bishop of Segovia's. The only difference being that this Virgen Morena stands suspended between heaven and earth, and thousands and thousands of leagues from Segovia.† It's a peculiar sort of Spain, though—the stars are so close you could touch them, but they're not the same stars: the Southern Cross instead of the Big Dipper. And in this part of the world November 4 is like April in Europe. Nevertheless, they toast the king's health and ceremoniously quaff large cups of a liquor that comes from the Islands, and strips the throat and corrodes the guts as effectively as "the soup prepared by the natives here, the color of which is akin to that of a *crème brûlée;* but what gives it this fine color is hot peppers ground into flour, and it scalds the throat as though one were swallowing fire. The more I drank of it," moans one inadequately briefed traveler, "the more violently it burned, and for nearly a week I felt this inflammation in my throat."[1] The Altiplano is no place for softies. Even the air you breathe lashes your heart.

Does Tupac Amaru's beat any faster as he prepares to make the decisive

---

*The Tupamaros of South America took this name in his memory.

†The entire central region of the Andes, called the Altiplano or high plateau, which is crossed today by the frontier between Bolivia and Peru and bisected by Lake Titicaca, is situated at altitudes ranging from 2,000 to 5,000 meters.

gesture? A file of travelers on muleback winds along the mountain path headed back toward the town of Tinta. Two separate groups: at the front, the bedizened Spaniards and black slaves of the stout and stately corregidor Don Antonio Arriaga, last in line on the finest mount. His eyes are sharp despite the intoxication of liquor and altitude, his hand lingers near his saddle holster from which protrudes the silver butt of a large pistol. Arriaga doesn't trust the second group, the "mountain Indians" in ponchos, wide trousers, and sandals. No weapons. Even their leader Tupac Amaru, cacique of Tungasuca, isn't allowed to carry firearms. We know all too well what such people are capable of doing with them.

But Don Antonio can't think of everything, and what he forgets this time are the ropes wound around the pommels of these stone-silent Indians' saddles. The *lazzo* is part of their equipment, and Tupac Amaru needs one even more than the rest, for he's a muledriver by trade, "which enabled him, without incurring the suspicion of the government, to visit the most divers places, working upon minds and sowing seeds of rebellion."[2]

Tupac Amaru? Who's Tupac Amaru? The authorities prefer to ignore the alias, all they know is José-Gabriel Condorcanqui, a young collaborator with the Spanish authorities, highly thought of in the schools of Cuzco and Lima where he learned their language so well. He has been so thoroughly integrated that they've even made him "Marquis d'Oropesa," after the name of a region near Lima. The road to Madrid is open to him. And, if it pleases him, when he's out on the plateau, to tell how he is a descendant of the last Incas* and thus of the sun, and to rechristen himself "Tupac Amaru," or in other words "Resplendent Snake," who cares? It's all grist to the colonial mill. A sacred cacique—what more could you ask? To him they'll pay taxes in kind, money and men without a murmur in the territory entrusted to him around his home village of Tungasuca in the district of Tinta, where Don Antonio Arriaga reigns as all-powerful corregidor of the province.

Corregidor and cacique—like governor and publican in olden days, like boss and foreman tomorrow. The eternal duet of slavery. The corregidor is the man from above, the cacique the man from below. The former comes from afar to extort everything extortable out of a people that has been domesticated by the latter, who is a local man. When the system works, everything purrs along. For the Spaniards there's gold and silver from the "Viceroyalty of Peru"; for the Indians there's purgatory on earth and paradise in the afterworld—if they worship the Black Virgin.

But Tupac Amaru's lasso is about to throw a monkey wrench into the

*Careful, the term is ambiguous; the word *Inca* means, first of all, the chief or sovereign whose dynasty goes back to the sun, like that of the Mikados. By extension, the people ruled by the Incas called themselves "Incas," too, as though all Japanese had taken the name of "Mikados" [or all Americans said they were "Presidents"—*Trans.*].

works. His inborn Indian impassiveness has enabled him to play a double game throughout his long youth. Now he's past fifty, and he's ready.

The Altiplano is prone to sudden changes of climate. The path pauses between two slopes, the sun is blotted out, one minute everyone is sweating and the next they're shivering. It's the moment to cross over to the slope of rebellion. We can't take anymore. The Spaniards have pushed us too far, since the mission of the *visitador* Areche back in 1777—oh, accursed "year of the three sevens," which children are taught to remember like the year of a great earthquake! That was the year Don José de Areche was sent out from Madrid to stiffen up the overliberal viceroy in Lima, to increase taxation on traders and miners, and to bring forth tobacco plants and metal bars from the earth—the Indian-kidnapper, the manhunter. "The *leva*, the *leva!*" The cry sped before him down the valleys and over the plateau when his soldiers rode up at dawn on market and fair days to cast their big net. "Troops were recruited by lot, as required. But in emergencies they resorted to the brutal practice of the *leva* [levy]. This was nothing less than a manhunt of Indians and Blacks, with full paraphernalia of ropes, chains, lassos; all that remained was to set the traps, and the authority took care of that. An officer, accompanied by a score of men armed and equipped with everything needed to overpower the recalcitrant, suddenly emerges at the end of a street, blocks all exits, and grabs the pass-ersby, who cannot escape. Only those whose dress or manner shows them to be members of the higher or middle social orders are allowed out. Not the Indians or Blacks."[3] The caciques can do nothing about it, not even those like Tupac Amaru who stand with folded arms during raids, and help the men from their districts "take refuge in the *pulqueros* caves,* where they remain hidden in the shadows, crouching behind barrels and sacks."

He's been less cooperative since 1777, the cacique of Tungasuca. He's losing his good name in Lima and in Tinta as well, where he didn't do much to help Arriaga put down the riots that broke out there—as at Juaraz, Lambayeque, Hyanuco, Pasco, Huancavelica, Moquegua, and all the other places where the corregidores have been given a hard time recently, but without any method or overall plan. Uprisings like sierra fires, easy to put out; you just beat them down as they catch. In Cuzco itself, a year ago, a network of conspirators was discovered and dismantled and Don Lorenzo Farfan—a *philosophe* in Peru, now we've seen everything—was thrown into the deepest dungeon; and along with him, the Indian cacique of the three villages nearest to Cuzco. And the other day at Christonovio some Indian children were innocently playing "you be corregidor" . . . It started with shrieks of laughter but they forgot it was a game, and the child who was "it" was found hanged.

The situation has remained tense. So tense that Don Antonio stubbornly

*A kind of community storehouse.

refuses to go to Tungasuca in person. He doesn't want to find himself on his subordinates' territory, like Louis XI at Péronne.* But he takes advantage of the priest's banquet on neutral ground to settle some business matters and give the underlings a look at their lord. He's in a good mood now, feeling relatively reassured, and he makes his one mistake when he agrees to observe the rules of protocol and take the lead along the summit path. They're coming to the fork. They're about to part, Don Antonio turning down the right-hand path toward Tinta and Tupac Amaru going left, to Tungasuca.

. . . In the end, Antonio Arriaga turns left, too. Mules and Indians aren't the only things you can catch with a lasso. Tupac Amaru's unfolds whistling through the limpid air like the white bird of rebellion. Snared around the neck and jerked off his monumental baldaquin saddle while the other Indians overpower his escort, the corregidor is dragged along the path behind the cacique's mule, and in this position he makes his entrance that same evening —Hail the conquered hero comes flayed, bleeding, and bellowing—into a topsy-turvy world.

November 10. They haven't wasted much time. Arriaga is put to death in front of a large crowd of people in the marketplace of Tungasuca, a big village built of clay under roofs of thatch and dried tiles, mounting in tiers up the sides of a fertile valley. A sort of Tartar town entrapped in gardens. The Incas are a sedentary people; what they love best is scratching at the soil, wherever they can find any in the folds of the Andes. Adventure and midnight rides aren't for them. But if you look hard enough you find those too. So much the worse for Don Antonio.

Hundreds of men and women with coppery skins and dead-black hair skinned tight and gleaming, protruding cheekbones, and eyes that are "elongated and rising upwards at the corner" have brought together, at the foot of the scaffold, the most gorgeous collection of noses imaginable, those noses that are "forward-projecting throughout their length, thickened around the nostrils, and opening downwards, as among the peoples of the Caucasian race."[4] A silent riot of color; every hue and tint of wool on brow and shoulder, and every nuance of eloquent muteness—the complete opposite to the clamor of a European mob attending an execution. There's dignity in the air, which is damp for once: it's the spring germa, that downpour that falls three times a year and sweeps away the earth so laboriously packed down on the terraces. Outlines are softened, and it seems as though the sea has climbed up the mountainside, as though a fog hampers people's

*He went there in 1468 to have an interview with Charles the Bold, who was on home ground. When Charles learned that Louis was making trouble for him elsewhere, he put him under house arrest, forced concessions out of him, and made him witness the quelling of the insurrection he had fomented. [Trans.]

movements—as few as possible because of the altitude.

Facing the gallows stands the throne of the Inca: two structures poised between the rattling gusts of wind. Atop a quickly-run-up platform of wood, covered with precious cloth and gold, *"Don José primero, par la gracia de Dios Inca del Peru, Santa Fé, Chile, Buenos Aires y Continente, de los mares del Sur,"** etc., presides over the execution of his lifelong foe.

What a lot of fancy titles Tupac Amaru has suddenly acquired! In vocabulary at least, the village feud has assumed the proportions of the continent. Emerging from its chrysalis, the butterfly glistens in accoutrements that would make a Merovingian jealous. He arrives on a white horse, supreme luxury in this land of mules, with a gold band stuck on top of his usual three-cornered hat; and although he's still wearing the *uneo,* the regulation Indian tunic, it is now pulled on over a scarlet cloak which in turn covers a blue velvet outfit. The golden sun on the end of the chain around his neck announces that he is the great-grandson of the sun and direct descendant of Manco Capac.† More than sufficient to talk man-to-man with the heir of Charles V, once he has chastised this miserable scum of a corregidor toward whom he now turns his eagle's beak.

"My person is the only one remaining of the blood of the kings of this realm.** My origin has incited me to strive, by every possible means, to end the abuses introduced by the corregidores and devised by the incompetent people in all the responsible posts and the ministries, who are guilty of all that has been wrought against the Indians and other persons, and who act in defiance of the measures of the kings of Spain themselves, whose laws, as I know by experience, are abolished or held in contempt."[5]

His grounds for negotiation are not ill-chosen, and Tupac Amaru shows some sense of diplomacy: appealing to the King of Spain against the exactions of his subordinates is not a crime of lèse-majesté. But in that case, maybe it would be better to keep this one as a hostage? Impossible; Arriaga has done too much. The ring of human hatred encircling his gallows is denser than the giant boulders of Machu Picchu. Tupac Amaru might prefer to spare him, but his little tribe of staff officers is packed around him as tightly as kernels on an ear of corn, and they can squeeze as well as protect. Micaëla, his young wife with the eyes like blue flames, Hippolyte, Mariano, and Fernand, his three well-muscled sons, and his daughters, and his brothers-in-law, and his brother Diego Cristobal, who is so skilled at taming eagles, and Julian Apaza the

---

*"Joseph I, by the grace of God Inca sovereign of Peru," etc.

†Manco Capac was the quasi-legendary founder of the dynasty of the thirteen Incas who made the grandeur of the famous empire that was cut off in full bloom by the Spanish conquest. Unlike Pugachev, Tupac Amaru was not a congenital wishful thinker, and his genealogy has never been questioned.

**From the letter Tupac Amaru sends to the Bishop of Cuzco.

hunchback, and Thomas Catari, who proudly styles himself "miner and grave-digger," and Cicenaro, who is so fond of killing; too many . . .

Cicenaro brings up the cart, and out of it steps the condemned man, bound up like a sausage but calm. He'll know how to die like a *caballero* in front of the gaggle of his terrified peers, the chiefs of Tinta— three other corregidores, the caciques, Captain Bernardo de la Madrid, Doctor Ildefonso Vegerano the tobacco administrator, and the Reverend Father Domingo Castro—trapped at Tungasuca, where, ostensibly to hold a council, they have been summoned by counterfeit letters from Don Arriaga . . . to witness his execution. They won't be hurt; they will simply tell the tale when they scatter hither and thither sowing fear. Eyes bulging, they now watch as the locally hired executioners—Negroes, the Indians won't demean themselves—bring a huge smoking stone chalice up to the poor man's face. It's been boiling over the live coals; but what have they put in it? Molten gold. They're going to make Don Antonio drink it before they hang him; shove down his throat an infinitesimal portion of all that gold the Spaniards have gouged out of the towns here to line the ceilings of their churches and fill their coffers.

Tupac Amaru turns away. He's not a cruel man. But he is the personification of the counter-horror. "From the conquest until now,* the Indians have never been allowed to improve their condition. The officials have labored only to despoil our unhappy race, never giving it a moment's pause. This is so notorious that no more conclusive proof is needed than the three hundred years of tears shed by these unfortunate souls." Who's that shouting "Mercy!" when the hell broth is brought up to Arriaga's mouth, now lower than the rest of his body, his jaws forced apart with hoes? It wasn't an Indian. A choked voice from the group of Spaniards tied up in the front row. But even if the "New Inca" made the sign of Caesar, thumbs up, he wouldn't be obeyed. The survivors of that long extermination have their thousands of slaughtered ancestors at their backs. Fifty years have passed since two gentlemen on a scientific mission to Peru dared write to Philip V that "corn is very scarce. The owners treat the Indians with unbelievable harshness. They even hoard the grain, which is the only form of food here, to sell it at a higher price, thus causing a high rate of mortality among the natives in all the provinces."[6] Since then, things have gone from bad to worse. Every Indian family in Tinta can count at least one child dead of starvation in the past ten years.

But it's not just the children: there are the Indians in the *obrajes* (cloth manufactures), who also "die of starvation, tools in hand," in front of their looms in the sunless holes where they're chained from dawn to dark; and the Indians who are dragged along the roads, "bound by the hair to the tail of a horse ridden by a half-breed who is taking them to the manufacture"; and the

*Same letter.

Indians who are deported to the Potosi mines, three days on muleback from Tungasuca, on the far side of hope . . .*

"The most important silver mines, those of Potosi and Pasco,† are situated at enormous altitudes, very near the snow line. To exploit them, men, supplies, and animals must be brought from afar. Water freezes there the year around and trees cannot grow. Only the hope of riches could make a free man abandon the exquisite climate of the valleys and go off alone to the spine of the Peruvian Andes."8 Ten thousand "free men" are in the grip of that madness, the silver-crazed Spaniards—but their whips need sixty thousand Indians. "There are mines whose locations the Indians conceal most carefully, for fear of being sent to do work they regard as dangerous to their health and very existence."9 "Each of the villages around was required to send a certain annual quota of Indians to Potosi to work in the mines. This was called the *mita*. The corregidores started the *mitayos* on their journey on Corpus Christi day. Most took their women and children with them" to the highest city on earth, the fortress–prison–forced-labor-camp of the *casa de la Moneda* adorned with the lion of Castille, where the King of Spain's silver beaters, who at least work in the open air, can consider themselves comparatively lucky. They survive two or three years; the miners last only a few months. Living underground and inhaling nothing but silver dust mixed with arsenic and antimony sulfide—you can't buy a pardon that'll save you from that. But there's been no pardon anywhere in Peru since Pizarro struck at the heart of the great people of the Incas. Atahualpa the emperor was lured into the main hall, where the Conquistador drew a mark on the wall:

"When the gold for your ransom reaches that mark you will be free."

In came the gold, draining out of the entire empire on the backs of men. The people ruined themselves for their Inca, whom Pizarro had strangled the day the gold reached the mark. People in the West never wearied of gloating over this exemplary conquest of an empire by 168 rascals. What dolts, those Incas! It would be a sin not to take advantage of them.

". . . In any event, it is certain that powerful emanations issue constantly from the mines: the Spaniards living above them are obliged to drink the Paraguay tea, or maté, very frequently to moisten their chests, for they are otherwise afflicted with a kind of suffocation. Within, however, the exhalations are far more noxious. Their effect upon a body unaccustomed to them is such that a man entering for a brief moment comes out as though rigid, feeling a

*In 1781 almost 900 silver mines are being worked in the territory of the Viceroyalty of Peru, along with 70 to 80 gold mines, for the exclusive profit of the mainland to which they bring, in the ten years from 1780 to 1789, the equivalent of 700 million new francs [$140 million].7

†According to Humboldt, who visits them twenty years later. The highest are at an altitude of 4,200 meters.

pain in all his limbs so intense that he cannot stir . . . The Spaniards call this
affliction *quebrantahuesos,* or that which breaks the bones. Even the Indians,
who are accustomed to it, must relieve one another almost every day."[10]
Which makes a big worry for the corregidores who have to find enough bodies
to keep up the work force of these weaklings. The circle of deportation spreads
in ever wider rings around Potosi. And it's impossible to operate without the
Indians: "They alone are fit for this work, at which Negroes cannot be employed, for they all die . . . The Spaniards look upon physical labor as something defiling for a white man. To be *hombre de cara blanca* is a dignity that
excuses Europeans from manual labor."

Don Antonio Arriaga, an *hombre de cara blanca,* held the record for the *mita.*
He was renowned as a supplier of men for the mines clear to Lima, and even
in Buenos Aires. He had eight gallows set up in Tinta (but not at Tungasuca:
the cacique was against it, which is one reason why they weren't on such good
terms), from which the dessicated corpses of deserting Indians swayed permanently.

Gold, in his case, kills literally. The advantage of this form of torture is
that it stifles the victim's cries . . . But it's no sight for Sunday school children,
that river of yellow fire in an open throat, the smell of singed pig, the sizzling,
the twitches. Tupac Amaru's rebellion begins with an atrocity on the scale of
the three atrocious centuries whose weight he is trying to shoulder. Is it ever
possible to overthrow a society without aping it? Not here.

They hang a dead body, a rigid cadaver, from a rope that breaks, of
course. The hanged man's neck has become an ingot of incandescent bullion.

TUPAC AMARU

53

MAY 1781

Even If Tupac Amaru Were to Perish

November 12, 1780. The news of Arriaga's execution reaches Cuzco, the most
important town in this immense backbone of the continent, brought by a
quaking corregidor from Quispicanchi, adjoining Tinta. He's had a close
shave.

In Cuzco it's the bishop who runs things, a bishop from the good old days of burnings at the stake and warrior monks. He has no trouble grasping the seriousness of the situation. The Spaniards in the American Empire are squatting on a powder keg. Four million whites, the masters, or at least that's how they regard themselves even when they are shopowners or innkeepers—but never laborers, never peasants; five million half-breeds and mulattos, the good-for-nothings, good-for-anythings; one million black slaves and zambos*—and eight million Indians. If they catch fire and carry the Blacks with them, and if they manage to win the half-breeds to their cause, Our Lady have mercy on all Spaniards! For a good many of them, molten gold and silver might well replace their breakfast chocolate. Things are even simpler in "the Viceroyalty of Peru," that fan whose foot is "the captainry general of Chile" and which spreads out between the Pacific and the upper Amazon along the western slopes of the Cordillera: four million Indians and half-breeds against two million Spanish. The latter's hope lies in the word *immensity:* "Most of the sierra Indians have never left their house and field, their travels hardly extend beyond the market of a neighboring pueblo. They live and die where they were born, and talk among themselves of Cuzco and Lima as inaccessible paradise."[1] Therefore, the spark of rebellion must be extinguished promptly, by piling into Tupac Amaru with all the resources at hand. The Bishop of Cuzco rounds up a thousand of the local militia, puts them under the command of Captain Cabrera, and sends them off to exterminate the rebels of Tungasuca.

To the rescue, ye shades and spirits of Pizarro!

December 8, feast of the Immaculate Conception. Down in the valleys, the warmth of June, flowers and birds. Spring leaning toward summer. But in this country everything changes with the altitude, and at a few days' march from these miniature Edens, Cabrera's thousand men find themselves back in the winter climate of the plateaus of Madrid, at the other end of the earth. They are harassed by ambushes in a blinding snowstorm that turns every rock into an Indian fortress. They can forget about nipping the insurrection in the bud. At Sangarara, eight leagues before Tupac Amaru's village, rebels are as thick as snowflakes. The punitive force finds itself shipwrecked in hostile waters. The other side have already got weapons, seized in local Spanish garrisons. Their aim with guns is as sure as it is with lassos, and when they don't have guns they turn stones into bullets. The encircled and famished Spaniards think they find salvation in one of those thousand and six churches that have sprung up like mushrooms all over the American soil. They're always the first building erected, in imitation of Christopher Columbus planting the cross on the first shore.

*The zambos were the product of intermarriage between Indians and blacks; the King of Spain had issued an order saying that "the men born of such admixtures, for the most part vice-ridden, shall never be authorized to bear arms or to live without the guidance of a master."

The church of Sangarara looks like all the rest, with its baroque mixture of cupola and steeple that would make the old barracks birds from Mogador and Ceuta think of Islam if it weren't for the brightly painted walls in the gaudy taste that was the fashion over here. But at nightfall the vivid hues fade in the icy gusts, and the church begins to look like a tomb. Inside, the soldiers are packed like sardines in a tin under the flickering light of the sanctuary lamp. Outside, several thousand Indians have emerged from the shadows to form a ring of death. Tupac Amaru isn't there, worse luck for the Spaniards. It's Cicenaro, Arriaga's executioner, who conducts the preliminary negotiations for the carnage:

"Surrender unconditionally."

"Will you give us quarter? Will you leave us our arms?"

"Surrender unconditionally. And remember Atahualpa."

All right, if they've got to die the Spaniards will die on their feet, they know that much. They think they're safe as long as the little lamp keeps flickering, because now that the Indians worship the same good Lord as themselves they wouldn't shed blood within sight of the holy altar. But the lamp goes out. Cicenaro orders the priest to remove the Christ from the tabernacle and put it in the presbytery.

"All those who want to serve our Lord the Inca Tupac Amaru, step forward at the church door."

Twenty or so Creoles* emerge, who've been driven to desperation all their lives by the officers from Spain. But whites in the service of the Inca? That's just what he's counting on. The rest of the men ration out their last powder flasks; they'll make the Indians pay for their skins, at any rate. They never get a chance: a sudden snapping and crackling announces the birth of an inferno. The Indians have heaped fagots all around the church and set fire to them. A few Spaniards try to break out and are mowed down. The next morning the charred bones of Cabrera's men are found among the smoking ruins. Strange cubic vestiges poke through them here and there, the foundations of a little temple of the sun razed two hundred years ago when the church was built. Two ripples on the sea of time.

A week later six hundred Spaniards are burned alive in the church of St. Peter of Bellavista. A few of them were soldiers, but mostly "priests, laymen, women, and children who had taken refuge in the church . . . At Caracoto the blood flowed so abundantly that they say the murderers' feet were bathed in it to their ankles,"[2] like those of the crusaders when the Moslems were massacred in the mosques of Jerusalem. Tupac Amaru has embarked upon a counter-

---

*Inhabitants of unmixed Spanish blood born in the colony. What the North Americans were to the English.

crusade. The Spain of the Inquisition wakes up on its gold heap in the glow of its infidel-burning stakes hurled back in its face by the servants of the Incas. It's dangerous to teach people to go around burning each other.

But by this time Tupac Amaru isn't seeing eye to eye with his staff anymore, not by a long shot. Bitter words pass between him and his henchmen. He looks further ahead than they do. He goes to the front lines in person to restrain Cicenaro from burying the Spaniards of Tapacari alive:

"This is not the time for such behavior. For the present our sole object must be to gain more and more ground.* Then we can consider how to remove any obstacles that may arise."3 What obstacles? Not the Europeans, because he's hoping to convert as many of them as possible to his side; certainly not the half-breeds, because his ultimate hold over the country will depend on them. Is he already thinking of eliminating the brutes serving under him, whom he can't for the moment do without? Cicenaro contradicts him openly:

"If we do not get rid of all who are not of our race, we shall remain subject to any man with a single drop of Spanish blood in his veins."

Quick, quick, we must march on Cuzco and capture that Mecca of the Incas, then hurry down to the sea, take Lima by surprise and the port of Callao, proclaim an amnesty, and negotiate with Charles III. Not for independence: for the viceroyalty. Tupac Amaru's goal is to be recognized as an emperor by divine right and heir of the Inca—and, at the same time, to be appointed Lieutenant General of Peru, which he will govern according to his own laws and with the consent of the people, and in the name of the King and God of all the Spains, which should keep everybody happy and forestall a reconquest. This implies that he must sooner or later get the upper hand of the Cicenaros and Apazas, the partisans of racist revenge.

"Since I first began to free the natives of this kingdom from the slavery to which they were reduced by the corregidores and other persons to whom all acts of charity are unknown, it has been my intention, insofar as lay within my power, to prevent murders and hostilities . . . Let none accuse me of wishing to cause the least damage to those who surrender, whatever class they may belong to . . . But those who obstinately persevere in unjust procedures will feel the full measure of severity exacted by divine justice."4

The justice of the Christian god, in other words, that creature of love and implacability whom the Incas received from their conquerors and now worship sincerely, their own gods having abandoned them with Pizarro. Not only do the New Inca's proclamations invoke the name of Christ, they pretend that he will be better served hereafter by the Indians, whose "condition has never enabled them to know the true God, only to pay the corregidores and priests

---

*Dialogue recorded on the spot by a Spanish spy and repeated verbatim at Tupac Amaru's trial.

the price of their sweat and labor. I have made a personal inquiry, throughout the greater part of the realm, into the spiritual and civil government of all its subjects. I have learned that those who make up that nation [Peru] do not know the evangelical law because, owing to the bad examples set them, there has been no one to teach it to them. What I did to the corregidor of Tinta was justice, for I assured myself beforehand that his actions did not conform to the Church; and this example was essential, to hold the other corregidores in check. It is my wish that the position of corregidor should be abolished entirely; that each province should have an *alcade* acting as mayor, who should be of Indian nationality but could even be some other person of good conscience, having no knowledge other than the administration of political and Christian justice in the Indies; that these persons should be paid a moderate salary and receive other benefits to be regulated in due course; that a royal audience should be established at Cuzco, where a viceroy shall live, so that the natives may obtain satisfaction more readily. At this time, I have no other motives. I acknowledge the supreme power of the King of Spain, dissuade no person from the obedience owing to him, and place no hindrance upon reciprocal trade, which is the principal fiber of the prosperity of this kingdom."[5]

A text which might more appropriately have been signed José-Gabriel Condorcanqui, former student of the faculty of Lima, than Tupac Amaru. "This is no revolution, Sire," his representatives could have told the king of Spain, "it is a reform." But its moderation is swept away along with everything else in the heat of the blaze. Tupac Amaru is talking about encouraging trade and the Christian mission at the head of forty or fifty thousand men (in mid-January) who are acting at a level of physical response that can only mean violence and massacre. It is a situation in which the reality gap is bordering on schizophrenia and his good intentions are paving the road to a hell of revenge.

He's about to meet its archfiend. Don Juan Manuel Moscoso y Peralta, Bishop of Cuzco, is a match for him: one of those Spaniards on whom a desperate situation works like a gallon of Malaga wine, carrying them on to triumph. As long as a Spaniard has a sword in his hand, anything can happen.

Cuzco* is in a state of siege this summer Christmas; the sun burns down fiercely on the heights but cannot warm the gray stones of the rectangular city rebuilt in checkerboard design by the Spaniards on the site of the old Inca town. "The lower part of the buildings may be called Inca and the upper part Spanish. The foundations of most of the houses are former Inca walls, made of enormous interlocking hewn-stone cubes which, though they are not cemented, have withstood earthquakes. This structure was decided by Pizarro

*At an altitude of 3,650 meters.

at the time of the conquest; to save time and labor, he merely removed the tops of the former buildings and added new stories to them, so that the city, which is Roman Catholic and modern* at its summit, has remained pagan at its base."[6]

Once its four gates have been shut in defiance of the cardinal points, that "pagan base" can supply you with some pretty formidable ramparts. You might think you were in an occupied Babylon, defended by a rather singular militia: "The priests are keeping watch at the towers†; they have organized rounds in the streets, are guarding the most dangerous posts and have neglected no detail of their military functions. The monks have undertaken to watch the churches, their monasteries and those of the nuns, in whose vestibules they mount an armed guard."[7] They are ceaselessly encouraged, harangued, and inspected by a mercurial little gentleman whose true nature surfaces as he takes command of his new recruits—men who used to imagine they were bishops and priests in another world, the world in which you carefully avoid seeing the nose on your face as long as nothing is happening. But let the storm come, and "My solicitude is extended to all, heedless of fatigue," modestly confesses the Monsignor of Cuzco. "We see the monks and priests more skilled with their guns than the half-breeds! They enlisted with the old men," most of the able-bodied having already gotten themselves slaughtered in the mountains, "and in a month and a half they have learned to maneuver like militia, while the Episcopal palace and collège have become a barracks for the Oropesa Indians"—that's right, the Indians from the plains region whose marquisate was given to Tupac Amaru, and who have been swiftly rounded up in a somewhat unusual *mita*—for war this time, instead of the mines. They've been warned that they will be tortured and hanged by their rebel brothers if they let themselves get caught, and it could happen, in the chaos of the sacking of a captured town, before the poor guys have time to sort themselves out . . . Now, commanded by monks, they are preparing to do battle against the army of their liberation. But just to be on the safe side, we'd better keep them out of the reach of Tupac Amaru, who is reported to be on his way.

In the evening of January 3 three Spanish hostages captured by the Incas after Arriaga's execution turn up looking sheepish at an outpost near Cuzco. They've got a letter for the bishop, from Tupac Amaru; are they going to be treated as traitors? No, only thrown into prison and put to the question, to punish them for not getting cut to pieces by the rebels. They can thank their lucky stars they aren't shot.

---

*That is, in the Spanish style of the sixteenth and seventeenth centuries.
†Account written by the bishop himself.

They're soon forgotten. The message from the Inca indicates that the decisive attack is imminent, and he even tries to play upon the terrorism which he is simultaneously struggling to contain. He pretends to believe, and maybe he does believe, that his partisans have already begun an insurrection inside Cuzco, and offers himself almost as a pacifier: "Since, in one part of the town, so many errors are being committed; since some are being hanged in my name and without confession, and others arrested, this news has caused me such pain that I find myself compelled to ask Your Excellency to put a stop to the abuses by allowing me to enter the town. For if this permission is not instantly granted I shall not be able to delay my entrance, which I shall make with fire and blood, sparing no person."[8]

A cheap Indian trick if ever there was one. Cuzco is quiet under the rule of its iron-fisted monks. Not quiet enough, though, to keep Tupac Amaru's supporters from sticking up broadsheets the next day, on the houses of the canons who form the *de facto* municipal government: "O King Charles III, by the grace of God, what perils now beset your kingdom of Peru, owing to the tyrannies of so many officials, visitors, corregidores, and other inventors of tyrannies! Draw your sword against those who have caused this perdition, and know above all that your Creole people is not content, because of the attempt to establish a salt monopoly and overburden these loyal subjects with taxes and duties. Even if Tupac Amaru were to perish, another would come in his place to oppose these tyrannous inventions and slay the cruel visitor and his accolytes, these persecutors of the kingdom."[9]

So he's trying to win over the Spanish natives, as well as the half-breeds. Well, why not? They're even worse off at the hands of their mother country than the North Americans used to be; the Royal and Supreme Council of the Indies tortures them with semicolons and numbered paragraphs that take years to reach them four thousand leagues away, telling them they can't sneeze without permission from Madrid and forcing their American lives into the Spanish mold, revised and supplemented by Austrian minutiae under Philip II. A continent hogtied by three or four superimposed thicknesses of restrictions. On this side of the Atlantic you can't appoint a notary public, a court registrar, or a vicar without the signature of the King of Spain. The mildest of reforms—those envisaged by Aranda—were strangled in the cradle. As for the economy of the colonies: why talk about something that doesn't exist? For a century the thin film of gravy, the few drops of initiative left to the native-born have been systematically siphoned off for the benefit of a few privileged companies which confiscate the entire commerce of the continent by order of the king. The South Americans are not allowed to manufacture so much as a toothpick; they have to buy everything from Spain. Corollary: they cannot freely export a single one of the products of their agriculture or mining. That's the work of "the monopolist traders,* whose political influence is increased by great wealth and sustained by intimate knowledge of the intrigue and momentary needs of the Court"[10]; *they* are Spain's true kings, and they have no faces and no ears to hear the wails of the flayed.

But the insurrectional strategy of a Tupac Amaru can't carry any weight with these people, who spend even more time hating each other than they do their oppressors in Madrid. No colonist could answer the call of an Indian. They'll find their own Washington, in their own ranks, mañana or the next day. And the lowest of the white ragpickers of Cuzco joins forces with the bishop and corregidores against the Inca's manifestoes —written, whether he likes it or not, in Spanish blood.

The tide turns on January 9. It isn't a real army laying siege to this Babylon, it's a horde of ill-equipped and ill-commanded bands who beat against the walls in disorderly waves, wearing out their wrath. The Indians overran the villages, but they can't capture a town in which their partisans have remained underground. Tupac Amaru's last letter to the bishop asks why nobody answers his letters? Why aren't his messengers sent back? His last ultimatum announces that he's going to reduce the city to ashes, slay all the Spaniards, make this into a stronghold solely for Indians . . . when he can't even prevent Spanish reinforcements from entering the town at night.

On the morning of January 12 seven hundred soldiers led by Colonel Laiseguillas make a decisive sortie, a battering ram in the direction of Tupac Amaru's headquarters, which are easy to identify because they form a homogeneous center in the bedlam of rebels, who are twenty times more numerous than the Spaniards but who scatter before them like flocks of sparrows—the Incas are not a warrior race, and the ease with which they abandon their leader shows how little ascendancy he has over them. That's what he gets for trying to be so lenient, no doubt. Not great enough for ferocity.

In a heavy hail of bullets and artillery shells, the white and yellow battalions of the "Lima Natives" charge up the little hill from whose crest Tupac Amaru was intending to flatten Cuzco. Worse, they are resolutely followed by the "Free White Mulattos" with black bands and gilt buttons, another regiment levied on the coast, whose presence confirms the fundamental failure of the rebellion: with a few exceptions, the mixed-bloods aren't stirring. The Inca has not been the federator of malcontents. All he can do now is break camp in a hurry, abandoning to the victors the beauti-

*According to Humboldt. Thirty years later this situation, exposed in the backwash of the European disturbances, produces the great uprisings of the *Libertadores,* led this time by Creoles: Bolívar, Miranda, Sucre, etc.

ful embroidered silk tent and gilt bed he appropriated at Tinta during the pillage of Arriaga's effects. He'll have had only two months to enjoy them in.

Then comes the odyssey of Tupac Amaru, already a ghost—like Pugachev, seven years ago on the other side of the world, lost between Don and Volga. The quarries of the great manhunts flash across the forestage of the end of the eighteenth century, a gold and satin theater whose curtain is still lowered. Prompt side and off side, blink once and they're gone. But the intermezzo has brought a frown to noble brows: really, such people should not be allowed in here, with their horses and dirty hands and wild airs. They leave spots. They smell. They kill. Faugh! They don't respect the rules of History played as a game. Let them join all the other clumsy oafs of failed revolutions, from Etienne Marcel to Thomas Münzer, and not forgetting Cola di Rienzo.* The harp and oboe can resume their tuning for the prelude to the little opera of reform with *ballets masqués*. But the curtain's begun to ripple. We can sense something in preparation behind it. On what setting will it finally rise? Not Russia, it seems, and now not Peru. He would be a clever man indeed, in 1781, who could predict the date and place.

But it's not so easy to bring down a ghost of this stature. It takes them a whole spring, or a whole Andean autumn. Returning to Tungasuca, the Inca tries to get his second wind among his loyal subjects. He still reigns as far as Tinta, which he fortifies, and he even manages to set up a rudimentary cannon foundry whose products fire balls of stone. Wasted effort: once a revolution loses the initiative, all it can have is a lingering death. Don José Antonio de Areche, the dread Visitor himself, has come up from Lima to Cuzco to relieve the bishop. Self-defense is the clergy's strong point; this man will take the offensive. In three months he doubles the vice-royalty's military forces. He outfits seventeen thousand men and sends them toiling up the mountain trails for the kill. The tide of repression waxes as the rebellion wanes. Unlike Pugachev, Tupac Amaru is not betrayed by a Judas. His lieutenants, simmering with dissidence ever since he criticized them for overdoing the reprisals, get themselves killed in disorganized skirmishes, or flee even farther away and higher, toward the peaks and inaccessible valleys. The attacking Spanish find the Tinta camp open on two sides. The Inca's most faithful followers die to cover his retreat, but he "escaped this day only because of the speed of his horse," by swim-

---

*Thomas Münzer: leader of the German peasants' revolt against the nobility in 1520; executed in 1525. Cola di Rienzo: head of an ephemeral Roman republic in 1347, massacred by his own partisans.

ming a river. It's the end, he's not the Inca anymore, he isn't even the leader of a revolt. José-Gabriel Condorcanqui, just another outlaw, leads his little band over vast stretches of salt pans between the raw sky and the short grass, where carcasses of llamas dead of hunger or thirst lie waiting for human corpses to join them, and the broad paved paths remind one that giants used to live in these parts. He writes his wife to join him; they'll try to reach that huge expanse of mysterious water forty leagues to the south, Lake Titicaca, the swimming pool of forgotten gods whose name means "stone of fire." A gray stone sea like an upside-down sky four miles above the ocean, their sea, their mother, the womb, refuge and consolation of the Indians, the place where the Spaniards are helpless as babes. But he moves too slowly, halfheartedly—maybe he doesn't care to survive as a loser. "Here come many valiant soldiers marching upon us. All that remains for us is to die."[11]

Tupac Amaru is taken prisoner on April 6, with his wife, Micaëla, his sons Hippolyte and Fernand, his brother-in-law Raphael, and sixty captains and soldiers of "his guard."*

We'll give them something to look at. When it comes to fancy executions you can't beat the West.

May 18, 1781. Tupac Amaru and his family are executed on the Cuzco parade ground bordered by Spanish homes with turned wooden balconies and Moorish arches. He dies in the setting he wanted to change, facing the cathedral built on the ruins of the palace of his ancestors. The huge stone book turns its greatest page toward the scaffold, the one showing the Last Judgment, when the Christ *"de los temblores"* opens his arms to the throngs ejected by the quaking earth. A platform covered with precious rugs has been erected across from it, for the Viceroy of Lima, the Visitor, and the bishop, at the foot of the governor's palace: here the house of God and the house of the king *(el cabildo)* stand face to face, as they do in every other big town in the New Indies, where the law imposes *uniformidad en todo* (uniformity in all) and where "from Mexico to the confines of Chile, the same right-angled streets and the same *plaza Mayor* were to be found."[12] Much farther away and at a much lower altitude, in Santiago, or St. James' town, a young Italian architect, Gioacchino Toesca, has been working for the past year on the Moneda, a copy of all the other huge edifices that have swarmed from Vienna to Madrid. It will be easier to strike pistoles there† than at Potosi, and they can be more

---

*Some 120 miles, as the crow flies, from the Churo gorge where seventeen guerilla fighters in Bolivia are betrayed and captured on October 8, 1967; their leader, Ernesto "Che" Guevara, is assassinated the following day on the orders of General Barrientos, Bolivian dictator.

†In 1842 this building, a pure marvel of eighteenth-century architecture measuring 150

quickly carried, bagfuls at a time, down to the ships in Valparaiso. The stone giant will bear witness to the triumph of a Spain hardly even singed by the fire of these Indians she swats down like flies in Cuzco.

Like flies whose wings are pulled off first; because they did after all give us a scare.

Standing in front of the officials' grandstand is a group of spectators, pale and erect; the condemned man's wife and relatives, privileged spectators—oh, very!—since they are to provide part of the entertainment. They know. They stand silent amidst the roaring of the crowd of colonists, lots of women in *sayas* and *mantos,* hooded from head to slippered feet but glittering with jewels, and all those men, every one in a uniform of his own devising: the colonial Spaniard will have no truck with civilian dress. Their joy is the joy of the bullfight at the moment of the final thrust, heightened by relief and weighted down by hatred. Nobody bears a grudge against a *toro;* but here . . . Eight executioners. One of them tears out Tupac Amaru's tongue, not that he'd have said anything anyway. The others prolong his drawing and quartering as long as they can, but his body must resist like the Andean stone because after lashing the four horses for an hour they weary of the sport. The viceroy makes a gesture. The head is severed from the already lifeless trunk, as it was done two centuries ago, almost to the day and on the same parade ground, to Tupac Amaru I, the "sixteenth Inca." "Mounting the scaffold he raised his hand to silence his subjects, whose mutterings troubled the crossbowmen. When his head fell under the scimitar of a Moor, the crowd uttered a long moan," on May 12, 1571[13] . . . Because of him, this one had insisted on calling himself "Tupac Amaru II." But this time the Indians have been driven away and certain refinements have been introduced. You can't stop progress.

A few formalities still have to be gone through. Micaëla is strangled. The brother-in-law and first son are decapitated. The mutilated corpses are hoisted on poles and the second son, Fernand—the youngest—is made to walk back and forth under them for his baptism by blood before his own head falls. He wasn't twenty. For the repose of the souls of the deceased, fat yellow wax tapers burn day and night for a year on the thousand-year-old paving stones, marking the bloodstains it is forbidden to wash, in front of an effigy of Our Lady of the Sorrows. They are called "the 18th of May lights."

---

meters by 115, becomes the official residence of the presidents of the Republic of Chile. It is totally destroyed on September 11, 1973, by the putschist air force bombardment; and it is in the "Toesca room," named after the architect, that Salvador Allende, constitutional president, gathers together his followers before dying, gun in hand.

For their bodies there will be no repose. The corpse of Tupac Amaru is dismembered and the limbs enclosed in leather bags, to be carried across the Andes on muleback and nailed to the gates of as many towns as possible. For good measure, the feet and hands of the rest of the family are also distributed among the corregidores. Will this form of lesson in submission, as old as mankind, work again? Mariano and Diego Christobal Tupac Amaru, a son and a brother, are already starting up something more like a jacquerie than a rebellion—but they are captured after being given safe-conducts. Before Diego Christobal is hanged his nipples are clamped in incandescent tongs. And the "vice-Inca" Julian Apaza, alias Tupac-Catari, is marching on La Paz on the far side of Lake Titicaca and laying siege to that other high-altitude center—the same terror as in Cuzco, and the same last-minute backlash.

But it really is too late: Spanish reinforcements are arriving from the Atlantic, by way of Buenos Aires and up the Amazon. The morsels of Julian Apaza,* which multiply as miraculously as relics from the Holy Land, serve to edify the populace for several weeks. To drive the point home, they are solemnly burned in two great fires, on the beautiful evenings of the Hallowe'en season.

The governors have learned one lesson from all this; they give up any further ideas of "Hispanizing the Indian mass."[14] We want no more of this integration nonsense. Peru is transformed for all eternity into an immense reservation for Indians corralled into timelessness. "All the descendants of the ancient Inca princes were hunted out and either put to death or deported to Spain. The titles and duties of the caciques were abolished in Peru . . . It was forbidden to wear clothes containing any allusion to the former Incan aristocracy." Ah, that old dream of the conqueror—to slay the past. It's possible, provided you seal every hairbreadth crack through which it might seep back into men's minds. So, war upon the rebel avant-garde, and upon yet another of those deadly books—"All the copies of the *Royal Commentaries* by the Hispano-Incan half-blood Garcilaso de la Vega"—from which Raynal and Diderot have just been borrowing—"a famous name in Spanish literature, were burned."

---

*Captured on October 17, 1781, the date that marks the official close of the revolt of the Peruvian Indians.

54

MAY 1781

But You Do Not Go to Mass

In France, Necker's execution that same 18th of May assumes a decidedly less bloodthirsty aspect; its ferocity is restrained. And yet this is no minor event. Five years after Turgot, a second reformer plummets through the trapdoor and the reign reaffirms its reactionary bent. Funny how this kind of fall always seems to come in May; Louis XVI's springtimes have an autumnal appearance.

As for the then unperceived link between what is going on in "the Indies" and at Versailles, the latest edition of the *Histoire des Deux Indes* is condemned on May 21, the moment Necker's protective hand is forcibly withdrawn from it. On the 22nd Raynal flees to avoid arrest, while over there in the other world the blood is still oozing from the segments of Tupac Amaru.

Since the publication of the *Account Rendered*, "informed circles" have been all at sea with their compasses spinning. On April 23 the "director general of finances is tottering" but by the 25th "everything has been patched up with regard to M. Necker: he appears to have won a total victory." On May 1 "the director general of finances enjoys the favor of the monarch with greater certainty than ever before"—about as much certainty as a weather vane, buffeted by every breeze from Marly, Choisy, or Compiègne, where travelers could smell something like an aroma of decomposing minister in the air. On May 16 "M. Necker's friends are trembling for him once again,"[1] and they're right. "It is said that the director general of finances has again complained to the king of the annoyances besetting him and has renewed his offer to tender his resignation, but that the monarch replied, 'Keep calm, and continue to merit my confidence by working for the happiness of my people . . .'"

In the mouth of a Bourbon this kind of reassurance is enough to make the most insouciant hair stand on end. Necker prepares for the worst. His showdown bid in January has put him within reach of both summit and abyss, and he can't remain suspended much longer between dismissal and the effective leadership of the government, to which public opinion is increasingly calling him. Unluckily for him, governments are not formed by public opinion.

An avalanche of epigrams, pamphlets, anonymous broadsheets. He ought to have expected it, really, but his hide isn't tough enough. The incense he's been inhaling in steady gulps at home has ruined his lungs. Who would have believed this big hunk of manpower could be so vulnerable? He tries to identify his enemies and parry their thrusts, and in doing so plays into their hands. He overplays his own, as in the case of a literary turd deposited on his doorstep by one Sieur Bourboulon, "formerly second clerk of a notary and now administrator of the finances of Monsieur, the King's brother. Monsieur Bourboulon has acquired, in the course of his progress from one of these extremities to the other, a vast experience of business.* He would never have claimed responsibility for a criticism of the *Account Rendered* that has aroused M. Necker's animadversion if he had not been certain of the support of a respectable protector. It is even said [on April 6] that Monsieur, whose enlightenment and devotion to study are well known, had a share in this work."[2] So the Comte de Provence is now perfecting his rope trick for strangling reformers at the right moment. Turgot was just a trial run. That's one way to build, on the cheap, a solid reputation as a bulwark of the overprivileged. Considering that Louis XVI can't stand his brother, that in itself might not be too bad, but Necker's going to have to contend with two otherwise highly accredited adversaries: Maurepas-Vergennes, the jealousy tandem.

On May 3 the Comte de Vergennes presents the king with a 200-line assassination, that *Mémoire* he's been polishing since January and has managed, with much mincing and blushing, to get himself "ordered" to produce. War is declared within the cabinet. From now on it's him or Necker. Knowing Vergennes's prudence, he must feel very sure of the king's ear to expose himself so far:

"Your Majesty, Sire, has ordered me to speak frankly; I obey. A battle has been joined between the government of France and the government of M. Necker."[3] The man who makes France's foreign policy sees the country as a perfectly level desert—the dream of Louis XIV: "Owing to the tireless efforts of so many wise ministers, there is no more clergy or nobility or third estate in France"; a classless society in other words, who'd have guessed it! "The distinction is fictitious, purely representative and without true authority. The monarch speaks, all the rest is the people and all the rest obey,"[4] that's the way to console Louis XVI, right on, there! Now throw in a pinch of xenophobia and a dash of intolerance: "If his ideas prevail over those established by long experience, M. Necker, following Law and Mazarin, with his Genevan and

*According to the author of the *Correspondance secrète*.

Protestant ideas, is perfectly prepared to institute in France a system within the world of finance, or a league within the state, or a Fronde against the established administration."* And since argumentation with Louis XVI consists in hammering away at a single nail, Vergennes does not hesitate to double-dot every *i*. "It is very dangerous to entrust the most delicate of the kingdom's administrations to the hands of an alien, a republican [*sic*], a Protestant."[5] And peeking over the rubble heap of his demolition, he submits his application for the post of principal minister of a 100-percent French France as soon as Maurepas has finally run out of wind.

But in the meantime, "Maurepas is still alive / And breaking wind like any five"[6]; and Necker doesn't despair of his support if only to checkmate Vergennes, whose machinations he is aware of although he doesn't know precisely where they're going to strike. After all, this basket case still holds the power of attorney for France, and Necker has somehow managed to gouge a few positive measures out of him in the last four years, at the cost of exhausting pilgrimages to what used to be Mme du Barry's little chambers:

"No one will ever know what steadfastness I had need of . . . I can still† recall that long, dark staircase of M. de Maurepas, which I mounted in fear and melancholy, uncertain of his response to some new idea I was working on in my mind, and which was most often designed to augment income by means of a just but severe intervention; I can still recall that little between-stairs office beneath the roofs of Versailles and above the King's own apartments, which, owing to its tiny size and its location, seemed like a distillate, a super-refined distillate, of every vanity and ambition; it was here one had to go in order to converse, with a minister who had grown old in ostentation and the usages of the Court, about reforms and measures of economy. I remember how many precautions were required in order to succeed, and how, after repeated refusals, I would ultimately obtain some small concession to the public weal; and I obtained it, it was plain to see, as a reward for the resources I contrived to find in time of war. I still remember the kind of shame that weighed upon me when I mingled with my words, and made bold to propound to him, some of the great moral ideas animating my heart."[7] A preacher! It must have given Maurepas a kick to hear him talking about his heart. At Versailles . . .

So, May 18. Necker goes back to put the question of confidence, "them or me," the cry of the man in extremis. It's dangerous. His friends advise him to wait. "They argued that he enjoyed the full trust of the King and all the good graces of the Queen,** and that he had only to possess himself in

*Of course, through his connections with the Protestant bankers, Necker has left himself open to this reproach.

†Written by Necker in 1795.

**According to Weber, Marie Antoinette's foster brother, who has just arrived from Vienna

patience for a time; that Maurepas, over eighty and in failing health, could not long trouble him."[8] But oversensitivity is not the only thing bothering Necker: they've also contrived to make it impossible for him to carry on his work. The publication of the *Account Rendered* was only the first stage in his plan of action, to be followed by various simplifications and economies carried out on the strength of public opinion, now at last "in the know." But Maurepas keeps putting off the decisions, and "public opinion," which doesn't know that, is blaming Necker! Talk, talk, talk, that's all you can do. "Public opinion" is beginning to cast a sullen eye upon his appeals for loans. So he's cornered; either he's got to go all the way or be called a coward.

The reason Maurepas can obstruct Necker's efforts is that the director of finances sees the king only when he is granted an audience. He's not allowed to sit on the Council, where everything can be settled by a word behind closed doors or a scrap of paper slipped under the sovereign's pen at the right moment. Even the unspeakable Turgot was able to talk to him face to face; but not Necker. It's too much, and it's got to stop. Necker asks Maurepas for the full powers and title of minister, and for admission to the Council. Or else . . .

M. de Maurepas's last joy is sweet. The hook has been well baited. The fish bites.

"Or else? . . ."

"Or else I shall find myself obliged to ask you to tender my resignation to His Majesty."

Those are the words Maurepas's been waiting for for months, ever since Necker had Sartines removed from office and pushed Castries and Ségur to the fore, and published his "blue fairy tale," as the old minister calls the famous "little blue book" in which, apart from one almost insolent doff of his hat, the author doesn't credit the Mentor with a single one of the good deeds attributed to the king. Therefore, Necker has to go. At the beginning of May Maurepas takes it upon himself to warn Louis XVI "that all the ministers were now determined to hand in their resignations should the doors be opened wide to this heretic." In a régime in which nobody says what he means to anybody, it's easy enough to make people talk by hearsay. Necker used the method against Maurepas, now he's getting it back. In fact, only Vergennes has said anything of the sort. The Marquis de Castries, to the contrary, is protesting "that all the ministers, including himself, might leave without harm; the King would always find a hundred more of the same caliber to replace them, whereas there is but one Monsieur Necker."[9] But he's careful not to say that to Louis XVI while it might still be of some use, and the king goes

---

to occupy a position as chamberlain at Versailles. His memoirs were written down by Lally-Tollendal from his own words.

on reigning in his cloud of silence interpreted by Maurepas, the sole spokesman of his harem—and, tonight, the monarchy's performer of acts of great
moment. Nobody can accuse *him* of kicking Necker out after Turgot; Necker
has put himself in the position of having to kick himself out.

"You, on the Council! But you do not go to mass! You know very well,
Monsieur, that the law of the state forbids the presence of a Protestant in the
Council . . ."

"Sully, who did not go to mass, sat on the Council, Monsieur."[10]

Thereupon Maurepas leaps at the opportunity to make a little witticism
on the conversion of Henri IV; admission to the Council is worth a mass or
two, after all; and Necker is too much of a philosopher to haggle over dogma.
Why, if he were to convert to the Church of Rome, there would be an end
of it . . .

Necker doesn't appreciate this form of humor. He quickly writes a few
words for the king:

"Sire, the conversation which I have had with M. de Maurepas does not
permit me to defer placing my resignation in your hands. My soul is profoundly distressed by this. I dare hope that Your Majesty will retain some
recollection of the years of happy but arduous work, and above all, of the
boundless zeal with which I have devoted myself to your service."[11]

What he's mostly daring to hope is that Maurepas is bluffing and the king
will refuse his resignation. He's counting on support from the queen, on a
surge of public opinion . . . The almost classic reflex of the disgraced minister
who thinks he's living through a nightmare and swears he's about to wake up,
it can't be true, they can't get along without me . . . And it's true enough that
he's asleep, but on quicksand. Before his turn comes, there were Turgot,
Choiseul, and Maurepas himself who have also sat up and rubbed their eyes.

On Saturday, May 19, Necker turns up the narrow pathway of the staircase of sorrows one last time, to take Maurepas's pulse in that beautiful box,
that rosewood attic under the eaves of Versailles in which one little man holds
France in his palm. Maurepas "bade him come in at once,* welcomed him with
customary affability and, with a placid countenance, informed him that the
King had deigned to accept his resignation. Necker staggered. Apart from a
few convulsive gestures, he remained speechless and motionless for some
moments. The Comte de Maurepas had to call his people and tell them to send
word to M. Necker's that the gentleman wished to leave at once."[12]

Fired like a flunkey.

---

*According to Bachaumont's *Mémoires secrets;* their author was presumably informed by
Maurepas himself, for it was to his advantage to intensify Necker's humiliation.

55

MAY 1781

Her Mind Raced Ahead

The news of Necker's fall hits Diderot like a bolt from the blue. He wasn't expecting it any more than three-quarters of the rest of the world. Here he is, suddenly at the mercy of the wolves, and not only him—everybody who's been trying to exist otherwise than on his stomach.

On March 1 he wrote a pretty little thank-you note to Mme Necker, who had sent him a socialite's pamphlet, unsigned but produced by herself, on the *Hospice de charité; Institutions, Règles et Usages de cette maison,* which she and her husband founded in 1778 on the premises of the Benedictines of Notre Dame de Liesse.* With no outside resources, the daughter of a Geneva pastor had undertaken a job which was supposed to be done by queens but which they always managed to wriggle out of, using alms as their alibi: the cleansing of the Augean stables, or rather hospitals, of the most Christian kingdom in which poor people died three to a bed. Mme Necker's hospital was the first ever to be opened to the poor with regulations stipulating one patient per bed. Diderot lets himself go slightly overboard about it: "I wanted a copy of the *Hospice* to have bound together with the *Account Rendered* and thus enclose within a single volume the two most interesting works I ever read or ever shall." This man from the east† never learned how to sing hymns softly: "The *Account Rendered* teaches sovereigns to prepare for a reign of glory, and teaches their ministers to justify their administration to the people. The *Hospice* teaches all hospital founders and directors their duties." Their authors will deserve "during their lifetime, or after they die, a dual monument that will display them to us, the one giving instruction to the masters of the world, the other uplifting their downtrodden servants."[1]

By way of a monument, two months later, it's the boot. And if anyone wanted to delude himself as to the significance of Necker's resignation he'd have had only one day, Sunday May 20, in which to do it. On the 21st the

*By modern numbering, 151 Rue de Sèvres; today, the Necker Hospital.

†Diderot was born in Langres in eastern France, where people are reputedly less subtle than in the center and south. [*Trans.*]

Parliament of Paris, to whom the Keeper of the Seals applied for emergency proceedings at the behest of the Comte de Maurepas, condemns the *Histoire des Deux Indes* and orders the Abbé Raynal placed under arrest.[2] Necker has never taken any official stand in support of the book, nor was he qualified to do so; but everybody knows that Raynal and Diderot are intimate friends of his, and that some of their source material came from Saint-Ouen. Even Parliament members who turned purple at the sight of the book would never have dared to attack it before, when they would also have been indirectly attacking the great financier of today and possible prime minister of tomorrow. Necker's mere presence created a climate of tolerance, even if he never reached a position in which he could try to have it translated into law.* This often happens when a man with a liberal reputation gains favor with the authorities in a monarchy. The weather vanes become a shade more lenient —not because they've been converted to liberalism, but because it's the diplomatic thing to do . . . one never knows. In this instance the atmosphere of the reign automatically becomes leaden overnight, all the fresh air in it having been forced out the door at Necker's back.

Séguier, the advocate general, yelps like a hyena in his final peroration, and his indictment is printed "by order of the King": "So this is their philosophy! It has just torn off the mask that concealed it from our eyes, and the deformity of its features will repel the universe . . . By some extraordinary singularity, Abbé Raynal's history, which was alleged to be purely philosophical and political, whose sole subject was the settlement of the Europeans in the two Indies, whose only goal was to be the increase and ease of trade; this account, I say, is so intermingled with impious statements and bitter reproaches, gross sarcasms and vulgar impostures, that one would think the author had undertaken the work for no other purpose than to unite every form of blasphemy in a single book."[3] Following this, the Parliament's decree stipulates "that the work shall be burned by the executioner's hand, that the said Raynal, depicted in the frontispiece of the book, shall be seized and taken into arrest, and conducted to the prisons of the Conciergerie there to be heard and questioned as to the matter of the said book, and his goods and chattels shall be seized and confiscated . . ." Simultaneously the Sorbonne declares "this delirium of an impious soul [to be] an abomination."

Raynal doesn't have to be told twice. His bags were packed the moment he got the news of Necker's fall. The police, who have no great desire to

*On August 24, 1780, he managed to get Louis XVI to endorse a proposal by Miromesnil to abolish the "preparatory question," that is, the torture inflicted upon the accused during preliminary hearings. But it had more or less totally lapsed in France anyway and wasn't even used against the murderer Derues. On the other hand, the ordeal of the "preliminary question," inflicted upon sentenced persons before execution, had been maintained in spite of Necker.

encumber themselves with a martyr, give Raynal ample time to leave his pretty house at Courbe-Voie (*curva via*, the bend in the old Roman road above the Seine beyond Neuilly), hidden among the trees near the rabbit warren of Colombes, from which this hermit of the easy life could amuse himself peering through his looking glass at the real hermits on Mount Valérien, farther away to the southwest. On the morning of May 23 a heavy vehicle crammed full of books (how could he survive without them?) carries two passengers away to exile: this outlawed man, whose fine features express "a capacity for mischief mingled with effrontery and an incontinence tempered by gluttony,"* and his nephew–secretary–special-pet Simon Camboulas, a tall, dark young man "whose deepset eyes, veiled by fleeting languors, illuminate a physiognomy of precocious majesty,"† imbued with that solemnity imprinted upon every Rouergue face almost at birth. To avoid the risk of a collision with the marshalcy, the runaways do not go through Paris. After crossing the Seine by the Clichy ferry, they take "the road of revolt" built to enable Louis XV to avoid his capital and, before moving on to the Low Countries, pause for a moment at Saint-Ouen to pay their respects to Necker.

They're not the only ones. What a crowd! There isn't enough room for all the visitors' carriages in front of the château, they have to line up along the avenues on the grounds. The departing Necker looks much more like Choiseul than Turgot, who left with his nerves in shreds, abandoned by all or almost, in a high dive from power to solitude. Whereas for Necker, "one would have said,** observing the universal expressions of astonishment, that no news was ever less anticipated. Consternation is written on every face; those whose feelings are contrary are too few. They would blush to show them. Promenades, cafés, all the public places are thronged with people, but an extraordinary silence reigns among them. They stare at one another. They sorrowfully clasp one another's hands, I would say as at the sight of some public calamity, except that these first moments of distress gave rather the impression of a grieving family which has just lost the source and mainstay of its hopes."⁴

Raynal and Camboulas mount three shallow steps and walk straight into that little jewel of countrified luxury, the Château de Saint-Ouen, bursting at the seams with Birons, Beauveaus, Richelieus, Choiseuls (of course), Noailleses, Luxembourgs, and even the Orléanses, senior and junior—the very same people who were waving their flags when Turgot fell. This time there's a split between the majority of the court nobility and the king. Seated beside

---

*According to Lavater, the celebrated "physiognomist" whom Raynal will visit in Zurich.

†Simon Camboulas, son of one of Raynal's sisters, was born near Rodez in 1760. He will represent the Aveyron district at the Convention.

**According to the *Correspondance littéraire* (text by Grimm), which sets the tone for enlightened Europe from June on.

Marmontel on a gray brocade sofa, the Neckers receive condolences "without dissembling their profound sorrow."[5] A strange little personage—is it an aged child or a precocious woman?—is taking in the scene, and will remember it for the rest of her days: their only daughter, Anne Louise Germaine,* and she's worthy of her role. Hasn't her two-act comedy *Les Inconvénients de la vie de Paris* already been performed at Saint-Ouen? Fifteen years old, a little bosom, a lot of lip, and an immensity of eye. "Mademoiselle Necker, obliged to sit up very straight, stayed close by her parents on a little wooden stool. No sooner had she taken her customary place than three or four elderly persons came up to her and spoke to her with the most affectionate interest; one of them, who wore a little round wig, took her hands in his and, holding them at some length, began conversing with her as though she were twenty-five years old. This man was the Abbé Raynal; the others were Thomas, Marmontel, and Baron Grimm.

"We sat down to eat. How Mlle Necker listened! She did not open her mouth yet she seemed to be speaking in turn, so expressive were her mobile features. Her eyes followed the looks and movements of those who were talking; one would have said that her mind raced ahead of theirs. She knew about everything, even political subjects which, at that time, were one of the main interests of conversation."[6]

But by this time Abbé Raynal is back on the road to Spa (decidedly the "in" gathering place that season), after passing on the torch to the young girl —a ceremony that all the Séguiers in the world can never prevent. The following day,

> the King was hunting in the plain of Saint-Denis, when Monsieur Necker crossed it on his way to the country.† Our punsters are inquiring:
> "And what game did the King raise?"**
> "Necker," they reply.[7]

---

*The future Madame de Staël, born in Paris on April 22, 1766. Her playlet was performed in the château in September 1778.

†According to the *Correspondance secrète*. We recall that Mesmer also went to Spa after his washout in Paris.

**In French, "Qu'est-ce que le Roi a chassé?"—a pun on "chasser," also meaning "to dismiss or discharge, as a servant." [*Trans.*]

ABBÉ MAURY

56

This Scarcely Evangelical Method

What's gotten into Louis XVI? Why, against the will of most of his entourage, has he allowed a minister who was thought to be efficient in matters of finance and who had a personality more or less compatible with his own to be driven to handing in his resignation? Against Necker are the king's two brothers, Maurepas, Vergennes, a number of members of the Parliament, and the parasitic overprivileged; for him are the snobs, the "progressive" nobility, the world of finance, the bourgeoisie, the queen—you heard me, the queen who, contrary to the line she took in Turgot's case, is now telling the world how she swung all her weight in the Genevan's favor, and if it had been up to her . . .

So? It's hard to make a dent in that noodle. Louis XVI's characteristic behavior, as we're beginning to know by now, is to wrap himself in so many layers of aloofness that nobody knows what he's thinking—or if he's thinking. This has a twofold advantage: he creates an illusion of mystery, and he revels in the ill-contained irritation that this attitude sustains in his entourage —the small, daily thorn in the skin. But ever since the publication of the *Account Rendered* he's been visibly out of sorts for the precise reason that in it Necker dared to raise his voice and Louis-the-Taciturn prefers people who don't talk, whence the favor enjoyed by Maurepas, who speaks only in epigrams, and Vergennes-the-totally-impenetrable. Within weeks the latter managed to forge a connection in the king's mind between the nearly simultaneous publication of the *Account Rendered* and the explosive new edition of the *Histoire des Deux Indes.* By stretching things a little, by mixing up the stories, the man who wrote about the budget could be turned into an accomplice of the two upstarts who were spouting nonsense about the established order. Then the Maury business crops up at just the right moment that spring to set a little alarm signal blinking in the king's eyes—danger of change, the catastrophe he fears worse than death. Now, if my certified preacher starts getting into the act . . .

From the *Correspondance littéraire,* April 1781:

> The *Lenten sermon preached before the King* by Abbé Maury will be most intriguing
> to read. The greatest reproach made at Versailles is that he brings too many
> things foreign to the Gospels into his sermons, too much discussion of politics,
> finance and administration; that he preaches TO the King rather than BEFORE
> the King.
>
> "What a pity," His Majesty said the other day on his way out of church. "If
> Abbé Maury had only said a word or two about religion, he would have covered
> every subject on earth."[1]

Yet there's nothing of the bel esprit in this Herculean priest. Abbé Maury
himself is still dazed by the wave of the magic wand that has snatched him out
of his father's little cobbler's shop in Valréas, in the county of Venaissin, and
whirled him all the way to the pulpit of the Chapel Royal. The Church is the
only fairy godmother capable of pulling off stunts like that, and Maury, now
within reach of the Académie Française and a bishopric, has no wish to deviate
from this gratifying trajectory. His frame may be ill at ease in his cassock, but
not his heart. A lumberjack remodeled into an athlete of eloquence. To
become awe-inspiring all he has to do is spread his huge arms as though to hug
his audience to his bear's chest and stifle it.*

His first lessons were learned in the school of fisticuffs under the good
priest of Buis-les-Baronnies, and he continued his studies in the humanities at
the Avignon seminary in the same spirit, moving on from battle to battle,
Latin, rhetoric, theology, every little bit helps in the fight for life. A charging
bull. As a citizen of a pontifical territory, he dreamed of Rome and imagined
himself pope. But the county of Venaissin was the Papal States' lost child;
everything there was left to rot, the people, the countryside, the town and its
priests, even if they were better off than a cobbler's son. Before he reached
the age of twenty Maury understood, like Sieys, that Paris was his only hope.
But, unlike Sieys, he doesn't balk at it, he pursues it—like one of those lovely
repentant sinners he's so fond of hearing confession from. He tutors, he
preaches to all and any comers, he frequents drawing rooms when he can and
convents when he must, society ladies when he has a chance and prelates when
he doesn't, he mouths the *Eloge de Fénelon* but only so he can say nice things
about Bossuet, he pays court to d'Alembert and court to the pious dauphin.† Beginning in 1767, he is grand vicar at Lombez and spends a few years

*Jean-Siffrein Maury, born at Valréas on June 26, 1746, is elected to the Académie Française
in 1785. Representative of the clergy at the Estates General, he becomes Mirabeau's most fiery
adversary in the royalist and clerical party during the oratorical jousts. First an émigré, he later
switches to Bonaparte, becomes a cardinal, and is Archbishop of Paris during the Empire.

†Louis XVI's father, that is.

maturing with the casks in Armagnac, before returning in 1772 to preach before the Académie for the feast of St. Louis:

"Well, gentlemen! Where would you be now without the Crusades?"[2]

This sally brings a smile to Voltaire's lips: "Reading the *Panégyrique de saint Louis* delivered by M. Maury before our illustrious Académie, I could believe myself listening to Peter the Hermit changed into Demosthenes or Cicero. He quite makes one long to see a crusade." And indeed, Maury belongs to the breed of crowd-movers, he's a total misfit in chapels that mute his stentorian voice whose Provençal accent he has rubbed off by sheer will power. Unruly locks, dark complexion, angular features: Peter the Hermit! People "clapped their hands in the chapel." Victory! "The Company unanimously decreed that as soon as the Cardinal de la Roche-Aymon* would be returned from Rheims, a deputation of three members of the Académie would call on him and ask him to be so good as to obtain assurance from the King that M. l'Abbé Maury would receive some mark of satisfaction."[3]

"Monsieur l'Abbé, next year you will preach before the King: the Last Supper† and Advent sermons, and Pentecost sermon for the ceremony of the blue ribbons. You are also to prepare yourself to preach before His Majesty at Versailles during Lent, beginning in 1775."

He expects an aging Louis XV, and might have preferred an undemanding listener of that ilk. But what he gets is a young Louis XVI for whom every word counts, a theologian-king perfectly at home in debates on sufficient grace, sanctifying grace, and their unfathomable attribution in the designs of the Lord. Religion is one of the six or eight subjects the king mastered thoroughly, with touching application, under the rod of the governor and almoners who accompanied him almost to the steps of the throne. So he looks upon this priest inherited from his grandfather with as much mistrust as all the rest of his legacy, but Maury's son-of-the-people side catches his fancy. Louis XVI likes simple folks. And the abbé manages to hit the right note in his very first sermons:

"Sire, your August Father commends your kingdom to you from the heights of heaven. Think, sometimes, what he would have done on the throne on which you sit. That is what you must do in order to restore to France the blessed reign she anticipated from him."[4]

That's the stuff! Louis XVI melts when you talk to him like that. But then Maury spoils it all. He's too eager to follow the fads. Like so many others this past year, he thought Necker's rise heralded a change of key in the reign, and he modulates just a quarter of a measure too soon. On March 14, 1781, the

---

*Grand almoner of France, completely doddering at the time. As such, he had control over the "roll of livings," and thus over all important ecclesiastical appointments.

†On Holy Thursday. The "ceremony of the blue ribbons" was to welcome those being received into the Order of the Holy Ghost.

champions of purity and immobility begin calling him to order: "M. l'Abbé Maury, a bold, intriguing churchman avid of success at any price, has taken advantage of the honor conferred upon him, of preaching before the King, to attract attention to himself, and people are quoting several of his sermons which have caused a stir at Versailles. In his efforts to be noticed he has chosen to sprinkle his discourse with historical references alluding to present-day events"—why, that's pure Raynal!—"or simply to embellish it with contemporary anecdotes. This scarcely evangelical method, which is rendered even less so by being heavily satirical, is extremely well suited to flavoring his speeches, but also to gaining enemies for himself. People affirm that the King is not well pleased with this orator on that account."[5] What account, though, when you come down to it? It's those mentions of the concrete that are causing the trouble, those nuggets of reality embedded in the gelatin of ecclesiastical verbiage on which Louis XVI has fed delightedly until now. His spirituality is no more Christly or apostolic than that of his epoch: to him Jesus is a dauphin, an associate in the empire of his Father, a sort of perpetual Joseph II. You address him in the manner prescribed by protocol, without concerning yourself with his Gospel. For the past six years the courtiers have sat and listened without raising an eyebrow while Maury lectured them about "the sublime philosophy of Christianity, that religion of unhappiness,* the God who is our father and our judge, the poor who will be our creditors and mediators before Him, the supremacy of a religion which never deceives and alone possesses the art of consoling, provided we prostrate ourselves at the sacred court of contrition and confess ourselves to a judge who instantly becomes our merciful mediator,"[6] etc. They've been swimming in sacred molasses. But now the abbé is shocking their socks off by bringing them back to themselves. We don't pay the man to wake us up!

April 16: "In a sermon on charity, he spoke of hospitals and observed that the multitude of foundlings was growing every day in Paris; that in 1780 there were thirteen thousand of them, seven thousand of whom died for want of care and good nurses." Really, Monsieur l'Abbé! The *Account Rendered* from the pulpit! He shows the tip of his tail at the worst possible moment, on April 30, "in a sermon on calumny, by quoting profane examples of ministers contending with the wicked. He evoked the names of Sully, Colbert, and, without naming him, alluded so pointedly to Monsieur Necker that no one could doubt the subject of his speech or the preacher's purpose." He's fumbled the ball: Louis XVI orders the grand almoner to give him a dressing-down:

"Avoid bringing foreign matter [*sic*] into your speeches, and things relating to the administration, of which you should have no knowledge, as should the public [*sic*]."[7]

---

*And to think that Chateaubriand later brags of coining this phrase!

Once is enough for Maury, who swallows his tongue for a year or two —but he has certainly helped to stir up Louis XVI, and not at all in the direction he was hoping. The king's religion is a form of obstinacy, not devoutness—Louis XVI is no mystic, he's a worrier, he needs certainties and a good conscience. Life and the world become intelligible to his eyes when he can find it natural that *he* and not his brother, his cousin, or the first idiot to come along should be the Anointed of God Almighty, God's image on the soil of France, the only layman in the kingdom entitled to commune both ways. If God wills, all will be well. But in order for God to will, all other hypotheses must be eliminated. Apart from the *Encyclopédie* and the various technical, scientific, or classical works selected for his library, Louis XVI possesses only two books: Tasso's *Jerusalem Delivered* and . . . *Robinson Crusoe.*[8] He has not read Voltaire or Rousseau or Helvétius, and studied Montesquieu only to condemn him. He knows less about the age he lives in than most of the craftsmen on the Place Dauphine. Many theological students are more curious than he is. But who cares, since he is the living keystone of an eternally stable universe?

Then you can judge his terror when, in the first days of May, Vergennes hands him, as an appendix to his *Mémoire* against Necker, a copy of the *Histore des Deux Indes* open to the page on which those boors—Raynal, Diderot, and why not Necker while we're at it, they're all the same man—address the king as "tu," as though they were talking to a stableboy: "Ah, if only, as I speak, two tears should steal from your eyes, we are saved . . ."

That'll be the day.

Louis XVI has long since memorized the maxims written for him in the year of his marriage by his confessor, Abbé Soldini, the priest who undoubtedly had the greatest influence over him: "I shall say nothing to you of the horror you must have of evil books, and your avoidance of those that are merely futile . . . The first must be burned, the second put from you. A prince will be no less a man of spirit for being ignorant of the sophistries of modern philosophers, when he is familiar with the other sources in history, belles lettres and true philosophy that can adorn him."[9] His duty is plain. His whole life long he will hear that voice: "You must read no book condemned by the Church without permission from the bishop of your diocese, and such permission will be granted only when necessary to you."*

So all Louis XVI has to do is leaf through these pages reeking of brimstone. It's already on his conscience that he sponsored the *Account Rendered.* A Protestant should never be allowed to write in France, not even numbers . . . After this, Vergennes and Maurepas only need to bring him a few subsidiary contributions such as the (alleged) *Letter from M. le Marquis de*

---

*Abbé Soldini was not a fanatic. He goes on at length, exhorting his pupil to reject "whatever is done in the defense of the Church but is lacking in the charity that must always go hand in hand with the truth."

Caraccioli to M. d'Alembert, [10] in which the Abbé Raynal is conveniently called the *"timbalier** of the Necker party." They point out to him that "however strict the orders sent out to every frontier post in the kingdom not to allow the new edition of the *Histoire des Deux Indes* to enter, some secret means has been found of bringing in a great many copies" and that "calumny has not hesitated to call into question the integrity of a minister who has encouraged this offense."

Just follow their gaze, Majesty . . . Louis XVI is already prone enough to imagine conspiracies against our holy religion and hence against his authority; say no more. Suddenly, beginning on May 18, the king is positively overflowing with good humor as the tide of consternation starts to rise around him. He is so grateful to Maurepas for sparing him the formalities of direct action. It has all taken place without sound and fury, much better than for Turgot.

But Vergennes is the big winner. He knew when to keep still and when to strike out. He'll be in the best seat for the post-Maurepas period, when Louis XVI will be looking for a principal minister of dyed-in-the-wool Roman Catholicism.

GRIMM

57

MAY 1781

You Have Got Gangrene

On May 25 Diderot blows up. "I hear the abbé's condemnation [Raynal's] cried up beneath my window.† I read it. I have read it. May the ignominy and curses that once rained down upon the Athenians who made Socrates drink hemlock fall now upon the heads of those infamous persons [the members of the Parliament] and the old imbecile they have served [Maurepas]." [1]

He feverishly scratches these few lines as a postscript to a letter written two months before and never sent. It's been lying around in his drawer because he couldn't make up his mind to humiliate the person to whom it is

*The *timbalier* rode in front of the dignitaries in an official procession, beating on a kettle-drum.

†On the Rue Taranne in Paris, where he has holed up like a weary old bear. He's fed up with Sèvres and no longer goes to see anyone in the country.

addressed. Now he can. It will put an end to his relationship with an old friend who has done him many a favor. Well, too bad. Or so much the better. He sends it, to Grimm. It's the final break—and not only with Grimm. That day Diderot quarrels with Diderot. The postscript goes on: "My friend, when one is incapable of a heroic action, one blames it; and one blames it for no reason other than that one is incapable of it."

They were bickering at the end of March, when Grimm was chasing Diderot from salon to salon trying to make him abjure his faith—at a friend's house, at his daughter's, at the home of the "inoculator-physician" Pierre Brasdor. An extension-cord quarrel. Grimm was one of the best-informed men in the part of Europe that read its news in his *Correspondance littéraire*. He got wind of Necker's fall and Raynal's condemnation ahead of time, and deplored them ahead of time, as he had deplored so many other things in the past thirty years between two pirouettes, before flitting off to console himself with a couple of dozen oysters. Since nobody can ever do anything about anything anyway, he thinks, the only thing that matters is to get your own irons out of the fire. So he imagines he's doing Diderot a favor by giving him early warning of the approaching storm. But if danger threatens, he personally means to be in the clear. Denis should stop running around with Raynal. He should loudly disclaim any part in the passages of the new edition that are creating all the scandal and that are—rightly—being attributed to him. Grimm puts him in the same predicament as he did Raynal:
"Either you believe that those you attack will not be able to take revenge upon you, in which case it is cowardly to attack them; or you believe that they can and will take revenge upon you—in which case it is madness to leave yourself open to their hostility . . ."
The eternal dilemma of the scribe, ever since he began coexisting with the high priest and the pharaoh. It's either silence (or writing as though one had nothing to say, simply covering paper)—silence, or cowardice, or madness. The well-meant words of advice stick in Diderot's throat.
"I understand you perfectly, and you have very unjustly and pointlessly hurt me very badly . . . You advise me to keep silent on the subject of Abbé Raynal? But is it really your design that I should follow your advice? If so, take care to speak of him more civilly than you did in my daughter's home. Is it not enough that the Visigoths have banned him; must he be attacked by his friends as well? There are so many impertinent parrots in society who talk, talk, talk without knowing what they say . . ."
His temper begins to rise: "The consequence of your wretched and insipid dilemma is to extinguish the race of famous men [ranging from Demosthenes to Voltaire, whom he mentions after Juvenal, Socrates, Aristotle, Montesquieu, and even Rousseau]; it is to create contempt for those

of our fellow citizens whose enemies have from time immemorial dwelled in the temples, palaces, and courts, the three lairs from which all the scourges of society have emerged. Oh, what a useful and commodious doctrine for oppressors!"

Must one then keep still and half live? In that case, all those "among the ancients and moderns who cared more to serve the world and their homeland than to spend tranquil and obscure days by their firesides, and thus neglected fortune, life, liberty, and even honor, were in your view fools—if they were unaware of the peril to which they exposed themselves; cowards—if they imagined there to be no peril; or madmen, when they have intrepidly awaited their glorious and fatal destiny?"

This is Denis white-faced and fuming, in one of those rages into which he worked himself two or three times a year at Sophie Volland's or the d'Holbachs'. A hailstorm on the plateau of Langres. Even the footmen fled. On those days this man, ordinarily so mild and droll, would hurl the dinner plates at the first face he saw. His big peasant's features are transfigured, his eyes start from his head, his hands tremble. He almost forgets about Raynal. This is his own quarrel. He speaks as one accused of the crime pedants hold most heinous of all: human warmth.

"Well, Raynal is a historian such as the world has never known before, and so much the better for him and so much the worse for History. If History had, from the outset, seized all civil and religious tyrants and dragged them through the streets by the hair, I do not know that they would have been the better for it, but they would have been more despised, and perhaps their unfortunate subjects would have become less patient . . . The book that I love, and that all kings and courtiers hate, is the book that gives birth to a Brutus . . . For my part, I shall but revere an author the more for having unreservedly abandoned himself to the violent motions of his heart . . .

". . . I am in no way displeased that the historian of the discovery of a new world, when coming to speak of an unprecedented phenomenon, should adopt a tone which is entirely his own. At least he will not be counted among the servile flock of imitators."

Coward? Madman? The two terms of Grimm's equation go straight to the nerve. Since the day he first put pen to paper he's been weaving back and forth between those two insults. Rousseau called him a coward twenty years ago. Today Grimm's telling him he's crazy. But, "how have we ever emerged from Barbary? The reason, happily, is that there have been men who have loved truth more than they feared persecution. Surely these men were not cowards. Shall we call them mad? You no longer know, my friend, how men of genius, men of courage, men of virtue, contemptuous of these great idols before which so many cowards are proud to fall upon their faces, you have forgotten how they wrote their books. Although I am not of their number I know, and I am going to tell you. The intention of pleasing or offending never entered their minds. They did not run after praise. They did not dread persecution. They wished to be useful. They wished to tell the truth."

He gives Grimm dilemma for dilemma:

> The people say, "Live first, philosophize afterwards."*
> But he who has donned the cloak of Socrates and loves truth and virtue more than life, he will say:
> "Philosophize first, and live afterwards . . . If you can." I seem to hear you laughing?

. . . The laughter of Frédéric Melchior, Baron Grimm, supreme pimp of men of letters, the despots' recruiting sergeant, the columnist of dowager duchesses. The man who tells all without ever saying a thing. Half a century of gossip, whispered by his painted mouth to the rhythm of his trotting scarlet heels. The one who'd be happier if Mozart had less talent. The friend who did Diderot so much harm by trying to do him good. The trip to Russia, that was Grimm:

"Ah, my friend, I see it, your soul has shriveled at Petersburg and Potsdam, in the Œil-de-Boeuf and the antechambers of the Great.† You tell me you have won the confidence of the Empress of Russia, that the King of Prussia deigned to speak to you, and that you can approach Vergennes if you [desire]** anything . . ."

It's getting-a-load-off-your-chest time between friends, and a cruel load it is. But the worst or best of friends is never the person one supposes. "Ah, friends! Friends! One there is, you may count with certainty upon him alone: the one whose benevolence and perfidy you have so long and so often experienced; who has done you so many good turns and so many bad, given you so much good advice and so much bad; who has filled your ears with so much flattery and told you so many unlovely truths, and whom you spend all your days praising and damning. You may outlive all the rest, but he will not abandon you until death: he is yourself; try to be your own best friend."[2] Has he followed his own advice? At the last minute Diderot recoils, when he sees his own image as he was eight years ago. Who is he berating now, Grimm or himself?

---

*"Philosophize" in the widest sense of the word, of course: love wisdom, seek out the why of things, then speak it.

†Potsdam: the Versailles of Frederick II; the Œil-de-Boeuf: the main antechamber at Versailles, which had "bull's-eye" windows.

**The word is illegible in the manuscript and has been established by deduction.

You caused me to feel great pity when you said to me, in Petersburg:

"Are you aware that although you may see the Empress every afternoon, I see her every evening?" . . .

My friend, I do not know you anymore. You have become, without suspecting it perhaps, one of the most secretive and yet one of the most dangerous of anti-*philosophes*. You live among us but you hate us . . .

My friend, be the favorite of the Great; serve them, I consent to it, although your talent and your years might be more worthily employed. But be their apologist neither in words, nor in mind, nor at heart—or else . . . fall into the cauldron in which all protectors and the whole accursed race of their protégés will burn for evermore.

My friend, you have got gangrene. Perhaps it has not yet progressed far enough to be incurable . . . It is not what I am brave enough to tell you, but what you will tell yourself that will make you well again.

We've strayed a long way from the Raynal pretext here, now we're getting to the heart of the matter, the knot of this dispute for three voices, the three voices of the century: Diderot, Voltaire, and that third who really cannot be omitted:

"I should never have become your friend if you had spoken at Jean-Jacques's, where I first met you, as you spoke yesterday in the house of the inoculator Brasdor . . ."

Jean-Jacques, standing with folded arms in a corner of Diderot's life ever since their quarrel in 1758, like the statue of the Commander. He only pretended to die three years ago, you know, so that he could come and stick pins into Denis every night: "I remained pure . . . You compromised." Easy to talk. Diderot swears he lied; but what a pedestal for posterity! And now their argument, previously known only to the initiated, is about to become public property. Rousseau's *Confessions* will be published by Moultou in Geneva within the year; perhaps no book has ever been so ardently awaited. "I have formed a project for which there is no precedent, and it will have no imitator. I want to show my fellow men a man, in the full truth of nature; and this man will be myself."* Excellent opportunity to show them a certain number of other men too, while he's at it—as seen by "this man," or in other words none too charitably. Denis Diderot, in the front row of the exhibit, knows about the passages in which Rousseau drags him through the mud: " 'And you too, Diderot!' I cried out to myself. Unworthy friend! . . ."³ "I had as yet"—when he began writing the *Confessions,* in the course of which his paranoia grew much worse—"no suspicion of the great conspiracy of Diderot and Grimm, otherwise I should easily have seen how enormously the former was abusing my confidence by giving what I wrote that harsh tone and bleak aspect it ceased

*Opening paragraph of the *Confessions.*

to have when he was no longer guiding my hand."[4] What Rousseau is saying is that Denis egged him on to defy the authorities and then left him holding the bag. Inevitably this is going to prompt a second glance at the Diderot-Raynal team. Has Diderot been up to his old tricks again? The trial will start, in any event, and it looks as though the hearings will drag on for centuries, before a gallery of millions of wide-eyed readers lapping up the expert testimony of their beloved professors: Diderot's fault, Rousseau's fault . . . The latter has managed to grab the tiller and he isn't about to let go. He is the plaintiff: "I loved Diderot tenderly, I loved him sincerely . . . But, exasperated by the tireless obstinacy with which he was forever contradicting me, in my tastes, my inclinations, my way of life, in everything that concerned only myself; rebelling to see a man younger than myself* so fiercely determined to govern me like a child . . . my heart was already filled with his repeated wrongs"[5]; but it took him years, he says, to grasp the full extent of the villainous plot woven against him by "the Holbachic coterie," which was at the root of all his woes. "Having withdrawn into solitude, I had no letters bringing news and no account of the world's affairs, I was informed of nothing and curious about nothing, living four leagues from Paris and as far removed from that capital by my indifference as though I had been on the island of Tinian,† with the oceans between us.

"Grimm, Diderot, and d'Holbach, meanwhile, were in the eye of the storm, spreading themselves about in the highest society and between them sharing out almost every sphere of it. The powerful, the clever, men of letters, men of law, women; they could unite and make themselves heard by all. One cannot fail to see how advantageous this position is to three men totally allied against a fourth, when he is in the circumstances that I was."[6]

"The Holbachic coterie" . . . the substance of the quarrel lies in those three words. Rousseau hadn't been able to stomach the atmosphere in the gentle Baron d'Holbach's home, the Château de Sucy-sur-Marne, a hidden paradise for men who had rejected the notion of God. A world of smiles and freedom where the wine was good and the women gay. Madame d'Aine's** laughter rained down on his shoulders and gave him chills as it went rippling through the halls. He had no taste for the schoolboy pranks of these big babies of forty and these beautiful full-blown women who used to frolic from bedroom to bedroom at the witching hour, without much attention to their language or attire. Rousseau's tight-lipped side made him a wallflower at this party. And their behavior jarred his nerves. How can it be possible to laugh so lightheartedly when you don't believe in anything?

*Rousseau was born in 1712, Diderot in 1713.

†In the Marianas archipelago; Rousseau had just read Captain Cook's voyages.

**Holbach's mother-in-law; he married her two daughters one after the other.

Their very existence was a persecution to him. He was preparing to dish
them out a vengeance as icy as his death.

Never mind; Diderot will answer back. He's not the type to faint away on
the witness stand: "Two hundred years ago Jean-Jacques would have been the
leader of a sect; or at any rate a demagogue in his country. Living in the
solitude of the forest was his undoing; the woods cannot improve the kind of
character he took to them."[7] These two certainly don't go about it daintily—
it's the karate-chop and the lumberjack's knee! And in order to have a sort of
"counter-*Confessions*" to leave when his turn comes, Denis has just started
reworking his *Essay on the Reigns of Claudius and Nero,* a "journey through time
and space, shuttling between Rome and Paris, the century of Nero and that
of Louis XV, a summons to the dead and a conversation with the reader,"[8]
in which he gives back blow for blow: "Rousseau is no more. Although for
many years he accepted every charitable service and every assistance friendship could render from most of us, and although, after acknowledging and
confessing my innocence, he insulted me perfidiously and in a cowardly manner, I have neither persecuted nor hated him. I respected the writer but I did
not respect the man, and contempt is a cold emotion, one that is not conducive
to violent actions."[9]

Having said that, he moves on to other matters. Diderot may have a
temper, but he's not one to flog a dead horse. His whole heart pardons the
kidney punches he has just delivered. Rousseau asked for it, so he got it; but
now it's Diderot's turn to go asking for it from a different clique: the men of
this age of Maurepas which is already beginning to be known as "the century
of Louis XVI," the men he's already worked over once in the *Histoire des Deux
Indes,* except that now he can't abide the mask of Raynal anymore, the anonymity; he doesn't want to deserve Rousseau's accusation. As soon as he finishes
the *Histoire des Deux Indes* he goes back to his essay, revising the whole massive
text and lengthening its title: *Essai sur les règnes de Claude et de Néron et sur les
mœurs et les écrits de Sénèque, pour servir d'introduction à la lecture de ce philosophe*
[Essay on the reigns of Claudius and Nero and on the manners and writings
of Seneca, to serve as an introduction to the study of that philosopher]. On
the literature of the past he builds a hymn to the future and a critical analysis
of the present. "Using the Latin philosopher as a pretext, he wrote magnificent
pages to the glory of philosophy; and everyone will recognize, in his portrayal
of the reigns of Claudius and Nero,* many of the brushstrokes that had painted

---

*Claudius: fourth Roman emperor, nephew of Tiberius and uncle of Caligula; succeeded the
latter after his assassination, reigned from A.D. 41 to A.D. 54. He had Messalina killed and married
Agrippina, and she imposed her son Nero, who thus became the fifth Roman emperor, as adopted
successor. Nero thanked her by having her killed five years later. He committed suicide before
being arrested in A.D. 66. Seneca (A.D. 3–A.D. 65) was Nero's tutor and played a role of some

the reign of Louis XV in such ghastly hues. The return to pagan philosophy and the idealization of the philosophers of Antiquity were universally seen as marking the triumph of the new thought, and as the ultimate rejection of the Judeo-Christian past."[10] It was also necessary to defend the honor of the "Holbachic coterie" in this work, which was virtually a team product: d'Holbach, Naigeon, and La Grange translated Seneca for Diderot so that he could show history repeating itself through his empathy with a brother seventeen centuries away. Because even back in A.D. 50 there must have been Rousseaus accusing Seneca of profiteering and compromise before Nero had him put to death. What was he supposed to do, retreat into purity? Didn't he forestall many dreadful things by taking action and making appearances at court as long as he still had some influence over the tyrant? Did he die any the less a hero because of it? Cowardice, madness, here we are again—as though there were any way of escaping them!

Except that when it came time for Seneca to take a razor to his veins, he found himself alone. And Diderot, in this surge of bravura, is naïvely tempted to identify with him.

"Ah, friends, friends" . . . Not only is Grimm trying to part him from Abbé Raynal and get him to forswear his own writings, but Naigeon,* the mainstay of their fraternity, now advises him not to publish his new version of the *Essay.*† That means Naigeon has to go too: "If you only knew how frivolous all things become when one is sixty-eight!"—in his fury he adds two years to his age—". . . and can hardly promise oneself more than another few years before handing oneself back to the elements, to dust . . . I will be insulted. But insults are not stones. Nothing hurts me. You have taught me only one thing, which is that it is virtually pointless to consult anyone . . . In all likelihood Grimm will judge as unfavorably as you, but however hard you beat a broken horse you cannot make him gallop . . ."[11]

. . . That revolting Grimm who, not content with trying to get him away from Raynal, is also endeavoring, through Meister, his second-in-command on the *Correspondance littéraire,* to stir up a quarrel between the Neckers, Abbé Raynal, and Diderot: "Nobody was more pained than Madame Necker by the indiscretion and, one may say, folly with which Abbé Raynal has just so

---

importance as a moderate and beneficent counselor during the first years of the reign, until his exasperated pupil sentenced him to death.

*Like Boulanger, Jacques-André Naigeon (1738–1810) is one of the little-known but important contributors to the *Encyclopédie;* he wrote many articles for it, chiefly on philosophy. "His anticlericalism had become a tic," said Diderot.

†Diderot could only see this as a coward's exhortation to prudence. But Naigeon may have thought—not without reason—that the *Essay* was still a shapeless clutter and could hardly add to Diderot's literary glory, however much it does him honor in other respects.

gratuitously jeopardized the happiness and repose of her old age [says Mei-
ster] . . ."[12] That is untrue.

It feels like the morning of Good Friday. The cocks are crowing. A great
lassitude has come over this old man who hates to fight, and especially to fight
alone. That's why his letter to Grimm has been left in his drawer "to be called
for"—until May 25. Seneca-Diderot has already said "What's the use?" so
many times . . .

But "I hear the abbé's condemnation cried up beneath my window"
. . . So I send the letter. "One must preach what is right and praiseworthy to
others, whether or not one is capable of it oneself."[13] "The philosopher shows
men their inalienable rights. He tempers religious fanaticism. He tells the
people that they are the strongest, and that if they are sent to the slaughter-
house it is because they have let themselves be led there. He prepares the
aftermath of revolutions, which always occur at the extremity of misfortune;
the aftermath that will make amends for the bloodshed."[14]

Now, after boxing the ears of all his false brothers, to which terrorist is
Diderot addressing this load of dynamite?

To Catherine II. The big carcass is straightening up again.

58

JUNE 1781

His Blood Is Still Warring with Him

On the banks of the Loire a broken young woman sits listening for the drop
of a pin in the north: Sophie de Monnier, hearkening for Gabriel-Honoré de
Mirabeau. He has just been "dedungeoned," as his father puts it; that is, let
out of Vincennes on a sort of parole; he is thirty-two. She is twenty-seven, and
in "partial confinement" at the convent of the Poor Clares at Gien. This will
be round two in a great love affair. Will it be a new surge of passion? Will
it be disenchantment? The late May springtime warms the gentle roads of
Sologne and the Gâtinais, intersected by the false frontier of the river; a season
passes in a small rustle of turning pages. Will this, at last, be something that
might resemble happiness? It's a month short of four years since he turned his
bleeding face to her and said, "I certainly have made you suffer." She was
pregnant. Now Gabriel-Sophie is dead. Victor too. Is their whole history
going to be written on children's tombstones?

The mail coach for Paris leaves Gien three times a week and returns three times. At every departure it carries a letter from her to Gabriel, but it does not always bring one back: answers come often, but not regularly. Even so, she has just calculated that they have exchanged 360 letters within the past year,* thanks to those fraternities of go-betweens they seem to have the knack of forming around them: turnkeys, wardens, and postmen on his side; a gardener, tavernkeeper, doctor, and notary on hers.[1] No question of corresponding directly. They have been firmly pinned down in a condition of prolonged infancy, and address their coded missives to postboxes. Gabriel's letters have grown rarer since he left Vincennes. A bad sign. She shows that she minds, with conjugal awkwardness: "I confess that I am madly weary of beginning all my letters with complaints of your silence."[2] But she doesn't despair because he has promised to make a break for Gien as soon as he sees the slightest chance of bringing it off. Therefore he still loves me, since he is prepared to risk, for my sake, a fresh crime of lèse-majesté, and above all of lèse-paternité, just when his fate is being officially restored to his butcher of a father. Sophie is brave enough to do anything except try to talk him out of coming. She's been living on the scheme for six months. Gabriel is already within reach, either at the Duponts' or at Bignon. All he needs to do is say he's going to Versailles and turn south instead: "I have inquired about the *turgotines*†; they pass through Briare on the way to Lyons. So you will be able to leave it there."[3] No; on second thought better avoid Briare where he might be recognized crossing the Loing: "Here is the way from Montargis to this place. From Montargis to La Commodité, two leagues. From La Commodité to Nogent-sur-Vernisson, two leagues. From Nogent to La Bussière, two leagues, and there is a detour from La Bussière to Gien that you can take without passing through Briare. The post supplies horses (there are about three leagues to cover). Almost everyone prefers it. I don't know whether there are post chaises, I presume not, but the road can be ridden at a gallop."[4]

And once he gets to Gien? She'll take care of that, provided it's after dark. He's to wait at the inn called the Madeleine, and for heaven's sake not at the other one, the Cage, where he would be denounced. Then he'll come for a stroll in the Chèvenières** along about midnight, and the kind Doctor Ysabeau will take his arm and lead him beneath my window in the convent wall. "As it is in the possibles [*sic*] that Ysabeau will be absent from Gien when you arrive, you should then ask for Lafleur [the tavernkeeper of the Madeleine], the process would be the same, but since it might also be too late for him to

---

*From June 18, 1779, to June 16, 1780.

†New rapid stagecoaches which Turgot put into service in 1775 on a few main routes, in this instance Paris–Lyons.

**Corruption of *Chènevières* [hemp fields]. Hemp used to be cultivated there; today it's the Rue Paul-Bert.

send word to me, then, as you are walking with him in the Chèvenières, you would call out 'Gabriel' aloud . . . I come to the window, then I drop the shutter and come down,''⁵ to open the door with a key stolen from the abbess, two previously manufactured keys having broken off in the lock.

Here is the very stuff of over-the-garden-fence conversation. Livening up small towns seems to be Sophie's mission in life—first Pontarlier, now Gien. There will even be the irreligious servant-nun accomplice in the person of the convent's extern sister Victoire, who isn't likely to denounce the lovers since she borrows Sophie's room when she wants to confess herself at length to the reverend father almoner, the Franciscan Père Maillet. Sophie has even promised this hulk of a priest that Mirabeau would recommend him to the court for a preacher's pulpit, nothing could be easier, because Gabriel is on the best of terms with the Princesse de Lamballe, why yes, didn't you know? This is the underground railway of confessionals, along which you advance as best you can from a roll-in-the-hay Victoire at the convent of the Poor Clares to the Superintendent of the Queen's Household. We can count on the almoner. The layout of the convent, an assortment of buildings scattered about the gardens, will make things even easier. "The house [Sophie's] is composed of one large pavilion, part of which overlooks the Chèvenières walk and the other part one of the gardens, and in addition to that there are a quantity of small buildings attached to all the corners. Our gardens are large. We go from one to the other.''⁶ One drawback: "My antechamber is so close to the place which everyone has a reason for visiting at any time that everything can be heard from it." They'll have to make love quietly. During the day that inconveniently large head can be hidden in an enormous clothes cupboard or rather closet, newly lined by an understanding carpenter. "Your apartment is finished and very comfortable. Everything has been made ready for you. Oh, how I wait for you!''⁷ And he won't starve to death, either: "Ysabeau will send me a cooked ham during the week, without anyone here being the wiser . . . Oh, dear husband, come quickly!''⁸

He's coming, but not to give her joy. She ought to have been on her guard. Those silences, those blank spots in his news . . . That long mid-April chat in the parlor with Dupont, more beaming and constipated than ever; it turns out he knows all about the scheme too, and promises to help . . . Monsieur Samuel Dupont, de Nemours, working for love? Oh, come now! And yet Sophie has had every opportunity to observe, letter by letter, the slow disintegration of Gabriel's morale, and even of his mind, at this man's hands. Last year it looked as though she had faced facts; she even signed a feeble letter to her doddering old husband back in his forests, begging him to have mercy on her and offering, for form's sake, to return to the conjugal fold, which she knew he no longer wanted. That was done to pacify the Ruffeys and show willingness before the property was divided up. But hope springs eternal

. . . In her, it positively pole-vaults. The instant Gabriel is outside the four walls of his cell, it starts bounding all over the place: "Brussels is not dead, although now, having no more child, I should be alone in the world there"[9]; she goes back to her old plan of fleeing to Belgium to await her lover before they move on to London together as soon as he can join her. That's what he's coming to talk to her about, it must be; but would she swear to it, on his oversized head?

Sophie: one of those soft, gentle women who are forever being trampled on by everybody, parents, brothers, friends, husband, police, and potentates, almost as a matter of course. She is waiting for the only man in the world who has never been nasty to her, the one who makes everything different. "You'll call out *Gabriel!*"

Alas. Brussels is dead.

From M. de Rougemont, governor of the prison of Vincennes, to M. Amelot, minister of the King's Household, on December 13, 1780:

> Monseigneur,
> I have the honor to report that, in pursuance of the King's order of this day, which has just come to my hand, I have forthwith released M. le Comte de Mirabeau *fils,* detained in the tower by order. There is no further news.
> I have the honor to remain, etc.[10]

Five years ago to the day, Sophie gave herself to him in "the Trollop's" bedroom in Pontarlier. "December 13. I was happy." She did not fail to notice, and celebrate, the coincidence: "December 13 will always be a memorable day for us, for that is the day we became husband and wife; it is also the day you were set free!"[11] Does it even cross his mind? For the first time ever, if his father's stool pigeons' reports can be trusted, the Marquis de Mirabeau has reason to be pleased with his son. On December 15 the Friend of Man is writing to his brother the bailli: "I account your nephew dedungeoned as from Tuesday or Wednesday, and although he is parked in the château [de Vincennes] in hands that will allow him so much and no more margin than they please, I shall be notified of everything . . . His letters to his sister now show some coherence of proper sentiments, and just and grateful thought."[12] He's finally got something to crow about: in the evening of December 13 Mirabeau writes Caroline du Saillant, the "robust laying hen"* and regent of Bignon, the few pitiful lines of the cowering hound:

> Dear friend, let your good heart leap for joy! I have embraced your husband, I clasped him in my arms, I felt myself caught in his. My irons have been struck

*An expression coined by her father.

off, and I am already enjoying the greatest comfort, I who scarcely dare beg for commiseration and indulgence.

I have kissed, read and copied out the instructions of my good father. I am going to thank him for them on my knees. I have added postscripts to all the enclosed giving the address of M. Honoré.* I have read them all to my brother and to Dupont. They approved them, and even with very marked satisfaction.[13]

The same pen that wrote the *Essai sur le despotisme* and *Des Lettres de cachet.* They've got him.

The day of his release he can't even stand up. Emotion, exhaustion, playacting? With him, it's always a bit of all three. In any event, Dupont has to give him an arm to lean on, and his brother-in-law himself, Caroline's fat husband, is impressed. "Du Saillant, who brought his brother-in-law out, is highly pleased with him in every respect, and he is a man who seldom enthuses," chortles the marquis. "He was expecting to find histrionics and pathos, and he found a deeply affected man, very penitent, very submissive, and above all converted, with his usual excess, to his father and family; at the same time, cheeky and sharp about everything else. Since he has the police at his beck and call, although he is not supposed to leave Vincennes, he was taken to Paris to get some clothes, for he was naked as a worm . . . He has grown considerably taller and stouter, and pretends that when I see this physical revolution it will give me some faith in the moral one. Yet his blood is still warring with him, for on the day of his release he drowned his bed in a hemorrhage from the nose . . . Well, du Saillant keeps telling me that Dupont must have hammered him devilish hard. Although I am quite prepared to believe in the efficacy of this treatment, I have even more faith in the force of locks and turnkeys."[14]

Naked as a worm between two hemorrhages, that of his incarceration and that of his emancipation: this is the man who was longing to shed his blood in America . . . And morally naked as well, defenseless, vulnerable as a newborn babe of thirty ejected from the womb of a prison designed to pummel him into a replica of the monster who put him in it. "On his father's part, his freedom was subject to three conditions: the first, that until further notice he should bear no other name than M. Honoré; the second, that he should make use of the cordial terms on which he had remained with his mother to end, without more scandal, the lawsuit pending between his parents since 1762; the third, that he should make approaches to his wife with a view to resuming their life together."[15] He could turn this into a supreme stroke of cunning, advancing behind lowered visor the better to skewer them with the weapon of his choice. That's what Sophie is counting on, and it's true that he thought of it

*The following day he explains to a friend: "I notify you that my name, and my only name, is M. Honoré."

himself about halfway through his term in prison. But the people he has to deal with are no choirboys. They don't open the cage door until the wings are well and truly clipped. For a while he's unable to fly at all; he can only take a few short hops, carefully calculated by his keepers. Such as this bolt from Montargis to Gien, which will be doing them a favor as much as himself: if you're going to liquidate Sophie de Monnier, you may as well hire a qualified killer for the job.

SOPHIE

59

JUNE 1781

I Shall Kill Myself . . . If I Am Pregnant

Six months of little hops—the physiotherapy of freedom—from the tower of Vincennes to its château, where he stays with Fontelliau the surgeon; then from Vincennes to Paris, where he stays with Le Noir's assistant Boucher, the "clerk of the secret" whom Sophie and he also call their "good angel"—in the letters submitted to him; then from Paris to Bois-des-Fossés, Dupont's home near Nemours, a quick flutter from Bignon where his father will not receive him or restore his identity until his period of probation is over.

To keep you up to date,* you must hear about the further adventures of Honoré. The scamp is winning his spurs, albeit somewhat tardily, and I believe he will yet end as a man. Those who see him say he has lost his spirit, but I asked Dupont, who has just called, and had gone back to the country after escorting him out of the tower, whether, in the month since he saw him last, he has grown more empty-headed, or seemed that way. He told me that, on the contrary, he found the head infinitely sounder than on his best days in prison. He reports twice a day, and has grown modest in his letters, but dark modest [*sic*], for he is seeing the world for the first time, and from underneath, and he is seeing some rum things . . . Today I have let him loose at Versailles, because of the Duc d'Ayen who has his quarter, and there, if he will heed me, he'll see ministers and all. Still the same object; humble profession of faith . . . When asked where he is living, where he is to be seen, he replies that a wretch who has been banished from his father's

*From father to uncle again, in their perpetual squawking owlery, on January 12, 1781. The aim was to get "Honoré" to take action against his mother through the Duc d'Ayen, La Fayette's father-in-law and chief of the Noailles clan, who was first gentleman of the chamber "by quarter," meaning that for three months he was the closest mouth to the king's ear.

household, and most deservedly so, has no dwelling place and must not appear save on obligatory occasions. This method is necessary for the finances,* and in order to avoid communication and frivolity, but it seems all the more so today, as it is the lads of eighteen who are running everything.[1]

One would hardly have guessed it, with Maurepas still at the wheel.

The Friend of Man beams more broadly with every passing month. In February:

> Honoré is still on the same path, and I do not spare him; in truth, he is docile and confiding, and never speaks of his father but great tears spring to his eyes. For the rest, I understand from the combined recitals of those who are seeing him for the first time or after a long interval that he no longer is the man we knew. He is now fully developed, contains himself, and is even imposing, despite that extreme vivacity which he has nevertheless mastered. He has made good use of his time in prison, having learned Greek, English, and Italian, devoted much study to the Ancients and especially Tacitus, whom he is translating. His mind, which was ever penetrating, has now become discerning, and has that gift of familiarity which lets him move the great about like sticks of wood; so that if only his head sat straight on his shoulders, which is the thing we are working at, but which he will find more difficult or at least a longer process of study than he supposes, he would soon be to the fore. Yet with that facility, that chameleon nature that takes coloration from everything that approaches it, you can sense what a conundrum it is for a father, whom he appears to accept as his absolute master, and consults twice a day . . . ,[2]

In writing, of course, since the father has still not deigned to see him. This may account to some extent for the fact that Gabriel hasn't always had time to write to Sophie, but he probably wasn't feeling too proud of himself, either. His relative silence enables him to hide the succession of little day-to-day weaknesses in which he is surreptitiously floundering as in the dormitory vices of some reform school. At this stage his only possible form of revenge consists of a few women caressed at last in the halls of the Château de Vincennes; Boucher's young and pretty wife, unceremoniously seduced by way of thanks for the couple's hospitality; favors extorted from soubrettes at Versailles and instantly transformed by his private mythomania into conquests of princesses; and last but not least, the sickening labyrinth of his flirtation with Julie Dauvers.

"I shall fuck no more, save for money" . . . It looks as though he's started taking his own hogwash seriously, and is spending his last months in captivity attempting to put into practice the precepts he expounded in *Ma Conversion.* Find a woman, any woman, and get paid. "Naked as a worm" . . . "M. Honoré" . . . Famished for life, and without a cent to his name. He knew that's

*That is, to keep him without money of his own.

how it would be once he was "liberated." Maybe if Sophie had some money . . . But she lives from hand to mouth on the interest from her dowry. So Mirabeau, in his cell, embarks on a crash correspondence course in gigolology. He's made friends with one of his companions in hell, Baudouin de Quémadeuc, who was incarcerated on the order of the Keeper of the Seals "for having purloined, after dinner in his home, place settings of gold and silver."* Like all prisoners, Baudouin boasts of his mistress Julie Dauvers, the daughter of a dentist employed by the Comte d'Artois, a lower-middle-class girl past the marrying age. Mirabeau gets hold of her address and begins an epistolary intrigue in which he can deploy all his considerable talents for duplicity. By the third letter (October 25, 1780) she is already "my worthy friend, my amiable friend, my most fair friend." By the fourth, "a magician, an enchantress, a siren, a divine friend."[3] On October 29 she becomes a "too noble and too tender woman" and on November 1, "the first after Sophie, the friend of my heart,"[4] but their positions are soon reversed because he's quickly swearing that he has told Sophie† how he has "found another soul worthy of yours, and henceforth your sex for me will be composed of two individuals." Licking his lips, he makes plans for an ideal orgy with Sophie and Julie to celebrate the prisoner's release; on November 30 she becomes "my darling Liriette, you whom I love like a second Sophie."[5] If she wants proof, before Christmas he is calling her "my Fanfan," like the other one. Poverty of vocabulary has ever been Don Juan's greatest failing. "No, I do not look upon you as one of my truest friends; I dare to regard you as my sole friend. Sophie is half of myself; that is different."[6] Does he imagine he made that up?

Julie Dauvers** seems to have had misgivings almost from the start. She keeps hanging back, although the amplitude of his inflationary imagination has impressed her. Mme de Lamballe is now back on the agenda, and he uses her as bait for the poor girl to whom he "confessed" what "he had not even revealed to Sophie" regarding his relations with that august person, and promises, the moment he is back at Versailles or Rambouillet and on intimate terms with the princess again, to get her a place at court: that old come-on, the carrot of Paris. But he tips his hand too soon by suggesting to Julie in June that he might stay "in her good papa's house" when they ease up on his restrictions. Their first—and last—interviews, at the beginning of 1781, are definitely not up to their letters. He finds her unaccommodating, she thinks him a nuisance. There is no ques-

---

*At least that was the official motive for his arrest, under a *lettre de cachet.* Baudouin denies it, and he was never brought to trial.

†This is unlikely. The sentence is found only in a letter to Julie, not to Sophie.

**Whose replies have been lost.

tion of giving him a place to stay, "for lack of space." However, Dauvers senior does make him a short-term loan of twenty-five louis,* just in case that place at Court might be for real . . . After all, Mirabeau really is going to Versailles now and then, this spring. But the most positive result of his trips there is to refurbish his repertoire of fairy tales.

To earn his pittance he actually does go to war in the Versailles antechambers, albeit halfheartedly—war against his mother and war against his sister, all the old alliances broken. But the credibility gap of this fresh convert to his persecutor's case is far too great. All he gets from the old minister Maurepas, decidedly in a lousy mood during this gestation period of his revenge upon Necker, is a bawling-out.

"There, on my desk, lie sixty letters or orders for the Mirabeau family! I would need a special secretary of state to deal with them. If all the people in Paris who lived on intrigue were driven out of the town, grass would grow between the paving stones. Your father takes me for his business agent. Is is not shameful that we still see no end to the scandals of this family?"[7] Gabriel can spy, ostentatiously displayed in the "Mirabeau file," a copy of the vicious *Mémoire* he published in Holland to demolish his father; and here he is trying to blame everything on his mother.† Maurepas is a spiteful man, but not cruel, and he's shocked by the medieval ruthlessness of the marquis's dealings with his family. "He sent word to advise me," admits the Friend of Man, "not to burden myself by laboring so hard over people who were ungovernable and had come of age, and to give up trying to carry out ideals of good domestic order similar to those I proposed for good social order.** I replied that I begged him to understand once and for all that, having openly done everything needful to prove that I have no connivance in the turpitude of my family, I will see without regret the mother on the boards and the son in the ranks of the unemployed, and will nonetheless walk with my head high and my chest bared."[8] Not, perhaps, the most tactful letter of introduction to accompany this son he is sending along as his last-chance lawyer.

Too late. Opinion has veered around to the marquise, still under house arrest with the nuns of the convent of St. Michel in Paris, and to her daughter, shut up at the Ursulines' of Sisteron. A couple of madwomen, maybe; but their treatment has been so arbitrary that it begins to look a shade obvious. Defending them means striking a blow against *lettres de cachet* issued on private grounds, and the wind from America is wafting through the Parliament, too, where the Grand Chamber finally has to decide, in the appeal against the

---

*2,500 new francs [$500].

†The *Mémoire* dates from November 1776.

**The allusion is to his "œconomist" doctrines, especially his *Theory of Taxation,* which earned him a few days in the Bastille under Louis XV.

judgment of May 1777, between the Mirabeaus, husband and wife, the
fishwives of Europe, this man and woman who have been scrapping over their
children's heads for the last twenty years like a pair of barroom brawlers. At
the hearing on May 3 the judges gawk when they see, next to du Saillant
and Coquebert the barrister, that large-headed man, the ghost new-risen
from the prisons of the king, who is beginning to be spoken of as a sort of
Cartouche or Latude.* They marvel at his audacity, but it also disturbs
them. They are having their first encounter with "Mirabeau *fils,*" "a convicted and effigized man† who dared to appear in the Palace [of Justice] in
his own name, and in the Grand Chamber, and at the tavern, and among
the judges . . . It is most singular that a man of this sort can impose upon
people to such a degree that he silences applause when it does not suit him,
and can say to the lawyers, 'Step softly, there, when you meddle in the affairs of the great!' "[9]

On May 18, 1781—really, what a number of things happen that day!—the
Parliament rules as requested by the celebrated Gerbier, the most expensive
lawyer in France, representing Mme de Mirabeau.** This time the decision
goes wholly and unconditionally against the Friend of Man, who is going to
have to cough up and restore to his wife goods and money to the tune of seven
hundred thousand livres.‡ Two days later she emerges from her convent††
and instantly lays siege to the mansion on the Rue de Seine with a battalion
of bailiffs. Her husband has fled to Bignon, which he's going to have to sell,
along with the mansion and everything else. Gabriel—perforce—chose
the wrong camp. His father is ruined, or worse: "From hair to toenails, I
am bound and pinioned at the bottom of the abyss . . . They killed me on
May 18!"[11]

On the 20th Gabriel-Honoré is allowed to prostrate himself at the feet
of his vanquished conqueror. Two of life's losers, two serious casualties on that
jousting ground called the family, will now try to keep each other warm among
the ashes. It's about time.

---

*Cartouche (1693–1721): a famous and notoriously flashy French bandit. Latude (1725–
1805): bastard of a noble family who sent an explosive to Mme de Pompadour and then warned
her, hoping for a reward; was imprisoned without trial and escaped three times. [*Trans.*]

†Sentenced to death in absentia by the court of Besançon in 1777 for "abduction of a married
woman," Mirabeau had been decapitated in effigy on the public square at Pontarlier. The sentence
had not been revoked.

**Necker was resigning the same day. The Parliament was about to condemn Raynal.

‡678,740 livres to be exact, or something in the neighborhood of 3.5 million new francs
[$700,000].[10]

††Louise de Cabris was also released, on May 28 at Sisteron, to the sound of bells, tambou-
rines, and the pop of harquebuses, in a little carnival of joy.

On March 31, 1779, Mirabeau wrote to Boucher: "You must understand that the eyes which the *Friend of Man** is casting upon me are those of a vulture awaiting its cadaver."[12]

A biblical scene, revised and corrected for the curtain of an act by Sedaine or Crébillon. One of the marquis's neighbors over from Montargis—the inevitable eyewitness standing on the forestage—plays the part of Greek chorus, exclaiming: "This is the return of the prodigal son!"[13] The father's changed a little since Jesus' time, though, and his son finds him changed, too, since he last saw him ten years ago:† a scrawny white plucked bird, brazening it out on the end of a rotten limb with his neck stiff as a poker. The marquis, meanwhile, was expecting the youth whose early years he could never find words enough to disparage, "Monsieur Hurricane, Baron Gusty-wind" . . . He finds a man, made and even unmade, the castaway of Vincennes. They've been tearing each other to shreds all this time without even being acquainted; and their present surge of affection is pure convention, but they're both good actors so they get carried away by their parts. Between perpetually lowered lids, like a warden, the marquis observes "that a great deal in my son's eruptions is physical . . . He is very quick to take offense, one can say nothing to him straight out without his eyes, lips and flush proving his discomposure, but the slightest show of affection causes him to dissolve into tears and he would throw himself into the fire."[14] "The slightest show of affection"—even from a vulture. "He has our form"—that of the Mirabeaus, as opposed to the Vassans—"build and aspect, save for his quicksilver; his hair is extremely fine, his brow has opened [*sic*], and so have his eyes. Much less vainglory than before in his speech, although some remains: a natural air, moreover, and far less ruddy," for he now has a prison pallor.

Somehow or other the summer lets them all transpire—humor, pity, remorse, contempt, and some not easily classifiable form of love, wearing the scent of this singular reunion. From his lair at Mirabeau another white-haired old man, the bailli, harangues his brother: "And so there you are, thanks to your posteromania,** spending your days trying to lay down the law to a thirty-two-year-old chicken! Are you gullible enough to believe you will ever make him into anything but what he is?" The marquis snaps back: "You don't cut off a son like an arm. If it were possible, I should have been one-armed long ago . . . I am trying to pour over this man my head, my soul and my heart," and he can't get over "the sight of a bloated barrel with a solemn

*His own derisive italics. He's talking about his father, remember.

†Gabriel's last stay at Bignon goes back to the spring of 1771; his father, who refused to attend his wedding in Aix, hasn't seen him since.

**Reminder: the marquis's existence and actions were motivated solely by the desire to perpetuate his name. As a Knight of Malta, the bailli had taken an oath to remain single.

and depraved demeanor, that says *papa* and does not know how to behave."[15]

After a few weeks of cohabitation, he roughs out this pretty amazing
portrait of Mirabeau at thirty-two:

> I have found in him nothing but as much wit as it is possible to possess, an
> unbelievable gift for grasping everything on every surface, but nothing, abso-
> lutely nothing beneath it, and in the place of a soul he has a mirror that temporar-
> ily reflects every image held up to it and retains not the slightest trace. It is
> impossible to talk reason or prudence to him without him saying it all a hundred
> times better than you, and none of it goes any deeper than the epidermis; he
> applies himself to nothing but he seizes everything; above all, he has a residue
> of anti-truth that occupies all his mental and physical faculties. Whatever art,
> science, literature, antiquity, learning or language you mention to him, he knows
> three times as much about it as you do, dashes everything off, mixes everything
> up, but he affirms things with convincing certainty and heat; he lies, in short,
> whether in matters great or small; affirmations, disappointments, stories of every
> description—nothing costs him, and all is forgotten and forgiven fifteen minutes
> later; mettlesome withal, and so unparticular that he will go off on the highways
> with thieves as soon as drink; no head, just a muddle, vexatious although uninten-
> tionally, unconsciously so, and only because he wants to say the right thing to each
> person; not a bad fellow when all is said and done, and naught but a phantom at
> bottom, for good as for evil; the pen golden and swift, taste, elegance, and an
> unbelievable talent for cadging everywhere.[16]

. . . "In a word, he is by instinct magpie and jay."[17]

May 29, 1781. Mirabeau is riding to see Sophie, the way one drowns a dog
after tying a stone around its neck. Those few hours can't have been much fun
for him. But it's no fun for the dog, either.

He doesn't need to take any risks at the inn or cry "Gabriel!" under the
windows; the kind Doctor Ysabeau is waiting for him at Nogent-sur-Vernisson
and gives him a lift over the last four leagues in his gig. At the end of the little
road between the flowering hedgerows he sees the gray and blue town dominated by the handsome château of Anne de Beaujeu, first Comtesse de
Gien.* The cherry trees are full of fruit, the smell of honeysuckle eddies in
wreaths. The poignant sweetness of the long Val de Loire evening falls like
anesthesia over this farewell. Suffering is less difficult here than in the Jura. At
least you can sleep by the river sands. Everything is misty.

He waits for night to come in a garden adjoining the convent. A gardener
leads him into the minute apartment where Sophie is expecting him, in the

---

*And daughter of Louis XI. She had the château built in 1490; today it houses the law courts
and sub-prefect's offices. The buildings of the Poor Clares' convent stood within a rectangle now
outlined by the rues Paul-Bert, Jeanne d'Arc, d'Orléans, and des Fossés.

state one can imagine. It's Tuesday night. He stays hidden there until Saturday, June 2. Four days. Four nights. Their last; about which these two people who were garrulous to the point of exhibitionism in happier days have remained utterly silent. This agony breeds so much shame, not only in him but in Sophie as well, that they do not, unlike so many other couples, inflict the ordeal of their breakup on anyone.

Breakup? No; but the right word doesn't exist. They love each other again, not as before but beyond words or gestures. She hasn't touched a man since their separation, and waits with embarrassing ardor for "that body, so beautiful, so white, so fat" which she has "always found a little stout when you are dressed. You are better naked. Then, you are superb."[18] . . . "Don't you remember how I used to say, in the beginning, that your eyes frightened me? You open them so wide, your whole face changes, pleasure oppresses you, you utter great sighs, and when you let your head fall upon my breast or arm, you are as beautiful as some lovely cupid."[19] He has hardly spent a day without a girl in the last six months, and is coming back to her with his tail between his legs like a soldier home to his wife. Sophie's dewiness has evaporated; she's lost that wild-strawberry look. Her hair is graying. She has cried so much that her red-rimmed eyes have worn away their lashes. She resembles some frightfully pious lady in "her very outmoded dress and her chignon that looks as though the rats had been nibbling at it."[20] But what about him? Fresh from his passage under the steam roller, "much heavier, especially in the shoulders, neck and waist,"[21] with his lachrymose popeyes and rotten guts and humbled air; did she find him the same as before?

Of all that they never say a word. Nor of the speeches he has prepared for her, and her own silences. Some things really are too sad to tell.

It undoubtedly comes as a relief when Dupont—him again—wings up on Saturday morning to warn Gabriel that he must flee, quick, hurry, they're after him, they're after him again. Because he left Bignon? Not exactly; here, a wink of complicity. For the first time ever his father is overlooking an escapade. He doesn't know what Gabriel is up to and he doesn't want to know. Shedding a mistress with this kind of boldness comes within his code of ethics. At last his son is beginning to behave like a gentleman. No, no; the reason he has to flee is that old Dauvers has lodged a complaint against Mirabeau to recover the twenty-five louis that have never been repaid. A sign that the Dauverses have punctured the windbag. Sophie panics. Is it debtors' prison next? No, no, madam, you are not to worry; even ruined, the marquis will pay; I will pay myself, everything will be all right, so long as your Gabriel stops acting like a baby; just make this one small sacrifice, you have made so many already, let him return to the fold, he'll be back to see you in a few weeks . . . I'll be back, I'll write every day, wait just a little while longer, just long enough for me to go to Besançon and get my sentence repealed, and then to Aix to reconquer my wife and, most of all, her estate, for honor and for cash, meanwhile you can reach some agreement with your husband, it'll only take a few months, and then Brussels, and London, and the cabin under the willows . . . hurry up, for heaven's sake, you're neither of you children anymore, can't you hear the horses coming down the Sully road?

Before she knows what's happening they're both far away, riding side by side almost like buddies. The next day she does her duty—a courageous letter. Is an abandoned woman ever asked to do anything else? "I love you as I loved you before." But this time without illusions. "They will all think we can't live without each other. Alas, my husband, they are wrong."[22] Only one brief protest against the amputation: "Oh, I am so oppressed, my heart is so heavy . . . Dear, dear friend, ah, I do believe we shall not see each other again for many a day."[23]

On June 6 she takes stock of her position: a lovelorn woman dumped by the riverside. Weep and be forgotten. "Here are many sorrows, many ills assailing us all of a sudden. Dear, dear friend, do not let your great heart and your beautiful soul be borne down. But, I swear it, if you are put in prison I shall kill myself. And also if I am pregnant."[24]

JEFFERSON

60

JULY 1781

The Boy Cannot Escape Me

By the skin of their teeth La Fayette and his men get to Richmond first, on April 29, footsore and weary. But they haven't seen anything yet. The Virginia campaign has just begun, and they're going to be needing some third and fourth winds.

Richmond (whose name the French write in their own style, Richemont), wasn't made a state capital until last year, dethroning Williamsburg as Williamsburg dethroned Jamestown before it: under cover of the big war, the war of the American town pump imperturbably pursues its course up and down the banks of that other Loire, greener than the French one, more heavily wooded and worse-tempered, but, like it, strewn with islands—the river of King James, which is momentarily becoming the frontier of the New World. If the English get across it, we may well find ourselves back on the Potomac with their swords in our buttocks.

From La Fayette to Steuben, whose soldiers are doing their damnedest a little farther east, retreating a foot at a time: "Richmond must be now the object for both parties . . . As long as we can keep the ferry at Richmond we might cross at that place . . . Could not some heavy cannon be put upon the river as floating batteries? . . . In case you find it is necessary to retreat up the riverbank, I wish the boats may get up in the same time, as I understand they cannot be replaced."[1]

He races around, he thinks of everything, he's got ants in his elegant breeches, and he's not the only one: The two old wolves who've been loosed against this cub also know that minutes count—the English general Phillips and the day-before-yesterday American general Benedict Arnold, the former in command and the latter doing all the commanding. Both want to get in as many licks as they can before the arrival of their top man, their liberal chief Cornwallis who's still delayed in the Carolinas. The main thing is to rob him of victory in Virginia at any price—the price of terror to be exact. War is never a picnic, but around here it's beginning to look even nastier than usual. For want of enough arms and men to intimidate all resistance, and for want of a warm welcome from the Virginians, most of whom have remained Whig in this cradle of Independence, the English are being forced to hang and burn —the two refrains to the old tune of dissuasion. "If Virginia had been hitherto favoured, it seems to have been determined at this time to inflict upon it a more than common portion of vengeance: And, so vulnerable is that province, by the joint operation of a land and naval force, that the British troops committed the greatest devastations without any serious opposition, or sustaining any loss."[2] Upon reaching Richmond, La Fayette finds a letter in General Phillips's best prose, brandishing a threat of reprisals against the ill-treatment being meted out to Tories here and there.* "Should any person be put to death, under the pretence of their being spies of, or friends to, the British government, I will make the shores of James River an example of terror to the rest of Virginia . . . I shall hope that you, sir, whom I have understood to be a gentleman of liberal principles, will not countenance . . . the barbarous spirit which seems to prevail in the council of the present civil power of this Colony."[3] Just you wait. La Fayette's answer, from the "American camp, April 30th, 1781":

"The style of your letters, sir, obliges me to tell you, that should your future favors be wanting in that regard due to the civil and military authority in the United States, which cannot but be construed into a want of respect to the American nation, I shall not think it consistent with the dignity of

---

*He wasn't making it up: whenever the Whigs identified an agent of this premature "fifth column" they tarred and feathered him, and sometimes he died.

an American officer to continue the correspondence . . . Such articles as the requiring that the persons of spies be held sacred cannot certainly be serious."4

Determination. That is all, or almost all, La Fayette has to pit against the English forces coming up the James River after seizing Yorktown, Williamsburg and Petersburg, "where they destroyed the tobacco warehouses . . . Their main object now, however, was to capture Richmond, as well on account of its importance as the capital of Virginia as because of the great mass of stores collected in the magazines at that city."5 La Fayette whips this square of the chessboard out from under their noses with no more than twenty-four hours to spare. On the morning of April 30 "they marched to Manchester, from whence they had a view of M. La Fayette's army, encamped on the heights of Richmond . . ."6 Them's big words.* La Fayette's entire "army" that day consists of nine hundred men; Phillips has over two thousand. Separating them, a roiling river in a dusting of islets, in front of the pink houses lined up like sacrificial victims along the edge of a quay dead with fear. "In the evening they returned . . ." Stalled. If they had attacked, La Fayette would never have had a chance to set up his second lines and there would be nothing left to cover Virginia. This is one of those blessed battles that decide a great deal without ever being fought.

There ensues a long game of hide-and-seek between the two armies on either side of the lower reaches of the James River, the main idea being not to give battle in open country but to let the other side get the lead so that it can be outflanked, cut off from its bases, and encircled. A grand old Indian game where all the work is done by horse patrols and riflemen. In it La Fayette wins his spurs as a strategist, by showing caution and refusing to follow too close on the heels of an enemy who far outnumbers him and keeps falling back with suspicious rapidity. "Had I gone on the other side, the ennemy [*sic*] would have given me the slip and taken Richmond, leaving nothing to me but the reputation of a rash, inexperienced young man."7 So English and French edge down toward the sea along parallel lines, each on his own bank hurling Trojan insults at the other. Both sides are waiting for reinforcements, and those of the English are much closer to hand, because all Cornwallis has to do is amble across North Carolina whereas Washington and Rochambeau are still riveted to New York and Newport by General Clinton's forces. Time, thus, is on Phillips's side, apart from the minor detail that he dies of an attack of fever on May 13, which momentarily benefits the traitor Arnold by rendering him omnipotent pending the arrival of Lord Cornwallis. Arnold takes advantage

---

*The same ones used at the mill of Valmy eleven years later [where the French finally checked the Prussians on September 30, 1792—*Trans.*].

of it to dig himself firmly into Petersburg, the biggest town on the south side
of the James, where La Fayette briefly contemplates taking him by surprise—
what a hanging that would be! Arnold, moreover, has few illusions, having just
questioned a captured American prisoner:

> "What do you think the Americans would do with me if they should succeed
> in making me a prisoner?"
> "We should cut off the leg which was wounded in the country's service, and
> we should hang the rest of you."[8]

The Frenchman's Americans do make one raid on the south bank, but
"my inferiority forced me to recross the river; but my position . . . will be such
as enables me to keep a post on this side, be within striking distance of the
enemy, and, without exposing Richmond, to recross if I choose . . . I request
everything that can do for crossing a river"—the one obsessive problem in this
American war—"boats, canoes, scows (a ferry boat excepted), and planks to
join two canoes, may be sent down from Richmond."[9]

May 15. Everything's going wrong. La Fayette fires off cries for help to
the four corners of Virginia. "The army under General Phillips [who he thinks
is alive], 2,300 rank and file at the lowest estimate, are for the present at
Petersburg, covered by Appomattox River on their front and on their right
flank by James River. They have an absolute command of the water [thanks
to their superiority in light craft and river-navigating equipment] . . . Lord
Cornwallis was at Halifax and probably is by this time on his way to Petersburg. There is hardly a man, or at least hardly a gun to oppose him." That isn't
literally true, but it's not so far off either . . . "We have some militia [recruited
locally] but are in such a want of arms that I dare not venture them into action,
for fear of an irreparable loss . . . Riflemen and Cavalry, or at least mounted
Infantry, are particularly wanting. No time ought to be lost, as the danger is
pressing."[10]

On May 20 Cornwallis reaches Petersburg. The English forces are almost
doubled. La Fayette, on his side, finally gets some reinforcements from
Wayne's detachment: eight hundred men. The eyes of all informed people in
America and even Europe begin turning toward Virginia. Are we finally going
to stop hearing about New York? Does this change of gaze mean that others,
more important, more decisive, are to come? 1781: the tectonic year. After
a glance at the gazettes the London bookmakers give five to one against La
Fayette. On May 17 he's made commander of all the forces in Virginia. But
where are they?

He feels as though he's been made commander of disaster. "I have been
long complaining that I had nothing to do; and want of employment was an
objection I had to my going to the southward. But for the present, my dear
friend, my complaint is quite of an opposite nature; and I have so many

arrangements to make, so many difficulties to combat, so many enemies to deal with, that I am just that much of a general as will make me a historian of misfortunes and nail my name upon the ruins of what good folks are pleased to call the army of Virginia . . . Their infantry is near five to one; their cavalry ten to one . . . To speak truth, I was afraid of myself as much as of the enemy. Independence has rendered me the more cautious, as I know my own warmth."[11]

He falls back to Richmond—for a start. What a waste of time it was saving the town two weeks ago! This time it'll have to be evacuated or the English will lay siege to it. Message after message to Washington, to Rochambeau, to all those people on some other planet who sit and twiddle their thumbs in the North while the English rip the South from his grasp and start chewing into the Center. Listen, you guys, do something to help me! To Washington, on May 24: "Were I anyways equal to the enemy, I should be extremely happy in my present command, but I am not strong enough even to be beaten."[12] Even so, he keeps a stiff upper lip; one thing he'll have learned from his American campaigns is that the "art of warfare" most often consists in retreating in good order. And it was no mistake on his part to gain half a month to get organized in: "Public stores and private property being removed from Richmond, this place is a less important object. I don't believe it would be prudent to expose the troops for the sake of a few houses, most of which are empty; but I am wavering between two inconveniences. Were I to fight a battle, I should be cut to pieces, the militia dispersed, and the arms lost. Were I to decline fighting, the country would think itself given up. I am therefore determined to skirmish, but not to engage too far, and particularly to take care against their immense and excellent body of horse, whom the militia fear as they would so many wild beasts." With good reason; facing La Fayette's forty horse cavalry, Cornwallis has eight hundred men mounted on the best horses in Virginia. His advance guard even have race horses, "like birds of prey."[13]

And what are the Virginians doing to help God and La Fayette to help themselves? Jefferson's total discomfiture is symbolic of that of the state entrusted to his care, whose fighting potential is officially reckoned at fifty thousand militia. Yet there's nothing of the braggart or the coward about Jefferson: it's just that he can't stand war. It upsets him, its flatly realistic everyday demands interfere with his midwifery of the New World, the future constitution, the abolition of Negro slavery. "When I left Congress in '76, it was in the persuasion that our whole code must be reviewed, adapted to our republican form of government . . . should be corrected, in all its parts, with a single eye to reason,"[14] whereas the aristocratic Virginia society in which he was born and has lived until now has been poured, bucket by bucket, from the wellspring of monarchy and "had a single eye to religion." Jefferson is in the process of shedding his skin and setting out, well ahead of the rest, on that quest for something beyond liberty, who knows by what name to call it, universal love, equality, the right to happiness? The name can come later. The main thing now is to get there. He is one of the first in either world to dream of pushing beyond the eternal bloodthirsty billiard game, I win–you win. He has just dumfounded the Virginia Assembly, a very grand name for a handful of local dignitaries garbed in black and baggageless, being driven from town to town and holding sessions in the few meetinghouses left standing—in Charlottesville for the moment, following Richmond, Williamsburg, and Jamestown. An ideologist, governor of Virginia? He'd be more at home among Bostonians.

He attacks slavery and in 1778 gets a bill adopted, almost by ambush, prohibiting the importation of slaves from Africa to Virginia. Oh, very well; but he's not to meddle with our own nice home-grown Negroes. It's very discouraging: "The bill on the subject of slaves was a mere digest of the existing laws respecting them, without any intimation of a plan for a future and general emancipation,"[15] that's all we need! Thomas Jefferson feels worse beaten by his own team than by the English. "Indeed, I tremble for my country when I reflect that God is just."[16] So, when it comes to running around looking for horses, boats, and wagons . . . He hasn't got what it takes to wage two wars at once, this one and the one to come. In fact, he's so incapable of looking after himself that the English advance guard, on their famous race horses, are about to fall upon Charlottesville unannounced while his assembly sits arguing about the Virginia of 1800. Jefferson and his colleagues have just time enough to decamp and hide in the woods. "Would anyone believe that that flight has become, in the hands of party men, the subject of I know not how many volumes of insult?* It has been sung in verse, and told in humble prose how, forgetting the noble example of the hero of La Mancha and his windmills, I refused to do battle alone against a legion."[17]

In disgust he abandons his post as governor of a shrinking Virginia to a military man, General Nelson, who'll be better at acting as deputy to the true governor of the state—the Marquis de La Fayette.

This is the moment for Cornwallis to rejoice and dream about victory parades. He writes to his supreme commander, Clinton, that "I shall now proceed to dislodge La Fayette from Richmond, and with my light troops to destroy any magazines or stores in the neighborhood . . . From thence I purpose to move to the neck at Williamsburgh [sic]."[18] La Fayette evacuates Richmond on May 27. Cornwallis crosses the James in force: "The boy cannot escape me." The chicken is hatched, true; but don't be too hasty about counting him.

*Written by Jefferson in 1820. His "flight from Charlottesville" becomes that good old tin can which any politician's opponents are always trying to tie onto his tail for good. It pursues him for the rest of his life.

61

JULY 1781

We're Off at Last!

But. On May 21 Washington and Rochambeau hold a second "summit conference" at Wethersfield, near Hartford, and they make up their minds to do
something. They're not going to waste another whole summer. La Fayette in
Virginia is only one of the players in the formidable game of hide-and-seek
that is about to begin, after so long a time out, over hundreds of leagues of
land.

In the North, Clinton holds New York facing Washington; Rochambeau
is in Newport; the Admiral de Barras,* sent from Brest to replace Ternay, is
cruising off Rhode Island with a small naval force. At the South-Center hinge
it's the La Fayette–Cornwallis skirmish. And down there in the Antilles, still
on the sidelines, Admiral de Grasse, the relief player who can change everything, rides at anchor in Cap Français.† What if we just shook it all up a little?
What if everybody finally got into the act?

The match opens at Wethersfield, within one of the opposing teams.
They agree on one point: the two army corps must be joined. They've had
enough of sitting like china dogs ten days' march from each other. America and France are—at last!—about to unite their puny forces. But to do
what? Here's where the play begins. Washington advances his usual pawn:
New York. He thinks this is a good opportunity to make that longed-for
attack, now that Clinton has exposed himself by sending reinforcements to
Cornwallis. Now, if de Grasse's ships could only lend us a hand at the
mouth of the Hudson . . . So sorry! Rochambeau cuts in. The harbor
channel is too shallow for heavy craft. He doesn't know what he's talking
about, but this is a firm and erroneous conviction among French sailors.
No; our best naval fortresses would not be able to pound the Brooklyn
batteries. But what if, on the contrary, de Grasse were to join us at the
entrance to the Chesapeake? How about if we struck our great blow in the

---

*Uncle of Paul de Barras, the future delegate to the Convention and member of the Direc-
toire.

†The northern port of the French part of Santo Domingo, today Haiti. In those days Cap,
or Cape, Français was more important than Port-au-Prince, the southern port.

South? Now there's a thought.* The idea of striking in Virginia was slowly seeping into the brains of the blockheads on the French senior staff just as La Fayette began putting up his noble defense in the vicious freshman hell-week he's been plunged into at the expense of the common cause. All alone there on the shore of the Chesapeake . . . the poor kid deserves better than to be eaten alive by Cornwallis, after all. And then, a victory over milord would be worth as much as Saratoga. People would be talking about it all over the world. In other words, they would be talking about our worthy selves.

Washington isn't dead set against this shift in the theater of operations. He's fond of his Virginia, and every day he grimly awaits news of a fresh raid on Mount Vernon. But he's intimidated by the daunting prospect of moving a large number of men and heavy equipment southwards over more than a hundred leagues, crossing the Hudson and the myriad rivers and streams that gave La Fayette so much trouble. Ah, if some French ships would only consent to come up the bay and load part of the combined forces at Head of Elk everything would be different! By the way, what exactly is de Grasse doing in Santo Domingo with all those cannons for such a little speck of land? Rochambeau promises to write to him. And whatever his answer, the French army will join Washington's, ostensibly to worry New York—which might give some indirect relief to La Fayette—but maybe to march south together if things look like turning that way.

May 28. The minute he gets back to Newport Rochambeau writes to de Grasse: "Such is the condition of affairs and the gravity of the crisis in America, especially in the southern states, at this moment. Your arrival may save the country; for none of the means within our control can be made available without your cooperation and without the naval superiority which you can bring here. There are two points at which to act offensively against the enemy, the Chesapeake and New York. The southwest winds and the state of distress in Virginia will probably lead you to prefer Chesapeake Bay, and it is there that we believe you will be able to render the greatest services, especially since you will require but two days to come from there to New York."[1]

The answer will get here when it can; by the time it takes a frigate to sail down to the Islands and back Rochambeau will be far from Newport at the appointed meeting place. But first he has to win a domestic battle against his associate, Admiral de Barras, whose orders when he left Brest were to take his eight ships up to Boston if Rochambeau marched inland. Now, now, my friend, you wouldn't want to do a thing like that—you just sit right here in Rhode Island with my siege artillery, and be ready to bring it down south if

*Prudently lisped out in the dispatches Rochambeau has just received from his new minister of war, Ségur, and new minister of the navy, Castries, the latter under the influence of letters from his son Charlus, La Fayette's companion.

de Grasse's arrival makes it safe for you to venture out on the high sea. I'm leaving you four hundred men to defend your moorings, and the Rhode Island militia will give you a thousand more.

Barras wavers. His orders are vague and leave him some latitude. In spite of the dribble of infantry he's being given, he has few illusions about escaping alive if the big English fleet should come to nail him in Newport. If he doesn't die on his quarterdeck, a council of war will settle his hash. But going to hole up in Boston, abandoning Rochambeau, imitating d'Estaing three years ago, taking the sailors away from the field of honor: the shame of it! . . . In these days the responsibility of a supreme commander is so immense: like Dupleix, like Lally, like Montcalm, somebody dumps half a continent in your lap and tells you to get on with it. There isn't time to wait for an opinion from the bureaucrats in Versailles before deciding. In the first days of June 1781 the fate of the American war is going to depend, not on Washington, Rochambeau, or La Fayette, but on the choice made by these two old chums from Provence, de Grasse and Barras, both offspring of the anthill of naval aristocracy swarming on the Mediterranean coast, brothers or cousins in their high-perched châteaus, barons of sea and boulder. There's a Sade threatening Gibraltar with what remains of the Toulon fleet; there's a Suffren on his way to the Indies to salvage what he can there. And if he weren't overage, there might be a Mirabeau commanding the fleet out here—not poor Gabriel, his uncle the bailli.

The council of war held in Newport on May 30 at Barras's request begins to look more like a little parliament, in which strategy will be settled by vote. It's the only way: Rochambeau and Barras have equal rank, neither has authority over the other. So Barras calls for a meeting of a joint council composed of the generals and senior officers of both armies, land and sea, "a recourse indicated in their instructions when circumstances compelled them to depart from them."[2] Is the fleet to go, or stay here in semi-safety? Everyone states his opinion in the most convoluted terms possible while waiting for the admiral to say his piece. All right, you asked for it: "No one is more anxious than I to see the Comte de Grasse arriving in these waters; he was my junior; he has just been made lieutenant general. The instant I learn that he is within reach I shall lay on all sail and hasten to place myself under his orders."[3] Impassive as he is, Rochambeau cannot restrain a cry of joy. It is a very lucky thing for America that day that the leader of the Newport fleet doesn't happen to hail from Brittany or Auvergne, and considers himself bound by regional solidarity. Charlus writes to his minister father: "I have not words enough to praise the admiral you have sent us. He is a good and worthy man."[4]

From Fersen to his "very dear father; Newport, June 3, 1781":

"We're off at last! In eight or ten days the army will be on the march. That is the outcome of the conference between the two generals. The plan of campaign, and our destination, are secret and should be so. I hope we shall see action, and are not being made to leave Newport in order to be garrisoned in some other small town. Our fleet is remaining here, guarded by the American militia and 400 of our troops. I am heartily sorry for those who will be ordered to stay in this detachment. The entire army is delighted to be leaving."[5] Not least of all Fersen, ever since he started taking a strong dislike to Rochambeau. He's come a long way from the welcoming and all-understanding-father image of the embarkation at Brest.

> I begin to find M. de Rochambeau rather tedious. He singles me out, it is true, and I am most appreciative of it, but he is disagreeably and even insultingly suspicious; he has more faith in me than in my comrades, yet that which he places in me is but mediocre; and he has no more in his general officers, who are highly displeased because of it, or in the senior officers in the army . . .
>
> His reputation as a general is made, but he will always be known as a bad politician. I believe him good as second-in-command, but undistinguished as leader of an expedition . . . He is a very narrow man; one can perceive this readily in conversation, and any doubts one may have are removed when one knows the people around him in whom he does place his trust. One is a brute, a former brigadier of hussars, or in other words a corporal, who has only been an officer for two or three years. The other is one of those people in whom gross common sense takes the place of wit; he was a spy in the Paris police when M. de Rochambeau took him on as secretary, because he speaks English and costs less than another and better man . . . He is extremely kind to me; he always singles me out from my comrades; he has made me his first aide de camp. I appreciate his kindness and am very grateful for it. I should do anything for him, but he bores me as he bores everyone else; I do not care for the company of animals, there is nothing to be learned from them.[6]

It really is time to be on the move.

Meanwhile, raids and counter-raids in Virginia. Three regiments of the Pennsylvania Line come to reinforce La Fayette, that's a thousand men to help him clamber up out of the trough of the wave. They've been marched to death, sunrise to sundown. Exhaustion sweats from the pages of their journals. June 8: "Took up the line March at Sun rise. Reach'd the North Branch Rappahanack [sic] at 10 oClock, troops waded the river and proceeded nine miles into this County. 9th Orange County. Took up the line of March at six oClock, cross'd the South Branch Rappahanack & proceeded Five miles into this County; country poor & buildings very small [for a native of Philadelphia]

10th. March'd at 5 oClock; a thin poor country. Join'd the Marquis's this day, made a march of 12 miles."[7] More bad breaks, meanwhile: the English against Charlottesville,* Jefferson does his famous flit and resigns from office, and, even worse, Steuben is surprised by another squadron of this ubiquitous English cavalry—all his wagons are taken off, with 2,500 pieces of arms, several casks of saltpeter and sulfur, flints, sailcloth, and upwards of sixty hogsheads of that rum and brandy without which nothing can happen in the state of Virginia.[8] La Fayette sticks up for his subordinate, just to sink him a little deeper: "The conduct of the Baron, my dear General [Washington], is to me unintelligible. Every man, woman and child in Virginia is roused against him. They dispute even his courage, but I cannot believe their accusations. I must, however, confess that he had 500 and odd new levies and some militia; that he was on the other side of a river which the freshet rendered very difficult to be crossed . . ."[9] Nobody's going to out-veteran La Fayette anymore.

Gilbert recovers what's left of Steuben's footsore forces—and faces around to fight. Cornwallis, following the good old English method, wastes time organizing himself along the James River. La Fayette, who's been able to catch his breath, takes advantage of his new reinforcements to bounce back from the first possible stream in the tangle of watercourses between Richmond and Fredericksburg—in this instance the North Anna, then the South Anna. It's as though he were crawling up the rungs of a ladder of water in order to pull open a trapdoor the English haven't had time to batten down. "From this time forward [June 10] the action of the Virginia campaign was reversed: the British were retiring, and La Fayette was following them."[10] The implication of pursuit is not quite justified, but at least the scales are even again. The threat of invasion in the central states is fading: Cornwallis doesn't dare venture very far from the mouth of the James and the tutelary fleet which is his umbilical cord at the entrance to the Chesapeake. "This was the nearest that the British army ever came to the reconquest of Virginia. From this point the tide began to ebb."[11]

How do you sense when a war is turning? Six hundred mountaineers troop in from the Shenandoah Valley, armed with hunting guns and one powder horn for every three of them. Are these the big birds that herald a change in the weather? Why is Cornwallis in such a rush to break his advance camp at Elk Hill on June 15? Cry of joy from La Fayette: "Lord Cornwallis is returning to Richmond, and we are following him."[12] There's a change in the real weather, too. The June heat has dropped like an eiderdown to smother the English and especially their German mercenaries, so unused to the almost tropical climate. This restores an advantage of habitat to the local militia, who

---

*This is only a raid of intimidation. The English cavalry are not strong enough to capture the town, and withdraw the next day.

begin to perk up. But weather alone cannot explain why Cornwallis abandons Richmond on June 20 without a fight, to withdraw farther east, closer to the sea, to Williamsburg. What's really happening is that the mechanism of the game of hide-and-seek is beginning to take effect. If Cornwallis finds it wiser to secure his rear guard rather than press his advantage, it's because Clinton's dispatches, which take only two days to come to him by sea from New York, have given him to understand that he might have to re-embark for the North in case a big battle should take place there, and have notified him that he will be getting no further reinforcements. Simply by emerging from his hole in Newport, Rochambeau has turned the tables.

Fersen keeps a little journal of the operations at that end: "After spending eleven totally inactive months in Newport, the army set out on June 12, 1781, leaving six hundred troops and a thousand militia under the orders of M. de Choisy, brigadier, to defend our earthworks there, protect our little squadron of eight ships which was to remain there, and cover our magazines in Providence, where we had all our siege artillery. The army crossed by sea from Newport to Providence, and then continued marching by land to Phillipsburg, fifteen miles from Kingsbridge, which it reached on July 6, and camped to the left of the Americans. Lauzun's legion was covering our left flank, marching nine or ten miles to the seaward of us. Our army was five thousand men, the Americans around three thousand." Bye-bye, Newport, the little town huddling among the waves under its pointed church spires and rusting arms, muscles, and minds. The Americans gape at the extent and majesty of the French army on the march, the parade of a military structure ten centuries in the sculpting.

And with the help of a private arsenal of wove paper, brushes, and colored inks, a pleasant little pink-cheeked chap with a round face and slightly turned-up nose, neatly dressed under carefully powdered and curled hair, is immortalizing it all, down to the last detail, in writing and sketches: Captain Louis-Alexandre Berthier, here beginning a long career as a maniac of warfare organized to the last buttonhole. Berthier's twenty-eight now but seems years younger, with his slight stutter and chubby suckling-pig aspect. His meticulousness relieves him of the need for imagination—but what a memory! What conscientiousness! He has made himself indispensable to the general staff simply by being around all the time. He has never been known to sleep. His pencils and notebooks are worth cannons. As Mathieu Dumas's assistant, he has spent weeks planning just where every French soldier would deposit his rucksack and find chickens and flour at each stage of his long perambulation through unknown territory. Every morning he's up before everybody else, setting up his easel off to one side and away from the bustle of reveille in order to paint a watercolor of the previous day's march, a little masterpiece of polished precision in pastel shades. If ever war could be pretty, it is in Berthier's paintings.[13] He is the child of that order. He was born at Versailles in the building that personifies it more than any other, almost opposite the château: the monumental "Hôtel des Ministères," four stories, one hundred windows on its façade, behind which a swarm of clerks stand scratching out fair copies of documents for the "Departments of War, Navy and Foreign Affairs." Inside it, therefore, Ségur, Castries, and Vergennes are cohabiting at this very moment, and can walk along the corridors and drop in on one another. His father, Jean-Baptiste Berthier, was governor of this building, and has bred into his very bones a horror of the overlooked speck of dust. We must not expect lyricism from his journal, but rigorous precision and a rejection of superfluity that verge upon abstract poetry.

> Providence is a small city of the second category, well-built and thickly settled. In peacetime it carries on a thriving commerce because of its situation, since frigates can come up to its docks. It is the residence of the Governor of the State of Rhode Island.
>
> The army halted here until the 18th. Meanwhile, the recruits from the convoy arrived. We made route marches to accustom the troops to the road and repaired all the wagons. Each company was allowed one of 1,500 pounds* capacity for all its baggage and the tents of the soldiers and officers; one wagon was assigned to the regimental staff, and each regiment was allowed a supplementary wagon, totaling twelve for each regiment.
>
> Owing to the difficulty of procuring forage and finding enough houses for the army staff and headquarters, it was decided to march the army in four divisions and distribute the artillery between them.[14]

Forward, march! Rochambeau and his son command the forward unit, a Vioménil and Charles de Lameth the second, another Vioménil and Victor Collot the third, Custine† and Berthier himself the fourth, Lauzun flanking them with his cavalry squadron. Eleven days on the march, through wood and swamp; in the evening they often pitch camp outside some inn whose name has become that of the place: Waterman's Tavern, Baron's Tavern, Barnes' Tavern. It's a real treat when they can lounge along the single street of a slightly more substantial burg such as Newton, which has fifty dwellings spaced around a meetinghouse. They all join up at Phillipsburg, in a Scottish setting: rugged hills with odd ruins lurking among them, narrow paths tumbling down through the woods to a broad, swift river in which the men would dearly love to bathe except that they can't because the noise of gunfire and cannons is too

*A scant ton in modern weight.

†Future commander of the Mainz garrison during Year II. [Mainz was occupied by the French in 1792 when a small group of citizens who were members of a Jacobin club and favored the ideas of the French Revolution collaborated with them. After a long siege and much damage the city was handed over to Prussian and Austrian forces in 1793.—*Trans.*]

loud—this is the Hudson, which everybody in the French camp calls the North River. The Americans, six hundred paces off, try to rival their allies in geometry and discipline. The officers exchange ceremonious and stiff-necked visits. New York is two leagues away, and everybody, both here and among the enemy, is still convinced that it is the chosen target for the summer's battles.

CORNWALLIS

62

JULY 1781

His Native Bravery Rendered Him Deaf

"Throughout the entire course of this war the English have appeared to be struck blind," observes Lauzun, who's playing the part of general busybody on this trip.* "They always do what should not be done, and always refuse to take the most obvious and certain advantages. Once the army was gone, all they needed to do, to destroy the entire scheme, was attack the French squadron in Rhode Island; but it never occurred to them. The French army marched across America in perfect order and discipline, a wonder for which neither the English nor the American army had ever set an example. I covered the army's march about fifteen miles to the east, and about forty miles from the North River."[1] Lauzun is one of the first high-ranking French officers to meet Washington near Phillipsburg, and is strongly impressed with him. "I found myself exactly at my assigned place, although the excessive heat and dreadful roads made this march infinitely trying. General Washington was well out in front of both armies, and told me he intended that I should lead a body of serious [sic] men, camping just outside New York, to surprise Fort Kniphausen, which was regarded as one of the key fortifications of New York." We now see our handsome duke promoted to his first command of a combined force, composed of his legion plus a regiment of American dragoons, a few companies of light horse, and a few American light infantry battalions. The whole caboodle begins skirmishing fiercely with the outposts of Clinton's entrenched camp, thereby confirming the idea that a general assault is about to begin. Washington's actions are so much in agreement with this hypothesis that nobody can

*Since his expedition to Senegal he has been building up a reputation as one of the court nobles best fitted to conduct military operations, which, along with diplomacy, is his highest ambition.

figure out whether he means it or not. He probably doesn't know himself, and is simply hanging on to all his trumps. "He wanted to seize the opportunity to reconnoiter New York from close up. I [Lauzun] accompanied him, with a hundred hussars. We received a great deal of gun- and cannon fire, but saw all that we wanted to see. This detachment lasted three days and three nights, and was extremely tiring, for we were on the move day and night, and had nothing to eat but the fruit we came across as we went. General Washington's letter to M. de Rochambeau was extremely decent about me; but my general forgot to mention it in his letters for France."[2] The French military command, we see, like the folks back at Versailles, are treating each other as handsomely as ever.

The shadow of these ten thousand men has already grown so tall that it falls upon Virginia before La Fayette does, and makes Cornwallis draw back. "Yesterday [June 21] morning the enemy evacuated Richmond, and seem to be bending towards Williamsburg. We are following them."[3] La Fayette is drunk with fatigue but this is a heady form of intoxication—it's the wine of retreat that makes you moody in your cups. He hasn't had his boots off for four days. Who cares? On June 23: "March'd at 2 oClock through a well inhabited country, though I can give no acc't of the people, as I have not been in a house for some days, though they look well [that is, Whig] on the road where they generally parade to see us. This day pass through Richmond, in 24 hours after the Enemy evacuated it,—it appears a scene of much distress,"[4] poor little bruised town, like a child battered in a fight between adults, with the pink bricks forming low mounds of coagulated blood. La Fayette, who hardly believes in God, lingers only long enough for the public formality of prayer in the "old church" in which Patrick Henry, in March 1775, pronounced the words of fire that burned America's bridges. The bench from which he harangued the Virginia Assembly, that assembly which has just scattered like a flock of pigeons in front of Colonel Tarleton's horsemen, is already being pointed out as a relic. "Give me liberty or give me death!" Well, we'll soon know which it is. La Fayette proves himself a good offensive general by not wasting time in Richmond and pressing his advantage, edging Cornwallis as far back as possible toward the Chesapeake. He multiplies his patrols to make his strength look greater than it is. He hoists foot soldiers onto the first nags he can lay hands on, so his cavalry will look twice as big. "At Six oClock in the morning we overtook a covering party, who retreated before us. We mounted a party of Infantry (Capt. Ogden's) behind lite [*sic*] Horse, who overtook their rear. We had a smartt [*sic*] skirmish Horse & foot in which we took some light Horse & Cattle & kill'd 30 on the spot with inconsiderable loss."[5] And Cornwallis makes his entrance into Williamsburg with the offended dignity of a gentleman whose poise has been shaken by a slingshot volley from a handful of hoodlum kids. The *Maryland Journal and Baltimore Advertiser* laughs out of La Fayette's side of the mouths of two states: "His Lordship is now in Williamsburg. His single tour to Virginia has cost his King more money, by the loss of Forts, men, cannon, stores, magazines, and supposed Carolina territory, than it would have cost the whole nobility of England to have made the tour of the world. His Lordship has had a most fatiguing march to the Point of Fork, and back again. The Marquis was to him what Fabius was to Hannibal.* Before Wayne made his junction he never lost sight of his Lordship, and when the junction was formed, by the single manoeuvre of opening a march through a wood, which intersected his Lordship, preserved the stores at old Albemarle Court-House, which the enemy had principally in view."[6] The forces are now equal; 4,600 men on either side, but Cornwallis's men are regular soldiers whereas the majority of La Fayette's are militia, who only fight when they feel like it. Nevertheless, things are looking so bright that La Fayette has a sort of premonition, on June 28: "General Greene [who's trying not to collapse in Carolina] demanded of me only to hold my ground in Virginia; but the movements of Lord Cornwallis may answer better purposes than that in the political line."[7]

A rainy July 4 can't quench the great "fudejoy"† which the Rebels light in camp to celebrate the fifth anniversary of Independence Day. "After that was over, Penn'a Line perform'd several maneuveres [*sic*], in which we fir'd."[8]

It's essential to do as much damage as possible before harvest time, when the American army is likely to melt away—it's not our good wives who'll get in the crops. But Cornwallis seems to have been stricken with ataxia. "His lordship has not thought proper to attack; though to my knowledge he has had it in his power several times, and to advantage."[9]

On the contrary, here comes another inexplicable turnabout. That same July 4 Cornwallis evacuates Williamsburg, where he might have fortified himself to withstand a long siege. He takes advantage of the few hours during which La Fayette has forgotten about heckling him to race down to the banks of the James and send his baggage across it to the south, continuing his southeasterly slide in the direction of Portsmouth—and re-embarkation?

La Fayette comes running. He doesn't mean to let the English cross the river as though they were on parade. Maybe he can pick up their rear guard? Let them get started and then fall upon the men left hanging on the north bank once the main body has crossed over . . . But Cornwallis is undoubtedly the best strategist the English have on this side of the ocean, and proceeds to execute a classic feint designed to make La Fayette think his moment has come.

---

*Fabius, a Roman general, retreated inch by inch around Lake Trasimenus in front of the invading Hannibal, so cleverly that Hannibal was already exhausted and weakened by the time he got to Capua.

†Captain Davis's stab at the French *"feu de joie,"* a bonfire celebration. [*Trans.*]

It's hot work, like stoking fires in a steam bath there in the swamps of Green Spring Farm where men and horses flounder and splash along a narrow dike that gives the English the advantage. The Americans come within an ace of falling into the trap. "Cornwallis had held back his whole army except the Queen's Rangers, and had disposed of his force in such a manner that it was concealed from the observation of La Fayette's advance guard.

"Into this trap the British commander expected to draw the Americans, whom he intended to annihilate at one blow after he should have them in his power. He disposed his outposts in a position where they would most likely be mistaken for a small force guarding his rear, and lay with his main body under arms, ready for the attack. Lieutenant-Colonel Tarleton went so far, in carrying out this stratagem, as to send false information into the camp of La Fayette, dispatching thither a negro and a dragoon, to whom he 'gave money and encouraging promises, to communicate false intelligence, under the appearance of deserters.' "[10] But La Fayette's been to school, too. You can't treat him like a greenhorn anymore. "Meanwhile, upon coming to the front, toward the middle of the afternoon, whilst Wayne's riflemen were engaged with Cornwallis's pickets, La Fayette observed that the British showed an unusual obstinacy in covering their position and in replacing the officers in command who were picked off by the deadly fire from the American rifles. This aroused his suspicion that these pickets were kept there to conceal from him some intention of the enemy. Thereupon he determined to make a closer examination in order to satisfy himself, although his own people were unanimously of the opinion that there was nothing of the British army left upon that side of the river but a covering party to guard the rear. Following the dictates of his own judgment in the matter, he rode forward alone to a point of land which extended into the river, to the right of his position, whence he could observe the movements of the enemy. There he discovered that the British forces were posted upon an open piece of ground a short distance from the river bank, at, or near, Ambler's Plantation, under protection of the batteries upon their ships, and evidently awaiting his attack."[11] He gives the order to fall back, too late to save Wayne and his regiments from being encircled, but they extricate themselves by means of "a brilliant exploit, which required all the daring of his nature to conceive: this was, as he quaintly puts it himself, 'among a choice of difficulties, to advance and charge them.' "[12] Wayne just manages to get free, but not his horse, which is killed under him in the charge. La Fayette also has a close shave, for two of his "hand horses"* are killed beside him. It really is very, very warm, that little overlooked battle of Green Spring Farm. "Our Field-Officers [according to Wayne] were generally dismounted by having

---

*That is, remounts held "in hand" by orderlies, to replace the horse mounted by an officer during combat.

their horses either killed or wounded under them . . . I will not condole with the Marquis for the loss of two of his, as he was frequently requested to keep at a greater distance. His native bravery rendered him deaf to the admonition."[13]

That's a wild understatement. He rushes into battle as though it were a debutante ball. "One cannot be equally gauche in every activity,"[14] he writes to his wife. The only time he can ever really come to terms with twenty years of self-doubt is when the shells start whistling around his ears.

63

AUGUST 1781

Without Consulting the Ministers

Eight days away by sea in a stiff breeze, way out there among the big sugar islands, the fate of the entire operation is about to be decided inside the ugly head of that grumpy giant, François-Joseph-Paul, Comte de Grasse du Bar. Once or twice a century some soldier's disobedience saves an empire. But it has to come at the right moment. This is it, everybody's telling the lieutenant general of naval forces of the King of France whose flag flies on a hitherto useless mastodon, the *Ville-de-Paris,* lying in the roads of Cap Français by order of Vergennes. De Grasse's mission is to protect the Islands and, if he wants some exercise, to attack Jamaica . . . on behalf of the King of Spain, to whom the English island has been promised in payment for his allegiance. As for America, we remember that he's not permitted to turn up there until the summer is over, and only then without taking any risks. This, obviously, will be too late.

What is it, at the end of a lifetime of standing at attention, that makes a great military chief live, move, act, exist—in other words, disobey? What is de Grasse's background that he can muster the guts to do it?

He was born in the seaside Alps, at the outlet of the gorges du Loup, almost sixty years before.* "Well born but insufficiently beaten," they say in the family[1] to explain his disagreeable temper. A childhood spent between extremes of cool shade and white sunlight, rock, the scrubby uplands, the

*On September 13, 1722, in the Château des Valettes where his mother was visiting, facing the Château du Bar on the other side of the gorge. It is still a scene of harsh splendor.

scorching cold mistral, and gravel underfoot. Hardly a book, except the ones he was forced to read. The Château du Bar was seven hundred years old and had oubliettes, underground passageways, and a regiment of servants to look after the little gentleman in rags. At thirteen—to his great joy, for sailing on the high seas was his one dream—he was dumped into the Knights of Malta (or, to be precise, of St. John of Jerusalem). To join this order of sea monks, of course, he had to go through the formality of taking the three vows. But poverty didn't frighten him since that meant the poverty of officers, whose ships were floating mansions with hundreds of footmen-mates, not to mention the fact that in those days the people you gave orders to were galley slaves. As for obedience and chastity, it's easy enough to choose them when you're thirteen. The Toulon Jesuits' mold had "set" him, like Suffren, into the perpetual infancy of an enraged overgrown schoolboy. The ceremonies in the gorgeous mantle adorned with gold and purple crosses initiate him into a military mandarinate apart from and superior to other men. "A minute shall be drawn up," stipulates the Statute of the Order, "supported by written documents, establishing the legitimacy and antecedents of the candidate, with testimonial, literal, local and secret proof of his father, mother, grandfathers, grandmothers, great-grandfathers and great-grandmothers extending back for more than one hundred years, and depicting his eight quarters.* The candidate shall show proof that his grandparents were recognized as gentlemen in name and arms."[2] At sixteen he already stood over six feet tall,† and once he grabbed an insubordinate deckhand by the jacket and slung him clear across the ship. He hasn't changed. Few men are more feared and less loved in the entire royal navy. One of his officers has just written a letter that sets every tongue in Versailles awag: "The almost universal hatred, on shipboard, of our commander, must be seen as the sole reason for the poor success of this campaign.** We might have captured and burned the enemy. Never has the chief been obeyed. Insolence has risen to such a pitch that one captain said aloud, 'That man must be made to feel all the fury and despair of a general who cannot rely upon his officers.' M. de Bougainville was put under arrest for two days. When they came to release him he was so infuriated that he refused to go, he was determined to avoid the command of his ship and division."[3]

But then, when did anybody ever teach de Grasse the art of loving and being loved? Naval officers are trained to be galley sergeants. He fired his first cannon, already against the English and already in support of Spain, on board

---

*Of nobility, four on the paternal side and four on the maternal.

†Six feet seven inches to be exact—a colossus for those days.

**This is nailing down the coffin lid before the patient is dead. The "poor success" he mentions is no more than an alleged apathy in the pursuit of English convoys; yet de Grasse did snatch the little island of Santa Lucia out from under Admiral Hood's nose, on the outward voyage.

the *Terrible* back in 1744. That means his hide has had more than thirty years to toughen in . . .

Toulon, Malta, the Indies, the Antilles. One incident: marriage, at the age of forty-two, and thus separation from his Order. Unlike Suffren, he wouldn't cheat on his vows and he wanted to found a family. Apart from that one detail, he remains a Knight of Malta to the tip of his whip. Morocco, Greece—to fight pirates when he ran out of English, whom he was overjoyed to meet again at Ouessant, under d'Orvilliers, and at Grenada, under d'Estaing. Now we see him in another incarnation, reborn into the nakedness of the supreme chief, under nobody. Able to *be*.

Three days ago he got Rochambeau's letter, which makes him sole arbiter of the summer. "I must not conceal from you, sir, that these people are at the end of their means; that Washington will not have half the troops he counted upon, and that I believe, although he is reticent about it, that he has not now six thousand men; that M. de La Fayette has not one thousand regular soldiers with the militia to defend Virginia, and about that many who are upon the way to unite with him; that General Greene lately was checked at Camden, upon which place he made an attempt, and that I do not know when or how he will join M. de La Fayette; that it is therefore of the greatest importance that you should take on board as many troops as possible; that four thousand or five thousand men would not be too many . . ."4 In other words, they're not just asking him for ships and guns, but also for the Santo Domingo-based regiments that the Spanish are counting on to conquer Jamaica. And money, Admiral, for the love of God, masses of money! Rochambeau is marching across a tight-fisted America on credit. On August 20 his treasurer Tarlé's coffers are empty. And it isn't Job Washington who's going to fill them. We see de Grasse transformed into an honorary Beaumarchais, implored to use "the influence of his credit and to demand aid from the naval army in the Antilles to a total of 1,200,000 livres in specie,* to be repaid here, including the costs and loss on exchange, by army treasury bills drawn on M. de Sérilly, treasurer general of the war."5

If he stays put, he's got absolutely nothing to lose. This war now three years old, this war of immobile commanders, is a mirror image of Louis XVI. All the blame will fall on those foolhardy daredevils Rochambeau, La Fayette, and Washington. Nobody will think about de Grasse. But if he bestirs himself and sails ships, men, and money all the way to the Chesapeake, far exceeding the terms of his orders, and maybe sinks them in the process, the boys back home will be gunning for him and they won't miss. He will have acted: the mortal sin.

---

*6 million new francs [$1.2 million].

But they're waiting up there. Everybody's waiting for an answer from this moodless, passionless man who neither reads, writes, nor talks. Service, service: the Comte de Grasse. How is he supposed to know?

Rochambeau and Washington are waiting in Phillipsburg, where the French army has encamped after marching two hundred twenty miles in eleven days "without losing a single man apart from two lovers from the Soissonnais regiment who went back to see their mistresses in Newport"; Rochambeau has asked Barras "to have a search made,"[6] and it won't be to pin any medals on them. The American army, also called the "Continental army," is crowding around the Hudson at the crossing known as Dobbs Ferry. On its left, the French are encamped in the hills, strung out in one long line clear to the Bronx. On July 6, for want of anything else to do, a fine ceremony is held in the field to celebrate their reunion. You'd think you were on the parade grounds at Sablons. Washington delivers himself of an official order in honor of the event:

"The Commander-in-Chief with pleasure embraces the earliest public opportunity of expressing his thanks to His Excellency, the Count de Rochambeau, for the unremitting zeal with which he has prosecuted his march, in order to form the long-wished-for junction between the French and American forces; an event which must afford the highest degree of pleasure to every friend of his country, and from which the happiest consequences are to be expected. The General entreats His Excellency, Count de Rochambeau, to convey to the officers and soldiers under his immediate command the grateful sentence he entertains of the cheerfulness with which they have performed so long and laborious a march at this hot season. The regiment of Saintonge is entitled to peculiar acknowledgments for the spirit, with which they continued and supported their march without one day's respite."[7] So much for the good old conscripts from Saintes, Cognac, and Barbezieux, who have indeed marched roundly and in remarkably high spirits, as though there were some affinity between the summer sultriness of the swamps of Saintonge and this New Jersey heat which is driving the rest of the men to their knees.

How handsome they look on their white horses, Washington and Rochambeau! All around them, in impressive array, stands the paraphernalia of a force that would fold at the first blow if they tried to storm the defenses of New York. Their cartridge pouches and shot bags contain powder for three days at most. The English ships, which can freely enter the Hudson, quadruple the firepower of General Clinton's forts, and the French siege material has been left behind in Newport. So the only effective thing they can do in this month of July is show themselves; and they do—while waiting for an answer from de Grasse.

That being the case, their seven or eight thousand men settle down to

make themselves at home, displaying the ineffable talent of the soldier—
similar to that of the cockroach—for adapting to any terrain. Ya gotta live. The
big event of July and August along this wooded riverbank is the grand game
of foraging for food, within the limits permitted by the officers. Every fowl and
porker, wild or not, is up for grabs; and so is—who would believe it?—every
woman. This period of compulsory inactivity gives one lieutenant of artillery
in the Auxonne regiment, Jean-François-Louis de Clermont-Crèvecoeur,* an
opportunity to conduct some admiring research into the unfettered mores of
the American female and the form of trial marriage she can contract. Crèvecoeur is from the Vosges; here he discovers a world that really is new, light-
years away from his native planet of Vaudréville, near Epinal. His interest,
bordering on envy, is patent:

> On August 11 a woman was arrested who had come from New York on the
> pretext of seeking her father who, she claimed, was a soldier in the American
> army; but doubtless her intentions were not so pure. She was put in a safe place
> to rest from her journey, which she had made on foot.
>
> "This anecdote leads me to make a brief observation on the subject of
> American women, or girls. In a country so new where vice should not be deeply
> rooted, why should there be such a large number of prostitutes? Only one reason
> seems to me to be the cause. Although the fathers and mothers keep an eye on
> their daughters during their childhood, once they reach the age when human
> nature demands that they know everything, they become their own mistresses and
> are free to keep company with anyone they wish. Among the country people (for
> today in the towns education has corrected the abuses of which I shall speak) the
> girls enjoy so much freedom that a Frenchman or an Englishman, unaccustomed
> to such a situation, straightaway seeks the final favors. It is actually the custom,
> when a young man declares himself to be in love with a young girl, without even
> mentioning marriage, to permit him to bundle with her. This permission is
> granted by the parents. He then shuts himself up in a room with the young lady
> to lavish the most tender caresses upon her, stopping short of those reserved for
> marriage alone; otherwise he would transgress the established laws of bundling
> . . . The truly virtuous girls, who are not governed by temperament, easily resist
> and conform to the letter of the law of bundling, but it is to be feared that those
> more amply endowed by nature in this respect succumb to the tender sport.
> Bundling, it would seem, is made for Americans only. The coldness and grav-
> ity of their faces proclaim that this sport suits them perfectly. The bundling
> period is not defined; you can play this game for five or six years before de-
> ciding to marry, and even afterwards if you wish, without committing yourself

*Crèvecoeur wrote a journal of the campaign, unpublished in France, which was found in
an attic in Providence, Rhode Island, in 1923. Made a captain in 1789, he emigrates and fights
against Napoleon in the service of Portugal before coming home to die, with a pension from Louis
XVIII, in his Château de Vaudréville. His observations on American women, related here, are
interspersed with a few lines from Berthier's journal.

finally to marry the girl after receiving these initial favors.

The women are generally very faithful to their husbands. You find few libertines among them. Yet some girls lead a most licentious life before they marry, though once married they, too, become good. The men are not fussy in this respect; they believe a girl should be free and do not despise her unless she is unfaithful after marriage. Thus a girl who has proved her worth, if she is pretty or rich, is quite sure of finding a husband; if she has had the misfortune to be seduced and the seduction bears its unfortunate fruit, it is not she who is disgraced, but the man. Respectable houses are henceforth closed to him, and he cannot marry into a respectable family.

It is rare to find a woman committing adultery here, though it does happen. In this situation the husband announces the delinquency of his wife and publishes it in the papers. No dishonor falls upon the husbands for the misconduct of their wives, and no one points the finger of scorn at a cuckold. Instead, they pity him. If the wife absconds with her lover, the husband announces in the gazette that his wife has quit his bed and declares that he will not pay her bills or be liable for any debts she may have contracted . . . This is no excuse, however, for dissolving the marriage, which rarely occurs, since their laws do not permit it. The husbands are quite patient about waiting for their wives to repent. If they do, their husbands take them back, forget the past, and live with them in perfect harmony. I leave it to the European husbands to ask themselves whether they are capable of doing as much.[8]

While the game treads water in the North, La Fayette continues rushing around in the South without much idea of what's really going on. After emerging unscathed from his very bad singeing at Green Spring Farm, in whose pastures a little cemetery of forty-two crosses has just been planted, he has gone back to Williamsburg and halted long enough to pull off his boots. At last, a town where he and his men can rest while he tries to figure out why on earth Cornwallis has made him a present of it, after Richmond. On the north bank of the James the English showed that they're still strong enough to make a stand. But after stopping La Fayette in his tracks and almost capturing or killing him, they then proceed to cross the river as though they were out on maneuvers. To draw him further on? To establish a sort of *de facto* armistice while waiting for fresh reinforcements to come to one side or the other? A sort of mock peace reigns in the little town, deserted by half of its two thousand inhabitants. Williamsburg smothers in a natural hollow bordered by hills flattened under the weight of a devouring, exhausting vegetation, you can't remember the names of even half the trees. La Fayette sends as many men as possible out to camp on top of Malvern Hill where, in the evenings at least, the sea breeze stirs up the sticky damp. He and his officers lounge in the houses grouped geometrically around the debtors' prison— crammed full of Tories at the moment—the parish church built in the year

Louis XV was born, and that pretty four-story college that bears the names of William and Mary, the royal couple in the days when it was still good to be English. Almost every Virginia gentleman has learned the few simple notions that pad out his common sense within its walls. The road running from the town's northeast exit is called York Way, and leads to the lovely, picturesque small port twelve miles away where La Fayette and Charlus wandered last spring, searching in vain for signs of French ships. Now he's not looking in that direction. He supposes, following the surprise retreat of the English, that he is firmly ensconced in the little peninsula he has just reoccupied between the James and the York, and can prepare—but for what, ye gods, in this crazy show? Are they going to ask him to take his five thousand men and reconquer the Carolinas? On July 20, with no news from headquarters, he has a brief, final attack of the blues, brought on by his eternal terror of being forgotten about. But he has excuses, one must admit. If Cornwallis is avoiding him, it must be so he can go and climb peacefully aboard his ships in Portsmouth, and if he's re-embarking, it can only be in order to lend Clinton a hand; and that means the decisive battle will be fought up there after all and without La Fayette, which is just what he's been dreading for the last three years, and especially the last three months. And what if Washington only sent him to Virginia at the request of his little playmates in Newport, who want to win all the laurels and leave him empty-handed? So he tosses a bottle into the sea in the direction of his adoptive father:

> When I went to the Southward, you know I had some private objections, but I became sensible of the necessity there was for the detachment to go, and I know that, had I returned, there was nobody there that could lead them on against their inclination. My entering this State was happily marked by a service to the capital. Virginia became the grand object of the ennemy [sic], as it was the point to which the Ministry tended.
>
> I had the honor to command an army and oppose Lord Cornwallis. When incomparably inferior to him, fortune was pleased to preserve us; when equal in numbers, tho' not in the kind of troops, we have also been pretty lucky [and modest].
>
> Cornwallis had the disgrace of a retreat and this State being recovered, government properly re-established, the ennemy are under protection of their works at Portsmouth, it appears an embarkation is taking place, probably destined to New York. The war in this State would then become a plundering one, and great manoeuvres be out of the question,—a prudent officer would do our business here and the Baron [Steuben] is prudent to the utmost. Would it be possible, my dear General, that, in case a part of the British troops go to New York, I may be allowed to join the combined armies?

By the time he gets to the end of his letter he's stopped bragging and started weeping. Washington must be the only man in the world to whom he can say: "No accounts from the Northward. No letter from Headquarters. I am utterly a stranger to everything that passes out of Virginia; and, Virginian operations being for the present in a state of languor, I have more time to think of my solitude. In a word, my dear General, I am homesick, and if I can't go to Headquarters wish at least to hear from them."[9]

But now's not the time for him to go to pieces. On the contrary, the game is about to start up again. Everything will soon be going his way, and Washington will be the only person ever to know how he very nearly lost heart at the last minute. From Cap Français, on July 28, the Comte de Grasse dictates to Rochambeau the letter that founds the United States of America as surely as the Declaration of Independence. On his own signature he has borrowed a million livres* from the Spanish bankers in Havana; because the French moneylenders, though closer at hand, weren't interested—which shows a lot about their sympathy with the Rebels and their confidence in victory. So much for the money. For the men, de Grasse decides to embark the Islands regiments: Gâtinais, Royal Marine, Agénois, Brissac, Barrois, Béarn, and Touraine, making three thousand infantry, a hundred artillery, a hundred dragoons, ten gunners and their siege guns and mortars—everything that's supposed to be on loan to Don Solano, the Spanish admiral, for the Jamaica expedition. So he'll have to use his soldiers well and quickly, and not get them turned into sausage meat before the Spanish complaints reach Vergennes.

> As this whole expedition has been undertaken at your request, and without consulting the ministers of France or of Spain . . . I have felt myself authorized to assume certain responsibilities in the interest of the common cause . . .
>
> I have learned with great chagrin of the distressing situation upon the Continent, and of the need of the prompt assistance which you call for. I have consulted with M. de Lilliancourt, who has taken charge of the general government, and prompted him to give me three thousand infantry and cannon from the Santo Domingo garrison.
>
> All will sail in twenty-five or twenty-six ships of war which will leave this place on August 3 and proceed to Chesapeake Bay, the point which appears to me to have been indicated by you, Monsieur le Comte, and by MM. Washington, de La Luzerne, and de Barras, as the one from which the advantage that you propose may be most certainly attained.
>
> From the efforts I have made to fulfill all your requests . . . you will conceive how earnestly I desire to change your present position and to put a new aspect upon the state of affairs.
>
> I leave you free to decide when you will join me on your side, for the furtherance of our common cause. Keep me informed, however, so that our maneuvers shall not interfere with each other.[10]

*Using the property he owns in Santo Domingo as part security.

There are only two or three authentic portraits of the Admiral de Grasse in existence. One, by somebody named Mauzaisse,[11] shows him as his subordinates saw him—with a fairly dreadful wild boar's leer. But a young portrait painter, Joseph Boze,* a debutant working the great homes of Provence, has recently taken advantage of a brief stopover in Toulon to catch, under coalblack brows, the penetrating eyes and big nose of a lover of the good life, and the little caustic smile of a man who's waiting to get even.

ROMME

64

AUGUST 1781

I Have Undertaken to Form a Man

Gilbert Romme is as far in the direction of the rising sun as La Fayette has sailed toward the setting, and while the name of the "hero of the New World" is becoming a household word, Romme is still totally unknown at the end of these three years spent pursuing his solitary adventure in Russia. America is pretty remote from the thoughts of most Frenchmen and seems to be totally absent from his. Circumstance has uprooted the son of the attorney of Riom just as thoroughly, albeit in the opposite direction, as it has his Auvergnat neighbor, the young marquis who spent his youth at Chavaniac. In this summer of 1781 Romme is an *outchitel,* that is, one of the horde of French tutors in the pay of the Russian nobility. But this tutor is something special. He has just set off on a monstrous journey "to the very gates of Asia" for the sake of Paul Stroganov, the little fellow whose destiny has been entrusted to his care. A continent will be the classroom for his lone pupil.

After Turgot's fall France seemed to offer Romme no outlet commensurate with his ambitions. He would never be given that professorship of physics he had had his eye on back in Auvergne. "I must not hope to see my country again in the capacity of physicist. M. Turgot's disgrace has removed that project as far from my grasp as the worthy minister has been removed from Court . . . All good citizens feel the nation's loss and can but bemoan the absence

*One of the great portrait painters of the Revolution. He paints—as we shall see—innumerable Marats, Dantons, Louis XVIs, and others. The pastel showing the unexpected side of the Comte de Grasse hangs in the museum at Blérancourt (Aisne), the home of Saint-Just.

of the person who put his master's confidence to such good use and who, perhaps before anyone else, truly understood how the arts and sciences must be of concern to governments, and deserve their protection. No doubt he was striding ahead too rapidly, however, and lost sight of the fact that the nation has so long been accustomed to creep snailwise toward the good. A person who does not think like the greatest number is in danger of becoming a victim of his sentiments."[1] At first he put little hope in "Monsieur Nêcre," as he spelled it, following the current fashion. Anything resembling a "bel esprit" was anathema to this hick-town boy dedicated body and soul to reality. "M. Nêcre has been made counselor of state [October 24, 1776] and given influence in the ministry, and the literary people driven from the throne by M. Turgot's disgrace are now being restored to it. As M. Nêcre's wife is a bel esprit, his home has become an academic gathering place frequented by MM. Thomas, Marmontel, Suard, Diderot, and all the wits whose reign is about to dawn. That of M. Turgot was the reign of good sense and reason: MM. d'Alembert, Condorcet, etc., were the most courted. Time will teach us what to expect of these new men."[2] Two years later he and a large portion of the enlightened third estate had made their peace with Necker, for want of anyone better. Necker was no Turgot, but "all his views bear toward relieving the suffering class of the nation [in 1778] at the expense of the rich and powerful, who should be the only people to pay taxes to the government. Someone has dared to think it, and M. Nêcre has had the courage to make it the guiding rule of his reforms."[3] So Romme came to trust him, but from afar and in a vague general way, not looking, as in Turgot's day, for a specific link between the reformist movement and his own future. As far as that was concerned, he was halfheartedly continuing his medical studies and abandoning himself to the unconscious intoxication of an unhoped-for social climb. He had begun hobnobbing with people whose company enlarged his vision of the world, liberal and Rousseauist aristocrats such as the Comtesse d'Harville and a self-exiled Russian nobleman, Alexander Alexandrovich Golovkin.

"M. de Golovkin could not be more kind. I eat at his home twice a week and he would have me come oftener. He is learned and will talk of nothing but sciences or scholars. I find his conversation infinitely satisfying"[4]—because it placed a stamp of approval, from a powerfully distinguished beyond, on the young Jansenist's obsessions: toughness and change. "He summons to his children all sorts of teachers who can guide their hands, train their bodies, and exercise or cultivate their minds; but he takes on the educating of their hearts himself. This last part of their schooling, ordinarily so neglected, has been wrought to the highest pitch of perfection in the count's method."[5]

"He confines his expenditure to the most reasonable necessities, decent care of himself, a house open only to quiet, sensible, and unfortunate people;

and the judicious education of his children. These do not consume the fourth part of his income; the remaining three-quarters he devotes to work in the country (undertaken to distribute earnings more widely no less than to improve his estates), to institutions and schemes which are useful to his neighbors and to the public and which, by procuring a living preferably for the destitute, save them from idleness and want. Also with that income, old people are cared for and their wants supplied, children are decently brought up, young people are married and given dowries, the sick receive treatment and assistance . . . It is not the quantity of money disbursed, but the way in which it is used, that distinguishes ostentation from its opposite . . . What is done with any surplus amount must be determined by the most pressing need, whether of one individual or of society in general."6

That even one being produced by such a rotten society can act as well as think this way, isn't that proof that man can be changed by man? Since the publication of *Emile* everyone has known which button had to be pushed in order for the process to become universal: the moral and civic education of every child. Golovkin didn't have to do much preaching to convert Romme to his own pet theories on the subject. "The child should be directed toward a trade that will be useful to himself or to others: mechanist [*sic*], gardener, draftsman, etc." He will study—in moderation—history, because "the sequence of past events will enable him to foresee in the future what evils or misfortunes are engendered either by vices which have become too widespread or by crimes against the social order which, by continually separating the cause of each individual from the general cause, inevitably place men of every condition and country in a state of perpetual warfare."7 But the real revolution—in the narrow sense of the word, meaning "a sudden, radical, or complete change"—in his theory of education consists in moving arithmetic, the poor relation in a Christian education, from the bottom of the pile to the top, making it the most essential subject. "The child begins with that, seeing its practical usefulness. Mathematics follows easily, and will lead our pupil, if we know our business, into its essential parts such as Mechanics, Hydraulics, Optics, etc."

Golovkin wrote all that in 1778, in a confidential brochure intended for that small group of acquaintances he had made on the desert isle of their collective intelligence, the refuge of all who live ahead of their time. In its pages the name of Gilbert Romme, teacher, appears for the first time in the beam of a fleeting ray of light: "This study is less difficult than is supposed; many observations have proved to me that progress in this science, so excellent at rendering the mind accurate, inventive and diligent, depends upon the way in which its basic elements are explained and demonstrated. M. Rome [*sic*], a worthy man of letters and profound physicist, has a work filled with philosophy, force, and erudition treating of this assertion; I adjure him, in the name of that part of the Nation to whom the sciences are precious, to give it to the public. His material has all been assembled and his work will be too useful for him to refuse to make it known."8

He never does, though. Romme is not an intellectual. Thanks once again to Golovkin, he dedicates himself to the practical application of his theories instead, through the education of a boy who might come to change the face of an empire one day—Paul Stroganov.

Romme met Stroganov senior at Golovkin's house in 1778, but also at the Lodge of the Nine Sisters, where Voltaire was received in triumph a few weeks before his death.* Stroganov was another refugee from Saint Petersburg, but he only came to Paris in gasps, when he couldn't get enough oxygen elsewhere. A Russian of the reign of Peter the Great rather than that of Catherine II. According to his friend Prince Czartoryski, "there was a singular mixture in him of the Encyclopedist and the old Russian boyar." This latter part of his personality occasionally drove him far from the Masonic lodge and into the Rue du Bout-du-Monde, where he treated himself to "encounters at twenty-five louis† a time with the demoiselle Macarty, one of our prettiest girls," in the opinion of an inspector working for M. Le Noir, "tall, well-made, brunette, with white skin, admirable teeth and a very pleasant face."9 "Beneath his brilliant worldly varnish" this Russian of the Enlightenment, "a constant companion of men like Helvétius and d'Holbach, was fundamentally uncouth"10; so that the finer points of his son's education** were somewhat beyond him. And in the spring of 1779 he absolutely had to go back to Russia, accompanied by wife and son, or be dispossessed of the vast estates which, unlike Golovkin, he had not been clever enough to shed in time. Well, at least he'd take a bit of France back with him in the person of this Jean-Jacques Rousseau II, alias Gilbert Romme, to provide some supplemental paternity for his boy. He offered a small fortune and carte blanche as far as educational methods were concerned.

"Would you like to come with us in the autumn?"

There followed three months during which this already old and excessively fastidious young man, for whom making up his mind to take the stage-cart from Paris to Versailles was a week's work, could imagine all the dreadful things that might happen to him. "I am not lighthearted," Diderot was saying in similar circumstances five years earlier, "my soul is troubled. It pains me to put half an earthly diameter between myself and my friends."11 But apart

---

*The name of this lodge, which plays an important role as a meeting place for the enlightened upper class rather than as a thinking club, refers to the nine muses of mythology.

†2,500 new francs [$500].

**Who was eight years old in 1779, when he was put in Romme's care. Paul Stroganov becomes one of the chief advisers of Czar Alexander I when he comes to the throne.

from the warmth of a few friendly houses there was nothing to keep Romme in Paris, no wife, no occupation. It was the chance of a lifetime, and it must be taken. He left feeling as though he had cast off for eternity, like one of Christopher Columbus's deckhands. "It is through travel that one learns to judge men, and I now have a twofold interest in knowing them, for I have undertaken to form one."[12]

The trip across Poland appalled him. That country was a bone-breaker for travelers, even those who could afford every convenience like the Chevalier de Corberon and his servants two years ago, "driven by wretched Jews' horses, for such are the post stations here. These consumptive creatures, being without either strength or will to pull, compelled us continually to push at the wheels. Moreover, the dreadful roads through the forests obliged us to light the postilions with pine or deal torches, which give off a very pale light. We multiplied this illumination as required or at our pleasure, and it afforded the loveliest views of the forest imaginable, but we were thoroughly wearied by that frightful night . . .

"The entire country is abominable; all one sees are pine trees and sand. The so-called towns are more like villages; the buildings mere wooden boards completely blackened by smoke and dust, thus adding the specter of uncleanliness to that of indigence. Furthermore, the inhabitants, most of whom are Jews, put a perfect finish to the tableau; the wretchedness of their condition, moreover, has by no means left the mark of misery upon the brows of these unfortunates. They are slaves, paupers, and content to be so. It is true that habit may soften the rigors of servitude; but at the same time it degrades men and destroys all force of character. Our people would beat these poor devils, but it only made them laugh and serve us with greater diligence; at the same time, they tried to rob us whenever they could."[13] Gilbert's friends in Riom, following his travels as wide-eyed as though he were going to the moon, also became well acquainted with "the turpitude of the Poles who rot in ignorance and drunkenness, treading upon ground which, in other hands, would make the wealth of all Europe."[14] Back in 1775 even Dupont de Nemours had given them up as a lost cause.*

Romme's first months in Saint Petersburg, on the other hand, seem promising in spite of the winter's bite; he becomes hardened to it, he thinks he's discovering a sort of Venice in Auvergne. "I arrived [in November] in a woollen coat and jacket, very thinly lined," to plunge into a fairy-tale world

---

*Dupont made an ill-fated attempt to found a national system of education in "this Republic without a republic." The recoil of the "enlightened" mind from a superficial contact with the Poles, who were kept in a state of utter brutishness by their masters, was a precursor of the contempt expressed by slum visitors at their first sight of the "clods who have never learned to wash."

that would have turned many another head: an apartment in the sumptuous Italian-style Stroganov palace on the banks of the Moyka, swarms of servants, gargantuan tiled stoves, and, entirely at his disposal and better than any palace, a natural history room, another for anatomy, another for physics, and a library of twelve thousand volumes. Every literate lord here builds himself a private museum to suit his own taste. Stroganov ushers him in as though he were St. Peter at the gates of Heaven: "This is your kingdom, my dear friend; I shall do everything in my power to see that you are happy in my homeland."[15] And he keeps his word, treating Romme with a respect and confidence that raise him far above the common run of *outchitels,* those table scrapings of France who are more often regarded as house servants or refugees. Here he is almost ennobled, and accredited at the court of Catherine in a way he could never dare hope to be at Versailles.

At first, though, the empress gives Stroganov a cold shoulder, partly because she does that to everybody who has the effrontery to desert Saint Petersburg, but mainly on account of those rather special motives that were increasingly coming to interfere in high politics. Rimsky-Korsakov, one of the prettiest boys in the imperial harem, had fallen in love with the delectable Countess Stroganov, *née* Princess Trubetskoy, and she had looked kindly upon him. Stroganov, as becomes a *philosophe*-husband, gave his wife free rein to invite whomever she pleased, and Rimsky-Korsakov in particular, to his estate outside Moscow. So Catherine was cross with him. But between true *philosophes* such petty resentments last no longer than one of the empress's infatuations, or, at this stage of her career, from three to six months. When the Rimsky-Korsakov liaison is over Catherine reaccredits Stroganov, and even allows him to accompany her on her trip to Mohilev in the spring of 1780, to meet Joseph II. The grand seigneur does not bear grudges and, during the trip, sings hymns of praise to "my dear Mistress whom I adore more every day"; hymns which, ricocheting off Romme, go to console the bourgeois of Riom who likewise worship at the shrine of the "Semiramis of the North."*

In May 1780 Romme is presented to this affable German lady in her eruptive fifties. The immense square, the palace with its hundreds of windows —everything in Saint Petersburg is oversized—the interminable staircases that leave you breathless, and way at the top, like a series of jewel boxes resting one inside the other, a succession of increasingly cosy and intimate drawing rooms lit by blazing crystal leading to the one in which you stand in a row in the most splendid attire you can find and watch a plump little *hausfrau* come trotting up, with a blotchy complexion and tight-skinned chignon, a stern expression belied by laughing eyes, dimples everywhere, "our little Mother

---

*The expression is Voltaire's. Semiramis was a semi-legendary queen of Babylon who may have reigned over the entire Middle East and who apparently had her husband slain. Catherine II, daughter of the Prince of Anhalt-Zerbst, was born on April 21, 1729, at Stettin.

Empress," an inimitable compound of voluptuousness and propriety. The smile she bestows upon the man with the blinking eyes, unalluring physique, and scant interest in women whose praises Stroganov is singing to her is a smile of convention. Romme, meanwhile, sees in her what he wants to see: the enlightened despot. A classic reflex in a meeting between "small" and "great": "The veneration and profound esteem she inspires in all who come to know her place this woman among the ranks of the extraordinary and privileged beings who enlighten men by making them happy and who are above their fellow creatures, even in their foibles, from which none is exempt . . . Seated upon the throne so often shaken by dreadful agitation, she, with her mildness and the affectionate concern she shows for her subjects, has been able to steady it . . . She is wholly engrossed in her people's happiness. Thus she has inspired confidence in all, and the political calm surrounding her extends to the farthest reaches of her vast empire, where the people vie with one another in blessing her name."[16] This might be known as the "Diderot reaction," the prefabricated one of 1773. And as with Denis, it doesn't take Gilbert long to snap out of it. The summer of 1781 finds him in the process of clearing his head, energetically digging himself out from under the Petersburg eiderdown in which his own unique vision of things might have been smothered.

CATHERINE THE GREAT

65

AUGUST 1781

The Finest of Actresses

"The more I study this nation," writes the Chevalier de Corberon, French chargé d'affaires in Russia, "the more difficulty I have in defining it. It is a mixture of beings so ill-matched to one another, among whom one cannot see the shades and degrees of difference, nor grasp the progress and trend of their ideas, principles, systems. At first glance you see a barbarian people and an enlightened and learned nobility with polite and winning ways; upon closer inspection, you perceive that that same nobility is, at bottom, nothing but those same barbarians dressed up and decorated, but differing only outwardly from the brutish part of the nation."[1] The French upper crust, with the belching and vomit of its Folies at Bagatelle or Mousseaux, is a totally different species from its rural underlings, of course . . .

To disenchant him with the Russian variety, Romme has had one of those little personal jolts that enable you to move on from an aching heart to cold, clear reason, from subjective to objective. In Count Stroganov's Saint Petersburg he is an honored guest; but in Moscow, when the time comes to take his pupil to visit the countess under the separated couple's terms of agreement, he is made to feel his status as a slightly superior domestic servant. He's not a man to let it pass. Gilbert's bread-and-butter letter to Mme Stroganov, thanking her for one such reception: "The discredit and almost dishonor attaching to the status of tutors in this country alarm my sense of delicacy too intensely for me not to take the greatest pains to inflict as little as possible of my presence upon those of your society who might feel a repugnance to breathe the same air as an *outchitel;* from my own experience I already sympathize wholeheartedly with any sensitive beings reduced to pursuing the same career here as myself."[2]

When Corberon first meets him, on August 20, 1780, Romme is beginning to have serious second thoughts about his vision of the empire of the latter-day Semiramis. He's sufficiently unlike these other people, with his look of always having something else on his mind, to make an impression on the flighty little chipmunk whose chief occupation is scampering through the exhausting thickets of high-society balls in pursuit of Natashas who are profoundly convinced, at the age of seventeen, that life has passed them by. "I was to supper with the Count Strogonof [*sic*] in a charming place at Kamenny Ostrov on the banks of the river; and during the play I chatted with Romme, the son's governor, who is a chap of thirty, most learned and curious, especially about natural history. He expounded quite an ingenious idea of his about the formation of comets and planets. He claims that, instead of being formed by a comet as Buffon maintains, these planets, and the comets as well, are splashes of igneous material from the sun which, by means of the centrifugal force imparted to it by its rotating motion, hurls portions of its inflamed liquid to great distances, and those portions imperceptibly cool, owing to the time of their birth, which agrees with Bailly's system . . ."*

"Romme advised me to call on the Comte de Golovkin in Paris; he lives philosophically [*sic*] there, for the education of two of his children."[3] Notwithstanding their differences of background and interests, Romme and Corberon agree on essentials. The Frenchmen exchange impressions like two shipwreck victims marooned on Russian soil sharing out their hardtack.

In this place you've got to know what's happening in order to survive. "Catherine the Great?" A woman past her prime, and a slave to her predilec-

---

*Jean-Sylvain Bailly has just achieved European renown by publishing his *History of ancient astronomy from its origins to the founding of the school of Alexandria.* As representative of Paris at the Estates-General, he plays a leading role in the Tennis Court Oath and is the first elected mayor of Paris.

tion for young men. That in itself wouldn't be so bad if she didn't also insist on bringing sentiment into it and idealizing the favorite of the day, or rather night, to the point of trying to turn him into a statesman. "There is nothing more natural than this feeling in a woman of her age who is ruled by this kind of passion; and at the same time there is nothing more regrettable, for it leads to petty weaknesses on the part of a sovereign. It would be desirable for her to take lovers for the physical side only; but that is rare among older people; and when their imaginations are not deadened, they are a hundred times more foolish than young men . . . Imagination and vanity ferment more in an old brain; it is a misfortune, to be sure, but at the same time it is a sign of some good qualities.

"By trying to make a statesman out of Lanskoy, the Empress shows that she is thinking of the State. It is a misguided good intention, but even a good intention counts for something and, if this sovereign were governed by some man of genius, she could be made to do the greatest and finest things; but such a man has not come forward, and as the illusions which she constructs for each of her favorites are being continually destroyed and renewed, the series of her weaknesses becomes innumerable and its consequences terrifying. With the broadest views and the best intentions, Catherine II is sending her country to perdition by her behavior, ruining it by her extravagance, and will ultimately be judged a weak and sentimental female."[4] This doesn't prevent the empress, at the great religious ceremonies, from making doubly certain of the support of the Russian clergy—the prime machine of power, stronger even than the army—"by prostrating herself repeatedly in front of the holy images, for our Catherine is the finest of actresses. She is pious, tender, proud, majestic, amiable, but at heart she is forever herself, that is to say, attached solely and exclusively to her own interests, and, to serve them, donning any mask that may seem fit and proper to her and necessary to her purposes."[5]

The prize cockerel of 1781, in any case, is Alexander Dmitrievich Lanskoy of the horse guard; he was twenty-two when Catherine "deigned to cast her eyes upon him" as a replacement for Rimsky-Korsakov, who was "the very model of fatuity, but of the most trivial sort, such as would not be tolerated even in Paris." "The poor Lanskoy is a trifle stupid, and his illustrious lady friend will alter him no more than she did Zoritz"—back in 1777—"whose mind she found sublime while he was in favor and whom she also wanted to turn into a person of note in the Empire."[6] Meanwhile, Lanskoy can't complain: he's already a general, chamberlain, and commander of cuirassiers. However, he would do well to keep an eye on "a certain Pazharsky, a captain in the army, who has been seen at the empress's gaming table these days. He is a young man built like a Hercules, about whom not another word has been said thus far."

Why bother with this kind of nonsense? Because here, a ripple in the bedspread is an affair of state. A change of favorites can bog down the train of Europe or send it off the rails. "In Russia one may observe a sort of interregnum coinciding with the displacement of one favorite and the installation of his successor. This event eclipses all others; it turns and fixes every eye in a single direction, and even cabinet ministers, affected by the general influence, suspend their operations until such time as a choice has been made, when minds can resume their natural preoccupations and the machine its wonted movements."[7] It is therefore just as essential for well-informed circles in both worlds to follow the scowl of the very high and very potent Prince Potemkin now as it once was to keep tabs on La Pompadour's caprices—for he, ex-champion among lovers, has now become their purveyor: "Saturday, the day of our supper in the country,* the Empress dined in a tent on the Nevsky islands as a guest of Potemkin, who has had a Cossack hall built in that place. This favorite, who plays the part of La Pompadour toward the end of her life with Louis XV, presented to her a certain Zoritz, major of hussars, who was made lieutenant colonel and inspector of light troops. The new favorite dined with her. He is said to have received one thousand eight hundred peasants for his first attempt.† After the dinner Potemkin drank to the Empress's health and went down on his knees. Upon leaving the table she went to the porcelain works, looking most merry, and even free; for they say the good woman was a little tipsy."[8]

And well she might be. Let's all drink to Catherine's health. She never stints on this kind of spending, even when, during one favorite's official reign, she treats herself to the equivalent of those little girls Louis XV used to have sent over to the Parc-aux-Cerfs. "Zavadovsky, who was the Empress's subsidiary favorite, received from Her Majesty fifty thousand rubles, five thousand as an annual pension and four thousand peasants in the Ukraine, where they are worth a lot. You will agree, my friend, that this is a profitable profession to exercise here."[9] Since then Corberon has become better informed. He is soon able to line up such figures for Gilbert Romme as can only put strange ideas into the head of a Jansenist dedicated to universal happiness: "In the end, Zavadovsky had six thousand peasants in the Ukraine, two thousand in Poland, eighteen hundred in Russia, eighty thousand rubles in jewelry, one hundred fifty thousand rubles in money, thirty thousand in plate and ten thousand as an annual allowance, in the space of eighteen months. Zoritz got land in Poland worth five hundred thousand rubles, an estate in Livonia worth a hundred thousand, five hundred thousand rubles in specie, two hundred thou-

---

*The scene Corberon is relating here took place on June 8, 1777.

†In other words, a fairly good-sized estate somewhere in Russia. In this country which had no land survey, the only way to arrive at even a general idea of the extent and importance of an estate was to count the number of serfs, or "souls" as they were called, which it contained.

sand in jewels, and a commandery in Poland worth twelve thousand a year. All that in one year. And these amounts are insignificant compared with those received by the Orlovs (seventeen million rubles), Potemkin (fifty million), Lanskoy (seven million two hundred sixty thousand) and the Zubov brothers (three and a half million)."*

All very well and good; but in that case who's running the country and how? Toward the end under Louis XV everybody knew it was Mme de Pompadour and the Duc de Choiseul, followed by the Duc d'Aiguillon. Under Louis XVI everybody knows it's Maurepas and Vergennes. But under Catherine? One day, after all, we'll have to guess which side of the fence Russia is likely to come down on if this war between France and England lasts much longer. Both are clearly manifested in the two men who are holding the reins of state so forcefully and harmoniously that the chariot is being pulled wildly in opposite directions. "In the Council [on September 22, 1780] there was a very fierce argument between Panin and Potemkin. The latter came out openly in favor of England and, wanting to intimate that Count Panin had sold himself to France, said straight out to the Council that effigies of Louis XVI make excellent whist markers. Panin retorted that if Potemkin had been in need of markers, he would have only to stretch out his hand to find it full of guineas. The quarrel became so envenomed that Panin went to fetch the Empress, who came and put a stop to it."[11]

Catherine's real job often consists of nothing more than this kind of exhausting arbitration between Potemkin, prince of favorites, and Panin, one of the few men in her court to whom she has delegated power without entangling it in her heartstrings, and who is thus able to steer in relative safety through the frequent storms. "What always surprises me is the way in which people work here. Count Panin, who is prime minister, lives as though he were some great noble who had no other condition but to be at Court, and no other occupation but to know what is going on there. He rises very late, amuses himself looking at new prints or books, makes his toilette, gives audience, dines, plays afterwards or sleeps, begins seeing more people and playing again, sups and retires very late."[12] "Sleep, gluttony and girls are his only activities." One can imagine how irate he was when the threat of insurrection compelled him, back in 1774, to bestir himself and go after Pugachev. A third man, Gregory Orlov—who assassinated Peter III—sometimes manages to save the day. He lives rather on the fringes of the court, but Catherine can hardly say no to him. He is still making and unmaking ministers with a word, from his enormous mansion on the Moyka quay not far from the Stroganovs', where he holds a levee worthy of a satrap. "It is an authentic court, one can have

*Historians of the reign of Catherine II estimate the total amount distributed among her favorites at over 100 million rubles, or some 2 billion new francs [$400 million].[10]

simply no idea of it in our European countries. Our princes of the blood and ministers receive fully dressed, and give their audience with the sort of consideration to which the public is always entitled. But here Asiatic customs have bequeathed that laxity of oriental despotism, and every man in high position receives the national public with opulence and indolence . . . The prince emerged from his chamber wearing a dressing gown, with unkempt, thinning hair and a long pipe in his mouth. We formed a circle, each person made his bow, and I [Corberon] came forward making mine, to tell the prince I had come several times without finding him in. He cut short my thanks, took me by the hand to tell me that he was charmed to have done what I desired, and was at my service for anything in which I might employ him. He sat in an armchair, had his curlpapers put on, smoked and continued conversing . . . After speaking to several persons, he gave orders that I was to be shown his paintings; as I was led out, the prince's entire suite bowed before me, for that is how much power favor and its reflection have over individuals here!"[13]

And so goes the Russia of the Enlightenment, with little prospect of change on the horizon. The heir to the throne might make it even worse. "Not only has the grand duke* a weak character, he may be said to have none at all; being by nature hard and cruel, his goodness results only from fear. He hates his mother, who looks down upon him and believes him unworthy of the station to which he is called. Moreover, his birth is not what is supposed. Peter III is not his father, it was a Saltykov who sired him."[14] He lives in retirement on his beautiful Pavlovsky estate on the banks of the Neva. Because of his terror of his mother, he sends his German guards out on ostentatious maneuvers every day, not without some effect on Catherine's nerves. Which will kill the other first? For more than a century Russia has been known as an "absolute monarchy tempered by assassination." To be on the safe side, Catherine has confiscated her two grandsons, Alexander and Constantine, who are destined to reign one day over Moscow and Constantinople respectively, and is bringing them up in her own way as part of a scheme to short-circuit that overexcited simian of a son. The only hope of 20 or 25 million men and women lies in the tiny fists of these two tots.†

Romme has seen the light. Why shouldn't he too manufacture a little king, the boy Stroganov has entrusted to his care to save him from that other plague? Gilbert decides that he will produce a true prince, that is, a free man—or at least free from *them*. But from himself?

"I have but one occupation here, which absorbs all my time, commands

---

*Paul Petrovich, born in 1754, who takes a long trip through Europe in 1781–82.

†In 1781 Alexander is four and Constantine one. In 1801 the former succeeds his father Paul I, who is indeed the victim of the traditional assassination, and rules over Russia until his own mysterious death in 1825.

all my actions and imperiously prohibits anything that might distract me from it. I have no recreations; I refuse all in order to devote myself wholly to my object."[15] It's you or me, little Paul—his name is the same as the grand duke's, but the happy-go-lucky boy who would undoubtedly just as soon not be used as a guinea pig for a new educational method is familiarly known as Popo. "My researches have borne principally on three points: physics, morals, and instruction. It is from my reading of Tissot, Rousseau, Locke, and the frequent discussions I have had on this subject with an enlightened friend, that I have drawn the ideas which I submit for your consideration,"[16] Romme writes to Stroganov in one of his regular reports.* Poor old Popo! "At this moment I am becoming a second father to him . . ." The kid must have been pretty resilient not to break his neck on all the good intentions paving his way through childhood. Romme appears to have put him in training as rigorously as if he had been a crown prince. Horsemanship, swimming, fencing, long walks, cold baths, a light and chiefly vegetarian diet, clothing that is "simple and coarse, possessing no elegance," forty winks on a bed of boards . . . Not exactly an imitation of St. Potemkin. Then, for the moral side: large doses of Plutarch, and Socrates in the front row. "The injustice of the Areopagus and the death of this wise man moved him deeply; and it was between two sobs that he said to me, heaving a long sigh, 'Does that mean that all good people are persecuted? And the most virtuous are most exposed to being tormented?' "[17]

Romme ruthlessly extirpates any reverence for the good Orthodox God from the child's mind and instills the worship of law in its place. The eternal refrain of his civics lessons is the inscription engraved in the Pass of Thermopylae by the last of the sacred battalion to die:

> Go tell the Spartans, thou that passeth by,
> That here, obedient to their laws, we lie.

But in accordance with Golovkin's precepts the pages of history are quickly turned. Make way for mathematics, physics, chemistry, natural sciences, and their practical applications. "I have made myself a law, to which I subordinate all pleasures. It is to edify my pupil at every instant, speaking nothing to him but the simple and highly unpoetical language of reason."[18] Jacques Démichel, a friend whom Gilbert brings from Riom to Saint Petersburg to become the *outchitel* of one of Popo's cousins, writes: "Romme has changed not a whit and never will. Always serious, always pondering, he lives

*The "enlightened friend" is Golovkin, of course. Tissot is the great hygienist doctor then in fashion, author of a treatise on *Onanism* and a formidable fanatic on the subject of sexual repression. John Locke (1632–1704), a nonconformist English philosopher, wrote some *Thoughts on the Education of Children* which make him a precursor of Rousseau. In the eighteenth century he is regarded as an apostle of freedom of expression.

only to think, to procure new knowledge for his pupil and add to his own. If he had not such a sensitive heart, which draws me closer to him, I believe I should be sorry to have expatriated myself. I know no one who carries circumspection so far. Absolutely nothing escapes him that can contribute to the edification of his pupil and the formation of his young heart."[19]

66

AUGUST 1781

The Last to Die

Master and pupil are about to take a closer look at that Russia of which little Paul will one day be, who knows, perhaps prime minister, and in which his father possesses estates that make Popo the heir to a monarchy larger than Holland and more feudal than the Dauphiné in A.D. 1000. Most of the "government"* of Tula belongs to Count Stroganov. It contains one of the largest armament factories in Europe. It also contains 340,504 serfs—that is, men, women, and children who are no less their owner's property than livestock, chickens, dogs, or American Negroes. The progress of the Enlightenment in Catherine the Great's Russia can be marked by the fact that they are actually being counted[1]; but as for changing their condition in any way, that's another story. The truth of the matter is that their condition *has* been changing during the last ten years, but only for the worse. Encouraged by the Czarina's "reforming" ukazes, the nobility has increasingly begun to dabble in industry and trade, with the result that the worker is tending to become welded to his factory or mine and the peasant to his soil. The laws against the "lower orders" have provided governors and managers with a vast arsenal of punitive and coercive measures, and they are taking full advantage of them, especially since the Pugachev uprising struck holy terror into the souls of the "enlightened" a few years back.

New towns are being built, agricultural companies are being formed, roads are being laid, and national wealth is on the rise. The revenue of the Russian state is in the process of climbing from 17 million rubles, at the beginning of Catherine's reign, to 78 million.[2] And Catherine, who is as

*A government was a very large territorial subdivision, more like a province than a county. [*Trans.*]

fanatical about exactitude as Frederick II, has just sent Grimm a balance sheet
covering the first fifteen years of her reign, which will be published all over
Europe at the risk of bringing a blush to her fellow sovereigns' cheeks:

Governments established according to the new regulations	29
Towns built	144
Conventions and treaties signed	30
Victories won	78
Memorable edicts embodying laws, or foundations	88
Edicts containing measures to relieve the people	123[3]

Grimm is under no obligation to peruse the gazettes published in Petersburg and Moscow; otherwise he might have had to supplement this front-page
story with a few of those humble news items that, taken together, give a far
truer picture. For instance, these advertisements which Romme has noticed in
the Saint Petersburg Gazette:

No. 38. For sale one wigmaker and a milch cow of good breed.
No. 46. For sale one complete family, or a young man and a girl separately.
The young man is healthy, strong and knows how to curl ladies' hair. The girl,
well-made and in good health, aged fifteen, can sew and embroider. Available for
inspection, to be had for a reasonable price.[4]

Saint Petersburg has no monopoly. In Moscow you get plenty of choice
every week in the *Moskovskie Vyedomosti:*

For sale one barber and four bedsteads, an eiderdown and other items of
furniture for good measure.
For sale two banquet cloths and also two girls able to serve and one female
peasant.
For sale one girl of sixteen, of good character, and a hardly used secondhand
carriage.
For sale one girl of sixteen, qualified as a lacemaker, knowing how to sew
linen, iron, starch, and dress her mistress; also fair of face and well-built.

On July 8, 1781, Romme and Paul Stroganov leave Saint Petersburg, that
balcony of the Occident overlooking Russia, and plunge into its immensi-
ties, heading toward the Urals and Siberia in the company of a "naturalist
scholar," Peter Simon Pallas, who is to help them identify minerals, plants,
and soil types and observe the stars. A voyage of exploration highly typical
of the age; the young Lavoisier, for instance, toured Alsace and Lorraine
before his marriage. "This trip will be made slowly and without strain.
Sole masters of our movements, my pupil and I, released from all protocol, have with us none but people of good will who are delighted to serve
us . . . An under-officer in Her Majesty's guards is accompanying us to as-

sist us on occasion and cover us with all the imposing dignity of a body-guard."[5] We can feel the sense of freedom and lightheartedness in Romme's letters, he's had his fill of the hypocrisy of the gilded cottages in which the Petersburg great are manufacturing their own Trianons—such as the "Empress's Divan": "This is a charming little country house two versts from Peterhof, near a brook in the woods. The outside is like that of any Russian peasant house, all logs; but inside, it is the prettiest thing imaginable. There is a drawing room, a dining room and a divan* covered in mirrors, affording a most delightful illusion. . . . This little retreat has been done with great taste, and the outside forms a perfect foil for the interior. Before the main entrance are what appear to be heaps of straw such as one may see in barns, but which are actually artfully painted doors, and the glass windows are covered by shutters with logs painted on them, and in the center a little dormer has been cut like those in thatched huts. We have reached such refinement in our opulence that people are going back to imitating the humble dwellings of the poor, so that our tastes, jaded by pleasure and profusion, may be whetted by the contrast."[6]

What Gilbert is now giving Popo is not this stage-set version of rustic simplicity. He has trained him "to love physical exercise, even when violent, long walks, fatigue. And travel is conducive to transforming these tastes into habits, and inuring him to hunger, thirst, heat, cold." Faithful to Count Golovkin's precepts, he chooses the simple *kibitka* as their vehicle. And he wants to take along the barest minimum in the way of provisions—milk, eggs, and fruit, which already formed his pupil's staple diet in Saint Petersburg, will be plentiful on the road. "Let misfortune and poverty assail him one day; they may take the fat from his body, but his soul will remain healthy, happy, and steadfast." Deprived of the thrills of the hunt, Popo will go exploring for rare minerals, "stonehunting." And even more than the works of nature, he will address his mind to those of man, chiefly his factories, foundries, and mines. "Popo will not grasp all the details in a process of manufacture, or all the elements in the series of operations which go to make up a trade; but I shall grasp them, I shall devote all my attention to them; he will be there, and one day I shall have only to remind him that cannons are cast in such a place and cloth printed in another . . . He will understand the conversations I shall have with him when he grows older."[7] This is the do-or-die of Rousseauism for a flesh-and-blood Emile: "The bad roads, bad beds, bad food, and our frequent walks have no ill effect upon either his health or his disposition."[8] "My plan entails giving Popo some rudiments of geography, agriculture, and natural history, and acquainting him with the customs and needs of the people by traversing the countryside with him, rather than by coldly expounding them in a study. And Russia and the

*Here the word means a small, intimate room. [*Trans.*]

Russian people are the first objects toward which I have sought to direct his initial learning, so as to multiply the ties that are to attach him to his fatherland."9

But when you go to read the Russian people like a living book you have to turn the pages with caution, for a beaten hound has a swift snap. On the way out of Saint Petersburg they cross a zone of perpetual insecurity. "This arises from the disruptions perpetrated around the town by a breed of vagabonds called *tavlinski.* They are servants with no places and no passports, deserters and vagrants who have banded together to live by theft. In the beginning the crown did not guard against these people, and even employed them to work in imperial houses and paid them handsomely for it, which caused a few noblemen's slaves to run away and, seeking to escape from their condition, come and ask for work for the crown, which tolerated and even defended them. But when the work was finished, having no more employment, they were afraid to return to their masters, and so joined forces with one another. Some say they are four or five thousand strong, others say thirteen thousand. This can become serious.

"There was another incident,* also quite serious. Four villages, sixty versts from the city, rose up against the exactions of their masters, who are a Colonel Albrecht, a Brigadier Gerdov, and Berkmann. The peasants came to complain to Volkov, the governor of Petersburg, who told them that under the new regulations they were free†; this excited them and drove them to such extremes that the troops had to be called out to put them down."10 Who'll save the peasants from freedom like this? "Instead of sending the troops to abduct the most resolute right away, the authorities wanted to issue ukazes; this was noised about, and the scoundrels' numbers swelled. No one would be surprised if this were to become a very grave matter. They say the Empress is afraid; she does not dare walk alone in her gardens, and has dismissed Volkov as head of the police department and domestic government of Petersburg, because he was so negligent."11 The worst of it is that the soldiers aren't any too reliable either. Are we about to witness a second Pugachev on the shores of the Baltic? "This brings no joy to the great lady, who was already out of temper. These *tavlinski* irritate her, and Potemkin has had a little spat with her on their account. He wanted to have them surrounded by the troops, and that was the right way to go about it; but the Empress would not hear of such a course. But others say that Potemkin, and above all Tolstoy"—commander of the imperial guard—"were opposed to sending out the guards because many people are discontent with the latter's monopoly; he is embezzling money and supplies intended for the guards, and it is feared that these men, far from

*In August 1780.

†This was not a general emancipation but "a few tradesmens' patents which the Empress doled out to petitioners."

striving to capture the bandits, might ally themselves with them."[12] Watches have been doubled, and the guards are carrying loaded guns, even in the corridors of the palace.

One can understand Romme's sense of release when he breaks out of this stifling atmosphere. A trip through Russia is a sort of spatial peregrination, you roll on over dead-level roads to the end of time, it's a "change of scene" in the purest form. "It takes a little over four versts to make one French league. Every verst is marked by a stake planted in the road with its number on it. The best way to travel in Russia is to keep going night and day, for there are no inns as in France; you cannot find a bed, and the houses in which you stop to eat the provisions you carry with you can supply nothing but plates and forks. This inconvenience is a result of the style of travel of the Russian noblemen: they take their entire household with them, beds, kitchen, and all. So there is no point in having innkeepers . . . Moreover, the peasants are naturally hospitable, they ask you into their homes whenever you want to stop; you give them whatever you like, and they are always pleased"[13]—those peasants whom Romme, in the euphoria of escape, initially sees as virgin-fresh and beautiful: "The peasant is accounted a slave; he is so because his lord can sell him or change him at will, but in most cases his slavery is preferable to the freedom of our laboring men. Here every man has more land than he is able to cultivate. The Russian peasant, once you get away from the towns, is hardworking, industrious to a fault, hospitable, humane, usually in comfortable circumstances, and once he has amassed the winter supplies for himself and his animals he can go to rest in his cottage, unless he is attached to some manufacture, of which there are many, owing to the rich mines in this country, or travels for his own enrichment or for his master."[14]

At first glance their lot strikes him as almost more favorable than that of the French peasantry. On his walks along the banks of the Ourcq with Mme d'Harville, Romme was appalled by the tyranny of the hunting rights that paralyzed the countryside around Paris: "Everywhere, beneath the walls of Versailles and a hundred leagues away, the peasants are treated with a barbarity that must revolt any sensitive soul. One might even say, and it would be perfect truth, that they are worse tyrannized here than in the remoter provinces. One might imagine that the proximity of the nobility would relieve their poverty, and that those gentlemen, witnessing their distress, must seek to alleviate it. Such would be the reasoning of any civilized heart, but it is not that of the Court people. The pleasures of the chase are pursued with such ferocity here that all else is sacrificed to them. The entire region around Paris has been divided into districts of the royal hunt, and as a result, woe betide the poor wretch who enters his own field to pull up the weeds choking his wheat: at most, he is permitted to sit up all night, every night, to frighten away the hordes of deer that devastate his vines, but he may not raise a finger to strike them. The worker borne down by craven servility often gives his time and labor for naught in the service of those pallid and gilded idols, and sees himself inhumanly shoved aside by them if ever he makes bold to ask for a wage."[15]

Here the muzhiks aren't bothered too much by the oppression of the hunt. Their lords seldom indulge in it and have limitless space to gallop over when they do. But as Romme comes to learn more, every time he can break the language barrier, his enthusiasm begins to wane. Count Stroganov seemed like such a progressive fellow back in Saint Petersburg; but seen from Tula . . . "On the Stroganov estates, whenever a peasant ran away, the steward was punished with the knout and the cost of searching for the runaway was deducted from his wages; if runaway serfs were found on the estate, he had to pay the cost of the inquiry, and of sending the men back to their village."[16]

In the end, his further observation of the true condition of the Russian people, especially the miners and Volga boatmen, would have cast a shadow over his determined high spirits anyway. But a letter that reaches him somewhere between Moscow and Nizhny Novgorod snuffs out the light for good. No more happiness for Gilbert. If he ever believed in it before he never will again; because on August 4, 1781, Golovkin dies in Passy.

"His death has turned everything around me to gall. In losing my hope of spending the rest of my days with him, I lose the sole object of all the pains I have been taking here; now they have become quite superfluous; if they prove fruitless as well, I shall be the most miserable of men. That worthy count was the rallying point for us all; it was to him that we each bore all our affection, and I felt that I loved you the better for being one of his worshippers,"[17] Romme writes to Mme d'Harville, the only true friend he has left in the world, or so he thinks—a clear measure of the extent of his loneliness in Russia. "There is none but you, you alone, to take pity upon the poor exile . . . Friendship! Only friendship can give me faith in virtue, can give me courage and fortitude in such sad circumstances. Oh, I give all to friendship! And I shall feel my isolation the less so long as I may rely upon the person who best perceived the qualities of the count. And if it be true that we can genuinely appreciate only those whom we resemble, then I must love you as dearly as I did him."[18] Does he mean *love?* Not a chance. Love scares him to death. Even in Petersburg Romme keeps it at a very safe distance, in the form of a sensitive and cultivated young woman named Mademoiselle Daudet, a granddaughter of the great actress Adrienne Lecouvreur who is Countess Stroganov's maid-in-waiting. If he had wanted . . . but he doesn't. They write each other beautiful letters, and that will be the end of it. What with his Jansenist childhood, the image of his mother, the shame he feels at the very thought of happiness, he's far too much of a Puritan. If his love ever ventures beyond the purely rational, it is directed toward one or two men or to inaccessible women such as the Comtesse d'Harville—because friendship is love without sex, love that offends neither reason nor virtue, at least according to his view of human relationships. But the sobs torn from his breast by Golovkin's death sound like those of a forsaken lover.

Romme at "the very gates of Asia" in 1781—a certain solitude. "Often, to maintain the sweet melancholy of my soul, I plunge into the dense forests . . . Only yesterday, fleeing the intrigues of the Court and the tumult of cities, I was wandering aimlessly over plains watered by the Neva not far from that famous city that bears its founder's name . . . Sensibility! Sweet gift of the gods! Ah, never forsake me! I love the very pain you make me suffer, and if there could be any good without you I should want none of it. May I ever rejoice in your delights, and may you accompany me even into the arms of death . . . Let me not survive the loss of my friends. Everything would revive memories for me a thousand times more dreadful than death itself. To die is nothing, but to be the last to die is the greatest torture. It is not that I wish to hasten the moment when my soul will quit its frail habitation. I await that dread moment with fortitude, and desire neither to advance nor retard it."[19]

LA FAYETTE
STORMING YORKTOWN

67

AUGUST 1781

A Very Happy Turn

On July 30 Washington sends La Fayette a soothing potion in the form of a letter—the habitual medication of their correspondence during the past three years:

> I take your private letter of the 20th in the light which you wish it, that of an unreserved communication from one friend to another; and I should be wanting in candor, were I not to expose my sentiments to you in as free a manner. I am convinced, that your desire to be with this army arises principally from a wish to be actively useful. You will not, therefore, regret your stay in Virginia until matters are reduced to a greater degree of certainty, than they are at present, especially when I tell you, that, from the change of circumstances with which the removal of part of the enemy's force from Virginia to New York will be attended, it is more than probable, that we shall also entirely change our plan of operations. I think we have already effected one part of the plan of campaign settled at

Wethersfield; that is, giving a substantial relief to the southern States, by obliging the enemy to recall a considerable part of their force from thence. Our views must now be turned towards endeavouring to expel them totally from those States, if we find ourselves incompetent to the siege of New York. The difficulty of doing this does not so much depend upon obtaining a force capable of effecting it, as upon the mode of collecting that force to the proper point, and transporting the provisions and stores necessary for such an operation. You are fully acquainted with the almost impracticability of doing this by land; to say nothing of the amazing loss of men always occasioned by long marches, and those towards a quarter in which the service is disagreeable. I should not, however, hesitate to encounter these difficulties, great as they are, had we not prospects of transporting ourselves in a manner safe, easy, and expeditious.[1]

So La Fayette can relax. The curtain in his theater isn't coming down for a while yet. On the contrary: the crowd of actors shuffling into the wings are beginning to produce quite a hum. Does this mean Washington has made up his mind at last? Far from it. He still doesn't know what de Grasse is doing. He is deploying his combined forces, based at Phillipsburg, on increasingly close reconnaissances outside New York, following the style newly inaugurated by Lauzun. "On the 19th, 21st and 22nd of July a series of reconnaissances was made under the skillful direction of MM. Desandrouin and du Portail, the chief engineers of the two armies, and M. de Béville, sergeant major of the French, which enabled the allies to identify the fortifications of the place and adjacent islands. The Chevalier de Chastellux and General Lincoln were protecting them, with a detachment composed of the Bourbonnais and Royal Deux Ponts regiments commanded by their respective colonels, two battalions of grenadiers and riflemen from the Bourbonnais and Soissonnais under the orders of the Vicomte de Rochambeau and Comte de Charlus, Lauzun's legion with its chief, and two thousand five hundred Americans. There was a quantity of cannon fire from all the New York works and all the small warships ringing the island, which produced no effect at all ... MM. de Lauberdière, de Closen, Berthier, de Vauban and de Damas, who had his horse killed under him, distinguished themselves particularly."[2]

It's all very lovely, it's all very brilliant, and it's all perfectly futile. Rochambeau, now in daily contact with Washington, is beginning to wonder whether he isn't working for some sort of Louis XVI of warfare, whose indecisiveness is rendered all the more irredeemable by its very majesty. Have the French abandoned Newport and their devitalizing inactivity only to exhaust themselves in a ballet of bloody maneuvers on the banks of the Hudson? Barras and Choisy, the commanders left in Rhode Island, are bombarding Rochambeau with shrill cries of "Now what?" He shoves them along to Washington, who preaches back, as though to some novice, his same old "wait and see" sermon: "It is almost impossible, in our present circumstances and uncertainty, to fix upon a definitive plan of campaign. The final measures will depend upon circumstances at the arrival of the Comte de Grasse and especially . . . the situation of the enemy at that moment, the reinforcements he will bring or the force we shall then have, the fleet's operations at the moment of its arrival and the advantages it will be able to secure, the length of time it will be able to remain on these coasts and the state of naval superiority while it is here."[3] The only items he's left out are the ages of the captains of the French fleet and the number of teeth of the crow's-nest lookouts.

Without de Grasse the war was about to sink back into immobility. The young Comte de Charlus, making a quite forgivable extrapolation, credits his father for this unhoped-for emergency exit. He writes to the marquis (who did, after all, prevent the worst by not completely paralyzing de Grasse): "But for you, I believe we should have remained on the defensive forever. The arrival of M. de Grasse, which we are told is to occur within a few days, is finally going to put us in a state where we can be of real use to America. Virginia will soon be relieved, and, if the English do not evacuate it, we must cover ourselves in glory there."[4]

But it'll also be because the English have jolly well asked for it. On August 1 La Fayette, still sitting in Williamsburg, learns to his stupefaction that Cornwallis is bringing his troops back across the James from south to north and fortifying himself at the extremity of the York River three leagues farther north, where he occupies the two towns controlling its mouth: York on the south and Gloucester on the north. The Yorktown equation is stated so clearly that it can be drawn without reference to a map.*

Has Cornwallis lost his mind? After months of marches and countermarches he's just quietly given up the conquest of Virginia, which was easily within the power of his army. He was perfectly all right on the south side of the James whether he wanted to occupy the area or to re-embark from Portsmouth unmolested. Yet here he is traipsing back up to Yorktown, where he could be cornered between the sea and his enemies at the tip of this peninsula formed by the courses of the two rivers, which the first English settlers baptized "Elisabeth City."

If he gets no help from his navy, and if it's the French ships that come instead and park themselves broadside across the entrance to the Chesapeake, thus plugging up the mouths of both rivers, Cornwallis will have dived head first into one of the neatest traps nature ever set to catch an army.

No, the poor lord is not off his nut—only obedient. Perforce: his supreme commander is within message range. Cornwallis would gladly have treated himself to a de Grasse-style insubordination, but Sir Henry Clinton has just

*However, the reader may prefer to glance at one [see next page], in case the author should turn out to be the only person able to understand his efforts to translate the military into the literary.

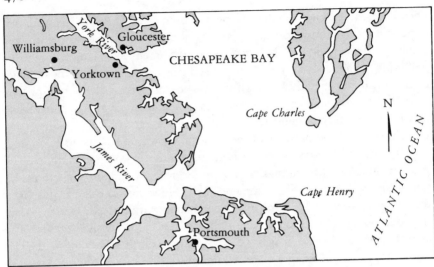

floored him with one of those dispatches that head every anthology of military botches. On July 8 Cornwallis wrote that he was withdrawing to Portsmouth to re-embark, that "a defensive post in Virginia could not have the slightest influence on the war in the Carolinas, and only protected some acres of unhealthy swamp, forever liable to become a prey to a foreign enemy."[5] In support of this view he evacuated Williamsburg. Whereupon Clinton reprimanded him like some second lieutenant for having made "so serious and mortifying a move as re-passing the James River, and retiring with his army to Portsmouth." Chesapeake Bay must be retained, it was of critical importance in the conduct of the war; and he therefore directed him, in His Majesty's name, to "take up a healthy station upon the neck between York and James Rivers." If he had already crossed the James he could just skedaddle back over it again, so as to "give the command of the lower, or Elisabeth country [sic], and deprive the rebels of the use of the two best settled rivers of the Chesapeak [sic], and deter an enemy from entering." To do this, he was authorized to "retain any or all of the troops who had been ordered to New York."[6]

About-face to the north, I said north. Order and counter-order, that's the first principle of military procedure. Cornwallis resignedly puts the whole machine into reverse, absolving himself of a future defeat. That's him in the clear. England really is having a run of bad luck. There, as in France, the vast apparatus of the army has produced the inevitable result, that of any large machine built on a hierarchical model: the worst possible commanding officers have emerged through the automatic promotion of nonentities. But the tip of the French pyramid is back in Versailles, whereas Britannia has transferred her crowning glory to New York. Too close to any generals worth their salt.

In the first days of August, La Fayette, already mollified by Washington's letters, learns that the English have indeed evacuated Portsmouth* . . . but not to go to New York; that they have entered the Chesapeake . . . but not to move up toward Baltimore or Annapolis; that they have disembarked at Yorktown and Gloucester . . . but are making no attempt, as they did in the spring, to push inland. "It would look as if they intended something permanent in this quarter."[7] He understands less and less about what's happening, but he senses that something is in the wind and that he'll have a hand in it, and that's all that matters. The vagueness of his dispatches, however, is not helping Washington to give birth to that famous decision. La Fayette sniffs cautiously at Cornwallis's tracks like a hound on the scent of a wild boar. "When a general has nothing but horse and foot to calculate upon, he may avoid useless movements. But when he is to guess at every possible whim of an army that flies with the wind and is not within reach of spies or reconnoitures [*sic*], he must forcibly walk in the dark." The fog begins to lift on August 6, when the information he sends to headquarters is clear enough to provide a first inkling of the victory at Yorktown:

". . . instead of continuing his voyage up the Bay, my lord entered York River and landed at York and Gloucester . . . You must not wonder, my dear General, that there has been a fluctuation in my intelligences. I am positive the British councils have also been floundering . . . York is surrounded by the river and a morass. The entrance is but narrow. There is, however, a commanding hill, at least I am so informed, which if occupied by them would much extend their works. Gloucester is a neck of land projected into the river and opposite to York. Their vessels, the biggest of whom is a 44,† are between the two towns. Should a fleet come in at this moment, our affairs would take a very happy turn."[8]

---

*The bulk of their army moves by sea, thanks to the transport ships which unload it in a single day at the mouths of the York. Clinton's decision was motivated by the "clutch" reflex, that determination to keep possession of strategic points on conquered ground in the event of a fresh offensive—the same reflex that has caused every other "pocket" and "hedgehog" catastrophe in the history of warfare.

†The forty-four gun *Choron.*

68

AUGUST 1781

There Is an Important News

And a fleet is coming. De Grasse weighs anchor at Cap Français on the morning of August 4, with twenty-six ships of the line and a few transports. On board, 3,289 men have been scooped out of those beautiful "great barracks" at the foot of the mountains alongside an honest-to-goodness "field of Mars" at the back of the town, far behind the quay running along the seafront. The little town, wedged between barracks and quay, has been conceived, built, and baptized in the French manner. The streets, straight as arrows, intersect perfectly square blocks of houses. The Rue d'Anjou and the Rue Dauphine run from the Rue de Rohan to the Place d'Armes, and the Place Royale is connected to the Place de Clugny by the Rue Saint-Louis. You might think you were in Aigues-Mortes except for the color of the faces in the crowd, which is like a chocolate-marshmallow sundae. The census reports that three thousand inhabitants live in the good-looking three-story stone houses with their wrought-iron balconies; but nobody's ever bothered to count the slaves, and with between three and ten of them for every resident townsman you get a total population of at least three times that number—a situation typical of all of the French part of the big island of Hispaniola, or Santo Domingo if you prefer, where twenty thousand Frenchmen make work for some hundred fifty thousand blacks and half-breeds imported from Africa on the seven hundred twenty-three slave ships that sailed this year from Nantes, La Rochelle, Saint-Malo, and Bordeaux. And we'll have to have more of them the minute this accursed war ends, because they're still dying off faster than they can reproduce—in spite of the "Black Code" enacted in 1685, which promises them "the practice of the Roman Catholic religion to the exclusion of all others, food and nursing."[1] Mme de Saint-Apremont, meanwhile, has just ordered her cook thrown alive into the rotisserie fire because he spoiled the steer she wanted to serve to Bougainville's staff officers—a fit of pique that slightly dampened the atmosphere at the party.[2] The bodies of slaves flogged to the bone by the foremen of silkworm plantations, or slaves dead of starvation because nobody feeds them when they get old, or slave girls made pregnant by a white, or unwanted slave children, are buried in huge pits dug every year, spaced far apart and well away from town in the desolate lands of Devil's Bluff.[3] Who could reckon the loss? De Grasse himself can't work out the accounts of the three island plantations in which he has invested the bulk of his fortune during the last ten years. His eagerness to precipitate events elsewhere is not totally divorced from a keen sense of his own best interest —he needs manpower.

The town has been a beehive of activity these last few days, with a great clatter of fine teams, officers, sailors, infantry, cavalry, and supply wagons all shoving and pushing through the swarm of blacks. On August 3 the bulk of the infantry goes aboard: Agenois, Tourangeaux, and men from the Gâtinais, commanded by a triumvirate of Saint-Simon brothers and cousins—marquis, count, and baron—all Picardy nobles descending more or less directly from the duke who was a figure of some importance at the court of Louis XIV and during the Regency.* On the morning of the 4th it's a wise man who can steer clear of Admiral de Grasse on his *Ville-de-Paris*. If the fleet is to "disembouque" from Cap Français unscathed, it has to catch the offshore wind that blows from nine to eleven and follow the only two channels deep-draft ships can take between the narrows bristling with reefs and sandbanks. You can't risk it two at a time, so the monsters of wood and canvas trail tamely along in single file in the wake of their giant leader through the "straits of the Caïques and Mogane," littered, like submarine speedways, with the wrecks of ships that tacked a shade too sharply once and never again. Noon and all's well, we can crowd on sail, nobody got lost on the Great Iguana, Little Iguana, Flat Islands, Etrilles, Samanas, or Kroo-ked, among a hundred others. It's because of all these obstacles that Cap Français is one of the least vulnerable fortresses in the Antilles. The only practicable passages are covered by the sixty cannons on Fort Picolet.[4] Anyway, thanks to the admiral's sea lore—and to the well-tried technique of Bougainville, whom de Grasse can't abide but whose navigating skill he is forced to acknowledge—the "disembouquement" is a success. The captains mop their brows. The ships can spread apart and catch the full force of the trade winds as they head westward, to America.

*And whom nobody at this point knows to be one of the greatest writers of all time, since the first edition of his *Mémoires* is not published until 1829. At this stage the marquis has top rank; he commands the entire body of troops being transported, and has put his brother the baron in charge of the foreign voluntaries, and his cousin Comte Henri—the future founder of "Saint-Simonism"—at the head of the gunners. ["Saint-Simonism" was a reaction against both the Revolution and Napoleonic militarism. Saint-Simon posits an industrial state directed by modern science; the aim of society should be to produce things useful to life. As a movement it was partly socialist, partly women's lib, and largely unorganized.—*Trans.*]

Meanwhile, La Fayette continues to observe the English who are settling in around Yorktown under cover of their ships' guns, and to "contain" them as best he can—you couldn't call it encircling yet, for Cornwallis's army outnumbers the Rebels two to one, in men and ammunition. Both sides wait, for "milord" to take the offensive or for reinforcements to come. Washington waits, too, until August 15, to write La Fayette the letter that changes everything. At last, some *news.*

> My dear marquis,
>   . . . The Concorde frigate has arrived at Newport from Count de Grasse. He was to leave St. Domingo the 3rd of this month, with a fleet of between twenty-five and twenty-nine sail of the line, and a considerable body of land forces. His destination is immediately for the Chesapeake; so that he will either be there by the time this reaches you, or you may look for him every moment. Under these circumstances, whether the enemy remain in full force, or whether they have only a detachment left, you will immediately take such a position as will best enable you to prevent their sudden retreat through North Carolina, which I presume they will attempt the instant they perceive so formidable an armament . . .
>   In the meantime, I have only to recommend a continuation of that prudence and good conduct, which you have manifested through the whole of your campaign. You will be particularly careful to conceal the expected arrival of the Count; because, if the enemy are not apprized of it, they will stay on board their transports in the Bay, which will be the luckiest circumstance in the world. You will take measures for opening a communication with Count de Grasse the moment he arrives, and will concert measures with him for making the best use of your joint forces until you receive aid from this quarter.[5]

Does that mean he and Rochambeau aren't coming themselves? And he still hasn't decided to throw in the full weight of the land forces to back up the navy? Who cares, La Fayette's in seventh heaven. On August 20 he writes to Wayne: "I am happy in this safe opportunity to open my heart to you. There is an important news which I communicate to you alone and which I request you to keep, Gen. Wayne, from everybody's knowledge. There is great reason to hope for an immediate aid by water."[6] The report he sends Washington the same day is a torrent of minute particulars in a cascade of effusions. Response and appeal.

> The greater part of the ennemy are at York which they do not as yet fortify but are very busy upon Gloster neck, where they have a pretty large corps under Col. Dundass. They have at York a 44 guns ship; frigates and vessels are scattered lower down. There is still a small garrison at Portsmouth. Should they intend to evacuate, at least they are proceeding with amazing slowness . . .

I shall today write to the gentleman.* Nothing as yet has appeared. I will take measures that he may hear from me the moment he arrives.

Taking whatever is in the rivers, and taking possession of the rivers themselves while the main body defends the Bay; forming a junction of land forces at a convenient and safe point; checking the ennemy, but giving nothing to chance until properly reinforced; this is the plan I mean to propose . . .

We may depend upon 2500 Continentals, rank and file, exclusive of artillery, and three, or if more are wanted, four thousand militia. Maryland would send 600 militia at least. I have 200 more dragoons and horses ready and am waiting for accoutrements.

There is such a confusion in affairs in this part of the world that immense difficulties are found for a proper formation of magazines. I have, however, strongly urged the matter . . . This State has a large quantity of beef, of corn, some flour, very little rum. Maryland ought to be early called upon. Water transportation will, I hope, ease our difficulties. Had we anything like money [*sic*], matters would go on very well. The dry season has rendered most of the mills useless.

We have no cloathing [*sic*] of any sort. No heavy artillery in order. Some arms will be wanting, some horse accoutrements and a great deal of ammunition. Nothing but your own entreaties may have a sufficient quantity of those articles transported to the head of the Bay.

In the present state of affairs, my dear general, I hope you will come yourself to Virginia, and that if the French army moves this way, I will have at least the satisfaction of beholding you myself at the head of the combined armies . . .

But when a French fleet takes possession of the Bay and rivers, and we form a land force superior to his, their army must soon or late be forced to surrender, as we may get what reinforcements we please.

Adieu, my dear General. I heartily thank you for having ordered me to remain in Virginia, and to your goodness to me I am owing the most beautiful prospect that I may ever behold.[7]

It's all happening. Their little game of hide-and-seek is approaching its climax. On August 21 bugles blow and snare drums roll all up and down and through the American and French camps near Phillipsburg. We're leaving! Everybody up in arms! Is it the big attack on New York? Guess again. We're going to cross the Hudson at West Point, where our formidable array of cannons will discourage the English from coming upstream to bother us while we get over. And then we'll carry on to the top of Chesapeake Bay across the fair land of the Jerseys. Everybody hopes we won't find an empty wilderness at Head of Elk, the way La Fayette did five months ago, and that there'll be an armada from de Grasse waiting to bundle us down to Yorktown in a hurry. Now it's Washington's turn to bend anxious ears in the direction of his French lieutenant; and it is now that their friendship assumes its historic, almost grandiose dimension. After endless delays and hesitations the big chiefs, Wash-

*He means de Grasse but doesn't mention the name in case his dispatch is intercepted.

ington, Rochambeau, and de Grasse, have finally set the ball rolling; but in order for it to make a strike and bowl over the English in Yorktown, La Fayette's two or three thousand forlorn Virginians are going to have to keep Cornwallis sewed up tight: "My dear marquis, Agreeably to my intentions communicated to you on the 15th instant, the troops destined for the southern quarter are now in motion. The American detachment is already on the west side of the Hudson. The French army I expect will reach the Ferry this day. Our march will be continued with all the despatch that our circumstances will admit. As it will be of great importance towards the success of our present enterprise, that the enemy on the arrival of the fleet should not have it in their power to effect their retreat, I cannot omit to repeat to you my most earnest wish, that the land and naval forces, which you will have with you, may so combine their operations, that the British army may not be able to escape. The particular mode of doing this I shall not at this distance attempt to dictate. Your own knowledge of the country, from your long continuance in it, and the various and extended movements, which you have made, have given you great opportunities for observation; of which I am persuaded your military genius and judgment will lead you to make the best improvement."[8]

Today General de La Fayette has finally become indispensable to the two worlds—for a couple of weeks.

69

SEPTEMBER 1781

A Child . . . Could Not Have Expressed a Keener Joy

August 30. Admiral de Grasse's ships reach the Virginia capes at the mouth of the Chesapeake without mishap. That's another stroke of luck. One side, anyway, manages to change position without getting caught. Because what with so many soldiers on board to slow down maneuvers and double the stakes, de Grasse has been chewing his nails nonstop at the prospect of interception at sea. And the English naval force is superior to his. But, like the French, it has had to be dispersed, to keep both the American coasts and the Antilles under surveillance at once. Grasp all, lose all, they say . . . In this summer of 1781 the English fleet is divided into two mighty squadrons: one under Graves, tied to Clinton's land forces in New York, and the other under

Hood and Rodney, the two best seamen in the world, the latter (vice-admiral) commanding the former (rear admiral) whenever they join forces.

De Grasse is still rabid on the subject of that old imbecile of a Maréchal de Biron, Lauzun's uncle, the senile dodderer in command of the Paris military forces, whom he has to thank for the last five months on his lonesome facing Rodney-the-Death, the most dreaded fighter on the high seas. Because four years ago Rodney was a prisoner on parole in Paris, brought to bay by a mountain of debt. A true man of the sea, a man of memorable broadsides. But Biron wanted to play tea-party war: "It is inadmissible that we should be deprived of an adversary of your quality. I shall stand surety for your debts." Rodney didn't need to be told twice, and since that day he has been spicing up George III's navy with that incomparable punch whose secret has been handed down in the heat of battle from every admiral since Drake to every midshipman in the Royal Navy: the art of striking at the right moment with the most force.[1] But it's de Grasse, not Biron, who's having to swallow the stuff; Biron is gazing at the flowers in the gardens of the Palais Royal.

In July Rodney's at Saint-Eustache des Antilles. His corvettes are keeping an eye on de Grasse's fleet, holed up at Cap Français, like a cat watching its mouse. But then Rodney falls ill—rheumatism, gout, the affliction of all great sailors whose systems are ruined by those brutal transitions from shipboard privation to overdoses of high life on shore. For two weeks it's touch and go with him, then the "surgeons" give their ruling: "You must go back to England, Milord, and get treatment there, or you will not live out the year." On August 1 Rodney turns over his command to Hood, who is no novice— but his instructions are evasive. Rodney is strong in battle, weak on paper. "If de Grasse weighs anchor, it will no doubt be to go to New York; in that case, try to get there before him, by way of the Chesapeake capes."[2] Hood does what he's told, but he does it too well—that eternal obsession with New York. The English cram on sail, abandoning the Islands the instant they hear that the French ships have moved off. But, starting from farther south (Antigua) and having better winds, they get to the Chesapeake ahead of the French, on August 25. Not a Frenchman in sight. Aha; they must be up there making trouble for Clinton and Graves; Admiral Hood streaks away to the north. And so, to his amazement, de Grasse sails up into an empty sea.

Finding release in action, Washington too is moving quickly and well; he makes a huge finesse as he goes, to keep the English stuck in their abscess of New York. "To cover West Point and the northern states, three thousand men under General Heath remained on the left bank of the Hudson, while for four days the French-American army, watched over by Washington, effected the long and difficult crossing of this river, with an inadequate number of fer-ryboats. They then descended the right bank as far as Chatham near Staten

Island, where M. de Villemanzy had most judiciously set up ovens and concentrated supplies with a view to an attack upon New York. Then, very suddenly, the generals veered sharply to the right, went up along the backs of the Jersey mountains, hurried toward the Delaware, which was at low water, forded it at Trenton and entered Philadelphia, honoring the president of Congress with a procession in the presence of a huge crowd,"[3] the kind of crowd that springs up out of the ground at the wave of a conqueror's magic sword. A month earlier Philadelphia was sitting tight and mute, like all towns that haven't made up their minds. Confirmation from Fersen: "Everything appeared to portend a siege of New York. The establishment of bakeries and other stores at Chatham, within four miles of Staten Island, our crossing of the North River and the march we made on Morristown all seemed to indicate that we were intending to attack Sandy Hook in order to facilitate the entrance of our ships. We soon perceived that it was not New York we were after, but General Clinton was completely duped and that is what we wanted. We crossed Jersey, which is one of the most beautiful of the American provinces and one of the best cultivated, and on September 3rd the army reached Philadelphia. It paraded through the town, and provoked the admiration of all its inhabitants, who had never seen so many people dressed and armed all alike, nor so well disciplined."[4] Like the crowds, the gods are also on the winning side; usually, crossing the Delaware poses serious problems, but "we were fortunate enough to find it at low water and forded it near Trenton,"[5] taking advantage of that blessed pause before the summer storms, taking over from the spring thaws, swell the rivers again.

For the foot soldiers, though, it's not quite such a fairy tale, because those summer storms are pouring down on them before flooding the Delaware. Poor Crèvecoeur! "One cannot imagine how many afflictions we had to endure during the six days it took us to march from Phillipsburg to King's Ferry on the Hudson River, a distance of 40 miles. It took us six days because of the terrible weather and incredible roads. We slept every night in bivouac. There was a terrific storm on August 20. I floundered in the mud and in a horrible marsh with all the wagons and the artillery train, not knowing where I was or how I could get out of it. Not until daybreak was I able, with great difficulty, to extricate myself. During the march from Phillipsburg I was in command of the rear guard of the artillery. I have no doubt that, had the enemy been able to predict our march, he would have caused us much anxiety."[6]

Rochambeau's eyes pop a little at the sight of the festive air of Philadelphia, its counting-its-chickens joy—because the game's not over yet. If those folks only knew . . .

The Continental "army" with which General Washington was thus setting out upon an expedition of greater magnitude and far wider military importance, from the boldness of its execution and the influence of its results, than any other in the war, was composed of but two thousand men. So far had the tide of the Revolution ebbed in this summer of 1781, and to such an extent was the country exhausted by the incessant demands of the preceding years of struggle, that the Commander-in-Chief could bring together, in the face of this impending crisis, only what naturally enough seemed to General de Rochambeau a mere "handful of men" . . .

Accompanying this little force were the well-equipped and thoroughly disciplined French troops, four thousand men, under General the Comte de Rochambeau.[7]

On the brink of his greatest victory, Washington fears he's on the brink of disaster, as is always the case in the great military suspenses of history. *If* Cornwallis lets himself be encircled and *if* de Grasse unloads enough reinforcements, he'll be in clover. But *if* the English can get back to the Carolinas and *if* their fleet, beating or outmaneuvering de Grasse's, comes up and transforms the trap into a countertrap, then the Continental army and the French expeditionary corps will fall into it together.

Now it's La Fayette's turn to comfort Washington. On September 1: "Upon a particular inquiry of the country, and our circumstances, I hope you will find we have taken the best precautions to lessen his lordship's [Cornwallis's] chances to escape; he has a few left, but so very precarious, that I hardly believe he will make the attempt; if he does, he must give up ships, artillery, baggage, part of the horses, all the negroes [*sic*]; he must be certain to lose the third of his army, and run the greatest risk to lose the whole without gaining that glory which he may derive from a brilliant defence.

"Adieu, my dear General, the agreeable situation I am in is owing to your friendship, and is, for that reason, the dearer to your respectful servant and friend."[8] For once his optimism isn't forced. He is no longer alone. Lieutenant Feltman of the Pennsylvania Line, under his orders, makes the following entry in his marching journal for September 2:

This morning at day-light, the troops took up the line of march and encamped opposite Jamestown, where lay a small English vessel under the sanction of a flag. We lay about two hours on our ground expecting every moment to see a glorious sight; at last a number of large boats appeared in sight with about three thousand French troops on board, and also three large armed vessels to cover the troops landing.

The troops landed on our opposite side, on James Island, and there encamped —which spread an universal joy amongst our officers and soldiers. Never did I behold a more beautiful and agreeable sight . . .

Took a walk to take a view of the French troops, who make a very fine soldierly appearance, they being all very tall men; their uniform is white coats turned up with blue, their underclothes are white.[9]

These are the Marquis de Saint-Simon's men, who've had time to freshen up their wardrobes at Cap Français. Saint-Simon, although considerably older than La Fayette and holding the rank of field marshal, places himself under his junior's orders—for the very good reason that he hasn't a clue about the terrain and knows nothing of the situation in the field. La Fayette spares this new French expeditionary corps, the largest after that of Rochambeau, the pain of feeling their way on unknown ground. "The squadron's longboats and barges went up the James and the troops from Santo Domingo disembarked at Jamestown on September 2, seven leagues from York and twenty from capes Charles and Henry, without being troubled by the English. Those same longboats then served to carry the Americans to the left bank of the river. Thus the two armies were united between the York and the James, Saint-Simon camping on the banks of the latter and La Fayette at Green Spring. When camp broke two days later the laborious work was undertaken, by manpower alone, of transporting the artillery to the mouth of the swamp. The devastation of the countryside would not permit of all M. le Marquis de Saint-Simon's hussars coming ashore. Only about half of them could be brought up. These first allied forces formed a body of some eight thousand men . . . The republican army was composed of four separate groups: six American regiments of regular and disciplined troops, trained and tried and in condition for line battle, forming a corps of about one thousand six hundred men; one hundred fifty dragoons, well mounted, trained and handling their mounts well; two thousand five hundred militia of the country and five hundred riflemen, a kind of mountaineer. The last two groups are not in uniform, they wear wide breeches with or without shoes; and the last, in particular, form a body of excellent chasseurs, fine shots, well suited for small warfare in the woods, but not for line fighting . . . Very few of these troops are tented [sic], almost all camp under a screen, a hut of grasses or leaves; all are sober and patient, living on corn flour, bearing privations and delays without a murmur, and being capable of fatigue and long marches, precious qualities which render an infantry truly light. They have a goodly air about them, moreover, and most are fine-looking men," according to the Chevalier d'Aucteville, captain in the royal engineer corps, one of the thousand and one who discover America and the Americans that day.[10]

"His army had now become formidable by the accession to it of three thousand regular troops with their equipment and artillery; and he was in a position to carry out effectually General Washington's injunction not to allow Cornwallis to escape. He began to throw his troops forward on the 4th of September; and by the night of the 7th he had taken up a strong position at Williamsburg with his combined army, almost within striking distance of the enemy."[11] And here is where two demons come to tempt St. La Fayette in the Virginia desert: de Grasse and Saint-Simon are begging him to launch an immediate attack upon Cornwallis, who is fortifying Yorktown as though the devil were after him but hasn't had time to finish yet. Let's snag the laurels before the others get here; let's have an 80-percent French victory. Equal shares for the three of us . . . The suggestion is so much in keeping with La Fayette's natural disposition and usual behavior that they can't get over his refusal. Has the command of a relatively powerful army suddenly inoculated him with the virus of prudence? Or is he so much a son of Washington that he wants to make the victory at Yorktown an event with political consequences for the America to come? THE victory? In any event, he does not succumb. "The admiral and the Marquis de Saint-Simon keep urging; they represent to me with repeated arguments that it is only fair, after so long and so fatiguing a campaign, which has now ended fortunately, that the glory of overthrowing Cornwallis should belong to those who had reduced him to his present extremity."[12] Please, gentlemen, please. La Fayette appears to have become parsimonious of soldiers' blood. The reason he gives for his refusal does him credit, even *a posteriori*. He replies that "General Washington and General Rochambeau would soon arrive; that it would be better to hasten their coming than to make a murderous attack which would waste much blood merely for the gratification of personal vanity; that they were certain to capture the enemy by regular approaches, after the succor arrived, and, in that event, to spare the lives of many soldiers."

Washington has given La Fayette a great deal since that day in 1777 when he singled him out and consoled him for his humiliations in Philadelphia, but today La Fayette pays him back with interest. That month of September finds them changing roles, La Fayette circumspect and Washington—who'd have thought it?—exuberant. At Chester, outside Philadelphia, the general receives, on September 5, "the agreeable news of the safe arrival of the Count de Grasse in the Bay of Chesapeake with 28 sail of the line and four frigates . . . The event is reported by those who were present to have produced an outburst of joy upon the part of the Commander-in-Chief which no one, up to that time, had suspected him to be capable of. Standing on the river bank at Chester, he waved his hat in the air as the Comte de Rochambeau approached, and, with many demonstrations of uncontrollable happiness, he announced to him the good news. The Duc de Lauzun says, 'I have never seen a man inhabited with a keener or more open joy than was General Washington,' and Colonel Guillaume of the Deux Ponts declares that, instead of the reserved and exceedingly dignified manner of the Commander-in-Chief to which they had grown accustomed, they then saw his face beaming with delight, and 'a child whose every wish had been gratified could not have expressed a keener joy.' "[13]

Oh, what they've gone through to reach this moment! . . . But now that the cards have been dealt, we can indeed predict that events will proceed according to the rules of the great cruel card game, the whist of war. Cornwallis is beaten before he begins. There remain only a few unpleasant formalities for the soldiers to go through—the men of Washington, Rochambeau, La Fayette, and de Grasse. They must fight and die so that the strategists can be proved right.

The seamen will be the first. In the morning of September 5 the united squadrons of admirals Graves and Hood, who have finally realized where the danger lies, sail up to the mouth of the Chesapeake, intending to enclose and, if possible, destroy the French fleet. This is zero hour for the great British empire in the Atlantic.

WASHINGTON

70

SEPTEMBER 1781

To Complete the History of Man

The Chesapeake. De Grasse carries the day with one bold decision taken before the first shot is fired—which is almost always the way with naval battles.[1] His fleet is lying at anchor inside the bay facing the mouths of the James and York on the morning of September 5, one of those luminous days in the early American autumn, when a French lookout ship coming hell-for-leather swings around Cape Henry and draws alongside the *Ville-de-Paris*. It announces that a fleet of at least ten sail is approaching on the open sea, coming from east-northeast—in other words New York—and making for the bay.

De Grasse is expecting reinforcements from Barras. But if this is Hood . . .

"Go take a closer look, confound you! Are you afraid it'll get you pregnant?"

The frigate scuttles away and gets close enough to the newcomers to be thoroughly peppered with shot. It returns an hour later, its sails hanging like the bedraggled ears of a spaniel after a scrap, to confirm the worst. It's not ten ships, it's more like thirty, and twenty of them ships of the line with two or three decks. This would appear to be the bulk of the English naval forces in America, having finally made contact at the mouth of the Hudson and now on their way to play double or nothing with the rest of us, abandoning Clinton to his fate for a few days.* The battle will be equal, but the English have the

*Unfortunately for the English, Admiral Graves, the senior officer, is commanding rather than Hood.

sea wind and capacity crews, whereas almost a thousand sailors and ninety officers of the French fleet are engaged on shore landing and installing Saint-Simon's troops.

But who says the English mean to enter the bay? Maybe they're only going to hang around outside the capes, waiting for an opportunity. Ah, but that's just the point: if Barras should turn up at this stage, and bring his little fleet into collision with them, he'll be in Davy Jones's locker before he has time to say ouch. De Grasse now performs his second historic act by deciding to give battle then and there. At ten in the morning he orders every man to his post. The land forces will have to lump it.

"But we need two hours to weigh anchor, Admiral!"

"Damn weighing. Slip the cables. We must get outside the capes by noon."

Winching the anchors free and stowing them manually is indeed a lengthy operation and requires a large number of hands. They abandon the anchors to the depths, by "slipping the cables," marking them with large buoys so they can retrieve them when they get back, if they get back. At eleven o'clock, obeying the saraband of signals run up by the flagship, the Comte de Grasse's fleet lays on sail and veers ponderously into the wind to leave the bay. You can imagine how La Fayette and Saint-Simon feel, and all the other men left ashore, in a garrison suddenly deprived of its heavy artillery and communications.

The first and maybe the stiffest battle is the one against the wind. It's blowing in from the sea so the sails have to turn sixty or seventy degrees into it, and every ounce of the men's strength is needed to steady the huge helms. And just to make matters worse, the tide's coming in and setting up a strong inshore current—thrusting the ships backward and giving them about as much agility as drunken giraffes while they tack cautiously back and forth—for "the usable passageway between capes Charles and Henry is actually but a few miles wide, owing to the presence of a dangerous sand bank in the middle."[2] But they can't wait for the tide to turn, that would give the English time enough to station themselves neatly around the only exit and pick off the French ships one by one like so many sitting ducks. So the first victory of the Chesapeake is a victory over the bay itself.

The *Auguste,* a wallowing eighty-gun pilot whale, is the first to win it, and as the principal ship of the vanguard she leads the whole procession; or rather her commander Louis de Bougainville wins it, that newlywed of fifty-two[*] for whom the war is just a pain in the neck because it keeps him from his work

---

[*]On January 27, 1781, he married a demoiselle de Longchamp-Montendre in Brest, and has a son by her at Christmas the same year.

of continuing and analyzing his explorations. At this rate, when will he ever get to the North Pole? When will he meet the survivors of the disaster that befell the man he respects more than any other—an Englishman as luck would have it—his colleague Captain Cook, so they can compare notes on the great seaways? When the war broke out Sartines, acting at his behest, ordered the French vessels to spare Captain Cook if they came across his ships, which were on their third trip around the world; but the natives of the Sandwich Islands took care of him instead.* Bougainville knows that the *Journal of Captain Cook's Last Voyage* has just come out in London, and is impatiently waiting to read it to find out whether or not that famous Northwest Passage really exists. Even if it doesn't, there are still so many islands in the world to be discovered, so many civilizations to be studied, by him and the young officer, twelve years his junior—Jean-François Galaup de La Pérouse—with whom he has just been spending long evenings in Brest and Cap Français dreaming of every sea in the world while their brutish comrades could think of nothing but polishing their cannons, the better to turn the English into mincemeat . . . Bougainville has a deadly hatred of weapons. He left the land army and his Rouergue regiment twenty years ago—thanks to Choiseul's protection—to join the navy and sail around the world because he wanted to navigate, to study the men of every skin and tongue. Not to conquer, to learn. "European customs in this respect are wholly absurd. The *philosophes,* no doubt, groan to see how some men, for no reason but that they have cannons and bayonets, reckon sixty thousand of their fellow creatures as naught;† how, with no respect for their most sacred rights, they look upon land which has been watered by the sweat of its inhabitants, and has housed their ancestors' mortal remains for centuries, as booty . . . The sole object of modern navigators, in describing the customs of new peoples, is to complete the history of man; the object of their navigation is to accomplish the exploration of the globe, and the unique goal of the enlightenment they seek to propagate is to enhance the felicity of the island-dwellers they visit, and increase their means of livelihood."³ Bougainville and La Pérouse disciples of Raynal? . . . The King of France is sending out some odd apostles to sail the high seas these days. After all, though, Bougainville did make him a present of the Malouines,** and is now preparing, grumbling and frowning over the geometry of currents, sun, and winds, to "complete the history of man" by extricating his squadron in some sort of order from its godforsaken moorings at Lynnhaven, where it almost runs aground between Cape Charles and Cape Henry.

*On February 14, 1779, Cook was killed on the beach in the course of a sordid squabble over provisions.

†Approximate estimated population of that part of the world which is just beginning to be called "Oceania."

**Today known as the Falklands.

He does it in three-quarters of an hour. The vanguard, at least, Bougain-ville's "blue and white squadron," is out: the *Languedoc, Citoyen, Glorieux, Souverain, Diadème,* and *Médée* in the wake of the *Auguste.* As all large fleets do, both English and French have divided their forces into three roughly equal groups, which makes for greater control over maneuvers. Even at the climax of a battle seven or eight ships can't get totally lost, and remain relatively mobile in the hands of their leader. Behind Bougainville's squadron, then, the two other groups of French ships—the "principal battle corps" or "white squadron" of nine ships with the *Ville-de-Paris,* carrying de Grasse, as its mother hen; and the nine other ships of the "blue squadron" commanded by Monteil—have to squeeze through and spread out opposite the twenty English ships of the line and seven frigates which are sailing straight at them "on the quarter," cutting their speed as much as possible in order to keep the wind. Hood is commanding the vanguard on the *Barfleur;* * Graves is on the *London,* in the center of the English principal battle corps; and Drake, a descendant of the grand old man himself, leads their rear guard on the *Princessa.*

Half past noon. The hour of greatest danger. Bougainville's squadron, the only one out of the bay, deploys for battle. The English are almost within firing range and outnumber the French three to one, since the rest of the fleet is still filing through the channel. If Admiral Graves sees his chance, he can take advantage of the following wind, charge the isolated French vanguard, turn it, and destroy or capture it . . . He "was in a position almost beyond the wildest dreams of a sea-commander."[4] But whether out of prudence or excess ambition (he may have thought the French force was smaller and could be destroyed totally), Graves orders his captains to engage in intricate conven-tional maneuvers, turning aside and then wheeling majestically back along a line parallel to the one which the wind is going to compel the French to take. In other words, it'll be a repetition of Ouessant, sailing past one another side by side and firing broadsides, only this time the forces are equal. At one forty-five the French officers heave a sigh of relief: their sacred elephant, the *Ville-de-Paris,* † lurches clumsily through the channel and comes to take her place in the line of battle between the *Destin* and *Victoire.* Standing head and shoulders above everybody else on the poop, visible from afar to the naked eye in his dress uniform with a wide scarlet band across his chest, de Grasse looks like some sort of seaborne ogre.

These immense manipulations proceed so silently! For another hour there's no sound but the breeze and bitten-off voices snapped up by the sea; the huge white and gilt masses slide along in obedience to mysterious laws.

*Ships captured in previous battles retain their original names; de Grasse, for instance, has a *Northumberland* in his squadron.

†Built under Louis XV by subscription among Paris merchants, in the days when private aid had to plug the holes in the budget of the royal navy.

But we're about to wake up the little fishies: the English have 1,410 cannons against 1,800 for the French, who stand to gain little by this slim advantage because of the men they've had to leave on shore—there's no crew to serve some of the pieces. And almost all the English hulls are copper-sheathed which means they'll take the impact better and make better returns as well, with their huge carronades—triple-power short-range cannons recently manufactured in the Bristol munitions works.

Half past two. Still confident despite his miscalculation as to the size of the French fleet, Graves orders his ships to engage. But a signaling error sends Hood's squadron out of reach, and for two hours it maneuvers desperately to get back into the battlefield, too late.

Three o'clock: the English center and rear guard begin exchanging fire with the French vanguard. Thunder, foam, and flames. Those few minutes of truth for which a naval officer's whole life is constructed, for which so many hands and arms labor and so much sweat drips in shipyards over so many miles of boards, iron, and canvas, and then that infinite patience of oceans crossed and recrossed . . . The ships roll like dice on a green baize sea. The first English volley kills M. de Bourdet, commanding the *Réfléchi;* eight English ships succeed in concentrating their fire on the *Pluton, Bourgogne, Marseillais, Diadème* . . . which begins to burn. The *Princessa* moves up to finish her off, but the *Saint-Esprit*—yes, that's right, the very ship on which Chartres gambled and lost his reputation three years ago—comes to the rescue and pumps so much metal into the *Princessa* that she breaks away crippled. As the two principal battle corps file past each other spitting out of scores of gun ports, things really get very warm. The *Shrewsbury* loses two masts, and her captain's leg. The *Intrepid* has its two topsail yards sliced off and the lower masts damaged. The *Montagu*'s three masts have got the shivers and she has to take in sail. The *Ajax* is leaking and beginning to heel. The *Terrible* as well, but worse,* under the fire pouring into her from Bougainville's *Auguste*—for a man who doesn't like war, he puts up a pretty good show. He's fuming just now because his foresail bowline† has been torn off and if he can't keep control of the wind his ship could start spinning like a top. He sends two hands out to re-rig the bowline and both are picked off by the English sharpshooters posted in the *Princessa*'s tops—for this vicious style of musketry is also part of the sport of naval warfare, with every marksman trying to bring home the biggest bag of game, his quarry of enemy officers or topmen, to offer to his mother ocean.

"My purse to whoever rigs that bowline!" shouts Bougainville.

A third topman scrambles out,** calling back as he goes:

"Admiral, we don't do this for money!"⁵

---

*She goes down four days later.

†Rope that keeps a sail close-hauled.

**The topman was the sailor who specialized in handling and servicing the rigging.

Five o'clock. The wind begins to drop. The French line has held up better than the enemy's; de Grasse, in other words, one of the outstanding naval officers of the century, has kept his ships in fairly good order through all the ups and downs of the battle. The admirals halfheartedly urge on their naval armies, if only for honor's sake. After all, no ships have been lost, it's a tie. But the sun will be down in an hour, and Admiral Graves, a bowed little man with a complexion so red it's almost blue, is being unnerved by the vindictive messages Hood keeps sending him by corvette. Just you wait, baby, back ashore it's you and me and a couple of pistols. Oh, if only Rodney had been here!

At six thirty they run out of wind and light, so it's cease fire. The English count ninety dead and two hundred wounded. Both sides stand as before: de Grasse within reach of the bay, Graves a little farther out to sea. Then who's the winner of this little battle which has such infinite consequences? It takes five days to find out. From September 6 to 10, through gale and calm, the fleets glare defiance at each other from afar, and on the 7th, 8th, and 9th they come so close that everybody gets ready for the second round. Not until the evening of the 9th does Admiral Graves run up the signal for a general retreat and sail back to the Hudson. De Grasse wouldn't dream of following him. France has won the day, since the code of war rules that whoever leaves the field first loses. The fact is, Graves has got too many sick ships and men to think seriously of trying again. To get water, supplies, ammunition, and medical care at Yorktown he'd have to force his way through the entrance to the Chesapeake, which is exactly what he has just failed to do. And for new masts and caulking, it's Charleston or New York. He plumps for New York. Cornwallis is doomed.

De Grasse goes back into the Chesapeake, where the Rebel and French soldiers think they're witnessing the miracle of the multiplication of the boats: twelve more ships of the line and eighteen transports loaded with men and the siege artillery left behind in Newport have come creeping down the shore under cover of the wrestling match between the two big fleets, like some scruffy coastal merchant line—it's Barras, keeping his appointment.

71

SEPTEMBER 1781

The Happiness of the Family

Then Yorktown. Another battle won before it was fought. The simple sum of an arithmetic problem, or two gears that finally mesh. Cornwallis's army, half the English military strength on the new continent, is about to be ground up like sugar cane in a mill. It was just a matter of getting all the wheels turning in the right direction at the same time. This time there's no chief engineer: events proceed in a sort of tacit understanding among the allied leaders.

In Philadelphia, we remember, the victory was celebrated a good month early with Washington and Rochambeau looking on and smiling and nodding despite their anxiety for news of La Fayette and de Grasse. The town, restored to its status as capital of the Independence and seat of a tranquilized Congress, is now beginning to feel like the pilot city of the future again. "The presence of the allied troops was an occasion for an extraordinary surge of activity among lower and upper classes; there was laughing, dancing, toasts. On September 3, M. de La Luzerne [the French ambassador] gave a dinner for Thomas M. Kean, the president of Congress, Washington, Rochambeau, and the chief French officers. On the 5th, during the day [day of the Battle of the Chesapeake], the Soissonnais regiment went through maneuvers for the inhabitants and was admired and acclaimed for its martial bearing."[1] The admiration is mutual: Clermont-Crèvecoeur hadn't imagined that there could be a town lovelier than Versailles, and yet!

> It took us an hour and a half to cross this large and beautiful city. We passed the State House where the members of Congress were assembled on the front steps. We saluted them, then passed the house of the Chevalier de La Luzerne, the ambassador of France to Congress, where the quality of the town were assembled. We then went to camp on the Schuylkill River a mile from town. This river flows into the Delaware below Philadelphia within sight of the city. If the Philadelphians continue to build, the city walls will be bathed by both rivers; I am told this is their plan. This will certainly be the largest

city in the world. It is built on a plain 10 to 12 miles in diameter on the right bank of the Delaware. Fairly big ships can come up to the city, which is extremely large and well-built.*

The houses are of brick, and the streets are wide and perfectly straight, with sidewalks for pedestrians on both sides. There is a large number of richly stocked shops. The city has a population of 40,000. In Market Street there are two immense brick markets, one of which is the meat market. I can find no fault with them except that they stand in the middle of a superb street, which they completely spoil. The port along the Delaware is about 2 miles long and consists simply of a quay, which is remarkable only for its length.

The State House where the Congress meets is quite a large building without ornament. There is nothing magnificent about the chamber where the members sit, which has no decoration. A long table covered with green cloth and some chairs are the only furniture. There are several very pretty Protestant churches, as well as two beautiful Catholic churches.[2]

And this, too, is something new for a Frenchman: a world in which different faiths live together and tolerate each other. Fersen, for his part, discovers the rustic side of Virginia:

Our canteens, well supplied with pâtés, ham, wine and bread, prevented us from noting the prevalent poverty of the inns, where there is hardly anything to be found but salt pork, and no bread at all. In Virginia, people eat nothing but a sort of cake made of Turkish wheat flour† which is roasted a little in front of the fire; this hardens the outside slightly, but the inside is uncooked dough. They drink only rum, which is spirits made of sugar mixed with water; this they call grog.

Apples were short this year, which means they have had no cider. Two hundred fifty miles from here, in the part of Virginia called the Mountains, everything is different. The land is richer, the main tobacco plantations are located there, and the soil yields wheat and every kind of fruit; but in the part along the coast, which is called the Plain, where we are, nothing but Turkish wheat is grown. Tobacco is the principal product of Virginia, not that this province, the largest of the thirteen, is unfit for other crops, but the sloth and vanity of the inhabitants are great obstacles to industry. The Virginians would truly seem to be a different breed of mankind; rather than looking after their farms and engaging in trade, every landowner wants to be a lord. No White ever works, but, as in the islands, all the labor is done by Negro slaves supervised by Whites, with a steward at the head of the whole. In Virginia there are at least twenty Negroes for every White man; this is the reason why the state sends so few soldiers to the army. All who engage in trade are regarded as inferior; the others say they are not gentlemen, and do not want to be seen in their company. They all have aristocratic principles and, when one sees them, one has difficulty understanding

*One such ship, the *Pennsylvania Packet*, unloaded Franklin there on May 5, 1777, after he was expelled from England. The city has now spread well beyond the junction of the rivers, and the metropolitan area has a population of over 4 million.

†That is, corn meal.

how they could join a federation and accept a government founded upon complete equality of condition; but the same spirit that prompted them to shake off the English yoke might well lead them on to other deeds, and I should not be surprised, when the peace comes, to see Virginia part company from the other states. In fact, I should not be surprised to see the American government transformed into a perfect aristocracy.[3]

"But do hurry, General," Captain du Portail, one of La Fayette's French officers, writes to Rochambeau, "Hurry; not that we should be tempted to take York without you. I do not believe we shall steal the project; we shall, I think, be content, and it will be glory in plenty for us, if we can succeed in preparing the triumph and preventing the enemy, in so far as possible, from assembling means of defense."[4] He can relax; neither Rochambeau nor Washington has mistaken Philadelphia for Capua.* The day after the festivities they're already far afield; preceding the army with their officers and a large escort, they reach the very top of the Chesapeake, Head of Elk, where a young man with fine features and large teasing eyes has been waiting for them for all of one hour: Captain de Saint-Césaire,† yet another heir to yet another huge naval estate in the south of France, one of the men in de Grasse's gang, bringing dispatches from his chief. They set the tone for the dialogue, the admiral's customary tone of gruff heartiness: "M. de Saint-Césaire, flag captain of my army [*sic*], is instructed to inform H.E. General Washington of the measures I am taking to facilitate his arrival. This officer's merit, intelligence, and my particular trust in him, whom I look upon as my second-in-command, are the grounds upon which I have chosen him, and I am convinced you will be satisfied with him. He precedes the arrival of the ships I intend to employ in this expedition . . . M. de Saint-Césaire is instructed to tell you how much I desire you [*sic*] and how great is my confidence. Your arrival is more agreeable to me than a reinforcement of four thousand men; this is not adulation, but the truth from a sailor to a brave man of war."[5]

Head of Elk is a crossroad bordered by fifteen or twenty houses near the place where the Susquehanna widens out and empties into that gray water, neither river nor sea, which is the Chesapeake. Pennsylvania ends there and Maryland begins, its full width, not to mention a fair share of Virginia, lying between Washington's troops and those of La Fayette. Only a little over half the big scramble southwards has been completed, starting in Newport for the French and in West Point for the Rebels. They've still got to get across the

*Capua (modern Santa Maria Capua Vetere), near Naples, whose connection with Rome was vaguely similar to that between the U.S. and Great Britain; but its uprisings were always severely quelled. Defected to Hannibal in 216 B.C., and at Cannae Carthage won by encircling the Romans, who fought in old-fashioned block formation. [*Trans.*]

†There is an attractive portrait of him, possibly by Fragonard, in the Fragonard Museum in Grasse. "Flag captain," we recall, means he was commanding a ship with an admiral on board.

toughest fifty leagues, that marmalade of solid ground and bridgeless rivers, a cross-country obstacle course running parallel to the west shore of the Chesapeake; and they've got to be quick about it. De Grasse and La Fayette, alone facing Cornwallis, might not be able to prevent a last-minute breakout. If de Grasse can only produce enough transport ships, the allies think they can save precious minutes and reach Yorktown in five days.

But the Head of Elk is also the seat of disappointment. De Grasse to Washington: "I am doing my utmost to hasten the arrival of your troops by sending six or seven ships of war to you, chosen among those which draw least water, to take aboard as many people as possible."[6] Six or seven: fat lot of good that'll be! "These ships will be followed by frigates and all other craft able to come up the river." When? Come Christmas, or when hell freezes over? With what they've got now all they can load is the vanguard, not even the wagon train. "In view of the impossibility of transport by water, the general-in-chief decided [on September 7] that the route of the main body would be from Baltimore to Williamsburg by way of Elk Ridge Landing, Bladensburg, Georgetown, Fredericksburg, Caroline Courthouse, and New Castle."[7] So the vanguard sets sail alone on the 9th, its canvas floppy and water-logged in the pouring rain—the weather's turning foul as it always does here around the equinox; but the infantry, moping at the thought of having to slog off through spongy Maryland cornfields on foot, are soon cheered when they learn how their seaborne comrades have been treated to every form of peril on that Chesapeake Bay which is readily mistaken for an artificial pleasure-pond but which is perfectly capable of producing a one-act version of the ocean fury unleashed. To cut a long story short, the rear guard gets to its destination almost as soon as the vanguard, and Clermont-Crèvecoeur's vexation is transformed into relief—at his friends' expense: "I did not embark at Head of Elk. Very much annoyed, I followed the army; but later I was consoled to have avoided all the misfortunes that befell the troops who had embarked there. They had to sail 300 miles in small boats virtually stripped of provisions. The weather was so terrible and the winds so adverse that the journey took them 18 days. We arrived almost the same time they did, without having suffered any inconvenience. The hardships the other detachment had endured were incredible. Several vessels, battered by winds and storms and on the point of shipwreck, had lowered their boats and sent their men to take refuge in the warships anchored at the entrance to the York River to blockade Cornwallis. They were expecting to rest there and spend a pleasant night after the bad experiences and the dangers of the preceding days, when Cornwallis sent fire ships to attack them. These rained firebrands down on the crews all night and spread terror among them. By the greatest good fortune they escaped injury, though they were attacked by no less than 7 fire ships"[8]—those fire ships which are Cornwallis's secret weapon, and which nearly do turn the tables on one particularly black night in late September.

Recipe—simplified—for a good fire ship: first you take some

> *flûtes* or pinnaces of approximately 150 or 200 tons, having a lower deck all of a piece, and another deck above it running fore-to-aft. Openings are cut at various points along the lower deck, measuring about a foot and a half square . . . A wide trap is made in the poop flooring, beneath which a swift-pulling launch may wait, so that when the helmsman has set fire to the leads, he may drop quickly down into it. Then the holds are filled with flares, that is, a certain amount of powder, say half [of a liter] to a quarter of saltpeter and half a quarter of common brimstone, the whole well mixed together and soaked in linseed oil but not too much, as this would delay ignition and the effect must be instantaneous. After that the holds are covered over with sulfurated cloth or heavy cartridge paper, and fagots are brought, small shavings, or other kindling soaked in whale oil . . . Empty spaces in the craft are also filled with pitch-coated casks loosely packed with those slender curling shavings that fall from the carpenter's plane.
>
> The rigging, yards, and sails are coated with pitch and brimstone; the ends of the main yard are garnished with iron grappling hooks, as are those of the foreyard and bowsprit. When fire ships are built of new timbers, only the softest and lightest are used, in which the fire will catch the more easily . . .
>
> To the fore, under the bowsprit, there is a stout grappling hook hanging from a chain, and another at each end of each yard, and each of these hooks is fastened to a rope running from that place all along the boat and on to the poop, to the place where the helmsman stands. The instant the fire ship has rammed the other ship, this rope must be cut by the helmsman before setting fire to the fire ship; he must attempt to collide with the enemy ship head on, and not broadside.
>
> Fire ships are crewed by ten or twelve men, who receive double pay on account of the risks involved.[9]

Such are the delectable devices that Cornwallis sends gliding along the York River at two in the morning toward de Grasse's thirty or thirty-five ships (counting Barras's reinforcements), which lie dozing in a semicircle at its mouth, sleeping the sleep of the just after a battle well won and a duty well done. Suddenly the night is rent by a pyrotechnical display spouting up from the depths of the sea and igniting the sixty-four-gun *Vaillant* so effectively that she drifts toward the *Réfléchi*—who doesn't deserve her name because her half-awake commander mistakes the *Vaillant* for the biggest fire ship in the world (decidedly, those English will stop at nothing) and starts pouring cannonballs into the poor ship whose mates, hanging naked in the tops, are dousing the flaming rigging with buckets of water. A lengthy stutter of flickering signal lanterns ensues, hard to see in all that smoke, before the two French ships manage to avoid sending each other to the bottom. "In the deep night it was heartrending," one sensitive sublieutenant observes, "to watch the fire burning the ships under sail while the current carried them away before our eyes."[10]

De Grasse, lying eight miles downstream on board the *Ville-de-Paris,* stands ready to weigh anchor. He writes Washington to announce "the lack of success obtained by the fire ships sent from York against our ships, which are blocking that river. Assuming that this operation was effected by Lord Cornwallis so that he might have the use of the York for one night at least— our ships being forced to cut their cables in order not to be set afire—and take advantage of that brief respite to come out of the river with his ships and, hurrying to the coast, cross and disembark on the right bank of the James, I immediately sent two frigates up to anchor at the mouth of the river and thus prevent so much as a barque from approaching. I hope that if this was the general's scheme, it may do him harm and turn to his disadvantage.

"Everything has reached the river today, including your artillery. It is time to begin closing in upon the enemy, and apprising him of our combined forces."[11]

Right behind you, Admiral. La Fayette, on the spot, has been dancing about like a cat on a hot tin roof. His last letter to Washington before their reunion announces that all is well, on land at any rate, notwithstanding the administrative rot in the state of Virginia—for which Jefferson cannot be held entirely to blame, he points out in passing—and notwithstanding the inevitable bickerings with de Grasse, who refuses to take La Fayette as seriously as *he* feels he ought to:

> . . . but if you knew how slowly things go on in this country; still I have done the best in my power; I have written and received twenty letters a day from government [of Virginia] and from every department. The Governor does what he can; the wheels of his government are so very rusty that no governor whatever will be able to set them free again. Time will prove that Jefferson has been too severely charged.
>
> The French troops, my dear General, have landed with amazing celerity; they have already been wanting flour, meat and salt, not so much, however, as to be one day without. I have been night and day the quarter-master collector, and have drawn myself into a violent head-ache and fever, which will go off with three hours' sleep, the want of which has occasioned it. This, my dear General, will apologise to you for not writing with my own hand [the letter is dictated].
>
> The French army [of Saint-Simon] is composed of the most excellent regiments: they have with them a corps of hussars, which may be of immediate use. The general and all the officers have cheerfully lived in the same way as our poorly provided American detachment. I think a letter from you on the subject will have a very good effect . . .
>
> I had recommended, with proper delicacy, to Count de Grasse to send some

naval forces up York River . . . No movement of Count de Grasse has as yet taken place . . .

Now, my dear General, I am going to speak to you of the fortifications at York. Lord Cornwallis is working day and night, and will soon work himself into a respectable situation; he has taken ashore the greater part of his sailors; he is picking up whatever provisions he can get. I am told he has ordered the inhabitants of the vicinity of the town to come in, and should think they may do him much good.[12]

He's being sarcastic: what he means is that opinion in Virginia is swerving back to true-blue Whig, the weather vanes have felt which way the wind is blowing, and Cornwallis may regret this decision because the civilians won't support the Yorktown garrison and a siege can last only as long as the town's inhabitants are boosting the soldiers' morale.

However, Cornwallis hasn't thrown in the towel yet. "He was hastening to complete his fortifications of Yorktown and Glocester,*and barring York River by mooring ships broadside on and sinking them. He had worked continuously at his defenses since the arrival of the army in Chesapeake Bay, with six thousand regular troops and the crews from the 40-gun ships and its frigates and transport ships, and an artillery of more than one hundred pieces."[13] England's last hope lies in Admiral Digby, who is said to be replacing Graves in New York and intending to sail down again "with a hundred sail and ten thousand men." In every siege, the besieged are always conjuring up such visions of hosts of liberating angels.

Meanwhile, the bulk of the combined armies is splashing down by forced marches through rain and mud, in greater danger of death by drowning and exhaustion than in battle, but with a sort of disciplined fury as though springs too long compressed were all being released at once. "Generals de Vioménil and de Béville went around the bay through Baltimore and, upon reaching that town, learned that M. de La Villebrune was awaiting them at Annapolis with the Romulus, five frigates and nine transports [sent by Barras]. They hurried thither, set their troops on board, except for the teams and administrative services which continued by land, and, on the 23rd, entered the James River to disembark at Hog's Ferry on the 24th and camp at Williamsburg on the 26th, within sight of Washington. The final part of the trip went without incident, but was quite trying in the James, which had to be negotiated, sounding line in hand, in rather poor craft." Grasse did apologize for the feebleness of the boats he had provided: "Not having been notified, I brought with me only such ships as could give me superiority over the united armies of England, and relied upon your resources for attacks, marches, etc., of which I could know nothing."[14] A small, snide rap on the knuckles administered in

*The name was written Gloster, Glocester, or Gloucester at the time.

passing by the Haves to those poor Americans who Have Naught.

Washington and Rochambeau reach Williamsburg on September 14, still ahead of the main body of their men. They have averaged sixty miles a day on horseback. La Fayette, as he says, has worked himself into a fever but crawls out of bed to welcome the two men he has been awaiting all summer long, all his youth long. The emotion of their reunion is one of those moments worth living for. It has an eyewitness, a wide-awake American eager to savor one of the first days in the life of a newborn world, after which nothing anywhere is ever quite the same again. Colonel Richard Butler, commanding one of La Fayette's regiments, did a good deed when he wrote in his diary that day:

> Sept. 14th—The Marquis Lafayette still continues ill of the ague.
>
> Yesterday the Marquis de St. Simon, and a number of his officers, paid a visit to our line, and the Baron Steuben and our good friend Gen. Wayne, whose wound and gout still continue ill.
>
> About 3 o'clock an express arrived, announcing the approach of our great and good Commander-in-Chief, Gen. Washington, and the Count de Rochambeau, the commander of the allied armies of France, now joining.
>
> At 4 P.M., the guns fired a royal salute as the General approached the camp, on which the two armies turned out on their battalion parades; His Excellency and the Count de Rochambeau, with their suites, attended by the Marquis de Lafayette, Maj. Gen. and commander of the American, and Maj. Gen. Marquis de St. Simon, commander of the allied army (lately arrived), and all their suites, visited the allied army first, and then the American army, and were saluted according to the custom; these ceremonies finished, the whole of the officers of the French army attended at the Marquis de St. Simon's quarters and were introduced to the *Illustrious Hero.* The field officers of the American army all attended to bid him and other Generals welcome.
>
> These ceremonies over, an elegant supper was served up, and the following great personages and officers supped together in the utmost harmony and happiness, viz—His Excellency; the Count de Rochambeau, commander of the allied army; Maj. Gen. Marquis de Lafayette, commander of the army in Virginia; Maj. Gen. Marquis de St. Simon, commander of the allied army in Virginia; Maj. Gen. Baron de Steuben, Inspector General of the American army; Count Dumas*(an officer of distinction in the French Guards, and one of the aids of Rochambeau); Count de Damas, another of his aids . . . and many other Cols. and Lt. Cols. and other officers of the allied army. To add to the happiness of the event and evening, an elegant band of music played an introductive part of a French Opera, signifying the happiness of the family, when blessed with the presence of their father, and their great dependence upon him.
>
> About 10 o'clock the company rose up, and after mutual congratulations and the greatest expression of joy, they separated.[15]

*Mathieu Dumas is no more a count than Butler himself, or at least not yet; Napoleon makes him Count of the Empire after Wagram, and Butler is anticipating.

On September 17 Washington has himself taken on board the *Ville-de-Paris,* not before going to no end of trouble to unearth, for honor's sake, a little English ship, the *Queen Charlotte,* which his men have recently captured. A symbolic visit by the beneficiary to the benefactor and purveyor of aid, men, and money. That day all power seems to lie with France, and de Grasse, possibly deliberately, commits a faux pas:

"On the American Chief's reaching the quarter-deck, the Admiral flew to embrace him, imprinting the French salute upon each cheek. Hugging him in his arms, he exclaimed,

" 'My dear little general!'

"De Grasse was of lofty stature; but the term petit, or small, when applied to the majestic and commanding person of Washington, produced an effect upon the risible faculties of all present not to be described. The Frenchmen, governed by the rigid etiquette of the ancien régime, controlled their mirth as best they could; but our own [this is written by Custis] jolly Knox, heedless of all rules, laughed, and that aloud, till his fat sides shook again."[16]

The effusions over, they have to work hard and get their cards down fast. Cornwallis is in the vise, now it has to be tightened. Arm in arm, Washington, de Grasse, and Rochambeau draw up their final plans and adopt their ultimate decisions. Behind them, three steps out of the limelight in the knot of officers, you can see a young man relieved of strategic responsibility and returned to the ranks, to whom nobody pays much attention—the Marquis de La Fayette, just another commander of one of the armies in the system Washington is now taking in hand.

In the middle distance. Thank you and good night, Monsieur de La Fayette, mission accomplished, back to the second string. There's too much to do just now for him to feel very hurt. But this day of the summit meeting for the three top men is the beginning of his relative subordination, and as soon as the smoke clears it starts to smart like a neglected wound.

72

War Itself Does Not Interest Me

September 24. Unforeseen crisis. Mini-crisis rather, but real enough to alarm Washington. De Grasse is talking about leaving. The man has just won the Battle of the Chesapeake, but he's so unconvinced of it that he takes the rumor of a return offensive by the English fleet far too seriously, and panics. He writes to Rochambeau: "Digby's arrival alters our operations. I am going to put to sea as soon as the weather permits, and remain outside the bay to prevent the enemy from entering . . . I shall leave M. de Saint-Simon's troops with you until success is ours or I shall be able to re-enter. If the winds force me to the leeward at the close of a battle and I am unable to return, please transfer the Martinique regiments onto the ships remaining in the river."[1] You can't mean it!

At times like this, it's useful to have a La Fayette on tap. He can be sent out to the *Ville-de-Paris* bearing a sort of plea which he will back up with all the weight of his experience in the field. Admiral, you can't do that to us!

> Give me leave, in the first place, to repeat to your Excellency, that the enterprise against York, under the protection of your ships, is as certain as any military operation can be rendered by a decisive superiority of strength and means; that it is in fact reducible to calculation; that the surrender of the British garrison will be important in itself and its consequences; and that it must necessarily go a great way towards terminating the war, and securing the invaluable objects of it to the allies.
>
> Your Excellency's departure from the Chesapeake, by affording an opening for the succour of York, which the enemy would instantly avail themselves of, would frustrate these brilliant prospects; and the consequence would be, not only the disgrace and loss of renouncing an enterprise, upon which the fairest expectations of the allies have been founded, after the most expensive preparations and uncommon exertions and fatigues, but perhaps the disbanding of the whole army for want of provisions.[2]

Can this distraught tone be Washington? That letter must have cost him plenty. There is, and will be from now on, a rift between the chiefs, with de Grasse on one side having whims and sulks, and Washington and Rochambeau on the other. The latter feels no pity for the poor admiral, and "borrows" eight hundred men "from his ship garrisons" to cross from Yorktown to Gloucester and besiege the other part of the English forces. De Grasse, wailing like Silas Marner, lets them go: "In order not to fail of the object which we have undertaken, I consent to give the eight hundred men you ask of me; but it is against my conscience, and perhaps to the dishonor of the King's flag . . . You are totally disarming my army."[3] But his ships stay where they are, and the land forces are at full capacity, and that's the main thing.

September 28. Washington has his reinforcements, the troops following him down from Head of Elk. Some even manage to embark at Annapolis and make their way through the Chesapeake squalls. The commander-in-chief leaves Williamsburg and takes up his position with the entire army two or three miles from Yorktown. His men are very weary and supplies are low. Poor "Elisabeth City" has been scraped clean by soldiers from both sides. The reinforcements arrive without their baggage. There's no more forage for the horses for ten leagues around. The soldiers' rations have been cut to biscuits and cheese. And they even have to beg flour from Shylock de Grasse. But they take comfort in the thought that the English have even less and no hope of more. The morale of the besiegers remains high, they feel that victory is at last within their grasp.

A few feet below the sixty houses of Yorktown lie the sand dunes, and there's a strip of swampy ground east of town, between the river and the dunes. Here Cornwallis has dug in as best he can, using every wrinkle of the terrain; but the English are beginning to tread on each other's toes under the watchful eye of the four or five ships whose artillery is covering them. Their protection on the inland side is ten or so hastily erected redoubts that house sixteen batteries totaling sixty-five cannons, manned by two hundred Germans and five hundred Tories—the last American royalists in Virginia.

September 29. The heads of the allied columns move forward "taking advantage of the woods, curtains of trees, bushes and creeks, so as to surround the enemy within firing range of their works."[4] More useful at this stage of the proceedings than any superior officer, a dozen American and French engineers divided into three groups sniff the terrain, feel it and taste it, and, working under heavy musket fire, assign the marksmen to the most strategic spots. How right he was five years ago, old Beaumarchais, when he screamed at Vergennes, "Monsieur le Comte, I beg you for gunpowder and engineers!"

September 30. The investment is complete. Cornwallis is shut in, except on the river side, where he can still communicate by boat with his lieutenant,

Tarleton—who is himself threatened at Gloucester, across from Yorktown, by the Comte de Choisy and the Duc de Lauzun. Fersen, at Rochambeau's side, is busily speeding up "the disembarkment of our siege artillery," which Barras has brought from Newport, "and manufacturing the quantity of fascines, sausages [*sic*], hurdles and gabions needed for the siege"[5]: those earth-filled wood and wicker contraptions of every shape and size that have been used for millennia to cover the assailants' approach to the walls.

The opposing forces are approximately equal: ten thousand men for Cornwallis, of whom only six thousand are English and the rest German or Tory. Plus six or seven thousand blacks who are used for hard labor on earthworks. They were picked up in the Carolinas along with the livestock and horses. Washington can line up about ten thousand to face them, half of whom are French—but the hinterland is with him, and there's de Grasse's formidable fleet artillery on the horizon playing its silent role of potential hellraiser. Opposite Yorktown, the French hold the left side and the Americans the right, all the way to the Chesapeake.

At dawn on October 2 the besieged are found to have abandoned their advanced works during the night and almost without a fight, even though they had been creating serious difficulties for Washington's engineers. Don't look a gift horse in the mouth. "We immediately took possession of them," notes Fersen, "and this greatly facilitated our works, by leaving us free to set up our first parallel on the far side of the ravine. If this was an error made by Lord Cornwallis it is excusable, for he had express orders from General Clinton to close himself within the body of the place, and a promise that he [Clinton] would come to his aid."

October 3. A bitter skirmish on the north bank, around Gloucester, where the English are trying to find an air hole and prepare an exit if things get really desperate. Colonel Tarleton, one of the despoilers of Virginia, decides to seize a position three miles from the center, where Choisy and Lauzun are setting up a camp for the eight hundred men de Grasse has just lent them. The two French chiefs vie with each other in their contempt for the local militia who have come to give them a hand. "M. de Choisy," says Lauzun, "is a good and brave man, absurdly violent, constantly in a temper, making scenes with everybody, and never showing any common sense. He began by sending General Wiedon and the whole militia to the devil, told them they were poltroons, and in five minutes had them almost as frightened of him as of the English, which is saying a good deal . . .

"I was not a hundred paces from there when I heard my vanguard letting off their pistols. I galloped away to find a piece of ground on which I could fight. As I came up I saw the English cavalry bearing down on me, three times more numerous than my own; I charged without pausing, and we joined. Tarleton picked me out and came toward me with raised gun. We were about to fight in single combat when his horse was thrown by one of his dragoons pursued by one of my lancers. I rushed over to take him, a body of English dragoons thrust between us and protected his retreat, his horse was left with me. He charged me a second time but did not break me; I charged him a third, overran part of his cavalry, and chased him back to his entrenchments outside Gloucester. He lost one officer and fifty men, and I took a fair number of prisoners."[6] And that's curtains for the cavalry, who have no more space to run in. The rest of this show is for the engineer corps and infantry.

October 6. The big day. Working by night the assailants open "the first parallel" six hundred yards from the English line; in other words, they dig a long row of trenches, like a slipknot, parallel to the town's defenses. In a siege, the essential weapon is the shovel, not the gun. To prevent the besieged from reacting, the French, on the left, simulate a night attack by firing in all directions. By morning the Americans, on the right, have already managed to dig a trench a thousand yards long, plant four improvised redoubts in it, cover them with palisades, and equip them with five batteries.* "The terrain, which was very heavily intersected by small ravines, greatly facilitated our approach and enabled us to reach our trench under cover, without having to dig an approach trench. Upon our left [this is Fersen speaking] we had opened another trench, supported by the stream on the left and a wood on the right; there we had a battery of four mortars, two howitzers and two twenty-four pounders that beat the stream, made communication between York and Gloucester hazardous, and greatly annoyed the ships in the river. The enemy did not fire much at night. On the following days we worked at perfecting the trench, palisading the redoubts and putting the batteries in order. They all fired during the day of the 10th. We had forty-one muzzles firing, counting cannons, mortars and howitzers. Our artillery was wonderfully well served, but the quality of the earthworks, all of sand, did not enable our cannon, well aimed though it was, to have as much effect as it would have done on another terrain; but we learned from deserters that our bombs were most effective, and the number of dead and wounded was rising appreciably."[7]

This is where the slaughter begins. Nobody's laughing now—but were they before? Five hundred yards from the fortified camp, the American and French guns have the entire enemy forces concentrated under their fire. Every shell is a hit. Elbow to elbow in the trenches, the riflemen pick off every suspicion of a red coat they see. The English projectiles, on the other hand, stray beyond the parallel or fall short of it. Space is on the besiegers' side.

*A battery is a group of cannons, variable in number.

October 10. Claude Blanchard, "principal commissioner of wars" (we might say chief supply officer) in Rochambeau's corps, notes that "the firing has become very active from the French trenches. We had an artillery of the first order, and the Americans, for their part, had large cannons and showed great activity; but they could not come near the perfection of our gunners, of whom General Washington was in admiration; it is true that they had, so to speak, perfect instruments: the cannons were new* and the balls perfectly matched to the bore.

"Going about some work connected with my occupation that day, I had occasion to enter the trenches at a place where a battery of mortars had been placed, which was firing upon an enemy redoubt; it countered with a few howitzers which did no damage. In that trench I found myself in the company of M. de Saint-Simon, who commanded it,"[8] and who is not quite just another officer. He is the third of the Saint-Simons in age and in rank. An intellectual turned loose among the fighters. Hardly twenty years old, keen eyes and a long aquiline nose in an interestingly pallid face. He's a good fighter himself, though, but an even better thinker: "I saw that the American Revolution marked the beginning of a new political era; that this revolution must necessarily bring about an important advance in civilization as a whole, and that, within a brief time, it would cause great changes in the social order then existing in Europe."[9] The young nobleman goes unnoticed among so many others more gaudy and Parisian or Versaill-ese than he. "War itself does not interest me, but the object of this war interested me keenly, and this interest enabled me to bear the work of it without repugnance. I want the end, I often told myself, so I must needs want the means . . . It was already clear to me what career I was cut out for and called to by my tastes and natural inclination. It was not my vocation to be a soldier; I was impelled toward a very different, one might even say contrary, form of activity,"[10] that is, working to change society by some means other than warfare—now there's a new thought, one that hasn't yet occurred to La Fayette.

Here begins Saint-Simon II, the man who tries to imagine the future. His ancestor, number I, did a first-rate job on the present. If anyone has been able to assassinate Louis XIV—in terms of people's assumptions about him—it was the Duc de Saint-Simon. But that's another story.

*These were the famous cannons forged from Gribeauval's designs.

73

OCTOBER 1781

The Play Is Over, Monsieur le Comte

All day October 10 gunfire pours from the allied trenches in a steady stream. "The French pieces were of the first order, new, in excellent condition, and firing accurately. The Americans had only solid, heavy, large guns of obsolete make, although they employed them with commendable energy."[1] The English answer intermittently, with guns of smaller caliber, because their fleet's cannon can't reach the besiegers' parallel.

After four days of pounding, October 6 to 10, half the houses of Yorktown are razed or fired, and the English nearly muzzled; they have to pull their guns back from the loopholes and shelter them behind merlons,* because the French gunners' aim has become too deadly accurate.

The French score another point: thanks to a few well-placed pieces at the far ends of their works, they manage to land some red-hot balls on the *Choron* and three more of Cornwallis's last ships anchored beyond the quay at Yorktown, and set fire to them. Nocturnal fireworks display. "Never had a more beautiful and ghastly sight been seen. In the pitch-dark night, the hatchways of the ships could be seen spitting sprays of fire while the shells rained down."[2] De Grasse, getting a bird's-eye view of the scene, is temporarily reassured. He writes to Rochambeau: "Last night I heard a considerable racket: no doubt you were measuring your instruments against those of Cornwallis. Make him dance me a pretty jig."

On the morning of the 11th Yorktown, seen from the tops of the little ocher hills two or three miles away, where Rochambeau's tall blue and gold gentlemen stand directing operations in the shelter of some ruined walls, is a semicircle of ceaseless explosions between sand and sea, a few pines and spruce shocked to find themselves still standing, a damp sun, some homeless birds, and, on the powdery road leading to the trench, battalions of impeccably geometrical white and blue soldiers marching five abreast to their deaths with their guns over their shoulders, shouting as they go either "Vive le Roi!" in the accents of Touraine, the Bourbonnais, or the Soissonnais, or "God and

---

*A merlon is a solid section of rampart between two embrasures.

Liberty!" in the Virginia drawl. From opposite them come oaths and battle cries in Scottish and Swabian. In this kind of warfare the men are hurled against one another in little regional distillates. It makes for greater cohesion in battle. You die among brothers. My widow will find out quicker if my next-door neighbor survives.

On the night of October 11–12, a new leap forward. The garrote in which Yorktown is slowly strangling is pulled several gasps tighter when the second parallel is opened, to bring the assailants within three hundred yards of the enemy's works, "the advance having been made with such secrecy, and so much sooner than the British had expected, that they did not suspect the movement until the morning light revealed to their pickets the men working in the trenches. The two parallels had been completed and occupied with very small loss to either the American or the French troops, and the fire of the besiegers now became destructive in the extreme."[3]

The English aren't answering back with marshmallows, however. Now that they can also see to aim at their attackers, the numbers of dead and wounded begin to assume the proportions of a small pitched battle. In Williamsburg and beyond, a hideous scene is being painted against that marine background, the reverse side of the glorious tapestries for war museums. The bodies of the wounded and ill—from exhaustion or scurvy—can be seen lying here and there on tent sheets spread on the ground, until somebody can give them better shelter. Wrapped in huge white aprons, a few men you would take for butchers are busying themselves nearby, on the treadmill of impotence. They're the army "surgeons," the bottom rung on the medical ladder, without assistance, order, bandages, or drugs, left to improvise the dying into life. In those days armies didn't give one-hundredth as much thought and money to the care of the wounded as they did to the grooms of the aides-de-camp. In 1781 it's a sin for a soldier to be wounded, a glory for an officer. The officer's servants nurse him and he gets the cross of St. Louis. The soldier's comrades try to keep his wounds from festering by urinating into them, and if he survives he may be entitled to live in the Hôtel des Invalides. "The infirmaries set up in the field are no longer sufficient; they have asked the Williamsburg hospital for assistance which it is unable to provide (meanwhile, five hundred are counted ill, and twenty officers among them). Nothing effective can be done to bind their wounds; the hospital equipment and staff, which set out with the army from Newport, are coming by slow day marches overland and have not yet arrived. To make matters worse, the few essential instruments and drugs brought with the troops on their forced marches had been left behind on the ships in the haste of disembarkation."[4] So, artisans of History, die without a fuss, please. This is war.

October 14. Surgery. The object is to remove two warts which disfigure and, more important, incommode the aesthetically satisfying second parallel: two English redoubts, about five hundred yards in advance of their fortified camp, are still holding out and pouring a hail of death upon the new trenches, into which they can now fire sideways. The engineers make their report, that's their job: they consider that the packed sand, wood, and men are ripe. The soldiers attack, that's their job. Washington orders the charge at dusk and, as though sensing that this is the last opportunity for movement before everything congeals, he sends out two detachments, one American and the other French, of about four hundred men each. The French grenadiers and riflemen are commanded by Major General Baron de Vioménil;* the Americans by . . . La Fayette, seconded by an Auvergnat, his fellow countryman de Gimat, and three Americans of note: lieutenant colonels Barber, John Laurens—back from Versailles to prove that verbal grapplings with Vergennes aren't the only kind of fighting he's fit for—and Alexander Hamilton, who has just left a most promising position as Washington's aide-de-camp because he could no longer put up with his beloved chief's chronic ill-humor. He's an oddball, a grumbler. His quarrel with Washington dates from February, when he decided to tell this latter-day Caesar that he'd better start looking for another bottle-washer. Washington had sent for him urgently, at a moment when Hamilton was busy at some important task. As soon as he finished he set off to answer the summons and, "instead of finding the General as usual in his room, I met him at the head of the stairs, where accosting me in a very angry tone, 'Col Hamilton (said he), you have kept me waiting at the head of the stairs these ten minutes. I must tell you Sir you treat me with disrespect.'—'I am not conscious of it Sir, but since you have thought it necessary to tell me so we part.'—'Very well Sir if it be your choice,' and we separated." Less than an hour later the commander-in-chief indicated to his aide-de-camp that he would like a word with him in private, so they could settle between them, in open speech, a matter that could be nothing more than a product of frayed nerves. But Hamilton stood firm on his refusal: "I always disliked the office of an Aide de Camp as having in it a kind of personal dependence . . . Infected however with the enthusiasm of the times, an idea of the Generals character which experience soon taught me to be unfounded overcame my scruples and induced me to accept his invitation . . . I was always determined, if there should ever happen a break between us, never to consent to an accommodation. I was persuaded that when once that nice barrier, which marked the boundaries of what we owed to each other, should be thrown down, it might be propped again, but could never be restored."⁵ Such is this man of liberty, who is more at ease this

*In the queen's coterie, but on the sidelines. He plays an important part in the emigration and Restoration, where he is on the side of the ultras.

evening serving under La Fayette than back at headquarters.

"La Fayette and the Americans were to try to take the right-hand redoubt and the French the left-hand one. Ten carpenters armed with axes, and fifty marksmen carrying fascines formed the vanguard ahead of four hundred grenadiers and riflemen, two companies of auxiliary riflemen and two cannons . . . The enemy's attention was to be drawn toward two secondary points while the attacks were being made simultaneously. The redoubt which was the Americans' objective put up little resistance and was carried by bayonet. At the other, our grenadiers came out with a fine flourish; the English [*sic*] grenadiers from Anspach and Hesse—some two hundred—fought back energetically and held their position, and our carpenters had to cut through the branches of the abatis and palisades in order to make a passage for the French who, notwithstanding the heavy fire, charged four hundred strong and carried the work at sword's point and took possession of the parapet. Thirty-nine men were taken and twenty-one put to the sword. The remainder fled and could not be caught. Our losses amounted to forty-six slain and sixty-two injured. One of the latter was the Chevalier de Lameth,* aide-major général des logis, and also Colonel de Gimat, La Fayette's aide-de-camp . . ."6 La Fayette doesn't miss this opportunity to get in a dig at Vioménil—one of the most virulent anti-Americans (anti-republicans would be more accurate) on Rochambeau's staff, one of those men who are fighting for their king but by no means for freedom. "The Baron de Vioménil had expressed some doubts at the outset whether La Fayette's troops would be able to perform the service required of them. Therefore, after his light infantry had made the assault with admirable courage, La Fayette . . . dispatched an aide-de-camp immediately to announce with his compliments that the American troops were in possession of their redoubt, and to say that if M. de Vioménil required any help the Marquis de La Fayette would have great pleasure in assisting him."7

What's the use of bickering? Both redoubts have been taken. Cornwallis's garrote fits like a collar. A collar of iron and fire.

October 15. The Yorktown garrison makes a final face-saving attempt, under cover of night, when the besiegers, exhausted and doped with the evening ration of rum that often does duty for soup in their diet, are sleeping soundly. "The English, counting six hundred of the best men, made a sortie which, by means of a subterfuge, might have succeeded. They came up before two batteries and called upon them not to fire, saying they were American; then they swarmed into the second parallel, spiked four guns, and seized M. de Beurguissant, captain of the Agenais regiment. It was the work of a moment. Chastellux countered with the reserves. The action became heated; the English

---

*This is Charles, oldest of the Lameth boys, and the one who will play the most important role in 1789–91.

paused, withdrew and were thrust vigorously back inside the town. Our losses were heavy. In the trench next day, the Marquis de Saint-Simon [commander-in-chief] was injured but refused to be relieved, and completed his twenty-four hours of duty."8 In the code of war etiquette that was almost a formality, a gesture of courtesy to twenty dead men.

Cornwallis is out of shells and out of food; he has less than two days' worth of cartridges, and his soldiers haven't had any biscuit for forty-eight hours. His wounded die where they fall. Where is he supposed to bury them?

October 17. The anniversary of Burgoyne's surrender at Saratoga in 1777, defeat in the North, the first English stumble at the top of the stairs. They haven't chosen the date on purpose; but now they're flat on their backs at the bottom. Around two in the morning a drummer appears on the ramparts of the fortress and hands a French officer a letter from Lord Cornwallis for Washington: "Sir, I propose a cessation of hostilities for twenty-four hours, and that two officers may be appointed by each side, to meet at Mr. Moore's house, to settle terms for the surrender of the posts of York and Glouces-ter."9 .

Moore's house, miraculously spared by the shelling, stands on one of the highest points in Yorktown, above the river. It is one of those capacious barn-and-house combinations, in the American style, all on the ground floor with a steep gabled roof. There's room enough inside it for a dozen men to sit around a big table—exhausted men who would far rather drink punch together than go on cutting one another's throats. There's precious little hatred between these adversaries. Every man has done all he could.* A sort of sporting spirit presides over the negotiations between plenipotentiaries in this modern-day Ys† submerged by the tide of war, in which hundreds of men lie on the ground outside the shattered houses waiting for somebody to give them food, watched by thousands of ghosts who have already starved to death but are still on their feet, God knows how—the Negroes. First article of capitulation:

"The garrison of York will march out to a place to be appointed in front of the posts, at two o'clock precisely, with shouldered arms, colours cased, and drums beating a British or German march. They are then to ground their arms and return to their encampments, where they will remain until they are dis-patched to the places of their destination. Two works on the Gloucester side will be delivered at one o'clock to a detachment of French and American troops appointed to possess them. The garrison will march out at three o'clock

---

*Cornwallis prudently sends Benedict Arnold to New York before he is encircled; his presence would have created complications.

†Ys: a legendary Breton city which was supposedly swallowed by the sea in the fourth or fifth century B.C. The king's daughter stole her father's key, opened the door, and let the water in. [Trans.]

in the afternoon; the cavalry with their swords drawn, trumpets sounding, and the infantry in the manner prescribed for the garrisons of York."10

And so it goes on October 19, 1781, with order and dignity to temper the exuberance of the victors and the chagrin of the defeated. The surrender at Yorktown is a sort of international parade in which each side makes it a point of honor to march better than the other. The English proceed in the appointed order between two lines of saluting victors almost two miles long, down the road that served to bring supplies to the trenches such a short while ago. On the horizon, whitecaps stipple the sea. The trees are weighted down by clusters of civilians who have walked or driven out from Williamsburg to watch, and who cheer so loudly that the trumpets nearly lose the beat. They're almost an impediment. The most arresting feature in this vast moving picture is the scarlet coats of thousands of Scottish troops—"stocky, vigorous, good soldiers"—pacing grimly forward: the red surrendering to the blue.

And the culmination of the movement is a group of men in unplumed bicornes and long dress coats over white vests and breeches, among whom Washington occupies the foreground without needing to ask for it. La Fayette —three steps behind, he's going to have to get used to it—stands among the senior officers. His name does not appear on the capitulation.

One false note: the English general cantering toward this group to perform the most humiliating act of all, the surrender of his sword, is not Cornwallis. He has announced that he is unwell and is keeping to his room. Maybe it's true. "Indeed," writes one of the officers, "there were grounds for sickness unto death, for a general of his quality to have allowed himself to be trapped in such a way after being abandoned by his own and held at the mercy of the man he had chased across New Jersey and pursued everywhere in vain five years before."11 De Grasse isn't there either: in fact, he never sets foot on American soil, and has barricaded himself on board the *Ville-de-Paris* as though aghast at the audacity of his act of insubordination, even though it has made him the midwife of a continent. He really is ill—with fatigue and gout; like Rodney he's got the "admirals' affliction." The public conquerors raised to the top of the flagpole on October 19 are Washington and Rochambeau.

General O'Hara, representing Cornwallis, heads for Rochambeau. "The English* invested this sad ceremony with much haughtiness and insolence. They were especially scornful of the Americans."12 O'Hara's gesture is quite deliberate and expresses the full significance of the moment. If Rochambeau consents to take his sword, then this is merely another incident in the thousand-year-old war between France and England. It's been a fight between gentlemen, played according to immutable rules, and the Insurgents standing there count for no more than Hessians or redskins: cannon fodder recruited for our

*According to Blanchard, the chief supply officer.

kings. But if King George's soldiers have to admit themselves beaten by the Rebels, then a whole world will be blasted by the wind from America, the world of monarchies and hierarchies.

Mathieu Dumas steps forward. He is standing next to Rochambeau, and prevents General O'Hara from completing his gesture. He turns toward Washington:

"You are mistaken, Sir. The commander-in-chief of our army is on your right."

And the sword of Yorktown is surrendered to America. How true it is that it is not the losing that hurts most, but to whom you lose.

The next day La Fayette writes to Vergennes: "Accept my congratulations, Monsieur le Comte, upon the good pen which has at last been cut for politics [in other words, you can finish off the war now that we have won it] . . . I am happy that our Virginia campaign has ended so well, and my respect for the talents of Lord Cornwallis gives his capture an additional value to my mind. After this attempt, what English general will undertake the conquest of America? Their maneuvers in the southern country have not been more successful than those in the North, and now the experience of General Burgoyne has been repeated."[13] And to Maurepas: "The play is over, Monsieur le Comte, the fifth act has just come to an end. I was somewhat disturbed during the earlier acts, but my heart rejoices exceedingly at this last, and I have no less pleasure in congratulating you upon the happy completion of our campaign. I shall not describe it to you in detail, Monsieur le Comte, but leave that to Lauzun, for whom I wish as great success in crossing the ocean as he has had in overcoming Tarleton's legion."[14]

For it's the handsome Lauzun whom Rochambeau sends to bear the glad tidings to Versailles. It's the least they can do for him. He'll hardly have time to hand the letter to its addressee, though: "I embarked on the King's frigate *Surveillante* and, after a crossing of twenty-two days, arrived at Brest and went to Versailles without losing a moment. I found M. de Maurepas on his death-bed; he was hardly conscious, yet he knew me and welcomed me most affectingly. He recommended me strongly to the King and his ministers, who promised him to carry out everything he intended for me. He died two days later, and M. de Castries and M. de Ségur treated me as ill as they were able."[15]

The Court is in a whirl about a very different victory: on October 22, 1781, the week of Yorktown, Marie Antoinette gave birth to a child—a real one, that is—a boy. Maurepas dead, Necker expelled, Vergennes in position as principal minister, Louis XVI beginning a second reign flanked by a dauphin and a won war. The heir who has just filled his lungs for the first time, at the same moment as America, should turn twenty in the year 1800. When will he succeed his father? The Bourbons are a long-lived tribe, and Louis XVI is in the pink of health. If the king lives as long as or longer than Louis XV, Louis XVII will come to the throne sometime in the mid-nineteenth century.

The king and queen are about to be welcomed officially by their good city of Paris, which is making ready a gala celebration in honor of the blessed event.

And these revels will take place on January 21, 1782.

Notes

Titles appearing in Volume I, where fuller descriptions will be found in some cases, are marked with an asterisk (*) upon first mention here.

I

1. Valentine Thomson, *Le Corsaire chez l'Impératrice* (Paris, Plon, 1936), p. 2 (for the crew) and pp. 31–5 (for events in the Irish Sea).
*2. Cuvillier and Bouin, *Essai d'un dictionnaire des principaux ports et mouillages du monde connu* (Paris, Librairie du Commerce, 1845), p. 50.
3. Janette Taylor, *Life and Correspondence of John Paul Jones* (New York, 1830), p. 42. [This quotation has been retranslated back from the French.]
4. According to Edward Fanning, one of his lieutenants, who published his *Narrative of the Adventures of an American navy officer under the command of the commodore Paul Jones* in New York in 1806.
5. According to one of his "friends" (?). See Thomson, *Le Corsaire chez l'Impératrice*, p. 11.
6. Archives nationales, M. M. 851, *Journal des services de Paul Jones*.
7. Don Carlos Seitz, *Paul Jones; his exploits in English seas during 1778–80; contemporary accounts collected from English news papers* (New York, Dutton, 1845), p. 46. [This quotation has been retranslated back from the French.]
8. *Life and Correspondence of John Paul Jones, including His Narrative of the Campaign of the Liman* (New York, 1830), pp. 89–92.

2

1. Letter from Anna Maria to Leopold Mozart, May 29, 1778. Quoted by Brigitte and Jean Massin in *Mozart* (Paris, Club français du livre, 1959). In this reconstruction I have followed the Massins step by step, and will borrow some of their quotations of Mozart and his family. How could I do otherwise? Their book is the definitive work on Mozart. When you build a monument, you mustn't be surprised if the Bedouins sneak in from the desert and rob a few stones from it.
2. *Ibid.*, p. 249.
3. On February 3, 1830. *Ibid.*, p. 30.
4. *Ibid.*, p. 32.
5. Letter to his father, July 31, 1778. Quoted by the Massins

(*ibid.,* p. 260), who comment:
"Many Frenchmen persevered in
this delusion, and insisted upon
seeing Mozart as an eternal child
. . . For Mozart, Paris was the
emotional symbol of this myth of
the child prodigy from which he
was furiously trying to escape."

6. Letters from Leopold to his son,
February 16 and 23, 1778. *Ibid.,*
p. 224.
7. February 28, 1778. *Ibid.,* p. 225.
8. July 3 . . . in the letter to his
father written on the day his
mother died! *Ibid.,* p. 252.
9. Grimm to Leopold Mozart, July
27, 1778. *Ibid.,* p. 262.
10. To his father, October 31, 1777.
Ibid., p. 174.
11. To his father, May 1, 1778. *Ibid.,*
pp. 236 and 239.
12. *Ibid.,* p. 235 (same letter).
13. To his father, May 1, February 7,
and June 12, 1778. *Ibid.,* pp.
239, 230, and 242.

3

1. G. Lacour-Gayet, *La Marine
militaire de la France sous le règne
de Louis XVI* (Paris, Champion,
1905, p. 119) [the work is
dedicated to my grandfather,
Admiral Manceron], (cited
hereafter as Lacour-Gayet, *Marine
française sous Louis XVI*).
2. According to *l'Espion Anglais,*
February 12, 1778.
3. Jacques Mordal, *Vingt-cinq siècles
de guerre sur mer* (Verviers,
Marabout-Université, 1959), I
(Au temps de la rame et de la voile),
129.
4. Lacour-Gayet, *Marine française
sous Louis XVI,* p. 96.

5. Letter of April 8, 1777. *Ibid.,*
p. 89.
6. *Ibid.,* p. 122.
7. Doniol, *Histoire de la participation
de la France à l'établissement des
Etats-Unis* (Paris), II, 34.
8. On April 12, 1777.
Lacour-Gayet, *Marine française
sous Louis XVI,* p. 54.
9. According to his letter of July 31
to the French ambassador to
Spain (Montmorin, Louis XVI's
future minister under the
Revolution). Doniol, *Histoire de
la participation de la France à
l'établissement des Etats-Unis,* III,
535.

4

1. Said by d'Argenson, quoted by
Amédée Britsch, *La Jeunesse de
Philippe-Egalité* (Paris, Payot,
1926) (cited hereafter as Britsch,
Jeunesse de Philippe). The mother
of "Louis-le-Gros" was a princess
of Baden.
2. Laurentie, *Histoire des ducs
d'Orléans* (Paris, 1832), III, 359.
3. *Considérations sur l'esprit et les
moeurs,* no author's name
(London, 1787), p. 106. In it,
Sénac de Meilhan collected the
notes he had been jotting down
in his spare time for many years.
4. Talleyrand, *Mémoires,* quoted by
Britsch, *Jeunesse de Philippe,* p. 40.
5. Details of this long sequence of
ceremonies have been preserved
in the Archives nationales
(K 142, 18) in twenty-nine
numbered notebooks: *Les
principales époques relatives à Mgr le
duc de Chartres, 1747–1777.*
6. Britsch, *Jeunesse de Philippe,* p. 48.

The first comment is by Talleyrand, the second by the Duchesse de Chartres (later d'Orléans), his wife.

7. *L'Espion Anglais, ou Correspondance secrète entre Mylord All'Eye et Mylord All'Ear,* III, 214.

8. *Paris sous Louis XV:Rapports des inspecteurs de Police au roi, publiés par* Camille Piton (Paris, Mercure de France, 1910), third series, p. 180. The original is in the Bibliothèque nationale, Manuscrits français, II, 360.

9. *Ibid.,* p. 187.

10. Britsch, *Jeunesse de Philippe,* p. 79.

11. V. Thomson, *Le Corsaire chez l'Impératrice,* p. 44. See also, in the *"Que sais-je?"* series (Paris, PUF), Paul Naudon, *La Franc-Maçonnerie,* p. 100.

5

1. Lacour-Gayet, *Marine française sous Louis XVI,* pp. 126 and 127.

2. Letter from d'Orvilliers to Sartines, January 2, 1778. *Ibid.,* p. 124.

3. *Ibid.,* p. 126.

4. *Ibid.,* p. 128.

5. *Ibid.,* p. 43.

6. Bachaumont, *Correspondance secrète,* I, 171.

7. According to the Chevalier de Charitte, flag captain of the *Duc-de-Bourgogne.* Lacour-Gayet, *Marine française sous Louis XVI,* p. 129.

8. No one has dissected the mechanisms of naval combat in those days more brilliantly than Jean de La Varende. See in particular *Suffren et ses ennemis*

(Editions de Paris, 1948), pp. 106–11 (cited hereafter as La Varende, *Suffren*).

9. There is a very complete file on the Battle of Ouessant in the Archives de la Marine, B/I, 136. See in particular folio 125, a most intriguing reproduction, on maps, of the four successive main positions of the fleets during the battle; folio 129 contains d'Orvilliers's letters to Sartines.

10. According to a letter attributed to Sartines and published in the *Courrier de l'Europe* and in *Nouvelles Extraordinaires* for August 1778.

11. According to the Chevalier and future Duc des Cars (then written d'Escars), formerly in the naval guards, gentleman of honor to the Comte d'Artois: he was one of the specialists in naval affairs whom Louis XVI trusted, and sent to Brest in September to investigate the alleged "cowardice" of the Duc de Chartres. See Duc des Cars, *Mémoires,* I, 181–2.

6

1. Duc des Cars, *Mémoires,* I, 179.

2. Britsch, *Jeunesse de Philippe,* p. 288.

*3. Lescure, *Correspondance secrète inédite sur Louis XVI, Marie-Antoinette, la Cour et la Ville, de 1777 à 1792* (Paris, Plon, 1866), I, 191 (cited hereafter as *Correspondance secrète*).

*4. Mercy-Argenteau, *Correspondance secrète entre Marie-Thérèse et le comte de Mercy-Argenteau, publié par* d'Arneth and Geffroy (Paris,

Firmin-Didot, 1875), III, 236
(cited hereafter as
Mercy-Argenteau,
Correspondance).

*5. François Fejtö, *Un Habsbourg
révolutionnaire, Joseph II* (Paris,
Plon, 1953), pp. 169–74 (cited
hereafter as Fejtö, *Joseph II*).

6. *Ibid.*, p. 175.

7. Mercy-Argenteau, *Correspondance,*
III, 231.

8. Fejtö, *Joseph II,* p. 178.

9. *Ibid.*, p. 179.

10. Mercy-Argenteau, *Correspondance,*
III, 233.

11. *Ibid.*, III, 230.

12. *Ibid.*, III, 227.

13. *Ibid.*, III, 227.

7

1. *Correspondance secrète*, I, 199.

2. *Ibid.*, I, 202.

*3. *Correspondance littéraire*, Grimm,
Meister, Diderot, etc. (Paris,
Garnier, 1879), XII, 136.

4. Britsch, *Jeunesse de Philippe,*
p. 283.

5. Bibliothèque nationale (ms. Z
492), Penthièvre Archives:
*Compliments et chansons composés à
l'occasion d'Ouessant.*

6. *Correspondance littéraire*, XII, 136.

7. *Correspondance secrète*, I, 199.

8. *Correspondance littéraire*, XII, 137.

9. Britsch, *Jeunesse de Philippe,*
p. 291.

10. According to d'Orvilliers. *Ibid.,*
p. 285.

11. *Correspondance secrète*, I, 200.

12. Duc des Cars, *Mémoires*, I, 179.

13. Britsch, *Jeunesse de Philippe,*
p. 292.

14. Archives nationales, K 154. Louis
XVI's consent to the creation of

the new rank is written in the
margin of the letter, in the king's
hand.

15. *Correspondance secrète*, I, 227
(September 29, 1778).

8

*1. A. Vallentin, *Mirabeau avant la
Révolution* (Paris, Grasset, 1946),
p. 183.

*2. Gilbert Lély, *Vie du marquis de
Sade* (Paris, Jean-Jacques Pauvert,
1965), p. 270.

3. A. Vallentin, *Mirabeau avant la
Révolution,* p. 194.

*4. Dauphin-Meunier, *La Comtesse de
Mirabeau* (Paris, Perrin, 1908),
p. 203.

5. *Ibid.*, p. 215.

6. Mirabeau, *Des Lettres de cachet et
des prisons d'Etat* (original edition
[falsely] dated Hamburg, 1782).
I am most grateful to our friend
Lucien De Meyer, the dynamic
Brussels publisher, for obtaining
this extremely rare edition for us
while [my wife] Anne and I
were working on *Mirabeau,
l'homme à la vie brûlée.* The
description of the prison of
Vincennes is on page 43.

7. *Ibid.*, p. 47.

8. Dauphin-Meunier, *La Comtesse de
Mirabeau,* p. 216.

9. *Ibid.*, p. 217.

10. *Dictionnaire des lettres*
(Laffont-Bompiani, 1961),
p. 196, entry for *"Cour d'amour."*

11. Mirabeau, *Des Lettres de cachet,*
pp. 13, 17, 20.

*12. Letter to Sophie, undated but
written in August 1778. *Lettres
originales du marquis de Mirabeau
écrites du Donjon de Vincennes*

pendant les années 1777, 1778, 1779 et 1780, contenant tous les détails sur sa vie privée, ses malheurs, et ses amours avec Sophie Ruffei [sic], marquise de Monnier, receuillies par P. Manuel, citoyen français (Paris, chez Garnery, 1792), II, 297 (cited hereafter as *Lettres de Mirabeau*).

13. *Des Lettres de cachet,* p. 52.
14. Letter to Sophie cited in note 12.
15. A. Vallentin, *Mirabeau avant la Révolution,* p. 194.
16. *Ibid.,* p. 190.
17. Letter to Sophie cited in note 12.
18. A. Vallentin, *Mirabeau avant la Révolution,* p. 191.
19. *Ibid.,* pp. 191–3.
20. *Des Lettres de cachet,* p. 99.
21. *Ibid.,* p. 100.
22. Letter from Emilie to Caroline du Saillant, September 6, 1776. Dauphin-Meunier, *La Comtesse de Mirabeau,* p. 214.
23. Letter to the Marquis de Mirabeau, October 23, 1776. *Ibid.,* p. 229.
24. *Ibid.,* p. 230 (same letter).
25. Letter to his brother the bailli. A. Vallentin, *Mirabeau avant la Révolution,* p. 199.
26. *Lettres de Mirabeau,* II, 347.

9

1. *Correspondance littéraire,* XII, 177.
*2. Bernard Faÿ, *Louis XVI, ou la fin d'un monde* (Paris, Amiot-Dumont, 1955), p. 179 (cited hereafter as B. Faÿ, *Louis XVI*).
3. *Correspondance secrète,* I, 168.
4. *Ibid.,* I, 170.
5. *Ibid.,* I, 171.
6. *Ibid.,* I, 256.

7. *Ibid.,* I, 179.
8. *Ibid.,* I, 233.
*9. This letter from the Comte de Provence to Gustavus III was found by A. Geffroy in the archives of the Court of Sweden (University of Uppsala Papers, Vol. XVI, no. 49) and published by him. See *A. Geffroy, *Gustave III et la cour de France* (Paris, Didier, 1867), I, 294, and II, 385 (cited hereafter as A. Geffroy, *Gustave III*).
10. See, in the Louvre, his portrait by Van Loo, *Le comte de Provence à la veille de son mariage.*
*11. *Mémoires* of the Prince de Montbarey (Paris, 1826), II, 29.
12. Comte d'Hezecques, *Souvenir d'un page,* p. 56.
*13. Dr. Galippe, *L'Hérédité des stigmates de dégénérescence dans les familles souveraines* (Paris, Masson, 1905), p. 268.
14. According to Théodore de Lameth, quoted by Gérard Walter, *Le Comte de Provence* (Paris, Albin Michel, 1950), p. 19.
15. *Ibid.,* p. 34. The first comment is by the Comte de Viry, ambassador of the King of Sardinia to France; the second by Mercy-Argenteau in a letter to Maria Theresa.
16. Letter of April 29, 1777. A. Geffroy, *Gustave III,* I, 294.
17. From a letter from Marie Antoinette to her mother. G. Walter, *Le Comte de Provence,* p. 47.
18. Jean-François Primo, *La Vie privée de Louis XVIII,* p. 73. See also Vicomte de Reiset, *Anne de*

Caumont La Force, comtesse de Balbi.

19. On the princes' households, see Guyot and Merlin, *Traité des droits, fonctions, franchises, exemptions, prérogatives et privilèges annexes en France à chaque dignité, à chaque office et à chaque état* (Paris, 1786 and 1788).

I O

1. *Correspondance secrète,* I, 243. The other quotations on the last days of Marie Antoinette's pregnancy for which no reference numbers are given are from the same source, pp. 245–51.
2. *Ibid.,* I, 246.
3. *Mémoires du comte Alexandre de Tilly, pour servir à l'histoire des moeurs de la fin du XVIIIe siècle* (Paris, Mercure de France, "Le temps retrouvé," 1965), p. 233. Beginning on that page, Tilly tries to push the alleged affair between Marie Antoinette and Coigny; this is the text used as evidence by historians seeking to claim that Coigny was her lover before Fersen. But Tilly was only fourteen in 1778, the year he first came to Versailles. However, his account does give an accurate idea of the explicitness of the rumors then circulating about the queen and Coigny, and also of what people thought of the duke.
4. Letter to a friend from Lindblöm, future Archbishop of Sweden, from Versailles, December 24, 1778. The original, in Swedish, is in the archives of the bishopric of Lïnkoeping.

5. Extracts from letters from Fersen to his father, in Alma Söderjhelm, *Fersen et Marie-Antoinette* (Paris, Kra, 1930), pp. 57–8.
6. *Ibid.,* p. 61.
7. Report by the Comte de Viry, ambassador of the King of Sardinia to France, on November 4, 1776. Quoted by Sabine Flaissier, *Marie-Antoinette en accusation* (Paris, Julliard, 1967), p. 144.
8. Attributed to him by Soulavie, in his *Histoire du règne de Louis XVI,* quoted in Flaissier, *Marie-Antoinette en accusation,* p. 144.
9. *Correspondance secrète,* I, 235.
*10. *Encyclopédie* (Paris, Cercle du Livre Précieux, 6 vols., 1967 [reprint of 1788 edition]), I, 81, article *"Accouchement."*
11. *Ibid.,* I, 82.
*12. *Mémoires inédits* [alleged] *de Mlle de Mirecourt* (Paris, Albin Michel, 1966), p. 105.
13. *Ibid.,* p. 106.
*14. A. Cheruel, *Dictionnaire historique des institutions, moeurs et coutumes de la France* (Paris, Hachette, 1855), II, 677, entry for *"Loi salique."*
*15. M. Marion, *Dictionnaire des institutions de la France au XVIIe et XVIIIe siècles* (Paris, Picard, 1969), p. 340, entry for *"Loi salique";* commentary taken from Le Bret's treatise of 1593, *La Souveraineté du Roi.* Cited hereafter as M. Marion, *Dictionnaire des institutions.*
16. B. Faÿ, *Louis XVI,* p. 180.
17. Mercy-Argenteau, *Correspondance,* III, 279.

18. Letter of June 25, 1779.
University of Uppsala Papers,
Vol. XVI, no. 50.

I I

1. J. B. Marcaggi, *La Genèse de
Napoléon, sa formation intellectuelle
et morale jusqu'au siège de Toulon*
(Paris, Perrin, 1902), I, 63.
2. *Ibid.,* p. 37. Other details in this
paragraph are from the same
source, pp. 20 and 46.
3. *Mémorial de Sainte-Hélène* (Paris,
Edition des Classiques Garnier,
1961), I, 682.
4. From Mirabeau's speech on the
status of Corsica to the
Constituent Assembly, November
30, 1789.
5. *Mémoires historiques sur la Corse
par un officier du régiment de
Picardie* (*Bulletin* of the Société
des Sciences historiques de la
Corse, 1889).
6. It has been said that Laetizia de
Buonaparte, *née* Ramolino,
granted her "favors" to Marbeuf.
At a stretch this is possible, for
they were "on social terms," and
she was only twenty-eight in
1778. But it is unlikely in view
of the prevailing modesty and
chastity of Corsican morality. In
any event, the myth that Marbeuf
was the father of Napoleon
doesn't hold water: In 1769,
when Laetizia was pregnant with
her second son, she was in
Paoli's camp, whose shaky
fortunes she and her husband
were following. Marbeuf had just
landed on the island with an
expeditionary corps. For Laetizia
to have had a child by him she

would have had to spend a night
in the French camp, like Judith
with Holofernes.
7. Ajaccio Archives, series A.A.
8. To reconstruct this maiden
voyage I have consulted my own
study of Napoleon's youth, *Le
Citoyen Bonaparte* (Paris, Editions
Robert Laffont, *"Plein Vent,"*
1969), pp. 11–38.

I 2

*1. *Mémoires du duc de Lauzun* (Paris,
Fayard, n.d.), p. 44 (cited
hereafter as Duc de Lauzun,
Mémoires). The next quotation is
ibid., p. 40.
2. Sartines's and Vergennes's
instructions to Lauzun are in the
Archives de la Marine, B/4 149.
Lauzun also kept an unpublished
diary from the time his squadron
came within sight of the African
coast until his return, and I have
followed this in my account of
events: Archives nationales, T
1527.
3. Text by Dumontet, quoted by J.
Saintoyant, *La Colonisation
française sous l'Ancien Régime*
(Paris, La Renaissance du Livre,
1929), II, 379.
4. Dumont d'Urville, *Voyage
pittoresque autour du monde* (Paris,
Tenré, 1834), I, 32.
5. Duc de Lauzun, *Mémoires,*
p. 138.
6. Dumont d'Urville, *Voyage
pittoresque,* I, 33.
7. *Ibid.,* I, 31.
8. Lauzun's record of the
expedition, Archives nationales,
T 1527.
9. *Ibid.*

10. *Ibid.*
11. Gaston Maugras and Croze-Lemercier, *Delphine de Sabran, marquise de Custine* (Paris, Plon, 1912), p. 27. *Ibid.* for the extract from the letter in the next paragraph.
*12. Gaston Maugras, *Le Duc de Lauzun et la cour de Marie-Antoinette* (Paris, Plon, 1913), p. 180.

13

*1. Charlemagne Tower, *The Marquis de La Fayette in the American Revolution* (Philadelphia, J. B. Lippincott Co., 1901), II, 41 (cited hereafter as Tower, *L.F. in America*).
2. *Correspondance secrète,* VII, 195.
*3. Federal Archives, Washington, *Papers of the Old Congress,* and La Fayette, *Correspondance,* p. 240. [The source of writings by La Fayette which were not originally in English or which do not appear in Tower in English is *Mémoires, Correspondance et Manuscrits du Général La Fayette, publiés par sa famille* (Paris, Fournier, 1838) (cited hereafter as La Fayette, *Correspondance* or *Mémoires*).]
4. *Papers of the Old Congress,* October 21, 1778.
5. According to La Fayette himself, in his correspondence. Tower, *L.F. in America,* I, 255.
6. *Ibid.,* I, 255.
7. According to Baron von Steuben, in Tower, *L.F. in America,* I, 323.
8. Letter to his father-in-law, the Duc d'Ayen. La Fayette, *Correspondance,* in Tower, *L.F. in America,* I, 256.

9. From Mauroy to the Comte de Broglie, November 1777. Quoted by Wladimir d'Ormesson, *La Première mission officielle de la France aux Etats-Unis* (that of Conrad Alexandre Gérard) (Paris, Champion, 1924), p. 87.
10. Tower, *L.F. in America,* I, 261–2.
*11. A. Maurois, *Histoire des Etats-Unis* (Paris, Albin Michel, 1943), p. 161.
12. These sham instructions, lengthy and detailed, are in the U.S. State Department Archives, *Papers of the Old Congress.* See Tower, *L.F. in America,* I, 274.
13. See his very long letter to the President of Congress, in Tower, *L.F. in America,* I, 277–80. In it La Fayette shows his loyalty to Washington and asks Congress to continue sending his orders via the general, even while he is in Canada, but apart from that he adopts the tone of a commander-in-chief and is slightly condescending to Congress.
14. Letter of February 9, 1778. La Fayette, *Correspondance,* in Tower, *L.F. in America,* I, 281.
15. To Washington and to Gates, February 18. *Ibid.,* I, 284 and 286.
16. Washington's reply, on March 10. *Ibid.,* I, 289.
17. Letter of March 6, 1778, from Eugenio de Galves, governor of Louisiana for the King of Spain, to Florida-Blanca. Doniol, *Histoire de la Participation de la France à la guerre d'indépendance des Etats-Unis,* III, 261.
18. According to Lieutenant Wickham, an eyewitness, in

Simcoe's Military Journal, I, 61 [and Tower, *L.F. in America,* I, 336].

19. Letter to his wife, November 6, 1777. Tower, *L.F. in America,* I, 345.

20. Letter to his wife, January 6, 1778. *Ibid.,* I, 266–7 (except the last two sentences, from his *Correspondance*).

21. Colonel Ogden's reply to Colonel Harrison, sent by Washington to inquire into the reasons for Lee's disobedience. *Ibid.,* I, 382.

22. La Fayette to the Comte d'Estaing, July 13, 1778. Archives de la Marine, B/4 144.

23. J. Simms, *Correspondence of John Laurens* (New York), p. 220 [and Tower, *L.F. in America,* I, 458].

24. Letter to the Duc d'Ayen, September 11, 1778. Tower, *L.F. in America,* I, 462. See also *Journal de M. de Cambis à bord du Languedoc,* quoted in Tower, I, 462.

25. Richard Amory, *Life of Sullivan* (Boston, 1862), p. 77.

26. La Fayette to Washington, August 25, 1778. La Fayette, *Mémoires,* I, 190.

27. Sullivan to Washington, September 8, 1778. Tower, *L.F. in America,* I, 490.

28. Letter to his wife, September 13, 1778, from Bristol (USA). *Ibid.,* II, 38.

*29. Letter to his wife, October 1, 1778. Charavay, *Le Général La Fayette* (Paris, Société de l'Histoire de la Révolution française, 1899), p. 24.

30. *Ibid.,* p. 41.

31. *Ibid.,* p. 38.

14

*1. Remark made to one of his companions, the Vicomte de Pontgibaud, in A. Maurois, *Adrienne, ou la vie de madame de La Fayette* (Paris, Hachette, 1960), p. 94 (cited hereafter as A. Maurois, *Madame de La Fayette*).

2. La Fayette, *Mémoires de ma main* (dictated by L.F. in 1828), I, 64.

3. *Ibid.,* I, 66.

4. A. Maurois, *Madame de La Fayette,* p. 98.

5. *Ibid.,* p. 99.

6. La Fayette, *Mémoires de ma main,* I, 65.

7. Bibliothèque nationale, manuscripts department, N.A.F., 22738, f. 6/7.

8. M. Rochon de Chabannes, *Théâtre* (Paris, Duchesne, 1786), I, 311.

9. Sparks, ed., *Works of Washington* (in French translation by Guizot) (Paris, 1832), III, 413 [and Tower, *L.F. in America,* II, 20–1].

10. La Fayette, *Mémoires de ma main,* I, 65.

11. Mercy-Argenteau, *Correspondance,* III, 315.

12. From Marie Antoinette to Maria Theresa, April 18, 1779. *Ibid.,* III, 309.

*13. Pierre de Nolhac, *Le Trianon de Marie-Antoinette* (Paris, Calmann-Lévy, 1924), p. 167.

14. Mercy-Argenteau, *Correspondance,* III, 309.

15. A. Söderjhelm, *Fersen et Marie-Antoinette,* p. 69.

15

1. Paul d'Estrée, *Le Père Duchesne (Hébert et la Commune de Paris)* (Paris, L'Edition moderne, n.d.), p. 14.

2. Paul Del Perugia, *La Tentative d'invasion de l'Angleterre de 1779* (Paris, Alcan-PUF, 1939), p. 117.

3. Arthur Young, *Travels in France,* (Cambridge, Cambridge University Press, 1950), p. 123.

4. Louis Jacob, *Hébert, le Père Duchesne, chef des sans-culottes* (Paris, Gallimard, 1960), p. 21 (cited hereafter as Jacob, *Hébert*). Subsequent particulars of Hébert's family are taken from this book.

*5. Reichard, *Guide des voyageurs en Europe,* Vol. II, *France* (Weimar, 1813), p. 130 (cited hereafter as Reichard, *Guide de la France*).

6. In a letter to his sister. Jacob, *Hébert,* p. 21.

7. *Ibid.,* p. 23.

8. *Colère du Père Duchesne sur le Départ de Monsieur Necker,* Monday, September 6, 1790. F. Braesch, *Le Père Duchesne d'Hébert,* complete critical edition (Paris, Librairie Sirey, 1938), p. 213 (cited hereafter as Braesch, *Le Père Duchesne*).

9. Jacob, *Hébert,* p. 25.

10. M. Marion, *Dictionnaire des institutions,* p. 383.

11. *Le Pape au Foutre, ou la Grande colère du Père Duchesne,* Sunday, March 27, 1791. Braesch, *Le Père Duchesne,* p. 639.

12. *Grande joie du Père Duchesne sur le décrit qui oblige l'Archevêque de Paris à rentrer en son diocèse et tous les calotins à prêter le serment civique,* Monday, November 29, 1790. *Ibid.,* p. 380.

13. *Dénonciation du Père Duchesne contre les marchands de vin, cabaretiers, limonadiers, bouchers,* etc., Thursday, October 14, 1790. *Ibid.,* p. 267.

14. *Souvenirs de la fin du XVIIIe siècle ou Mémoires de R.D.G.* (Paris, Sillandre, 1835), II, 247.

15. Jacob, *Hébert,* p. 24.

16. *L'Indignation du Père Duchesne contre l'indissolubricité* [sic] *du mariage et sa motion pour le divorce,* Monday, December 6, 1790. Braesch, *Le Père Duchesne,* pp. 391 and 392.

17. Jacob, *Hébert,* p. 26.

18. Del Perugia, *La Tentative d'invasion de l'Angleterre en 1779,* p. 117 (taken from the *Gazette des Deux-Ponts,* July 8, 1779).

19. Arthur Young, *Travels in France,* p. 124.

20. *Grande joie du Père Duchesne à l'occasion des scellés mis au Palais et du déménagement des juges du Parlement,* Sunday, October 17, 1790. Braesch, *Le Père Duchesne,* p. 270.

16

*1. *Lettres de Madame Roland, publiées par* Claude Perroud (Paris, Imprimerie nationale, 1913), new series, I, 544, to Sophie and Henriette Cannet, December 24–28, 1776. I must renew my thanks to Mr. J. Guillermet here for the loan of this irreplaceable monument on the psychological development of one of the most attractive characters of the

Revolution. For convenience this will hereafter be shortened to *Lettres de Mme Roland.*

2. *Ibid.,* I, 371, to Sophie, February 5, 1776.

3. *Ibid.,* I, 399, to Sophie, April 15, 1776.

4. *Ibid.,* I, 412–15, to Sophie, May 17, 1776.

5. *Ibid.,* I, 483, to both sisters, September 18, 1776.

6. *Ibid.,* II, 53, to Sophie, March 29, 1777.

7. Bibliothèque nationale, *Papiers Roland,* ms. 6244, folios 290–6. In 1864 the first editor of the complete text of Mme Roland's *Mémoires* wrote, on the subject of these pages: "This is a profession of moral and religious faith written in terms worthy of a thinker and author of the highest order."

8. *Lettres de Mme Roland,* II, 57, to Sophie, April 12, 1777.

9. *Extrait de mon âme,* final folio (see Note 7).

10. *Lettres de Mme Roland,* I, 542, to both sisters, Christmas Day 1776.

11. *Ibid.,* I, 406, to Sophie, May 2, 1776.

12. *Ibid.,* I, 468, to Sophie, September 1, 1776.

13. *Ibid.,* I, 406, to Sophie.

14. *Ibid.,* I, 424, to Sophie.

15. *Ibid.,* I, 433, to Sophie.

16. *Ibid.,* I, 428.

17. *Ibid.,* I, 452, to Sophie.

*18. Georges Huisman, *La Vie privée de Madame Roland* (Paris, Hachette, 1955), p. 99.

19. *Mémoires de Madame Roland* (Paris, Plon, 1905), II, 237.

20. *Lettres de Mme Roland,* I, 505, to Henriette, October 16, 1776.

21. M. Marion, *Dictionnaire des institutions,* p. 524.

22. *Lettres de Mme Roland,* I, 511, to Sophie, October 27, 1776.

23. *Ibid.,* I, 492, to Sophie, October 2, 1776.

24. *Ibid.,* I, 513, to Sophie, November 10, 1776. The previous quotation is from the same letter.

25. *Ibid.,* II, 97, to both sisters, July 19, 1777.

26. *Ibid.,* II, 87, to both sisters, June 21, 1777.

27. *Lettres d'amour de Roland et Marie Phlipon, publiées par* Claude Perroud (Paris, Picard, 1909 [loaned by Monsieur Guillermet]), p. 107, from Manon to Roland, May 7, 1779. Cited hereafter as *Lettres d'amour des Roland.*

28. *Lettres de Mme Roland,* II, 142, to Sophie, October 4, 1777.

29. *Ibid.,* II, 244, to Henriette, March 31, 1778.

30. *Ibid.,* II, 106, to Sophie, August 7, 1777.

31. *Ibid.,* I, 507, to Sophie, October 20, 1776. This quotation refers to another match proposed the year before, a rich young man "from way across the Marais" [district of Paris].

32. *Ibid.,* II, 73, to both sisters, May 23, 1777.

33. *Ibid.,* II, 54, to Sophie, March 29, 1777.

34. *Ibid.,* II, 116, to both sisters, August 19, 1777.

35. *Ibid.,* II, 110, to both sisters, August 9, 1777.

36. *Ibid.,* II, 105, to Sophie, July 28, 1777.

37. *Ibid.,* II, 114, to both sisters,

August 19, 1777. The previous quotation is from the same letter.

17

1. Saffais Municipal Archives, in the Meurthe-et-Moselle Archives, G.G.2.
2. Pierre Marot, *Recherches sur la vie de François de Neufchâteau* (1966), p. 17 (cited hereafter as Marot, *Recherches sur F. de N.*).
3. The rumor was unfounded and Pierre Marot demolishes it. *Ibid.*, p. 20.
4. *Pièces fugitives de M. François, de Neufchâteau en Lorraine, âgé de quatorze ans* (Monnoyer, Neufchâteau, 1765), p. 8.
5. *Almanach des Muses* for 1767, p. 95.
6. Roger Tisserand, *L'Académie de Dijon de 1740 à 1793* (Vesoul, 1936), p. 139.
7. *Almanach des Muses* for 1767, p. 104.
8. *Mercure de France,* December 1767, p. 195.
9. Marot, *Recherches sur F. de N.,* p. 41.
10. According to Cubières, in an *Essai sur François de Neufchâteau* which came out in Paris in Year VII.
11. Marot, *Recherches sur F. de N.,* p. 43.
12. Gaston Lenôtre, *Sous le bonnet rouge* (Paris, Grasset, 1936), p. 270.
13. *Lettres de Mme Roland,* II, 175, to Henriette, December 17, 1777, relating the Abbé Bexon's descriptions of the Vosges.
14. *Lettre de M. François de Neufchâteau à M. l'abbé Drouas, à l'occasion des bruits répandus contre le séminaire de Toul* (no date or place of publication, fifty-six pages).
15. E. Buisson, *"Un collaborateur de Buffon, l'abbé Bexon,"* *Bulletin de la société philomatique vosgienne* (1888–89), p. 275.
16. Marot, *Recherches sur F. de N.,* p. 57.
17. *Ibid.,* p. 59.
18. Bachaumont, *Mémoires secrets,* VIII, 148 (July 29, 1775).
19. On Contrexéville before the Revolution, see sheaf C 18 of the Vosges Archives, concerning the hot-springs resorts; in the collection of the Intendance de Lorraine. The other details in this paragraph are from the same source.
20. *Almanach des Muses* for 1777, p. 227.
21. Marot, *Recherches sur F. de N.,* p. 91.
*22. Linguet, *Annales politiques* (London, 1778), II, 7.
23. Voltaire, *Correspondance,* Vol. XVIII, or Vol. L of the *Works,* no. 10107.
24. *Correspondance secrète,* V, 171.
25. *Almanach des Muses* for 1778, p. 19.
26. *Lettres de Mme Roland,* II, 192, to Sophie, February 9, 1778.
27. Letter to his friend Poulain-Grandprey, June 29, 1778. Marot, *Recherches sur F. de N.,* p. 102.

18

1. *Lettres de Mme Roland,* II, 82, to both sisters, June 21, 1777.

2. *Ibid.*, II, 319, to Henriette, October 6, 1778.

3. *Ibid.*, I, 450, to Sophie, July 22, 1776.

4. *Ibid.*, I, 335, to Sophie, October 31, 1775.

5. G. Lenôtre, *Existences d'artistes* (Paris, Grasset, 1940), p. 188.

6. *Ibid.*, p. 189.

7. Alfred Leroy, *La Vie intime des artistes français au XVIIIe siècle* (Paris, Julliard, 1949), p. 274.

8. *Lettres de Mme Roland*, II, 133, to Sophie, September 19, 1777.

9. *Ibid.*, II, 207, to Sophie, February 24, 1778.

10. *Ibid.*, II, 96, to Sophie.

11. *Ibid.*, II, 174, to Sophie.

19

1. *Lettres d'amour des Roland*, p. 35, from Roland to Manon, September 17, 1777.

2. *Lettres de Mme Roland*, II, 144, to Sophie, October 4, 1777.

3. *Lettres d'amour des Roland*, p. 39.

4. *Mémoires de Mme Roland*, II, 228. These lines were written fifteen years later, when she was living under the shadow of death and still reeling from the shock of her passion for Buzot. This will account for their disenchanted tone. But after comparing them with the letters dating from the time of their engagement, a ring of truth remains.

5. *Lettres de Mme Roland*, II, 200, "to Sophie *alone*," she specifies, February 17, 1778.

6. *Ibid.*, II, 223, quoted by Manon in an interminable letter to Sophie written in "March 1778."

7. *Lettres d'amour des Roland*, p. 54,
from Manon to Roland, August 12, 1778.

8. *Lettres de Mme Roland*, II, 321, to Henriette, October 6, 1778.

9. *Ibid.*, II, 342, to Sophie, December 12, 1778.

10. *Lettres d'amour des Roland*, pp. 63 and 64, from Manon to Roland, January 3, 1779.

11. *Ibid.*, p. 66.

12. *Ibid.*, p. 69.

13. *Ibid.*, p. 158, from Manon to Roland, June 10, 1779, alluding to what happened in April.

14. *Ibid.*, p. 82.

15. *Ibid.*, p. 87, from Manon to Roland, April 21 and 23, 1779. The following quotation is from the same source.

16. *Lettres de Mme Roland*, II, 377, to Sophie, April 28, 1779.

17. *Lettres d'amour des Roland*, pp. 93 and 95, from Manon to Roland, April 25, 1779.

18. *Ibid.*, pp. 98 and 99.

20

1. Walter Markov, "*Jacques Roux avant la Révolution,*" *Annales historiques de la Révolution française,* XXXV (1963), 458.

2. "*Jacques Roux à Marat,*" complete text of the sixteen-page pamphlet published three days before the latter's assassination and reprinted by A. Mathiez in *Annales historiques de la Révolution française,* VIII (1916), 533.

3. *Voyage d'une Hollandaise en France* (Paris, Jean-Jacques Pauvert, 1966), p. 51.

4. Markov, "*Jacques Roux avant la Révolution,*" p. 458.

5. "*Jacques Roux à Marat,*" p. 533.

6. *Ibid.*, p. 534.
7. Abbé Mazière, *"L'Affaire Mioulle et le séminaire d'Angoulême en 1779,"* *Bulletin et Mémoires de la Société archéologique et historique de la Charente*, eighth series, Vol. VII (1916).
8. Arthur Young, *Travels in France*, pp. 62–3.
9. Charente Archives, B 1141. This file also contains five pages of interrogation of Jacques Roux: his first words for posterity.
10. *"Jacques Roux à Marat,"* p. 535.
11. Pranzac Parish Records (the entries for 1751 and 1752 are in the village town hall; all other years are in the Charente Archives).
12. Markov, *"Jacques Roux avant la Révolution,"* p. 459.
13. *"Jacques Roux à Marat,"* p. 533.

21

1. La Varende, *Suffren.* I have taken the physical description from this book; the personality profile has been revised in the light of contemporary memoirs.
2. Letter from Suffren to Madame d'Alès, April 3, 1779. Quoted by Jean-Jacques Antier, *L'Amiral de Grasse* (Paris, Plon, 1965), p. 129. I take this opportunity to thank Yvette and Jean-Jacques Antier for their hospitality at Cannes and Saint-Cézaire, sites haunted by the naval or political personalities that flowered there —de Grasse, Suffren, Isnard, and, of course, the Mirabeaus. J.-J. Antier, that authority on naval matters, has helped me greatly by the loan of works

otherwise impossible to obtain and by giving me invaluable information on questions of navigation.
3. Las Cases, quoted by La Varende, *Suffren*, p. 20.
4. La Varende, *Suffren*, p. 75.
5. *Ibid.*, p. 80.
6. From a "candid shot" by an English officer. *Ibid.*, p. 200.
7. Lacour-Gayet, *Marine française sous Louis XVI*, p. 187.
8. Letter from d'Estaing to Sartines, January 3, 1779. *Ibid.*, p. 189.
9. La Varende, *Suffren*, pp. 38 and 40.

22

1. This letter from Aristide to his uncle, who got him into the navy, was written in November 1778 on board the *Gloire*, where he took part in the Battle of Ouessant. Admiral Bergasse du Petit-Thouars, *Aristide Aubert du Petit-Thouars, héros d'Aboukir* (Paris, Plon, 1937), p. 17.
2. *Ibid.*, p. 6.
3. From a brief autobiography by Aristide du Petit-Thouars. *Ibid.*, p. 8.
4. *Ibid.*, p. 12. Unfortunately, the manuscript of *Barbogaste-le-Hérissé* was lost during the Revolution.
5. *Ibid.*, p. 15.
6. "It was at this moment [when Chartres was trying to set the example for attack] that M. d'Orvilliers, restrained by the timid instructions he had received and loyal to his system of circumspection . . . , decided, at nightfall, to give the woeful signal [for retreat]." From a

Précis de la guerre de 1778 à 1783 composed by the Chevalier de Lostange on the basis of du Petit-Thouars's papers and published by Dentu for the latter's sisters in 1821. The sole remaining copy is in the Bibliothèque Nationale.

7. A letter from Aristide telling Commander de Colomieu about the battle of Grenada six years later. Admiral B. du Petit-Thouars, *Aristide Aubert du Petit-Thouars, héros d'Aboukir*, p. 25. Unnumbered quotations on the same subject are from the same source.

8. *Ibid.*, p. 24.

9. Lacour-Gayet, *Marine française sous Louis XVI*, p. 199.

10. *Ibid.*, p. 200.

11. J.-J. Antier, *L'Amiral de Grasse*, p. 131.

12. *Annales maritimes et coloniales* (Paris, 1822), II, 204.

13. Bibliothèque nationale, Cabinet des Estampes, *Histoire de France*, year 1779: plan of the naval combat of Grenada.

14. Letter from Suffren, July 10, 1779. Lacour-Gayet, *Marine française sous Louis XVI*, p. 206.

*15. Roger Lafon, *Beaumarchais, le brillant armateur* (Paris, Société d'éditions géographiques, maritimes et coloniales, 1928), p. 135.

16. Admiral B. du Petit-Thouars, *Aristide Aubert du Petit-Thouars, héros d'Aboukir*, p. 26.

17. Letter from Suffren cited in note 14.

18. Lacour-Gayet, *Marine française sous Louis XVI*, p. 207.

19. Archives de la Marine, B/4, 164.

20. J.-J. Antier, *L'Amiral de Grasse*, p. 132.

23

1. Bachaumont, *Mémoires secrets,* July 19, 1779.

2. Chevalier de Metternich, *Lettres historiques, politiques et critiques* (London, 1792), III, 201. This socialite "observer" was a cousin of the future chancellor of Austria.

3. *Correspondance secrète*, I, 272 (July 5, 1779).

4. Lacour-Gayet, *Marine française sous Louis XVI*, p. 265.

5. *Lettres de M. de Kageneck au baron Alströmer, sur la période du règne de Louis XVI de 1779 à 1784, publiées par* L. Léouzun le Duc (Paris, Charpentier, 1884), p. 1.

6. From Montmorin to Vergennes, July 27, 1779. Archives des Affaires étrangères [Foreign Affairs], Spain, folio 124.

7. *Ibid.*, Spain, Vol. 590, folio 141.

8. *Correspondance secrète*, I, 272 (July 5, 1779).

9. *Lettres de Kageneck*, pp. 10 and 14 (August 1779).

10. *Ibid.*, p. 12.

11. Archives des Affaires étrangères [Foreign Affairs], Spain, Vol. 595, folio 387.

*12. Charles de Chambrun, *Vergennes* (Paris, Plon, 1944), p. 168.

13. From an undated letter from Vergennes to his wife. *Ibid.*, p. 244.

14. *Ibid.*, p. 303. Also for the following quotation.

15. Archives des Affaires étrangères [Foreign Affairs], Spain, Vol. 595, folio 387.

16. Letter from Vergennes to his wife. Chambrun, *Vergennes,* p. 233.
17. Letter from Vergennes to the Comte de Guines, then French ambassador to London, June 23, 1775. Archives des Affaires étrangères [Foreign Affairs], England, Vol. 510, folio 297. This is more than an incidental note in a text: Vergennes has just taken up his post and is making initial contact with his ambassadors. It is a manifesto.
18. *Correspondance secrète,* I, 358 (January 13, 1779).
19. Archives des Affaires étrangères [Foreign Affairs], Spain, Vol. 589, folio 302.
20. *Ibid.,* Vol. 589, folio 60.
21. *Ibid.,* Vol. 591, folio 316.
22. *Ibid.,* Vol. 590, folio 355: Florida-Blanca's position as summed up by Montmorin, September 7, 1778.
23. *Ibid.,* Vol. 590, folio 226.
24. *Ibid.,* Vol. 590, folio 418.
25. For details of their deployment, see Jacques de Broglie, *Le Vainqueur de Bergen et le secret du Roi* (Paris, Editions Louvois, n.d.), p. 425.
26. *Gazette des Deux-Ponts,* June 27, 1779.
27. John Almon, *Parliamentary Register* (London, July 1779), XIII, 419. Burke made the statement on June 16 [*Trans.*].
28. Archives de la Guerre [War], A/I, Box 3732/10. [This quotation has been retranslated back from the French.]
29. Letter from Beaumarchais to Vergennes, August 31, 1779. Archives des Affaires étrangères [Foreign Affairs], England, Vol. 538, folio 90.
30. *Revue contemporaine* (1865), p. 388.
31. Remark made privately by Vergennes and reported by M. Hennin, one of his secretaries. Paul Del Perugia, *La Tentative d'invasion de l'Angleterre en 1779,* p. 34.
32. Archives des Affaires étrangères [Foreign Affairs], Spain, Vol. 591, folio 422.
33. Archives nationales, A.F. III, 186 *b* (memorandum of an espionage report of February 15, 1779).
34. From Montmorin to Vergennes, June 11, 1779. Archives des Affaires étrangères [Foreign Affairs], Spain, Vol. 594, folio 240.
35. From Vergennes to Montmorin, May 29, 1778. *Ibid.,* Vol. 594, folio 178.
36. Bachaumont, *Mémoires secrets,* May 13, 1779.
37. Metternich, *Lettres historiques,* II, 262.
38. *Correspondance secrète,* I, 179 (October 24, 1779).

24

1. From a *Mémoire* by d'Eon, dated February 2, 1779, against Beaumarchais. Bibliothèque municipale de Tonnerre, R. 30.
2. *Lettre de la chevalière d'Eon à M. le comte de Maurepas,* from Versailles, February 8, 1779. *Correspondance littéraire,* XII (February 1779), 213.
3. Archives des Affaires étrangères [Foreign Affairs], England, Vol. 516.

*4. Pierre Pinsseau, *L'Etrange Destinée du chevalier d'Eon* (Paris, Clavreuil, 1945), p. 209 (cited hereafter as Pinsseau, *D'Eon*).

5. Letter from d'Eon to Vergennes, October 2, 1777. Archives des Affaires étrangères [Foreign Affairs], England, Vol. 517.

6. Pinsseau, *D'Eon*, p. 210.

7. Bibliothèque municipale de Tonnerre, R. 34.

8. Pinsseau, *D'Eon*, p. 212.

9. *L'Espion anglais, ou Correspondance secrète entre Mylord All'Eye et Mylord All'Ear*, January 4, 1778.

10. Bibliothèque municipale de Tonnerre, R. 28.

11. Published on February 10, 1778. *Ibid.*, R. 32.

12. Bibliothèque municipale de Tonnerre, L. 58, September 12, 1778. *Ibid.* for the following quotation.

13. Bibliothèque municipale de Tonnerre, R. 34.

14. *Correspondance littéraire*, XII (February 1779), 213.

15. F. Fromageot, *"La Chevalière d'Eon à Versailles,"* Carnet historique et littéraire* (1900), p. 67.

16. Bachaumont, *Mémoires secrets* XIV, 12.

17. *Pétition et mémoires de la chevalière d'Eon à l'Assemblée Nationale de France* (London, 1792). Archives des Affaires étrangères [Foreign Affairs], England, Supplement, No. 17.

25

1. From Fersen's *Journal*, in A. Söderjhelm, *Fersen et

Marie-Antoinette, p. 59. Subsequent statements by Fersen are from the same source.

2. Léon Mention, *L'Armée de l'Ancien Régime* (Paris, Henri May, n.d.), p. 11.

3. From a royal decree of 1743. *Ibid.*, p. 13.

4. *Ibid.*, p. 14.

5. *Ibid.*, p. 51.

6. J. de Broglie, *Le Vainqueur de Bergen et le secret du Roi*, p. 428.

7. Letters from the Duc de Broglie to Louis XVI, May 25 and 26, 1778. *Ibid.*, p. 414.

8. *Correspondance littéraire*, XII (May 1770), 248. *Ibid.* for the following quotation.

9. From Rochambeau, *Mémoires*, in J. de Broglie, *Le Vainqueur de Bergen et le secret du Roi*, p. 440.

10. *Mémoires du général Dumouriez* (Paris, Didot, 1862), p. 207 (cited hereafter as Dumouriez, *Mémoires*).

11. *Ibid.*, p. 86. Also for the following quotation.

26

*1. Chateaubriand, *Mémoires d'outre-tombe* (Paris, Edition des Classiques Garnier, 1946), I, 77 and 80.

2. Duc de Lauzun, *Mémoires*, p. 135. The following quotations are from the same source.

3. Doniol, *Histoire de la participation de la France à la guerre d'Indépendance des Etats-Unis*, IV, 231.

4. *Voyages en France de François de la Rochefoucauld, publiés par* Jean Marchand (Paris, Champion,

1933), I, 51 (cited hereafter as *Voyages en France de La Rochefoucauld*).

5. *Ibid.*, I, 54.

6. Archives des Affaires étrangères [Foreign Affairs], United States, Supplement I, no. 182 *a*.

7. Britsch, *Jeunesse de Philippe*, p. 297.

8. Dumouriez, *Mémoires*, I, 214.

9. J. Hippeau, *Le Gouvernement de la Normandie* (Paris, 1882), II, 37.

10. Paul Del Perugia, *La Tentative d'invasion de l'Angleterre en 1779*, p. 75. Subsequent unnumbered particulars of fleet movements are from the same source, especially chapters 6 and 8.

11. Lacour-Gayet, *Marine française sous Louis XVI*, p. 256.

12. *Ibid.*, p. 254.

13. From a diagram in the Archives de la Marine, G/4, 155, folio 3.

14. Archives des Affaires étrangères [Foreign Affairs], Spain, Vol. 598, folio 273.

15. Lacour-Gayet, *Marine française sous Louis XVI*, p. 260.

16. Letter from the Marquis d'Héricy, July 21, 1779. Hippeau, *Le Gouvernement de la Normandie*, II, 35.

17. Lacour-Gayet, *Marine française sous Louis XVI*, p. 50.

18. From d'Orvilliers to Sartines. *Ibid.*, p. 269.

19. Figures calculated by the author, based on Lacour-Gayet: ships' crews as altered by Sartines's new regulations, p. 49; table of the "grand combined army of d'Orvilliers," p. 639.

20. Littré, entry for *"mousse,"* quoting from *Le Siècle de Louis XIV.*

21. Lacour-Gayet, *Marine française sous Louis XVI*, p. 46.

*22. Letters from the bailli to the Marquis de Mirabeau, May 1763. Loménie, *Les Mirabeau* (Paris, Dentu, 1879), I, 257–9. These images date from the end of the Seven Years' War, but every naval war painted them afresh.

23. Anonymous *mémoire* from 1780. Archives de la Marine, B/1, 93.

24. Jean Aigrit, *Les Registres paroissiaux de la Basse-Bretagne* (Nantes, 1890), p. 31.

25. *Encyclopédie*, XIV, 802, article *"Scorbut."* Subsequent unnumbered quotations on scurvy are from the same article.

26. Lacour-Gayet, *Marine française sous Louis XVI*, p. 641.

27. Archives des Affaires étrangères [Foreign Affairs], Spain, Vol. 594, folio 463 (July 23, 1779).

28. *Ibid.*, Vol. 594, folio 462.

29. Lacour-Gayet, *Marine française sous Louis XVI*, p. 271.

30. *Gazette des Deux-Ponts*, August 26, 1779.

31. Lacour-Gayet, *Marine française sous Louis XVI*, p. 274.

32. *Ibid.*, p. 275.

33. To the Duc d'Harcourt, August 28, 1779. *Ibid.*, p. 277.

34. According to d'Estaing in his *Journal de Cadix.* Archives de la Marine, B/4, 177.

35. To Vergennes, August 20, 1779. Lacour-Gayet, *Marine française sous Louis XVI*, p. 280.

36. Chevalier de Mautort, *Mémoires, publiés par* the Baron Tillette de Clermont-Tonnerre (Paris, Plon, 1895), p. 101.

37. Bachaumont, *Mémoires secrets,* September 17, 1779.
38. Mercy-Argenteau, *Correspondance,* III, 355.
*39. François Métra, *Correspondance secrète* (London, 1784), July 29, 1779.

27

1. Paul Bastid, *Sieyès et sa pensée* (Paris, Hachette, 1970), p. 31 (cited hereafter as Bastid). The ordination took place at the Lazarists' house in the Saint-Victor district of Paris.
2. Albéric Neton, *Sieyès* (Paris, Perrin, 1901). This is an extract from the *Vues sur les moyens d'exécution* written by Sieys for the Estates General in 1789, in which he copied almost page for page the notes he had written in his youth, between 1770 and 1780 (p. 27).
3. Letter from Sieys to the Convention, 20 Brumaire Year II. Bastid, p. 345.
4. *Voyages en France de La Rochefoucauld,* I, 213.
5. Neton, *Sieyès,* p. 18.
6. Archives nationales, M. M. 494.
7. *Annales historiques de la Révolution française* (1933), note by Henri Calvet on page 538. This note ends a long uncertainty among historians, which filled no fewer than four articles in those same *Annales* and occupied the thoughts of Albert Mathiez himself. There is also a minute of the Constituent Assembly sitting of June 10, 1790, no. 331, corrected in the hand of the man

himself: "Read Sieys not Sieyès."
8. O. Teissier, *Documents inédits: la jeunesse de l'abbé Siéyès* (Marseilles, 1897 [from the *Nouvelle Revue*]), quoted by Bastid, p. 24.
9. Archives nationales, Siéyès Collection, 284 AP/I.
10. Letter to his father, June 25, 1773. Bastid, p. 30.
11. *Notice sur la vie de Sieyès, membre de la première Assemblée nationale et de la Convention; écrite à Paris en messidor, deuxième année de l'ère républicaine (vieux style, juin 1794)* (Paris, chez Maradam, Year III). This *Notice,* the work of his German friend Oelmer, contains a series of reminiscences by Sieys himself put in chronological order, and may be taken as an autobiography. The following quote is from the same source.
12. L. Bertrand, *La Bibliothèque sulpicienne,* Vol. III, quoted by Bastid, p. 30.
13. Bastid, p. 31.
14. In particular, this was the design of Abbé Emery, already the most notorious Sulpician in the Order. *Ibid.,* p. 290.
*15. Talleyrand, *Mémoires* (Paris, Jean de Bonnot, 1967), I, 20.
16. *Notice* on Sieys, p. 7.
17. According to his friend Fortoul. Bastid, p. 32.
18. Neton, *Sieyès,* p. 25.
19. All of which are to be found in the Siéyès Collection in the Archives nationales, together with the scheme for a library written in 1770 and mentioned farther on.
20. Archives nationales, Siéyès Collection, 184 AP/2.
21. Bastid, p. 293.

22. Paul Hazard, *La Pensée européenne au XVIIIe siècle, de Montesquieu à Lessing* (Paris, Boivin, 1946), I, 55.

23. *Corpus général des philosophes français: Condillac,* Georges Le Roy edition (Paris, PUF, 1947), p. xi.

24. *Ibid.,* p. xxv.

25. This essential text was used by Sainte-Beuve in his study on Sieys. See Bastid, p. 294.

26. Hazard, *La Pensée européenne au XVIIIe siècle,* II, 142. On Adam Smith's influence on Sieys and his subsequent borrowings from the *Wealth of Nations,* see Bastid, p. 312.

27. Renan's famous text on his birthplace, published in his *Souvenirs d'enfance et de jeunesse* and quoted by Neton, *Sieyès,* p. 29.

28. Abbé Sicard, *L'Ancien Clergé de France: Les Evêques avant la Révolution* (Paris, Lecoffre, 1905), p. 279.

29. *Notice* on Sieys, p. 9.

30. Bastid, p. 17.

31. *Ibid.,* p. 39.

32. Letter published in full by Neton, *Sieyès,* p. 37.

33. *Ibid.,* p. 39.

34. Letter written by Sieys on February 8, 1783, to Clément de Ris, a former Parisian lawyer, now tax collector at Tréguier. De Ris later becomes a senator in the Consulate and the hero of Balzac's *La Ténébreuse Affaire,* and remains close to Sieys from 1781 on.

35. Neton, *Sieyès,* p. 22.

28

1. *Voyages en France de La Rochefoucauld,* II, 133 and 134.

2. Abbé Christian Moreau, *Une mystique révolutionnaire: Suzette Labrousse, d'après ses manuscrits et des documents officiels de son époque* (Paris, Firmin-Didot, 1886), p. 17 (cited hereafter as Moreau, *Suzette Labrousse*). The unnumbered quotations that follow in this passage are from the same source.

3. From a letter from Suzette Labrousse to the Abbé de St. Gérac, October 1779. *Ibid.,* p. 15.

4. Bibliothèque nationale, 13851, folios 210–11, G 9/46.

5. Pierre Pontard, *Recueil des ouvrages de la célèbre Mlle Labrousse* (Bordeaux, Brossier, Year IV), p. 50. We shall be meeting the author, Pierre Pontard, later on; he becomes constitutional Bishop of Dordogne and in that capacity tries to propagate the cult of Suzette Labrousse.

6. Moreau, *Suzette Labrousse,* p. 4.

7. Lairtullier, *Les Femmes célèbres de la Révolution* (Paris, 1867), article "Labrousse."

29

1. Moreau, *Suzette Labrousse,* p. 66.

*2. Daniel-Rops, *L'Eglise des temps classiques* (Paris, Fayard, 1958), II (*L'Ere des grands craquements*), 337.

3. *Ibid.,* II, 365.

4. *Ibid.,* II, 368. This is Jean Lapeyrie, a Capuchin whose

religious name is Ambroise de
Lombez (1703–1778).

5. J. Bremond, *Le Courant mystique
au XVIIIe siècle* (Paris, 1943), p.
206. (The author of this work is
Abbé Bremond's brother, who
vainly sought to carry on his
kinsman's work after his death.)

6. Daniel-Rops, *L'Eglise des temps
classiques*, II, 405, *"Saint Alphonse
de Liguori. La religion des temps
nouveaux."*

7. Anonymous, *Histoire de Saint
Alphonse de Liguori* (Paris,
Poussielgue, 1877), p. 601.

*8. G. Lacour-Gayet, *Talleyrand*
(Paris, Payot, 1933), I, 51.

9. *Ibid.,* I, 41.

10. *Ibid.,* I, 11.

11. Talleyrand, *Mémoires*, I, 9.

12. *Ibid.,* I, 24 and 33.

13. *Prophéties* of Suzette Labrousse,
quoted by Moreau, *Suzette
Labrousse*, pp. 29, 31, and 39.
There are hundreds more, even
less coherent.

14. A fragment of the *"grande
prédication de Suzette Labrousse aux
frères Chaminade,"* three priests
who were running the Mussidan
collège as a family business. *Ibid.,*
p. 25.

15. Draft of a letter kept among
Suzette Labrousse's papers and
dated September 19, 1779. *Ibid.,*
p. 20.

30

1. Letter from Colbert to de Seuil,
July 19, 1760.

2. These two extracts from Mme
Renaudin's letter to her brother,
Joséphine's father, are quoted by
Frédéric Masson, *Joséphine de
Beauharnais, 1763–1796* (Paris,
Ollendorf, 1901), pp. 78 and 79.

3. Quoted by André Castelot,
Joséphine (Paris, Perrin, 1964),
p. 25.

4. Mademoiselle Avrillion, *Mémoires*
(Paris, Mercure de France, *"Le
temps retrouvé,"* 1969), p. 178.

5. Slaves' names culled by André
Castelot from the archives kept at
La Pagerie, Martinique, *Joséphine,*
p. 18.

6. F. Masson, *Joséphine de
Beauharnais,* p. 95.

7. J. Saintoyant, *La Colonisation
française sous l'Ancien Régime,* II,
142.

8. Letter from the "Marquis" de
Beauharnais to Mme Renaudin,
June 26, 1760. Quoted by F.
Masson, *Joséphine de Beauharnais,*
p. 36.

9. *Ibid.,* p. 73.

10. Letter, March 11, 1778. *Ibid.,* p.
75. The following quotation by
the marquis is on page 77.

11. Raphaël Barquissau, *Les Isles*
(Paris, Grasset, 1941), p. 162.

12. Arthur Chuquet, *Dugommier*
(Paris, Fontemoing, 1904), p. 5.
Other information on
Dugommier comes from the
same work, or from the
*Dictionnaire historique et
biographique de la Révolution et de
l'Empire,* by Robinet, Robert, and
Le Chaplain.

13. According to a note by one
Thouluyre-Duchaumont,
Dugommier's classmate at the
Colin school, quoted by
Chuquet, *Dugommier,* p. 2.

14. F. Masson, *Joséphine de
Beauharnais,* p. 80. *Ibid.* for the
next quotation.

15. Clemente Fusero, *Joséphine, plus que reine* (Paris, Pierre Waleffe, 1967), p. 14.
16. F. Masson, *Joséphine de Beauharnais*, p. 63.
17. Arthur Young, *Travels in France*, p. 127.
18. F. Masson, *Joséphine de Beauharnais*, p. 65.
19. *Ibid.*, p. 81.
20. These three extracts from letters from Alexandre de Beauharnais to Mme Renaudin are quoted by A. Castelot, *Joséphine*, p. 27.
21. F. Masson, *Joséphine de Beauharnais*, p. 87.
22. Adolphe Joanne, *Les Environs de Paris* (Paris, Hachette, 1868), p. 401.
23. Confidential remark made by Napoleon, on St. Helena, to Grand-Maréchal Bertrand; see Bertrand, *Souvenirs*, transcribed by Paul Fleuriot de Langle (Paris, Sulliver), Vol. I. The word was not written out by the decipherer, who told me verbally what it was.

31

1. *Lettres d'amour des Roland*, p. 113. In this instance only I shall not give detailed references for every quotation, especially as they may be identified by the dates of the letters, which are usually given in the text.
2. *Lettres de Mme Roland*, II, 357, to Sophie, February 1, 1779.
3. *Ibid.*, II, 365, to Sophie, February 23, 1779.
4. Recopied in Roland's hand, letter by letter, just to rub salt in Manon's wounds. *Lettres d'amour des Roland*, p. 268.
5. *Ibid.*, p. 311, but this time in Gratien Phlipon's hand.
6. *Mémoires de Mme Roland*, II, 53.
7. *Ibid.*, II, 79.
8. For Sister Sainte-Agathe, see Claude Perroud's appendix at the end of Vol. II of the *Lettres de Mme Roland.*
9. *Mémoires de Mme Roland*, II, 248.
10. *Ibid.*, II, 249.
11. *Ibid.*, II, 238 and 252.
12. *Ibid.*, II, 250.

32

1. C. Vatel, *Vergniaud, manuscrits, lettres et papiers* (Paris, Dumoulin, 1873), I, 22 (cited hereafter as Vatel). This letter, undated save for "Tuesday," immediately precedes that of January 1, 1780. It was written in November or December 1779.
2. January 1, 1780. *Ibid.*, p. 23.
3. Lamartine, *Histoire des Girondins*, illustrated edition (Paris, Le Chevalier, 1865), I, 422. Henri Guillemin called my attention to the veritable gold mine of first- or secondhand biographical information in this work, wrongly misprized by historians. One need only come to terms with the shimmer of Lamartine's style: the shimmer of fire.
4. Copied by Vatel, I, 174.
5. *Ibid.*, I, 175.
6. Reichard, *Guide de la France*, p. 129.
7. *Voyages en France de La Rochefoucauld*, II, 131.
8. *Ibid.*, II, 132.

9. *Notice sur Vergniaud,* written around 1842 by M. François Alluaud *fils,* his nephew, in Vatel, I, 1.

10. Letter, November 1, 1778. *Ibid.,* I, 15.

11. Undated letter, but written in the winter of 1778–79. *Ibid.,* I, 16.

12. In his letter of January 3, 1779.

13. Letter dated Shrove Tuesday, that is, February 16, 1779. Vatel, I, 18.

14. *Ibid.,* I, 191. Papers from Vergniaud's youth, found in his home after his arrest in 1793. The lines of poetry may not be by him; if they are copied from someone else, their author is unknown. In the sheaf there are over twenty-five fragments recopied in his hand, always giving the author's name: Laborde, Favart, Sedaine, Marmontel, etc.

15. *Notice* by his nephew, in Vatel, I, 3.

16. *Ibid.,* I, 4.

17. Lamartine, *Histoire des Girondins,* I, 114.

18. *Voyages en France de La Rochefoucauld,* II, 132.

19. Vatel, I, 74 and 137. *Ibid.* for the following quotation.

20. Arthur Young, *Voyages en France,* II, 564. [Retranslated from French edition (Paris, 1794) used by author.]

21. Letters to François Alluaud, April 22 and May 6, 1780. Vatel, I, 24.

33

*1. *Mémoires* of the Abbé Morellet (Paris, Ladvocat, 1821), I, 287, where the complete text of the song can be found.

*2. Bernard Faÿ, *Benjamin Franklin,* (Paris, Calmann-Lévy, 1929), II (*Benjamin Franklin, citoyen du monde*), 219 (cited hereafter as B. Faÿ, *Benjamin Franklin*) (Volume I: *Benjamin Franklin, bourgeois d'Amérique*). Franklin's wine cellars came from d'Eon's brother-in-law, the Chevalier O'Gorman.

3. *Ibid.,* II, 179.

4. *Ibid.,* II, 218.

5. From a letter from Franklin to a friend in Philadelphia. [Retranslated from French edition used by author.] *Ibid.,* II, 221.

6. *Mémoires* of the Abbé Morellet, I, 295. *Ibid.* for the following quotation.

7. *Ibid.,* I, 289.

8. *Mémoires* of the Baronne d'Oberkirch on the court of Louis XVI (Paris, Mercure de France, *"Le temps retrouvé,"* 1970), p. 416. *Ibid.* for the following description of the cats' dinner.

9. B. Faÿ, *Benjamin Franklin,* II, 227.

10. Quoted by Guy Besse in his introduction to Helvétius, *De l'Esprit* (Paris, Editions Sociales, *"Les classiques du peuple,"* 1959), p. 26.

11. *Ibid.,* p. 27.

12. *Correspondance littéraire,* XII, 385.

13. *Mémoires* of the Abbé Morellet, I, 135.

14. B. Faÿ, *Benjamin Franklin,* II, 225. *Ibid.,* II, 228, for the following quotation by Turgot.

34

1. Tower, *L.F. in America,* II, 83.
2. The original of this memorandum from La Fayette to Vergennes, dated July 18, 1779, is in the Archives nationales, I, IX, 42, folio 154.
3. A. Maurois, *Madame de La Fayette,* p. 107.
4. Letter from La Fayette to Maurepas. Archives nationales, United States, Supplement I, 239 *a. Ibid.* for the following quotations.
5. A. Maurois, *Madame de La Fayette,* p. 109.
6. Archives de la Marine, B/4, 143.
7. Rochambeau, *Mémoires* (Paris, Le Jay, 1809), I, 13.
8. *Ibid.,* I, 31.
9. Maurice-Charles Renard, *Rochambeau, libérateur de l'Amérique* (Paris, Fasquelle, 1951), p. 36 (cited hereafter as Renard, *Rochambeau).*
*10. Vicomte de Noailles, *Marins et Soldats français en Amérique* (Paris, Perrin, 1903), p. 146. The other unnumbered quotations or details in this passage are from the same source, pp. 147–73.
11. Instructions from the Prince de Montbarrey to Rochambeau. Archives historiques de la Guerre [War], Box 3733.
12. Unpublished letters included by A. Maurois in *Madame de La Fayette,* pp. 109–13.
13. Lacour-Gayet, *Marine française sous Louis XVI,* p. 295.
14. Accounts of the storekeeper general, Martin de Permon, for April 9, 1780. Archives historiques de la Guerre [War], Box 48.
15. Archives de la Marine, B/4, 183.

35

1. *Instructions remises à M. de La Fayette,* March 5, 1780. Archives des Affaires étrangères [Foreign Affairs], United States, Vol. II, no. 69.
2. *Correspondance secrète,* I, 300.
*3. Comte de Ségur, *Mémoires ou Souvenirs et anecdotes* (Paris, Lecointe, 1842), I, 206 (cited hereafter as Comte de Ségur, *Mémoires).*
4. O. G. de Heidenstam, *Marie-Antoinette, Fersen et Barnave* (Paris, Calmann-Lévy, 1913), p. 14.
5. Mercy-Argenteau, *Correspondance,* III, 409.
6. From Rochambeau to Montbarrey, April 20, 1780. Archives historiques de la Guerre [War], Box 3733.
7. From the same to the same. *Ibid.,* Box 3746.
8. A. Söderjhelm, *Fersen et Marie-Antoinette,* p. 69.
9. Letters from Fersen to his sister, June 30, 1778, and to his father, November 19, 1778. *Ibid.,* pp. 54 and 55.
10. O. G. de Heidenstam, *Marie-Antoinette, Fersen et Barnave,* p. 16. *Ibid.* for the next quotation.
11. Comte de Ségur, *Mémoires,* I, 407.
12. Letter from La Fayette to his wife, May 6, 1780. A. Maurois, *Madame de La Fayette,* p. 116.
13. Rochambeau to Montbarrey, May

3, 1780. Archives historiques de la Guerre [War], Box 3734.

14. The Comte de Wittgenstein (letter to Montbarrey, April 17, 1780). Archives historiques de la Guerre [War], 1780, Box 48.

15. Rochambeau to Montbarrey, May 3, 1780. *Ibid.*, Box 3733.

16. *Correspondance secrète*, I, 302.

36

1. *Journal de Paris*, April 6, 1780. Bibliothèque nationale.

*2. Dr. Cabanès, *Marat inconnu* (Paris, Albin Michel), p. 161.

*3. Extracts from Marat's *Plan de législation criminelle*, quoted by Gérard Walter, *Marat* (Paris, Albin Michel, 1933), p. 60.

4. *Ibid.*, p. 62.

5. Letter written in November 1779. *Ibid.*, p. 65.

*6. Description (for other details as well, and the probable etymology of "Trahoir") taken from Thiéry's *Guide des amateurs et des étrangers de Paris*, 1787, I, 412.

7. "*Souvenirs d'un témoin oculaire*," the mineralogist François Sage, in *Analyse chimique et concordance des trois règnes* (Paris, Panckoucke, 1786), I, 117. Also for the next quotation.

8. G. Walter, *Marat*, p. 63.

9. *L'Ami du Peuple*, January 27, 1791. [This is Marat's paper.]

10. Published in full by Dr. Robinet, *Vie de Condorcet* (Paris, Librairies-·Imprimeries Réunies), p. 20.

11. *Journal de la République française*, No. 98, fragment from Marat's autobiography, quoted by Robinet, *Vie de Condorcet*, p. 24.

12. Bibliothèque de l'Institut, M. *b/2/3x*.

13. *Lettre sur le charlatanisme académique; les Charlatans modernes, par M. Marat, L'Ami du peuple* (Paris, 1791), quoted by Robinet, *Vie de Condorcet*, p. 21.

*14. On an unspecified Thursday in August 1774. *Correspondance inédite de Condorcet et de Turgot* (Paris, Charavay, 1883), p. 189.

15. Bibliothèque de l'Institut, unpublished manuscripts, R. 69 g 1.

16. From Condorcet to Turgot, September 1777. *Correspondance inédite de Condorcet et de Turgot*, p. 297.

*17. Edouard Grimaux, *Lavoisier* (Paris, Alcan, 1896), p. 131.

37

1. According to G. Walter, *Marat*, p. 66.

*2. J. P. Brissot, *Mémoires, publiés par* Claude Perroud (Paris, Picard, n.d.), I, 186 and 212 (cited hereafter as Brissot, *Mémoires*).

*3. Jean-François Primo, *La Jeunesse de Brissot* (Paris, Grasset, n.d.), p. 87.

4. Brissot, *Mémoires*, I, 197 and 202.

5. G. Walter, *Marat*, p. 66.

6. Brissot, *Mémoires*, I, 102. Unnumbered quotations that follow in this passage are from the same source.

7. Sainte-Beuve, Introduction to the *Lettres de Madame Roland à Bancal des Issarts*, p. xlii.

8. Advertisement in the *Courrier de l'Europe*, October 2, 1778, Boulogne edition.

9. Expression used by Brissot in his avenging pamphlet of 1781, "*Un*

indépendant à l'ordre des avocats," mendaciously marked "printed in Berlin." "I desired to learn the discipline and principles of the Order of Lawyers and I donned their grotesque harness."

10. Primo, *La Jeunesse de Brissot,* p. 90.

11. Dialogue recorded verbatim by Brissot in his *Mémoires,* I, 96.

38

1. From the record of deaths in the parish church of Notre Dame de Deuil for the year 1780, "collated to the present instant and issued by myself, the undersigned parish priest, on June 6, 1780; Sevoy, priest of Deuil." Published by Manuel in *Lettres de Mirabeau,* IV, 279.

2. A. Vallentin, *Mirabeau avant la Révolution,* p. 184.

3. More confidential remarks from the marquis to his brother. *Ibid.,* p. 201. *Ibid.,* too, pp. 223 and 227, for the following two references.

4. *Ibid.,* p. 201.

5. *Lettres de Mirabeau,* III, 253.

6. *Ibid.,* IV, 221.

7. To Sophie. *Ibid.,* III, 251.

8. A. Vallentin, *Mirabeau avant la Révolution,* pp. 204 and 205.

9. *Lettres de Mirabeau,* III, 343 and 357.

10. Dialogue reconstructed from an exchange of letters between Mirabeau and Dupont, recopied by the former, with commentary, for Sophie. *Lettres de Mirabeau,* III, 343–8.

11. *Ibid.,* III, 362.

12. *Ibid.,* III, 391.

13. *Ibid.,* III, 408. Same source for the "last word."

14. *Ibid.,* IV, 73.

39

*1. Letter from Le Noir to Amelot (minister of the King's Household, and in that capacity responsible for *lettres de cachet*), September 10, 1777. Quoted by Paul Cottin, *Sophie de Monnier et Mirabeau* (Paris, Plon, 1903), p. 61. This book contains some of Sophie's letters, while Mirabeau's are in Manuel's 1792 edition. These officially authorized letters had to be handed over to the prison officers once the correspondents had read them; which is how Manuel, when he becomes chief of the Paris police after August 10, discovers them and later publishes those of Mirabeau.

2. *Lettres de Mirabeau,* III, 284.

3. Undated, in a packet of thirty-five items of *Lettres de Madame de Monnier,* Ref. 92, 1780, kept in the Mirabeau Collection at the Bibliothèque Paul Arbaud in Aix-en-Provence. The Duc de Castries made some singular discoveries there during the exhaustive exploration which preceded the writing of his *Mirabeau.* See the detailed catalog of this material, much of it still unpublished, which he gives in the appendix to his *Mirabeau,* p. 562.

4. *Lettres,* II, 396. *Ibid.* for the next quotation about Fourcroy.

5. *Ibid.,* III, 260.

6. *Ibid.,* IV, 426.

7. Letter from Sophie to Boucher, September 17, 1779. P. Cottin, *Sophie de Monnier et Mirabeau,* p. 133.

8. To Sophie, February 21, 1780. *Lettres de Mirabeau,* IV, 228.

9. *Ibid.,* IV, 102.

10. To Sophie, February 20, 1779. *Ibid.,* III, 98.

11. To Sophie, July 19, 1779. *Ibid.,* III, 307.

12. Dauphin-Meunier, *Autour de Mirabeau, documents inédits* (Paris, Payot, 1926), p. 36.

13. A. Vallentin, *Mirabeau avant la Révolution,* p. 211.

14. Dauphin-Meunier, *Autour de Mirabeau, documents inédits,* p. 42.

15. To Sophie, of course. *Lettres de Mirabeau,* IV, 235.

16. *Ma Conversion, roman scandaleux par C. d. M.* (Paris, Editions du Golem, 1970), p. 17.

17. To Sophie, May 8, 1779. *Lettres de Mirabeau,* III, 182.

18. P. Cottin, *Sophie de Monnier et Mirabeau,* p. 122.

19. *Lettres de Mirabeau,* IV, 170.

20. *Encyclopédie,* XV, 428, entries for "Spasme" and "Spasmodique."

21. A. Vallentin, *Mirabeau avant la Révolution,* p. 222.

22. The scene is diligently reconstructed, as always, by Gilbert Lély, *Vie du marquis de Sade,* p. 327.

40

1. Tower, *L.F. in America,* II, 107.

2. The description of headquarters, including quotations, is from Chastellux, *Voyages dans l'Amérique septentrionale pendant les années 1780, 1781 et 1782* (Paris, Panckoucke, 1788), I, 220.

3. Tower, *L.F. in America,* II, 109.

4. Chastellux, *Voyages dans l'Amérique,* I, 226.

5. Letter from Washington to Joseph Jones, Representative of Virginia to Congress, written May 31, 1780, in Jared Sparks, *The Writings of George Washington* (Boston, Little, Brown and Company, 1855), Vol. VII, p. 68. It is significant of the centralizing clearheadedness of Washington, in opposition to the particularist anarchy of the individual states. We see the Year II conflict between Jacobins and Federalists foreshadowed here.

6. Tower, *L.F. in America,* II, 111.

7. La Fayette to Rochambeau and Ternay, July 9, 1780. Archives historiques de la Guerre [War].

8. Letter from La Fayette to Mr. Reed, president of the Supreme Executive Council of Pennsylvania, May 31, 1780. *Life and Correspondence of Joseph Reed* (Boston, 1818), p. 320 [and Tower, *L.F. in America,* II, 116].

9. Tower, *L.F. in America,* II, 125.

10. Duc de Lauzun, *Mémoires,* p. 140.

11. This and the following quotations, when unnumbered, are extracts from letters by Lauzun quoted by G. Maugras in *Le Duc de Lauzun et la cour de Marie-Antoinette,* pp. 206–11.

12. Vicomte de Noailles, *Marins et Soldats français en Amérique,* p. 179.

13. According to his *Mémoires,* quoted by Renard, *Rochambeau,* p. 105. The story of Rochambeau's reception in

Newport is taken from this
source, but also from G.
Maugras, *Le Duc de Lauzun et la
cour de Marie-Antoinette,*
pp. 212–15.

41

1. La Fayette to Washington, July
   26, 1780. La Fayette,
   Correspondance, I, 468.
2. G. Maugras, *Le Duc de Lauzun et
   la cour de Marie-Antoinette,* p. 213.
3. Same letter as in note 1. The
   following quotation is from a
   postscript added the next day.
4. Letter from La Fayette to the
   Prince de Poix, "at the light
   division camp near the island of
   New York, September 3, 1780."
   Maurois, *Madame de La Fayette,*
   p. 119.
5. La Fayette, *Correspondance,* I, 345.
6. Original text in the Library of
   Congress, Washington. Quoted
   by Tower, *L.F. in America,* II,
   151.
7. La Fayette, *Correspondance,* I, 362.
8. *Ibid.,* I, 365.
9. *Lettres d'Axel Fersen à son père*
   Paris, Firmin-Didot, 1929), p.
   73. The next three quotations
   are from the same letter, written
   September 8, 1780.
10. Tower, *L.F. in America,* II, 141.
11. *Lettres* of Fersen, p. 77.
12. *Ibid.,* p. 76.

42

1. G. Maugras, *Le Duc de Lauzun et
   la cour de Marie-Antoinette,* p. 220.
2. *Lettres* of Fersen, p. 74.
3. Rochambeau, *Mémoires,* quoted
   by Renard, *Rochambeau,* p. 115.
   Ibid. for the following quotation.

4. *Lettres* of Fersen, p. 82.
5. Tower, *L.F. in America,* II, 184.
6. Renard, *Rochambeau,* p. 118.
7. Letter from La Fayette to the
   Chevalier de La Luzerne, West
   Point, September 25, 1780.
   Published in full in the *Revue de
   la Révolution,* Vol. V (1885). *Ibid.*
   for the following unnumbered
   quotations.
8. Tower, *L.F. in America,* Vol. II,
   pp. 168–9.
*9. Jared Sparks, *American Biography*
   (New York, Harper & Brothers,
   1902), Vol. 3, "Benedict
   Arnold," pp. 278–9.
10. Jared Sparks, *The Writings of
    George Washington,* Vol. VII,
    pp. 256–7.
11. To his father, October 16, 1780.
    Lettres of Fersen, p. 85.
12. La Fayette, *Correspondance,* I, 376.

43

1. From *Le Poète malheureux, ou le
   génie aux prises avec la fortune,* in
   Gilbert, *Poésies diverses* (Paris,
   Quantin, 1882), p. 104. The
   texts by Gilbert quoted in this
   passage are from the same work
   unless otherwise stated. The
   famous verse *"Au banquet de la
   vie,"* etc., is in *Ode IX imitée de
   plusieurs psaumes,* p. 96, his last
   work, written when he knew he
   was doomed, but three months
   and not eight days before his
   death in the Hôtel-Dieu, as
   erroneously alleged on a plaque
   which can still be seen in the St.
   Louis ward of that hospital.
2. Gilbert's biographers have both
   exaggerated and underestimated
   this scene. By cross-cutting, it can

be reconstructed as here. See
Ernest Laffay, *Le Poète Gilbert*
(Paris, Bloud et Barral, 1898),
p. 273.

3. *Correspondance littéraire,* XII
(December 1780), 459.

4. J. A. Schmidt, *Notice sur le poète
Gilbert* (Nancy, Sidot, 1890),
p. 18.

5. Colin, *Vie et Mort de Gilbert,*
quoted by Laffay, *Le Poète Gilbert,*
p. 42.

6. Charles Monselet, *Les Oubliés et
les Dédaignés,* literary figures of
the late eighteenth century
(Paris, Poulet-Malassis, 1859), p.
162. The two previous
quotations are from the same
chapter, on Baculard d'Arnaud.

7. From some anonymous verse
published in *Siècle,* which was La
Harpe's paper. Quoted by Laffay,
Le Poète Gilbert, p. 109. The next
two insults are also by La
Harpe.

8. Letter published in full in the
Amateur d'autographes, February
10, 1877.

9. Laffay, *Le Poète Gilbert,* p. 62.

10. P. Courbe, *Promenades historiques
à travers les rues de Nancy au
XVIIIe siècle* (Nancy, 1833), p.
167. *Ibid.* for the following
quotation.

11. *Correspondance littéraire,* XII,
460.

44

*1. C. L. Morris, *Marie-Thérèse, le
dernier conservateur* (Paris, Plon,
1937), p. 305. *Ibid.* for the
following quotation, from a letter
from Maria Theresa to the
Comte de Greiner.

2. Mercy-Argenteau, *Correspondance,*
III, 384.

3. *Ibid.,* III, 364.

4. *Ibid.,* III, 444.

5. From Marie Antoinette to her
"chère maman" on July 13,
1780. *Ibid.,* III, 445. The
sentence makes the queen's
opinion of the Rebels extremely
clear.

6. *Ibid.,* III, 404.

7. Fejtö, *Joseph II,* p. 189.

8. *Ibid.,* p. 193.

9. Mercy-Argenteau and Maria
Theresa, *Correspondance,* III, 453.

10. *Ibid.,* III, 394.

11. *Ibid.,* III, 416.

12. *Ibid.,* III, 398.

13. *Ibid.,* III, 437.

14. *Ibid.,* III, 473. Also for the next
quotation.

15. *Ibid.,* III, 364.

16. *Ibid.,* III, 396.

17. *Ibid.,* III, 442.

18. *Ibid.,* III, 482. Also for the next
quotation.

19. November 3, 1780. *Ibid.,* III,
485.

20. Mercy-Argenteau, *Correspondance,*
III, 492. The death of Maria
Theresa has been reconstructed
on the basis of the books by
Fejtö and Morris and, above all,
the on-the-spot account by her
elder daughter, the Archduchess
Maria Anna, who is
hunchbacked, remains unmarried,
and retires to the Ursuline
convent at Klagenfurt.

21. Fejtö, *Joseph II,* p. 197. The
emperor takes a morbid delight
in his bon mot, which is repeated
in his first letter to Louis XVI
after his coronation on
December 6, 1780.

45

1. *Lettres de Marie-Antoinette à Joseph II et Léopold II, publiées par* von Arneth (Leipzig, Kohler, 1866), p. 22.
2. *Ibid.,* p. 25. Next quotation from p. 26.
3. A. Bonstetten, *Lettres à Fredericke Brun, publiées par* Matthisson (Geneva, 1841), I, 205.
4. *Ibid.,* II, 18.
*5. Lady Blenerhasset, *Madame de Staël et son temps* (Paris, Westhausser, 1890), I, 13.
6. An expression of Harbert Lüthy's, in *La Banque protestante en France de la révocation de l'Edit de Nantes à la Révolution,* Vol. II: *De la Banque aux Finances (1730–1794)* (Paris, SEVPEN, 1951 [one octavo volume, 861 pages!]).
7. Jean Bouvier, review of the book by Lüthy cited in the preceding note, *Annales historiques de la Révolution française,* XXXIV (1962), 373. *Ibid.* for the next two quotations.
*8. Sénac de Meilhan, who as intendant of Marseilles was in a position to know, accuses Necker of fraud on this subject. See Pierre Jolly, *Necker* (Paris, "Les oeuvres françaises," 1947), p. 50. *Ibid.* for the following quotation.
9. J. H. Meister, *Mélanges de philosophie, de littérature et de morale,* II, 58.
10. *Mémoires* of the Abbé Morellet, I, 154.
11. For an introduction to the picturesque personality of the Marquis de Castries, I recommend his biography, based on unpublished material and on his diary in particular, by the Duc de Castries, *Le Maréchal de Castries* (Paris, Fayard, 1956).
12. B. Faÿ, *Louis XVI,* p. 198.
13. On February 18, 1781. See P. Jolly, *Necker,* p. 185.
14. Dominique Joseph Garat, *Mémoires historiques sur la vie de M. Suard, sur ses écrits et sur le XVIIIe siècle* (Paris, "chez A. Belin, imprimeur-libraire," 1820), I, 270. *Ibid.* for the following unnumbered quotations.
15. P. Jolly, *Necker,* p. 186. *Ibid.* for the following unnumbered quotations.
16. Jean-Jacques Antier did me the very great favor of lending me the original copy of the *Compte Rendu* [Account Rendered] so that I could study it page by page. All the extracts from it in this passage are taken from that copy.
17. B. Faÿ, *Louis XVI,* p. 207.

46

1. Letter printed in full in *Magnétisme animal,* writings of F. A. Mesmer, *publiées par* Robert Amadou (Paris, Payot, "Sciences de l'homme" collection, 1971). This work is essential to an understanding and reassessment of Mesmer, and turned up just at the right time for me to write this passage. Unnumbered quotations by Mesmer are from this source, and in particular the extracts from his long *Mémoire,*

composed at the same time as his letter to Marie Antoinette and entitled *Précis historique des faits relatifs au magnétisme animal jusqu'en avril 1781.*

2. *Mémoires* of the Comte Dufort de Cheverny, *publiées par* Robert de Crèvecoeur (Paris, Plon, 1901), I (*L'Ancien Régime*), 444. *Ibid.* for the rest of the description of the buckets.

3. Lescure, *La Princesse de Lamballe* (Paris, Plon, 1864), p. 139.

4. Letter from Marie Antoinette to Marie Christine, February 26, 1781. *Ibid.,* p. 132.

5. From the *Mémoires* of Madame de Genlis. *Ibid.,* p. 82.

6. From the *Mémoire sur la découverte du magnétisme animal,* published by Mesmer in 1779 (Amadou, *Magnétisme animal,* p. 59). *Ibid.,* for the following quotations.

7. December 20, 1780. Arneth, *Lettres de Marie-Antoinette à Joseph II,* p. 26.

8. The terms used by Mesmer in reply to Maurepas, in the long account of their interview in his *Précis historique des faits relatifs au magnétisme animal jusqu'en avril 1781 (Magnétisme animal,* p. 183). *Ibid.* for the following quotation.

9. *Magnétisme animal,* 189.

10. *Ibid.,* p. 102.

11. *Les Amusements des eaux à Spa,* no date or author's name, undoubtedly published shortly before the Revolution (Paris, Panckoucke), p. 18.

12. From a letter from Mozart to his father. Brigitte and Jean Massin, *Mozart,* p. 333.

47

1. Tower, *L.F. in America,* II, 227.

2. La Fayette, *Correspondance,* I, 370.

3. September 17, 1780. *Lettres* of Fersen to his father, p. 78.

4. October 16, 1780. *Ibid.,* p. 80.

5. January 9, 1781. *Ibid.,* p. 98.

6. *Ibid.,* p. 102.

7. Tower, *L.F. in America,* II, 171.

8. "Light division camp, October 20, 1780." *Ibid.,* II, 172.

9. "Headquarters, October 30." *Ibid.,* II, 175. He was stung, and so answered immediately.

10. From New Windsor, December 13, 1780. *Ibid.,* II, 188.

11. From camp at Harrington, New Jersey, October 4, 1780. *Ibid.,* II, 189.

12. A. Maurois, *Madame de La Fayette,* p. 122.

13. Tower, *L. F. in America,* II, 270.

14. Dispatch from Vergennes to the Chevalier de La Luzerne, the king's ambassador to the United States, May 11, 1781. *Ibid.,* II, 281.

15. Franklin to the Comte de Vergennes, Passy, February 13, 1781. *Ibid.,* II, 272.

16. In Washington's letter of instructions to La Fayette, February 20, 1781. *Ibid.,* II, 228.

17. February 24, 1781. *Ibid.,* II, 231.

18. *Ibid.,* II, 236.

19. Rochambeau's instructions for M. le Baron de Vioménil, March 5, 1781. *Ibid.,* II, 237.

48

1. From New Windsor. Tower, *L.F. in America,* II, 266.

2. Letter from Vergennes to La Luzerne, February 15, 1781: two days after receiving Franklin's letter. *Ibid.*, II, 197.

3. De Witt, *Washington*, p. 179.

4. From a long letter from Vergennes to La Luzerne, March 9, 1781. Tower, *L.F. in America,* II, 276–7.

5. *Ibid.*, II, 285.

6. Same dispatch as in note 4. *Ibid.,* II, 277. Also for the next two quotations.

7. March 21, 1781. *Ibid.*, II, 283.

8. La Fayette to Washington. *Ibid.,* II, 243–4.

9. To Washington, March 23, 1781. *Ibid.*, II, 244.

10. To Washington, April 8, 1781, from Head of Elk. *Ibid.*, II, 248.

11. Jared Sparks, *The Writings of George Washington,* Vol. VIII, pp. 32–3.

12. According to Rochambeau in his *Mémoires.*

13. J.-J. Antier, *L'Amiral de Grasse,* p. 172.

14. From New Windsor, April 6, 1781. Tower, *L.F. in America,* II, 254–5. *Ibid.* for the following quotation.

15. *Ibid.*, II, 258.

16. From La Fayette to Washington at the Susquehanna ford, April 15, 1781. *Ibid.*, II, 259.

17. La Fayette's report to Congress, April 22, 1781. *Ibid.*, II, 261. Congress adopts a vote of congratulations to the Baltimore merchants for their civic spirit.

18. To Washington from Baltimore, April 18, 1781. *Ibid.*, II, 286–7.

19. To Washington, April 23, 1781. *Ibid.*, II, 187.

49

*1. Letters from Turgot to the Duchesse d'Enville. Quoted by Edgar Faure, *La Disgrâce de Turgot* (Paris, Gallimard, 1961), p. 521. *Ibid.* for the following quotation.

2. C. J. Gignoux, *Turgot* (Paris, Fayard, 1945), p. 260.

3. Henri Laboucheix, *Richard Price, théoricien de la révolution américaine* (Paris, Didier, 1970), p. 25.

4. *Ibid.*, p. 27.

5. *Ibid.*, p. 147. Also for the following quotation.

6. *Mémoires* of the Abbé Morellet, quoted by Gignoux, *Turgot,* p. 269.

7. Adam Smith, *The Wealth of Nations* (London, Dent, Everyman's Library, 1971), II, 430.

8. Gignoux, *Turgot,* p. 270.

9. *Ibid.*, p. 271.

10. *Ibid.*, p. 273.

11. Letter from Dupont to Malesherbes, April 17, 1781.

12. *Correspondance littéraire,* XII, 527.

*13. Pierre Grosclaude, *Malesherbes, témoin et interprète de son temps* (Paris, Fischbacher, n.d.), p. 447.

50

1. Guillaume-Thomas Raynal, *Histoire philosophique et politique des établissements et du commerce des Européens dans les Deux Indes* (Geneva, 1780), Book IV, Chapter XVIII. This is, of course, the fourth edition, Diderot's. There are four quarto volumes, one more than in the previous (1776) edition, to

which Diderot contributed little. This one is dated 1780 but does not cross the Swiss border into France until the following year.

2. *Correspondance secrète,* XI, 42.

*3. J. de Norvins, *Mémorial, publié par* Lanzac de Laborie (Paris, Plon, 1896), I, 22.

4. Marc de Vissac, *Les Révolutionnaires du Rouergue: Simon Camboulas* (Riom, Edouard Girerd, 1892), p. 43 (cited hereafter as De Vissac, *Simon Camboulas*). *Ibid.* for the following quote.

5. *Ibid.,* p. 48.

*6. Malouet, *Mémoires* (Paris, Plon, 1874), I, 199.

7. Denis Diderot, *Essai sur les règnes de Claude et de Néron,* in *Oeuvres complètes* (Paris, Assezat-Tourneux, Garnier, 1875), III, 400.

8. Quoted by de Vissac, *Simon Camboulas,* p. 49.

9. Quoted by Anatole Feugère, *"L'Abbé Raynal et la Révolution francaise,"* Annales historiques de la Révolution francaise, VI (1913), 311.

10. Léon Beclard, *Sébastien Mercier, sa vie, son oeuvre, son temps* (Paris, Champion, 1903), I, 451.

11. Michèle Duchet, *Anthropologie et Histoire au siècle des Lumières* (Paris, Maspero, 1971), p. 478. *Ibid.* for the following quotation.

12. Feugère, *"L'Abbé Raynal et la Révolution francaise,"* p. 310.

*13. Denis Diderot, *Correspondance, publiée par* Georges Roth and Jean Varloot (Paris, Editions de Minuit, 1968), XV, 190.

14. Letter from Diderot to Catherine

II, June 29, 1779. *Ibid.,* XV, 149.

15. Yves Benot, *Diderot, de l'athéisme à l'anticolonialisme* (Paris, Maspero, 1970). The author of this major work is also a teacher who, in 1969, suffered a form of persecution at the hands of the French government in the true tradition of those inflicted upon the *philosophes* by Louis XVI; he has given researchers a timely reminder of the revolutionary radicalization of Diderot's thinking in his last years. The two sentences, quoted here in reverse order, are from pages 258 and 16.

51

1. To M. and Mme de Vandeul, May 31, 1779. Diderot, *Correspondance,* XV, 146.

2. To abbé Gouttes, January 25, 1780. *Ibid.,* XV, 169.

3. This quotation and the following extracts from Diderot's texts for the *Histoire des Deux Indes* are from Vol. XV of his *Oeuvres complètes* (Paris, Club français du livre, 1973), pp. 419–570, where the exact reference to the 1781 edition is given in every instance.

52

1. *Un journal de voyage inédit au long des Côtes du Chili et du Pérou* by Vincent Bauver, *publié par* Régine Pernoud, in *"L'Amérique du Sud au XVIIIe siècle," Cahiers d'histoire et de bibliographie,* No. 3 (1942), p. 29.

*2. François Rousseau, *Le Règne de*

Charles III d'Espagne (Paris, Plon, 1907), II, 236 (cited hereafter as F. Rousseau, *Règne de Charles III*). This work contains one of the best accounts of the insurrection of Tupac Amaru; I have used it for the atmosphere and chronology of events (pp. 236–47). For further particulars, see Boleslao Lewin, *La rebelión de Tupac Amarú y los origenes de la emancipación americana* (Buenos Aires, 1957).

3. Jean Descola, *La Vie quotidienne au Pérou au temps des Espagnols, 1710–1820* (Paris, Hachette, 1962), p. 195 (cited hereafter as J. Descola, *Vie quotidienne au Pérou*). *Ibid.* for the following quotation.

4. Charles Minguet, *Alexandre de Humboldt, historien et géographe de l'Amérique espagnole* (Paris, Maspero, 1969), p. 377.

5. F. Rousseau, *Règne de Charles III*, II, 240.

6. Jorge Juan and Antonio de Ulloa, quoted by J. Descola, *Vie quotidienne au Pérou*, p. 50. *Ibid.* for the next two quotations.

7. J. Descola, *Vie quotidienne au Pérou*, p. 238.

8. *Ibid.*, p. 239.

9. *Ibid.*, p. 240. Also for the following quotation.

10. Amédée François Frezier, *Relation du voyage de la mer du Sud aux côtes du Chili et du Pérou*, quoted by J. Descola, *Vie quotidienne au Pérou*. *Ibid.* for the next quotation.

53

1. J. Descola, *Vie quotidienne au Pérou*, p. 46.

2. F. Rousseau, *Règne de Charles III*, II, 238.

3. *Ibid.*, II, 245.

4. From Tupac Amaru's letter to the bishop of Cuzco, January 3, 1781. F. Rousseau, *Règne de Charles III*, II, 239–41. *Ibid.* for the next quotation.

5. The original of this text, undoubtedly in Tupac Amaru's hand, is in the Royal Archives in Madrid, Estado leg. 4200.

6. J. Descola, *Vie quotidienne au Pérou*, p. 101.

7. Quoted by F. Rousseau, *Règne de Charles III*, II, 238. *Ibid.* for the next quotation.

8. Same reference as for note 4, above.

9. There is a copy of the broadsheet in the Royal Archives of Madrid, Estado leg. 4200.

10. C. Minguet, *Alexandre de Humboldt*, p. 235.

11. Letter to his wife, April 2, 1781. In Danvila y Collado, quoted by F. Rousseau, *Règne de Charles III*, II, 243.

12. J. Descola, *Vie quotidienne au Pérou*, p. 90.

13. *Ibid.*, p. 244.

14. Michel Deveze, *L'Europe et le monde à la fin du XVIIIe siècle* (Paris, Albin Michel, 1970), p. 470. *Ibid.* for the following quotations.

54

1. These four items of "information" are given by Lescure on the dates stated, in his *Correspondance secrète* for 1781. *Ibid.* for the following quotation, dated May 16.

2. *Correspondance secrète*, I, 383.

3. B. Faÿ, *Louis XVI*, p. 207.
4. Joseph Droz, *Histoire du Règne de Louis XVI*, I, 225. *Ibid.* for the next quotation. This text by Vergennes may well plunge theoreticians of the "Capetian monarchy" into a cruel dilemma, even though he was one of its demigods.
5. Lady Blennerhasset, *Madame de Staël et son temps*, I, 155. This *Mémoire* is so damning to the memory of Vergennes that his biographers or the royalist historians of Louis XVI have always tried, like Noah's sons, to cover it in its nakedness.
6. May Paul Claudel forgive me for appropriating his last poem and changing a word: "Maurepas" in place of "Claudel."
7. Necker, *De l'administration de M. Necker*, by himself, in *Oeuvres complètes* (Geneva, 1808), VI, 13.
8. *Mémoires* of Weber, quoted by P. Jolly, *Necker*, p. 197.
9. P. Jolly, *Necker*, p. 198.
10. Dialogue related by Necker. Same reference as for note 7, p. 15.
11. *Ibid.*, VI, 17.
12. B. Faÿ, *Louis XVI*, p. 209.

55

1. Diderot, *Correspondance*, XV, 206.
2. Note by the editors of *ibid.*, p. 240: "P. Vernière has pointed out this 'exact concomitance' (*Oeuvres philosophiques*, p. 637). With one blow, thus, Maurepas was striking two adversaries known for their inability to compromise. (Compare Métra, *Correspondance secrète*, XI, 256)."

3. De Vissac, *Simon Camboulas*, p. 53. *Ibid.* for the following quotation.
4. *Correspondance littéraire*, XII (May 1781), 510.
5. According to Marmontel, related by P. Jolly, *Necker*, p. 218.
6. Observed by Mme Rilliet, then Mlle Huber, who was one of her intimate friends, in Lady Blennerhasset, *Mme de Staël et son temps*, I, 183.
7. *Correspondance secrète*, I, 399 (May 25, 1781).

56

1. *Correspondance littéraire*, XII (April 1781), 498.
2. Mgr. Ricard, *L'Abbé Maury avant 1789* (Paris, Plon, 1888), p. 85 (cited hereafter as Ricard, *L'Abbé Maury*). *Ibid.* for Voltaire's pleasantry.
3. Records of the Académie Française, August 27, 1772, quoted by Ricard, *L'Abbé Maury*, p. 87. *Ibid.*, p. 89, for the grand almoner's words.
4. Sermon on the third Sunday in Lent 1778. Ricard, *L'Abbé Maury*, p. 101.
5. Bachaumont, *Mémoires secrets*, March 14, 1781. *Ibid.* for the next two quotations, both dated April 30.
6. Sainte-Beuve, *Causeries du lundi*, "L'Abbé Maury et l'éloge de Fénelon," IV, 166.
7. Ricard, *L'Abbé Maury*, p. 106.
8. Pierrette Girault de Goursac, *L'Education d'un roi: Louis XVI* (Paris, Gallimard, 1972), p. 217. The author has expended mines of erudition and hard labor on

unpublished material in an
attempt to prove that Louis XVI
was brought up by a genius, but
manages to double-kill him with
her kindness even so.

9. *Ibid.,* p. 216. Also for the next
quotation.

10. Quoted in *Correspondance littéraire,*
XII (April 1781), 498. *Ibid.* for
the following quotations.

57

1. Diderot, *Correspondance,* XV,
227. Owing to the remarkable
quality of the annotations, all the
unnumbered quotations in this
passage have been taken from
the same edition. The long *Lettre
apologétique de l'abbé Raynal à Mr
Grimm* (the title is in Diderot's
writing), written on March 25
but not sent until May 25, is no.
925 in this series, pp. 210–27.

2. Diderot, *Essai sur les règnes de
Claude et de Néron,* in *Oeuvres
complètes* (Club français du livre
edition), XIII, 451. Diderot was
polishing the final pages of this
essay all the while his letter to
Grimm was sitting in his drawer.

3. J.-J. Rousseau, *Les Confessions*
(Paris, Club des Amis du Livre
progressiste, 250th-anniversary
edition, reproducing the
complete text of the Geneva
manuscript), p. 474.

4. Note by Rousseau in the margin
of the Geneva manuscript. *Ibid.,*
p. 368.

5. *Ibid.,* p. 433.

6. *Ibid.,* p. 470.

7. Diderot, *Essai sur les règnes de
Claude et de Néron,* p. 358.

8. *Ibid.,* XIII, 275, from Roger

Lewinter's outstanding
introduction to this edition.
Lewinter adds, "The *Essai* . . .
brings Diderot's speech to a
close exactly as the *Confessions* do
that of Rousseau. Both texts are
self-portraits painted *sub specie
aeternitatis,* and they reveal all
the difference in the itineraries
followed by the philosopher and
the citizen."

9. *Ibid.,* XIII, 361.

10. Pierre Naville, *D'Holbach et la
philosophie scientifique au XVIIIe
siècle* (Paris, Gallimard,
"Bibliothèque des Idées," 1967),
p. 129.

11. From Diderot to Naigeon, July
28, 1780. Diderot,
Correspondance, XV, 178.

12. *Correspondance littéraire,* XII, 499.

13. By Diderot, quoted by Yves
Benot, *Diderot, de l'athéisme à
l'anticolonialisme,* p. 40.

14. Diderot, *Mémoires pour Catherine
II,* quoted in *ibid.,* p. 152.

58

1. P. Cottin, *Sophie de Monnier et
Mirabeau,* p. lxxii. All
unnumbered quotations in this
passage are from this work, a
good quarter of which is taken
up with the "meeting at
Gien."

2. A. Vallentin, *Mirabeau avant la
Révolution,* p. 228.

3. From Sophie to Gabriel,
December 23, 1780. P. Cottin,
Sophie de Monnier et Mirabeau,
p. 207.

4. From Sophie to Gabriel, March
19, 1781. *Ibid.,* p. 236.

5. From Sophie to Gabriel, March

31, 1781. *Ibid.,* p. 241.

6. *Ibid.,* p. ccxxiii. Also for the following quotation.

7. Already, on February 15! *Ibid.,* p. 126.

8. March 27, 1781. *Ibid.,* p. 238.

9. From Sophie to Gabriel, undated but certainly from February 1781. *Ibid.,* p. 221.

10. Archives nationales, K 164.

11. December 23, 1780. P. Cottin, *Sophie de Monnier et Mirabeau,* p. 298.

12. This is an unpublished extract from one of the marquis's letters to his brother, interpolated into the correspondence. Dauphin-Meunier, *Lettres de Mirabeau à Julie Dauvers* (Paris, Plon, 1903), p. 245.

13. From Mirabeau to Caroline du Saillant. *Ibid.,* p. 243. The explanation about the identity of "M. Honoré" (footnote on page 420) comes from a letter to La Fage, *ibid.,* p. 247.

14. From the marquis to his brother, December 20, 1780. *Ibid.,* p. 244.

15. P. Cottin, *Sophie de Monnier et Mirabeau,* p. cxciv.

59

1. From the marquis to his brother, January 12, 1781. Dauphin-Meunier, *Lettres de Mirabeau à Julie Dauvers,* pp. 257 and 258.

2. From the marquis to his brother, February 13, 1781. *Ibid.,* p. 270.

3. *Ibid.,* p. 42.

4. *Ibid.,* p. 63.

5. November 30, 1780. *Ibid.,* p. 192.

6. October 29, 1780. *Ibid.,* p. 56.

7. Dauphin-Meunier, *Louise de Mirabeau, marquise de Cabris* (Paris, Emilie-Paul, 1914), p. 240.

8. Loménie, *Les Mirabeau,* II, 613.

9. Letter from the marquis to his brother, May 8, 1781. *Ibid.,* II, 632.

10. *Ibid.,* I, 478.

11. *Ibid.,* II, 637.

12. Dauphin-Meunier, *Lettres de Mirabeau à Julie Dauvers,* p. 284.

13. A. Vallentin, *Mirabeau avant la Révolution,* p. 237.

14. *Ibid.,* p. 235. Pages 237 and 238 for the next three quotations.

15. From the marquis to his brother, July 21, 1781. Dauphin-Meunier, *Lettres de Mirabeau à Julie Dauvers,* p. 340.

16. Letter from the marquis to one of his Italian "disciples," the Marchese Longo, from Bignon, September 4, 1781. Loménie, *Les Mirabeau,* II, 640.

17. From the marquis to his brother, September 2, 1781. Dauphin-Meunier, *Lettres de Mirabeau à Julie Dauvers,* p. 340.

18. Letter of July 27, 1780. P. Cottin, *Sophie de Monnier et Mirabeau,* p. 165.

19. December 14, 1780. *Ibid.,* p. 201.

20. *Ibid.,* p. 118.

21. A. Vallentin, *Mirabeau avant la Révolution,* p. 237.

22. *Ibid.,* p. 229.

23. Letter of Sunday, June 3, 1781. P. Cottin, *Sophie de Monnier et Mirabeau,* p. 263.

24. Letter of June 6, 1781. *Ibid.,* p. 268.

60

1. From La Fayette to Steuben, from Bowling Green Tavern, April 27, 1781. Steuben's Papers, New York Historical Society [and Tower, *L.F. in America*, II, 289].

2. Charles Stedman, *The History of the Origin, Progress, and Termination of the American War*, vol. II, printed for the author (London, 1794), pp. 383–4.

3. La Fayette, *Correspondance*, quoted by Tower, *L.F. in America*, II, 302.

4. *Ibid.*, II, 303.

5. *Ibid.*, II, 292 (Tower's note).

6. Military Journal, in *ibid.*, II, 293.

7. Washington's Papers, Department of State, Washington, in *ibid.*, II, 298.

8. Autobiography of Arnold, in *ibid.*, II, 340.

9. Sparks's Papers, Harvard College Library, in *ibid.*, II, 308.

10. Letter from La Fayette to General Wayne, who was commanding the Pennsylvania Line and from whom La Fayette was hoping to get prompt relief. Wayne's Papers, Historical Society of Pennsylvania, in *ibid.*, II, 310.

11. Letter from La Fayette, on May 23, to his friend Alexander Hamilton, a future personality in American politics and at this point Washington's aide-de-camp. *Ibid.*, II, 315.

12. La Fayette, *Correspondance*, I, 438. *Ibid.* for the next quotation.

13. La Fayette, *Mémoires*, I, 270.

14. Adrienne Koch and William Peden, eds., *The Life and Selected Writings of Thomas Jefferson* (New York, The Modern Library, Random House, 1944), p. 44 ("Autobiography").

15. *Ibid.*, p. 51 ("Autobiography").

16. *Ibid.*, p. 279 ("Notes on Virginia").

17. [The author was working from a French translation of an edition of Jefferson's works; the translator has retranslated this passage.]

18. Cornwallis to Clinton, from "Byrd's Plantation, North of James River, May 26, 1781." Tower, *L.F. in America*, II, 319–20.

61

1. Copies of letters from Rochambeau in the Library of Congress, in Tower, *L.F. in America*, II, 390.

2. Archives historiques de la Guerre [War], Box 3734 / 4.

3. Vicomte de Noailles, *Marins et Soldats français en Amérique*, p. 220.

4. From the Comte de Charlus to the Marquis de Castries, June 5, 1781. Archives historiques de la Guerre [War], Box 3734 / 4.

5. *Lettres* from Fersen to his father, p. 117.

6. May 17, 1781. *Ibid.*, p. 113.

7. Journal of Captain John Davis, in *Pennsylvania Magazine of History and Biography*, Vol. V, No. 3.

8. Tower, *L.F. in America*, II, 332.

9. Private letter from La Fayette to Washington, from "Allen's Creek, 22 miles from Richmond, June 18, 1781": "I request you, my dear General, to remember

that this communication is not to the Commander-in-Chief." Federal Archives, Washington.

10. Tower, *L.F. in America,* II, 334–5.

11. *Ibid.,* II, 337.

12. Letter from La Fayette to Steuben, June 15, 1781. Steuben's Papers, New York Historical Society [and Tower, *L.F. in America,* II, 338].

13. His *Journal de la campagne d'Amérique,* written in the form of a letter to two brothers back home in France (who also become generals during the Empire), has been published in English in full, with numerous facsimiles, in H. C. Rice and A. S. K. Brown, *The American Campaigns of Rochambeau's Army, 1780, 1781, 1782, 1783* (Brown University Press and Princeton University Press, 1972). All of Berthier's maps and sketches are reproduced in Vol. II with remarkable wealth of color and attention to typographical detail. I follow them closely in describing the episodes leading to the capitulation of Cornwallis at Yorktown.

14. *Ibid.,* I, 246.

62

1. Duc de Lauzun, *Mémoires,* p. 146. *Ibid.* for the following quotations.

2. *Ibid.,* p. 147.

3. From La Fayette to Colonel Davis, June 22, 1781. Tower, *L.F. in America,* II, 341.

4. Journal of Captain John Davis, in *ibid.,* II, 342.

5. The following day. *Ibid.,* II, 347.

6. Issue of July 17, 1781, in *ibid.,* II, 349. The article is signed "a gentleman in the army of the Marquis de La Fayette."

7. La Fayette, *Mémoires,* I, 441.

8. Journal of Captain John Davis, in Tower, *L.F. in America,* II, 354.

9. Said by Colonel Febiger, quoted in *ibid.,* II, 355.

10. *Ibid.,* II, 358.

11. *Ibid.,* II, 361–2.

12. *Ibid.,* II, 363.

13. *Ibid.,* II, 368.

14. La Fayette to his wife, August 24, 1781. A. Maurois, *Madame de La Fayette,* p. 126.

63

1. J.-J. Antier, *L'Amiral de Grasse,* p. 27. Unnumbered quotations in this passage are from the same source.

2. *Ibid.,* p. 38.

3. *Correspondance secrète,* I, 316 (September 27, 1781).

4. Archives historiques de la Guerre [War], Box 3734.

5. *Ibid.,* Box 3734 / 16.

6. Letter from Rochambeau to Barras, July 8, 1781. Library of Congress.

7. Tower, *L.F. in America,* II, 395.

8. Clermont-Crèvecoeur, *Journal des guerres faites en Amérique pendant les années 1780, 1781, 1782, 1783, avec quelques dissertations sur les moeurs et coutumes des Américains,* etc., in *The American Campaigns of Rochambeau's Army,* I, 38–9.

9. La Fayette, *Correspondance,* I, 445.

10. Letter from de Grasse to Rochambeau, Cap Français, July

28, 1781. J.-J. Antier, *L'Amiral de Grasse*, p. 204.

11. *Ibid.*, p. 48.

64

*1. From Romme to Dubreuil, October 15, 1776. Museum of the Risorgimento in Milan, Box 8, quoted by Galante Garrone, *Gilbert Romme, histoire d'un révolutionnaire* (Paris, Flammarion, 1971), p. 68 (cited hereafter as Galante Garrone, *Gilbert Romme*).

2. *Ibid.*, p. 70.

3. From Romme to Dubreuil, undated, but written in late 1778. *Ibid.*, p. 73 (Box 27).

4. From Romme to Dubreuil, February 16, 1775. *Ibid.*, p. 38 (Box 7).

5. Same reference as for note 3.

6. From a text by Golovkin himself, in a pamphlet published in London in 1778, *"Mes idées sur l'éducation du sexe, ou Précis d'un plan d'éducation pour ma fille."* *Ibid.*, p. 60.

7. *Ibid.*, p. 55 of pamphlet. Also for the next quotation.

8. *Ibid.*, p. 57 of pamphlet.

9. C. Piton, *Paris sous Louis XV: Rapports des inspecteurs de Police au roi*, III, 364.

10. Galante Garrone, *Gilbert Romme*, p. 81.

11. A. Lortholary, *Le Mirage russe en France au XVIIIe siècle* (Paris, PUF, 1951), p. 213.

12. Letter from Romme to Dubreuil, May 11, 1779. Galante Garrone, *Gilbert Romme*, p. 89 (Box II).

13. L. H. Lalande, *Journal intime du chevalier de Corberon, chargé d'affaires de France en Russie, 1775–1780* (Paris, Plon, 1901), I, 52 (cited hereafter as *Journal de Corberon*). This traveler's impressions and observations on Saint Petersburg society tally so closely with those of Romme that it has sometimes been supposed that they must have exchanged writings; but in reality, they only compared reactions.

14. Letter from Romme to Dubreuil, December 1, 1779. Galante Garrone, *Gilbert Romme*, p. 93 (Box II). *Ibid.* for the following quotation.

15. *Ibid.*, p. 98.

16. Romme's notes in his private notebook and thus a true reflection of his own opinion. *Ibid.*, p. 104.

65

1. *Journal de Corberon*, I, 257.

2. Galante Garrone, *Gilbert Romme*, p. 107.

3. *Journal de Corberon*, II, 293.

4. *Ibid.*, II, 329.

5. *Ibid.*, I, 362.

6. *Ibid.*, II, 328.

7. Dispatch from Corberon to Vergennes, September 17, 1778. Archives des Affaires étrangères [Foreign Affairs], Russia, Vol. 101, folio 319.

8. *Journal de Corberon*, II, 137.

9. *Ibid.*, II, 151.

10. *Ibid.*, II, 152 *n.*

11. *Ibid.*, II, 370.

12. *Ibid.*, II, 319. The following quote is by Corberon's predecessor, J. Durand, in a dispatch to Vergennes in 1772.

13. *Ibid.*, II, 114.

14. *Ibid.*, I, 245.
15. From Romme to Dubreuil, February 17, 1781. Galante Garrone, *Gilbert Romme,* p. 100 (Box 13).
16. Undated letter to Count Stroganov. *Ibid.*, p. 100.
17. *Ibid.*, p. 101 (Box 41). Also for the next quotation on Lacedaemon.
18. Letter from Romme to an unidentified correspondent. *Ibid.*, p. 102 (Box 67).
*19. Marc de Vissac, *Romme le Montagnard* (Clermont-Ferrand, 1883), p. 76.

66

1. Michel Confino, *Domaines et Seigneurs en Russie vers la fin du XVIIIe siècle,* a study of agrarian structures and economic attitudes (Paris, Institut d'études slaves de l'Université, 1963); figures based on the fourth population census, taken in 1782, p. 187.
2. In the devaluated money of 1796. See Leon Gershoy, *L'Europe des princes éclairés* (Paris, Fayard, 1966), p. 119.
3. Zoé Oldenbourg, *Catherine de Russie* (Paris, Gallimard, 1966), p. 340. *Ibid.*, p. 295, for the advertisements in the *Moskovskie Vyedomosti.*
4. Michel Denis and Noel Blayau, *Le XVIIIe siècle* (Paris, Armand Colin, 1970), p. 209.
5. Letter from Romme to Dubreuil. Galante Garrone, *Gilbert Romme,* p. 128 (Box 16).
6. *Journal de Corberon,* II, 271
7. Galante Garrone, *Gilbert Romme,* p. 129.

8. Grand Duke Nicholas Mikhailovich, *Le Comte Paul Stroganov* (Paris, Plon, 1905), p. 163.
9. Letter from Romme to Mme d'Harville, January 28, 1785. Galante Garrone, *Gilbert Romme,* p. 134.
10. *Journal de Corberon,* II, 302.
11. *Ibid.*, II, 289.
12. *Ibid.*, II, 311.
13. *Ibid.*, I, 125.
14. Letter from Romme to Dubreuil, August 1781. Galante Garonne, *Gilbert Romme,* p. 111.
15. Letter from Romme to Dubreuil, September 15, 1778. *Ibid.*, p. 75 (Box 10).
16. M. Confino, *Domaines et Seigneurs en Russie Vers la fin du XVIIIe siècle,* p. 67, note 1.
17. Letter from Romme to Mme d'Harville, December 31, 1781. Galante Garrone, *Gilbert Romme,* p. 114.
18. From Romme to Mme d'Harville, February 17, 1782. *Ibid.*
19. *"Elégie sur la mort d'une parente aimée,"* kept among his papers and intended for himself alone. *Ibid.* (Box 39). The text dates from 1784 but is not out of place here: it expresses an unswerving trend in Romme's views on and reactions to friendship.

67

1. Tower, *L.F. in America,* II, 406.
2. Rochambeau, *Mémoires,* quoted by the Vicomte de Noailles, *Marins et Soldats français en Amérique,* p. 225.

3. Rochambeau to Barras, July 21, 1781. Archives historiques de la Guerre [War], Box 3734 / 65.
4. *Ibid.,* Box 3732 /82.
5. Letter from Cornwallis to Clinton, July 8, 1781. Tower, *L.F. in America,* II, 408.
6. From Clinton to Cornwallis, July 15, 1781. *Ibid.,* II, 408.
7. From La Fayette to General Wayne, August 2, 1781. *Ibid.,* II, 413–14. Also for the following quotation.
8. La Fayette to Washington, from camp at Pamunkey, August 6, 1781. *Ibid.,* II, 415–16.

68

1. J.-J. Antier, *L'Amiral de Grasse,* p. 181.
2. P. Bernard, *La France à Saint-Domingue avant la Révolution* (Paris, Hachette, "*Petite collection illustrée*"), p. 62.
3. (Unsigned) report from the intendant of Santo Domingo, in 1768, to the minister, Bourgeois de Boynes. Archives de la Marine, 1822 / Q 37.
4. Berthier scrupulously transcribed the layout of the town of Cap Français and its "*disembouquements.*" See *The American Campaigns of Rochambeau's Army,* II, nos. 176 and 177.
5. Tower, *L.F. in America,* II, 419–20.
6. *Ibid.,* II, 418.
7. *Ibid.,* II, 420–3.
8. From Washington to La Fayette, August 21, 1781. *Ibid.,* II, 427.

69

1. G. Maugras, *Le Duc de Lauzun et la cour de Marie-Antoinette,* p. 208.
2. J.-J. Antier, *L'Amiral de Grasse,* p. 211.
3. Vicomte de Noailles, *Marins et Soldats français en Amérique,* p. 233.
4. *Journal des opérations* kept by Fersen and sent to his father on October 23, 1781, in *Lettres* of Fersen, p. 126.
5. Rochambeau, *Mémoires,* I, 287.
6. Clermont-Crèvecoeur, *Journal,* etc., in *The American Campaigns of Rochambeau's Army,* I, 40.
7. Tower, *L.F. in America,* II, 426.
8. La Fayette, *Mémoires,* I, 460.
9. Tower, *L.F. in America,* II, 431.
10. Chevalier d'Aucteville, *Journal de la campagne de la Chesapeak* [*sic*], Archives de la Marine, B/4 184–144.
11. Tower, *L.F. in America,* II, 432.
12. La Fayette, *Mémoires,* I, 277. *Ibid.* for the following quotation.
13. Tower, *L.F. in America,* II, 440.

70

1. The Battle of the Chesapeake has been reconstructed down to the smallest detail by J.-J. Antier in *L'Amiral de Grasse.* See also Lacour-Gayet, *Marine française sous Louis XVI;* R. Weed, *The Battle of the Capes* (Norfolk Museum, 1959); and Karl Tornquist, *The Naval Campaigns of de Grasse* (Philadelphia, John Ryes, 1942). I have also taken a few details from the text of

Admiral Barjot's 1957 lecture to the Academy of the Var on "The Battle of the Chesapeake."

2. J.-J. Antier, *L'Amiral de Grasse,* p. 231.

3. Jean-Etienne Martin-Allanic, *Bougainville navigateur et les découvertes de son temps* (Paris, PUF), II, 1481. This text, taken from an account of La Pérouse's voyages, echoes a sentiment of Bougainville, by whom La Perouse was influenced intellectually and philosophically at least as much as in scientific matters.

4. According to Commodore James, *British Navy in Adversity* (London, Macmillan, 1926), p. 290.

5. *Ibid.* [This passage has been retranslated from the French.]

7 1

1. Vicomte de Noailles, *Marins et Soldats français en Amérique,* p. 234.

2. Clermont-Crèvecoeur, *Mémoires inédits,* in *The American Campaigns of Rochambeau's Army,* I, 46.

3. Fersen, *Lettres* to his father, p. 132.

4. From du Portail to Rochambeau, from Cape Henry, September 2, 1781. Archives historiques de la Guerre [War], Box 3734.

5. From de Grasse to Rochambeau, September 4, 1781. *Ibid.*

6. From de Grasse to Washington, from Cape Henry, September 4, 1781. *Correspondance du général Washington et du comte de Grasse* (Washington, D.C., Institut français, 1931). *Ibid.* for the following quotation.

7. Vicomte de Noailles, *Marins et Soldats français en Amérique,* p. 237.

8. Clermont-Crèvecoeur, same source as for note 2, p. 52.

9. *Encyclopédie,* II, 449, article "*Brûlot*" (fire ship).

10. J.-J. Antier, *L'Amiral de Grasse,* p. 250; also in Tornquist, *The Naval Campaigns of de Grasse.* The fire-ship episode takes place during the night of September 22–23, 1781.

11. From de Grasse to Washington, from Cape Henry, September 22, 1781. Same source as for note 4.

12. La Fayette, *Mémoires,* I, 465.

13. According to the Chevalier d'Aucteville, one of the first historians of the campaign, who published an initial account of it in 1784. See Vicomte de Noailles, *Marins et Soldats français en Amérique,* p. 237.

14. Vicomte de Noailles, *Marins et Soldats français en Amérique,* p. 237.

15. From Colonel Richard Butler's marching journal. *The Historical Magazine,* Washington, VIII, 102.

16. Charles Lewis, *Admiral de Grasse and American Independence,* (Annapolis, U.S. Navy Institute, 1945), p. 174.

7 2

1. Archives historiques de la Guerre [War], Box 3734 / 104.

2. Tower, *L.F. in America,* II, 447.

3. Archives historiques de la Guerre [War], Box 3734 / 110.

4. *Ibid.,* Box 3734 / 105 (Journal of Operations).

5. *Journal des opérations* of Fersen, in *Lettres* to his father, p. 128. *Ibid.* for the following quotation.

6. Duc de Lauzun, *Mémoires,* p. 150.

7. *Journal des opérations* of Fersen, in *Lettres* to his father, p. 129.

8. *Journal de Claude Blanchard pendant la guerre d'Amérique* (Paris, Plon, 1886), p. 236.

9. Comte Henry de Saint-Simon, *Lettres américaines* (Paris, 1826), p. 9.

10. Maxime Leroy, *La Vie du comte de Saint-Simon, 1760–1825* (Paris, Grasset, 1925), p. 94.

73

1. Vicomte de Noailles, *Marins et Soldats français en Amérique,* p. 241.

2. Eyewitness account by an anonymous English officer. J.-J. Antier, *L'Amiral de Grasse,* p. 260. *Ibid.* for the following quotation by de Grasse.

3. Tower, *L.F. in America,* II, 449.

4. Vicomte de Noailles, *Marins et Soldats français en Amérique,* p. 241.

5. Harold C. Syrett, ed., *The Papers of Alexander Hamilton* (New York and London, Columbia University Press, 1961), II (1779–1791), 563–6.

6. Archives historiques de la Guerre [War], account of the siege of Yorktown, Supplements, 1781.

7. Tower, *L.F. in America,* II, 450.

8. Vicomte de Noailles, *Marins et Soldats français en Amérique,* p. 245.

9. Tower, *L.F. in America,* II, 454.

10. *Ibid.,* pp. 456–7.

11. Robert Hughes, reported by J.-J. Antier, *L'Amiral de Grasse,* p. 263.

12. *Journal de Claude Blanchard pendant la guerre d'Amérique,* p. 310.

13. October 20, 1781. La Fayette, *Correspondance,* I, 470.

14. *Ibid.,* I, 471.

15. Duc de Lauzun, *Mémoires,* p. 151.

Index

A

Academy of Sciences, 259–64 *passim*, 270

Account Rendered to the King (Necker), 323 and *n.*, 327–32 *passim*, 348 *n.*, 363, 394, 395, 397, 399, 403, 407

Adams, John, 236 and *n.*

Africa, 69, 71 and *n.*, 72 and *n.*, 74; *see also* Senegal; slavery and slave trade

Aiguillon, Duc d' (Emmanuel-Armand de Richelieu), 464

Ailly, d', 230, 231

Aine, Mme d', 413 and *n.*

Alembert, Jean d' (Jean-Baptiste Lerond), 31 *n.*, 262, 270 and *n.*, 311, 312, 404, 408

Alès, Mme Marie-Thérèse de Saillans d', 134

Alexander I, Czar of Russia, 457 *n.*, 465 and *n.*

Alluaud, François (father), 226, 227 and *n.*, 230, 231, 233

Alluaud, François (son), 227 *n.*, 229 *n.*, 231 *n.*

Almanach des Muses, 111, 114

Alströmer, Baron, 149

Ambroise, Brother, 200

Amelot, 313 *n.*, 419

American Revolution, 76–84, 246–56, 287–307, 340–56, 429–54, 473–514

army (British), 77–81 *passim*, 289, 290, 295–6, 297, 304, 340, 349 *n.*, 353, 359 *n.*, 430, 433, 477 *n.*; German mercenaries, 246, 289, 295–6, 349 *n.*, 504, 505, 511; *see also* Clinton, Gen. Sir Henry; Cornwallis, Gen. Lord Charles

army (Continental Army), 77–81 *passim*, 287–8, 342–3, 439, 444, 449, 486, 504, 509; *see also* Washington, George

army (French), 241–56 *passim*, 288–303 *passim*, 340, 342, 345–50 *passim*, 435–42 *passim*, 448–53 *passim*, 474, 485, 499–514 *passim; see also* La Fayette, Marquis de; Rochambeau, Gen. Comte de

battles, 78–9, 80, 81; Yorktown, 452, 475–6, 477, 480, 482, 485–8, 493–514 *passim; see also* New Jersey; New York; Rhode Island; Virginia

Congress, 7, 77, 236, 289, 494, 495

Dutch loan, 344 *n.*

flag adopted, 7

and France, 7, 17, 87–8, 236, 289 *n.*, 344 and *n.*, 348–9, 354 *n.*, 355 *n.;* Franklin as representative, 7, 233–41 *passim*, 259, 260, 264, 345, 348, 349; Louis XVI's attitude, 30, 87, 243, 245, 250, 349; treaty of alliance, 86; *see also* army (French) *above;* navy (French)—and England

navy (American), 3–8 *passim*, 17, 22, 85, 256

navy (British), *see* Royal Navy

navy (French), *see* navy (French)— and England

and Spain, 3, 154

see also United States

Ancellet, André Eloy, 129–30

André, Maj. John, 304, 305, 306–7

Angoulême, Duc d' (Louis de Bourbon; later Louis XIX), 61 *n.*, 129

Apaza, Julian (Tupac-Calari), 379–80, 393 and *n.*

C

D

N

O

P

A NOTE ABOUT THE TRANSLATOR

Nancy Lipe Amphoux was born in Rockford, Illinois, and was educated by the corn-fields there, at Vassar and Carnegie-Mellon, and in Europe, where she has lived since 1959. Her interests and activities include teaching and social work, horses and tropical fish, and Zen. Some of the books she has translated are Henri Troyat's biographies of Tolstoy, Pushkin, and Gogol; Edmonde Charles-Roux's biography of Chanel; and François Ponchaud's *Cambodia Year Zero*. She now lives in Strasbourg, France.

A NOTE ON THE TYPE

The text of this book was set, via computer-driven cathode-ray tube, in Garamond, a modern rendering of the type first cut by Claude Garamond (1510–1561). Garamond was a pupil of Geoffroy Tory and is believed to have based his letters on the Venetian models; it is to him we owe the letter we know as old-style.

This book was composed, printed, and bound by The Haddon Craftsmen, Inc., Scranton, Pennsylvania.

The book was designed by Earl Tidwell.

087673